Praise for Jon Pessah's

THE GAME

"A poignant account of the power struggle between three men: MLB Commissioner Bud Selig, Yankees owner George Steinbrenner, and players union leader Don Fehr."
— Robert Birnbaum, *Daily Beast*

"This might be the definitive account of how front offices control Major League Baseball.... Pessah crafts freeze-frame descriptions of the most critical backroom moments of the modern era."
— Rob Fischer, *Men's Journal*

"There are lots of fresh notes, quotes, and anecdotes in *The Game*, but its chief value for those who care is its meticulous reconstruction of the fraught era.... The most compelling parts of *The Game* deal with baseball's abject failure to confront the steroid plague."
— Edward Kosner, *Wall Street Journal*

"A gritty and sensational history of America's national pastime.... A juicy and engrossing story that reads like a thriller, with a star supporting cast.... Pessah calls the game perfectly."
— Marilyn Dahl, *Shelf Awareness*

"A compelling, high-stakes look at baseball.... Pessah does a great job of providing glimpses of conversations fans were not privy to while placing them in context by describing what was happening on the field in that moment. Essential for fans of 1990s- and 2000s-era baseball."
— Matt Schirano, *Library Journal*

"Fascinating.... This juicy read focuses on three men who shaped [baseball's] history over [the last] two decades—Selig, union head Don Fehr, and Yankees owner George Steinbrenner.... The most surprising part of the book is without a doubt the portrait of Steinbrenner. While still rendered as an insatiable tyrant, the Boss—and his willingness to put his money where his mouth is—is a breath of fresh air."
— William O'Connor, *Daily Beast*

"In clear, accessible prose, *The Game* covers strikes, steroids, and everything in between. Not an easy task. The most memorable sections are about Steinbrenner. Pessah deftly captures the man's heavy-handed—and often underhanded—leadership."
— Michael S. Schmidt, *New York Times*

"A sweeping and comprehensive investigation of the business of baseball over the past three decades.... Fascinating."
— Anthony L. Fisher, Reason.com

"Serious baseball fans will appreciate the author's deep research and his ability to weave multiple stories together into a graceful narrative."
— *Kirkus Reviews*

THE
GAME

INSIDE THE
SECRET WORLD *of*
MAJOR LEAGUE BASEBALL'S
POWER BROKERS

JON PESSAH

BACK BAY BOOKS
LITTLE, BROWN AND COMPANY
New York • Boston • London

Back Bay Books / Little, Brown and Company
Hachette Book Group
1290 Avenue of the Americas, New York, NY 10104
littlebrown.com

Originally published in hardcover by Little, Brown and Company, May 2015
First Back Bay paperback edition, May 2016

Back Bay Books is an imprint of Little, Brown and Company, a division of Hachette Book Group, Inc. The Back Bay Books name and logo are trademarks of Hachette Book Group, Inc.

The publisher is not responsible for websites (or their content) that are not owned by the publisher.

The Hachette Speakers Bureau provides a wide range of authors for speaking events. To find out more, go to hachettespeakersbureau.com or call (866) 376-6591.

ISBN 978-0-316-18588-2 (hc) / 978-0-316-18589-9 (pb)
LCCN 2015901927

10 9 8 7 6 5 4 3 2 1

RRD-C

Printed in the United States of America

To Suzi,
and in memory of Harriet

CONTENTS

THE
GAME

Prologue

THE BESPECTACLED 66-YEAR-OLD man in the blue blazer, white shirt, and red tie is walking across the thin stretch of grass between the first baseline and the home-team dugout. His name is Bud Selig, and it's several hours before his favorite team takes the field for batting practice. Selig usually enjoys being surrounded by people, but this quiet period before a baseball game is one of the Commissioner's favorites. It's April 6, 2001, and only a few stadium workers dot the stands. He's not sure if it's the serenity of the moment, the simple beauty of the manicured field, or the sweep of the grandstand that evokes the game's past. But for a man who has a lifelong love affair with baseball, it feels like walking into a cathedral.

He glances over at the pitcher's mound, his blue eyes squinting, and marvels at just how high it rises and how gosh-darn close it feels to home plate. He looks beyond the mound to the green walls stretched across the sprawling outfield. Even on his best days growing up on Milwaukee's ball fields, he could never knock a ball over those fences. No; the players who could do that were gods.

There's much about the game he cherishes, though maybe not as much as he did in the '70s, when he was a young owner and the game seemed simpler. So much has changed, so many battles have been fought, so much blood spilled. He often finds himself thinking back to 1992, when he led the revolt against his friend Commissioner Fay Vincent, took control of the game, and saved it. The game was in chaos back then. Yes, he'd sacrificed a World Series, but it was his good judgment, his innovations, and his political skill—especially his political skill—that brought the game back to life. He's sure of that.

Baseball is too important a social institution to fail—isn't that what he's told every fan, reporter, and lawmaker ever since? If that weren't true, how had he been able to help raise billions in taxpayer money to build baseball stadiums? The game has 11 sparkling new stadiums because Selig persuaded local governments to give him what he wanted—what he *needed*—to keep baseball alive in their cities.

Nowhere is that more true than here in Milwaukee, where the stadium closest to his heart is finally ready. In a few hours the first pitch will be thrown at the $414 million Miller Park. There are still many in this town who bitterly resent bailing out his debt-ridden team, but even the harshest critics admire the architectural wonder he's given them.

Selig's eyes roam his team's new home. The one-of-a-kind fan-shaped retractable roof. A plaza lined with restaurants, shops, and luxury suites. Soaring brick archways that keep the promise voiced in the Brewers' new promotional video: *Miller Park, where a fan can't help but feel the reincarnation of baseball's romantic past.*

Selig walks a few steps down the baseline, his hands in his pockets, his slight slouch familiar to any baseball fan. How many times has he already watched the six-minute promo? He loves the clip of Hank Aaron and the Braves winning the '57 World Series and the celebration that followed—the first and last the town's enjoyed during its 50 years of baseball. And the clip of Robin Yount getting his 3,000th hit in a Brewers uniform. He's especially fond of the final passage, which will soon play on the 48-foot-wide screen in center field.

Miller Park will create a barn fire of passion for the team. The eyes of the baseball world will focus on Milwaukee, and talk of the inadequacies of small market baseball will give way to praise and the recollection of a time when fans lived and died with their team and the team waged battle for their fans. A time when loyalty to the grand old game was shared equally between players, owners, fans, and corporations.

Selig smiles. He was the town's 35-year-old boy wonder when he brought baseball back to Milwaukee in 1970. His reward: a team to run as he saw fit. Now he stands in his new stadium, running not just his team but also his entire sport.

Selig takes one more look around the park, then walks slowly into the Brewers dugout. He ambles through a series of tunnels and onto an elevator that brings him up to the .300 Club, where his friends and the city's leaders are gathered to celebrate the place that took him almost 15 years to build. He spends a few hours there, shaking hands and accepting congratulations, until word comes that he is needed back downstairs.

It's time to greet the man who once believed he would become the Commissioner of baseball.

President George W. Bush is working his way through Miller Park's visitors locker room surrounded by Secret Service agents and White House reporters. Just 24 hours earlier, Bush was in D.C., where the popular new President pushed Congress closer to passing his $1.35 trillion, 10-year tax cut. He'd promised his old friend Buddy that he'd throw out the first pitch the night Miller Park opened, and it was a promise he planned to keep.

So he'd flown into Milwaukee on Air Force One earlier this afternoon with Laura, National Security Advisor Condoleezza Rice, and his Health and Human Services Secretary Tommy Thompson, the former Wisconsin governor who helped build Bud's stadium. And now Bush is doing what he loves — hanging with major league players, sharing stories of his days running the Texas Rangers, and autographing a baseball for Hall of Famer Rod Carew, now the Brewers hitting coach.

"Something's wrong with this picture, me signing this for you," Bush tells Carew as he hands him the baseball. Everyone laughs. Bush is radiant in his black cowboy boots and dark slacks, a blue satin Brewers warm-up jacket pulled over a 40-pound flak vest. He's smiling broadly as he shakes hands with player after player.

"You've got my support on the tax cut," Cincinnati Reds pitcher Scott Sullivan tells him.

"It's going to be a heck of a lot bigger than anyone thought," Bush shouts back.

Bush is clearly enjoying himself, Selig thinks as he follows the

President on his tour of the clubhouses. The two men developed a bond when Bush joined baseball in 1989, a few months after helping his father win the White House. They had much in common. Both grew up close to their mothers and wanted desperately to impress their fathers. Both were accustomed to being underestimated, something each uses to his full advantage.

And both have an abiding love for baseball. As a boy in grade school, Bush carried a bat to class every day, idolized Willie Mays, and talked about owning a baseball team, just like his uncle, one of the original owners of the Mets. But his real dream, one of Bush's best friends told a magazine writer just before the 2000 election, was to become baseball's Commissioner.

"He wanted to be Kenesaw Mountain Landis," the friend said. "I'm still convinced that's his goal."

Chances are Selig has seen that article. There isn't much concerning baseball that he doesn't read, listen to, or watch. While some scoffed at the notion after Bush was elected President, Bud and others inside baseball know how much George W. Bush wanted to be Commissioner. And how close he had come.

It was one of the many challenges Selig faced after Vincent's removal in September of 1992. Vincent is a longtime friend of the Bush family, and George openly supported the Commissioner right down to the day of his forced resignation. Selig assumed control two days later, but the last thing he wanted was to alienate a friend. Especially one with such powerful connections. So Selig made Bush a promise: he would support his dream to become baseball's next Commissioner.

It was a promise Selig would never keep—there was just too much at stake, and Bush wasn't battle-tested. The owners were preparing for another war with their players and union leader Don Fehr, a war Vincent was not prepared to fight. "The Commissioner should represent the players and the fans as well as the owners," Vincent kept telling Selig. That's when Selig knew Vincent had to go.

No, this was not the time for someone else to run his game—no matter how often he told Bush the job could be his.

Selig is sure he made the right decision back in 1992. And he is even more certain now, in 2001, for history seems ready to repeat itself. The labor deal he accepted after the 1994 strike was a truce, not a peace plan. Players are still making too much money. George Steinbrenner—with four titles in the last five seasons and a cable channel soon to launch—is still spending too much money. And Don Fehr is still in charge of the union. The power struggle between Selig, Steinbrenner, and Fehr—which in many ways has defined this era—has not abated.

Billions are again on the line, but this time there is a difference. Selig has made the owners even richer, doubling the value of their franchises and tripling their revenues with new stadiums and television deals. He's growing rich, too, thanks to this new stadium and the $3 million salary—plus bonuses—he now earns as Commissioner.

And he has far more power, too. Last time his main focus was bringing the owners together—a task once thought near impossible. Nothing, he knew, could ever get done without a united front. That accomplished, he now has complete control of labor negotiations. He's spent millions lobbying Congress to get to this moment, and he has a popular friend and ally in the White House, one who's just passed a landmark tax bill favoring many of the rich men who own baseball teams.

How could things have worked out any better?

Every one of the 42,024 seats at Miller Park is filled with fans who've already splurged on overpriced hot dogs, beer, and Brewers merchandise. They've watched the huge bald eagle leave its left-field perch next to Bernie Brewer and swoop down to the pitcher's mound while kids from every county in the state held the edges of a giant, outfield-covering flag. They've listened to longtime Brewers announcer Bob Uecker's well-worn but oddly entertaining jokes and paid equal attention to the introductions of Yount and Rice. Now they're ready for the main event.

"Mr. President, Mr. Commissioner, it's time," a Brewers official says just minutes before the first game's scheduled start.

Bush practiced pitching for an hour with White House spokesman Ari Fleischer a day earlier while waiting out the tax vote. He entertained reporters earlier that night by telling them he was still deciding between throwing a split finger or a straight fastball to Brewers manager Davey Lopes, who is now standing behind home plate ready to catch the first pitch. The President and the Commissioner, still chatting away, follow their escorts into the Brewers dugout.

The two men pause, then Selig climbs the steps and strides to the top of the pitcher's mound. He will throw out the first pitch. The President will have to wait his turn.

Selig is, after all, the Commissioner.

And this is his game.

PART I

CHANGING OF THE GUARD
(1992–1994)

Chapter 1

IN BUD WE TRUST

September 3-September 9, 1992

IT'S THE THIRD day of September in 1992, and Milwaukee Brewers owner Allan "Bud" Selig turns his black Lexus sedan south on Interstate 94 for the short drive to Chicago that's been a long time coming. He's called a meeting to decide the future of Commissioner Fay Vincent, the man he now considers the most urgent of baseball's many problems. Most of the game's other 27 owners want Vincent to resign, a rare display of unity, but Selig isn't sure their resolve will hold. Nor is he certain they can fire Vincent without an ugly fight.

What Selig does know is this:

He has to persuade Yankees owner George Steinbrenner to share his rapidly growing revenues, which Selig's Brewers have no hopes of ever matching.

He has to force union leader Don Fehr to accept a cap on the players' rapidly growing salaries, which his Brewers have no real hope of paying.

And he has to twist the arms of Wisconsin politicians to build a new stadium so he can pay off his rapidly growing debt.

There's only one way to make sure all this happens: take control of the game. Now. The survival of his baseball team—and every other small market team—depends on it.

Vincent didn't have to be shoved aside like this, Selig thinks as his car barrels down the highway. He's been warning Vincent for months that his Commissioner's job was in jeopardy if he didn't agree to stay out of the upcoming labor negotiations.

Sure, there are other issues that have put Vincent's job at risk. American League owners are still irate that Vincent gave them less than a quarter of last year's $190 million expansion fees—$42 million to the National League's $148 million—even though both leagues supplied the same number of players to stock the new Colorado and Florida teams. Of course the owners somehow forgot they'd asked Vincent to decide the split after they couldn't agree among themselves.

And the Tribune Company is now taking baseball to court over Vincent's decision to move their Chicago Cubs to the NL West along with the St. Louis Cardinals. Again, it was the NL owners who asked Vincent to make that call. But by next season the Tribune Company will pay seven teams for their broadcast rights, so that request was easy to forget, too.

Truth is, Vincent was never a comfortable fit for the game's owners. He was already a wealthy man when he was swept into office two days after his close friend and Commissioner Bart Giamatti died of a sudden heart attack on September 1, 1989, after only five months in office. He was elevated to stardom a month later for the calm hand he displayed after a 6.9 earthquake hit minutes before Game 3 of the Giants-A's World Series, killing 63, injuring 3,700, and paralyzing the Bay Area for days. Working with local authorities, Vincent and baseball played a key role in guiding a crippled San Francisco back to life. A dedicated baseball fan and star athlete until a fall in college left him hobbled, Vincent felt the Commissioner should tend to the interests of the owners *and* the players and fans. And that meant wading into labor negotiations when they stall, as they have like clockwork for almost two decades.

But the labor contract holds the key to fixing the owners' problems, and labor talks have been Selig's domain ever since he took over the Player Relations Committee, the owners' bargaining unit, in 1985. Going up against Fehr and the union was *his* job. And Selig desperately wants Vincent out of the way.

Selig and his allies have no intention of allowing a replay of 1990, when they felt Vincent double-crossed them by meeting secretly with Fehr at his Greenwich, Connecticut, home during the owners' long spring training lockout. Vincent undermined management's position during that visit, taking their salary cap proposal off the table and giving in to union demands. At least, that's the way the owners saw it. The resulting agreement left free agency intact and player salaries continued to climb.

No, Selig isn't taking any chances this time around. Not when he has so much at stake.

Quite simply, Selig knows he can't keep things going in Milwaukee unless the game's economics change—and change dramatically. He already has so many liens on his franchise that he was forced to take $35 million from baseball's line of credit just to pay this season's bills. He's certain to lose a host of players to free agency in a few months, including his team's biggest star. And he needs a new stadium, but those talks are going nowhere with the game's financial structure in doubt.

Fehr's solution: move the Brewers to a bigger market. Selig was a 31-year-old car dealer and the largest nonvoting shareholder of the Milwaukee Braves when his team packed up and moved to Atlanta for the 1966 season. It took four years for him to beg, borrow, and all but steal a team out of a Seattle bankruptcy court to bring Major League Baseball back to Milwaukee. He'll be damned if his hometown will lose a baseball team for the second time.

Selig's mind turns to his relationship with Fehr. Nothing infuriates baseball's owners more than the media calling Fehr the game's most powerful man. Selig believes all Fehr really cares about is getting big money for his players. And that's why he has to be stopped, if not driven from the game completely.

Not that Selig hasn't already tried and lost. It was Fehr who took the owners to arbitration—*three times*—after they stopped bidding on free agents for three seasons in the late '80s. Each time Fehr accused the owners of collusion, and each time an arbitrator agreed. It cost the owners $280 million—almost $11 million each—to settle all cases. Selig is still working to pay off that bill.

Selig glances in his rearview mirror and sees the man who negotiated that settlement, Foley & Lardner lawyer Bob DuPuy, sitting in the backseat of the Lexus, behind Bud's daughter Wendy. DuPuy looks a bit nervous, and Selig jokes that they both need to relax instead of worrying about how fast he's weaving his car through traffic.

Was it only last May that he instructed DuPuy to work with a growing number of owners who wanted to sack Vincent? What began as a group of six teams grew to 18, and Selig had DuPuy monitor their meetings, coordinate with their lawyers, and report everything back to him. When Vincent got word of these meetings, he told them what they were considering was meaningless—the game's constitution clearly states that a sitting Commissioner cannot be removed. It became DuPuy's task to find a hole in Vincent's argument, a task that turned into a full-time job.

Selig glances over at his daughter. He's been grooming Wendy to run his team almost since the morning his then 10-year-old little girl burst into his bedroom, tears streaming down her cheeks, demanding to know why her father had traded pitcher Marty Pattin—her favorite player!—while she was fast asleep. Now 32, Wendy is smart, driven, and as big a Brewers fan as her 58-year-old dad.

Milwaukee was a great baseball town when Selig was young, setting attendance records and celebrating Hank Aaron and Warren Spahn when the Braves won a World Series title back in '57. But that was before free agency made winning far more complicated—and a whole lot more expensive. And long before the size of a team's television market mattered more than the number of tickets sold.

The cable television explosion in the late '80s changed everything. Steinbrenner's record-setting $486 million, 12-year deal with the MSG Network in 1988 was just the canary in the mine, warning owners like Bud of the trouble that lay ahead. Now, in 1992, 60 percent of America is wired for cable, a number that's growing fast. The cable monopolies are in need of programming to fill their 24/7 systems, and baseball offers 162 reality shows a season.

But Milwaukee, bound by Chicago to the south, Minnesota to the west, and Lake Michigan to the east, is an old Rust Belt town with a shrinking population. Cable television will bury Milwaukee, not save it—unless Selig can persuade the Steinbrenners of baseball to share their growing profits.

Selig thinks about the clashing agendas he'll encounter in Chicago. Most of the owners don't care much for each other—too much wealth, too many egos—but Bud is a friend to them all, a skill he learned long ago as a salesman for his father's Ford dealership. He doesn't mind the dysfunction—hell, he's learned to benefit from it—but he does hate the way most of them do business.

Seven teams—the Yankees, Mets, Dodgers, Red Sox, Blue Jays, Cubs, and Orioles—earn the lion's share of baseball's bounty, a record $1.2 billion this season. And they want to keep it that way; revenue sharing isn't in their vocabulary. Teams in the middle—the Cardinals, Rangers, Indians, and the like—spend wildly when they think they can win. But too often, they simply get burned.

Seven others—the Pirates, Expos, Twins, Padres, Royals, Mariners, and Bud's Brewers—have just about given up hope. With the wealth gap growing ever larger, Selig would just as soon follow the advice of his close friend, White Sox owner Jerry Reinsdorf, and use a lockout to shut down the game and force a change rather than continue fighting a losing battle.

Selig's thoughts shift back to Vincent. *He's been in baseball for all of three years, and thinks he has all the answers.* Bud's been in baseball for 32 years, longer than all but three owners, and no decisions are made without his blessing. Yes, baseball's constitution allows the Commissioner to weigh in on any issue, but all Vincent's predecessors understood they worked for the owners. Rarely did a Commissioner cross them. And when they did—"Commissioneritis" is what the owners call it—they were dismissed at the end of their terms.

Damn, Vincent just never listened.

Vincent is already threatening to take them all to court if they try to fire him. But he's crossed so many owners in his three years that most of them have been calling Selig regularly for months, demanding Vincent's head. *Let him sue,* they're telling Bud. *We'll take our chances.* The Commissioner still has his supporters, including one whose father sits in the White House, but as Selig and his two passengers approach Chicago, he knows a tipping point has been reached.

It's time for Fay to go.

And time for Bud to take charge.

Selig looks around the Hyatt Regency O'Hare suite Reinsdorf rented for a pre-meeting strategy session. About 18 owners are present, lawyers in tow, all of them ready to move on Vincent. Everything is proceeding as planned.

Bud's happy to see his mentor, 77-year-old Twins owner Carl Pohlad, among the arrivals. The two men grew close soon after the billionaire bought the Twins in 1984, and it's become Pohlad's practice to send a new suit, dress shirt, and ties to Selig every Christmas in a valiant attempt to improve the younger man's appearance. The two men spend at least an hour on the phone every Saturday morning, talking business, politics, and baseball.

For most of the past year, the conversations have focused on how poorly their byzantine game is run. The American League office manages its league, the National League office oversees its 12 teams, and any efforts to get the two to work together and maximize profits are feeble at best.

Selig knows that no matter how much money Carl has—Pohlad's net worth is an estimated $765 million—he's tired of owning a franchise he insists is bleeding money despite winning its second championship in five years last October. And that's why he refused to match Toronto's two-year, $10.85 million offer to his star pitcher, Jack Morris, last December. Morris claimed a place in World Series history last fall when he shut out the Braves for 10 innings to win Game 7 and the title. Pohlad was furious when the 37-year-old pitcher turned his back on the Twins' offer in favor of bigger bucks in Canada.

Pohlad hired the accounting firm Arthur Andersen this spring to draw up a better business model and soon started holding meetings with a handful of owners. The Pohlad Group, as it came to be called, began with six owners—with Selig as a cofounder—and soon grew to 20. The mission was to alter the game's business plan, focusing on capping player salaries and creating equitable sharing of local television revenue.

Although Pohlad started this uprising, Selig knows it's Reinsdorf who's led the charge. Reinsdorf lost faith in Vincent well before this season. He still talks about sitting in the Commissioner's Park Avenue office in the final days of the 32-day lockout in '90, when Fehr delivered what he called the union's best and final offer. Selig, Pohlad, and three other members of the bargaining team were there, too. "I'm begging you to take this deal," Vincent told them. "I'm begging you."

Pohlad and Reinsdorf stood up, excused themselves, and walked slowly down the hall and into the men's room. Standing at the urinal next to Reinsdorf, Carl turned to Jerry and said, "We have to get rid of this guy."

Vincent keeps pointing to Article 9 of baseball's constitution, which states there can be "no diminution" of a Commissioner's powers, as proof that he cannot be fired. Fact is, the constitution contains no mention of removing the Commissioner from office before his term expires. Reinsdorf and Selig have been talking about how many votes they need to oust Vincent, and they settled on a minimum of 18. They also scheduled this meeting six days ahead of the already planned quarterly meetings in St. Louis to give Vincent time to realize that a fight against two-thirds of ownership would be fruitless.

At least, that is their hope.

The media often portrays Selig as Reinsdorf's puppet—the two friends are convinced it's Fehr who pushes the story, hoping to drive a wedge between them—but the truth is the two men complete each other. No one questions Reinsdorf's intellect or his detailed grasp of the business of baseball, something few other owners have taken the time to learn. But Reinsdorf lacks political skills, which are Selig's stock-in-trade.

Yes, Reinsdorf can be charming, but he's far more comfortable being combative. Selig also has a temper—as anyone who's stood next to him when his Brewers are losing will attest—but he understands the value of relationships and is willing to work hard to maintain them. If it's Reinsdorf who crafts the deals, it's Selig who knows how to close them.

Reinsdorf will rarely call an owner—other than Bud—unless he has something important to discuss. Selig could not be more different. Before there were cell phones and the Internet, there was Bud on his office phone for hours on end, talking to one owner after another, casually but carefully gathering up information. No one knows more about what is happening in this game than the man in Milwaukee.

And no one knows the value of money—and the credibility and power that come with it—better than Selig, who has far less of it than any owner in baseball. The son of a baseball-crazy schoolteacher mom and a father who owned Wisconsin's largest Ford dealership, Selig now lives a comfortable life in one of Milwaukee's leafy upper-middle-class suburbs. He earns $463,000 a year running the Brewers, along with what amounts to spare change as president of Selig Leasing Company, Inc., the company his father started years ago to cater to local businessmen.

His most valuable asset is his stake in his beleaguered baseball franchise. But if the sport's economics are not tilted more in Selig's direction, he'll either have to sell or move the team. Neither option is palatable. And that is why Selig is at the Hyatt Regency O'Hare today.

Reinsdorf was an early supporter of the Pohlad Group, even though he turns a nice profit while his team plays second fiddle to the Cubs. The Brooklyn-born son of a sewing machine salesman made his money fashioning tax shelters for doctors and lawyers when the top tax rate was 70 percent. He sold his practice to build an investment company that soon raised $650 million to buy up real estate in Chicago, more than enough to partner with TV executive Eddie Einhorn and buy the White Sox for $19 million in 1981.

Reinsdorf sold his investment firm to American Express for $102 million a year later, then spent $9 million to buy the Chicago Bulls in '84. As luck would have it, the team drafted a kid named

Michael Jordan later that summer, and they've already given Reinsdorf two NBA championship rings.

But it's a World Series title Reinsdorf wants most. Pushing Vincent out and ushering in Selig—with his anti-union and pro–small market stances—is all part of making sure the teams with the biggest payrolls don't always have the best shot to win. Or the only shot. Reinsdorf wants the next Commissioner to be the game's CEO, reporting directly to the owners. For the last 10 years, others have been suggesting that Selig take the job, and Reinsdorf has now joined the chorus.

All they have to do is get rid of Vincent first.

A pack of baseball writers is already assembled in the Hyatt Regency's lobby when Selig and his friends arrive. "No comment" is all they get from the owners attending the pre-meeting strategy session, but that changes when Rangers minority partner George W. Bush strolls through the doors.

Bush loves his role in baseball, but he arrives in Chicago a man conflicted. George was a kid when Fay, the best friend of his uncle Bucky, worked in his family's oil fields. George H. W. called from the White House to congratulate Vincent when he was named Commissioner, and both father and son count Fay as a good friend.

Neither Bush wants to see Vincent forced out of office. But if Vincent is no longer the Commissioner, Junior would love to have the job.

Bush's Rangers partners know political operative Karl Rove is using their baseball team as a marketing tool for George's eventual run for governor of Texas, just as he will later use a ranch in Crawford to market W's run for the White House. But Bush has often told Vincent that he'd rather sit in the Commissioner's chair than the governor's mansion.

Many in baseball have heard him say similar things. And while most of the owners resent the attention Bush attracts from the media, they all recognize his rare social intelligence—a certain magnetism—which draws even the most successful men to his side. Still, as Vincent's fate grew uncertain, a few owners were already whispering that George was not sharp enough to run their game.

Reporters flock around Bush, who's accompanied by his team of Secret Service men, and he slows just outside the meeting room to enjoy the attention and state his case. "Vincent is my friend, but I happen to also believe this guy is a good man who's being made a scapegoat," Bush tells them. "Generally the scapegoat is not the solution. We have to get our own house in order."

Bush has been trying to help save his friend's job for months, defending him to the owners while encouraging Vincent to stay on the sidelines in the upcoming contract talks. A majority of owners now want a salary cap and increased revenue sharing, Bush told Vincent, and they appear willing to shut down the game to get their way. Vincent told his friend he considered it his job to make sure all sides—the owners, the players, and the fans—are treated fairly. He didn't think a salary cap was fair—or attainable—and had reservations about Bud and Jerry's revenue sharing ideas. And shutting down the game was clearly not in the best interest of the fans.

The odds are clearly against the Commissioner, but Bush warned the owners that this man wasn't going to leave without a fight. Vincent has already hired Brendan Sullivan, senior partner of the elite Washington law firm Williams & Connolly, to take his case to court if necessary. Sullivan received wide acclaim when he successfully defended Colonel Oliver North in the Iran-Contra affair five years ago. Word is he's relishing going up against the so-called Lords of Baseball.

And that's not the owners' only worry. There's talk that baseball's banks might freeze their credit if they move on Vincent, which is especially worrisome to those owners counting on loans to bankroll their forays into this winter's loaded free agent market. It was Vincent who closed the deal on their line of credit a year ago, when the agreement almost fell apart, and the thought of a protracted legal battle is already making some of baseball's bankers nervous.

It's almost time for the meeting to begin, but Bush is taking a small bit of delight in the fact that some of the anti-Vincent forces are annoyed watching him publicly defend the Commissioner. "It doesn't matter what the vote is," Bush says. "We're dealing with a man of integrity. He's not going to leave."

The doors to the large ballroom swing closed as each owner walks to his or her assigned seat. Breaking custom, the National League and American League owners are intermingled, a move Selig and Reinsdorf made to separate Vincent's allies. Toronto Blue Jays President Paul Beeston, the man they've chosen to chair this meeting, stands behind the head table, a league lawyer on either side, and gavels the proceedings to order.

The league lawyers have drawn up a resolution of no confidence, the Blue Jays executive tells the owners, calling on Vincent to step down immediately. "Each of you will have a chance to speak," says Beeston, who's been given a carefully crafted order of speakers. This meeting will last almost four hours, and it will be quite some time before anyone has a chance to speak in Vincent's defense.

Beeston calls upon Pittsburgh chairman Doug Danforth to speak first. It's a strategic choice. Danforth is widely respected for the four years he spent running Westinghouse, where he shed divisions, doubled profit margins, and tripled its stock price. Danforth led a group of local executives who bought the Pirates seven years ago, and their team is on its way to its third straight NL East title and drawing 2 million fans.

But Danforth says the team can no longer afford to pay its stars. Last season it was All-Star third baseman Bobby Bonilla who bolted for the big market Mets. Already this year, star pitcher Doug Drabek and left fielder Barry Bonds, the game's best player, have told Pirates management they will be gone at season's end. No small market owner could miss this message.

The 70-year-old Danforth likes Vincent and just a few weeks ago visited the 54-year-old Commissioner in New York, trying to convince the younger man to walk away. But Vincent wouldn't hear of it, and now Danforth is calling for his removal.

"I personally have no confidence in Fay's leadership," Danforth says. "Players' salaries are too high. Clubs are on the verge of collapse. Media leaks come out of his office, and he's intervened in areas he had no business getting involved in."

And then the dagger.

"Baseball cannot move forward under his leadership," Danforth says.

Four more of the game's elder statesmen—Fred Kuhlmann of the Cardinals, Bill Giles of the Phillies, Stanton Cook of the Cubs, and Peter O'Malley of the Dodgers—all rise and echo Danforth's words. Soon it's Pohlad's turn.

"All Fay is interested in is having the spotlight on himself," says Pohlad, reminding his fellow owners of Vincent's frequent visits to ballparks and his routine of sitting in a golf cart on the field talking to players, answering questions for the media, and signing autographs for fans. How will any of that solve the owners' problems?

"Fay's incompetence," Pohlad declares, "is a cancer."

Nine men speak before Beeston recognizes Bush. "You all are inconsistent as hell," says Bush, reminding them they've all changed their minds about Vincent depending on the issue. "I don't agree with the first nine speakers. Fay makes tough calls, and even if Bush doesn't agree with them, he respects them.

"Fay doesn't play politics. He'll go to court to keep his position, I assure you of that. There's no point in firing him, because he's not leaving."

Boston's Haywood Sullivan and Baltimore President Larry Lucchino also come to Vincent's defense. "He can't be fired," insists Lucchino, citing the game's constitution, "and he won't resign." Mets co-owner Fred Wilpon, who sees the Commissioner as the firewall between his franchise and owners with revenue sharing agendas, pitches a compromise. Rather than fire Vincent, they should convene a committee to restructure the Commissioner's role and the way the game is governed.

None of this makes any difference to Reinsdorf, who pulls out a list he's been compiling for months entitled "Bad Things Fay's Done" and begins reading. He's botched our labor negotiations and George Steinbrenner's suspension. He leaks stories to the media. He even refused to allow Minnie Minoso to come to bat for the White Sox and become the first man to play in five different decades.

"Vincent has done a terrible job," Reinsdorf says. "He's simply incompetent."

On and on Reinsdorf talks, his voice rising and his words coming faster, until almost 20 minutes have passed. Finally, a sheepish look creeps across his face. "I've probably talked too much," he says, sensing that everyone in the room thinks he reached that point long ago.

"That's right," Selig says. "Give him the hook."

Selig rises and turns serious. "This is a very traumatic day," he says, the emotion clear in his voice. "I wrote a memo after the 1990 negotiations which was very critical of the Commissioner. [Houston owner] John McMullen called me and said I was far too easy on him.

"Fay has had an opportunity to propel us forward, but instead he's held us back. I was one of the last to come to the conclusion that Fay must go, but he really doesn't care for the institution. There will be less damage if we make a change and move on so we can propel the industry forward."

When Mike Illitch, the new owner of the Tigers, and Mariners CEO John Ellis speak in favor of the resolution, Selig and Reinsdorf know they have their 18 votes. Beeston collects and counts the secret ballots, though he never doubted the outcome. He's been around Selig long enough to know Bud never brings anything to a vote without first knowing the result.

The final count is 18–9 in favor of demanding that Vincent step down, with one abstention. If Vincent refuses, the Executive Council will decide the next step at the owners meeting in St. Louis six days from now.

National League President Bill White is asked to call Vincent with the news. The conference room doors swing open again, and all Vincent's supporters rush past reporters without commenting—including Bush, who marches quickly behind his wall of Secret Service agents, anger etched on his face.

Beeston emerges and says he'll read the resolution but won't take any questions. The most damning passage: "The major league clubs do not have confidence in the ability of the present Commissioner, Fay Vincent, to carry out the responsibilities of the office of the Commissioner, and under his direction it is impossible for baseball to move forward effectively and constructively."

Done reading, Beeston folds the document in half and excuses himself. "That's all, boys," he says, with a wave of his hand.

The vote may have been secret, but the lobby is abuzz with how it all went down. The Cubs, White Sox, Yankees, Dodgers, Angels, Giants, Cardinals, Phillies, Pirates, Brewers, Twins, Indians, Blue Jays, Rockies, Padres, Mariners, Tigers, and Braves all asked for Vincent's removal.

The Mets, Orioles, Astros, Rangers, A's, Marlins, Red Sox, Royals, and Expos voted against the resolution. Cincinnati's Marge Schott, who got up and walked out of the meeting early, abstained.

"It would certainly be difficult if 18 clubs are asking you to resign," says Joe Molloy, appointed the Yankees managing partner until his father-in-law, George Steinbrenner, returns from suspension in March. "The industry is paralyzed. The hope is that Fay recognizes that."

Several other owners linger in the lobby, speaking with reporters, none more eagerly than Reinsdorf. "Now, for the first time, Vincent can see the numbers against him," says Reinsdorf, who can't restrain a smile while holding court in the center of the lobby. "Before this, he may very well not have realized there were 18. Now he knows."

The questions come fast, and Reinsdorf is happy to answer every one of them. Could the owners fire Vincent in St. Louis if he refuses to resign? "We didn't discuss that today," he says, "but I see no grounds for compromise."

Vincent has already announced he plans to attend the quarterly meeting in St. Louis. What happens then? "He will not be permitted to preside."

And how will this affect the next labor talks? "When we go to war with the union," says Reinsdorf, "I want the Commissioner to have an obligation only to the owners."

True to form, Selig is more reserved—and evasive—than his partner. "I don't have any reaction other than to say the resolution speaks for itself," Selig says. "It was a very, very constructive meeting. There was a discussion of real issues and not personalities."

A reporter asks if today's outcome is a big step toward solving baseball's problems. "Only history will tell," says Selig. "I'm always optimistic."

Another reporter relays the news that Vincent has issued a press release in New York, vowing to remain in office. Selig sighs, answers a few more questions, then gathers up Wendy and DuPuy for their drive back to Milwaukee.

He thinks about how all their lives are about to change. Wendy has been the Brewers' general counsel for the past two years, and she'll soon pick up more of her father's work, especially the negotiations for the new stadium. Bud's still telling the Milwaukee media he'll build a new ballpark himself, but both Seligs know they'll be asking taxpayers to build it once baseball gets its house in order.

He'll send more of baseball's legal affairs to DuPuy when Vincent comes to his senses and resigns. And he'll assume the role of Commissioner, focusing first on picking up the pieces from today's meeting, where there were many bruised feelings. Then he'll start selling his strategy for the coming confrontation with Fehr, this time without worry about interference from Vincent.

Bud is cruising on I-94 when he reaches for his car phone. It's long past time to check in with Lori Keck, his assistant. Keck has been with him since '72, doing the same job she did for Vince Lombardi before the Packers coach left Green Bay for Washington. No one in the Brewers organization, maybe not even Wendy, knows Bud better.

For 20 years, Keck has sat outside Bud's cramped, cluttered office, screening his calls, keeping him on schedule, telling him when his bills are due—and overdue. Keck still remembers the early years when she would pull out a step stool so Bud could peer out the windows along the top of his office wall and count cars as they entered the County Stadium lot, hoping there would be enough paying customers to cover the team's bills.

She knows all the owners who come in to see Bud—Steinbrenner, a frequent visitor, is one of her favorites—and because Selig never closes his door, she knows just about everything that's going on in the game. And Keck already knows the news coming out of Chicago—and what it means—when she picks up her boss' call.

"Good afternoon," says Keck. "Commissioner Selig's office."

She could swear she hears Bud almost swerve off the road.

*   *   *

It's been four days since the owners meeting in Chicago and still no word from Vincent. It's Labor Day afternoon, and Selig's legal counsel Bob DuPuy is spending the holiday sitting at his kitchen table, a telephone pressed to his ear. He's on a conference call with Reinsdorf, Bill Giles, and lawyer David Boies, debating what to do should Vincent show up at the owners meeting in St. Louis two days from now.

All the four men know for sure is that Vincent went off to his summer home in Harwich Port, Massachusetts, to ponder his next move. They've heard Bush, Marlins owner Wayne Huizenga, and a few others are urging Fay to fight. If he does, they all consider Brendan Sullivan a formidable opponent and know a court battle could linger well into next year.

There's another conference call scheduled for later today, and DuPuy is hoping it doesn't completely wipe out his day. Like many in Milwaukee, he's caught up in their baseball team's magic season, and he'd like to catch at least some of today's game on TV.

The Brewers, picked to finish in the bottom half of the AL East, are the surprise team of baseball and enter today's game in third place, just 5½ games behind division leader Toronto with 26 to play. But the future of the team's two best players—designated hitter Paul Molitor and pitcher Chris Bosio, both free agents at season's end—has also been a big part of the team's story for the last few months.

Everyone knows about the team's money problems—heck, Bud and Wendy talk about it almost every day. It was driven home again just a few days ago, when Toronto acquired Mets ace David Cone—and the pitcher's big contract—off waivers. Bud could only tell his players and fans it was a deal he couldn't afford.

Still, pennant fever is alive and well in Milwaukee, and Robin Yount's pursuit of his 3,000th hit has been a nice bonus. DuPuy has been a Brewers fan since coming to Milwaukee's Foley & Lardner in 1973. It's been 10 years since the Brewers made their lone World Series appearance, and, like every other Milwaukee fan, he's hanging on every game.

But DuPuy and the other three men on the line still have an unwanted Commissioner to deal with. They are debating the merits of the strategy baseball's legal team has suggested—Vincent can be replaced, they say, if the owners pay off the $1 million and change left on the last 18 months of his contract—when Giles starts shouting. "Fay's quit!" he yells. "I just saw it on ESPN. It's all over!"

DuPuy hangs up, then dials Selig's number to give him the news. Vincent decided a win in court would be a Pyrrhic victory. Too many of his employers, Vincent wrote in his letter of resignation, "want the Commissioner to represent only owners and to do their bidding in all matters. I haven't done that, and I could not do so." So he decided to resign.

One could almost hear the collective sigh of relief across baseball. In the absence of a Commissioner, the game's Executive Council is now in charge. The Council will appoint a chairman to serve as Acting Commissioner, and it's no secret Selig will fill that role. All that remains now is the formality of the Executive Council vote in St. Louis.

Selig tells DuPuy he is no longer needed in St. Louis, and the lawyer is happy to cancel his flight. There is a pennant race to watch. Yount is three hits away from 3,000. And DuPuy has tickets for the next three games.

What could be better?

The large black limo comes to a stop, the back doors swing open, and out comes Bud Selig and his daughter. They walk briskly to the County Stadium owners' entrance with fellow travelers George Bush, Padres owner Tom Werner, and American League President Bobby Brown trailing close behind. It's September 9, and a few hours ago they were all at the Adam's Mark Hotel in St. Louis, where baseball's Executive Council voted Selig the game's Acting Commissioner. Then they hopped on a private plane and flew to Milwaukee.

And now Bud, Wendy, and their friends are rushing to Selig's suite to see if Yount will rap out his 3,000th hit. The Brewers' average attendance is just under 23,000 a game—16th in baseball—but 47,589 fans jam into rickety County Stadium tonight, hoping to witness history. Selig hasn't seen the place this alive in years.

Yount bats second, and everyone, teammates included, rise to their feet as Robin steps in against Cleveland right-hander Jose Mesa. Milwaukee fell in love with "The Kid" back in '74, when the 18-year-old shortstop hit a game-winning home run in his sixth game. The owner fell in love, too, doting on him as though he were the son he never had. Selig even forgave Yount for threatening to retire and play pro golf in '78 unless he got a big raise. Bud gave him the money, and Robin paid him back, winning one MVP playing shortstop, another playing center field, and later turning down better offers from other teams to remain in Milwaukee.

Yount works the count to 3–2, then fouls off two pitches as flashbulbs pop all around the stadium. Mesa throws his ninth pitch, and this time Yount grounds out weakly to first. Almost instantly, reporters shift gears and swarm Selig's suite in search of details from the meeting in St. Louis.

The game's new leader walks them to the alcove at the back of the media center for an impromptu talk. After years of strolling up and down press row, Selig knows most of the journalists by name, even the national writers in town to watch Yount, and loves the interaction. Tonight the local writers jump in first, asking how he plans to juggle running the game and his team.

"There will be some demands on my time," Bud says, "but it's something that I'm not overly concerned about."

Why would he be? Selig already chairs most of the game's important committees, from labor to ownership changes—almost a dozen in all—something even many of the owners didn't know. "How can he be in charge of so many things?" the Dodgers' Peter O'Malley asked earlier today.

Another reporter asks if the owners plan to lock out the players next spring. "I've heard those stories, and I don't understand the logic of that," Selig says. "But I don't have any further comment."

When will a new Commissioner be named? "I can't predict a time. We're dealing in uncharted waters."

Will he be moving to New York? "My heart lies here, it always has and always will. I'm basing myself right here."

Werner and Bush stand off to the side, watching Selig's performance. Much of the rancor between owners dissipated today in St.

Louis when two Vincent supporters, Boston's Haywood Sullivan and Baltimore's Eli Jacobs, seconded Selig's nomination. Bush, who was livid for days after the September 3 meeting, has also come to terms with Vincent's demise. He'll give Selig a little time, let things settle down, then talk to him about becoming baseball's next full-time Commissioner.

"Bud's got a lot of experience," Bush tells the media. "He has the type of personality that can take a very difficult situation, smooth it over, unite baseball, and move forward."

Selig continues fielding questions until the bottom of the 3rd, when a Brewers official lets Bud know that Yount will be hitting again soon.

"That's it, guys," says Selig, who heads for the owner's loge, just in front of the press box, where he'll pace the aisles—a scene Milwaukee players and fans have grown accustomed to watching for years.

Yount strikes out on five pitches with the Brewers trailing, 3–0, and again in the 4th. Now hitless in his last seven at bats, Yount flings his bat in frustration as his boss continues to pace.

The Brewers have come back to lead 4–3 in the 7th when Yount again walks to the plate. A week shy of his 37th birthday, he entered tonight's game hitting .257, no longer the player he was three years ago, when he went 21–103–.318 and won his second MVP. But he can still hit a mistake, and when Mesa makes one on an 0–1 pitch, Yount times it perfectly, lacing a line drive to right that sends the Brewers flooding out of their dugout the moment Robin touches first base. Reporters can see tears in Selig's eyes as he walks back to his suite to hug his wife Sue and Wendy.

Paul Molitor and Jim Gantner are the first to grab Yount, which is only fitting. The three Brewers have played together for 15 seasons, tying a major league record. A giant "3,000" flashes on County Stadium's scoreboard, and every Brewers player, coach, and trainer gets their chance to congratulate Yount. Of the 17 players to reach 3,000 hits, only Ty Cobb and Hank Aaron did it at a younger age.

It's nine minutes before the fans settle down to watch their team close out what they hope will be its 76th win. But this night will not end sweetly. With two outs in the top of the 9th, reliever Darren

Holmes' back leg slips as he fields a bunt and throws wildly to first. The ball sails past Molitor at first and two runs score, giving Cleveland a 5–4 lead. The Brewers go down quietly, with Yount lining out softly to short to end the game.

The loss drops the Brewers 5½ games behind first-place Toronto with 23 games left. Selig takes Bush down to the clubhouse to meet his players and sip Champagne the team brought in for Yount. In a few hours, Selig and his group will fly back to St. Louis, where tomorrow Bud will begin work on reversing Vincent's realignment decision to move the Cubs out West. And tell Bob Lurie he can't sell the Giants to the group in Tampa.

But Selig wants to hold on to this night as long as possible. They've just witnessed the kind of game that turns a fan into a kid again, worrying only about the fate of his favorite team. The kind of game that brings an entire community together as almost nothing else can. This is the best of baseball, Selig tells Bush as they reach the elevator. This is why baseball can't leave Milwaukee.

And this is why Selig is determined to change the way the business of baseball is played.

Chapter 2

A WHOLE NEW WORLD

October 24–December 9, 1992

GEORGE STEINBRENNER IS in his 14th-floor suite at the Regency, the Manhattan luxury hotel on 61st and Park, where he's lived for the past 25 years when he's not in Tampa. He's sitting at a small table, his diamond-studded 1978 World Series ring flashing on his right hand, a lunch of club sandwiches and skim milk between him and a *New York Times* business writer. It's October 24, 1992, two years and 86 days since Fay Vincent banned him from running the New York Yankees.

Steinbrenner is pleased the *Times* sent over a business writer instead of a sportswriter. It's a sign of respect for his business skills—respect he feels Vincent never showed him. Not even this past July, when Vincent told George he could return to baseball but made him wait until March 1, 1993.

But now Vincent's gone.

"I've never accepted March 1 as the date," he tells *Times* writer Douglas Martin. "Fay made a unilateral decision. Bud knows that."

"When will you ask Selig to change the date?" Martin says.

"Oh, I haven't wanted to bother him," Steinbrenner answers. "He's my friend, and I respect the pressures he's under. But I will. I think I could be a help with the labor negotiations."

Especially since the other owners are going after his money. Again. No, George is not going to talk about *that* with Martin. Steinbrenner hasn't forgotten that Orioles President Larry Lucchino led the revenue sharing charge to grab the Yankees' cable money the minute George was suspended. Nor will he forget that plenty of owners were thrilled when Fay banned him for paying two-bit gambler Howie Spira to get damaging information about his star Dave Winfield.

Fucking hypocrites. The Executive Council knew all about Spira for years and never said a word. And it's not like Steinbrenner was the first owner who paid to get leverage against one of his players. The players union's first leader, Marvin Miller, made that clear when he defended George on the editorial pages of the *New York Times.* Miller wrote about the Yankees' threats to tell Mickey Mantle's wife about the other women in Mickey's life if the star didn't agree to a pay cut.

Of course, this wasn't the first time George was kicked out of baseball. Bowie Kuhn banned him in 1974, when Steinbrenner was caught making illegal campaign contributions and obstructing justice in the Watergate mess. The government fined him $35,000, took away his right to vote—he was a convicted felon—and Bowie sentenced him to 15 months. Ronald Reagan was kind enough to pardon George as he was leaving office, a favor for his friend and fellow former Hollywood actor, Angels owner Gene Autry.

George takes a sip of his skim milk and listens to Martin's questions. Why did you pump cash into your troubled shipbuilding business this summer instead of declaring bankruptcy? "Bankruptcy signifies failure," he says.

People say you used Yankees money. "Absolutely not!"

Will you be voting for President Bush next month? "I haven't decided yet."

What about hosting *Saturday Night Live* last week? "Loved it," says George, remembering when he walked into rehearsal and everyone ignored him. *SNL's* executive producer Lorne Michaels put his staff up to that, eager to see how Steinbrenner would react. George burst out laughing as soon as he caught on.

Steinbrenner shifts the conversation to his hobbies—playing

piano, watching wrestling, driving harness horses. "Driving that thing was the scariest feeling I've ever had," he says. Martin pokes at his sandwich, then asks about the story floating around last March, the one about Steinbrenner selling the Yankees to Paramount Communications.

It was Paramount that gave him the $486 million, 12-year deal for the Yankees' TV rights in 1988, the record-breaking contract that showed baseball what local broadcast rights would be worth in the new world of cable television. "I listened to them," he says about Paramount, "but the deal was aborted."

Martin brings up life in exile again. Vincent hadn't allowed Steinbrenner to set foot inside Yankee Stadium—or any other stadium in baseball—though the Boss was permitted to attend the team's quarterly meetings. Steinbrenner insists he had to learn about player trades in the newspapers. And he still can't believe his employees were forced to sign pledges saying they did not speak with him and submit the documents to Vincent every six months.

It was so bad, he says, that he couldn't even talk about the team to his son-in-law Joe Molloy—the last of his three replacements—at the dinner table last Christmas.

"We sat like two mummies," he says, waving his arms.

Steinbrenner smiles to himself. Of course any decision of consequence flowed through him—George wasn't about to let general manager Gene "Stick" Michael sign free agents or make trades without his approval. And he kept a pretty tight lid on spending during his banishment—he's still fuming about his shouting match with Michael over the $1.5 million signing bonus they gave No. 1 pick Brien Taylor in the summer of '91, then the highest in baseball history. Stick stood his ground, yelling that Steinbrenner drove up the price by talking about the deal to the media.

Steinbrenner put his foot down this past June, paying only half as much for the high school shortstop they drafted, a kid named Derek Jeter. Steinbrenner is still mad as hell at Michael, but he respects his GM for standing up to him. Not many in his organization have the balls to do that.

Certainly not Hank, who was Steinbrenner's first choice to run the team when he was banished. But when Vincent made a fuss about handing off to a family member, George's older son took the opening to cut and run instead of insisting the job should be his. *Typical Hank. If he thinks I'm tough, he should have lived with my father.* George is 62, and still remembers being unable to please Henry Steinbrenner, a man who struck fear in even the toughest hands in their shipyard.

Steinbrenner went through two Yankees minority partners before installing Molloy, a former schoolteacher who married his younger daughter, Jessica, in 1987. Joe's done a good job, and George plans to keep him involved—as involved as anyone is when George is running the show. He also thinks highly of his other son-in-law, Steve Swindal—who's married to Jennifer Steinbrenner—but Swindal is busy running the family's tugboat company in Tampa.

The man Steinbrenner is really grooming is his younger son, Hal, who just graduated from Williams College—George's alma mater—last spring. "He's going to run the Yankees one day," he told the team's chief operating officer David Sussman at last spring's quarterly meeting. "Teach him everything you know."

Steinbrenner and Martin continue talking sports and business over lunch until it's just about time to end the interview. Just one more thing, Martin says. "Will we see a new Boss?"

Steinbrenner leans back in his chair. He is not a stupid man. He still remembers how the fans in Yankee Stadium cheered the night his suspension was announced. He knows he has to tone down the act, if not what he really does behind the scenes. And he still has to persuade Selig to move up the date of his return.

But he's a winner, damn it, and the free agent market is loaded. Barry Bonds. David Cone. Greg Maddux. Jimmy Key. He's going after every one of them. This, however, is not the time to lay out his plans.

"I'm not sure yet what my role will be," says Steinbrenner, who talks instead about the younger men in his family. "I'm very blessed at having four good men to step forward.

"And at least now I will have something to say about how they spend my money."

The Boca Raton Resort and Club sits on a 324-acre stretch along one of Florida's most exclusive coastlines, with a private beach, a championship golf course, tennis courts, and six swimming pools, three of which sit along the beachfront. The lobbies have soaring archways, rows of palms trees, and grand, sweeping stairways that lead guests to world-class restaurants and opulent rooms with ocean views.

It's December 1, 1992, and it's here that Don Fehr will spend the next four days mapping out battle plans for the war he has been fighting with baseball's owners since 1985. This is the union's annual Executive Board meeting, and 47 players—including rising stars like Tom Glavine and Larry Walker and veterans like Tim Raines and Scott Sanderson—sit at tables arranged as a horseshoe, ready to hear Fehr's take on the changes rippling through their game.

"Thank you all for coming," says Fehr, dressed in his usual button-down shirt, jeans, and sneakers. "Before I start, I want to remind everyone here that this is your meeting. The decisions made here are yours, not the staff's."

The owners like to paint Fehr as a pied piper, leading the game's players over the cliff to the ruination of baseball. But the players here think otherwise. Fehr lays out their options, gives his opinion, and they make the decisions. As always, Fehr has good news and bad news for them. The good news: the amount of money pouring into the game has never been greater. A decade ago, baseball was a $300 million business. This season it will bring in $1.6 billion. And the projection for next season is $1.75 billion.

Attendance, at record levels the last several years, dipped slightly with the recession this past season. But union economists think it will rebound nicely, especially with new teams in Colorado and Florida for the '93 season. "With all this good news," says Fehr, "why are the owners so unhappy?"

One answer lies in the packet of information the players are thumbing through: the average player salary hit $1 million this season, up from $371,000 in 1985.

Fehr is famous for speaking in long, dense paragraphs, and some players poke fun by keeping a running total of the esoteric terms he uses, then showing him their lists. Many turn to union lawyers Lauren Rich and Michael Weiner for translation. But Fehr speaks with more clarity as the situation becomes more dire, and right now he cannot be more clear.

The game and the owners are in turmoil, Fehr tells them, and ticks off the self-inflicted wounds: The Vincent mess. The botched realignment. The aborted Giants sale. For all the change Selig promised after he took over, Fehr says, baseball's central office simply "doesn't work."

All the players here know Fehr's low regard for the game's owners — especially Selig — and the reason why. It was 1985 when Fehr, negotiating his first contract as the union's executive director, ended the players' two-day strike and agreed to cut salary arbitration eligibility from three years to two. It was a major concession, costing players not yet qualifying for free agency hundreds of thousands of dollars. But the owners told Fehr they were going broke and gave the union a limited look at their books — an industry overview, without team breakouts — to support their case.

The deal brought swift criticism from Marvin Miller, still very much the union's godfather, both behind closed doors and in the pages of the nation's newspapers. Miller, who plucked Fehr out of a Kansas City law firm to handle the case that secured free agency in 1975, thought the owners had deceived the new union leader.

It turned out Miller was right. Almost instantly, the owners worked together to shut down the free agent market, an act of collusion that went on for three years until the owners settled the cases for $280 million. An act, the union believes, that was led by Selig and Jerry Reinsdorf.

At the same time, the owners responded to the cocaine scandal involving 13 players in 1985 by inserting drug testing clauses into every player's contract. It was a clear violation of the collective bargaining agreement, and Fehr quickly filed a complaint. When baseball's arbitrator Tom Roberts ruled the testing clauses had to be removed, the owners fired him. (He was reinstated a year later.)

Fehr won all three collusion cases and the respect of the players, who from that point forward always thought they had the smartest man in the fight. And Fehr has grown even more cynical about the people on the opposite side of the bargaining table, especially the man leading them now.

Fehr arrived in Boca Raton all but certain that Selig and his allies would soon invoke their option to re-open labor contract negotiations. He tells the players that Selig's negotiator Richard Ravitch is proposing a revenue sharing plan and a salary cap. Not that he's heard this directly from Ravitch—the two men have yet to meet. No, Fehr read about it in the *New York Times* article now sitting in front of each player.

Fehr finishes by laying out the agenda for the next four days. Yes, there will be time for the players and their wives to enjoy the resort. And the annual golf tournament is Wednesday, when Fehr will play in the final foursome to make sure—the players laughingly tell him—his scattershot drives won't slow down play.

But there's a lot of work to be done. They'll all be briefed on attendance figures, television contracts, merchandising money, and a host of other data. They'll leave with the responsibility for briefing teammates and reporting back with any concerns.

The year ahead could be difficult, Fehr warns them. "Expect the owners to test you," he says. The Players Association is in good shape, but the owners are making a mess of their game. And that isn't good for anyone.

Our job, he tells the players, "is to save the owners from themselves."

It's December 9, and Selig is sitting at the head table in Louisville's Galt House Hotel ballroom, where the final session of baseball's Winter Meetings has started. Selig has been coming to these meetings for 22 years, but never has he endured anything as chaotic or troubling as this.

The game's Acting Commissioner opened the meetings three days ago by preaching the need to be fiscally responsible, but clearly no one was listening. Just yesterday, 16 free agents signed big new contracts, making it the busiest day in the 17-year history of free agency. Toronto gave four-time 20-game winner Dave Stewart a two-year, $8.5 million deal. Royals owner Ewing Kauffman, fighting a losing battle with bone cancer, handed David Cone a record $9 million bonus—payable at the end of this month—as part of a three-year, $18 million contract.

And word is out that the Braves will make the Cubs' Greg Maddux the game's highest-paid pitcher later tonight, when they offer him a five-year, $28 million deal.

In the past three days, more than 30 free agents signed contracts worth $225 million, bringing the total for this year's signing period to $365 million. That doesn't include the four-year, $24 million contract extension Seattle gave Ken Griffey Jr.—and he's still two years from free agency.

It does include the six-year, $43.75 million contract San Francisco bestowed upon Barry Bonds, making him the game's highest-paid player. The deal is causing Selig all sorts of headaches: supermarket magnate Peter Magowan has not yet been approved as the new owner of the Giants, prompting outgoing Giants owner Bob Lurie to loudly tell the Acting Commissioner he has no intention of honoring the Bonds deal if Magowan is not approved by the owners. And given the hostile reception the Bonds deal received—Magowan raised the salary bar right after promising not to increase the Giants' payroll—who knows? That just might happen. Selig blessed the deal only after getting Magowan to promise to pay Bonds even if the owners vote to block his bid to buy the Giants.

The record signings also included the three-year, $13 million deal Paul Molitor struck with Toronto—the one that gave Selig nothing but heartache. His team had already lost 16-game winner Chris Bosio to Seattle and second baseman Scott Fletcher to Boston. But Molitor's departure was personal, bringing an end to 15 years of shared experiences—the spectacular play (.303 career average; 412 stolen bases), the countless injuries that cost Molitor more than 500 games, and the support Bud provided when Paul's cocaine habit became public in the mid-'80s.

Of course, losing Paulie was no surprise. Not when Selig offered him a pay cut—twice—after Molitor hit .320, drove in 89 runs, and stole 31 bases this past season. Not when he refused to offer his best player arbitration until just minutes before Toronto announced the deal, a move that got the Brewers a first-round draft pick as compensation. No, Selig knew the minute he decided to cut his team's $30 million payroll by $8 million that there wouldn't be enough money to bring Molitor back.

But that doesn't mean Selig won't mourn his loss. Or that Moli-tor understands. The newest Blue Jay went on the radio in Milwau-kee yesterday and shed tears while talking about leaving town, then held a press conference later in the day and told the media he might still be a Brewer had management acted sooner. That stung. Bud told local reporters he was confident his team would be competitive, but he has no idea how that will really happen.

Selig also doesn't know what to do with Marge Schott. News broke in late November that the Reds owner keeps a swastika armband in her home and has made racist and anti-Semitic remarks around her employees. She showed up unannounced in a near-empty press room today at 8:30 a.m. and read from a short prepared statement that was both apology and challenge. "For any such remarks which were insensitive, I am profoundly sorry and I apologize to anyone I hurt," Schott said.

"But in fairness to me, I wish to add that while I am not without blame in this matter, I am also not the cause of the problem. Minor-ity issues have been present in baseball long before I came to the game."

Selig is sure Schott's comments will make great fodder for the Senate hearing he has to attend tomorrow in Washington. A hand-ful of Senators are once again threatening to revoke the sport's anti-trust exemption, this time demanding that baseball name an independent Commissioner. Baseball is the only pro sport with this exemption, a mistake made by the Supreme Court in 1922 and embodied in the unanimous decision written by Justice Oliver Wendell Holmes, who declared that baseball is not interstate com-merce and therefore not subject to the Sherman Antitrust Act. The exemption essentially allows baseball to operate as a monopoly, granting it many rights, none more important than control over open markets. Keeping a market open allows teams to use reloca-tion as a threat to get taxpayer financing for new stadiums. It also keeps the best markets available for expansion, which attracts the hundreds of millions of dollars so many men are willing to pay to join this exclusive club.

The courts have since left it to Congress to correct that mistake, but everyone in baseball understands that will never happen. If

Congress revoked the sport's prized exemption, what excuse would lawmakers have to hold hearings that give them invaluable face time on ESPN and headlines in the *New York Times*? Still, few owners want to take the chance, so they all play along with Washington's Kabuki theater.

Appearing before Congress is always painful, but nothing can be worse than the secret ballot held two days ago on re-opening the labor deal, a vote that laid bare the internal divisions the Acting Commissioner faces. The big market teams want nothing to do with Selig's revenue sharing plan and strongly oppose re-opening the contract. The small market teams, led by Selig, Reinsdorf, and Pohlad, insist they won't survive another season without both a salary cap and revenue sharing. After several hours of rancorous debate, the owners voted to re-open the contract by the slimmest of margins, 15–13, a vote that sparked immediate speculation they would initiate a lockout—literally shutting down their operations—come spring training.

The final meeting of the week has just stretched past its second hour when Marlins President Carl Barger gets up suddenly and walks quickly toward the ballroom doors. A startled Selig can see that Carl is sweating profusely. Just then, Barger collapses. In a blur, AL President Bobby Brown, a cardiologist, is at Barger's side, performing CPR and mouth-to-mouth resuscitation. Selig quickly gavels the meeting to a close while others race to call an ambulance.

It's a visibly shaken Selig who stands outside the ballroom moments later, speaking to the media. He tells them what little he knows about Barger, who is being rushed to the hospital as they speak. "This is another dizzying event of the last 90 days," he says. Selig tries to focus on business, telling the media that yes, they are discussing realignment, and no, they haven't decided if they will add any teams to the postseason yet.

Selig answers a few more questions when a reporter asks what he thinks about media stories saying his sport is in chaos.

"Anyone who has been in any of our committee meetings knows that is not true," Selig says. "This is not an industry wobbling around aimlessly."

Selig calls an end to questions and rushes off to the car waiting to take him to the airport. The last three months have felt more like three years. Selig won't learn that Barger died that night from an aortic aneurysm until he reaches his hotel in Washington. But no one would blame him if he is already wondering whether his new role is really worth all this trouble.

Chapter 3

INEXTRICABLY LINKED

February 17, 1993

Sue Selig has always known her husband's life revolves around baseball. She knew it when he was "Bud from the West Side" in their high school days, growing up together in Milwaukee in the early '50s. She knew it when Bud's first wife Donna stood up in divorce court in 1976 and said Selig was "married to baseball." And she started living it when she and Bud were married a year later.

Sue jokes with friends about her husband's obsession, telling them when she kisses Bud good night before going to sleep, Bud turns over, dials Jerry Reinsdorf, and starts talking baseball all over again.

But Sue knows her husband well enough to know that this really isn't a joke.

Especially now.

Sue Selig has never seen baseball take over Bud's life—their life—the way it has since he became Acting Commissioner in St. Louis five months ago. It's been baseball all day every day, at home and, more often than not, on the road. She's helped him pack for one owners meeting after another—in Chicago, St. Louis, Louisville, Dallas, Phoenix—and for several trips to baseball headquarters in New York. She's listened to the phone ring nonstop, overheard heated conversations, and witnessed calls that stretch more than an hour at a time.

Bud told her he'd only be Acting Commissioner for six months, not the "two or three months" he told everyone else, but that time is just about up. And she knows he'll never leave the job now, no matter how many times he says he doesn't want it. She's known that all along.

Why should he give it up? Bud's been the unofficial Commissioner for years, as far as she could see. When the other owners had a problem, they turned to Bud first, not the Commissioner. And they always came running to Bud when they wanted someone to talk some sense into George Steinbrenner.

Sue's been Bud's sounding board through all of it, Selig's kitchen cabinet alongside his daughter Wendy and Reinsdorf. They all have their roles to play, but it's Sue who usually hears things first. And she's the one with the hair trigger, firing off an opinion almost the moment her husband stops talking. Bud is the one who takes forever to make a decision, mulling over every problem, slowly pushing everyone toward his position while rarely telling anyone what he really thinks.

The two of them have talked often the last few months about how to convince Steinbrenner and the rest of the big market teams to share their revenue with less profitable franchises like the Brewers. George is one of Sue's favorites, has been since Steinbrenner and Selig were the young turks of baseball back in the '70s. So it pains her when George and Bud go at it over business. When Bud asks her, "Why doesn't George understand it's the only way some of us can survive?" she really doesn't know what to tell him.

She knows Bud will be looking for an answer today. It's February 17, and he's asked the owners to fly out to Arizona, where he has a winter home, for their second meeting of 1993. It's their sixth meeting in the past six months, but this time Selig has put revenue sharing on the agenda. Which must mean he's confident he'll get the answer he wants. Like everyone else, Sue knows her husband never puts anything to a vote until he has enough owners behind him to ensure victory.

Revenue sharing is not the only thing on Bud Selig's mind as he drives toward Phoenix this late winter morning.

Support has grown for making the postseason field larger, so there'll be plenty of discussion about a three-division format for each league and another round of playoffs, one worth millions in TV rights fees. Bud wasn't a big supporter of the idea, but he's come around. Interleague play, an idea proposed by the American League back in the '70s, is also on the table. Bud's dropped his opposition to this as well.

The search committee for a new Commissioner is finally scheduled to hold its first meeting. A host of names have been floated the last few months, including media darlings Colin Powell, George Mitchell, and George Bush. The first two were never in the conversation, but Selig and a few others continue to tell Bush they will back him when the time is right.

After five months and several talks with Vincent, Bush is beginning to understand "the right time" may never come. Selig has the patience to wait for a problem to solve itself, and that strategy appears to be working now with Bush. Karl Rove and many influential Texas Republicans are pushing hard for Bush to run for governor against popular incumbent Ann Richards. The former President's son can't put off that decision too much longer.

Selig's also getting help from his friend in Minnesota, Carl Pohlad, who is leading a group of small market owners determined to put off selecting a new Commissioner until after a new labor deal is done. Given that negotiations with Fehr and the union have yet to even begin, a new deal won't happen until early next year, and Bush can't put off his decision nearly that long.

At least Selig won't have to think about Marge Schott for a while. Two weeks ago, the Executive Council recommended a one-year suspension to discipline Schott for her racially insensitive behavior, and Selig quickly made the ban official. But his difficulties with racial issues are far from over. He was embarrassed three days ago when a *Milwaukee Journal* report showed the Brewers lagging behind most of baseball in hiring minorities and women. And now Jesse Jackson is talking about staging protests on Opening Day in cities around the country—including Milwaukee—if baseball doesn't take concrete steps to improve its lackluster record on minority hiring.

As if Bud doesn't have enough problems on his hands already.

And then there's Howard Metzenbaum. The Ohio Senator, who owned a small piece of the Cleveland Indians back in the '70s, said he will again go after baseball's antitrust exemption if a new Commissioner isn't named soon. *That damn exemption.* Some owners have openly wondered why they just don't give up the exemption and avoid these headaches altogether.

But that's just not going to happen. Certainly not as long as Bud needs leverage for replacing County Stadium, one of the oldest and least profitable venues in the game. Reinsdorf keeps telling Selig he should threaten to leave town, just as Jerry did when he flirted with Tampa five years ago to get a sweetheart deal in Chicago. But Selig prefers to be less direct, telling the media he can't survive in Milwaukee without a new stadium while letting others spread rumors about interest from other cities.

Either way, it will be the taxpayers who will foot the bill. But Wisconsin politicians have told Selig they want baseball to get its financial house in order before spending political capital to help his Brewers, leaving Bud's stadium plans in limbo.

No one wants — or needs — a labor deal more than Selig, and this time he's determined to get it right. No disasters like 1990. He's repeatedly told the large market teams they will have to share their fast-growing local television revenues — something Fehr has been telling baseball, too. But unlike Fehr, Selig insists the large market owners will get these revenue sharing dollars back — and then some — with the money they'll save on players' salaries once a salary cap is in place. And they all know franchise values will rise at least 10 percent, maybe more, with the cost certainty a cap provides, just as they did in the NFL and NBA.

Selig simply turns a deaf ear when big market owners point out the obvious: a salary cap kills their advantage to spend whatever it takes to sign a player. But truth be told, that's Bud's hope and dream. He wants to stop the likes of Steinbrenner from poaching the best players from the less wealthy teams, just as the Blue Jays did when they swooped in and signed Molitor.

Selig knows the union will fight a salary cap, just as they've done successfully in each of the last two labor negotiations. But that's a battle for another day. All he wants today is for the owners to accept the concept of linking revenue sharing and a salary cap, and Selig is determined not to leave this meeting at the Ritz-Carlton without that agreement.

He's convinced the future of Milwaukee and other small market franchises may hang in the balance.

Selig's labor negotiator walks into the hotel's conference room, a briefcase full of memos and charts under one arm, ready to give yet another presentation to baseball's 28 owners. Dick Ravitch gave them an in-depth proposal on revenue sharing late last fall, and all he's heard since then are complaints. You're asking us to share too much money. You're not asking Steinbrenner to share enough money. Who the hell are *you* to tell us what to do with *our* money?

And the owners wonder why they can't beat the union at the bargaining table. Ravitch can hardly believe it's only been 16 months since he signed on as the owners' chief labor negotiator. Some days it feels more like 16 years.

It's not like Ravitch hasn't tackled big jobs before. He ran his family's construction business in the rough-and-tumble New York City real estate market, developing prominent housing projects for low- and middle-income families. He rescued the Urban Development Corporation from insolvency, building tens of thousands of apartments and houses. He turned around a broken-down Metropolitan Transportation Authority, getting the trains to run on time. And he put the Bowery Savings Bank back on its feet before selling it and making an unsuccessful run for mayor of New York.

In the fall of 1991, Ravitch was 58 and mulling over his next move when a headhunter came calling. Baseball is interested in hiring him to change the game's economic system, the headhunter said. Would Ravitch be interested? So he met with Selig, Reinsdorf, and a few others, and they all told him the same thing: their business was broken.

The more he listened, the more interested he became. He bought their idea that a salary cap and revenue sharing would make the sport more competitive and more profitable. And he saw the logic in forging a partnership with the game's players. Yes, a cap meant the players would get a smaller piece of the pie, but increased competition would make the pie bigger, making them all better off. That's the way it works in the NFL and NBA, and both sports were booming.

Ravitch asked what Vincent's role was in all this. "Oh, the Commissioner has agreed to stay out of labor," said Selig, and Ravitch bought that, too.

That was his first mistake.

"Don't think you are going to be able to accomplish anything," Vincent told Ravitch soon after he was hired. "In the end, I'm going to have to come in and settle it."

And Vincent had another warning for Ravitch. "They're going to pull the rug out from under you."

Ravitch ignored Vincent's warning — Mistake No. 2 — then blundered again when he met with Fehr. In previous lives, Ravitch cozied up to union leaders and cut backroom deals that each man would then sell to his own side. But when he pitched the idea to Fehr over lunch a few months into his new job, his negotiating partner bristled. That's not the way we do business, said Fehr, who walked away amazed that Ravitch thought the owners would allow him to make any real decisions.

Ravitch began to understand what was really happening soon after Vincent was fired. He was dismayed to learn how often his new employers would lie to him — and to each other. It's the rare owner who gives an honest account of what his franchise earns. Teams owned by TV networks underprice their rights fees. Teams run by breweries somehow have little or no income to show from beer sales. Teams barter tickets to games for seats on airline flights without reporting the seats as income — at least not to MLB. And the list goes on.

No wonder the owners pushed back so hard when he suggested they share all their financial information.

And now, little more than a year on the job, Ravitch is starting to feel the slight pull on that rug beneath his feet, just as Vincent had predicted. First came the whispers about Selig having talks behind his back soon after Vincent was forced out. Today there's a story in the *Los Angeles Times* that Ravitch's job may be in jeopardy.

But Ravitch and Selig still share a common goal: they both need a path to a deal. So Ravitch arrived in Phoenix telling the media it would be "catastrophic" if the owners could not agree to share revenues, and that's the message he delivers when Selig turns the meeting over to him.

Their game is in trouble, he tells them, and one major reason is clear: the years of labor wars and owners publicly bashing their players have taken a toll. The game's national television ratings are dwindling. The demographics are going in the wrong direction—baseball fans are increasingly older and poorer than those following the NFL and the NBA. A recent Gallup poll shows Americans favor the NFL over their game by a 2–1 margin, and Michael Jordan is lifting basketball over baseball in the hearts and minds of the young and hip.

Baseball, once considered the "affordable sport," is losing that appeal, too, with the cost for a family of four to attend and enjoy a game now $100 or more. And of course the owners' costs are skyrocketing. Payrolls are taking 55 percent of their revenues. By 1994, Ravitch tells them, 263 players will be making at least $3 million— an average of nine on each team. How many small market teams will be able to afford that?

Simply put, it's time they changed the way they do business.

"The union has consistently said that the way to solve baseball's problems is for ownership to get its own house in order," Ravitch tells the owners. "If you want a salary cap, you have to give them something in return, an act of good faith. You *have* to give them revenue sharing."

Ravitch is not a great salesman. Some in this audience find him arrogant and abrasive, his presentations more like demeaning lectures. Few are willing to concede that it's the message they dislike rather than Ravitch himself.

But the man who hired Ravitch knows how to use his negotiator as a foil, and Selig's worked the room well enough to finally get the owners to agree—in principle—to tie revenue sharing to a salary cap. The vote is unanimous. Ravitch has already left the hotel when Selig meets with the media to announce the news.

"It's often been said by the Players Association, 'Let them solve their own problems first. Let them go to revenue sharing,'" Selig says. "We don't have a specific plan—I'd say it's more philosophical. But the clubs took a step today to acknowledge there is a direct linkage between revenue sharing and a salary cap.

"One can't exist without the other. The two are inextricably linked."

Don Fehr is in his corner office at the players union in Manhattan when the flood of media calls from Phoenix begins. Few of the callers are surprised by his response.

"The real linkage is the big market owners won't share with small market owners unless the players give them back the money," Fehr tells Murray Chass of the *New York Times*. "That's the only linkage we've heard about."

He has another sharp-tongued comment for Ross Newhan of the *Los Angeles Times*. "Heck, if Jerry Reinsdorf is such a good friend of Selig's, why doesn't he just write him a check? I'm dumbfounded as to who they think they're impressing."

Fehr hangs up, knowing he's just thrown the owners' plan back in their faces. But he knows something else, too. The union was prepared to go to court to argue that revenue sharing and wages are linked, which, under labor law, makes revenue sharing a mandatory subject of collective bargaining. Selig just saved him the trouble. Now, any change the owners want to make in their revenue sharing plan must also be approved by the union.

The owners don't realize it yet, but they've just given Don Fehr a seat at their table.

Chapter 4

RESURRECTION

February 22–June 13, 1993

IT's been almost seven months since George Steinbrenner answered the late-night call in his suite at the Barcelona Olympics he'd been waiting so long to get. It came from Randy Levine, the last in the long line of lawyers Steinbrenner hired to get him back into baseball.

"What the fuck do you want?" Steinbrenner said to Levine that late July night.

"Boss, I have great news," Levine told him. "You've been reinstated."

"Great," Steinbrenner said. "When?"

"You're back March 1," Levine said.

"March 1! It should have been January 1," Steinbrenner said. "Terrible job."

Steinbrenner called back the next day, praising Levine and his partner, Arnie Burns. Levine had offered Steinbrenner an intriguing proposition when he signed on: If I fail, the brash young lawyer said, you owe my firm nothing. If I succeed, I'm your new outside counsel. George kept his word, and Levine gained an important new client.

And now it's the last week in February, only a matter of days until Steinbrenner's ban officially ends, and the media can't get enough of him.

The slow buildup of interviews that began last October is now a full-blown blitz, with the Yankees sorting through upwards of 400 interview requests. New York papers are running a daily countdown to March 1, and the team takes out full-page ads to trumpet George's return — a picture of a dozen Yankees with their 62-year-old owner standing smack-dab in the middle. There's no mistaking this message.

Steinbrenner promises WFAN he'll spend the first two hours of his return — from midnight to 2 a.m. — talking and taking calls. He sits down one night with CNN's Larry King and in the morning with *Today* show host Bryant Gumbel, telling both that Yankees fans will see a kinder, gentler George Steinbrenner.

He talks about the 11 pounds he dropped from his six-foot-one frame by trading glazed doughnuts for freshly juiced fruits and vegetables. "It's done wonders for my energy," George says. And he makes sure to mention that he starts every day wearing the black terry-cloth robe that former Yankees catcher Rick Cerone gave him at Christmas, the one with THE BOSS IS BACK emblazoned in white stitching across the back. "A very thoughtful gift," he says.

Writers for national media outlets flock to New York and Tampa, and the Boss assures all he'll be different this time around. "I'm going to be less involved," he says. Of course, "less" is a relative term. With spring training already under way, Steinbrenner says he wants to find a place in the organization for retired Yankees Tommy John, Willie Randolph, and Reggie Jackson.

Sports Illustrated asks the question on everyone's mind: WILL THE BOSS BEHAVE HIMSELF? The magazine's cover is an instant classic: a grim-faced Steinbrenner sitting atop a white horse, posed as Napoleon in full uniform, right hand half tucked into his jacket. Yes, George has left his Elba.

"This is the most ballyhooed return since the Resurrection," Jerry Reinsdorf tells *SI*.

A handful of Yankees officials hope so. They've spent weeks in secret meetings, hatching ideas for Steinbrenner's grand reentry. Several options were tossed around before they decided on a two-pronged approach: a limousine carrying a look-alike of former President Bush would roll into the parking lot at the same time a helicopter landed in center field, where a Marilyn Monroe look-alike would pop out with hoops she'd hold up for a pair of dogs to jump through.

All the while, Steinbrenner will be in the stands in disguise, which he'll shed when fans and the media are instructed to look his way.

"You never can tell if there will be a surprise," Steinbrenner tells reporters. "You don't think I'm going to let you guys rest, do you?"

On February 26, the Yankees planning committee is still deciding whether George should dress as a clown or a bearded usher when terrorists explode a car bomb in a parking lot beneath the World Trade Center, killing six people and injuring more than a thousand. Steinbrenner immediately scratches the reentry plan — "It would be inappropriate," he says — and decides to simply fly into Fort Lauderdale from his office in Tampa. The only special touch: pinstriped THE BOSS IS BACK media badges for the 200-plus reporters requesting credentials.

Down in Fort Lauderdale, Steinbrenner's team awaits his return with a mixture of relief, excitement, and dread. Relief that life in limbo — three managing partners, no direction for two-plus years — is finally over. Dread that the turmoil that led to five straight losing seasons — including a 67–95 record in George's last year before the ban, the team's worst since 1913 — might return.

But there is real excitement, too. The Yanks signed free agents Jimmy Key and Wade Boggs, and trades for Paul O'Neill and Jim Abbott have everyone in the organization believing they can contend. "The beautiful part of it is that Mr. Steinbrenner goes to spring training with one purpose — to win it all," Yankees captain Don Mattingly says. "It's a great feeling."

Buck Showalter, the team's young second-year manager, boldly tells Yankees beat writers he looks forward to working for the man who has changed managers 20 times in 20 years. Showalter brought discipline to the lethargy that gripped the Yankees in Steinbrenner's absence and was rewarded with a three-year contract extension last July.

But the team still finished 76–86, just five games better than they did in '91, and everyone knows that won't cut it with George. "I don't think he can put any more pressure on me than I already put on myself," says the 36-year-old Showalter, who's spent his entire minor league playing and coaching career in the Yankees organization. "I'm sure a lot of people will see that as naïveté, but I don't think so."

General manager Gene Michael knows better. The day before Steinbrenner arrives, a reporter walks into Michael's spring training office. "So," Michael says, "are you here to do a story on me getting fired?"

No one understands Steinbrenner better than Michael. A slick-fielding, light-hitting shortstop on George's early teams, Michael has served as a Yankees scout, coach, manager, or general manager for most of the past 25 years. Michael is the rarest of Yankees: he can stand up to George, and he can make the Boss listen—sometimes.

No one is a better judge of talent, and Steinbrenner made Michael his GM for a second time right before leaving in 1990. And the Boss has been criticizing him ever since. Michael wasn't surprised a few days ago when Steinbrenner told reporters, "I'm not real sure about Gene's future." This is nothing new.

Whatever George decides, Michael knows he's built the foundation for a very good team. He signed low-budget free agents Mike Stanley, a big bat behind the plate, and Steve Farr, who flourished as the team's closer last season. He sent Steve Sax to the White Sox before last season for Melido Perez, who became the ace of the staff, and Bob Wickman, who was 6–1 as a spot starter.

He's excited about the trade for Jim Abbott, the 25-year-old left-hander who was born without a right hand and with a 90-plus mph fastball. But it's November's Paul-O'Neill-for-Roberto-Kelly deal that Michael thinks will transform the team. He loves O'Neill's bat and his intensity, and thinks Lou Piniella's attempt to turn the left-handed O'Neill into a dead pull hitter was a big mistake.

"Either he'll hit 40 home runs or he'll hate me," the Reds manager told Michael a year ago. Piniella's experiment was a bust: O'Neill hit just 14 homers and ended up with a career-low .246. After feuding with the Reds manager all last season, O'Neill is thrilled to be in New York.

Best of all, Michael overhauled the roster without disturbing the farm system, which has already produced Bernie Williams, now their starting center fielder. Michael knows that youngsters Derek Jeter, Andy Pettitte, Mariano Rivera, and Jorge Posada all have a good shot at making it to the Bronx. Soon.

"I'd like to be the general manager—I think I've done a decent job," Michael tells the reporter in his office. "But once George gets back, he'll be his own general manager. I'll become more of an aide."

It's almost midnight on February 28, the end of his last day on the outside looking in, and Steinbrenner is about to say hello to WFAN's Suzyn Waldman. Out in Milwaukee, Bob DuPuy leaves his house and climbs into his car, where he will sit for the next few hours. Bud Selig asked him to monitor Steinbrenner's appearance, and DuPuy is hoping his car radio can catch WFAN's signal some 700 miles away.

At 12:01 a.m., DuPuy hears Steinbrenner's voice, and the show is on. George tells Waldman it's great to be back and how much he's enjoyed all the attention. He gives Michael a tepid endorsement, says he expects big things from his team, and tells Waldman he admires Showalter's attention to detail. Then he adds a detail of his own: "Buck was hired because he was affordable."

Welcome to the Boss, Mr. Showalter.

Waldman opens the show to callers, and DuPuy cringes when a man says he holds Steinbrenner responsible for the death of manager Billy Martin, his frequent sparring partner who died in a car crash on Christmas Day three years ago. Several other calls are taken—some welcoming George back, others asking him not to meddle—before a caller comes on and identifies himself as a Mets fan.

"I want to tell you how happy I am that you're back," the caller tells Steinbrenner.

"That's what I love about New York!" George says. "It's a big city, a melting pot, and you can be a Mets fan and *still* be happy that I'm coming back."

"No, you missed my point," the caller responds. "I know how badly you'll screw up the Yankees. And that will make all Mets fans happy."

DuPuy can't help but laugh. And when the two hours are over, he walks back into his house ready to tell Bud he has nothing to worry about from George.

At least not yet.

The sun has barely risen in the sky over Tampa the next morning when David Sussman walks into the headquarters of the American Ship Building Company and finds his way to George M. Steinbrenner's office. This is where Steinbrenner conducts the Yankees' business, and the Boss wants to get an early start with the team's chief operating officer. After his 31-month suspension, Steinbrenner has a lot on his mind.

"Tell me about our sales from signage," he asks Sussman.

"What is the rate card for hot dogs and beer?"

"Give me the breakdown on last year's attendance."

"Are we selling out our suites?"

The questions come, one after another, as an hour ticks away. The punishment Fay Vincent laid down restricted Steinbrenner to the team's quarterly meetings and discussions on major media deals, financing, and any negotiations with the city. No one had been permitted to give George the information he was asking for now. Sussman ought to know—he was the one charged with collecting signed cards from Yankees employees pledging they had not spoken with the Boss.

"Let's start looking at our advertising numbers," Steinbrenner says. "Then we have to leave for Fort Lauderdale."

All Sussman's numbers tell the story of a team struggling to break even. Every owner in baseball is envious of the Yankees' $486 million, 12-year cable deal, but Steinbrenner and his partners took a chunk of that money up front when the deal was signed in 1988. A few years later, the Boss sold off a piece of the contract to a bank for another one-time payout. The two deals left less than $20 million per season from TV—more than enough for most teams, but making it a challenge to bankroll one of baseball's highest-paid rosters.

Still, Sussman loves being part of the Yankees. Like many boys who grew up in New York, Sussman dreamed about playing for his favorite team. Reality was law school, though, and Sussman graduated from Columbia in 1980. He jumped at the chance to become the Yankees' legal counsel in early fall of 1989, despite warnings he received from every team executive during his five-hour interview.

"Let me tell you about George," he heard at the beginning of each conversation. Followed by: You don't want this job. He is abusive. He will treat you like shit. People here live in fear.

One of those warnings came from general manager Bob Quinn—George's 10th GM in his first 15 years as owner. Quinn told Sussman he was the right guy for the job and thought they'd have a great time together. But Quinn—speaking of himself—guessed he wouldn't be around when Sussman started.

"I'm at the end of my rope," he told Sussman.

Quinn quit in mid-October.

Sussman was still in his honeymoon period with Steinbrenner when Vincent started his investigation in March of 1990, but that was long enough to understand what the warnings were all about. Steinbrenner managed through fear and humiliation, and paranoia permeated the hallways of Yankee Stadium, even though the Boss was only in the Bronx for about 10 games a year. When Steinbrenner was at home in Tampa, everyone worried about leaving their desks—even for lunch or a trip to the bathroom—for fear of missing one of Steinbrenner's many calls.

Most Yankees employees understood that Steinbrenner learned all about fear from his overbearing father, Henry, who towered over his son's life until his death in 1983 at the age of 79. George always knew he was rarely the smartest man in the room, but he had a deep understanding of power and the most effective ways to wield it. One of his favorites: giving employees overlapping responsibilities, believing that the inevitable tension between them produced the best results.

It's no different at AmShip, the company Steinbrenner merged with the one he bought from his father in 1963 and built into a powerhouse of Great Lakes shipping. But AmShip's glory days are long gone. The move to Tampa in 1983 could not stop the bleeding, and Sussman can feel the desperation hanging in the air about its uncertain future.

But those worries are for another day. Today is all about being the boss of the Yankees, and there's a private jet waiting to take the Boss to Fort Lauderdale.

It's just after 10 a.m. when Steinbrenner's plane touches down at Fort Lauderdale Executive Airport. "We're walking," Steinbrenner tells Sussman and his other passenger, Tom McEwen, his close friend and sports editor of the *Tampa Tribune,* and the three men head down the quarter-mile path to the Yankees complex. Steinbrenner gets within 30 feet of the main gate before he's recognized, setting off a chain reaction that sends 200 reporters, two dozen camera crews, and several hundred fans scrambling his way.

The two Fort Lauderdale policemen assigned to protect George do all they can to keep him from being crushed. Steinbrenner, dressed in tan pants, a white shirt, and a blue V-neck sweater, answers questions and signs autographs as he slowly makes his way to the field a hundred yards away. A smile never leaves his face.

"I knew there would be a lot of attention," Steinbrenner says. "It makes me feel good. Nobody remembered me when I was a shipbuilder. There's no owner who isn't in it because of his ego. At least I admit that."

The media begins asking questions, and Steinbrenner easily falls back into character. He calls Showalter a rising star who "has no worries." He declines to say the same about Gene Michael, but steps on the rumor that Reggie Jackson will soon become the new GM. "That's not happening," George says. He talks about his interest in Jack Clark, a former Yankee recently released by the Red Sox, and declares his team will challenge the Blue Jays for the AL East crown.

It takes a full 61 minutes for Steinbrenner to shuffle onto the field, where he ducks into the dugout and resumes grilling Sussman. But the briefing session is soon put on hold so George can jump back onto the field, where he's greeted by cheers and a few "George must go" chants. He interrupts the team's pregame workout to pose for pictures with an uncomfortable-looking Don Mattingly, Michael, and Showalter, who wisely says he doesn't mind the interruption.

"I think he kind of brought everybody's intensity level up," says Showalter, showing he's a quick study.

Steinbrenner tells Showalter he plans to address the team tomorrow, then brings 75-year-old Mary Homer, a waitress at one of his favorite local restaurants, out onto the field for a hug. That done, he wades back into the stands, kissing babies and signing autographs, all the while peppering Sussman with questions. There's an owners meeting in Phoenix in two days, and the owner of the Yankees has a lot of catching up to do.

"Go on ahead, I have a phone call to make," Steinbrenner tells Sussman. "I'll catch up with you at the meeting."

The two men have just finished lunch at the Phoenix Ritz-Carlton, where Sussman briefed Steinbrenner on the many issues he'll confront in his first owners meeting since 1990. Sussman understands that the timing of his boss' return is no coincidence. The Yankees executive is sure that revenue disparity is about to force big changes in the game, and there's no way these changes are going to be made with the owner of the game's most lucrative franchise sitting on the sidelines.

And Sussman knows full well that all the talk about revenue sharing centers on George's money. That's what preoccupies Sussman as he walks into the hotel ballroom for the American League meeting and suddenly stops short. Sitting around a large conference table is every AL owner, each wearing gray flannel slacks, a navy blue blazer over a white shirt, and identical red, white, and blue ties—Steinbrenner's trademark outfit. The Angels' Jackie Autry, the lone woman in ownership, is wearing a gray skirt instead of slacks.

Sussman shakes his head and catches the eye of George Bush, who holds a finger to his mouth in a gesture that says, Don't tell him! "Typical Bush," Sussman says to himself.

Steinbrenner blows into the room five minutes later and sits down next to Detroit's Mike Illitch, oblivious to the scene playing before him. Steinbrenner immediately starts talking to Illitch, but he'll be damned if he understands why Mike keeps pointing to his tie. Finally, George takes the full measure of Illitch, quickly looks around the table, then searches for Bush.

"You did this!" he shouts, pointing directly at Bush as everyone breaks up laughing. "I know you put everyone up to this."

But even Steinbrenner can't keep a straight face.

"Welcome back, George," says Bush, with a wide grin.

The idea did indeed come from Bush, who has a knack for getting people to do what he asks them to do. It's one of the reasons he's convinced he'll make a great Commissioner. And yes, everyone has a good laugh. But the joke aside, most of the game's owners feel the same way about Steinbrenner.

They despise him.

Or worse.

And the feeling is mutual. Steinbrenner may not understand the complexities of revenue sharing—that's Sussman's job—but he certainly knows these owners resent his success, even as it puts money in their pockets. None will deny that a strong Yankees team means bigger national TV and merchandising dollars, among other benefits—they are just loath to admit it.

Or have it shoved in their faces. Steinbrenner treats his fellow owners as badly as he treats his employees, and his angry outbursts are legendary. He has called them liars, cheats, and frauds to their faces.

But these are just words. Steinbrenner has given them real reason to detest him. It was George who handed the union its victory in the first collusion case when he was the lone owner to give arbitrator Tom Roberts intimate details of their plan not to bid on each other's free agents. And no one's banged on the table more loudly than Steinbrenner to end every labor stoppage, no matter what it took. (And no one lost more money when the game shut down.)

The owners hate the way he's bid up prices of free agents, though plenty of them have done that, too. But it's the big money Steinbrenner throws at role players that truly angers them. It's a killer when their players point to those inflated contracts to justify big raises when they go to salary arbitration. George simply shrugs it off as the price of doing business—unless, of course, he's the one losing an arbitration case.

The only owners Steinbrenner counts as friends are Selig and Reinsdorf. And it's Selig the others turn to when they hope to stop George from doing something destructive. "So they asked the Golden Boy to call me again," George will say when Bud telephones him to discuss his latest transgression. Selig and Steinbrenner came into the game three years apart, and the two midwesterners have developed a warm relationship over the years.

It was Bud who helped broker peace between Steinbrenner and Reinsdorf when the two men went at each other soon after Reinsdorf joined the game. "How do you know when George Steinbrenner is lying?" Jerry asked a crowd at an All-Star Game event in Chicago in 1983. "When his lips are moving." More egregious was Reinsdorf's suggestion that baseball put a third team in the New York market. The reason: he was steamed about Steinbrenner signing one of his players after promising he wouldn't.

Steinbrenner fired back by calling Reinsdorf and his partner, Eddie Einhorn, the Katzenjammer Kids publicly—and much worse privately.

Both men were fined for their words, which they would laugh about in the years to come. They became dinner companions when Reinsdorf came to New York, though Steinbrenner always remained wary of his former adversary. And in the spring of '84, that wariness cost him. The two were dining in Manhattan when George began complaining about the cash calls he kept getting from his partners in the Chicago Bulls.

"Your partners don't know what they're doing," Reinsdorf told Steinbrenner. "That team should be making money."

"Well, would you be interested in buying it?" asked Steinbrenner, who owned 10 percent of Chicago's basketball team.

Reinsdorf said sure, but didn't give it much thought until he received a call from one of Steinbrenner's partners a few days later asking if he were serious about buying the team. Negotiations quickly ensued, and as Reinsdorf was closing the sale, he kept telling Steinbrenner to keep his stake.

"No, all I do is sink money into that team," he told Reinsdorf. "I'm getting out."

Not long after Steinbrenner sold his stake, the Bulls drafted Michael Jordan, who would transform both the Bulls and the NBA. And now, whenever the subject comes up, Steinbrenner quickly tells people, "Damn Reinsdorf—he fucked me out of the Bulls."

But it's the money his Yankees make that concerns George now, and while he thinks both Bud and Jerry have his back, he also knows that the two men are pushing the hardest for revenue sharing and a salary cap. One measure takes money out of George's pocket, the other all but eliminates the advantage he holds in free agency. There will be plenty of arguments ahead for these friends.

The owners hold two votes before leaving Phoenix. The first endorses the idea of three divisions and a wild-card team. The second approves Ravitch's request for sharing detailed financial information to better understand the need for a salary cap and revenue sharing.

The only one to vote against the latter measure: Steinbrenner.

Every player in baseball has heard the horror stories about playing for the Boss, but it's another thing to actually experience it. Most players on the Yankees roster weren't around the last time Steinbrenner was in charge, so Don Mattingly isn't surprised when one concerned teammate after another asks him how life is going to change. Just play hard every day, Mattingly tells them, and you'll be fine.

But the Yankees captain knows better. Much better. There are only two kinds of relationships you have with George Steinbrenner: love-hate and just plain hate. There is no third option. It's something Mattingly learned the hard way.

If one player appeared destined to be spared George's cruelties, it was Mattingly. Steinbrenner all but fawned over the quiet kid from Indiana during the player's first four seasons, and for good reason. Mattingly won the batting title in 1984, just his second full season, hitting a robust .343. He was the MVP the following season—batting .324, belting 35 home runs, and knocking in 145. In '86, he hit .352, leading the league with 53 doubles and 238 hits—both Yankees records—and won his second straight Gold Glove.

Fans worshipped the 25-year-old player they called Donnie Baseball, and the media routinely called him the best player in the game. Steinbrenner boasted that his young first baseman already ranked with the all-time Yankees greats. Mattingly, it seemed, could do no wrong.

Until February of 1987. That's when Mattingly took the Yankees owner to salary arbitration, a process in which both sides submit a figure, state their case, and an arbitrator decides the winner. Every owner hates the system—which the owners themselves put on the table in 1974—and Steinbrenner is no different. For months, Steinbrenner told writers that no player was worth $2 million a year, the figure most thought Mattingly would request and receive. It was a level reached by only five future Hall of Famers—Jim Rice, George Brett, Eddie Murray, Mike Schmidt, and Gary Carter—and Royals superstar reliever Dan Quisenberry.

Mattingly's just a kid, George kept saying, one who had suddenly gotten greedy. Of course, that's not what he told Mattingly just before the arbitration deadline. "No matter what happens, it's nothing personal," George said. "It's just a business, so don't be offended."

But when the arbitrator decided in favor of the player's record $1.975 million request—Mattingly kept it below $2 million on the slim hope of pacifying his boss—the Yankees star became the highest-paid player in franchise history and George's newest whipping boy. "I'll expect him to carry us to a World Series championship," Steinbrenner declared. "He's like all the rest of them now. Money means everything to him."

Steinbrenner began hurling barbs almost daily, saving his harshest attacks for Mattingly's biggest moments. When Mattingly tied a major league record by hitting a home run in eight straight games in '87—despite a sprained wrist—Steinbrenner claimed the injury occurred because his star put records ahead of winning. When Mattingly was named to the All-Star Team in '88, Steinbrenner called him the "most unproductive .300 hitter in baseball."

The more the Boss beat on Mattingly, the more the fans turned on George. Their anger reached such heights that only minutes after Vincent banned Steinbrenner on July 30, 1990, the news spread through Yankee Stadium like wildfire, with the crowd of 24,037 standing and roaring in approval.

Like most Yankees, Mattingly was stunned by Steinbrenner's suspension. And relieved. But it wasn't long before the calm turned to boredom. Playing for the Yankees was then like playing for most any other team: win some, lose some, go home, do it all over again the following season.

He couldn't live with George, Mattingly discovered, but he couldn't live without him, either.

And now that George has returned, no one is happier than the Yankees first baseman. Mattingly's tired of hearing that he's the only Yankees star never to play in the postseason, and with George back—and spending money—Mattingly feels that streak could end soon. "I know we're going to try to win it all," says Mattingly as training camp draws to an end. "I know that it will be that way as long as Mr. Steinbrenner is around."

Mattingly opens the '93 season strong, batting .328 and rapping out 20 hits in the first 14 games. Mattingly will turn 32 on April 20, and his back problems have ended the days when he regularly lashes doubles and home runs. He hit 14 homers last year—the first time that figure exceeded single digits in three seasons—and with former doubles hitters like Sammy Sosa and Paul Molitor joining the McGwires and Palmeiros as home run threats, Mattingly's lack of power is far more glaring.

Showalter's team is playing good ball in mid-May when Mattingly pulls a rib-cage muscle that sidelines him for 25 games. The team is in third place, four back of Detroit, when he returns June 10 in Milwaukee for a series between two teams going in very different directions.

Mattingly picks up five hits in the four-game series—including his third home run—raising his average to .264. But unlike the last few seasons, he now has plenty of support. O'Neill—shooting line drives to all fields, just as Michael predicted—Stanley, and Boggs are all hitting .300. The Yankees win three of four, and the losses leave Bud's team in sixth place at 27–33. Only one hitter in the Brewers lineup is batting .300—34-year-old backup infielder Dickie Thon. And the heart and soul of last season's second-place team is starring in Toronto.

Steinbrenner's Yankees leave Milwaukee on a high, the heart and soul of their team back and hitting, and all their new players making big contributions. It's the middle of June, and barely a negative word has been spoken by or about Steinbrenner.

The same cannot be said about his good friend in Milwaukee.

Chapter 5

SYSTEM FAILURE

June 25–October 23, 1993

Paul Molitor walks out of the Pfister Hotel in downtown Milwaukee, stops to sign a few autographs, then slides into a cab for the short ride to County Stadium. He's made the trip to the Brewers home field more than a thousand times, but never from the visiting team's hotel. And never with the sense of anxiety now rattling around in the pit of his stomach.

It's Friday, June 25, a date Molitor circled more than six months ago. "I looked at Toronto's schedule right away and saw that was the first time we come to Milwaukee," Molitor told a Brewers beat writer a few days ago. Batting third for the defending-champion Blue Jays before 50,000 fans every home game is easy. But leaving the place he'd spent his entire adult life, where he played ball for 15 years and built a good life for his wife Linda and their eight-year-old daughter Blaire, had been a lot harder than anyone knew.

Molitor thinks about his new life as the cabbie turns onto I-94, County Stadium now just two miles away. He was relieved to face the Brewers for the first time in Toronto back in late May, when he rapped out seven hits, scored three runs, and knocked in two. By the end of the four-game series, Molitor was hitting .340 with seven home runs and 34 RBI.

He'd taken a few hard swings at Brewers management, too. Molitor wondered aloud why Selig waited five weeks to make him an offer last fall and why the offer was almost a million dollars less than he earned the season before. "I just felt they were prepared for me to leave," Molitor told Milwaukee writers.

He swung even harder a week later. "When there's talk that your club's future is in jeopardy and you have a six-year stadium controversy, it doesn't breed confidence," Molitor said. "I don't miss that uncertainty of the future."

Molitor knew his words would only increase the finger-pointing going on in Milwaukee. Disappointed with a team that quickly fell to the bottom of the AL East, Brewers fans are regularly ripping Bud, Wendy, and GM Sal Bando. The normally laid back Bando has been criticizing fans and the business community for not supporting their team, warning that Milwaukee might even lose its baseball team again.

Molitor's harsh words stung Selig, who is in his office now, waiting for his former star. The two men, who haven't spoken since Molitor left town, agreed to meet before tonight's game. It's 2:30 p.m. when Paul strolls through the players' gate and up the ramp to the executive offices on the main level.

"Come on in, Paul," says Selig when he sees Molitor enter secretary Lori Keck's tiny adjacent office. Molitor closes the door as he steps into Selig's office.

"How are you, Paul?" asks Bud.

"I'm doing well, very well," Molitor says as he sits down in one of the two chairs in front of Selig's desk and nervously looks around the cramped, cluttered room. Not much has changed. Bud's desk is still covered with newspapers and half-opened envelopes.

There were many angry letters from Brewers fans when Molitor left for the Blue Jays, some blaming Selig for letting their hero leave, others calling Paul just another greedy ballplayer. And it's no secret there were hard feelings on both sides.

But the two men have always respected one another. That certainly was the case when Molitor acted as the go-between for Selig and Don Fehr during the 1990 lockout. The Brewers even ran a picture of both men on the cover of their monthly magazine headlined PEACEMAKERS—as the labor battle neared an end. Paul has always liked Bud. That's part of what made last fall so painful.

Now it's time to clear the air.

They agree that maybe they said things out of anger they really didn't mean. They talk about the strategy—or lack of strategy—on both sides that probably made the situation worse. But most of all, they agree that the growing wealth gap between the small and big market teams is too often driving the decision making. Especially when a star player in a small market wants to stay but the team just doesn't have the money the big market teams have to pay him. "I miss a lot of things about Milwaukee and playing with the Brewers," Molitor says.

"In many ways it was more difficult for me to let you go than it was for you to leave," Selig says.

"Maybe we could have changed some things," Molitor says, "but there was little any of us could do to prevent what happened."

Both Selig and Molitor are relieved to be talking instead of arguing, and soon they are trading ideas about how to solve the small market problems. They talk about how the television deals for the big market teams dwarf those the small market teams are looking at. They agree that revenue sharing is inevitable. Selig raises the idea of a salary cap, Molitor talks about the players having a say in business decisions if the compensation system is changed.

Almost 30 minutes have passed, and so has much of the tension between them. Molitor reminds Selig that he has a media conference with local writers. "You know, I have a much better understanding now of what you went through last fall," Molitor says as he gets up to leave.

"Paul, I want you to know the door is still open for you to come back and work here when you are finished playing," Selig says as the two men part ways.

A crowd of 39,308, the largest since Opening Day, has filed into County Stadium, eager to see their former star play ball. Many are wearing Molitor's old No. 4 Brewers jersey. Others hold up signs that say things like PAUL, YOU'RE STILL A BREWER IN OUR HEARTS. Some are not as forgiving, including one fan who carries a sign that says SEASON'S GREEDINGS, TRAITOR on one side and MONEY OVER LOYALTY IS THE ONLY REASON on the other.

Molitor is having nothing short of a career year, batting .332 with nine home runs and 49 RBI in 72 games as the team's primary designated hitter. He's stolen 13 bases in 15 tries, stealing the hearts of Blue Jays fans as well. "The calls we get about Paul are overwhelmingly positive," Toronto sports talk show host Dan Shulman tells the *Milwaukee Journal*.

There's a runner on second with one out in the 1st inning when Molitor finally steps into the batter's box. A huge roar washes over the stadium, forcing Molitor to step back out. Clearly moved, he taps his heart and points to the crowd, then up toward Selig's box, and finally into the Brewers dugout.

A full minute later, Molitor digs back in against Milwaukee's Jaime Navarro. The Brewers right-hander gets ahead in the count, 1–2, then fires a pitch that Molitor rifles back up the middle for a run-scoring single. The crowd erupts once again, and Molitor cannot hold back a smile as he stands on first, his heart pumping hard.

The Brewers spoil Molitor's return when pinch hitter Dickie Thon singles in a run with two out in the 9th for a 6–5 win. The ovation for Thon is the loudest of the night. Still, "It's a night I'm always going to remember," Molitor says in the crowded postgame locker room.

More than 45,000 fans are on hand for each of the next two games and watch both Molitor and the Brewers struggle. Molitor manages just a pair of hits, but his offense is barely missed. Joe Carter slams a game-winning home run in the 9th inning on Saturday that moves the Blue Jays into sole possession of first place.

Carter homers again in the Blue Jays' 5–4 victory on Sunday. It's Toronto's 10th win in its last 12 games, lifting the Jays to a season-high 16 games over .500.

The loss is the Brewers' 13th in their last 18 games, leaving them in sole possession of last place in the AL East, and it's the off-the-field games that are most important to Selig now. Watching his former star playing for one of the game's richest teams before huge crowds reminds Selig of what he needs most to keep baseball alive in Milwaukee: other people's money.

And lots of it.

There is help on the horizon. Wisconsin Governor Tommy Thompson has privately told Selig he'll give him what he needs, pledging to use taxpayer money to finance most of a new $207 million stadium. But the help won't come until after the '94 elections. Using public funds for stadiums is never popular with voters, and the constant squabbling between baseball's owners and players has made the idea toxic.

So all Selig can do is tell fans that everything's on hold until the owners agree to his plan for a salary cap and revenue sharing. None of this will be an easy sell. Selig has already summoned the game's owners to the small, upscale town of Kohler, 60 miles north of Milwaukee, to make his next pitch. He has been working the phones nonstop to win over the dissenters—and there are many.

And all Selig has to do is pick up his local paper before the Brewers' final game against Toronto to see Don Fehr already lobbying against his plan. If the owners insist on a salary cap, Fehr warns, the players will walk. Given the wealth and war chests on both sides, he says, the next break in play could last a very long time.

Many Milwaukee fans might not mind if *this* season came to an early end. The Brewers stumble into July's All-Star break at 37–49, last in the division standings and league attendance. When Milwaukee opens the second half losing four straight to Chicago, it's clear Selig's team will remain in the basement for the rest of the season.

Less clear is what the future holds.

"Everybody's wondering if we are going to be playing here next year," says center fielder Darryl Hamilton, the team's union rep. "And I hate to say it, but if we leave, Milwaukee will never have another baseball team."

Selig has few reasons to be optimistic about getting his revenue sharing and salary cap deal in the days leading up to the owners' August 11–12 meetings at Kohler's plush American Club resort.

There have been constant phone calls from George Steinbrenner tearing into Bud's labor negotiator Dick Ravitch, shouting about socialism, and threatening to sue. Steinbrenner is always threatening to sue, but there are whispers about others mounting legal challenges as well.

The truth is, none of the 10 big market teams are interested in sharing more of their local revenues, leaving Selig at least three votes shy of the 21 he needs for an agreement. Bud's good friend Fred Wilpon, co-owner of the Mets, is one of the fiercest opponents. Peter Angelos, the lead investor of the group that paid $173 million for the Orioles, has also argued loudly against revenue sharing. Colorado owner Jerry McMorris, whose Rockies haven't even completed one full season yet, is worrying about creating a welfare state.

"People tend to lose incentive and pride when you make it easy for them to survive," McMorris says.

Fehr, of course, is doing his best to kill Selig's efforts to unite the owners. In late July, the union leader sent a letter to every player, proposing a strike on Labor Day if the owners emerge from what he calls their "evangelical retreat" in Kohler with a salary cap plan. The players rallied around the threat, putting the owners' $260 million postseason payday from CBS in jeopardy. "The only time you can get them to negotiate seriously," Molitor says, "is to have the possibility of a work stoppage this fall."

Selig pushes all this from his mind as he walks up to the podium to open the meetings. "This is an historic occasion," says Selig, repeating his oft-used opening line. Dressed in a somber dark blue suit, Selig keeps his brief remarks focused on the Darwinian choice he says small market teams face every season: do they lose their best players and pile up big losses on the field or pay them and pile up big losses off the field?

The system is broken, he says again. And it must be fixed to give baseball fans what they deserve: hope and faith that their teams can compete. Or even survive. "Change is never easy," Selig says, "but we have to do this for the good of the game. The purpose of coming to this off-site is to put aside our differences and find common ground."

Selig turns the meeting over to Dick Ravitch, who ambles to the podium clutching the notes for his presentation. Ravitch and his staff have spent the last two months compiling baseball's financial data and sending out a series of proposals. The owners, lawyers, and financial experts now sitting in this amphitheater have all had ample opportunity to weigh in.

"This is just a starting point," Ravitch tells his audience.

But a few minutes later, many in the group make their position abundantly clear. Ravitch is barely past his introductory remarks when the owners of the big market teams stand, as if on cue, and walk toward the amphitheater's exit, their clusters of lawyers and financial experts trailing closely behind.

Steinbrenner, gone.

Wilpon, gone.

McMorris, gone.

George Bush, gone.

Paul Beeston, gone.

Selig can only watch in stunned silence as the others file out, one after the next, his hopes for an agreement fading fast.

Common ground?

These people can't even share a common room.

Selig can't help but feel betrayed. Have they listened to anything he's been saying since he took over for Vincent? Isn't this why they keep losing to the union at the bargaining table? All Fehr has to do is hold his players together and wait for the owners' differences to pull them apart. That strategy has worked every time.

But Selig is convinced the players won't risk losing the big salaries they now make by staging a long strike. This is our chance to change the system, he keeps saying. All we have to do is stand together.

Evidently, Selig still has a lot more persuading to do.

Just how much more is clear once the large market owners settle into their own conference room and take turns bashing their small market brethren. Why should these franchises be guaranteed a profit? If they can't run their businesses properly, why should we have to bail them out? Most of them are taking the money we're already giving them and stuffing it in their pockets instead of improving their teams. Why should we give them more?

To no one's surprise, Steinbrenner speaks up loudly and often. And with good reason—it's George who stands to lose the most under any version of Ravitch's plan. The Yankees owner will soon be putting his shipbuilding company up for sale, making his baseball team his family's main business. And Steinbrenner is determined to protect his interests.

Damn it, George says, league rules already give AL teams 25 percent of his cable money for every game they play in New York. They all get big crowds when the Yankees come to town. The AL rules give visiting teams 20 percent of the gate for every game (as opposed to 46 cents for every ticket sold in the NL). Isn't that revenue sharing? Yankees merchandise is always a big seller, and they all share in those profits, too.

"I'm a charitable guy, but I don't like the idea of a socialist state," George shouts. "The Yankees shouldn't be punished for their success."

Every one of the big market owners agrees with Steinbrenner. We're the ones developing new ways to market our teams, they tell each other. We're the ones out there taking all the risks. Where is this sense of entitlement coming from?

Just about the only time the warring factions see each other the rest of the day is when they get hungry and head for the buffet tables set up in the main hall. And when that happens, insults fly and shouting matches begin.

"Remember, it takes two teams to play a baseball game," Montreal's Claude Brochu says loudly enough for everyone grabbing food to hear.

"Maybe we'll just start our own damn league," Boston's John Harrington shoots back.

"When you're walking down the street and someone asks you for money and you give him a dollar," Beeston yells, "he doesn't turn around and then ask you for five dollars."

Harrington and Beeston are considered the reasonable men among the big market group, which now includes the Yankees, Mets,

Red Sox, Cardinals, Marlins, Rockies, Orioles, Blue Jays, Dodgers, and Rangers. Some are surprised to see Texas aligned with the big market teams, but Bush and Rusty Rose, the Harvard-trained brain behind the Rangers, expect a big surge in revenues when the Rangers' new stadium opens next year. And they plan to keep as much of that revenue as they can.

Not every team making money stands with the big market teams. The Cubs and Braves side with the small market caucus, a strategic decision they hope will persuade those owners to hold down the royalties their superstations pay for broadcasting their games across the country in return. Then there's Jerry Reinsdorf, whose White Sox turn a nice profit. Reinsdorf, the hardest of the hard-liners, loves the cost certainty the NBA cap provides for his Bulls. He wants a salary cap in baseball so badly he's publicly stated his willingness to shut down the game for a year—even two—to get it.

It's late the first night when Selig, Reinsdorf, and Ravitch head over to the large market conference room, leaving a trail of reporters at the door as they walk inside. Selig lets Ravitch do the talking, and the result is not pretty. Ravitch can barely get a sentence out before one or another of the owners shouts an angry retort. None of them are buying his ideas.

A half hour later the three men emerge, silent and downcast. They push past the reporters, who watch Ravitch put his arm around Selig's shoulders as they walk back to the small market caucus room empty handed. The reporters soon hear laughter from the room the three men have just left.

Both sides continue their internal discussions well into the early morning hours. At midmorning the next day there is some movement. Each big market team agrees to write down an amount it is willing to put into a revenue sharing pool. The total comes to $43 million—only half of what the small market teams want—and the offer is quickly rejected.

It's late that afternoon when Beeston and Bush walk over to the small market room with another offer: $54 million. The kicker: the $11 million increase from their first offer would be paid by three teams—the White Sox, Braves, and Cubs. All 18 owners in the small market caucus quickly vote it down.

As the last few hours of the meeting slip away, a half dozen black vans pull up to the side entrance of the American Club and leave their motors running. It's 11 p.m., and a handful of local folks have gathered outside the resort hoping to see the famous men who run America's National Pastime. A glimpse is all they get. The owners slip through the double doors and jump into the vans, leaving Selig and Ravitch to explain what went wrong.

"When you're changing established patterns of life, a certain amount of trauma and a certain amount of time are needed to effect those changes," Selig tells reporters before ducking into his car.

Ravitch delivers the only news: the owners will make no attempt to unilaterally impose new contract terms this winter, nor will they lock out the players next spring. Both are empty gestures. A lockout has little support. And management can't change contract terms without first bargaining in good faith—and the two sides have not held a single bargaining session. A court challenge by the union would be a slam dunk.

"Though I'm obviously disappointed that we didn't achieve closure on a plan today, I believe an enormous amount of progress has been made," says Ravitch, looking weary. "Baseball will be played, and I hope everyone enjoys the rest of the season."

Selig has already made calls to several owners by the time he sits down for breakfast with his wife the next day and sifts through the fallout from the disaster in Kohler. He's also spoken with local reporters asking about Milwaukee Mayor John Norquist, who says he's willing to use taxpayer money to build a new stadium. The disaster at Kohler, the mayor says, makes it obvious that Selig won't have the money to build one himself.

Norquist and Selig have clashed for years, and the mayor's offer is nothing new. Norquist wants the stadium built downtown as part of his efforts to revitalize the city. Bud wants it right next to County Stadium, in an empty valley three miles outside the center of town, where food sales and parking fees maximize his profits.

Tell the mayor thanks but no thanks, Bud says to reporters. We'll take care of the stadium ourselves.

"You wouldn't believe how nasty things got in Kohler," Selig tells his wife. But there is a glimmer of hope. The big market teams hate the very idea of revenue sharing, but their meager offer gave Selig at least a toehold, something to work with. And the owners still support him. Indeed, at baseball's quarterly meeting next month in Boston, the Executive Council will tell ownership they've awarded Selig $1 million for his work as Acting Commissioner—more than double what he's earning as president of the Brewers.

And why not? Selig may be preaching gloom and doom, but business this season has never been better. Toronto and Colorado are on pace to draw 4 million fans; five teams will draw more than 3 million, and no team will fail to attract at least a million paying customers. Revenues should approach an all-time high of $2 billion, and the record sale price of the Orioles has raised the value of all their teams. And as long as Bud is in charge, there is no risk of a Commissioner siding with the union in contract talks.

Still, the rebuke at Kohler stings. For the first time Selig can remember, he hadn't locked up the votes before opening a meeting. He won't make that mistake again, certainly not next month in Boston. It's clear Ravitch has a lot more work to do and less clear that he can handle it, so there will be no revenue sharing vote on the agenda. Instead Bud will celebrate his first full year as Acting Commissioner by announcing a new format for 1994: three divisions and a wild-card team to expand the playoffs by another round.

Selig knows he has the votes for that. Even the union is saying it will approve the changes, though why the owners need the union's consent to make changes to their game is something Selig still can't understand.

There is nothing subtle about Lenny Dykstra.

Not the big chaw of tobacco in his cheek, the one he uses to spit streams of brown liquid everywhere he goes. Not the red Mercedes he wrapped around a tree after a night of drinking two summers ago, a crash that kept him out of the Phillies lineup for nine weeks with a broken cheekbone and collarbone and several broken ribs. Not the high-stakes poker games that forced Vincent to investigate the center fielder's after-hours activities.

And certainly not the extra 15 pounds of muscle layered onto his five-foot-ten frame when he walked into spring training this season. Whoa—what did you do in the offseason? the writers all asked when they first saw Lenny in February. Took a lot of good vitamins, he told them, and that was the end of the discussion. Everyone knows that what you see with Dykstra is what you get.

Except for Dykstra.

"I'm a lot different than I appear to be," he's told writers in every city as his performance gets better and better over the course of the season. The writers know how much Lenny loves to entertain, and the line is always good for a laugh.

Who knew Dykstra was also telling the truth?

Kirk Radomski does. Dykstra told the Mets clubhouse man he was using steroids back when Lenny was still playing in New York in the late '80s.

So does Darren Daulton. The Phillies All-Star catcher and Dykstra's after-hours running mate is also on the juice.

And Jeff Scott certainly knows. The weight lifter has been shooting up Lenny with the anabolic steroid Deca-Durabolin since 1991, when the two men met at a bar near the Phillies' spring training camp and became fast friends. Scott partied hard with Dykstra from January through March, charged the ballplayer $100 for each Deca injection, then gave him enough of the steroid to last the season when the Phillies headed north.

But this past winter, Dykstra—now 30 and entering the last year of his contract—told Scott he wanted something stronger. "I want size, dude," Dykstra told him. So Scott gave the Phillies outfielder a new cocktail—two oral steroids and three injectables—monitored Lenny's diet, and pushed him hard in the weight room. Then Scott sat back and watched the buddy he called his "science experiment" blow up.

And Dykstra did just that. After playing fewer than 100 games in each of the last two injury-riddled seasons, the Phillies' leadoff hitter went to the plate more times this season—773 in 161 games— than anyone in major league history. He led the National League in hits (194), walks (129), and runs (143)—something no NL player had done in 79 years. He batted .305 and set career highs in home runs (19), doubles (44), RBI (66), stolen bases (37), and on-base percentage (.420).

Dykstra is sure he isn't the only player using. Jose Canseco has been open about his use of steroids since 1988, when he became the first player to hit 40 home runs and steal 40 bases in a single season while playing for the A's. It was the same year Red Sox fans serenaded Canseco with chants of *"Steroids, steroids"* after a *Washington Post* columnist went on CBS' *NewsWatch* and claimed the outfielder was using steriods.

Congress made anabolic steroids a controlled substance in 1990. A year later then-Commissioner Fay Vincent put the drug on baseball's banned substance list and the A's made Canseco the highest-paid player in the game. Players know that plenty of the new, big bodies they are seeing this summer are on the juice. Their only question is how many.

Pitchers are wondering the same thing. It wasn't long ago when a pitcher escaped trouble if he could hit the corner down and away. Sure, a hitter might get lucky with an opposite-field flare, but paint that corner and you were usually rewarded with a routine ground out. Now even the little guys like Dykstra are rifling those pitches on a line to the opposite field. And some are taking those pitches deep.

Third base coaches are also marveling at what they see. Why do so many fly balls look like something you see at the driving range, hitting a second gear and taking off instead of settling into an outfielder's glove? A lot of scouts are wondering, too. Players they thought were washed up a few years ago are now playing better than they did in their prime. Others who couldn't stay healthy as young players are suddenly iron horses in what used to be the twilight of a baseball career.

(The FBI isn't wondering, though. Canseco, Mark McGwire, and a handful of other Oakland players turned up as users during a four-year investigation that ended in '93 with the arrests of 70 steroid dealers. But athletes weren't targets of their investigation, so the feds saw no reason to talk about steroid use in baseball.)

Home runs are up everywhere this season—33 percent over last year. Bush's Rangers crushed 181 homers, tops in the majors, with

Juan Gonzalez belting a league-leading 46 and Rafael Palmeiro smacking 37. In all, five players hit 40 home runs, and 22 players hit 30 or more home runs—double the number from a year ago. Some baseball execs insist home runs are up because expansion has thinned out pitching, the new parks are smaller, and the baseballs are harder. Or maybe it's all the protein shakes and creatine the players are taking. Seems like every hitter has a blender in his locker this season.

Popping amphetamines—greenies, as the players and coaches call them—has long been an accepted part of the game, a much-needed pick-me-up to get through a grueling season. Most clubhouses have two pots of coffee for players—"leaded and unleaded"—one with amphetamines, one without. But now there are so many sample boxes from supplement companies lying around that some clubhouses are beginning to look like GNCs.

Whatever the reason, 1993 is a season filled with spectacular hitting performances and tight pennant races. Barry Bonds puts up big numbers—46–123–.336—and earns his second straight MVP. Ken Griffey, all of 23, wallops 45 home runs for Seattle, while 24-year-old Sammy Sosa hits 33 home runs for the Cubs, matching his total for the previous three seasons combined. Reinsdorf, who traded Sosa after '91, can't help notice how much bigger Sammy looks in a Cubs uniform. His own 25-year-old star Frank Thomas outperforms both, hitting 41 home runs, knocking in 128, and hitting .317, leading Chicago to its first division title in 10 years.

It is a good season for young and old alike. In Colorado, 32-year-old Andres Galarraga leads the majors in hitting at .370, a full 103 points above his career average, which thrills the 4,483,350 fans— a major league record—who flock to watch the Rockies. Toronto's Joe Carter, who turned 33 during spring training, has another superb season with 33 home runs and 121 RBI. And Carter's new teammate Molitor turns in a career year at 37, batting .332 and leading baseball with 211 hits. His 22 home runs and 111 RBI are both career highs.

Selig is still searching for revenue sharing votes as the regular season melts into the playoffs and the Phillies and Blue Jays advance to the World Series. The business of baseball is broken, the Acting Commissioner says. But there is nothing wrong with the game once the beefed-up players take the field.

Molitor and Dykstra are the most compelling players on two World Series teams that could not be more different. The Phillies, who finished last in the NL East a year ago, are a bunch of rough-and-tumble players who revel in their image as the game's so-called Wild Bunch. The defending-champion Blue Jays are the quintessential professionals, as polite and wholesome as the country they call home.

But pennants are not won on style points, and both teams have strong rotations, star closers, and tough lineups that outscored opponents by more than 100 runs. As for Selig's competitive balance concern, it's a toss-up: the Jays have the sport's highest payroll at $47.2 million; the Phillies have the tenth lowest at $28.5 million—just $4.7 million more than the Brewers.

The teams split the first two games, and with the Series shifting to Philadelphia, Toronto manager Cito Gaston opts to play Molitor at first and bench John Olerud, the AL's leading hitter. Molitor rewards Gaston with a triple, a home run, and three RBI in a 10–3 Toronto rout. Dykstra belts a double and a pair of home runs to give the Phillies a 14–9 lead through seven innings in Game 4, but a run-scoring double by Molitor brings in Mitch Williams. The Phillies closer faces six batters and coughs up five runs, the lead, and the game, leaving Toronto one win shy of a repeat.

Curt Schilling shuts down Toronto, 2–0, in Game 5, moving the Series back to Toronto and Molitor back to DH. The former Brewer smacks an RBI triple in the 1st and a solo home run in the 5th as Toronto jumps to a 5–1 lead. But Dykstra blasts a three-run homer in a five-run 7th to put the Phillies up, 6–5. And that's where the game stands in the 9th when Molitor steps in against Williams with one out and Rickey Henderson on first.

Molitor singles on Williams' third pitch, bringing up Joe Carter, who's been quiet all Series. But there is nothing quiet about this at bat. Williams unleashes a fastball down and in, and Carter rips the ball deep down the left-field line. Carter is racing to first when the ball sails just to the right of the foul pole and into the stands, and 52,195 fans erupt. Their Blue Jays are champions again.

Dykstra walks slowly off the field, his four home runs, eight RBI, and .348 batting average reduced to a footnote. But he'll get his reward soon enough. The Phillies are already discussing a four-year, $24.9 million contract extension, which will make Dykstra the highest-paid leadoff hitter in the game's history.

Molitor's reward is more immediate. He got exactly what he wanted—the chance to play on the big stage—and no player came up bigger. The ex-Brewer hit .500, scored 10 runs, and drove in eight. There is little suspense when the MVP is announced: who else could it be?

Molitor is just about to enter the Toronto clubhouse when he's met by Selig, and the two men embrace. "I know how much you wanted to experience this," Selig whispers into Molitor's ear. "I'm happy for you."

"Thank you, Bud," is all Molitor can get out before the tears begin to flow. He thanks Selig once more, then walks into the clubhouse, where Champagne is being sprayed everywhere.

Molitor is still sitting in his uniform at 2 a.m., soaked with sweat and Champagne, the celebration now going on in venues outside the stadium. A reporter who covered Molitor for many years in Milwaukee is one of the few still working the room. "I was overcome by my emotions," Molitor tells the writer, his voice a raspy whisper. "I'm not embarrassed to admit it. A lot of guys went out of their way to tell me how much it meant to them to see me win."

The two men talk about Molitor's life with the Brewers, the good times and the bad. They talk about what it would have been like to win it all in Milwaukee and how unlikely that would have been.

"I didn't want to say anything before, but now that we've won it I can say it's the best year I've ever had," Molitor says. "I can't explain why at 37 that happened, but my timing was good.

"It just all worked out."

Chapter 6

FOR THE GOOD OF THE GAME

November 8, 1993–January 19, 1994

Gᴇᴏʀɢᴇ W. Bᴜsʜ sits in the back of a black limousine on his way
to a downtown Houston hotel, the notes for his short speech close
at hand. He peers out the window at the glass office towers of the
city's skyline, fidgeting as he tries out nicknames for his new personal assistant, Israel Hernandez. "And your name is now...Izzy,"
he tells the 22-year-old Hernandez. Bush leans back, a satisfied
smile crossing his face as he begins to sing. "Izzy fuzzy? Wazzy
fuzzy? Izzy?"

It's November 8, and Houston is the first of four stops today for
the managing general partner of the Texas Rangers, who will officially announce what everyone has known for months: he wants to
be the next governor of Texas.

Bush toyed with the idea of running four years ago, but the family felt the timing wasn't right. His father was President, and W's
résumé was too thin and his past too checkered. He needed to craft
a new image, and everyone told him running a baseball team was
the perfect solution. They didn't have to push George very hard;
baseball has always been his first love.

And now the time to enter politics is right, but the job is all
wrong. The truth is, Bush would much rather be the Commissioner

of baseball than the governor of Texas. But it didn't take long for him to realize the job was never really available.

Not that Bud Selig ever told George that directly. Instead, the whispers around the game were loud enough for Bush to know he no longer stood a chance of getting the job.

So back to politics it is, and Bush is confident he'll beat Ann Richards come this fall, despite the incumbent's high approval rating. Texas is rapidly turning Republican, and Karl Rove, Bush's chief strategist, has already put Republicans in office all around the state. Rove was the last to give up on Bush's run in '90, but now he sees that four years of being the face of the Rangers have wiped away W's negatives — the failed oil ventures, the unsuccessful run for Congress, the drinking problems, and the rumors of drug use.

The Rangers have never been more popular, and with a talented young team and a gorgeous new stadium to open next spring, the team's future has never looked so bright. And much of the credit is going to Bush, the rare owner who is every bit as popular as his team's many stars.

Not a bad return on a $500,000 investment.

That's how much Bush kicked in when he joined the group that bought the team for $89 million back in March of 1989. The deal gave Bush a 1.8 percent stake in the franchise, with an escalator clause pushing his share to 11 percent once his partners recouped their original investment. He also earned $200,000 a year to team with Rusty Rose, a financial wiz who worked his magic behind the scenes while Bush was out front, selling tickets to fans and cutting deals with business leaders and politicians — the same people he'd need in his corner when he ran for governor.

It was a perfect fit for Bush, whose love affair with the game dates back to his days as a catcher for his Little League All-Star team in Midland, Texas. Baseball was all that mattered to young George, who collected baseball cards, memorized trivia, and told friends he'd own a baseball team one day.

And when he got his chance, Bush threw himself into the role. He pored through media guides and studied statistics in the *Baseball Register* as if he were still a kid. He ate lunch with manager Bobby Valentine several times a week, mixing talk of baseball strategy with questions about the game's other owners and the powers of the Commissioner. He was a frequent visitor to the club-house, where he felt so comfortable that some of his talks with Valentine took place while Bush used the toilet in the manager's office, door open, a copy of *Baseball America* in his hands.

"How's this Double A pitcher in Huntsville?" he'd shout from his seat in the john. "You guys know anything about him?"

He arrived at Arlington Stadium hours before each game, chatting up ticket takers and concession vendors he knew by name. He'd welcome fans at the gate, schmooze the beat writers, then stroll onto the field to trade stories with his players during batting practice. By game time, he was in his seat behind the Rangers dugout, shirtsleeves rolled up and a baseball cap atop his head. He'd root loudly, spit sunflower seeds just as his players did, and sign baseball cards bearing his likeness for fans lining up to meet the owner of the Rangers.

It all paid off handsomely, too. Before Bush, the Rangers had never attracted more than 1.8 million fans in their 17 years in Texas. With Bush, the team's attendance never fell below 2 million. The fans loved the big bats of Rafael Palmeiro, Juan Gonzalez, and Ivan Rodriguez, and they adored living legend Nolan Ryan and hard-throwing Kevin Brown.

And attendance is sure to rise when the Rangers move into their new 49,292-seat ballpark in Arlington next spring—as will revenues, thanks to the new park's luxury suites, club seating, restaurants, and shops. Another work stoppage should be the only thing that can keep Bush and his partners from reaping franchise-record profits.

The deal for a new stadium had come together quickly. In October of 1990, with the Rangers' popularity surging and rumors flying about a possible move to Dallas, the city of Arlington agreed to spend $135 million to build a new stadium, paying the bill by adding half a cent to one of the highest sales taxes in the nation. The Rangers agreed to kick in $56 million, all of it coming out of future revenues from the new stadium.

The stadium deal increased the value of the Rangers franchise by at least $40 million, but there were more gifts to come. Bush and his partners wanted more than 200 acres surrounding the stadium for commercial development, and they soon began making offers to the landholders, most of them farmers and homeowners. If anyone balked, the local government seized the land under eminent domain and handed it to Bush and his partners for pennies on the dollar.

For years, the Republican Party in Texas had held closely to a policy stating that "public money (including taxes or bond guarantees) or public powers (such as eminent domain) should not be used to fund or implement so-called private enterprise projects." Suddenly, the party developed a severe case of amnesia.

Critics of the stadium deal cried "Corporate welfare!" but that did little to damage Bush or his team's rising popularity. Indeed, the sales tax referendum passed by a 2–1 margin. And with Rove making sure reporters always referred to Bush—and only Bush—as the owner of the Rangers, the strategist capitalized on W's popularity in order to pass off the future candidate's business failures and personal indiscretions as part of his "nomadic" years, allowing no further questions to be asked.

By late 1990, everything was going according to plan; George had shaped up to be a strong candidate for governor.

But to Bush, the only thing better than being a baseball owner was being the game's Commissioner. So when Fay Vincent was forced to resign in the fall of '92, running for governor suddenly turned into Plan B.

It was a month or so after Vincent left office when Bush placed a call to his old friend. "Fay, what do you think of me becoming Commissioner?" Bush asked.

"I think it's a great idea," Vincent answered. "You're smart; you love baseball. Is it something you want?"

"Well, I've been thinking about it. Selig tells me that he'd love to have me be Commissioner."

Vincent went silent for a moment. He recalled a conversation he'd had with Chuck O'Connor, then baseball's chief labor lawyer, not long after Vincent was named Commissioner. Selig thinks baseball Commissioner is one of the most important titles in American life, O'Connor told Vincent. He thinks it makes whoever holds the position a historic figure.

"Watch out for him," the lawyer advised the new Commissioner. "He wants your job."

Vincent considered Selig a friend and ignored the warning. Now he knew better, and he didn't want Bush to make the same mistake.

"George," Vincent said, "my guess is that Selig wants the job himself."

A few more weeks passed when Bush checked in with Vincent again. Bush still yearned for the Commissioner's job, but there were people pushing him hard to run for governor, he told Vincent. He was going to have to make a decision about running soon.

"George, I'm worried," Vincent replied. "I still think Selig wants the job for himself."

Bush kept waiting for the right words from Selig, but they never came. And by late February, Bush realized Vincent had been right all along. Bush saw himself as another Kenesaw Mountain Landis, but Selig was standing firmly in his way, and it was time to move on. Rove quickly got the campaign up and running, and by early September Bush announced his intention to run for governor.

Still, there were tears in George's eyes when he was back in Section 9, Row 1 on October 3 for the final home game of the Rangers season. He'd grown close to Nolan Ryan over their years together, and the future Hall of Famer was being honored in what would be the last home game of his career. Damn, George was going to miss being owner of the Rangers.

But now Bush is standing at the podium in a Houston hotel ballroom, a crooked smile on his face as he pauses while delivering his first official campaign speech. He looks out at the roomful of political reporters, confident he will charm them just as he's charmed the baseball writers the last four years.

"The best way to allocate resources in our society is through the marketplace," says Bush, letting his voice rise to drive home his point. "Not through a governing elite, not through red tape and overregulation, not through some central bureaucracy."

Unless, of course, you happen to need some help getting land and a stadium for your baseball team.

*   *   *

Bud Selig arrives at the owners meeting at the Marriott Harbor Beach Resort in Fort Lauderdale on Monday, January 17, with two priorities. He's hoping to celebrate his 17th wedding anniversary the next day with a revenue sharing deal and the Commissioner's job in hand. Now that the Bush problem has solved itself, the Commissioner's post is the easier goal to accomplish, and a plan is already in place to close the deal.

Bud wants the job on his own terms. He wants to keep ownership of his team a while longer—he's promised Wendy a shot at running the Brewers and building the new stadium. Besides, the team is carrying so much debt, a sale would almost be a net loss.

Selig also wants to remain in Milwaukee. And he wants a longer trial period than the year-plus he's already served before making the appointment official, to see how the fans and media feel about having an owner as Commissioner of baseball. His allies have promised to fulfill his every wish.

But a revenue sharing deal is proving elusive. Selig thought he nailed it down a little more than a week ago when two teams—the Marlins and the Rangers—bolted the big market coalition, leaving his opposition with eight votes, the bare minimum necessary to block a deal. Selig's plan called for three times the current amount of revenue sharing and had the full support of the owners' bargaining team. But when the votes were counted, the plan fell one vote short.

One damn vote!

The defeat led to much hand-wringing in Milwaukee, where rumors of the Brewers moving to Charlotte, Tampa, or Portland continue to fly. Selig fanned those flames yesterday at the Brewers' annual Fanfest, telling fans and the media—once again—that the Brewers cannot remain in Milwaukee without help. "We won 92 games two years ago and drew 1.857 million and we didn't even finish in the black," Selig said. "We can't keep piling millions of dollars into the team that we have no chance of recouping."

This is why Selig has no intention of stepping down as Commissioner—and giving up control of the agenda—no matter how many times he insists he doesn't want the job. And he knows this part of his plan is secure, even as he calls a meeting of the Executive Council this Monday night in Florida with search committee chairman Bill Bartholomay prepared to present recommendations for Commissioner.

More than 100 people expressed interest in the job, says Bartholomay, who personally interviewed 46 of them. The list, he says, is pared down to Harvey Schiller, the head of the U.S. Olympic Committee, and Arnie Weber, the outgoing president of Northwestern University. Both men have heavyweight sponsors: Schiller is backed by Steinbrenner, who is a member of the Olympic Committee, and Weber is backed by Reinsdorf and Cubs President Stanton Cook, who both sit on the Northwestern Board of Trustees.

But before Bartholomay can open the discussion, Twins owner Carl Pohlad speaks up, setting in motion a plan hatched by several small market owners. "There are many of us who don't think we should name a new Commissioner until we agree on revenue sharing," says Pohlad. The Council agrees to table the matter for the night, then spends the next several hours debating the structure of the Commissioner's job. When the meeting breaks up at 12:15 a.m., they've decided that the new Commissioner will be in charge of labor negotiations—the very thing they took away from the last Commissioner.

Pohlad ups the ante when the Council meets again Tuesday morning. "I move that we do not bring in a Commissioner until we have a new labor agreement with the union," the Twins owner says. The motion once again ends any discussion of Bartholomay's candidates. And when the meeting adjourns, Pohlad instructs Twins President Jerry Bell to draft and circulate a resolution. By the time the full owners meeting opens a few hours later, Bell produces a sheet of yellow legal paper containing one handwritten sentence:

"The following clubs prefer to delay any action on appointing a new Commissioner until revenue sharing and pending labor issues are resolved."

The resolution is signed by 11 teams—three more than are needed to block any nomination. Six more teams quickly sign up after seeing Bell's list. Given the events of the last few hours, Selig tells the owners, he has little choice but to accept their decision "for the good of the game."

One goal reached, Selig starts the revenue sharing discussion when the owners reconvene. They've all heard Bud's bargaining plan. Get the revenue sharing deal, agree on a salary cap structure, hand it to players, and bargain on the edges, not the fundamentals. Selig knows Don Fehr will have to agree to revenue sharing — he's been asking for it for years. It's the cap Fehr will reject, and Selig's plan is to hold firm, dare Fehr to take the players out on strike, then continue to hold firm.

Selig doesn't think the players will stay out long, not with their average salary now $1.19 million. But if they do, the owners should be prepared to lose the season. And if negotiations still go nowhere, he says, we'll declare an impasse and implement the salary cap and revenue sharing over the union's objection. That is our legal right.

And then the shocker: if the players don't report to spring training, Selig says, they should be prepared to bring in replacement players. It's the same strategy the NFL owners successfully used in 1987 to break the players' strike and install their salary cap.

"But first," Selig says, "be united in our labor strategy."

And the revenue sharing debates begin again. It's midafternoon when Cardinals President Stuart Meyer proposes a compromise that combines the demands of the big and small market teams. The owners in each coalition talk among themselves, then to each other, then back among themselves as one hour blends into the next. Florida owner Wayne Huizenga's wife has prepared an elaborate dinner for them all on a yacht, but there's no way Selig will allow this meeting to end without a decision.

Shortly after 9 p.m., a weary and nervous Selig calls for a vote. This time it's clear that the big market teams have finally consented to a deal. The reporters waiting outside can hear the cheering when the measure finally passes. Selig checks his watch at the final vote: 9:25 p.m. All 28 teams have voted yes.

The doors swing open even as Selig is mixing congratulations with a plea to show up at the pier for Mrs. Huizenga's much-delayed dinner party. Steinbrenner walks out briskly and passes reporters without breaking stride. The Yankees owner decided to be a team player, but he isn't happy about it.

No one is happier—or more relieved—than Selig. His Brewers and the six other small market teams will receive somewhere between $5 million and $9 million a season under this revenue sharing plan. Nearly half the teams will pay between $1 million and $5 million. It's not everything Selig wanted, but it's enough.

"It's a gigantic step forward," Selig tells the media, his wife Sue at his side. "It was hard at first for clubs to understand other clubs' problems. Even this morning, if you had told me I'd get a 28–0 vote I wouldn't have believed it."

There are tears in Selig's eyes as he describes what happened behind closed doors only moments ago. "An industry that has been portrayed as rudderless and aimless did something that had never been done," he says. "I can't tell you the feeling I have inside."

A Milwaukee reporter asks Selig what tonight's vote means for the Brewers' ability to finance a new stadium. "I don't want to get into that now," Selig says. "This is the first step. You can't have any other steps without it."

Another reporter asks about the Commissioner search. "We just agreed on a revenue sharing plan," says Selig, clearly annoyed, "and you're already asking about a Commissioner."

There are more questions, but Selig waves them off. After 16 months, he's won the revenue sharing battle and every owner in baseball now stands behind him as Acting Commissioner. There will be more time to answer questions tomorrow. What's left of this night will be spent in celebration.

"Have a good night, boys," Selig says as he walks away with his wife.

All the owners have left the Marriott when *New York Times* writer Murray Chass takes the elevator up to his room and dials Fehr's home number. The union leader is not surprised to hear from Chass, who fills him in on what he knows of the owners' plan.

"There's nothing like predetermining the end of negotiations before you start," says Fehr, the sarcasm in his voice impossible to miss. "For two years, they've been saying that if they reach such an agreement, the next step is for players to accept a cap. There has not been the slightest suggestion that the players were invited to do anything except say, 'Yes, sir.'"

Which is exactly what Selig just told his fellow owners.

The second day of the owners meeting is reserved for announcements. Each league will have three divisions and an expanded postseason. The playoffs will begin with four best-of-five series, with the winners advancing to a best-of-seven league final. The pennant winners will then meet in the World Series.

The owners have decided that any new labor agreement requires 21 votes—a 75 percent supermajority—instead of a simple majority. This is a crucial change that makes it far easier for Selig and his partner, Reinsdorf, to get their way. All they need now is eight votes in order to block any deal they don't like. And the rumor from the previous night is true: Selig has been drafted to remain Commissioner.

"In no way, shape, or form do I want to be Commissioner or will I be Commissioner," Selig says. "If this promotes stability, it is in the best interests of baseball."

It is left to Bartholomay to call the two finalists. His first call is to Schiller, who is not surprised. During the interview, Bartholomay had asked Schiller why he wanted to be Commissioner. "With all due respect, it already looks like you have your Commissioner," Schiller answered, nodding in Selig's direction. When Steinbrenner checked in after the interview, Schiller told George what he had said.

"I know, I know," the Boss told him, "but please don't withdraw your name. It will make us look bad." Schiller assured his friend he would keep up the pretense, so it is easy to be gracious when Bartholomay calls.

Weber, who was so confident the job was his that he's been leaking his selection to the media, is not nearly as understanding. A stream of invective is launched at Bartholomay after he delivers the news.

The courtesy calls done, Bartholomay goes out to spin the media.

"It has become increasingly clear that we could be best led through this critical time by the only person who fully understands the journey, its pitfalls, and its dreams," he announces. "We have prevailed upon Bud Selig to continue as chairman of the Executive Council, the titular head of Major League Baseball, fully charged to make the leadership decisions this game needs."

As for his search committee going forward?

"I would think the committee would review what we have done," he says, "evaluate where we are at that time, and decide how the process should work."

Or as Schiller said, they already have their Commissioner.

Chapter 7

EVERYTHING TO LOSE

June 14–July 28, 1994

IT'S MIDAFTERNOON, AND, like clockwork, Bud Selig walks through the owner's gate at County Stadium. He's just completed his usual lunchtime routine: the 2.4-mile drive up to Gilles Frozen Custard stand for his regular hot dog with sauerkraut and a Diet Coke, back to his Lexus to eat while reading the local sports section, the short drive to Selig Leasing Company to say hello to his oldest daughter Sari, who manages the family car leasing business.

Then back to County Stadium.

"Hello, Lori," Selig grunts as he walks past secretary Lori Keck and into his cluttered office. It's June 14, and though the Tigers are in town to begin a three-game series, tonight's game is barely on his radar. The biggest game of Selig's career is beginning 700 miles away in New York, where Dick Ravitch is delivering the owners' contract offer to Don Fehr. Twenty-one months after replacing Fay Vincent, Selig is taking his first real shot at reshaping the economic landscape of Major League Baseball.

The final piece of Selig's plan fell into place last week when he nailed down the structure for the salary cap at the owners' quarterly meeting in Cincinnati. By the time the owners and baseball execs finished riding the elephants shipped in by Reds owner

Marge Schott for their annual summer party, most agreed that Bud had done the impossible—he'd united all 28 owners. In the last six months, Selig got them to agree on revenue sharing, a salary cap, and a measure requiring 75 percent approval for any labor deal.

And now he is sitting in his office, waiting to hear Fehr's response to his contract offer. Selig thinks the deal is a good one: a seven-year contract, with the players getting 50 percent of the game's revenues—a lot more than many of his hard-line allies wanted to offer. That translates to $1 billion a season, a sum that will increase as revenues grow. And when was the last time revenues haven't grown?

We want this to be a partnership with the players, Selig instructed Ravitch to tell Fehr. And this is a partnership that should make Fehr happy.

But Selig knows it won't. Reinsdorf always says that Fehr is driven only by the specter of Marvin Miller and a psychopathic hatred of baseball owners. Both Selig and Reinsdorf think Fehr is a danger to the game—and either the union leader will be beaten this time around or he'll wind up putting many of them out of business.

Selig isn't about to let the latter happen, especially in Milwaukee, where he currently has his hands full. Milwaukee Mayor John Norquist has used baseball's shaky labor situation to push harder for any new stadium to be built downtown. It was hard to argue with Selig over the location of a new stadium when everyone believed he was going to pay for most of it. But if Selig insists he needs revenue sharing and a salary cap just to survive, how can he keep his promise to build a stadium with money of his own? And if the taxpayers will be paying most—if not all—of the bill, Norquist thinks it's only right that they have a say where the stadium is built.

Selig is also annoyed with *Milwaukee Magazine* writer Bruce Murphy, who recently wrote that the Brewers were $50 million in debt. "Absurd," Selig told the *Milwaukee Journal*. Murphy implied that a significant portion of the losses came as the Brewers bought back stock from many of Selig's original partners, purchases that gave Bud control of the franchise and boosted his share in the team from 2 to 16 percent. Selig called the higher figure nonsense but did not dispute that he's the largest shareholder. Nor that he's the man in charge.

But what good is having controlling interest when your hands are tied? The average player's salary has gone from $512,000 to $1.19 million in the past five years, a change Selig says makes it all but impossible for small market teams like his to survive. Bud won't open his books like Baltimore's Peter Angelos recently did, but he insists he's lost millions the past three years.

By mid-May, the low-budget Brewers had already suffered a franchise-record 14-game losing streak and enter tonight's game last in the new AL Central division at 27–34. Only one regular is hitting .300, and the pitching staff is in shambles.

But while Milwaukee's season is heading in the wrong direction, the rest of baseball is bursting with great stories. Ken Griffey Jr. (26 home runs), Matt Williams (23), and Frank Thomas (22) are all mounting challenges to Roger Maris' single-season home run record. Thomas is a triple crown threat, batting .368 with 52 RBI, while his team goes toe-to-toe with Cleveland and star outfielder Albert Belle (16–49–.356) for the AL Central title.

Second-year catcher Mike Piazza (13–56–.342), the Dodgers' former 62nd-round draft pick, is headed back to the All-Star Game. Molitor, who'll turn 38 in August, is hitting .342, and Tony Gwynn (.386) looks primed to make his second run at .400. In Montreal, 22-year-old sensation Pedro Martinez (5–3, 86 strikeouts in 80 innings) is keeping the small market Expos just two games behind Greg Maddux (10–2, 1.38 ERA) and the Braves.

Paul O'Neill's superlative hitting (12–42–.417) and Jimmy Key's pitching (9–1, 3.14) have pushed the Yankees into first place, and the AL's best team is once again baseball's biggest draw.

Historic is one of Selig's favorite adjectives, one he uses a bit too often, but no one understands the value of a run on Maris' record or a .400 season—or a winning team in the Bronx—better than the Acting Commissioner. His sport is built on history, and this season is shaping up to be one for the ages. Is he really prepared to give it all up to get what he wants at the bargaining table?

The truth is, no matter how often he tells his fellow owners—and himself—that the players are making too much money to mount a long strike, Selig knows Fehr will attempt to take the players out if the owners don't drop their salary cap demand. That message was delivered once again by Paul Molitor. "If they're banking everything on a salary cap, then I don't think we'll see 1994 having a World Champion," Molitor told Selig's hometown paper. "The only optimism I can find is they've always shown they can make a deal in the 11th hour."

Selig can only shake his head. Baseball needs the changes he's proposed. Yes, the cap eliminates salary arbitration. But this deal gives players free agency after four years instead of six, though teams will have the right of first refusal for those two years. Yes, the deal requires the union to put half their licensing money into the revenue sharing pool—the very money it uses for its strike fund—but Fehr is always talking about partnership. How can they be partners when everything isn't shared?

Fehr will disagree, Selig is sure of that. So the real question is not *if* but *when* the players will strike. Selig is determined to keep the owners from folding this time, and passing the 75 percent rule all but ensures he'll succeed. Losing this season will be a high price to pay—a very high price—but if that's what it takes to change the game's economic system, so be it. How else can teams like the Brewers survive?

Selig takes a small bit of solace knowing the blame for all this will fall on Fehr. He's the one who'll be turning down $1 billion—or more—while taking the players out on strike. And if the fallout breaks Fehr's hold on the players, what could be better? Yes, losing a season would be awful, but this time the reward would be worth the price.

It's late afternoon when reporters begin to call Selig, relaying the union's response to the contract offer and asking for the Acting Commissioner's reaction. "They eliminate salary arbitration, add a cap, and pose all kinds of limitations on free agency," Fehr told reporters. "Put those three things together, and you've cut the heart out of the player compensation system."

Fehr's lieutenants are even more pointed. From the union's

associate general counsel, Gene Orza: "How could the owners believe we could be happy? The revenue they're sharing is the players' revenue." From assistant general counsel Lauren Rich: "If they thought we would be pleasantly surprised, there's a real communication problem here."

Selig listens thoughtfully, lets a few moments pass, then replies. "I think the clubs could have made a much more difficult and arbitrary proposal," he says. "They didn't, and believe me, there were some clubs that really had to strain to vote for this."

Selig hangs up. He's thrown down the gauntlet, and this time he's confident the owners will hold firm.

Let's see how Don Fehr deals with that.

Donald Martin Fehr lives to solve problems. That's what makes him happy, and there isn't a problem he doesn't think he can figure out. On a recent All-Star tour through Japan, he sat down with a group of writers and laid out his plan to solve Tokyo's suffocating traffic woes. No one was surprised. They know he reads almost 200 books a year, most of them scientific studies of how things work. Pull the puzzle apart, then put the pieces together again — problem solved. It's the way his mind works.

Which is why he feels such a deep sense of futility on July 18, when he makes the short walk from union headquarters to the InterContinental Hotel in New York for another meeting with Dick Ravitch and his staff. A cloud has enveloped Fehr's entire team for the past several months, a feeling of being pulled into a black hole with no way of breaking free. A problem without a solution.

It has been five weeks since the owners delivered the contract offer that threatens to stop this season dead in its tracks. This is not a battle over money; that would be easy. This is about competing philosophies.

The owners want to dramatically change the economic system, installing a salary cap that would give them control over costs.

The players want to maintain the status quo, preserving the free market for their services once they play six years in the majors.

Neither side is going to alter its position unless forced to do so.

So there will be a strike.

Will the owners really cancel a season and a World Series? The union's sources among management, agents, and baseball's business partners say yes. The readiness to try the NFL's 1987 strategy is especially strong among the seven small market teams, these sources say. And a few have singled out Reinsdorf as being almost eager to give it a try.

Given the steps the owners have taken—no independent Commissioner, hard-liners dominating the decision making, a supermajority required for any deal—it's easy to see that baseball is rushing toward its eighth straight work stoppage.

Until that point is reached, any negotiating session is little more than theater, designed to preserve legal positions and influence public opinion. They've all been down this road before, and given the history—continued distrust and resentment on both sides over collusion and the $280 million it cost the owners—this battle promises to be especially long and ugly.

That's pretty much what Fehr explained to the union's Executive Board in Chicago on June 16, two days after Ravitch delivered ownership's offer. The owners are talking about wanting a partnership with you, he told them, but that is little more than a smoke screen. "They're trying to provoke you," he said, advising them to be prepared for a worst-case scenario.

Then he handed the owners' 27-page proposal to Lauren Rich. Search hard for any common ground, Fehr told her, no matter how small. Fehr has two goals: he wants to keep the players on the field, and he wants a counteroffer strong enough that any attempt by Selig to declare talks at an impasse and implement his new system would be rejected by the National Labor Relations Board. At that point, the owners would either return to the bargaining table or suffer stiff penalties.

Every union worries about implementation, especially since Ronald Reagan made busting unions acceptable when he replaced the striking air traffic controllers in the early '80s. Unions have been trying to save jobs by offering concessions ever since. If Selig and the owners succeed in getting their terms, it would reverse almost all the rights players have gained in the past 20 years.

Rich, a veteran labor lawyer with a National Labor Relations Board background, spent the better part of a month poring over the report, consulting with economists and accountants, hoping to find something that might lead to a deal. On July 16, she gave Fehr a report that was sharp and to the point: This is nothing new, she wrote. It's the same deal the owners have been trying to get for years. And once again, their reasoning makes little sense.

Rich tore apart their proposal point by point. Management claims the game lacks competitive balance, but only five teams—including the two expansion teams—have fallen short of the post-season in the last 15 years. In all, 19 teams have won a pennant and 12 have won the World Series.

The owners publicly claim 19 teams are losing money, but in truth the sport is doing well. Very well, says Rich, no matter how you look at it—and that's according to the confidential numbers given to them by the owners themselves, numbers the union agreed to keep private. Baseball has turned a profit for eight straight years, clearing almost $800 million. Last season's record $1.9 billion in revenues is 50 percent higher than just five seasons ago. Franchise values have never been higher and will continue to grow, given the twin booms in cable television and stadium construction.

Despite all this, Rich told Fehr, the owners are seeking huge concessions. The 50-50 split of revenues—down from the players' current 55 percent share—and a salary cap would cost the players as much as $1.5 billion over the life of the seven-year deal. Selig is even asking players to hand over half their licensing money, a gift of at least $25 million a season.

And forget about a free market for players. There are now 15 teams at or near the proposed cap, she wrote, meaning more than half the clubs would not be able to bid on free agents. Granting free agency after four years increases the supply of players at the same time the cap is decreasing demand. You don't have to be an economist to know this would be bad news for the players.

The question for teams won't be "Will this player help me win?" she concluded. It will be "How much can I spend?" A salary cap won't promote competitive balance. Or innovation. And management's revenue sharing plan is so poorly constructed it will do little to grow the game's profits.

Given all this, what's in it for the owners?

"The clubs," she wrote, "would have guaranteed profits."

A black convertible pulls into the players' parking lot on the west side of Yankee Stadium, and Don Mattingly pops out and walks over to the players' entrance. He says hello to the guards, takes the stairs down to the clubhouse level, and makes his way to the home-team locker room. He's made this walk for 12 years, but his pulse still quickens every time he enters the Yankees clubhouse. Walking into any major league clubhouse is special; walking into the clubhouse Ruth, Gehrig, and DiMaggio called home is a walk into history.

It's been a good season in the Bronx, a special season. Other Yankees teams over the past dozen seasons may have had more talent, but this one works hard and plays the game right. The Yankees have just returned from a West Coast road trip where they won 10 of 11, the last game a dramatic, come-from-behind victory over the Angels on a Mattingly three-run homer in the 9th. It's July 28, and the Yankees are an AL-best 61–37. Mattingly's first trip to the postseason is a lock.

The home run was Mattingly's sixth of the season. He's more of a singles and doubles hitter now, and after batting third every season since 1984, he's given way to Paul O'Neill, now the team's best hitter. "I would have made the switch a long time ago," he told Buck Showalter eight days ago, when the Yankees manager told the first baseman he would be batting fifth.

The Captain hasn't told anyone yet, but if the Yankees go all the way, this will be his last season. He's now 33, he's tired of working hard just to be an average player, and most of all, his three boys are growing up without him. Mattingly's gone by mid-February and isn't home again until October, so he's missed the basketball and Little League games, the birthday parties and Fourth of July barbecues. He's missed all the things he can never get back.

Mattingly has one more year left on his contract, a year worth $4 million, but he's making $3.62 million this season and has always been careful with his finances. Money will not be an issue. His right wrist is throbbing and his back is sore; the fact is, his body never really stops hurting anymore.

He's had a good career—a great career until injuries stole his bat speed—and if he finally gets to the World Series, he's ready to call it quits. Would he feel different if he were still averaging 27 homers and 114 RBI while hitting .327—Hall of Fame stats— the way he did in his first six full seasons? Who knows?

But his plans could all change soon. Yesterday the owners formally rejected the union's counterproposal for a new collective bargaining agreement. And at the very moment, Fehr is on a conference call with the union's Executive Board, talking about when—not whether—to set a strike date. Given everything Mattingly knows, the players are ready to walk whenever the Board selects a date.

That's why he has already reserved a house on Kentucky Lake in Tennessee. He'll take the summer vacation with the kids he never gets to take. He's not sure how long they'll be out, but Mattingly doubts a strike will be short. He might as well start making up for lost time.

Mattingly walks to his locker—in the far corner, reserved for the team's veteran stars—where columnist Ira Berkow of the *New York Times* is waiting. It's 10:45 a.m., and Mattingly doesn't feel like talking. It's going to be a long day: last night's game against the Red Sox was suspended with a score of 3–3 in the 8th thanks to a persistent rainstorm, and the two teams will finish that game before starting the one already scheduled for this afternoon.

But he agreed to the interview a while back, and this is an opportunity to send a message to fans who think the players are greedy and to any owners who doubt the players' resolve. It's also a chance to remind the younger players that others have sacrificed for them. So he sits down, changes out of his black polo shirt and jeans, pulls on the No. 23 Yankees jersey, and starts telling his story.

"What would playing in a World Series mean to you?" Berkow asks.

"I picture myself making the great play—diving for a ball, getting a big hit with men on base, wanting to know if I could take my game to another level," Mattingly says. "Like Paul Molitor did in last year's Series.

"But where I am now, and how I got here, is more important than me being in a World Series. I have to look at the big picture, not just at the small picture, which is me."

He tells Berkow how the union does a good job teaching players about the game's labor history and how players pass that knowledge along from generation to generation. Former Yankees star Goose Gossage told Mattingly he made $7,500 as a rookie in 1972; now the minimum salary is $109,000. Current Yankees reliever Steve Howe, a rookie with the Dodgers during the 50-day strike in 1981, told him the owners were crying poor then, just as they are now.

"Same story," Mattingly says. "Same script."

And, of course, there's Curt Flood.

"I met Curt last year at a banquet in the offseason, and we talked about how he stood up to the owners to seek free agency," Mattingly says. "He was blackballed, but he opened the door for Dave McNally and Andy Messersmith to sue baseball for free agency."

The two men chat a bit more about the season. Mattingly is having a solid year, batting .295 with 18 doubles and 47 RBI to go with those six home runs. His fielding is once again flawless—there's little doubt he'll take home his ninth Gold Glove.

But the game isn't about stats and awards, Mattingly says. It's about wins and losses. It's so much easier when you are winning. Every play is important. Every game is a big game.

And a strike could wipe that all away.

"I think I'm like most of the players," Mattingly tells Berkow. "If it has to be, it has to be. We can't wait to make our stand after the season. We'd have no leverage then.

"We have no choice but to act now."

Mattingly knows he's signed his last contract. The next labor agreement is for the game's young players and for those who come after them. But Mattingly would never turn his back on them. And he knows the same is true for all the union veterans.

Mattingly is dressed and ready to walk out to the field when word from the union reaches the Yankees clubhouse. The Executive Board voted to strike on August 12 if an agreement hasn't been reached. None of his teammates are surprised. Mattingly's talked to Fehr enough to know that his chance to play in a World Series just took a big hit.

At least now he knows when he'll be driving out to the house on Kentucky Lake. When—and if—he'll be coming back to Yankee Stadium is anyone's guess.

Chapter 8

FEHR STRIKES

August 1–September 14, 1994

It's ALREADY BEEN a long day when Don Fehr walks into his corner office at union headquarters and plunks down behind his cluttered desk. He's just come from taping the *Charlie Rose* show, where he barely controlled his disdain for Dick Ravitch for the 60 minutes that baseball's lead negotiators sat at their host's round table and debated the reasons why baseball is about to go over the cliff.

This was their third television appearance together in the past week, and baseball writers, bored and annoyed with following another baseball labor battle, have dubbed this the Dick and Don Show. A few of the more clever writers are calling the appearances Fehr and Loathing, which, given the nature of their talks, is far more fitting.

It's Monday, August 1, exactly 17 years to the day since Fehr joined the staff of the Players Association, and he's never felt more frustrated. Or helpless. The strike date is just 10 days away, and he's convinced Selig is all but daring the players to walk out.

Fehr also knows that many of the owners are confident the players will give up and agree to their demands, no matter how many times they've been proved wrong. It's always been the owners who cave, but this time there is a difference. This time Selig and Reinsdorf only need six more owners to join them in blocking a deal—and they have those from the small markets alone. Fehr is convinced these owners are all willing to sacrifice this season to get what they want.

Barring a miracle, this season is soon going to end.

Fehr flips through the letters in front of him until he sees one from Ravitch's office. *That's strange,* he thinks as he slices through the top of the envelope and pulls out the two-page letter. He and Ravitch just shared a limo back to their respective offices, which are just a few city blocks apart. If Ravitch had something to say, Fehr wonders, why didn't he just bring it up then?

The letter is dated July 29, just one day after the players set their strike date. And it's addressed to Leonard Gray, the players' pension fund administrator, with a copy going to Fehr. *What the hell?*

As Fehr begins to read, he can feel his anger mount.

"As you know, the agreement to contribute to the Major League Baseball Benefit plan expired March 19," he reads. "Thus, there is no existing contribution obligation on the part of the Clubs.... We are now providing notice that the Clubs are temporarily suspending contributions to the Benefit Plan pending the outcome of negotiations with the MLPBA."

Fehr is stunned. The pension plan, the very thing that prompted players to unionize four decades ago, provides for the health care of players—past and present—and their families. This payment—$7.8 million—is historically the quid pro quo for the players' participation in the annual All-Star Game. A game they played 20 days ago.

How long have Selig and Ravitch known about this? How many times has Ravitch sat across from Fehr without bringing this up? Charlie Rose had asked Fehr about the lack of trust the players have for the owners. "There's a long history of bad dealings" by the owners, Fehr told him.

The owners just added another chapter.

If this is yet another ploy to undermine Fehr, it's an ignorant one at best. Nothing unites Major League Baseball players more than their pension.

Fehr marches down the hall to the union's main conference room, where he finds Lauren Rich and Michael Weiner. Mark Belanger and Tony Bernazard, former players now working for the union, and Gene Orza hear the commotion and arrive moments later. All are as outraged as their boss when they hear the news.

"Dirty pool," Weiner calls it.

"True, but this is a gift," says Orza. "The players will never listen to them now."

Fehr discusses trying to move up the strike date (doubtful) and filing a complaint with the National Labor Relations Board (absolutely). He asks his staff to set up a conference call with the Executive Board for tonight, so he can break the news to the player reps.

Two days later, Fehr sits down and writes a pair of letters. One is to all the players, assuring them the union can and will cover the missed payments and continue their benefits.

The other is to Ravitch, for whom he has lost what little respect he ever had. He accuses the owners of purposely misleading the players about their All-Star Game participation, only to take their money and run. Far worse, he says, the owners are guilty of playing with the health and well-being of the players and their families.

"Why the players would want to be 'partners' with people who do that is beyond imagination," he writes.

Don Mattingly sits in the Yankees dugout, arms spread across the ledge of the cushioned blue bench. The Yankees captain's eyes are fixed on his two oldest sons, Taylor and Preston, who are running around the Stadium's lush green outfield. It's four hours before the Yankees' game against the Orioles, early even by Mattingly's standards, but he wants to give his sons a chance to enjoy the Stadium.

It's August 9, and Mattingly's not sure when—or if—they'll have this chance again.

"It could be my last game," he tells a few reporters who ask him what he thinks will happen if the players strike. "If this thing goes through the winter and into the spring, and they do something I don't agree with, I don't know if I would play. This could be my last day of baseball."

The sense of shared uncertainty is clear two days later when

Mattingly walks into the clubhouse, where all his teammates are emptying their lockers into large cardboard boxes. Players are milling about, trading phone numbers, exchanging autographed baseballs. It looks and feels like a clubhouse on the day a season ends.

George Steinbrenner and Buck Showalter walk into the room, and all activity comes to a halt. "Men, I don't want you to take this dispute personally," Steinbrenner tells his players. Nineteen of them do not have a contract for next season, and many of them are wondering if today is their last day as a Yankee. "This is business," their boss says. "Just stay in shape in case there is a settlement."

Showalter, an intense, driven man in the best of times, is a tight fist of emotion as he steps forward. "I want to thank you all for playing so well this season," the manager says. "This is the best chance this organization has had to play in the postseason since 1981. You all should be proud of what you have done here, even if the strike prevents us from going any further."

A crowd of 37,333 shows up on this gloomy, gray afternoon and watches a seesaw game destined to go extra innings. Toronto jumps ahead, 2–0, then Danny Tartabull belts a three-run, 3rd-inning homer after a Wade Boggs sac fly to put the Yankees up 4–2. The lead changes hands twice more before the Jays tie it at 6–6 in the 8th. But it's the music playing over the Stadium sound system that tells the real story:

The Clash's "Should I Stay or Should I Go."

KWS' "Please Don't Go."

R.E.M.'s "It's the End of the World As We Know It," the Beatles' "We Can Work It Out," and Elton John's "Don't Go Breaking My Heart."

Writers work the phones as the innings slip by. Baltimore owner Peter Angelos tells the *New York Times* he thinks there's a little bit of movement, but says, "I don't know where it's coming from." Colorado owner Jerry McMorris says he believes the salary cap is negotiable. Bud Selig says McMorris is dead wrong.

A handful of writers walk over to the owner's box to seek out Steinbrenner, who creates a mini stir. "Ravitch needs to drop the competitive balance argument given [that] Montreal has the second-lowest payroll and the game's best record," says Steinbrenner. But the Yankees owner is beginning to get worked up when he's asked if he's breaking ranks with Selig.

"I do not intend to show any split in this group," says George. "Bud Selig is leading this ship, and I'm tired of the harpooning and hits he's taking. My interests are being represented."

The game is almost four hours in when Ed Sprague leads off the 13th with a line drive over the wall in left, putting Toronto up, 8–7. When New York's Matt Nokes flies out to center, the Yankees walk off the field with their fifth loss in the last six games. Still, if this is the end of the season, their 70–43 record is second only to Montreal (74–40) for the best in baseball.

The players and coaches finish packing in a quiet clubhouse. O'Neill, whose .359 average leads the league, stuffs baseball cards in his duffel bag and leaves. Showalter asks writers if he's supposed to give away his hat, a season-ending baseball tradition. Mattingly puts three gloves in his bag, looks around the clubhouse one last time, and walks out.

The scene is the same in clubhouses across the country, a season full of sterling performances cut short. In Denver, Greg Maddux wins his 16th game, a three-hit shutout that lowers his ERA to 1.56. In Houston, the Padres' Tony Gwynn raps out three hits to raise his average to .394, the highest since Ted Williams hit .406 in 1941.

Matt Williams, who hit his major league–leading 43rd homer in the Giants' final game in Chicago yesterday, cleans out his locker in a somber Candlestick Park clubhouse. Frank Thomas is doing the same in Chicago. Thomas' line: 38–101–.353. "I picked the wrong season to have a career year," he says.

The Mariners-A's game, last on the schedule, gives baseball fans one final glimpse of what they will be missing. Seattle's Ken Griffey Jr. is the game's crown jewel. Already a six-year veteran at 24, Junior has 171 career home runs, putting him on track to join the big three: Mays (660), Ruth (714), and Aaron (755).

Home run No. 172 comes in style: a grand slam to deep right-center field, giving him 40 home runs and 90 RBI to go with his .323 batting average. The runs are more than enough to nail down Randy Johnson's 13th victory. The Big Unit strikes out 15, giving him a major league–leading 204 in 172 innings.

It's 9:45 p.m. PDT when Ernie Young swings and misses John-son's final pitch. As the fans file out of Oakland Coliseum, no one knows when they'll see another pitch thrown. But most of them know whom they will blame for laying waste to this terrific season.

Bud Selig and Don Fehr.

Nothing Selig and Fehr do over the next few weeks will endear them to baseball fans. Selig immediately issues a gag order—enforceable by a $100,000 fine—to keep his side in line. He sees no reason to give Fehr any help holding the players together. Nego-tiators on both sides agree to bring owners and players to a meeting in New York with federal mediator John Calhoun Wells in late August, but after two days the discourse is so rancorous that Wells says he has no intention of holding another meeting any time soon.

Selig ratchets up the pressure on September 2 by declaring he'll have to cancel the season and World Series unless a deal is reached within the next seven days. Four meetingless days later, Fehr announces he's filing a complaint with the National Labor Relations Board over the owners' failure to make their $7.8 million pension fund payment.

"It is not unexpected," says the owners' outside counsel Chuck O'Connor. Though Ravitch has not been formally fired, Selig has pushed him aside in favor of O'Connor, a lawyer from Morgan, Lewis & Bockius. "We feel we are well within our legal rights," O'Connor says.

As time runs short, Selig shoots down rumors that 19 owners are ready to drop their salary cap demand—two less than the num-ber needed to end the strike. On September 7, he sends a small contingent to New York to meet with Fehr. Most of the talk focuses on a luxury tax plan, an idea that first emerged in late August as a replacement for the salary cap. The plan penalizes teams with pay-rolls over a predetermined threshold, with much depending on where the threshold is set and the size of the tax. Some on both sides leave the meeting believing—praying?—that a hint of prog-ress may be emerging.

At 11 a.m. the next day, Dodgers pitcher Orel Hershiser, Pittsburgh shortstop Jay Bell, Texas pitcher Kevin Brown, and Oakland catcher Terry Steinbach meet Lauren Rich, Michael Weiner, and Steve Fehr at union headquarters. Together they walk the four blocks to MLB headquarters at 245 Park Avenue—the media in tow—and hand-deliver a new proposal. The offer places a tax on payrolls and revenues, transferring about $50 million from big market teams to small market teams. There is no mention of a cap.

But what little optimism these talks generate quickly fades. Selig flies into New York the next day—September 9, his deadline for a new agreement—and attends his first bargaining session. He listens while Colorado owner Jerry McMorris, Boston's John Harrington, and others discuss the tax plan with Fehr and his lawyers.

When he's heard enough, Selig tells Fehr he's not ready to cancel the season, but the union's offer just isn't good enough. Moments later, Selig says the same thing to the media. "Unfortunately," he says, "it's our judgment that this proposal was unresponsive to the long-term interests of baseball."

Then he slips off for a private meeting with Fehr, Molitor, and Rich. But he has nothing new to say. "We want cost certainty," Selig tells Fehr. "You have a few more days to give us what we need. If you don't, the season is over." The meeting lasts a matter of minutes.

His message delivered, Selig leaves for the airport, where a private jet awaits to take him back to Milwaukee. His wife only has to look at the stress etched on Bud's face when he arrives home to know where things stand. Selig is determined to win, but going down in history as the man who shut down baseball—even though he thinks it's Fehr who deserves the blame—weighs on him heavily.

Selig spends the last weekend of the baseball season at football games. He's at the Packers game on Sunday, telling reporters that fans at County Stadium are urging him not to give in. One night later, he's interviewed at halftime on *Monday Night Football* and delivers the bad news.

"We're either very close to the end or within a day or two," Selig tells Al Michaels.

Selig continues to work the phones, making sure his side remains united while keeping track of back-channel talks between Fehr and McMorris over a luxury tax plan. The Rockies owner carries the conflicting hopes of both sides—Selig thinks McMorris can talk sense into the union leader; Fehr thinks McMorris can talk sense into the Acting Commissioner. Sadly, McMorris never bridges the gap.

Fehr spends Monday in a four-hour meeting in New York with the players on the Executive Board. He makes sure the first checks from the $200 million strike fund—as much as $10,000 to almost 1,400 current and former players—are ready to go out on September 15. He double-checks that the conference-call network will remain intact when the season is shut down and that players know about the meetings he'll hold across the country in the coming weeks.

When this meeting comes to a close, Fehr delivers his own message. "It doesn't matter what I say—Bud will do what he wants to do," he tells the media. "The notion that he cares the slightest about what we say is nonsense. It's all pretense.

"It'll be tragic if the playoffs and World Series go down. But this has not been of the players' making."

With Yom Kippur, the Jewish day of atonement, looming on Thursday, it is obvious the owners will cancel the season on Wednesday, September 14. Selig makes two important calls on September 12. One is to Steinbrenner, letting George know the Executive Board is preparing a statement announcing that the season will be canceled the next day. He tells Steinbrenner how disappointed he is that it's come to this, especially with the Yankees in first place.

The other call is to Fehr. It's over, he tells the union leader. We've run out of time.

"I'd like to make this a joint announcement," Selig tells Fehr.

"Bud, I'm not going to help you do this, you have to do it yourself," Fehr says. "Our job is to get an agreement. If you want to pull down the World Series, that's your responsibility, not mine."

All that remains now is a conference call with Selig's fellow owners. In an effort to shield Bud, they decide to issue a joint statement from New York and then conduct media conferences in their own cities. One thing they won't discuss: Harrington's suggestion in the *Boston Globe* that ownership will use replacement players next spring if the strike isn't over. There will be time for talk like that soon enough.

It's just past noon on September 14 when Selig walks into the Gilles Frozen Custard stand and orders his hot dog and Diet Coke. This meal will be eaten on the drive back to his office at County Stadium. By now the four-paragraph statement announcing the end of the season has been released, signed by 26 of the 28 clubs. Marge Schott refused to sign; she wanted to finish the season with minor leaguers. Angelos refused as well, explaining in a letter to Selig that while he agrees with the decision, he feels it is counterproductive to place all the blame on the players.

Which is precisely what Bud does.

The clubs, Selig says in the statement, made a reasonable offer to the players for $1 billion in salary and benefits. "The union refused to bargain with us over costs and took a hard-line position that the clubs would fold, as they had in past negotiations," Selig says. "That was a terrible mistake, one for which all of us must pay."

Selig makes his way to County Stadium's executive dining room, the only place in the ancient building large enough to hold all the reporters and camera crews who showed up to record history. Players have missed 669 games. The sterling seasons by Gwynn, Griffey, and so many others are now faded memories. Upwards of $800 million has already been lost by both sides combined, with far more losses to come.

And for the first time since 1904, the World Series will not be played.

"It is very hard to articulate the poignancy of this moment," Selig says. "This is a failure of so much. Lest anybody not understand, there can't be any joy on any side."

The Acting Commissioner insists that the game could not go on without solving its problems. Yes, the short-term pain is intense. But when a solution is finally found, it will all be worth it. And no, shutting down the season was not the owners' strategy from the start.

"Despite the view that it was some predetermined plot, it was far from that," Selig says. "We have to make a deal soon and start playing baseball again."

In New York, the man Selig blames for baseball's problems is delivering his version of what's just transpired. It's hard to escape the irony of the location Fehr has chosen—the InterContinental Hotel, site of so many fruitless bargaining sessions. The union leader walks up to the podium, shakes his head, and wraps up the day's event succinctly.

"Anticlimactic," says Fehr, squinting into the bank of TV lights. "Anticlimactic in the extreme."

No, Fehr is not surprised. He's been planning for this day for months—years, really—hoping it would never arrive. But now that it has, it's almost impossible to think that what happened today was not inevitable.

"Bud Selig's words and behavior in the last several days have been accompanied by such expressions of finality that it's obvious he wants you and I—and all the fans—to understand the Lords of Baseball have had their say," says Fehr, sounding more resigned than angry.

"When people think back to what the final image of the 1994 season will be, it may be Bud Selig at a press conference in Milwaukee, protesting pain and gnashing teeth, but nevertheless going ahead and dashing the hopes and dreams of so many people."

PART II

ART OF THE DEAL
(1994–1996)

Chapter 9

ENDGAME

November 8, 1994–February 7, 1995

As THE FIRST autumn without a World Series in 89 years gives way to the final two months of 1994, Americans shift their attention to events that will reshape the nation. On November 8, an unknown backbencher from Georgia ushers in the first Republican majority in the House of Representatives in 40 years. New Speaker of the House Newt Gingrich will go toe-to-toe with President Bill Clinton, shut down the government in a battle over the budget, and turn compromise into something akin to treason.

On the same day, George W. Bush topples popular incumbent Ann Richards to become the 46th governor of Texas. It's not even inauguration day before W's chief strategist Karl Rove is talking about putting another Bush in the White House. The newly elected governor announces he'll place all his assets into a blind trust except his $600,000 stake in the Texas Rangers, which just four years later will be worth $14.9 million, the down payment on turning Rove's prophecy into reality.

But it's the trial of former football star O. J. Simpson, charged with the gruesome murder of his ex-wife Nicole and her friend Ron Goldman, that grabs the nation's attention. The case puts America's race relations squarely on trial, and views on Simpson's innocence or guilt often break down along racial lines. And it's Judge Lance Ito's decision to allow cameras into his courtroom that turns the Simpson trial into must-see TV, transforming nightly cable news shows into cultural heavyweights. The era of televised celebrity prosecutions is born, a phenomenon that will one day envelop several of baseball's biggest stars.

But right now, no one is happier to escape the daily media scrutiny than Bud Selig, who is greatly disappointed to discover that many Americans blame him for the abrupt end to the baseball season. He gives baseball's public relations man Rich Levin a standing order to comb the media for stories that lay the blame at the Acting Commissioner's feet. Levin doesn't have to look too hard.

In San Diego, the *Union-Tribune*'s Wayne Lockwood writes, "Bud Selig? Canceled the World Series. Hardly the way any of us would choose to be remembered." Steve Milton of Ontario's *Hamilton Spectator* tells Canadian readers that Selig "killed the World Series. Gunned it down in cold blood and plain daylight, then mourned its passing with crocodile tears."

No writer cuts deeper than *San Francisco Chronicle* columnist Bruce Jenkins. "It wasn't Hitler, the Depression or a major earthquake that killed the national pastime," Jenkins writes. "It was Bud Selig."

But as hard as the thin-skinned Selig takes the criticism, he can't dwell too long on these attacks. Not when his long battle with Fehr is about to reach a tipping point.

It's been clear for months—if not years—that the union will not accept a salary cap. And it's increasingly obvious that the same is true for the luxury tax plan the owners offered up as an alternative in mid-November, a scheme it took the union all of one day to reject. The tax was just a cap in another form, the union said, one that would have cost the Yankees $20 million—on top of their $47 million payroll—had it been in effect for the 1994 season. With penalties that steep, who needs a cap?

By now, both sides know it is inevitable that the owners will declare an impasse and implement their salary cap and revenue sharing plan. And the union will answer by taking the owners to court. So as Selig's second full year as Acting Commissioner enters its final month, only three real questions remain:

Can Selig keep the owners united until they decide to implement their cap?

Will a federal judge agree that MLB has bargained in good faith?

Will the players end their strike when Selig brings in replacement players?

If the answer to all three questions is yes, Selig will have his new economic system, the owners will have control over their game, and the union — for all intents and purposes — will be crushed.

This is why Selig so eagerly embraced Bill Usery, the well-regarded mediator President Clinton inserted into this dispute back in mid-October. A genial 70-year-old who favors loud sweaters and insists on keeping both sides tied to the bargaining table until a deal is done, Usery has a long history of resolving difficult labor disputes.

Not that Selig thinks Usery can broker a deal. There's no reasoning with Fehr, he's sure of that. But Selig understands the politics of Usery's position and has worked hard to curry favor. Turning down the mediator's services — $120,000 a month, split evenly with the union — would only have hurt the owners' chances of beating the unfair labor practices charge the union is sure to file. And gaining Usery's support can only make it easier to bring back the players once the owners implement their new system.

Selig is quick to follow the mediator's advice in early November and replace Dick Ravitch at the bargaining table, handing the reins — at least publicly — to Red Sox CEO John Harrington and Rockies owner Jerry McMorris. Selig had quietly brought back Chuck O'Connor as his main adviser anyway, so cutting Ravitch loose was no real sacrifice. Ravitch will submit his resignation December 5, effective at year's end, and he'll be gone a day later.

But Selig decides he's given Usery enough care and attention by late November, and he's ready to make his big move. Jerry Reinsdorf, Carl Pohlad, and Kansas City's David Glass have been lobbying hard for implementation, and on November 29, Selig authorizes Harrington to make two big announcements. First, the owners will implement their salary cap and revenue sharing plan, effective December 5. Second, they will hire replacement players if the union remains on strike.

What happens next will stick in the craw of many owners—especially the one who lives and dies with his White Sox—for years to come.

Usery begs Selig for more time, and the Acting Commissioner gives the mediator until December 15 to get an agreement. When Usery gets nowhere, both the owners' negotiating team and Executive Council meet in Chicago to plot their next move. Clinton's mediator again asks for one more chance, and this time he receives support from O'Connor, Harrington, and McMorris.

O'Connor lays out his case for granting Usery's request. The NLRB just announced it would issue an unfair labor practices complaint against the owners for withholding the pension payment back in August, giving the union an edge in proving the owners bargained in bad faith. And Lauren Rich, the architect of the union's proposals, called O'Connor's junior partner Rob Manfred late last night with word that the union was preparing another offer, which argues against an impasse.

Then there are financial risks to consider. If you lose in court, O'Connor explains, the players will be owed wages they would have earned under the old contract, a bill that will be tripled by the contract's anti-collusion provision. That, he says, would dwarf the $280 million the owners paid for collusion.

"We are at an impasse, and you have the legal right to implement now," O'Connor says. "But it's my recommendation that we tell the union they have another week to make a deal or we will implement."

Reinsdorf speaks up immediately. "What if the union makes some minor moves?" he asks. "Don't we run the risk of losing the impasse?"

"No," O'Connor answers. "We only lose the impasse if they make a significant move."

"I'm not a labor lawyer," Reinsdorf says, "but I think we risk losing the impasse and we should implement now."

Reinsdorf is full of passion and fire, and his attacks on Fehr usually rally the owners. But not this time. Selig sees where the consensus lies, sides with the moderates, and sets one more dead-line: 12:01 a.m. on December 23. "If there is a scintilla of a chance to have a reasonable solution at the table, for God's sake we've got to do it," Selig announces. "If not, a week passes quickly."

It's left to McMorris to meet with Fehr to find a solution. The two men sit down in Washington on December 20, with the Rock-ies owner offering a two-tier tax plan, the second tier designed to hit the Yankees and other big spenders. But the two men part without an agreement, prompting McMorris to complain that the union has failed to offer a plan of their own. Fehr disagrees.

"There's a difference between 'They won't give us a counter-proposal' and 'They won't give us what we want,'" he says.

At 2 p.m. on the day of Selig's deadline, the union delivers a proposal: a three-tiered tax plan that hits the highest spenders the hardest. It takes Selig's bargaining team six hours to pull it all apart, and when they're done, all optimism disappears. The com-bined taxes, McMorris says, would generate $600,000 from all 28 teams—a mere $57 million less than the owners' proposal.

The hard-liners are irate. Everyone else is just tired of it all. "It's very clear there is no basis for an agreement or even meaningful dialogue," says Wendy Selig-Prieb, who's been part of these talks from the start.

Selig says he will not put together a counteroffer; the time to make a deal is over. And this time, no one on his side is suggesting otherwise. It's been six months since Selig put management's first offer on the table, and they're no closer to an agreement now than they were when the players walked out 133 days ago. All they've done is run up almost a billion dollars in losses from both sides.

"Make the announcement," Selig tells Harrington after every-one has had their say on a tension-filled conference call.

Selig hangs up. *Reinsdorf was right—Fehr was never going to agree to anything.* Now they'll implement the system they wanted four years ago, the one they thought they could have had if Vincent hadn't undercut their lockout by dealing directly with Fehr behind their backs.

Not that this is going to be easy. No one is eager to use replace-ment players. But Selig is betting that using replacements will be a short-term solution, if this thing even gets that far. The players are approaching $300 million in lost wages. Even with the union's $200 million strike fund to help mitigate their losses, how much more can they afford to lose? And how will the players react when they see other men taking the field wearing their uniforms?

It's almost 11 p.m.—midnight on the East Coast—and Selig is just about done with his marathon of phone calls. He's thanked the negotiating team for its hard work. He's shared his disappointment with the media. "To get the kind of offer we got is extremely disappointing," he says.

And he's heard all about Fehr's tough talk at the union's press conference. "The owners will come to regret this sooner than they realize," Fehr defiantly told reporters. "Not only is this not over, it may not even be halftime yet."

Halftime, indeed! Selig knows he's done what no one thought possible—pulled the owners together and kept them united. And because he did, there will be a new system in place tonight at one minute past midnight, 19 years to the day since the introduction of free agency. Let the writers say whatever they want now. When history is written, they will look back on this day and realize it was Bud Selig who saved Major League Baseball.

A tired Don Fehr is sitting in the plush lobby of the Mayflower Renaissance hotel in Washington, D.C., suffering from the flulike symptoms that always hit him during a long and stressful labor crisis. And none has been longer or more stressful than the current crisis, now in its 178th day. It's late on Sunday afternoon, February 5, six weeks since Selig made his big move. With Fehr is his inner circle: his younger brother Steve, Gene Orza, Lauren Rich, and Michael Weiner. The union officials are picking apart the bizarre turn of events of the last few days when a hotel clerk approaches Fehr.

"Mr. Fehr?" the young clerk says. "We have an envelope for you."

"Okay, thanks," Fehr says as he rises. He gives a "Now what?" look to his staff and follows the clerk to the front desk.

It's been five days since President Clinton called both sides to Washington for one more try at a negotiated settlement. The President had a warning for them, too. If the owners and players could not come up with a solution, Clinton said, he'd ask Bill Usery to find one for them.

But Fehr arrived in Washington unconcerned. He had sent word through sources close to the President that the union had little confidence in Usery. Clinton signaled back that he had no plans to pressure the union into a settlement. Fehr was content to wait for the NLRB ruling, confident his contract proposal from December 22—and the owners' failure to counter—eliminated any chance of an impasse.

He'd met with Harrington last Wednesday, February 1, listened to the owners' latest plan—another luxury tax scheme—and simply shrugged. The tax rates, he said, are "extraordinarily heavy." The next day, Harrington announced that the owners would make good on the missed $7.8 million pension payment. That didn't draw much of a reaction from Fehr, either.

But what happened on Friday did.

That's when NLRB general counsel Fred Feinstein summoned O'Connor to his office to deliver important news. "I'm going to issue an unfair labor practices complaint against the owners," Feinstein told O'Connor. Left unsaid was whether Feinstein would also be seeking an injunction to stop management from implementing and hiring replacement players, but O'Connor knew the chances of that coming next were high.

But Feinstein also offered O'Connor a way out: reinstate the terms of the last contract, return to the bargaining table, and he'd withdraw the complaint. It was nothing short of a giant do-over. O'Connor relayed the news to the owners, who quickly voted to comply, effective Monday, February 6.

And just like that, everything the owners put in place on December 23 disappeared. "We're back under the old system," Fehr told reporters on Friday.

It was a huge win for Fehr and his staff. There was just one problem: not one of them believed the owners would keep their word.

Which is what they were discussing just moments ago, when the hotel clerk interrupted. Fehr is convinced there's no chance Selig will allow baseball to play another season under the old contract.

And with spring training set to open in nine days, they all expect his next move will come soon.

Just how soon is clear the minute Fehr returns from the front desk, a plain white envelope in hand. It's from O'Connor, addressed to "Donald M. Fehr, Esquire." Fehr tears it open and pulls out the letter.

It is all of three paragraphs, but it's a shocker.

> *This letter is to inform you that the Major League Baseball Player Relations Committee—the PRC—shall be the sole authorized representative of the 28 Major League clubs.*
>
> *The MLBPA is now on notice that individual clubs are not authorized to negotiate or execute individual player contracts.*
>
> *Consequently, the MLBPA should notify its players and certified agents that the PRC is the Clubs' exclusive bargaining representative and they may not lawfully attempt to negotiate with the individual clubs.*

Fehr always believed the owners would try to break the union. Now he's convinced the proof is in his hands. Individual teams are no longer allowed to sign players. Only Selig, still head of the PRC—the owners' labor committee—can do that, putting an end to the free market for players. The owners are also eliminating arbitration, as spelled out in a memo accompanying O'Connor's letter. Both actions violate the agreement made with Feinstein only 48 hours earlier.

None of this will hold up in court, Fehr thinks, but he doubts the owners care. It took the NLRB six weeks to evaluate the union's charges and issue the first complaint. With the maneuvers of this weekend, Selig has reset the clock. The legal process will start over again when the union files new charges tomorrow, giving the owners five weeks, maybe more, to use replacement players in spring training games.

Fehr can all but hear Selig telling owners the strike will end just as soon as the players see replacements take the field. This is exactly what the NFL owners did in 1987, when the players ended their strike after fans showed up and tuned in to watch replacement games.

This is a war of attrition. And Fehr doubts there is anything the President and his mediator can do about it.

"What am I supposed to tell the 95 players who just lost their arbitration rights?

"Am I supposed to tell them you have gone blind?

"Am I supposed to tell them you forgot how to read?"

The union's Gene Orza may be short and a bit round in stature — a shade over five feet six, pushing 200 pounds — but his sharp mind and acid tongue make him the perfect weapon when Fehr wants to launch an attack. And that time is now, in a crowded guest room in the Mayflower Hotel. And as Bill Usery, the target of Orza's assault, absorbs each blow in stunned silence, Fehr lets his deputy unleash one more punch before calling him off.

"What am I supposed to tell them?" repeats Orza, his voice dripping with indignation. "That you have gone senile?"

Fehr motions Orza to stop, leaving Usery staring numbly around the tense, silent suite filled with union officials, players, Usery's two assistants, and the man Fehr most wanted to witness Orza's performance — Steven Rosenthal, an adviser to Clinton's Secretary of Labor Robert Reich.

The union had been briefed on Usery's proposal just before walking into this room to hear it from the mediator himself. Fehr's instruction to Orza was clear: once Usery finishes his presentation, leave no doubt that the union will never accept these terms.

Orza did his job well.

And now it is Fehr's turn to drive home the same point. When Fehr is angry, as he is now, his voice doesn't rise. Instead, he is controlled and speaks firmly, with an ever-increasing level of sarcasm.

"How much would be raised by this tax?" Fehr asks.

"I'm not sure, Don," Usery says.

"How do you come up with these numbers?"

"I don't know about that."

"How much money do the players lose or gain? How much money do the clubs lose or gain?"

"I don't know, Don. I'm not an expert in economics."

The questions keep coming, rapid fire, until it is painfully obvious that Usery relied on his assistants to craft the proposal. Fehr knows there is a very good chance the NLRB will issue another complaint *and* seek an injunction. Feinstein has already announced that the owners are implementing their new plan "at their own peril."

And Fehr is also confident the players will hold together, all of which means there is zero chance he would ever accept this proposal—whether Usery can explain it or not. Satisfied that Rosenthal's report to the White House will accurately reflect the union's position, Fehr has one last thing to say to Usery.

"You're not helping these negotiations," Fehr tells the veteran mediator. "You're setting them back. I think it's time you should leave."

The large, windowless Roosevelt Room in the White House dates back to 1902, when the West Wing was built. Now situated across from the Oval Office, it occupies the original site of the office of the President. Richard Nixon gave the room its current name to honor Teddy Roosevelt, who built the West Wing, and FDR, who expanded it. Portraits of both men decorate the room, along with the Nobel Prize given Teddy for brokering peace between Russia and Japan in 1906, the first Nobel for an American.

On the evening of February 7, the room serves as the nerve center for President Clinton's last-ditch attempt to settle baseball's labor crisis. The meeting starts shortly after 6 p.m., with Vice President Al Gore offering ideas while each camp sits on opposite sides of the conference table—Don Fehr, Gene Orza, Tom Glavine, Cecil Fielder, Jay Bell, David Cone, and Scott Sanderson on one side; Bud Selig, John Harrington, Jerry McMorris, Chuck O'Connor, Rob Manfred, and St. Louis' Stuart Meyer on the other.

Clinton arrives at 7:20 p.m. It hasn't been an easy few months for the President. The sting of the midterm election disaster is still palpable, with his failed health care plan being blamed for the Democrats' loss of both the House and the Senate. He continues to be dogged by Kenneth Starr's ever-widening Whitewater investigation. And just yesterday he delivered a $1.6 trillion budget he knew was dead on arrival.

He's aware the polls show Americans think he should stay out of the baseball conflict. And his handpicked mediator has saddled him with a plan Selig's grudgingly accepted but Fehr rejected completely. When was the last time a Democratic President went against a union, even one as rich as the MLB Players Association?

All he has left is the prestige of his office and his considerable powers of persuasion. But even Clinton has to know that finding a solution tonight is a long shot.

"I am a believer in collective bargaining, and I don't want to impose a solution on anyone," says Clinton, his raspy southern drawl dragging out the sentence for maximum effect. "And I know that I am getting criticized for getting involved in sports. But there are a lot of Americans who really love baseball, and I feel an obligation to them."

Clinton pauses, letting the 13 baseball men take in the full force of their surroundings. Baseball players are used to a big stage, but sitting in the Roosevelt Room with the President and Vice President of the United States can be more than a little intimidating. And Clinton needs every edge he can find.

"So I am urging all of you," he says. "Let's try to figure out a way to solve this tonight."

As if on cue, chief of staff Leon Panetta, communications director George Stephanopoulos, and other administration officials march in. Small groups form around the room, each reviewing the many proposals rejected by one side or the other over the past six months. None of the groups includes anyone from the opposing side.

Eventually, Selig and his people move into Panetta's office, Fehr holds forth in the Roosevelt Room, and members of Clinton's staff go back and forth between the two camps, engaging in baseball's version of shuttle diplomacy. Usery hasn't said much, but Selig only has to look at the downcast mediator to realize Clinton is not going to support his proposal in the face of union opposition. And if any doubt remains, all Selig has to do is glance out into the hallway, where Glavine is helping the President with his golf swing.

As the discussions approach the four-hour mark, the President has a few basic questions:

Will the union reconsider Usery's proposal?

No, says Fehr.

Will both sides accept binding arbitration?

Yes, Fehr says.

Absolutely not, Selig answers.

Will both sides play this season while a presidential fact-finding committee crafts a framework for negotiations at season's end?

Once again, Fehr agrees.

Once again, Selig refuses.

There are no more questions to be asked and answered, so Clinton calls everyone back to the Roosevelt Room. "I'm going to ask Congress to pass legislation to settle this dispute through binding arbitration," says a clearly exasperated President.

But everyone knows it's an empty gesture. Even before this meeting was called to order, Senate Majority Leader Bob Dole and House Speaker Newt Gingrich put out a statement making it clear they wanted no part of this problem. "We maintain our view that Congress is ill-suited to resolving private labor disputes," they said. No, the Republicans have little intention of giving Clinton a high-profile victory. Baseball's players and owners are not the only ones at each other's throats.

"Both of you have a lot at stake," Clinton tells them. He takes the measure of the 13 men sitting at the table, then says he has rarely seen the level of hostility he's witnessed tonight.

"I'm afraid you are all going to wind up losers," he says.

There is nothing left to do now but meet with the media in the White House briefing room, admit defeat, and make a public plea for Congress to save baseball from itself.

"I had hoped that tonight I'd be coming out to tell you that baseball was coming back in 1995," Clinton says as the hour approaches 11 p.m. "Unfortunately, the parties have not reached an agreement. Clearly they are not capable of settling this strike without an umpire. Congress has to step up and pass the legislation.

"Unless they do, we may not have baseball in 1995."

Chapter 10

FEHR'S DAY IN COURT

February 16–April 4, 1995

Don Fehr leans against the front of the dais, arms folded loosely across his chest, watching the long lines of striking baseball players file into a big ballroom in Orlando's Hyatt Regency Grand Cypress Resort. It's just about time to call this meeting to order, but 260 players put their names on the sign-up sheet, and many are still searching for one of the few empty seats at the tables spread out before him.

This is one of several meetings Fehr scheduled to keep players informed, telling them what the owners are up to, explaining the union's decisions, and answering their questions. And since this meeting takes place on February 16—the first day of spring training—it was always going to be a big one. But then Lenny Dykstra went on ESPN last week, said mediator Bill Usery's proposed 50-50 split of revenues sounded good, and promised to round up 20 of the game's top players and figure out how to end this strike. Once word got out that Lenny was coming to Orlando—and Fehr told Gene Orza to make sure he was—this was destined to be the biggest meeting in union history.

Fehr knows Dykstra's stand is exactly what Selig is counting on—when a star player breaks ranks, can the others be far behind?

And the union leader wouldn't be surprised if Phillies President Bill Giles, one of Bud's close allies, is the man pulling Lenny's strings. Indeed, the rumor flying around the ballroom is that Lenny was seen huddling with Giles at a local bar last night, scribbling down notes as the Phillies executive spoke.

But Fehr isn't all that concerned about Lenny as he calls the meeting to order. The union filed another unfair labor practices charge four days after leaving Washington, and Fehr is certain the law is once again on their side. That's what his team has been telling the players. And the players believe it, too. A $280 million collusion settlement buys you a lot of credibility. So does refusing to take a salary during the strike, something Fehr and his staff have done during every work stoppage—and this one is no different.

And now Fehr is ready to deliver his message. The owners refuse to drop their demand for a salary cap, so negotiations are at a standstill, he tells the jam-packed room. The owners think they can get the cap because they believe you'll cave once you see replacement players wearing your uniforms. They still don't understand you.

"We will win this," the union leader says, "if we remain united."

Fehr knows the owners are pressuring players to cross, especially young players who haven't made their money yet. And veterans who failed to put money aside and now have big bills to pay. And Latin American players worried about getting their work visas to come back to the United States.

Which is why Dykstra is such a gift.

Dykstra, flanked on either side by teammates Darren Daulton and Dave Hollins, rises from his seat, pulls a sheet of paper out of his jacket pocket, and begins to read. "Now is the time to make a deal," he says, keeping his eyes down. "This can get really ugly. The union is going to get broken when people start crossing the line. We're all losing so much money every day."

Roger Clemens is the first to interrupt. "Put that fucking paper down and tell us what you really think," Clemens says. "Don't tell us what your owner thinks."

"Yeah, tell us what you think," others repeat across the room.

"You don't know what the fuck you're talking about," some of them shout.

Cecil Fielder stands and looks at Lenny as the room quiets. Everyone knows the big first baseman is a carefree spirit, but there's little of that in evidence now. "All the guys who came before us and gave so much so that we could do what we're doing now, and some of you guys don't want to do the right thing," Fielder says. "If you all don't want to do the right thing, well, fuck you."

Dykstra struggles through a few more talking points before he puts the paper down and finally looks up. It's time to rejoin the team. "You all know that I've had some problems with this process," Lenny says, "but I just want to make sure you all know that I am behind this union. I want to get back on the baseball field, but I'll stick with you as long as I have to."

More players stand up, one at a time, repeating Fielder's call for solidarity, vowing to do for tomorrow's players what previous generations of players did for them. Then it's time for union leadership to speak up. Michael Weiner tells the players that management's offer wipes out most if not all the gains the players have fought for and won, going all the way back to Curt Flood. The freedom to market your skills, to play where you want to play and who you want to play for, and the right to salary arbitration—all of it, Weiner says, will vanish.

David Cone, who's been lobbying Congress alongside Fehr to repeal baseball's antitrust exemption, tells players they simply can't trust the owners. "They say they want to split profits 50-50, but they won't show us their books," he says. "How will we ever know if we really got 50 percent?"

Scott Sanderson, another Executive Board member, applies the finishing touch. "The central question is very simple," says Sanderson, an 18-year veteran without a contract for the coming season. "Can I have a show of hands: Which of you players here think we should give the players who come after us less than we received from the players who came before us?"

The room is hushed as everyone looks around. Not a single hand is raised.

The owners thought turning Lenny to their side would tear us apart,

Fehr thinks as the gathering takes on the feel of an old-time revival meeting. But they never get it right. And they never will. Not as long as the Mattinglys, the Fielders, and the Sandersons remember all they've gained and how easily it could all slip way. These players are as united now as they were the day they went out on strike, a message the owners will soon receive from the media waiting outside the ballroom doors.

Fehr knows he has Lenny to thank for that.

It's been a bad few months for the game's Acting Commissioner. In January, he finally had to tell the good people of Milwaukee that he can no longer afford to pay for a new stadium, which now includes plans for a roof and a brand-new price tag: $250 million. The team lost $10.7 million in '94, he admits, including $4 million in loan payments alone.

Selig tries to jump-start baseball's stalled labor talks, convening a meeting in Scottsdale on February 28. But the talks crash and burn three days later when Paul Molitor shreds Selig's revenue sharing and luxury tax plans before a roomful of owners, executives, and players. Embarrassed and frustrated, Selig issues a threat on his way out the door: he just might turn negotiations over to Jerry Reinsdorf and union-busting lawyer Bob Ballow and "let them blow the whole thing up."

Meanwhile, his replacement player scheme runs into trouble right from the start. Sparky Anderson, the game's most successful manager, tells the Tigers on February 17 that he won't manage replacement players. Detroit, which had already paid Anderson $350,000 of his game-high $1.2 million salary, puts its manager on an unpaid leave of absence.

Which is more than the Red Sox do for their hitting coach and former major league star Mike Easler, who also refuses to work with strikebreakers. Boston promptly fires him. Toronto allows manager Cito Gaston and his coaches to work with its minor league teams instead of replacement players, but Canadian lawmakers tell the team to find a new home field—in another country—if replacements are used. Canada does not allow strikebreakers, though the government makes an exception for the Expos, fearing the cash-strapped team might fold and cost Canadians their jobs.

Orioles owner Peter Angelos — worried in part about protecting Cal Ripken's consecutive game streak — makes good on his promise not to field a replacement team. Selig threatens Angelos with fines, suspension, and the possible loss of his franchise. And Washington, D.C., makes a sudden appearance on the list of markets being considered for another soon-to-be-announced round of expansion. When Angelos refuses to buckle, Selig is forced to cancel all 32 Orioles exhibition games.

"Selig's methods to resolve baseball's problems are — how should I put it? — amateurish, ineffective, and doomed to failure," Angelos tells the *Los Angeles Times.* "Watching him is like watching a person put his hand in a buzz saw. You want to shout, 'You're splattering blood all over the rest of us!'"

Selig's attempt to use top minor leaguers as replacements is foiled when Fehr warns the young stars they'll be considered scabs and forever banned from the union if they cooperate. When promises of bonuses and threats of demotions fail to induce any of the top prospects on each team to play ball, the owners kick them out of camp. Fehr smartly steps up and pays the players' way home.

Many of the players who do take the field are laughable. Mets center fielder Marcus Lawton came to camp straight from a riverboat casino, where he was a card dealer. Their new second baseman Bubba Wagnon left his job at B&B Landscaping in Alabama. At Yankees camp, George Steinbrenner watches his team of truck drivers and cabbies lose its first two games, then fires six players and cuts his staff's salary by 10 percent. Then he tells Gene Michael to put a better team on the field.

Yankees beat writers keep asking George why he's been silent about the strike all spring, but Steinbrenner simply repeats what he's said all along: he supports Selig. What else could he say? Even after Selig put him on the powerful Executive Council in late February, George knows any plan Bud proposes is going to cost him dearly. So what is Steinbrenner going to tell reporters — that he's pulling for Fehr to win this fight?

On March 2, the Indians trade five replacement players to the Reds without getting a single player in return. "Cleveland got the better deal," says Cincinnati manager Davey Johnson, who watched 48-year-old Pedro Borbon—a spot starter when the Reds won back-to-back titles in the mid-'70s—fall down from exhaustion while jogging around the Reds complex.

After the Brewers replacements lose to the Rockies 24–2, starting pitcher Tim Dell tells Milwaukee manager Phil Garner, "We just haven't peaked yet." In the Mariners' camp, manager Lou Piniella sees his new recruits gain so much weight from feasting on the free breakfasts, lunches, and postgame ice cream that he puts them all on diets.

Through it all, the owners keep telling fans and the media that this is the only way to save a game facing dire economic problems. But it all sounds laughable on March 9, when the owners vote to add expansion teams in Phoenix and Tampa for the '98 season. How can baseball be in such bad shape, reporters ask, if there are people competing to give them $150 million per team just to join their club?

But the really bad news comes on March 14. That's when NLRB general counsel Fred Feinstein announces he will issue yet another charge against the owners, accusing MLB of failing to bargain in good faith when Selig implemented the new system. And it gets worse three days later: Feinstein says he's asking the NLRB for permission to seek an injunction in federal court. If issued, an injunction would force the owners to dismiss the replacement players and restore the terms of the old contract.

As he waits for the NLRB to render a decision, Selig knows the players will never break ranks now. The ruling comes on a Sunday afternoon nine days later, and it's more bad news for Bud. In a 3–2 vote, the Board's three Democrats clear Feinstein to seek an injunction.

After a 227-day strike, Selig and Fehr will face off in federal court.

The nation's baseball fans tune in the next day to learn the identity of the judge who they hope can do what the President, the Vice President, two federal mediators, and countless lawyers have failed to do: put Major League Baseball back on the playing field. In Manhattan, a court clerk turns the hand crank that rotates a thin, boxlike drum containing cards bearing the names of 38 federal judges. Then he stops, opens the drum's latch, pulls out a card, and reads three words aloud: Justice Sonia Sotomayor.

Born a Yankees fan in the South Bronx and raised by a single mother, Sotomayor graduated from Princeton in 1976 and was appointed to the federal court by President George H. W. Bush. She is considered thoughtful, thorough, and exceptionally bright, and her decisions in her 2½ years on the bench tend to tilt left. Now 40 and still the federal court's youngest judge, she's on the fast track, many say, to be the first Hispanic named to the Supreme Court.

Sotomayor tells both sides of baseball's dispute that she doesn't know any more about the case than the average reader of the *New York Times*. But it's clear she understands its time-sensitive dynamics: Opening Day is Sunday, six days hence, so she instructs management to file its briefs by Wednesday, less than 48 hours away. The NLRB will have until 5 p.m. Thursday to respond. Meanwhile, she will read the voluminous filing the NLRB lawyers delivered today.

"The hearing is set for Friday at 10 a.m.," says Sotomayor, who sends the lawyers off with one final thought. "We would like to see the two sides settle this thing without our involvement."

No one involved thinks there's even a remote chance of Sotomayor's wish coming true—least of all Don Fehr, who has to be feeling good about how things are playing out. Both the NLRB and the union are relieved the judge selected to hear this case is not a conservative—the kind of judge who tends to favor management. As an added bonus, the judge is a woman. The union is weary of seeing many of Sotomayor's male counterparts turn into little boys when presiding over cases involving baseball—and delivering judgments to match.

The next three days are a blur. Steinbrenner and Mets co-owner Fred Wilpon spend Tuesday rounding up the eight votes needed to block a lockout. On Wednesday Fehr announces that the players will end their strike and return to work if Sotomayor grants the injunction blocking the use of replacements. Selig holds a conference call on Thursday, and all but three owners vote to start the season with replacement players.

"I want it on the record that I think it would be a tragic mistake to go ahead with this plan," says Steinbrenner, who joins Baltimore and Toronto in opposition. But as the hour-long call draws to a close, Steinbrenner tells Selig he'll change his vote if the Orioles and Blue Jays change theirs.

Neither will bend.

"Bud," Steinbrenner says, "just do what you want with my vote."

"George," says Selig, "you have to make the call."

"Okay, then," an exasperated Steinbrenner says. "I'll go with you."

Sotomayor steps into courtroom 101 of the U.S. District Court in Manhattan early Friday morning. There are four tables before her bench, two on each side. The room is filled with reporters and baseball officials, leaving very few seats for curious New Yorkers wanting to sit in on history.

Sotomayor compliments both sides for doing an excellent job of educating her on the details of the case, then says she hopes no one thought she was not a baseball fan. "You can't grow up in the South Bronx without knowing baseball," she says.

Her first question is to Dan Silverman, the regional director for the NLRB in New York, asking him to explain why the owners' action causes the players irreparable harm if it isn't stopped now. Silverman explains that changing the contract unilaterally is illegal, and that only a speedy trial will prevent the owners from benefiting from their illegal activities.

Sotomayor next turns to George Cohen, who represents the players. There is a long-standing principle, Sotomayor tells everyone in the courtroom, that if harm can be remedied by money, "you don't issue an injunction." Why, she asks Cohen, can't any harm caused by the owners be solved by monetary means?

" 'Competitive bids,' Your Honor, does not just mean money," Cohen says. "It means an intense variety of personal considerations. Where does a player want to play? Does he want to go back to his home team? Does he want to go to a team he thinks is going to be a pennant contender? Does he want to go to a team where he believes he will be a regular player?"

There are 115 players who are free agents this season, Cohen tells the judge. "Each one of these 115—approximately 20 percent of our bargaining unit—are being deprived of that opportunity," Cohen says.

The judge then asks what this has to do with arbitration, and it's clear from the way she frames her question that Sotomayor thinks the arbitration issue can be settled monetarily. Cohen explains how each class of player is connected to the others, how one superstar on the market can raise the bar for everyone—including players in arbitration—and how that changes from year to year.

It is not unlike collusion, he says, when the owners changed the system illegally. And the union is still trying to apportion the money fairly—five years later. "It's like trying to unscramble an egg," Cohen says.

Sotomayor's questions for owners' lawyer Frank Casey have a much harder edge. "What right do you, as any other employer in this system, have to change wages unilaterally?" she says. After Casey says the expired contract affords management the right to change wages, the judge tells him, "What you can't do…is change the salary until you have reached an impasse in bargaining." There are more questions, but it is already clear that the judge knows where she is heading.

The court proceedings are finished in 98 minutes. "Thank you," Sotomayor says as she prepares to leave for her chambers. "Let's take a break. In 15 minutes we will come back and I will tell you what I am going to do."

She returns to the bench in 18 minutes, and every lawyer involved understands the decision they are about to hear was written in advance. Given the judge's questions, they also know whatever final changes she just made did not change the result: the players have won. Now they are all about to hear why.

"This strike has placed the entire concept of collective bargaining on trial," Sotomayor says. "It is critical, therefore, that the Board assure and that I protect its assurance that the spirit and the letter of federal labor law be scrupulously followed."

Her conclusion: "The Board has reasonable cause to believe that the owners have committed an unfair labor practice and that an injunction is just and proper."

Sotomayor takes 47 minutes to read her entire decision, and it is a blistering indictment of management. The owners, the judge says, simply "misunderstand the case law." She says their argument for centralized bargaining is "superficial" and "misguided," adding that "the right to join collective bargaining units belongs to employees, not to employers."

The only remedy to all this, says the judge, is "to issue an injunction and thereby restore the status quo."

The result: the owners have to reinstate salary arbitration, competitive bidding for free agents, and the anti-collusion provision of the free-agency rules. In addition, Sotomayor rules that neither side can declare an impasse in negotiations unless they receive her approval first.

It is a complete repudiation of the owners' actions. All that was left was for Casey to request a stay of Sotomayor's decision.

"Denied," Sotomayor says. "You can go across the street."

Casey and his team quickly rush across the street to the Court of Appeals for the Second Circuit. But the confidence the owners' lawyers had coming into court today is gone. And so is any optimism that a decision by the appeals court will be any different from what they've just heard.

Fehr calmly collects his notes and heads to a brief meeting with the media. Sotomayor's ruling "provided every bit of relief we asked for," he says. Would it surprise him if the owners resorted to another lockout? Nothing the owners do surprises him, he says. "However, it would be an obvious indication they want to continue the dispute."

The winning side celebrates by gathering for lunch at a nearby tavern. Fehr does not attend; instead he takes the subway back to his office with his brother Steve. He has a letter to write to Selig, telling the Acting Commissioner he is ready to start bargaining again. "Please give me a call when you want to start," he writes. Michael Weiner leaves lunch when he learns the appeals court will hear the owners' petition for a stay and an expedited appeal of Sotomayor's decision next Tuesday, and heads back to court to collect the papers.

Gene Orza, Lauren Rich, and the rest of the staff lawyers are already at the union's office when the Fehrs arrive. There are no speeches, and few congratulations are exchanged. Instead, there's a meeting to review the back-to-work agreement and discuss their options should the owners do the unexpected and lock out the players. There are almost 800 players with unsigned contracts and several dozen players to prepare for arbitration hearings. There's also a plan under way to set up camp in Homestead, Florida, for the 115 free agents to work out while their agents broker deals.

Sotomayor's injunction does not rule on the merits of the unfair labor practice charges the players filed against the owners, but it's clear from her written decision that she thinks the owners are in the wrong, just as Feinstein, Silverman, and the majority of the NLRB had already concluded. Nor does her ruling order the players back to work. Indeed, the owners do not immediately accept the union's offer to return.

In a statement released soon after the ruling, Selig says, "The injunction may represent a step backward in our negotiations. Obviously we will appeal." The owners, he says, will meet on Sunday in Chicago to decide their next move. Left unsaid: arrangements are already being made to iron out back-to-work rules with the union tomorrow.

Two days later, Selig is at the O'Hare Hilton, meeting with the owners he's spent the past three years holding together. They want him to stay on as Commissioner—he has no intention of stepping down—but whatever sense of common purpose they held these last seven months is gone. It was always a fragile bond—they are, after all, in business to beat each other—so Selig is not surprised when the accusations and recriminations fly.

Why did Selig keep assuring them the players would cave?

Why did he think Clinton would back Usery's proposal?

And why wasn't there a fallback strategy?

Asks Marlins owner Wayne Huizenga, "Why are we folding after all this time instead of locking out the players?"

The lawyers present have already explained the financial risks of the lockout route, and few owners want to take that chance. Many in the room are just weary of it all and ready to put the game back on the field. But Huizenga, Reinsdorf, and a few other hard-liners don't want to quit.

"You're cowards," Huizenga says in disgust.

But Selig has already counted the votes and knows that those favoring a lockout don't have the 21 votes they need to keep the players out of camp. The 75 percent rule Reinsdorf pushed through in '94 to keep the owners from folding is working against him now. Selig doesn't even ask for a vote—no reason to stir the pot.

When their anger is spent, Selig reviews the back-to-work plan the two sides just reached. The players will be welcomed back to camp on Wednesday. Spring training will last three weeks, with Opening Day on April 26. The season will be 144 games rather than the regular 162. Rosters will be set at 28 until May 15, when they return to the normal 25.

After 234 days, the longest strike in sports history is over. As Selig walks out to meet the media, he knows he has nothing tangible to show for all his efforts. But despite the pain of the lost season, the lost World Series, and the hundreds of millions in lost revenue, Selig understands a few things were gained.

He now knows the big market owners will accept more revenue sharing.

He knows the players will accept a luxury tax, albeit one not nearly as large as he would like.

And he knows the fans will accept an owner as the game's full-time Commissioner.

"The clubs are delighted to announce we have accepted the union's unconditional offer to go back to work," a weary Selig says. "The players are back, the game is back, and we are very happy about that."

Frank Casey wishes he weren't here. It's Tuesday, April 4, one day before players report to spring training, and the owners' lawyer is listening to three judges in the Court of Appeals for the Second Circuit shred his request for a stay of Sotomayor's decision. He's already been told that he's "in the wrong court" for this motion, that his strategy is poor, and that he's "going around in circles."

And Casey thought listening to Sotomayor was rough.

Chief Justice Jon Newman asks Casey why he claims the injunction gives the players an incentive not to negotiate when Fehr has now sent Selig not one but two letters to the contrary. "When you're telling us that the injunction is stopping you from negotiating a collective bargaining agreement, you're telling us something that isn't so," Newman says.

It goes on like this for an hour, and near the end Casey hears something he will dread telling Selig. Two of the judges wondered why the owners withdrew their first implementation on February 3, when the NLRB said it would issue a complaint. "You could've fought that in court, and you would've had a heck of a case," says Judge Ralph Winter, considered the expert in this field. "You didn't."

The three judges are unanimous in their decision: the stay is denied.

Selig declines to answer questions when reporters call about the court decision, and his day only gets worse from there. The results of the vote to finance a new Brewers stadium with a lottery come in late Tuesday night, and the news is awful. Voters rejected the lottery, with 348,009 saying yes and 616,685 voting no.

No revenue sharing.

No salary cap.

No stadium.

Bud Selig is back to where he started three years ago.

Chapter 11

BACK TO WORK

April 25–September 6, 1995

Redemption will not come quickly—or painlessly—for those who run and play Major League Baseball. After a rushed three weeks of spring training, Opening Day is the chance for baseball fans around the country to let all concerned know just how they feel. One fan in Cincinnati sums it up when he rents a plane to fly over Riverfront Stadium with a banner reading owners & players: to hell with all of you! trailing behind.

The Marlins and Dodgers line up along the baselines in traditional Opening Day fashion, then they all take off their caps and wave to the crowd as the PA announcer tells them to "say thanks to the loyal and patient fans of South Florida." The loyal and patient fans treat the players to a long and loud chorus of boos. "I wanted to boo, too," says LA first baseman Eric Karros.

Three fans pay a Shea Stadium usher three dollars to let them rush the field, where they sprinkle 147 one-dollar bills at the feet of Mets infielders. All three are wearing T-shirts reading greed across the front and wind up at second base, fists raised, as the crowd of 26,604—16,000 less than a year ago—stands and roars. The picture runs in newspapers across the nation.

The PA announcer in Pittsburgh has to warn of a forfeit to make fans behave after they shower the field with sticks taken from flags the team handed out in the Pirates home opener against the Expos. In Detroit, fans use Indians center fielder Kenny Lofton as their target for baseballs, Coke bottles, whiskey flasks, beer cans, and a napkin dispenser. The outburst causes a 12-minute delay, and MLB is so concerned it sends in security director Kevin Hallinan to coordinate policing efforts for the next few games.

Both management and the union ask players to make an extra effort to connect with the paying customers, and players sign autographs for long lines of fans before and after games. No one shows more gusto than the newest Red Sox Jose Canseco, who stands in front of Fenway Park at 8:15 a.m.—almost five hours before game time—shaking hands and welcoming early-arriving fans to Opening Day.

Milwaukee management recruits 60 Little Leaguers to throw a "first pitch" to the Brewers and visiting White Sox players, who autograph each ball right there on the field. And after all the Brewers are introduced, every player and coach tosses his cap into the stands. But the game draws only 31,426—Milwaukee's smallest Opening Day crowd in 22 years—and one fan dumps beer on Chicago center fielder Mike Devereaux while Acting Commissioner Bud Selig takes it all in from his box.

Even the Yankees fall 7,300 short of a sellout, despite the regal presence of Joe DiMaggio, there to throw out the first pitch, and the eagerness to see Don Mattingly resume his quest to reach the postseason—now 1,657 games and counting. Don Fehr and Gene Orza draw loud boos when they're spotted walking onto the field. "You ruined the game," one fan shouts at Fehr as he stands at the batting practice cage. When Fehr walks off the field, another fan holds up a sign saying SHAME ON YOU! Fehr gives him the finger.

George Steinbrenner, recovering from surgery to repair a detached retina, misses the Yankees home opener, but his involvement with his team has never been greater. On April 5, he personally sends a marginal outfield prospect and just shy of $1 million to Montreal in exchange for John Wetteland, the game's top closer. The Expos—battered by losses from the strike—can no longer afford Wetteland's $2.4 million contract or the raises he's sure to get in arbitration the next two seasons. And Steinbrenner already cut a deal in December with his old friend Jerry Reinsdorf to bring Chicago's former Cy Young winner Jack McDowell to New York. George's expectations have never been higher.

And that's bad news for manager Buck Showalter and his players when a slew of injuries drops the Yankees into last place in the AL East on June 6. Steinbrenner responds by making daily calls to Showalter to demand changes and results, reinstating the ban on facial hair he'd partially lifted and singling out Danny Tartabull for special abuse.

Steinbrenner questions Tartabull's honesty when the outfielder— who hit .195 with no home runs and three RBI during the team's recent 4–16 tailspin—complains of back spasms and Showalter pulls him from the lineup. The Boss asks reporters why the criticism hasn't motivated Tartabull, in the fourth year of a team-record five-year, $25.5 million deal, the way it once did Reggie Jackson. The relatively calm owner of the past two seasons—the one who agreed in late 1994 to be regularly lampooned on the hit TV sitcom Seinfeld—is officially gone.

"I haven't softened," Steinbrenner says, in case anyone is wondering. "I am just as tough as I was before."

George puts on a show in Detroit on June 13, sitting behind the Yankees dugout scribbling notes one day after his team dropped an error-filled game to the Tigers to fall to 16–25, the fourth-worst start in Yankee history. He then stands in the middle of the post-game locker room and complains to reporters while the players look on. "I came to find out what the problem is with this team," he says. "I'll tell you one thing—it's not the payroll."

Steinbrenner, whose $47 million payroll trails only Toronto's $50 million roster, is never shy about spending money. And on June 19 he opens his checkbook to give Darryl Strawberry $675,000 and a $100,000 bonus if the troubled player follows his aftercare program for drug abuse. The same day he tells Doc Gooden's agent the Yankees want to talk when the pitcher's season-long suspension for cocaine use ends.

"I think Darryl can turn things around and be a great lesson for young people," says Steinbrenner, defending a decision that draws widespread criticism.

The constant media circus erases the baseball-only atmosphere Showalter worked so hard to cultivate. And the manager can't help but feel it's contributing to his team's poor play. As does the team's captain. "We went two or three years where it was just baseball news," Mattingly says. "Now we've got this other stuff again. It's disruptive."

Disruptive? George's father taught him to manage by fear, and the way this overpaid team is performing, these Yankees have plenty to be fearful about.

Finally.

For the last several years, *Los Angeles Times* baseball writer Bob Nightengale has been pitching a story on the rising yet under the radar use of steroids by baseball players, but the idea never garnered much interest with his editors. Now it's the second week of July, and Nightengale's just been given the weekend baseball column to write, and he's free to choose his subject. Well, he figures, might as well take a shot at the steroid story.

Finally.

Nightengale, a tall, gregarious young writer who makes friends and develops sources easily, has listened to baseball people talk about steroids almost from the moment he began covering the Royals for the *Kansas City Star* back in 1986. Coaches point out a player whose bat speed has suddenly increased with age and know something's up. Scouts complain to him about losing credibility when a lightly regarded player not only makes the bigs but plays like a Hall of Famer. Players joke about the new vitamins making the rounds when a teammate shows up to spring training 25 pounds bigger — all of it muscle — than he was when the season ended just three months earlier.

No one mentions names, but it's not hard for Nightengale — or most anyone on the baseball beat — to pick out Mark McGwire and Jose Canseco, or the A's and the Rangers, as prime suspects. First it was the game's hitters who drew suspicion, then the relief pitchers throwing 95 mph for three, four, even five days in a row. And it isn't just the new muscles, players tell him: it's the sense of confidence the suspected users seem to develop—confidence that translates into the focus needed to hit these 95 mph fastballs.

Back when the *Los Angeles Times* hired Nightengale to cover the Padres in 1989, San Diego superstar Tony Gwynn began sharing his concerns about the rising use of performance-enhancing drugs. And when the players came to their abbreviated spring training three months ago, there were more big bodies than ever—and fewer players joking about it. Nightengale listens to home run hitters like Ken Griffey and Fred McGriff complain about being suspected of using drugs at the same time the drug users are posting numbers as big—if not bigger—than theirs.

So Nightengale starts with those he knows best. One of his first calls is to Gwynn, hoping the future Hall of Famer has seen enough. Gwynn is cautious, but he does want the story to get out.

"It's like the big secret we're not supposed to talk about, but believe me, we wonder just like the rest of people," Tony tells him on the record. "I'm standing out there in the outfield when a guy comes up, and I'm thinking, 'Hey, I wonder if this guy is on steroids.'"

Nightengale reaches out to Randy Smith, the Padres general manager. Smith is a baseball lifer, the son of longtime baseball executive Tal Smith, and he's already told Nightengale how troubled he is by what's happening to the game. When Nightengale tells him the story he hopes to write, Smith says he's all for it. Like Gwynn, Smith wants the story out of the shadows.

"We all know there's steroid use, and it's definitely become more prevalent," Smith says for publication. "The ballplayers all know the dangers of it. We preach it every year.

"But because there's so much money to be made these days, guys are willing to pay the price now and will pay the piper later. I can understand it's a difficult choice for some players. They know it can take five years off their lives, but then they say, 'Okay, so I die when I'm 75 instead of 80.'"

Nightengale asks Smith how many players he thinks are using steroids.

"I think 10 percent to 20 percent," Smith says. "No one has any hard-core proof, but there's a lot of guys you suspect."

Nightengale thanks Smith for his time—and his honesty—and hangs up, knowing he has a story. He calls an American League general manager, who won't go on the record but tells Nightengale he thinks Smith's estimate is low. "I wouldn't be surprised if it's closer to 30 percent," the GM says. "We had one team in our league a few years ago where the entire lineup may have been on it.

"Come on, you just don't put on 50 pounds of muscle overnight and hit balls out of stadiums. I'm seeing guys who were washed up five years ago and now they've got bat speed they've never had before. It's insane."

Frank Thomas tells Nightengale he'd love to see drug testing in baseball. Expos GM Kevin Malone agrees. "If it can be done in every other sport, why not ours?" he says. "You hear the rumors that usage is way up, and it would be nice to know if those are accurate." Dodgers reliever Todd Worrell tells Nightengale, "We've got guys out there willing to risk their lives just for a piece of glory. Until we have a set policy, we'll continue to have problems, finger-pointing, and controversy."

Nightengale has left Selig for last. He tells the Acting Commissioner what he's hearing, leaving out the names but letting Bud know he's heard a number of players and men in management say they're worried about rising steroid use. Selig does not sound alarmed, nor does he have much to say. He tells Nightengale he spoke with the owners about steroids "a year, maybe 18 months ago," and no one felt there was any evidence that steroid use should be a concern.

"If baseball has a problem, I must say candidly that we were not aware of it," Selig says. "It certainly hasn't been talked about much. But should we concern ourselves as an industry? I don't know. Maybe it's time to bring it up again."

His reporting done, Nightengale writes his column and turns it over to his editors on the morning of Friday, July 14. The story runs the next day under the headline:

Steroids Become an Issue.
Baseball: Many Fear Performance-Enhancing Drug Is Becoming
Prevalent and Believe Something Must Be Done

Nightengale is at Dodger Stadium by late afternoon to cover the team's night game with the Marlins. The Dodgers have lost seven of their last nine and enter the day's game at 35–36, despite another sparkling season from Mike Piazza. The 26-year-old catcher, who played in his third straight All-Star Game four days ago (and homered), is hitting .367, with 13 home runs and 38 RBI in 44 games.

Nightengale is standing at the batting cage when Piazza approaches him. "Hey, dude, I saw your column in today's paper," Piazza says. "Do you really think that many players are using steroids? That there are that many players juicing?"

"Yeah, Mike," Nightengale says. "I do."

"Wow, really?" says Piazza, who pivots and walks away.

As batting practice ends, Nightengale makes his way up to the press box, where hardly a word is spoken about his story. Despite the best intentions of Smith, Gwynn, and the others who hoped their words might spark a reaction, Nightengale's story receives little attention.

It's clear only a handful of those in the game want to talk about its growing drug problem. Nightengale files the story away, and it remains largely unnoticed until a certain Senator from Maine brings it back to life 12 years later.

No matter which direction Bud Selig looks as he makes his way through his third summer as baseball's Acting Commissioner, all he sees are problems. Big problems.

His labor situation is a mess. Once Sotomayor ruled against the owners, Selig's dream of a salary cap died. So did the owner solidarity he worked so hard to achieve. Everyone reverted to form, especially Steinbrenner, who scoops up David Cone in late July for three minor leaguers and pushes his payroll to a game-high $55 million while the small market crowd keeps cutting costs. Selig's $16 million payroll—down from $23.5 million a year ago— is now the lowest in the AL.

Baseball's lawyers appealed Sotomayor's decision, but no one expects it to be overturned. Selig gives his blessing for Foley & Lardner's Stan Jaspan to reach out to the union's Lauren Rich, and back-channel talks begin again in late summer. But Selig knows the negotiations won't go anywhere. Why would the union want to cut a deal when they've got everything they want right now?

In the meantime, Selig is talking to old friend Randy Levine, the man who helped get Steinbrenner back in baseball, about leaving his job as Rudy Giuliani's labor commissioner to take over baseball's negotiations. Selig tells Levine he needs a deal, and he needs one soon. Come September, Levine will announce he's taking baseball's labor job.

The players are back, but many of the fans aren't. Selig's Brewers are among the hardest hit, playing before six crowds under 10,000 by the All-Star break. They'll barely draw 1 million fans for the season, despite a team that's overachieving. The Brewers are 52–52 on August 19, just one game behind the free-spending Yankees and squarely in the first-ever wild-card hunt, forcing Selig to explain his team's success in a system he insists dooms it to failure.

"I'm delighted we're in the wild-card race so far, and I hope it continues," Selig says. "But it is very hard to compete this way on a sustained basis."

It's the same message he delivers daily in Milwaukee, telling fans and politicians how desperately he needs a new stadium to pump up his bottom line. Selig never threatens to leave, he simply takes every opportunity to say the Brewers can't afford to stay in Milwaukee without a new stadium.

It appears Selig may finally get his wish when, with little advance notice, he and Governor Tommy Thompson announce a stadium plan on August 19. The Brewers' proposed new home will have 42,000 seats and 75 luxury suites and will be built in the County Stadium parking lot. It will have a first-of-its-kind natural grass field under a retractable roof. The latter is a necessity if Selig is going to expand past the shrinking Milwaukee market: it's awfully tough to persuade fans to make a two-plus-hour drive if the weather is going to wash away the game.

Under this plan, Selig's team will own 36 percent of the new stadium and receive all the profits from every game and every event they can book, from rock concerts to tractor pulls. In return, the Brewers will contribute $90 million of the proposed $250 million construction cost. They'll also pay $33 million in rent over 30 years, a deal Selig can't break without losing his share of the building and facing legal action. If all goes well, the new stadium will open in 1999.

"Major League Baseball means you're a major league player," Governor Tommy Thompson says, "and Wisconsin cannot afford to lose its major league status."

New taxes will pay the bulk of the cost: a tenth-of-a-cent sales tax increase in Milwaukee and Waukesha Counties and a 1 percent bump in hotel and motel room taxes in the same two locales. To further help the Brewers, Thompson says the quasi-public Wisconsin Housing and Economic Development Authority (WHEDA) will grant Selig a $50 million low-interest loan. The Brewers owner hopes the sale of naming rights will cover the $40 million balance of his obligation.

Selig, Thompson, Milwaukee Mayor John Norquist, and Milwaukee County executive Tom Ament began work on this plan four months ago, after state voters crushed the lottery proposal to fund the stadium. The negotiations were done privately in an attempt to keep opposition to a minimum. The proposal goes to the legislature in September for approval, but critics begin tearing it apart almost the minute the deal is announced.

Senate Majority Leader Mike Ellis, a Republican and longtime Selig critic, calls it "the biggest rip-off of the taxpayer in the history of Wisconsin," and other legislators follow his lead. Ellis wonders how Bud can pay the rent and the WHEDA loan—an estimated $6 million a year—when he was late on his $600,000 rent payment *this* year.

The director of WHEDA, an agency that usually loans money for low-income housing and small businesses, wonders the same thing. Fritz Ruf, a Thompson appointee, says he can't commit to the loan until he inspects the Brewers' books and is assured that they can meet their obligations and have collateral if they can't.

No one is tougher on Selig than the residents of the two counties directly affected, many of whom get their say in a series of public hearings before state legislators. About 400 of them show up at a hearing September 6 to listen to the Brewers owner state his case and to offer up their own.

"Other baseball teams that have built new stadiums have experienced unbelievable success," says Selig, who sits rocking back and forth in his chair while addressing the lawmakers. He reminds them what it felt like to lose the Braves in the '60s and how difficult it was to bring baseball back to his home state.

"We could go elsewhere and do much better," Selig says. "We want to stay here."

Selig's last comment is a mistake, drawing boos and shouts of "Go!" from the crowd. The reaction is so heated that the Waukesha County sheriff's deputies warn protestors to calm down or be escorted out of the building. Many in attendance say they want the Brewers to stay, but most are against the tax hike.

"I'm tired of hearing about how Bud Selig is suffering," says one woman.

"The Brewers are an entertainment industry," another woman says. "I can choose to go or not. The sales tax I have no choice on."

The hearing lasts for several hours, and Selig tells reporters he understands some of the negative reactions. "It's part of getting this package done," he says before rushing off to the airport, where a private plane awaits to fly him to Baltimore.

Selig is on his way to see Cal Ripken play in his 2,131st straight game, breaking Lou Gehrig's record for most consecutive games played. In a few hours, the Acting Commissioner will be sitting in a suite with President Clinton, witnessing history at Camden Yards — the gem of a stadium the people of Maryland built to keep their baseball team from leaving town.

Most of the 46,272 fans are already inside Camden Yards by the time Selig arrives, though those parking closest to the stadium are being delayed by Secret Service agents, who ask them to exchange their car keys for a receipt. With the President and Vice President, a few Supreme Court justices, and dozens of congressional representatives in attendance, every one of these cars will be searched. The keys will be returned when the fans leave.

More than 600 members of the media are also inside. Many

have followed Ripken for more than a week as the Orioles icon approached Gehrig's magic number of 2,130 consecutive games played, a record that has stood for 56 years. It's very different from a year ago, when Camden Yards sat dark, the players were on strike, and Selig was seven days from canceling the World Series. But no one is talking about that now. Baseball connects best with its fans when there's a player chasing history, allowing one generation to share something special with another.

And few moments are more special than this. The entire country's been caught up watching Ripken as he washes away memories of greedy owners and selfish ballplayers one game at a time. It's this very record—showing up for work, day after day, since May 30, 1982—that transforms a millionaire shortstop into a working-class hero.

The Orioles have underachieved all season, but Ripken has performed magnificently in the run-up to this night, hitting .364 and two homers in the eight games of this home stand. The pregame locker room is mobbed with media and Secret Service men, who surround Clinton, his daughter, Chelsea, Vice President Gore, and his son Albert III as they chat with the Orioles star.

"You're a great role model for the young people of the country," Clinton tells Ripken.

Ripken autographs baseballs for Clinton and Gore and writes a message on his signature-model black Louisville Slugger bat for the President: "To President Clinton. Thanks for being here on this special day. Cal Ripken."

It's soon time for the nationally televised game. Ripken charges onto the field, and everyone stands to cheer, including the 260 fans who paid $5,000 each to sit in the two rows flanking the Orioles dugout. The proceeds from the temporary seats—more than $1 million—will fund research for Lou Gehrig's disease at nearby Johns Hopkins.

The Orioles have a 2–1 lead in the 4th inning when Ripken comes to bat for the second time against Shawn Boskie. The young Angels right-hander runs the count to 3–0, and the fans boo. Ripken then scorches Boskie's next pitch halfway up the stands in left field, and the crowd goes wild as Ripken rounds the bases.

But that's nothing compared to what comes next. The first two Angels go down in the top of the 5th, then Damion Easley lofts a soft fly ball to short right field. And when O's second baseman Manny Alexander squeezes the ball tightly at 9:20 p.m., the game is official, and all of Camden Yards erupts.

Banners hanging from the B&O Warehouse behind right field unfurl to show the number 2,131. Black and orange balloons are released and streamers fly everywhere. Sparklers are lit on the stadium's roof, and fireworks explode in the night sky.

Members of the Orioles bullpen run in as the scoreboard flashes IT'S OFFICIAL. Players on both sides hold video cameras as Ripken emerges from the Orioles dugout, points to his parents watching from a luxury box, taps his heart, and waves to the crowd. He takes off his uniform shirt and hands it to his wife Kelly, who's sitting near the dugout.

Teammates Rafael Palmeiro and Bobby Bonilla grab Ripken and shove him onto the field, and Cal jogs down the right-field line, shaking hands and high-fiving fans along the way. Ripken stops in left center and embraces bullpen coach Elrod Hendricks, who has seen every one of the 2,131 games. He approaches the Angels dugout, hugs Rod Carew and Chili Davis, then shakes hands with every player.

He finally reaches the Orioles dugout, but the crowd begs for more. Ripken obliges, patting his chest and mouthing the words, "I can't take any more." After 22 minutes and 15 seconds, Cal finally takes his seat.

The rest of the game—a 4–2 Orioles win—is a formality, a necessary delay before postgame ceremonies. Ripken strolls out to the makeshift stage, flanked by his mother and father. His teammates shower him with gifts, including a 2,131-pound rock for his garden. Orioles owner Peter Angelos hands him the keys to a new Chevy Tahoe.

The clock shows midnight when the regal Joe DiMaggio walks to the microphone. The crowd goes silent. "All records are made to be broken," says DiMaggio, a rising Yankee star when Gehrig played his last game on April 30, 1939. "Wherever my former teammate Lou Gehrig is today, I'm sure he's tipping his cap to you, Cal. You certainly deserve this."

And now it's time for Cal. The 35-year-old star singles out his parents, his wife, and former teammate Eddie Murray for praise. He thanks the Baltimore fans for the support they've shown him in his 15 seasons as an Oriole.

"Tonight I stand here, overwhelmed, as my name is linked with the courageous Lou Gehrig," Ripken says. "I know that if Lou Gehrig is looking down on tonight's activities, he isn't concerned about someone playing one more consecutive game than he did. Instead he's viewing tonight as just another example of what is good and right about the great American game."

Up in Angelos' box, Selig exhales for what feels like the first time in a year. His game still has no labor contract, nor does he have any assurance his team will have a Camden Yards to call its own. But it turns out no matter how many times the owners and players shut down the game in a battle over money, or hustle tax dollars to build new stadiums, the fans keep coming back. And Cal Ripken just showed them why.

It's the game they love.

Chapter 12

NEW FOUNDATIONS

October 5–December 30, 1995

A STUNNED AND tired Wisconsin Senate Majority Leader Mike Ellis walks to the podium to make an announcement he did not think he would be making. The bill to finance a new stadium for the Brewers has just been defeated, 16–15. It's the second failed vote—by the same margin—of this session, one that started 12 hours ago, on Thursday, October 5.

It is 12:38 a.m. on Friday, and it is now dawning on everyone in this chamber that there's a very real chance the Senate will not approve this bill. Which could very well mean that, for the second time in the city's history, Milwaukee could lose its baseball team. And this time for good.

The room turns to chaos as reporters rush into the hallway to get reactions before filing their reports, trying hard not to trip over the cables from the dozen television stations broadcasting live. Milwaukee Mayor John Norquist tells them the stadium plan is "dead." Aides to Governor Tommy Thompson are predicting the Brewers will pack up and leave Wisconsin.

Bud Selig, his face flush with anger, brushes past reporters, refusing to talk. It's a smart decision, given what Selig wants to say. Taking no chances, Selig's public relations man Carl Mueller pulls

Bud down the hallway and into the Assembly wing of the State Capitol.

"How the hell did we lose this vote?" Selig says when he's out of earshot of reporters. "What the hell is Thompson doing now? He can't get us one more damn vote?"

It wasn't supposed to play out this way after the Assembly passed the stadium bill nine days ago. That was a hard-fought win, one that also went deep into the early morning hours. Selig and his daughter Wendy had literally gone door-to-door at the Capitol earlier that day, talking to each Assembly representative, lining up votes. It's the kind of retail politics Bud does best, and in the end he secured approval for the $250 million domed stadium by a comfortable margin, 52–45. Even Ellis, the stadium's fiercest opponent, conceded Selig would have smooth sailing in the Senate.

Now this.

Selig had hoped to ride a winning season into the stadium vote, but his team collapsed down the stretch, losing 25 of its last 32 games to finish far out of the wild-card race. The Yankees won 22 of their last 28 to grab the first-ever AL wild-card ticket to the postseason, and they've just won the first two games of the best-of-five playoff series against the Mariners.

But it's the Indians who grab Selig's attention. Flush with cash from record attendance at their two-year-old stadium—they've sold out every game since June 12—the Indians have a bevy of young stars, went 100–44 to run away with the AL Central, and hold a 2–0 lead on Boston in the American League Division Series, their first postseason appearance in 40 years.

Selig envisions a new stadium energizing his franchise in just the same way. But now all that is in doubt. Earlier in the week, Thompson and other stadium supporters were stunned to learn they were at least three votes short. Hank Aaron made an appearance to ask for support, and so did Robin Yount, but the Democrats remain staunchly opposed to raising taxes. They still want the ballpark built downtown. And Racine's George Petak, who is managing the bill for the Republican majority, changed his vote to no when his district became the fifth to be hit with an increased sales tax to pay for the Brewers' new home.

Assembly leader David Prosser tells Bud to use his office and says Ellis will call for a third vote soon. It's almost 2 a.m. when word reaches Selig that the Republicans are working on an amendment to allow each of the five districts to hold a referendum on raising their sales tax. But that falls apart, too. "Let's get the hell out of here," Selig says to his wife. But Sue preaches patience. "We can't leave now," she says.

Selig is pacing the hallways when he tells Carl Mueller he wants to see Norquist. Though the mayor has lobbied for the stadium, he's always wanted it to be built downtown. As the hours slide by, Selig is beginning to think Norquist is working against him. By the time Norquist arrives, he's sure of it.

"You're the one who's going to be held responsible for this!" Selig yells. "You killed baseball in Milwaukee!"

Norquist is shocked. Yes, the two men don't care for each other. And yes, he wants the stadium built downtown. He's pushed through a host of projects that have pumped new life into Wisconsin's largest city. The ballpark could be the centerpiece, if only Selig would get on board.

But Selig has never changed his mind. And Norquist has worked hard to get this bill passed. It's been a long day— and night— and Selig's attack has a liberating effect on Norquist.

"You're ripping the people off!" Norquist shouts back.

The two men continue trading verbal punches for several minutes before they're pulled apart by aides worried the media will hear the angry exchange. Norquist storms off, leaving Selig to wait for news of his fate.

Ellis calls for a third vote at 4:56 a.m., and he has to concentrate to hear the votes being cast over the voices of TV reporters doing live reports from the chamber. It's going to be tight again, but Petak has suddenly had a change of heart, and his yes vote swings the balance. The bill passes, 16–15.

When Selig gets the news, he walks quickly through the halls and into the Senate chamber, shakes Petak's hand, and hugs several other Senators. There are tears in Selig's eyes as he keeps repeating, "This is a great day, just a great day."

Selig is soon talking to a throng of reporters. It's been seven years since he started down this road. It was never a sure thing, no matter how obvious it was to him that a new stadium was the only way he could keep his team in Milwaukee. Thank God for George Petak.

"I had a different speech prepared about an hour ago," Selig jokes as he finishes up. "You'll never know how grateful I am I didn't make that speech."

There are going to be changes.

Big changes.

It's the final game of the playoffs' opening round, and one only has to watch George Steinbrenner squirming in his seat at Seattle's Kingdome to know that change will soon be sweeping over his Yankees. Or listen to his angry words, as the men forced to sit in this suite with him— Gene Michael, Brian Cashman, David Sussman, and Reggie Jackson— have done for the past three days.

Manager Buck Showalter has been the focus of Steinbrenner's anger, as he's been for most of the season. Steinbrenner tortured his manager with near-daily second-guessing and threats about his contract, which runs out at the end of this month. Only on the final day of the season, when his team clinched the wild-card spot in Toronto—the Yankees' first postseason berth in 14 years—did George relent.

"Buck has been simply brilliant at the end of the season," a teary-eyed Steinbrenner said in the SkyDome locker room. "I don't know what the future holds, but I know firing Buck was never considered."

Steinbrenner's sudden affection aside, Showalter knows full well he is managing for his job against the Mariners. Things looked good when the Yankees won the first two games in New York. But Randy Johnson beat them when the series shifted to Seattle for Game 3, and they blew a 5–0 lead in Game 4 and lost 11–8. Now Game 5—and most likely Showalter's job—seems to be slipping through his fingers.

Mariners manager Lou Piniella—a former Yankees player, GM, and manager—has been the club Steinbrenner has used to beat Showalter with for the last three games. He didn't have much reason to use it tonight until Ken Griffey Jr. slams a monstrous home run off David Cone—the pitcher's 124th pitch—with one out in the bottom of the 8th.

"Piniella's fucking pulling Buck's pants down," Steinbrenner grumbles as he watches Griffey circle the bases after his fifth homer of the series. "This isn't even close."

The Yankees still lead 4–3, but Cone is clearly shaken by Griffey's blast. He gets Edgar Martinez to ground out but loads the bases on a single and two walks. Piniella sends up Doug Strange, a .236 hitter, to pinch-hit for catcher Dan Wilson. Showalter stays riveted on the bench, choosing to go with Cone, who's now thrown 142 pitches, over closer John Wetteland, who gave up a game-winning grand slam in Game 4.

Cone throws a strike, then three straight balls. A called strike brings the count full, but his next pitch is a splitter that bounces at Strange's feet for ball four, forcing in the tying run. Cone all but falls over exhausted, Steinbrenner throws up his arms and curses, and Showalter finally makes a move.

In comes rookie Mariano Rivera, who's been a revelation. Rivera gave up 11 home runs in 67 innings this season, had a 5.51 ERA, and is no one's idea of a rising star. But he was brilliant in the 15-inning Game 2, keeping the Mariners scoreless over the last $3^{1}/_{2}$ innings while striking out five for the win. He tossed another scoreless $1^{1}/_{3}$ innings in Game 4.

And now Rivera strikes out Mike Blowers on three pitches, leading to the instant second-guessing of Showalter for not lifting Cone sooner.

Both managers go to their Game 3 starters to get out of jams in the 9th, and it's soon clear they're going to let Randy Johnson and Jack McDowell determine who advances and who goes home. Johnson cracks first, allowing a run on a walk and a single in the 11th to give the Yankees a 5–4 lead.

But McDowell gets in trouble immediately when Joey Cora and Griffey both single to put runners on the corners for Martinez. Seattle's DH has 11 hits and eight RBI in this series, but Showalter stays with McDowell, again ignoring Wetteland, who throws up his arms in frustration. Steinbrenner sits in his cramped suite, arms folded across his chest, jaw clenched tight.

McDowell gets the first strike, but Martinez rockets the next pitch down the left-field line, and the race is on. Cora scores easily, and here comes Griffey, charging around second and third, cutting each bag in perfect stride. Yankees left fielder Gerald Williams fields the ball cleanly, but Griffey is a blur as he gallops the final 90 feet, sliding in well ahead of the relay throw. The Mariners pile on top of Griffey at home plate, fireworks explode inside the dome, and 57,411 fans go wild as the shell-shocked Yankees trudge off the field.

The celebration is still audible inside the somber Yankees clubhouse when Showalter orders the room cleared to address his team. It was a spectacular series, filled with terrific performances and dramatic moments that quieted the critics of baseball's new playoff format. It's a series many will credit with saving baseball in Seattle when the King County Council approves a new stadium 15 days later.

But it does little for Showalter's job security or that of many of the 20 Yankees without a contract for next season. More than a few have tears in their eyes as Buck walks to the center of the room. "I want to thank you all for everything you did for me," says Showalter, struggling to choke back tears of his own. "Who knows where we'll be next year? But I want you to know how proud I am of everything we have done."

Steinbrenner walks in and heads directly to Mattingly, who played brilliantly in the first postseason games of his career, hitting .417 with five extra-base hits and six RBI. The Boss and the Captain speak quietly for a few moments before Steinbrenner reaches over, puts his hand on the back of Mattingly's neck, and squeezes gently.

It's almost midnight when the Yankees board their plane for the long flight to New York. Once inside, the jet's cabin grows as quiet as their Kingdome locker room. Cone and McDowell are sitting in the back, drained and pitching arms aching, when Mattingly walks down the aisle. He settles into the seat between the two pitchers and puts an arm around each of them.

"I just want to thank you for everything you did this season," Mattingly tells them quietly. "We wouldn't have reached the playoffs without everything you two did, and I wouldn't have had this experience. This really meant a lot to me."

The three men then sit in silence, wondering if this is the last time they will call each other teammates.

When things go wrong, Steinbrenner always feels the need to mete out punishment. The first to be summoned is general manager Gene Michael, who arrives in Tampa nine days after the Yankees' loss in Seattle. Michael's always had a special relationship with Steinbrenner, who values Stick's judgment, respects his backbone—their shouting matches are legendary—and enjoys his company. But this team underachieved, damn it, and there's a price to be paid.

Michael, the architect of a team that's 41 games over .500 the past two years, earned $550,000 this season. He has an option for next season, with a raise to $600,000, but Steinbrenner tells Michael he'll only bring him back as GM under one condition: "I'm cutting your salary to $400,000," he says.

"George, I don't deserve that and you know it," Michael says.

"Well, I'm not going to pay you $600,000 just to fight with you all the time," says Steinbrenner. He then makes Michael another offer.

"You should go back to scouting," he says. "You won't have to be in the office as much, I'll pay you $150,000, and you can sit with me and second-guess everyone, too."

It doesn't take Michael long to agree. He, too, is tired of fighting, and truth be told, evaluating talent is what Michael loves, and freedom from the office—and George's endless phone calls—is what he craves. On October 17, Stick agrees to a two-year deal for $300,000 as director of scouting and a seat at the decision-making table.

But before Michael can leave his current position, says Steinbrenner, there are two more things he has to do: One, find his replacement. Two, put together a list of candidates to replace Buck Showalter.

Michael's not surprised Steinbrenner wants to ax Showalter. Steinbrenner has never felt comfortable with the tightly wound manager. And Michael's heard George complain about all the credit Buck has received for turning the Yankees into a winning team. That's never a good sign for anyone working for the Boss.

But Steinbrenner is also aware that Showalter is popular with the fans, and ditching him is going to require a bit of finesse. So Steinbrenner lets Showalter twist in the wind for 11 days—never once speaking with him—while he gauges the reaction to stories he's planted about Buck's possible departure. He also gets a little help from an October 12 episode of *Seinfeld*, when the back-to-the-camera Steinbrenner character blurts out to George Costanza that he's firing Showalter as the comedy show's credits roll.

He finally brings Showalter to Tampa on October 20, and the two men spend the next two days talking about what went right last season, what went wrong, and how to improve the team. Showalter asks for a three-year deal with a meaningful raise, and wants to know who the next GM will be before making any decision. Steinbrenner offers him a two-year deal for $1.05 million—a nice bump over the three-year, $1 million contract Buck just completed—and tells Showalter he'll consider adding a third season.

But there's a catch: Steinbrenner wants the freedom to dismiss any of Showalter's coaches, at any time, without objection. And he doesn't want to bring back hitting coach Rick Down. It's a poison pill, designed to push Showalter into rejecting the deal. And George can see by Showalter's struggle to remain calm that the ploy is working. "Think it over," George tells him, "and let me know your decision."

Meanwhile, Steinbrenner also wants to know who his next GM will be. "I know you won't believe this," Stick told him last week, "but no one wants the job." What does Stick mean, no one wants the job? *This is the Yankees!* Michael told him that experienced execs like outgoing Tigers GM Bill Lajoie and top assistants like the Angels' Mike Port said no without hesitation. Joe Torre was in last week and told Michael that all the headaches of dealing so closely with Steinbrenner aren't worth the $400,000 the Yankees are offering.

But on October 22, Stick calls Steinbrenner with good news: he's spoken with Houston's Bob Watson, and the game's only black GM is interested. George is intrigued. Watson, a two-time All-Star first baseman, played for the Yankees for two of his 19 seasons. He's produced a winning team in his two years as GM in Houston—on a tight budget—and he knows baseball.

"Offer him the $400,000 you turned down for two years," Stein-brenner says.

Michael and George's son-in-law, general partner Joe Molloy, spend five hours on the phone the next day banging out a deal with Watson. Steinbrenner phones in late in the talks to add an important detail. "Bob, it's time for me to take a step back," Steinbrenner tells the 49-year-old Watson. "You and Joe Molloy will run this team. I will only be involved in the major decisions."

Watson knows full well that Steinbrenner has burned through 15 general managers in 23 years. But Watson enjoyed his two seasons in New York. He was grateful in 1982, when Steinbrenner had three trades lined up for him and allowed Watson to choose where he wanted to go. (He chose Atlanta, so he could play under Joe Torre.)

And these are the Yankees. *How can you turn down a chance to join the Yankees?*

He tells Steinbrenner he wants the job, and that's when George gives Watson his first assignment. "Give me a list of who you want as your manager," Steinbrenner says. "Buck Showalter is not coming back." There has been no announcement about Showalter's future, so Watson asks how this will be handled. "I've had some conversations already, and Buck and I have a long-standing relationship," Steinbrenner says. "Let me handle it."

Watson is soon on a conference call with the media from his home in Houston, describing his new position as the most prestigious in baseball, and telling reporters he wouldn't have taken this job if he didn't think he could handle the pressure. Watson's whirlwind day complete, the Yankees' new GM gives Molloy his list of managers—with Torre's name at the top—and flies to Cleveland for the World Series.

Steinbrenner checks in on Showalter a day later. We've named a general manager, the Yankees owner tells him—it's time to make your decision. "I need more time, Mr. Steinbrenner," Showalter says. "I'll give you an answer tomorrow." And when Showalter calls Steinbrenner the next day, the conversation focuses on Buck's coaching staff. Showalter still wants to protect them all.

"I'm sorry, but I can't agree to that," Steinbrenner tells him. "Some of them have to go, especially Rick Down."

Showalter is not willing to sacrifice his hitting coach. Or any of his coaches. "I can't agree to the contract as it is structured," he tells Steinbrenner, who can almost hear the door of his trap snap shut. "Mr. Steinbrenner, I'm sorry, but I have to turn down this offer."

"Well, if that's the way you feel, I understand," says George, and their 10-minute conversation is over. And so is Showalter's 17-year career with the Yankees organization.

Baseball instituted a rule a while back mandating that no major announcements be made during the World Series. Steinbrenner already ignored the rule on Monday when he announced Bob Watson as his new GM. Now it's only an hour before the Braves and Indians take the field for Game 5 in Cleveland when the Yankees release a statement:

Buck Showalter, last season's AL Manager of the Year, has resigned as manager of the New York Yankees.

"We tried but were unable to dissuade Buck," Steinbrenner says in the statement. "I have nothing but praise for Buck and the job he did for us, and I told him I am very upset by his leaving. I wish Buck and his fine little family nothing but the best."

At first glance, baseball executives think the release they've been handed is a joke. Watson knows otherwise and remains silent. Showalter's wife Angela hears the news from reporters, then calls her husband as he's driving home from a round of golf. Showalter is incredulous when he returns reporters' calls.

"I have never resigned a job in my life," Showalter repeats to each reporter. "I thought all I'd done was reject the offer on the table."

The war of words is still raging the next day—Steinbrenner insists Buck resigned; "Heavens, no," Showalter tells reporters—when Watson flies into Tampa to sign his contract and meet the Boss. Steinbrenner welcomes him to the Yankees and once again tells Watson that he'll be stepping back. "It will be you and Joe Molloy who will be running the team," George repeats.

And now he wants to talk about the man who will replace Showalter. Watson and Gene Michael are pushing for Torre. The Boss has reservations about the manager who was fired by St. Louis in June, has an 894–1,003 career record, and not a single postseason win to his credit. Hell, despite making nine All-Star teams in his 18-year playing career, Torre's never once played in the postseason.

"The guy's a loser," George tells Watson. "He hasn't won a World Series."

"No, he's not a loser. A lot of people haven't won a World Series," Watson says. "I've played for him, I've coached for him, and if we put the right people around him, he'll do a great job for the Yankees."

"All right," Steinbrenner says. "But if this doesn't work, it's on you."

It's only a matter of days before the 55-year-old Torre, comforted by having his friend Watson between him and George, agrees to a two-year contract that will pay him $500,000 the first season and $550,000 the second. Torre and Watson both meet the media on November 2 at Yankee Stadium, and their reception is less than warm. Steinbrenner is absent, and both men are grilled about working for a man who fires general managers and managers seemingly on a whim.

"This is a once-in-a-lifetime situation," Torre says. "When you walk into Yankee Stadium, you get goose bumps."

"What about when you walk into Steinbrenner's office?" he's asked.

"When you get married, do you think you're always going to have a great relationship?" says Torre, whose third wife is pregnant with the couple's first child. "To have an opportunity to win is worth all the negative sides you want to talk about."

Then it's Watson's turn. Yes, says Watson, he's aware this is the 20th time Steinbrenner has changed managers. Yes, there were other managers on his list. But he's convinced Torre is the right man. "I did not bring in any other candidates after speaking to Joe," Watson says. "I really feel this is the right man to lead the Yankees."

"When Bob called me, the realization of what the Yankees organization means hit me," Torre tells the skeptical media. "I was in the office where the World Series trophy sits. That's the missing piece in my career."

What about working for a man who will often treat you as a

child? another reporter asks. "We all have bosses," Torre says. "I can't be concerned until something happens I think isn't right."

Headline writers and columnists have a field day in the papers, especially the *New York Daily News,* which runs a picture of a smiling Torre under a big, bold headline: CLUELESS JOE. The subhead reads: TORRE HAS NO IDEA WHAT HE'S GETTING INTO.

"He thinks he knows, but he has not a clue," columnist Ian O'Connor writes. "It is always a sad occasion when a man becomes a muppet."

But Torre and Watson shrug off the media and get to work. Their first move is trading for defensive-minded catcher Joe Girardi. Wade Boggs re-signs for two years and $4.05 million on December 5. Two days later, the team replaces the retiring Don Mattingly with Tampa native Tino Martinez, who Steinbrenner personally signs to a five-year, $20 million extension after acquiring the 27-year-old power hitter in a five-player trade. Watson signs veteran infielder Mariano Duncan on December 11.

Steinbrenner signed Doc Gooden, another of his rehab projects, in mid-October, but the team still needs pitching. The Yankees and Cone are close to a deal when Steinbrenner, frustrated that his ace is taking so long to decide, tells Watson to reduce their offer. An angry Cone renews talks with Baltimore. Alarmed at the news, Steinbrenner calls the pitcher from a pay phone in a Tampa hospital, where he's visiting a friend.

"David, there must have been miscommunication—our original offer stands," Steinbrenner tells him. "I will also include a no-trade clause.

"And David, you have to understand that New York is where you belong. Mattingly is retired, and you are going to be Mr. Yankee. You're a leader, and that is what this team needs. I want you to play for the Yankees for the rest of your career."

The deal also includes two option years, which would keep Cone a Yankee through 2000. He agrees on the spot. Steinbrenner calls Watson soon after he finishes with Cone.

"Well, you got him," Steinbrenner says.

"Got who?" Watson asks.

"You got Cone," Steinbrenner says. "I gave him a no-trade clause, and he signed."

"No, George—you got him," says Watson, who's beginning to understand that George will always be his own GM.

The Yankees trade for Tim Raines, then sign free agent left-hander Kenny Rogers to a four-year, $19.5 million deal before the year is out. The spending spree pushes the Yankees' payroll well past the $39 million budget Steinbrenner gave Watson, prompting Bud Selig to complain to his friend that he's once again out of control. Watson learns two more things about his new boss: the man ignores budgets, and he ignores the Acting Commissioner.

In the space of three months, Steinbrenner has opened his wallet and pulled together many of the ingredients that will soon turn his Yankees into the finest franchise in the game. "Oh, don't worry about the money," Steinbrenner tells his GM.

Especially when it is money well spent.

Chapter 13

TRUE LIES

January 25–August 31, 1996

G‍EORGE STEINBRENNER IS sitting, back to the camera as always, in the cramped Queens home of Frank and Estelle Costanza. In this January 1996 episode of *Seinfeld,* a series of missteps convinces the faux Steinbrenner that Frank and Estelle's son George, an assistant to the Yankees' traveling secretary, is dead. And the Boss is there to deliver the news personally.

"But he was so young," says Estelle, wiping away a tear. "How could this have happened?"

"Well, he was logging some pretty heavy hours," Steinbrenner says. "That kid was a human dynamo."

Frank is sitting next to his wife, slowly shaking his head, eyes toward the floor. Grief-stricken? Well, yes, but...

"Why the hell did you trade Jay Buhner?" Frank suddenly says to Steinbrenner, his voice steadily rising. "He hit 30 home runs and over 100 RBI last year. He has a rocket for an arm."

Pause.

"You don't know what the *hell* you're doing!"

"He was a good prospect, no question about it," the Boss says. "But my baseball people loved Ken Phelps' bat. They kept saying, 'Ken Phelps, Ken Phelps.'"

This episode is every Yankees fan's nightmare: their team's impulsive owner trading prospects for aging veterans or journeymen he mistakes for stars. (Buhner would have three straight 40 home run, 100 RBI seasons, and Phelps was gone after 131 nondescript games.) Even die-hard fans can't remember who George got when he shipped out future Cy Young winner Doug Drabek, two-time NL batting champ Willie McGee, and two-time NL home run champ Fred McGriff, all products of the Yankees fertile farm system.

That George was easy to hate. But Jerry Seinfeld's send-up of Steinbrenner—this is George's seventh appearance since May of 1994—has done wonders to soften his image. And in the spring of 1996, this George, now 65, is different. Maybe not a lot, but enough.

The first to pick up on it is David Cone, now in his first spring training with the Yankees, who realizes what Steinbrenner really wants is for his players to treat him as part of his own team.

"George wants us to talk to him, to ask his advice," Cone tells his teammates. "He wants to have a *relationship* with us."

Cone's wit can be as sharp and disarming as his deep array of pitches, and in a clubhouse full of introverts, his ability to connect with the team's owner is almost as valuable as his resilient right arm. Especially on days when Steinbrenner decides to stroll or storm into the clubhouse.

"George, I don't think Paul [O'Neill] is ready today," Cone will tell Steinbrenner. "He needs a pep talk from you."

And Steinbrenner beams.

"You better be ready today," George will tell Cone.

"Just don't fuck anybody up," Cone shoots back.

And George will walk away smiling.

Joe Torre gets it, too. The son of a New York City police detective who emotionally abused Joe and his four older brothers and sisters, Torre understands only too well what Steinbrenner endured with his own father. Like Cone, Torre knows the right buttons to push, too, and he's confident enough to defer to the Boss without losing the respect of his players.

"Mr. Steinbrenner is the owner," Torre tells reporters when camp opens on February 15, "and he can say what he wants to say."

Torre's relaxed approach is welcomed by his players, who'd grown tired of Showalter's micromanaging. Torre tells the Yankees he won't manage through the media — a favorite practice of George and many of his previous managers — and tells reporters he won't engage in the game of dueling quotes with his owner. "You can talk to him or you can talk to me," Torre tells the beat writers. "You decide. Don't try to play us off each other."

Torre shares Steinbrenner's high expectations for this $54 million team. Veterans Cone, Jimmy Key, Wetteland, O'Neill, and Tino Martinez are in their primes. Aging stars Wade Boggs and Tim Raines can still perform. And up-and-coming Bernie Williams and Andy Pettitte are ready to blossom.

But it's two more of George's kids — one considered a sure thing, the other a mystery — who will truly change the face and future of the franchise.

It was Gene Michael who first saw something special in Mariano Rivera. It wasn't just the control and the fastball that jumped from the high 80s to mid-to-upper 90s after arm surgery in 1994. It was Mo's preternatural calm, no matter what the situation, that Michael found so intriguing.

But convincing everyone about the newcomers this spring has not been easy. Torre, a former All-Star catcher, wonders how the slender Panamanian can succeed using just one pitch, a fastball with little movement. So does general manager Bob Watson, who watches Rivera give up six runs and five hits in $1\frac{1}{3}$ innings of an intrasquad game on February 26 and dangles the 25-year-old reliever in front of half a dozen teams. He finds no takers.

Michael has an easier time convincing everyone it's time to move aging Tony Fernandez to second and start rookie Derek Jeter at short. "He's going to make mistakes, but he's ready," Michael tells Steinbrenner. "We put him at shortstop and don't even think about making a change until May."

Jeter does indeed make mistakes early, throwing the ball away in the 1st inning of his first game at Legends Field in Tampa, the Yankees' new spring training home. The 21-year-old goes hitless in his first 11 at bats, too. But he soon settles down, impressing Torre with his range and an inside-out swing that sends line drives flying to all fields. "If he hits .240 and plays solid defense, he'll be fine," Torre is soon telling everyone.

But on March 24, Fernandez dives for a ball and fractures his right elbow, putting Steinbrenner in panic mode. Fernandez was Plan B if Jeter flopped. When Michael walks into camp later that day, Watson grabs him. There's a meeting in Torre's office, the GM says. The Boss is talking about sending Jeter down and bringing in another veteran.

"George, you promised we weren't going to do this," Michael says as soon as he enters the room.

"I know, I know, I was supposed to stay away until the end of May," Steinbrenner says.

But the Boss is worried. Will Jeter hit? Will the errors end? Can he handle New York? "Are we sure this is the right thing to do?" Steinbrenner asks.

Yes, says Michael. Torre agrees, and so does Watson.

Then Willie Randolph, Torre's infield coach, speaks up.

"As long as we keep him off the Columbus shuttle, he'll keep his confidence up," says Randolph, using Yankee-speak for George's habit of shuttling players between New York and their top minor league team in Ohio. "The kid is a hard worker, and I'll work with him every day."

"Yeah, well, you think so?" George says, still nervous. "I don't know this kid."

"We have a good supporting cast," says Randolph. "We can afford to find out if the kid can play."

George backs off, and he's not disappointed. Jeter opens the season with a home run and a dazzling over-the-shoulder catch in the Yankees' 7–1 win on a freezing cold day in Cleveland. The kid raps out three more hits and scores three runs as the Yanks take two straight from the defending AL champs. Torre bats Jeter ninth to lessen the pressure on his young shortstop, but it's Derek who walks up to his manager before their home opener as Yankees on April 9 and asks, "So are you ready for this?"

Jeter is almost too good to be true. The son of an African American father who works as a drug counselor and a white mother who works as an accountant, Jeter is boyishly handsome and wonderfully respectful. He refers to the owner as Mr. Steinbrenner, calls his manager Mr. Torre, and his team-first approach is vital to transforming these Yankees into a team most fans will find hard to hate, no matter how much money the owner spends.

Confident without being cocky, he also charms the New York media, which is already talking him up as Rookie of the Year by the time the Yankees move into first place on April 28.

If Jeter is a pleasant surprise, Rivera is a revelation. Installed as the set-up man for Wetteland, Rivera allows just three runs in his first 16 appearances—an 0.88 ERA—and strikes out 32 in 30⅓ innings. Mo's still using his one pitch, but his rising fastball reaches 98 mph and is all but unhittable.

Most surprising of all is how the Yankees are winning. While home runs again dominate baseball this spring, Steinbrenner's men are playing small ball. No Yankee will hit 30 home runs in a season when a record 17 players will hit 40 or more. Instead, Torre's team relies on advancing runners, sac flies, and two-out singles.

The starting pitching is solid, but it's the Rivera-Wetteland combination that makes this team's staff special. The two relievers are so dominant that opponents soon realize the game is over if they trail after the 6th inning. Indeed, the Yanks will finish 70–3 when holding a lead after six.

Steinbrenner has little to worry about this spring until Cone goes down suddenly in early May. Despite pitching well—Cone starts 4–1, with a league-leading 2.02 ERA—the 33-year-old ace has been fighting numbness in the fingers of his pitching hand since training camp. Doctors had to run two sets of tests before they found a small aneurysm—a swelling of a blood vessel that can burst if left untreated—in the front of his right shoulder.

On May 7, Watson tells the team their emotional leader will have surgery the next day and may miss the rest of the season. The players are stunned. George responds by driving Watson batty—he wants to bring back Darryl Strawberry. Again.

"We just lost the ace of our staff," Watson tells George. "We need a pitcher, not another hitter."

"I want to sign Darryl," Steinbrenner insists. "We need someone who can hit home runs."

Now Watson is stunned. His team is set at DH with Ruben Sierra and Tim Raines. The Yankees didn't pick up Darryl's option last winter, thinking his occasional big bat did not make up for his poor outfield play, and Strawberry had to find work in the independent Northern League in hopes of landing another big-league job.

"We don't need Strawberry," Watson tells his boss.

"I want Darryl," Steinbrenner repeats.

A frustrated Watson tries to find a trump card. "I thought you agreed that Joe Molloy and I were going to run this team," he says.

"Not anymore," George answers. "I'm taking back control."

It's an hour before Mark McGwire and the Oakland A's play the Brewers on the night of June 14, and Bud Selig is walking among the fans in the parking lot of County Stadium. Selig likes chatting with fans, but he's Commissioner now, and there just don't seem to be as many hours in the day.

Tonight, however, Selig isn't here to swap stories about his old Brewers teams or ask fans what they think about the current crew. He took two punches to the gut earlier today, and he's ready to fight back. The first hit was delivered by the consulting firm Evensen Dodge, which was hired by the Board overseeing the construction of the Brewers' new stadium. The consultants issued a report calling Selig's team a risky investment that will bleed money for years to come.

The Stadium Board itself delivered the second blow, rejecting Selig's latest plan to finance his team's $90 million contribution to the new stadium. The Board told Selig he had two weeks to come up with another plan or it would stop collecting the sales tax increase needed to pay the state's $160 million share of the project.

This confrontation has been brewing since February, after Selig once again told state officials that he did not have collateral for the $50 million low-interest WHEDA loan Governor Tommy Thompson arranged to help finance the team's share of the $250 million domed stadium. Without collateral, said WHEDA director Fritz Ruf, he had no choice but to withhold the loan, leaving Selig fuming and scrambling for another plan.

Thompson was adamant that the state pull the $50 million loan when he learned Selig could not put up any collateral. Selig insists Thompson and the state knew he had no collateral well before they committed to making the loan. Thompson says Bud has to pay his fair share and vows not to spend a nickel more than the $160 million he already promised.

The deeper examinations of Brewers finances that followed did not help Selig's cause. The state auditor who reviewed the team's books claimed he wasn't shown the extent of the Brewers' debt on his first pass. It was only after he agreed not to tell legislators what he found, the auditor said, that he was given a full look at the team's books.

Selig insisted he'd hidden nothing, but taxpayers, lawmakers, and the media stopped listening. Work on the stadium was halted, and Selig was peppered with ideas about how to solve his financing problem. Milwaukee Mayor John Norquist again offered a $50 million loan if Selig agreed to build the stadium downtown. Others called for Selig to sell a piece of the team to raise the money he needed.

"I've never in all my years in baseball watched public officials engage themselves in the internal operation of a baseball team," Selig said. "And it isn't going to happen here."

Republican politicians had their own reason to be unhappy with Selig. On June 4, the voters of Racine recalled George Petak, the Republican State Senator who cast the deciding vote in favor of financing Selig's stadium. Petak's recall, the first in Wisconsin history, flipped control of the Senate to the Democrats, thereby crippling Governor Thompson's third-term agenda. Supporting Selig had cost the Republicans dearly.

Today's Stadium Board ultimatum leaves Selig furious, and he decides it's time to go straight to the team's fans. And there are a few thousand of them now in County Stadium's parking lot, crowding around a makeshift platform as a visibly angry Selig walks up to the microphone. He wants them all to know their team may not be playing in their town too much longer.

And he wants to make damn sure they know who's to blame.

Selig's lips are trembling as he begins his pitch. "I've witnessed the sadness of seeing gates closed," he says. "Then we brought baseball back to Milwaukee, and I didn't think we'd ever have to worry about these things again. But we've been forced to do things that no other team in any sport has ever done. I find that very troubling."

Bud's not a polished speaker, but his passion comes across and the crowd is behind him. These are the fans who arrive hours before a game for tailgate parties, the ones Selig says won't go to a downtown stadium. These are the die-hards who would truly miss the Brewers if Selig were to actually make good on his threat to leave.

"If there is anybody left in Wisconsin who doesn't believe that this was political and had nothing to do with economics," says Selig, his voice rising, "then they haven't followed the story."

While Selig's story in Milwaukee grows bleak, the story of baseball everywhere else is bright—even without a labor deal. The new Fox contract is paying each team $11 million, almost double what they each received a year ago. Fox's up-tempo style and fresh camera angles bring an air of excitement—and the all-important 18–34 male demographic—to its baseball broadcasts. Nike's ad campaign is making Ken Griffey Jr. the smiling face of baseball, and attendance is up across the game.

Things are even looking up on the labor front. Hiring Randy Levine back in September was a sign to the union that Selig wanted a deal, not another confrontation. Levine is a dealmaker, not a hard-liner. Selig also persuaded the owners to approve a new revenue sharing plan, one that would send an additional $3.5 million to small market teams like his. And he won approval for interleague play, which will be another boost to revenues when Levine and Don Fehr finally reach an agreement.

All of which makes Selig's messy stadium battle even more galling. And it's killing business—in 30 home games, the Brewers have drawn less than 10,000 fans a dozen times. Worse, Thompson has already announced that Selig's financing problem has pushed back the opening of the stadium to 2000, costing Milwaukee the '99 All-Star Game and the revenue bump it brings to the host city and team.

The 14,404 fans who bought tickets for tonight's game had no idea they'd also be watching Selig, who right now is wrapping up his 30-minute appeal as game time nears. All that's left, Selig says, is to sit down with Thompson next week and try to save baseball in Milwaukee one more time.

"I want to meet with the governor—alone—and determine where this project is," Selig says.

But he has no intention of waiting quietly. Just a few hours later he slips into the Brewers television booth for an interview, where he tells listeners he has no idea why the politicians are trying to force him out of Milwaukee. The stadium cameraman is ready when Selig leaves the booth. An image of Selig pops onto the scoreboard video screen, just above the bold-lettered tagline: COMMITTED TO KEEPING BASEBALL IN MILWAUKEE. Selig waves as the sparse crowd stands and cheers. He holds his two thumbs up when the fans start chanting "Bud! Bud! Bud!"

Two days later, Selig does a Q&A with the *Journal Sentinel,* thanking Brewers fans for their support and criticizing his opponents. At midweek, the paper reports that an unnamed baseball owner says Charlotte is MLB's top choice for the Brewers' new home if a stadium isn't approved.

Selig gets his private meeting with Thompson at County Stadium on June 22. It's the first time the men have spoken in two weeks, which is no accident. Thompson long ago tired of Bud's act and is appalled that Selig is still complaining even as the governor spends precious political capital to help him. We'll get the stadium built, Thompson tells Selig, but we'll need time to work out the details. And it would be great if you could tone down the rhetoric.

But there's no way Selig is shutting down his PR blitz, not with another event scheduled later that night. This time there are 10,000 fans in the County Stadium parking lot for a rally. And the fans are chanting Selig's name when it's Bud's turn to speak.

"Someday our children and our children's children are going to be able to watch major league baseball in Wisconsin because of what you did here today," Selig tells them.

Watching all this play out is Mike Joyce, the longtime director of Milwaukee's ultraconservative Bradley Foundation. Joyce, a former aide to President Ronald Reagan, has used Bradley's nearly half-billion-dollar endowment to promote supply-side economics and advance the careers of conservative jurists Robert Bork and Antonin Scalia. He's currently donating freely to those attacking President Clinton in the Whitewater investigation.

Joyce is also a baseball fan and has an 11-year-old son who lives and dies with the Brewers. On June 25, Joyce meets with Bud and Wendy, spending an hour listening to everything that's gone wrong. "Thanks for your time," is all he says as the Seligs leave. A day later, Joyce has an announcement to make.

First he calls Selig and tells him he's offering a $20 million loan to build a stadium. Next he calls Thompson and tells the governor he'll grant the loan at almost no interest to "break the political logjam." Minutes later, he's sitting in the conference room of his foundation explaining his decision to reporters.

"Forget the politics; forget the players' strike; forget the whining of the few but loud malcontents," Joyce says. "Remember this: major league baseball is an authentic, unifying, and eloquent expression of American tradition that is played in our greatest cities.

"We seek no ownership. We do not wish to be an equity partner. We're doing this for this community."

Joyce's announcement does, indeed, break the logjam. And three days later, on June 29, Thompson is standing with Selig to announce they finally have a deal. The state will take on the $20 million loan from the Bradley Foundation and a $1 million loan from Milwaukee's Helfaer Foundation. Both loans—which have to go through the state to protect the organizations' tax-exempt status—will be covered by Brewers rent payments.

Norquist pledges a $15 million loan from the city, and a group of local businessmen put up another $14 million in loans. The American League will extend a $10 million line of credit to cover any increased costs. And Selig will use the $41.2 million deal he just signed with the Miller Brewing Company for the stadium naming rights to cover the balance of his $90 million responsibility.

Thompson concedes the state is now on the hook for an additional $21 million should the Brewers default—a position he was unwilling to be put in by the WHEDA loan—but Joyce covers for Thompson. "Don't put too much emphasis on repayment," he says.

"It's a charitable investment." (In fact, the loan will be forgiven after $6 million is repaid.)

"This deal has been a long time in coming," Thompson says.

And for Selig, it's been well worth the wait. The team is now taking loans for $29 million instead of $50 million, cutting its borrowing costs almost in half. Bud doesn't have to sell off a piece of his team to raise money, and the stadium will be built exactly where he wants it.

"On behalf of the Brewers, I thank everybody," Selig says. "I think Major League Baseball will be pleased with this deal because it allows us to become a viable ball club in this market."

But not just yet. Four weeks later Brewers fans are hit with bad news. Greg Vaughn, who leads Milwaukee with 31 home runs and 91 RBI, has been traded to San Diego for three young players who'll never see the inside of Miller Park wearing a Brewers uniform. The 31-year-old Vaughn will be a free agent at season's end, and the Brewers have decided they don't have the money to sign the team's best player.

Looks like the financial wizards at Evensen Dodge weren't too far off the mark.

Ken Caminiti knows it's time.

It's June 24, eight weeks since the Padres' star third baseman dove for a ball, fell hard on his left shoulder, and tore his rotator cuff. Two cortisone shots in early May haven't stopped the pain. Nor has the fistful of prescription painkillers he knocks back with a large cup of vodka and a hint of orange juice.

The 33-year-old star hasn't been able to lift his left arm over his head without intense pain, much less drive the ball the way he did a year ago, when he hit .302, belted 26 homers, and drove in 94 runs, all career highs. He's already missed 15 games, and he's been all but invisible in the 38 games he's played, hitting .204 with just six homers.

Caminiti's reckless disregard for his body has left him with numerous scars and a reputation for playing through pain during his 10 seasons with the Astros and Padres. But this time the pain is too great, his play too subpar, and the results too clear: the Padres are

23–29 since Caminiti wrecked his shoulder, and their chances of winning the NL West, so bright when the season began, are already beginning to fade.

Yes, Caminiti knows it's time.

So on this rare day off, Caminiti drives the 20 miles south to Tijuana. He pulls up to the first pharmacy he sees, walks in, and tells the man behind the counter he wants anabolic steroids, a drug both legal and easy to buy once you cross the border. *"Testosterona,"* the man says. Caminiti nods yes and purchases enough to last him through October.

Caminiti is no stranger to using drugs to dull his pain. He'll often take two or three times the prescribed dose of painkillers to soothe the aches from his many injuries. Teammates marvel at his ability to empty the hotel minibar, mix alcohol with cocaine, party all night, and be ready to play the next day. Close friends Jeff Bagwell and Craig Biggio convinced Caminiti to enter a 12-day alcohol rehab program in the 1993 offseason. A sober Caminiti went on to make his first All-Star team the following season. Sadly, he's back to drinking again.

Caminiti's never used steroids, but he's hardly unaware of the impact they've had on the game. He's watched steroid use build for years and reach critical mass this April in a big way. The Mariners hit a record 44 home runs in the first month of the season, the best of five teams that broke the record of 38. The Twins broke another record by scoring 175 runs in their first 25 games, three teams scored 20 or more runs in a single game, and the Expos hit a record six grand slams.

Barry Bonds, Gary Sheffield, and Brady Anderson all tied the major league record with 11 home runs in the season's first month. Anderson, the Orioles' 32-year-old leadoff hitter who's averaged 14 home runs the last three seasons, homered to open four consecutive games, yet another record. Orioles execs used to jokingly blow hard whenever Brady hit a fly ball, trying to "nudge" it over the fence. They rarely have to pucker up this season.

And the home run barrage didn't slow after April. The White Sox hit seven home runs in two late-May games against the Brewers. The Braves belted six against the Reds on May 31, the same day the

Expos' Henry Rodriguez hit his 20th home run, reaching that number earlier than anyone in National League history.

Sammy Sosa hit three home runs against the Phillies on June 5, the seventh player this season to hit three in one game. The Cubs outfielder was one of three players to hit two home runs in the same inning this season.

Everyone has a theory for the jump in offense, but not everyone is as frank as Royals pitcher Tim Belcher, who told the *Los Angeles Times*, "Everybody's blaming the pitchers, but it's smaller strike zones, smaller parks, and steroids. That's not a good combination." Nor as blunt as Pittsburgh manager Jim Leyland. "I'd swear on a stack of Bibles we don't have steroids on this team," Leyland said. "But I wouldn't know about the rest of baseball."

There are other numbers to consider, too. Despite horrible weather in the East and Midwest, attendance in April was up 7 percent. ESPN's baseball ratings jumped 19 percent. Sales of licensed merchandise are up 40 percent, and apparel and hat sales are up 86 percent.

All Caminiti cares about is the pain in his shoulder, and he's hoping the steroids do the trick. In a hurry—and, unlike experienced users, with little idea about cycling on and off the drug— Caminiti begins injecting steroids and doesn't stop. The results are immediate. He hits safely in the last six games of June, rapping out 12 hits in 25 at bats—a .480 average—with three home runs and 11 RBI.

The steroids not only make Caminiti feel better, they help him add several pounds of muscle on his six-foot, 200-pound frame in a matter of weeks. Sure, he's worried about how much his testicles have shrunk, but not enough to stop using the drug. Not when the ball is flying off his bat.

And not when the Padres are winning again. Caminiti is nothing short of stellar in July, hitting six home runs with 26 RBI and a .357 average while playing a flawless third base. With their cleanup hitter back and better than ever, the Padres go 15–12, finishing July in first place in the NL West, a half game ahead of the Dodgers.

"He lifts everyone on the team to a higher level," Padres GM

Kevin Towers says. "Teammates see him playing with a torn rotator and other injuries and they give a little more effort."

Padres fans cannot get enough of their hero, whose toughness is celebrated with the song "Where Have All the Cowboys Gone?" every time Caminiti walks to the plate. The buff third baseman is videotaped warming up with his shirt off, and the Padres run the clip regularly on the Qualcomm Stadium scoreboard. Fans are turning out in record numbers, putting the Padres on pace to surpass 2 million in attendance for the first time since 1985. And local politicians, who've been blocking funds to upgrade Qualcomm, are now talking about building an entirely new stadium.

Caminiti blazes through August, hitting 14 home runs to reach a career-high 31. Pumped up on his *testosterona*, Caminiti gets stronger in the season's dog days, hitting .449 over the last 14 games of the month — 11 of them Padres wins. National writers are talking about Caminiti as the MVP favorite in profiles, lauding his willingness to play through pain and his dedication to the nutritional supplements he carries around in a little black bag.

No more painkillers. Not as much booze. A bag of pills and powders for the writers to see, a bag of syringes and steroids to use when he's alone. As baseball enters the stretch run, Caminiti is the leader of a first-place team and the best third baseman in the game.

And he is living a lie.

But then, who in baseball isn't?

Chapter 14

DYNASTY

August 8–October 26, 1996

GEORGE STEINBRENNER CAN only smile when he reads the *New York Times* on August 8. FOR THE BOSS, A CHANGE FOR THE BETTER is the headline atop the column about the kinder, gentler Yankees owner, the latest in a season-long series of stories marveling at the new George. And this one carries the stamp of approval of two men who played for the Boss and are now on the front lines.

"It's not like it was in the real needy days, where he was always being quoted in the papers and stuff," coach Willie Randolph says. "His opinion is obviously strong...but it seems he's really listening to what Joe and Bob need and want."

Bob Watson agrees. "He has mellowed," says George's 12th GM. "During the interview process he said he was not going to be involved in a lot of the decision-making process and, for the most part, he hasn't."

All of which would be fine...if it were true.

But it's not.

This is: George is still George, only wiser. Instead of regularly howling in the media, Steinbrenner has stayed behind the scenes, focusing his rants almost exclusively on one man—Watson, whose life he's made a living hell since the day they locked horns over Strawberry.

What makes this especially maddening for Watson is there's so little reason for Steinbrenner to complain, given what his team's accomplished in the face of unrelenting adversity. First there was Cone's surgery. A month later Bernie Williams' 5-year-old son had lifesaving surgery to stop a rapidly spreading ear infection. Torre's 64-year-old brother Frank has been battling serious heart problems since May, and his 68-year-old brother Rocco died of a heart attack at home on June 21 while watching a Yankees game.

With all that, the Yanks reach the All-Star break at a league-best 52–33 and hold a six-game lead over Baltimore in the AL East. Torre coaxes a breakout season from the introverted Williams, who reaches midseason hitting .326 with 16 home runs. Andy Pettitte is 13–4, and Rivera allows only 38 hits and strikes out 70 in 60 innings. "I just know this team is going to the World Series," says the normally reserved Rivera.

It sure looks that way after the Yankees open the second half with a four-game sweep of the Orioles. Steinbrenner did indeed sign Strawberry, and it's Straw's walk-off, two-run homer that beats the Royals on July 28. The win pushes New York's AL East lead to a season-best 12 games.

Watson pulls off a coup three days later, sending malcontent Ruben Sierra to Detroit for Cecil Fielder. Big Daddy has 26 home runs and gives Torre the right-handed bat he's wanted since spring training. Fielder's so happy to join New York that he agrees to defer $2 million of the $7.2 million he's set to earn next season to finalize the trade.

But none of this has stopped Steinbrenner from calling Watson two, three, four or more times a day to criticize whichever player he thought was coming up short. Why did Bernie throw to the wrong base? Why didn't O'Neill reach a bloop single to right? How could Bob Wickman blow another save? Steinbrenner wanted this player benched, or that player sent to Columbus, or every coach fired at one time or another.

George is calling Torre, too, though Watson does his best to shield his manager and players from most of Steinbrenner's outbursts. But there's little Watson can do to fend off George when an injury to John Wetteland in mid-August and a trade gone bad sends the team into a tailspin.

Steinbrenner first turns up the volume after left-handed reliever Graeme Lloyd, acquired from the Brewers, reveals he received a cortisone shot for elbow tendinitis four days before the August 23 trade. That may explain why the six-foot-eight Australian has been hammered for 10 runs in his last five appearances.

The Yankees lose 26 of 44 games, chopping their 12-game lead over Baltimore to four, and the Boss needs someone to blame. So he tells Watson his job is on the line unless Lloyd rebounds. He tells reporters the team's playoff hopes all rest on Torre. He singles out Kenny Rogers, who's 0–3 with a 14.13 ERA in his last three starts: "They'll fry him in New York if he keeps that up."

And then he goes after his friend in Milwaukee.

"There are paths in baseball to settle these things, but it's difficult when the Commissioner owns the other team," Steinbrenner says. "I'm for Selig keeping the job. I never thought it would come to the point where it bothered me, but it has become a concern."

George is momentarily pacified when Cone returns in spectacular fashion on September 2, throwing seven no-hit innings in Oakland before Torre lifts him. But the Yankees lose three of their next six, slicing their lead over Baltimore to 2½ games on September 11. And that's when a New Jersey paper cites a "source in the Yankee organization" saying that Watson "is already out of here."

The story touches off the kind of media frenzy that Watson and Torre have avoided all season. "It doesn't surprise me that he would do this, but it surprises me that he would leak it without telling me," says Watson, who sees Steinbrenner's fingerprints all over the newspaper report. "I hope he would be enough of a man about it to come and tell me."

Speculation over the fates of both Watson and Torre fill the media for a full seven days while Steinbrenner privately tells each man everything they've done will be wiped away if they don't win the division. Then George provides a bizarre twist at the Stadium on September 18, the opening night of a pivotal three-game series with the Orioles. He walks into the clubhouse a few hours before the game and asks reporters to gather around.

With his players looking on, the Boss has an announcement to make:

Joe Torre will be back next year, Steinbrenner says, no matter what happens the rest of this season. "I like everything he's done," he says. "There's no reason not to tell him to relax and he'll be back."

When Steinbrenner pauses, he's asked about Watson, who, like Torre, has a guaranteed contract through next season. "I can only jump one hurdle at a time," says George.

It's their young shortstop who shows how to quiet the owner. Jeter scores the winning run in the 10th inning of the first game against Baltimore. One day later, he singles to knock in the first two runs of a 9–3 win, stretching his hitting streak to 11 games and restoring order in the Bronx.

So much for that .240 bar Torre set for the rookie in March.

The division clincher comes four days later in the first game of a doubleheader in Milwaukee. The Yankees score four in the 1st and 10 in the second en route to a 19–2 win and their first AL East title since 1981. Torre remains in the dugout, tears streaming down his face, while the players rush the field to join the celebration at the pitching mound.

"I got very choked up," Torre says in his office between games. "At this stage of my career—which I thought was over last year—this could be the start of my greatest experience in baseball."

Torre touts the performances of his many veterans, then pauses before talking about the two players who truly changed the team. Rivera, the pitcher he wanted to trade, will soon finish an astonishing season: an 8–3 record, 130 strikeouts, and just 73 hits in $107^{2/3}$ innings. Then there's Jeter, whose final line—.314, 10 home runs, 78 RBI, 104 runs scored—will earn him Rookie of the Year honors.

"No question," Torre says. "Derek Jeter and Mariano Rivera were our biggest X factors."

Torre doesn't discuss his boss, but Steinbrenner's role—his late-season antics notwithstanding—cannot be overlooked. It was Steinbrenner who gave Watson and Gene Michael the money to build much of this team in December. He opened his wallet again to bring in Fielder, who hit 13 home runs in 53 games. He gave second chances to Dwight Gooden, who threw a no-hitter in May, and to Strawberry, who's been a model citizen while contributing 11 homers as a role player.

Yes, he pounded on Watson so much the writers joked about adding "Beleaguered" to the GM's name. But unlike in past seasons, Steinbrenner did not derail his team. He's eagerly waiting for the playoffs, even as he keeps his eye on the revenue sharing battle still being waged between the small market owners and the players union. He's already told his business staff that they must come up with ways to make back whatever revenue the Yankees are certain to lose in any new labor agreement.

George is convinced he's done his part. Now his team just has to win it all.

Steinbrenner is a one-man welcoming committee before Game 1 of the American League Championship Series, walking the corridors of the Stadium in his standard blue blazer, white turtleneck, and gray slacks, greeting fans and signing autographs. He even helps one young woman find her seat.

"Hey, that's a nice owner," shouts a fan.

"Hey, she's a nice-looking girl," George shouts back.

Fan after fan stops to thank him for bringing a winner back to the city, and George beams. The Boss has brought the swagger back to New York, and right now he can do no wrong.

Even two ugly incidents in the AL Division Series win over Texas put little more than a few small dents in George's new public image. With his team on its way to a 6–2 loss in the opening game at the Stadium, Steinbrenner left his box, found the Rangers wives, and chastised them for celebrating too boisterously. "People in the other box couldn't see, we asked them not to ruin it for everyone else," he told Dallas reporters, who criticized him sharply. The next day he started a petty argument with Reggie Jackson on the team bus to the airport. The fight escalated into such an angry exchange that Joe Torre and Willie Randolph had to pull Reggie away from George, and the story received wide play.

But Bernie Williams (.467) and Derek Jeter (.412) helped engineer two come-from-behind wins in Texas to take the series, and all is forgiven and forgotten.

Steinbrenner is every bit as excitable for the first game of the ALCS. He sees Steve Palermo, the umpire turned motivational speaker after he was shot and injured stopping a robbery five years ago, and insists Steve and his wife watch the game from the owner's box. He gets a hug from talk show host Regis Philbin when he enters his box, and escorts the wife and daughter of the late Yankees catcher Elston Howard to their seats. He shakes hands with Robert Merrill, the former opera star who has just sung the national anthem. The Yankees are playing for a ticket to the World Series, and all is right in Steinbrenner's world.

"This is where we should be," he says.

George is delighted when the Yankees jump out to an early 2–1 lead, but it doesn't last. Brady Anderson, who slugged 50 home runs during the regular season—nine more than his last three seasons combined—rifles a homer into the right-field seats in the 3rd to tie the game 2–2. Andy Pettitte coughs up the lead on another solo shot by Rafael Palmeiro in the 4th.

The Yankees trail 4–3 in the 8th, and Steinbrenner is in his box fretting. But his rookie shortstop walks calmly to the plate and lofts the first pitch he sees from Armando Benitez to right field, where it bounces off the top of the fence and into the stands for a game-tying home run. Or so it seems. Replays show what veteran umpire Richie Garcia failed to see: the ball deflected off the glove worn by a 12-year-old named Jeffrey Maier and bounced into the stands.

The Orioles argue, but to no avail, and the run stands. Two innings later Bernie Williams wallops a no-doubt-about-it home run to left, and the Yankees have the victory. "Do I feel bad?" says Jeter when asked about Garcia's call in the postgame interview room. "We won the game. Why should I feel bad?"

The Orioles win Game 2, but the Yankees sweep the next three games in Camden Yards to win their first pennant since 1978. Williams, blossoming into a truly dominant player, hits .474 with a pair of home runs and six RBI and is named MVP. Jeter hits .417 and seems to ignite every big Yankees inning.

Steinbrenner left Baltimore before Game 5. He wants others on center stage, so it's his younger son Hal on the TV podium with Torre and Watson. Hal, who worked hard on the family's hotel business this season in order to stay out of his father's line of fire, is still on the podium when Wade Boggs sneaks up and pours Champagne over his head. The 26-year-old blinks and laughs.

Sitting quietly off by himself is Mariano Rivera, who has yet to allow a run in $8^2/_3$ innings over four postseason games. "I'm just sitting here meditating and thanking God for what we've done," he tells a reporter. "Because He helped us do it."

Many feel Steinbrenner's team will need divine intervention to beat the Braves, who three days later club the Cardinals, 15–0, to win a thrilling seven-game NLCS. The oddsmakers install the defending champs as heavy favorites: the Yankees are a nice team, everyone agrees, but the Braves are making their fourth trip to the Series in the last five full seasons, a budding dynasty with the perfect blend of youth and veterans, power hitting and superb pitching.

All but one Braves regular finished the regular season with 10 or more home runs, and the heart of the order—Chipper Jones (30 homers), Fred McGriff (28), and Ryan Klesko (34)—is arguably the game's best. But it's pitching that truly makes the Braves special. Greg Maddux is the game's best pitcher, the winner of his league's last four Cy Young Awards. Left-hander Tom Glavine won the award in '91 and has three 20-win seasons on his résumé. John Smoltz, who won 24 games and struck out 276 this season, is certain to be Atlanta's sixth straight Cy Young winner. Closer Mark Wohlers and his 99 mph fastball leads a bullpen that can match New York in depth and strikeouts.

It's hard to know if Steinbrenner is bluffing or a believer when he warns everyone not to take his team lightly. "I believe we have a good chance of upsetting these fellas," he says. "This is not the first time we've been the underdog. I like lying in the weeds."

But Watson and Torre know better. Steinbrenner is a world-class worrier in need of constant reassurance, a man who panics at the first sign of trouble. And plenty goes wrong in Game 1. The Braves are up 8–0 after three, with Andruw Jones slugging a pair of home runs, rendering the rest of the 12–1 debacle an afterthought. Except for Watson, who is wondering why the Yankees threw fastballs to Jones when their scouting report stressed never to throw the 19-year-old a fastball for a strike.

It's the first question he asks Torre as soon as the game mercifully ends. Torre shrugs and calls in catcher Jim Leyritz, who explains he thought they could trick Jones.

"Did you think you could trick him twice?" Watson says.

"Yeah, I did," Leyritz says.

The player leaves his manager's office, and Watson looks at Torre. "You know George is going to ask what happened, and I'm going to have to tell him the truth," Watson says. Torre nods, and sure enough, when Steinbrenner finds Watson, he demands answers. When Watson tells him Leyritz ignored the scouting report, George erupts.

"I spend hundreds of thousands of dollars on scouting, and your dumbass players don't follow instructions!" he bellows. "I want Leyritz traded. Right now!"

Watson remains calm. "George, it's after midnight; we can't trade him," he says. "Besides, we can't replace him on the roster. That would leave us with 24 players and one catcher."

"I don't care!" Steinbrenner snaps back. "I want you to trade him!"

"Look, we'll trade him as soon as the World Series is over," says Watson, who will ship Leyritz to the Angels six weeks after the Series. "And we'll make sure to follow the scouting reports."

Steinbrenner storms out, and he's no calmer when he walks back into Torre's office before Game 2. He's also worried and embarrassed. "This is a must-win; it's a must-win!" he keeps repeating. "What are you going to do?"

Torre calmly searches for something to tame Steinbrenner's temper, and he finds a gem. "Hey, we'll probably lose tonight, too, George," he says, barely looking up from his lineup card. "But Atlanta's my town. We'll sweep them there and win it back home."

Caught off guard, Steinbrenner pauses before speaking again. "Are you sure?" he says. "I don't know. Really? Okay, but are you sure?"

Maddux and the Braves win Game 2 in dominant fashion, 4–0. The Yankees have been outscored 16–1, and now George isn't the only one who's embarrassed. The clubhouse boys tell Game 3 starter David Cone and a few other Yankees that the Braves are whooping it up in their clubhouse, acting as if the Series is already over.

"It's like we're a prop," Cone tells a few friends as the team prepares to fly to Atlanta.

Game 3 is a reprieve: Williams homers and knocks in three runs, and Cone and the bullpen keep the Braves in check for a 5–2 win. But that's soon forgotten the next night, when Atlanta jumps out to a 5–0 lead after three innings. The Braves are up 6–3 and are five outs from taking a 3–1 Series lead with Wohlers on the mound and two runners on base. In steps Leyritz for his first at bat since being benched after Game 1. The Yankees catcher works the count to 2–1, then fouls back two straight 99 mph fastballs.

Seeing that Leyritz has his fastball timed, Wohlers throws a slider, and the entire Series pivots. Wohlers hangs the pitch, and Leyritz sends it sailing well over the left-field wall. The three-run homer energizes the Yankees, who all rush out of the dugout to greet Leyritz, and drains the life from the Braves. And when the Yankees piece together a pair of runs in the 10th on a bases loaded walk and an error, the Series is tied.

Standing in the Yankees clubhouse after the game, Steinbrenner gushes about everyone in a New York uniform. He calls the homer by Leyritz the biggest of the season. He praises Graeme Lloyd, who got McGriff to ground into a double play to end the 9th and is credited with the win.

"Did I lose hope? No," says George. "You never lose hope with these guys. We'll do okay tomorrow with Andy Pettitte. Just you watch."

Pettitte is better than okay, throwing 8⅓ shutout innings to outduel Smoltz, 1–0. The Yankees head back to New York with a chance to do what only two other teams in history have ever done: win four straight World Series games after losing the first two. Starting pitcher Jimmy Key asks his girlfriend Karin Kane to marry him before leaving for the game, then goes out and holds the Braves to one run in 5⅓ innings. The Yankees support Key with three runs in the 3rd, and the Stadium starts rocking and never stops.

Rivera blows away the Braves for two innings, then hands the game over to Wetteland. There are two outs and runners on first and second when Wetteland runs the count to 3–2 on Mark Lemke. The Stadium is literally shaking, with all 56,375 fans on their feet, shouting and clapping, as Lemke fouls a ball toward Charlie Hayes. The third baseman drifts under the pop-up, squeezes it in his glove, and it's pandemonium in the Bronx.

Every Yankees player and coach rushes the mound, which is soon a pile of hugging, laughing, and crying men in pinstriped uniforms. Torre finds Leyritz, the only player left from the team that lost 95 games six years ago, and asks him to lead the team on a victory lap around the Stadium. The fans, who are hugging, laughing, and crying as well, cheer as the champs jog around the field while police on horseback set up around the field. Wade Boggs hops aboard a horse and takes one lap around the Stadium before being the last Yankee to leave the field.

Atlanta manager Bobby Cox stops to hug his friend Torre before walking into the hushed Braves clubhouse, where his players struggle to explain what happened to them the last five days. General manager John Schuerholz says he knows. The difference between the two teams, Schuerholz says, is the $18 million Steinbrenner spent on bench players.

There is only joy and more tears in the packed Yankees clubhouse. Watson stands in one end of the room, his wife Carol at his side, relieved and satisfied. The manager he wanted and the club he helped build have won the Yankees' 23rd World Series title. There were days when Steinbrenner all but crushed his spirit, but the Boss also gave him the money and freedom to bring in the players he needed all season, with seven of the 25 men on the field tonight arriving after June 11.

He's asked if he'll be back next year. "That's up to Mr. Steinbrenner," answers Watson. "It's been a tough road," he concedes, but he's proud to be the game's first minority general manager to win the World Series. He admits he's exhausted, saying all he wants to do now is "smoke a cigar, drink some Champagne, and enjoy this." And with that he walks out of the clubhouse, ending the night without speaking a word to the man who employs him.

That man has been practically babbling ever since the game ended. "Great, great, these guys deserve it, and so does the city of New York," Steinbrenner keeps repeating as he crisscrosses the crowded clubhouse. "This city never gives up, and neither did these guys. This is great, great."

Tears stream down Steinbrenner's face as Selig hands him the championship trophy as the TV cameras roll. Selig is choked up, too. The two men have grown up together in this game, and Selig is truly happy for his friend. "I have been the one constant in his baseball life since 1973, the one who brought him back from suspension," says Selig, forgetting that it was Fay Vincent who ended George's ban. "After all we've been through together, it's a very emotional moment for both of us."

What Selig doesn't mention is the yelling match he had with Don Fehr only hours earlier in an office adjoining Steinbrenner's box. The issue: baseball's unsettled labor deal. George knew about that heated exchange. He also knows that no matter what kind of deal Selig eventually gets, it is certain to cost him a large chunk of money.

And that's not lost on Steinbrenner, even on this night. George spent $67 million by season's end building this team, but he's sure you have to spend money to make money, and there's a lot of money to be made now. He has a talented team filled with marketable players like Cone, O'Neill, and Williams. And it's already clear that Jeter and Rivera will be truly special players.

No, this isn't the time for Steinbrenner to pull back. There's a new stadium to be built, a new TV deal just a few years away, and sponsors lining up to be paired with his attractive young stars. This team is going to make Steinbrenner a lot more money—and even more famous.

Atlanta's Schuerholz and everyone else in baseball can complain all they want.

George has only just begun to spend.

Chapter 15

DEAL!

November 6–November 26, 1996

It's been 14 long, hard months for Randy Levine, who is standing in the ballroom of Chicago's Hyatt Regency O'Hare on November 6 with the owners of baseball's 30 teams, all of them about to engage in an exercise in futility. Levine's done what he was hired to do—negotiate a deal with the union and begin the healing process between the owners and their players—only to see his friend and his boss Bud Selig throw him under the bus.

Levine is disappointed he can't stop the owners from doing what they always do: misread the union. *Turn down this deal, Fehr will panic, and we'll get a much better deal,* hard-liners like Jerry Reinsdorf keep insisting. Selig agreed, withdrew his support for an agreement he seemed ready to approve, and effectively killed the deal the owners will be voting on in just a few minutes.

This is going to end one of two ways, Levine thinks as he listens to Selig open the meeting. Either the owners suddenly change course and accept this deal and continue on the road to recovery—one that was jump-started this season with the Yankees championship and the surplus of power hitters—or they will stand firm and reject the deal, see their game crash and burn once more, then start the process all over again next year.

And they'd be starting over with a new negotiator. There's no way Levine is doing this again, even if the owners beg him to return. New York Mayor Rudy Giuliani wants to make him a deputy mayor, and Levine can't get back to the Giuliani administration fast enough.

It's time for Levine to state his case, and though today's outcome is predetermined, the curly-haired, 41-year-old lawyer is not ready to fall on his sword—despite rumors that he is quitting or about to be fired. Why should he leave with a stain on his résumé? Instead he gives it one last try, explaining that this deal gives the small market teams the revenue sharing they need. And there's a tax leveled on the game's five biggest spenders to rein in salaries.

The union signed off on interleague play, which will start next season, and the players are kicking about $150 million of their own money into the owners' revenue sharing pool in each of the next two years.

"Is this deal everything you wanted? No, but it gives you what you need," Levine says. "It breaks new ground, and you can come back and make adjustments in your next negotiation."

Levine runs through the terms and numbers on the deal sheets sitting in front of every owner, but he can see most of these men have already tuned him out. He asks for questions, gets a few, and when the last question is answered, Levine says he has one more thing he wants them to consider.

"If you do not approve this deal, there is no way the union will bargain with you again," Levine warns them. "We are no longer at impasse. We will keep living under the old agreement you all hate, and there is a very good chance we will be hit with another unfair labor practice complaint. It will be World War III."

A dour-looking Selig thanks Levine. The Acting Commissioner polled every owner the night before, so he knows what will happen next. Still, he asks Levine to leave the room so he can take a roll call vote. Levine nods, collects his papers, and walks out to the hallway, where he'll spend an hour waiting for the owners to make their next mistake.

Levine is used to waiting. It's about all he's done since the weekend of August 9, when he and his assistant Rob Manfred spent three very long days and nights banging out an agreement with the union. The two sides found common ground on revenue sharing, and Fehr finally said yes to a luxury tax—the first time the union agreed to any form of payroll restraint since free agency changed everything in 1976. By the early morning hours of Saturday, Levine had reason to believe a deal was finally within reach.

Why not? Levine had stopped negotiations almost hourly so he and Manfred could call Selig with updates. At each step they heard nothing but encouragement. After only bad news for more than a year, Fehr was cautiously optimistic when he spoke with reporters that Saturday in a break from the marathon sessions. "It's certainly true that the differences have been substantially narrowed," Fehr said that day. "We're encouraged."

Selig's support was vital for Levine, who is no stranger to the owners or the union. He'd dealt with both sides during his time as Steinbrenner's outside counsel. He'd done a little private work for Selig and Reinsdorf, too. Levine's wife Mindy grew up with Selig's eldest daughter Sari, and the two remain close to this day. His mother-in-law is close to Sue Selig, and Mindy's father is Bud's internist as well as the Brewers' team doctor.

"When Randy tells you something, he's speaking for me," Selig told Fehr on more than one occasion. By the time Levine and Fehr called it quits early Saturday evening, August 10, the two men were confident they had a groundbreaking agreement. Things were looking so good that the Phillies' Dave Montgomery, a well-respected member of the bargaining team, called Levine early that Sunday morning to wish him luck. "We hear you're close to a deal," Montgomery told him. "That's great. Everyone is excited."

But not for long. After telling Levine to "keep going" all Sunday morning, Selig suddenly reversed course. Early that afternoon the Acting Commissioner called his chief negotiator and shut down the talks. Again. "Bud, we're on the one-yard line here," Levine told Selig. "This is a great deal."

Selig didn't budge. "I'm not ready to support this deal," Selig said. "It's not good enough."

Fehr was incredulous when Levine gave him the news. "Fuck you, Randy," the union leader told him. "We have a deal. We're not going to give you a thing."

What changed for Selig? There's little doubt Reinsdorf wanted more, and for the White Sox owner, it wasn't just money. Reinsdorf wanted Fehr brought to his knees, and this deal didn't come close to doing that. Instead Fehr has never appeared stronger. No one gets into Selig's head better than Reinsdorf, who doesn't tell his close friend what to do, as the media often suggests—he just knows the right buttons to push.

"We spilled all this blood and this is the deal we are getting?" would be enough to get Selig thinking. "You're getting fucked by the union" would be enough to start Selig second-guessing himself. And Reinsdorf had plenty of support. It was clear once news of a deal spread that Selig was getting pushback from his friends Carl Pohlad, David Glass, and all the other hard-liners.

Whatever his reasons, Selig pulled the plug on any meaningful talks for the next six long weeks. On September 24, Fehr reached out and told Selig he was sending out a deal memo for his members to ratify based on his agreement with Levine. He had no choice, he told Selig, the season was almost over, and the players were soon to scatter.

A few days later the two men and Levine met for lunch in Milwaukee, and Selig told Fehr he needed to make four changes in the deal. Fehr calmly told him the time for doing that had come and gone. He wasn't quite as civil when the two men met at Levine's office on October 21, hours before Game 2 of the World Series. And for good reason: Selig told him he had changed his mind again. The deal was off.

"You told me Randy had the authority to make a deal, and now you're undermining him," Fehr shouted at Selig. "We might just pull this whole deal off the table!"

But that was merely a warm-up for their confrontation during Game 6 at Yankee Stadium on October 26. Fehr had made a few minor concessions to reach another agreement and had shaken hands with Levine in Atlanta two days earlier. Frustrated that Selig refused to publicly acknowledge their new deal, Fehr told reporters on the field during batting practice that negotiations were over and an agreement was at hand.

"Bud just has to decide if he wants it," Fehr told them.

An hour later, Selig gave reporters a different story. "I regard the negotiations as ongoing," he said. "I don't think there's anything more than that."

When Levine pulled the two men together during the game in an office outside Steinbrenner's suite, Fehr confronted Selig. "What the fuck are you doing?" Fehr thundered. "You're wasting my time! You don't want to do a deal. I am prepared to stay where we are. I will fight you in court. What the fuck is wrong with you?"

Then he turned to Levine. "How can I trust you, Randy?" Fehr shouted. "You should fucking quit. How can you work for these people?"

When Selig could take no more, he shot back. "Don't fucking talk to me that way," Selig yelled. "There is no deal. I'm going to try to get there, but we have issues."

"You have issues?" Fehr shouted, the veins in his neck beginning to bulge. "We agreed to a fucking deal in Atlanta! What are you trying to do?"

The two men were still yelling at each other when a door to Steinbrenner's suite opened and out charged the Boss. "What the hell is going on in here?" said Steinbrenner, his anger rising with each word. "I have 30 guests in there, and you are disturbing them. Shut the fuck up!"

Steinbrenner looked over at Selig, who was clearly shaken. "Are you all right?" he asked Bud. "Look, just take this out of here."

Steinbrenner returned to his party, but Fehr was still not finished. "How is this going to end?" he asked Selig. "I can't trust Randy anymore. You are the only one I am going to sit down with. You are the Commissioner. There is nobody else I can make a deal with."

Selig ignored Fehr's final barrage as the two men walked away and said nothing to reporters who had gotten wind of the meeting. When the media turned to Levine, he gamely tried to convince everyone that things were still on track. But nothing was further from the truth, and everyone knew it. Another fiery meeting after the game did nothing to improve the situation.

Selig then took four days before calling today's vote, giving opponents ample time to lobby against the agreement and the two men who crafted it.

One particularly mean-spirited attack in the *Chicago Tribune* told Levine exactly where his deal stood. "What we should do is put Randy against the wall, blindfold him, and shoot him for treason," one anonymous NL owner said. "Randy wants to make any deal," another unnamed owner told the *Tribune*, "so he can be the hero."

And an unnamed member of the Executive Council made it personal, dragging Selig and Levine's family ties into the story. "What Randy has done is horrendous," the owner, widely believed to be Reinsdorf, told the *Tribune*. "Bud is bleeding and very hurt, but there isn't much he can do."

Selig announced he had no intention of firing his negotiator, but his silence on the merits of Levine's proposal was all that really mattered. Publicly, Selig declined to comment on the deal, insisting he did not want to influence anyone's vote. Privately, he made it clear that this was not the deal he wanted.

And that is what he is telling the game's owners today as soon as Levine walks out of the ballroom at the Hyatt Regency. "We should reject this deal and go back to the union and get what we need," Selig tells them. "We have not waited this long to accept an agreement like this."

The roll call vote is 16–14 in favor of the deal, far short of the 23 votes needed to pass. Seeking leverage for the next round of talks, Selig urges more owners to reject the proposal. Two votes later, it's 18–12 against the deal, with the Reds, A's, Orioles, and Cardinals doing what Selig asked.

Next, Selig tells Bob DuPuy, his personal lawyer who doubles as the outside counsel for the Executive Council, to form a committee with Baltimore's Peter Angelos. Their task: do a risk/reward analysis of each provision in Levine's proposal, and lay out the risks of making no deal at all.

"We look forward to expeditiously getting together with the union and bring closure to a labor agreement," Selig tells reporters at the end of the seven-hour meeting, "an agreement that will bring long-term peace and labor harmony to the game."

Levine is on his way to O'Hare Airport after his stinging defeat when Fehr reaches him on his cell phone. "You thought you were different, but I fucking told you this is what would happen," Fehr says. "You should quit now. There is no way we are going to change anything in that deal."

Especially not the changes the owners are demanding. Fehr and Levine agreed to limit the number of teams paying the luxury tax to five and for the tax to be in place for three of the five years of the deal. The owners want no limit on teams hit by the tax, plus a fourth taxed season.

Both changes are nonstarters, Fehr tells Levine, and that's the message he's ready to deliver when Selig leads a small contingent of owners and lawyers to the union's office the afternoon of November 11. The two sides meet in the union's conference room, where a painting of Marvin Miller stares down at Selig, John Harrington, Fred Wilpon, Claude Brochu, Levine, Rob Manfred, and Bob DuPuy as they takes seats at the long conference table. Sitting opposite them are the union's Gene Orza, Lauren Rich, Michael Weiner, Tom Glavine, David Cone, and B. J. Surhoff.

When everyone is settled, Fehr begins. "This is a sad day for the players, for the union staff, and for baseball," he says. "I would like to describe the events that brought us here today."

And with that, Fehr launches into a 45-minute lecture about how Selig lied to him, misled the players, and undermined the entire negotiation process. They all sit in uncomfortable silence as Fehr tells them how he begged Selig to keep negotiating after Dick Ravitch was fired. How he begged Selig to keep bargaining after the NLRB announced it would seek an injunction. And how he begged yet again after Judge Sotomayor's ruling.

Each plea was treated the same way.

"I never heard back from you," says Fehr, looking directly at Selig. "You said you would resume negotiations in the fall when you hired a new negotiator who would have full authority to make a deal. Randy entered as your negotiator in November, and you told me to trust Randy as if he were you."

So we did, Fehr said, and after a series of negotiations we reached an agreement. "But you were not willing to endorse the deal," Fehr tells Selig. He rattles off one meeting after another, all about getting a deal, all ending with Selig's refusal to act.

"A clear signal that you did not want a deal," Fehr says.

Fehr talks about reaching another deal with Levine in Atlanta, about their bitter confrontation at Yankee Stadium, about the deal the owners voted down five days ago in Chicago. "You broke your promises," Fehr says to Selig. "You never intended to make a deal."

Why? Fehr says he can only guess.

"Perhaps it's the only way you can remain Commissioner and keep your salary," he says.

"Perhaps it's because you have your new stadium."

"Perhaps you just cannot handle it."

Selig has no reply, nor does any of his team, and the room goes dead silent. "Let's take a short break," Fehr finally says. Fifteen minutes later, everyone gathers around the conference table again. Fehr makes it clear the union will never grant the owners their two big demands, that all he's willing to do is tinker around the edges. And with the day's newspapers thick with rumors that Levine plans to resign at the stroke of midnight tonight, Fehr ends the meeting with one last question.

"Bud," says Fehr. "Who is your negotiator now?"

After an uncomfortable silence, a sheepish Selig says, "I guess I am."

It's clear to all but the most passionate hawks that Fehr and the union aren't going to move. And in the days following the meeting at union headquarters, Mets owner Fred Wilpon bangs away at Selig to make a deal. Paul Beeston pleads with him to do the same. Selig is hearing from Steinbrenner almost every day, too. Enough of this nonsense, they tell him: just make the damn deal.

About the only reprieve Selig had came on November 9, when 15,000 Brewers fans braved a raw, windy day to celebrate the formal groundbreaking for Miller Park. Hank Aaron and Robin Yount were there to thrust shovels into the ground in the center-field parking lot, where Bud's new $250 million money-making machine is scheduled to open in 2000.

Maybe they'll have a labor agreement by then.

DuPuy and his group finish their risk/reward analysis, and it's not pretty. Baseball's bankers are worried about getting repaid if there's another work stoppage, and they're talking about jacking up their once-favorable rates. The TV networks are unhappy, and a host of sponsors are holding back almost a billion dollars in deals until a labor agreement is signed. Interleague play will remain on hold—a new revenue source lost. Small market teams in need of revenue sharing, like Bud's Brewers, will sink deeper into the red.

As Thanksgiving approaches, Selig realizes it's time to take Fehr's deal. He just can't go another season without some form of increased revenue sharing, and Fehr is more than willing to play under the current agreement, which favors the players. So Bud starts calling the hawks, working hard to talk them off the front line. This war has to end, he tells them; there's too much at stake. He gets the biggest pushback from Reinsdorf, who still isn't ready to stand down. But this is one time the White Sox owner can't find the right button to push.

The tipping point comes on November 20. Levine is in his office at MLB headquarters when a clerk pops in and tells him Reinsdorf just signed Albert Belle. All contracts are filed with MLB before they're announced, and this one, the clerk tells Levine, is the richest in baseball history: $10 million a season for five years, with a $5 million signing bonus. Yes, the same Albert Belle who's been suspended five times in eight seasons for actions such as throwing baseballs at fans and verbally abusing a female TV reporter during the '95 World Series.

The kicker: Reinsdorf added a clause ensuring the hard-hitting Belle will remain one of the three highest-paid players for the life of his contract.

The owner who's railed the loudest and longest about curbing player salaries has just broken the bank. Levine rushes into the hall, where he sees Manfred, who's just heard to same news. "What the fuck?" says Levine, and both men run back into Levine's office to call Selig.

"Bud, have you heard the news?" Levine asks. Selig has not. Levine fills him in, and there is silence on the other end of the line. "Thank you," Selig says.

Selig is soon on a conference call with the game's owners, and one thing quickly becomes clear: Reinsdorf's stunning decision has broken any remaining resistance to the deal they'd just rejected. Another vote will be held in Chicago in six days. But first, Selig wants to talk to Reinsdorf, who has spent the day telling reporters that he's just trying to win.

"It doesn't mean I like the system," he tells every reporter who reaches him.

And that's what he tells Selig when the two speak later that day. "But Jerry, all you've done is preach about getting spending under control," says Selig, who knows there is little reason to discuss this much further. What's done is done, and Reinsdorf has done what every owner in baseball always does: whatever's best for his team.

Reinsdorf has one request for Selig. "Please don't work the owners," he asks. "Let's get to Chicago and have an honest discussion." But it's not long after Reinsdorf walks into the O'Hare Hilton ballroom on November 26 that he realizes Selig has the votes he needs to approve the deal. "I can't believe he fucked me," Reinsdorf mutters, and he's still muttering when the roll call reaches him. "No," he says, but only Cleveland, Kansas City, and Oakland join him, and the deal is approved, 26–4.

"It gives me great personal pleasure that baseball fans can finally look forward to five years of uninterrupted play," Selig tells the media. "We can now work together to bring peace to the game and reconnect our sport to all of our fans."

Fehr issues a statement soon after he receives Selig's concession speech. "While we are pleased with the owners' action today, the successful conclusion of this negotiating process represents only the very first step in the rebuilding process," it reads in part. "Much work remains to be done."

For once, Fehr and Selig are in agreement. Their deal is a work in progress: the luxury tax will start next season and end two seasons later. Revenue sharing will begin retroactively with the '96 season but will be phased in over the life of the contract: $42 million in local revenue is expected to be sent from the top 12 teams to the bottom 14 in each of the first two years—the Marlins and Rockies will be exempt from revenue sharing until 1998—and the amount will increase to $70 million in 2000. The players will be taxed 2.5 percent of their salaries for the next two seasons to help fund revenue sharing.

The subject of random testing for steroids, briefly discussed in 1994, never made it back to the bargaining table and is another subject to review for the next contract. Owners can still test their players if they have reasonable cause, but no one was tested this past season, even though some middle infielders looked like middle linebackers and home run records fell by the bushel. That option figures to remain on the shelf.

Besides, neither side is too concerned about the level of steroid use in the game. These things tend to run their course. As long as steroid use doesn't get out of hand, the drug will take its place beside amphetamines as an accepted part of baseball, something to help players make it through a long season, recover from injuries, and maybe add a year or two to their careers.

The labor agreement covers five years, with a players' option for a sixth, and both sides will watch carefully to determine how each provision will change the game. Especially the team in the Bronx. Steinbrenner soon learns he'll have to shell out $5.8 million in revenue sharing for this season. George has already turned up the heat on his business execs to find big deals that will maximize the Yankees brand and make up for lost revenue.

But cut back on spending? Not likely, especially with players like Roger Clemens hitting the open market. Steinbrenner is already planning his trip out to Houston to personally deliver a big offer to the star pitcher.

Fehr meets with the players over the next few months to explain what the new deal means to them, and it's something different for each group. The minimum salary will more than triple, to $190,000, by '98, and it's important for veterans to understand that the more young players are paid, the better chance older and well-paid players will have to keep their jobs. Make the minimum too low and owners will stock the end of their bench with younger players every time.

"You're all connected," says Fehr, who reminds players that their determination to remain united when Selig and the owners shut down the game was the major reason management didn't get the salary cap it so desperately wanted.

Fehr also tells his players how important it is that baseball find an independent Commissioner, though he knows Selig won't be leaving the job any time soon. The owners don't even have a search committee, much less a search under way. Selig continues to say he doesn't want the job, but the office is his to keep, and there's no way he's walking away now. The revenue sharing deal he just accepted will hand the Brewers $4.6 million for this past season and an estimated $30 million–plus over the life of the contract, but that's a fraction of what Selig wanted—and still wants.

That's just one reason this labor war was a huge victory for Fehr and the union—and why it's never been more accurate to call the labor leader the most powerful man in baseball. The owners never got their salary cap or any changes to free agency or salary arbitration. Fehr's credibility among the players has never been higher.

No, Selig won't be stepping down as Commissioner.

Not when he still has so much work left to do.

PART III

SECRET OF SUCCESS
(1997–2000)

Chapter 16

SETTING UP SHOP

January 1–December 15, 1997

It's hard to imagine a people more full of hope than Americans in the opening days of 1997. As President Bill Clinton takes his second oath of office, jobs are plentiful, home values are rising, and the stock market has almost doubled in the last two years. Fed chairman Alan Greenspan mumbles about irrational exuberance while the pundits joke about a market on steroids, but no one seems to mind.

Seinfeld, again featuring a larger-than-life baseball owner, keeps the country laughing as TV's top-rated sitcom. For sentimental souls like Bud Selig, it's all about the Green Bay Packers, the NFL's third-oldest team, who vanquish the New England Patriots to win their first Super Bowl since 1968. Selig also has a vested interest in the Packers, given his seat on their Board, his boyhood allegiance to the Green and Gold, and his admiration for a league in which even the team from the smallest market can win it all.

Milwaukee, the 17th-largest market in the country when Selig brought the Brewers to town in 1970, is now 32nd in America and dead last in the major leagues. So Selig remains determined to make MLB as small market friendly as the NFL, and despite losing to Don Fehr at the bargaining table, he enters the new year on a roll. He has money in his pocket, thanks to the new revenue sharing agreement. He has a new stadium on the way. Just a few hundred yards from his County Stadium office, workers are finally pouring the foundation for Miller Park, which has already doubled the value of his franchise years before the ceremonial first pitch is thrown.

And he has a job that's taking him places. There's an unspoken acceptance inside baseball that Selig is now the Commissioner, the only "acting" being when he denies he wants to keep the job. Congress has lost interest in pushing for an independent Commissioner, and media and the fans have grown accustomed to an owner living in Milwaukee while occupying the game's top post.

Selig also wants his election to be unanimous, which won't happen as long as Peter O'Malley—whom Bud has marginalized the past four years—still owns the Dodgers. But there are few other detractors. If anything, support for Selig after the labor talks is as strong—if not stronger—than ever.

Sure, there are a few owners who aren't enamored of Selig's ways. Some of the hard-liners are still angry with the way the labor negotiations ended—especially Reinsdorf, who took Bud's eventual support for the deal as a personal affront.

But no one denies that Selig has delivered: the owners now have revenue sharing, and their new luxury tax is the first restraint on salaries since the start of free agency. There are double the number of teams playing for postseason money, a product of the wild-card and three-division format, and the hotly anticipated interleague play will debut this season. They enjoy a lucrative national television deal and, most important, their franchise values are growing higher and higher.

So they'll indulge Bud's need to be courted, they'll spend the money on a search firm for appearances only, and they'll take turns publicly paving the way for his coronation. Many of them have pushed Selig to relocate to New York, but that's never going to happen, no matter how much sense it makes and how often his wife Sue begs him to make the move. Instead Bud's all but convinced Paul Beeston to leave his post as president and CEO of the Blue Jays and move down to New York to be his right-hand man.

That move will free Selig to pursue his vision to centralize baseball under an all-powerful Commissioner. On this year's agenda: a dramatic realignment of the American League and the National League to build more rivalries and cut travel costs; building the rationale for even more revenue sharing in the next contract; and a game plan to finally market baseball on a national level.

Selig already persuaded the big market boys to support the formation of Major League Baseball Enterprises last January. The unit's mission is to centralize marketing of all uniforms, jackets, and caps bearing team logos and—most important—distribute revenues equally among all 28 teams. It is yet another attempt to socialize the profits of the Yankees, whose apparel is almost always the game's top seller.

Selig settled on Kraft Foods executive Greg Murphy as CEO last June, but it quickly became apparent that the Naval Academy grad had little feel for baseball and even less for dealing with its owners. Selig is already working on an exit strategy when Murphy presents his underwhelming plan for the coming season at the Waldorf Astoria on March 3. Entitled "March to Opening Day," it's a combination of public relations events—Kodak's 100 Memorable Moments in Baseball exhibition tops the list—$150 million in unspecified marketing deals, and promises of more dollars from former sponsors. Murphy can't show any of baseball's new TV spots—they were not finished in time for this meeting.

What he shows instead to the handful of reporters sitting in the cramped conference room is the helmet cam, a lipstick-size camera Fox plans to insert into catchers' masks during the season. Longtime baseball executive Bill Murray tries on the mask in a moment that is truly cringeworthy.

When Murphy's presentation mercifully ends, his day goes from bad to worse. Most of the reporters present have spent the past two days chasing rumors of a big deal brewing between the Yankees and German apparel giant Adidas. It turns out the rumors were true, and while Murphy was showing off his helmet cam, Steinbrenner was issuing a statement laying out the details.

The deal is a stunner: Adidas will pay the Yankees $95 million over the next 10 years for the exclusive right to put its trademark three stripes on just about everything it can: the outside stadium walls, the outfield and backstop fences, the dugout roofs, ticket stubs. It will also advertise heavily in Yankees publications and TV and radio broadcasts. And the release states that the partners will "collaborate on joint programs involving certain athletic equipment and apparel, within the Yankee rights." Whatever that means.

The deal is a staggering sum of money, more than teams like the Brewers earn each season from their TV deals. Selig thought he'd prevented just this sort of inequality by creating MLB Enterprises. *Damn it, all apparel with team logos is MLB property!* But Steinbrenner claims this deal doesn't fall within those parameters, and under the new revenue sharing rules, he only has to share 20 percent of his take instead of half.

The reporters all have the same question for Murphy: Does the Yankees-Adidas deal undermine MLB Enterprises? "We do not have the details, and until we do, it's very difficult for me to share what our views are," is all Murphy can say. "As soon as we do, we will tell you what we think the situation is."

Selig is getting the same question on call after call to his office in Milwaukee. "Obviously, we haven't seen the deal," Selig says. "Until I see the terms, it would be unfair to comment or speculate on it."

Selig instructs his outside counsel Bob DuPuy to ask Yankees lawyers for a copy of the contract. Their answer? "We'll consider the request." *What the hell?* Selig has already received calls from Reinsdorf, Pohlad, and others who are furious with Steinbrenner. And they don't yet know that Beeston's Blue Jays and other teams are already talking about reaching out to Adidas for deals of their own. So much for Bud's national marketing plan.

"How could he do this to me?" Selig mutters as he reaches for the phone to dial Steinbrenner's number. *George promised he'd let the new system work, and he won't even give it a chance to get off the damn ground.*

Just last week George unleashed a profanity-laced tirade at Selig during an Executive Council meeting. The reason: Bud's opposition to George's pursuit of Japanese pitching star Hideki Irabu. Under baseball's rules, San Diego received the exclusive bargaining rights to Irabu, but Steinbrenner wants in. Since when do rules apply to George?

Steinbrenner shouted about baseball's conspiracy to hold back the Yankees that day. Now he does this. Selig doesn't know what's worse—the new Yankees deal or that George did it behind his back. But one thing is certain: things will get ugly in a hurry.

Steinbrenner's decision to keep the Adidas deal a secret until he was ready to announce it wasn't a tough one. "There's a good chance baseball will try to block this deal if they know about it in advance," David Boies told George soon after the Boss hired the famous litigator to help craft the Adidas contract. "MLB might be displeased with a fait accompli, but it's probably better to seek forgiveness than permission."

The decision to make the deal was even easier. Steinbrenner always says you have to spend money to make money, and after winning it all last October, he's been forced to ante up to keep winning. Joe Torre wanted a raise and an extension; he got both, with two more years at $2 million per. Bernie Williams, a free agent after the '98 season, settled for $5.25 million to avoid arbitration. Agent Scott Boras immediately set the cost of an extension at $9 million a year, and the center fielder's long-term future as a Yankee is suddenly in doubt.

Cecil Fielder wanted a two-year extension or a trade, his right as a veteran traded in midseason. He'll eventually drop his trade demand, but Steinbrenner still has to pay him the final year on his Tigers contract, a Yankees-record $7.25 million.

The youngsters want to be paid, too. Andy Pettitte ($600,000) and Mariano Rivera ($550,000) were easily satisfied, but Jeter, the AL's unanimous Rookie of the Year, rejected Steinbrenner's offer for $450,000—$100,000 below the young star's asking price— on March 5. The two reconcile five days later at $540,000, plus $25,000 in performance bonuses.

All this drives the Yankees payroll to $62 million, the highest in baseball history. George expects a big return on his investment, and he's never asked more of his management team than he's demanding right now. Indeed, GM Bob Watson will check in to a hospital complaining of chest pains in late April, and doctors will tell him to reduce his stress, lose 20 pounds, and cut his 105-hour workweek to a manageable 80.

The truth is, the Boss was on a rampage even before the owners finally approved the new labor deal, publicly stating that revenue sharing and the luxury tax "can't be something that goes on and on forever." If it does, he says, "then perhaps we should move the game to Russia."

He's even more strident in private, ranting about owners who aren't using the money to improve their teams as promised. Some, he says, are taking their newfound dollars and paying down debt incurred during '94, when Bud shut down the game with George's Yankees on their way to the World Series. Some are using it to pay off the loans they needed to buy their teams. And others are simply stuffing the cash into their pockets.

Steinbrenner is right on all counts, and the Commissioner is supposed to make sure none of this happens. But George suspects that Selig's doing the same thing with the Brewers' revenue sharing checks, so how can he expect Bud to tell the other owners to stop? No, Steinbrenner says, these men aren't his partners. They are his competitors, and he will do everything in his power to bury them.

Besides, they ought to be thanking him. Steinbrenner has once again shown them that they are all grossly undervaluing their franchises, just as he did with the landmark cable deal in 1988. The sneakers war is raging, with Nike, Adidas, and Reebok showering teams and athletes with money just to wear their shoes and display their logos. If nothing else, George's Adidas deal just upped the ante for sponsorship rights for every team in baseball.

George has always understood the value of the Yankees brand, and he's charged COO David Sussman and marketing director Derek Schiller with maximizing the team's name and its recent success. Adidas is just the first of many deals the Yankees have in the pipeline—from computer companies to cars—all deals that will challenge what MLB controls and what each team can call its own.

The Yankees turn over a copy of their Adidas contract and supporting documents a few days after the deal is announced, and it's not long before Selig hands down a ruling: Steinbrenner cannot sell Yankees T-shirts—or any other items of clothing—that bear the Adidas logo. They can't even outfit their grounds crew in Adidas apparel.

This is just the kind of thing George's lawyers warned him would happen, and after a few weeks of fruitless negotiations, Steinbrenner raises the stakes: the Yankees and Adidas sue each of the other 29 teams, MLB Enterprises, and 14 officials, owners, and lawyers, challenging the new revenue sharing agreement on antitrust grounds while charging that all of baseball is conspiring against his team.

"At least since the Yankees purchased Babe Ruth from the Boston Red Sox in January 1920, many clubs have expressed envy and enmity towards the Yankees for their aggressive competitiveness... both on and off the field," litigator David Boies writes in the 91-page suit he files on May 6. The lawsuit is especially critical of one franchise—the Milwaukee Brewers—citing Selig's team for "mismanagement" that has resulted in 14 straight years without a division title, the longest drought "of any current Major League Club."

Baseball's reaction is predictable. Steinbrenner is quickly kicked off the powerful Executive Council in a unanimous vote by its other nine members. He's also removed from the realignment committee, among others, and there is even talk of a third suspension. Two hundred days after his team won the World Series, George Steinbrenner is once again persona non grata in baseball.

"This is sad," says Selig when he announces the moves. "All of us recognize our responsibilities when we come into baseball and while we're in baseball. Most of us believe very strongly we have a responsibility to act like partners."

Most, but not all. The owner in New York is still playing by his own rules.

Selig's troubles with the Boss notwithstanding, it's turning out to be a very good season for the man from Milwaukee. Interleague play, the season's big experiment, is a smash hit—attendance for the first 84 games is up 35 percent. The Yankees drew 168,719 when they won two of three from the Mets, the biggest crowds since Yankee Stadium was remodeled in 1976 and a 115 percent increase over their season average.

There are legitimate pennant races in every division, and a few teams in each league are battling for wild-card slots. Even Bud's Brewers have been surprisingly competitive, holding on to first place in the AL Central as late as June 4, despite having the game's fourth-lowest payroll.

Many owners are intrigued by Selig's "radical realignment" idea, in which as many as 15 teams would shift leagues along geographic lines to increase rivalries and cut down travel costs. (The plan's biggest opponent is the union, which thinks this break from tradition is a big mistake.) It appears likely that Milwaukee will move to its old home in the National League, a shift needed if Arizona and Tampa are to be placed in different leagues when they debut in '98. The proposed move polls well with Brewers fans.

Hitters are again racking up home runs at a record rate, with Mark McGwire, Ken Griffey, Barry Bonds, and Tino Martinez among a dozen players on pace for 40 homers. Seattle is poised to break Baltimore's record of 257 homers in a season, set just last year. Pitchers are putting up big numbers, too, none better than Clemens, who's experiencing a rebirth in his first season with Toronto. With one start left in July, the 34-year-old Rocket is a game-best 16–3, with 173 strikeouts in 163 innings and a 1.54 ERA.

The Commissioner has received high marks for the season-long celebration of the 50th anniversary of Jackie Robinson breaking the sport's color barrier. It kicked off when Selig joined Rachel Robinson and President Clinton at Shea Stadium on April 15, the date of Jackie's first game. Stepping up to the microphone, Selig told the 54,047 fans, "No single person is bigger than the game. No single person other than Jackie Robinson," and then announced that baseball is retiring Robinson's number. "No. 42 belongs to Jackie Robinson for the ages," said Selig.

But the Commissioner hasn't been able to slow the disappearance of black players from his game. This season, black players make up 17 percent of baseball, down from the high of 27 percent in 1975; by 2012, their numbers will fall to 8 percent.

To Bud's delight, there's constant chatter about Selig taking over the Commissioner's job. And his desire to be drafted with unanimous consent is falling into place now that Peter O'Malley is deep in talks to sell his Dodgers to News Corp's Rupert Murdoch. O'Malley was part of the old guard who dismissively referred to Selig as Bud Light when he forced his way into baseball in 1970. Selig knows O'Malley resents how effectively Bud relegated him to the sidelines.

And now the time is right to centralize baseball. It's July 23, and Selig is on a media conference call to announce Paul Beeston as the game's first president and chief operating officer. Bud has nothing but praise for the man he's forgiven for signing Paul Molitor four years ago, and points out they already have a strong working relationship from Beeston's time as chairman of MLB's budget committee.

Most of the 75 writers on the call are well acquainted with Beeston, the first person ever hired by the Blue Jays. The Toronto native started as a team accountant back in 1976 and climbed to president and CEO, overseeing the rise of one of the game's model franchises. But Labatt, the beer company that has owned the team from the start, was bought by Interbrew in June of 1995, and the Belgium-based company has little interest in baseball. Beeston is ready for a change.

It's a shrewd hire by Selig. Beeston is respected and well liked by all the owners, and may be the only man on good terms with Selig, Steinbrenner, and Don Fehr. Now he'll run baseball's day-to-day operations in New York and report directly to Selig. "We have the best game in the world, and that is sacrilegious for a Canadian to make that statement," Beeston says. "But I believe in this game."

The reporters are done quickly with Beeston and spend the next hour asking Selig if this move means he's going to make his own role official. Many of Bud's media enablers are on the call, and they take turns telling Selig how much everyone wants him to accept the job.

Beeston plays right along. "It's no secret that I hope Buddy takes the job," he says. "I will go down there, and if I can make his job easier, I think perhaps he will put himself in a position where he can at least consider it."

Selig basks in the attention. He insists he's never wavered from his decision that the job he's held for nearly five years is temporary. But he's also careful to leave the door open. "I can't help speculation," he says.

The *Chicago Tribune*'s Jerome Holtzman asks Selig if he can comment on *just the possibility* of becoming the permanent Commissioner.

"Jerry, I think I have," Selig replies. "There is just nothing more I can say, and I sort of...I just...I don't even focus on these things anymore."

But Holtzman keeps pushing. "It would be easy for you to say, 'I am not interested.' I don't know if you are saying that."

"I think I am," Selig answers. "And all I'm saying is that I have been very clear, very lucid for five years. I don't see any need to say any more, and I am not going to."

But he will address how the job has changed in the five years since he's taken charge. "I think the Commissioner of baseball has as much authority and power," the Commissioner says, "as any human being in America."

Mark McGwire takes one last practice swing, shifts into his batting stance—back straight, knees slightly bent—and looks intently out at the Giants' young All-Star left-hander Shawn Estes. It's the top of the 3rd in a 2–2 game in San Francisco on September 10, and with the Cardinals' season all but over, their fans back in St. Louis are thinking about only two things:

Will McGwire hit another home run today?

And will the free-agent-to-be sign to play for their beloved Cardinals next season?

The answer to the first question comes on Estes' next pitch, a 79 mph changeup that catches too much of the plate. McGwire lashes the bat with his 19-inch biceps, and the ball rockets on a line into the first deck in left field, 448 feet away. The solo shot is McGwire's 50th home run of the season, making him only the second player in baseball history to hit 50 in back-to-back seasons.

The other player?

Babe Ruth.

The 12,623 fans at 3Com Park stand and cheer for the man who until August 1 had spent his entire 10-year career playing across the bay in Oakland. But the A's are rebuilding, and new owner Steve Schott said he could not pay Big Mac more than the $7 million he is earning this season. So on July 31, Oakland sent its biggest star to St. Louis for three young pitchers of modest potential.

McGwire hit 34 home runs before leaving Oakland, many of them towering shots that evoked memories of Mickey Mantle's tape-measure homers in the '50s. After going without a home run in his first seven games as a Cardinal, McGwire started doing things neither Ruth nor Mantle had ever done. His homer today is his 16th in his last 80 at bats—one in every five official trips to the plate. Ruth's career average of a home run every 11.76 at bats is the best in baseball history. McGwire is now second at 11.94— and falling.

Of course, neither Ruth nor Mantle had ever used anabolic steroids.

McGwire first took steroids with teammate Jose Canseco in 1989, the year before Congress made it illegal to use the drug without a prescription, then started using again after the 1993 season to combat injuries. He took them last season, when he hit 52 home runs after missing the first 18 games of the season, and again this season, his walk year.

Like most juicers, McGwire rationalizes his decision by telling himself that using steroids is not against baseball's rules. And, like all those players, he's wrong. Steroids were first put on baseball's list of banned drugs in 1991 by then-Commissioner Fay Vincent, who sent out a memo announcing the ban to every team. That same memo was reissued this season on May 15, this time carrying the signature of Bud Selig. Clubs were instructed to post the six-page memo in their clubhouses, but most general managers didn't remember receiving it.

But even if the GMs had posted it, would it have mattered?

Certainly not in San Diego, where general manager Kevin Towers is pretty sure he knows what's really in the little black bag Ken Caminiti has carried with him all season. Or in Oakland, where

Canseco isn't shy about telling teammates which steroids to use and how to use them.

Or in New York, where first-year Mets GM Steve Phillips remembers seeing players shoot up in minor league locker rooms when he was a player in the '80s. Phillips asks the Mets doctor to speak to his team about the dangers of steroids use, and the young GM wants a clean game. But he also wants a level playing field and knows his job is to win. He's not about to search every shoe box and bathroom stall to find out who on his team is using performance-enhancing drugs. And he is not alone.

And would it really matter in St. Louis, where the team opens concession stands early for the droves of fans showing up to catch McGwire go yard in batting practice? St. Louis certainly has been good to Big Mac. The media cover him with breathless adulation, and Cardinals fans cheer him wildly before every at bat, all but begging the big first baseman to commit to their team.

And six days after matching the Babe, the 33-year-old McGwire answers their prayers, announcing that he's accepted the team's three-year, $28.5 million offer to remain a Cardinal. He is immediately lionized for taking less money than he was sure to get on the free agent market. He's even deferring some of the money in order to give Cardinals management more flexibility to improve the team, which will finish fourth in the NL Central this season.

"I'm happy here," he says. "That's what matters."

The Cardinals end the season at home with three games against the Cubs, whose right fielder, Sammy Sosa, is finishing up his own fine season: 36 home runs, 119 RBI, and 22 stolen bases. But all eyes remain on McGwire, who thrills the home crowds with a pair of home runs in the season's penultimate game and another in the final game.

His season-high 58 home runs are the most since Hank Greenberg hit 58 in 1938, leaving Cardinals fans counting the days until next season. McGwire averaged a homer in every other game with the Cardinals, but asking for another season of 50 would be a bit greedy. Even Ruth, who hit 50 or more home runs four times, never did it in three straight seasons.

Besides, McGwire will be in St. Louis for three more years. He even has an option for a fourth. How could any Cardinals fan possibly ask for more?

There will be no parade down the Canyon of Heroes in Manhattan this fall. Moments after Bernie Williams' deep fly ball to left-center field is caught by the Indians' Brian Giles to end the ALDS and the Yankees' season, Steinbrenner emerges from his suite on the first level of Jacobs Field and meets the media.

It's been a strange year for the defending champions. The Yankees led the league in pitching and finished second in runs, with Tino Martinez hitting 44 homers and emerging as a major force. They won four more games than last season's team but never spent a day in first place, settling instead for the AL wild card.

Gene Michael had the season's biggest save when he calmed George after Mariano Rivera blew three of his first six save chances as the replacement for closer John Wetteland. "He can't handle it," Steinbrenner said.

"Just leave him alone," Michael told him. "He'll be fine."

Rivera was fine, converting 17 of his next 18 save opportunities. And that was before Mo found what he called his "gift from God," the cutter he discovered in a mid-June catch with teammate Ramiro Mendoza. Rivera insists he changed nothing in his grip, but he suddenly had a late-breaking cutter that broke bats — and the backbone of rallies. He finished with 43 saves, six wins, and a 1.88 ERA.

To the chagrin of many, Steinbrenner succeeded in landing Hideki Irabu, sending two minor leaguers and $3 million to San Diego for the Japanese star. And to the delight of most, Irabu had a difficult first season, going 5–4 with a 7.09 ERA. The Yankees' best personnel move was one they didn't make. Watson convinced Steinbrenner not to send Jorge Posada and Mendoza to Boston to bring back Mike Stanley.

But the defending champs fell far short of a repeat, falling in the first round to Cleveland in five games. "All I have to say is I'm proud of them," says the Boss, a tight smile on his face. "We battled them all the way. A few breaks here, a few breaks there . . . we'll win it next year."

Steinbrenner's friend in Milwaukee is also looking forward to next season. Union opposition shelved radical realignment, so Selig will have to be content with the Brewers moving to the NL Central. The move to the National League sits well with Milwaukee fans, and Selig is hopeful the shift will help bring fans back to County Stadium after just 1.44 million came out to watch this season's 78–83 Brewers.

It's lame-duck owner Wayne Huizenga's Marlins who emerge as World Series champions, beating the Indians in seven games in just their fifth year in baseball. Huizenga, who spent $89 million to bring in free agent third baseman Bobby Bonilla, outfielder Moises Alou, and pitcher Alex Fernandez, announced his plans to sell the team earlier this season. Any chance that winning would change his mind was quickly dispelled when the Blockbuster Video founder immediately announces he'll cut the team's payroll to the high teens while continuing to shop his ball club.

The reason: Huizenga insists the Marlins can't pay for star players and turn a profit unless the taxpayers of Miami build the billionaire's team a baseball-only, retractable-roof stadium like the one now being built in Milwaukee.

"Unless a new stadium is built, where luxury suites and all other revenue go directly to the team, I do not believe the Marlins will ever be in a World Series again," says Huizenga, who claims he lost $34 million while playing in Pro Player Stadium, which he happens to own. He also owns the stadium's other tenant, the Miami Dolphins. "I sincerely doubt that someone will lose $30 million a year again in order to win the World Series."

Alou, who hit 23 home runs and drove in 115 during the regular season and sparkled in the World Series, is shipped to Houston on November 11 for three journeymen pitchers. A month later, the team sends Kevin Brown, its best pitcher, to San Diego for rookie Derrek Lee, who played 22 games in '97, and two minor league pitchers.

The sell-off won't be complete until the spring, when six more stars are sent packing, but it's clear even now that next year's Marlins will bear little resemblance to the team that just won baseball's biggest prize. The Florida fire sale reminds veteran baseball writers of 1976, when A's owner Charlie Finley sold off the stars from his championship teams only to have Commissioner Bowie Kuhn use his "best interests of the game" powers to void the deals. One of Kuhn's vocal supporters was the young owner of the Brewers, Bud Selig.

But this is a different time and a different Bud Selig. Earlier this fall, Selig and the Executive Council gave Carl Pohlad permission to explore selling the Twins to buyers who would move the franchise to Charlotte. The reason: Minnesota voters said no to a taxpayer-financed stadium. It won't be the last time Selig considers shafting baseball fans in the Twin Cities.

Protecting the home team now has strings attached, and Selig remains silent as the best team in his game is dismantled. But his message couldn't be any clearer: build new stadiums for our teams or suffer the consequences.

Chapter 17

ALMOST PERFECT

January 4–July 9, 1998

On the fourth day of 1998, New York's newspapers all run stories about the unknown shipbuilder from Cleveland who, 25 years ago to the day, was introduced as the new owner of the New York Yankees. "I won't be active in the day-to-day operations of the club at all," George Steinbrenner, now the longest-tenured Yankees owner, promised that day. "I can't spread myself so thin. I've got enough headaches with my shipping company."

George has a good laugh as he's repeatedly reminded of the biggest understatement of his career. Sure he meant what he said all those years ago, but he didn't understand how bad things were. "There were things that needed fixing," he tells one reporter after another.

One month later, Steinbrenner is sitting in a booth at the Regency Bar & Grill on Park Avenue, waiting for Brian Cashman. If all goes well, the 30-year-old Cashman will become his 13th general manager. Gene Michael, who hired the serious, hardworking Cashman as his assistant GM four years ago, says he is ready. So does Bob Watson, who told George just last night that he should promote his young assistant. That was just moments after Watson quit, ending two successful but stormy years as the team's GM.

It's no surprise that Watson resigned, not after he told people at a public seminar a few weeks back that the baseball people George listens to are "little people that run around in his head." Steinbrenner knew Watson had been upset since last fall, when George picked up the option on the GM's contract without giving him a raise. Watson was voted Executive of the Year in 1996, and the Yankees won 96 games last season. But George thought Watson took too long to get things done, and felt he had to get into the middle of trade talks to bail out his GM — which he often did without telling Watson.

George had desperately wanted the Expos' Pedro Martinez, and blamed Watson when Montreal dealt the ace right-hander to Boston for two minor leaguers. He somehow forgot that Expos GM Jim Beattie, who Steinbrenner publicly ridiculed when Beattie was a rookie pitcher for the Yankees two decades ago, swore he'd never do a deal with the Boss if he could help it.

Now the Twins have put Chuck Knoblauch on the market, and George wants the All-Star second baseman. Badly. So on the first weekend in February, the Boss, in town for the annual Baseball Writers' Association of America award banquet, called Watson and ordered his GM to offer Bernie Williams and Andy Pettitte for Knoblauch.

"I'm not making that deal," Watson said.

"Are you defying me?" George roared back from his hotel suite.

"Yes," Watson answered. "Bottom line, you cannot trade Bernie Williams and Andy Pettitte for Chuck Knoblauch. I'm not going to hurt the team."

By now, George was furious. "If you don't do it, you're fired."

"You don't have to go that far," Watson said. "Instead of you firing me, I quit."

Steinbrenner shot right back. "I'll ask Stick to do it, then."

Now Watson was angry, too. "You do that, I *am* leaving," he told Steinbrenner. "I suggest you hear this. Here are the keys hitting the table." And Watson dropped his keys on his desk.

"Here is my cell phone and my pager hitting the desk."

Bang, bang.

"This is going to hurt me because these are the keys to the

House That Ruth Built," said Watson, who then stood up and walked out of the room. He made it official when he told George he was quitting in person at the Baseball Writers dinner last night.

It was early Monday morning when Watson slipped into Cashman's office and told him the news: I've resigned for health reasons, he told Cashman. And I've told George to give the job to you.

"George is going to give you a call later today," Watson said. "You've got a lot to think about, buddy."

George made that call, and now he is sitting impatiently in his booth at the Regency, waiting for Cashman to arrive. But naming a new GM may not be the most important thing on Steinbrenner's mind today. Cable magnate Chuck Dolan, his old friend from Cleveland, is preparing a bid for the Yankees. It was a few months back when Dolan told Steinbrenner that Cablevision, which airs as many as 150 Yankees games a season to its 2.9 million customers, wanted to buy the team rather than pay for the TV rights, which expire after the 2000 season. "You'll have an offer in March," Dolan told him, and the Boss didn't reject the idea out of hand.

Now 67, George would much prefer to hand the reins of the franchise to one of the younger Steinbrenner men, especially 28-year-old Hal, who occupies the office down the hall from his at Legends Field. But Steinbrenner knows his relationship with his younger son has never been rockier. The more George pushes, the more time his son spends working on the family hotel business. Hal bristles every time his father mocks his suggestions or reverses his decisions, but George can't help himself. Damn it, Steinbrenner thinks, what he dishes out is nothing compared to the grief his father put on him, and look where he is now.

But Hal doesn't respond the same way. Working for George makes Hal dread the days when his father comes to visit Hal's daughters, and he doesn't want that. Keeping his distance is the only way he sees to keep their relationship sane. Expecting Hal to take a bigger role with the Yankees is not going to happen any time soon.

Son-in-law Joe Molloy was filling the void, but he asked for a year off last August. By January, Molloy and George's younger daughter Jessica decided to separate, and they will file for divorce next month.

Steinbrenner has now turned to Steve Swindal, husband of his older daughter Jennifer, to help him manage the team.

Jennifer married Steve in 1983, and told her husband he was free to work for any of her father's companies that interested him— except the Yankees. She didn't want that kind of pressure to be part of their new marriage. Swindal ran the family's tugboat company for 11 years, until Steinbrenner sold it last September. George then asked Steve to join the Yankees as a general partner, and Jenny gave her blessing. Intelligent, genial, and sixth-generation Tampa, Swindal quickly won the respect of the Yankees' front office and is the family's new representative in the team's day-to-day operations.

The future of the franchise is weighing on George's mind, but he knows he will have to hear Chuck Dolan's Cablevision offer before he makes any decisions for the long term. The short term is taxing enough.

And now Cashman is walking into the Regency, dressed in a suit and clearly nervous. Cashman wears glasses, is five feet nine with thinning hair, and the guys around the office call him Costanza, befitting his resemblance to the character who works for the Yankees on *Seinfeld*. Steinbrenner has watched Cashman grow up since giving him an internship 12 years ago as a favor to Brian's father John, a fellow horseman and a longtime friend. The nickname aside, Steinbrenner knows there's a toughness about the kid who played second base and set a single-season-hits record at Catholic University.

The question is, will he be tough enough?

"I've talked to a lot of people about you, and they say you're capable of doing this job," Steinbrenner tells Cashman. "I can go outside the organization and recycle somebody else, someone who has done this job before, but I've been told you can do it.

"So, what do you think?" George says. "Do you want this job?"

Cashman stares at the bear of a man he's witnessed berating Yankees employees more times than he'd like to remember. It was not long ago when Steinbrenner looked at Watson and him and called them office clerks. "You're clerk one," he told Watson, then turned to Cashman. "And you're clerk two." He's seen seven general managers during his time with the Yankees, each one of them crushed and humiliated before they left, and Cashman's always told himself he never wanted this job.

Now Steinbrenner wants an answer.

"Yes, sir," Cashman says. "I'm your man."

"Good, let's talk about your contract," says Steinbrenner, looking satisfied but impatient. "What do you want?"

What do I want? Well, Cashman thinks, *it would be great if I could stop shaking.* Steinbrenner seems ready to give him a two-year deal, maybe three. But is that really a good idea? He's not even sure he can do this job. The fans are going to wonder who he is, and the media's going to kill him.

Cashman has a better idea. "Let's just do a handshake," he tells Steinbrenner. "I guarantee you that I will work hard. Let's see how it goes."

"Deal!" George shouts, reaching over to shake Cashman's hand, never for a moment thinking he's just hired his last general manager as owner of the New York Yankees.

Cashman wants to make one thing perfectly clear. "If someone wants to reach out to the Yankees, and they're wondering who to reach out to, that man is me."

That's what Cashman tells the media at Yankee Stadium on Tuesday, February 3, right after Watson told them he had resigned and introduced Brian as George's next GM. And if anyone thinks Cashman's statement is naive, he wants to clear that up, too.

"I'm going into this with my eyes wide open," Cashman says. "I know there will be phone calls when I don't want them. I understand this is one of the most difficult jobs in sports, if not *the* most difficult. I understand what George wants."

And he knows George wants Knoblauch, so the next day Cashman kisses his still-stunned wife Mary good-bye, hops on a plane for Tampa, and joins negotiations to land the Twins star. Two days later, Cashman completes his first trade, sending Eric Milton—the team's top pitching prospect—three more minor leaguers, and $3 million of Steinbrenner's cash to the Twins for the four-time All-Star second baseman. George is already feeling good about the kid GM he's paying just $130,000.

George stays happy as spring training gets under way and his team—and business—only gets better. Hideki Irabu, a disappointment last season, shows up with a trim build and a live fastball. He strikes out seven of 12 Braves in a mid-March outing, never reaching a three-ball count. "You can't get any better than that," Joe Torre says.

On March 20, the Yankees sign Cuban star pitcher Orlando Hernandez, who escaped his homeland on a flimsy raft in December and now owns a four-year, $6.6 million contract. The pitcher they call El Duque throws in the low 90s, has an array of pitches rivaling that of new teammate David Cone, and should be ready by midseason. Cone is rebounding nicely from his shoulder surgery and will take his place in the rotation by Opening Day. Knoblauch pleases Steinbrenner by reaching base in all 24 preseason games, batting leadoff in a lineup that hit .314 in spring training and may be the best in baseball.

A lineup like this costs plenty, too. The Yankees head into the season with a $66.8 million payroll, second only to Baltimore's $72.5 million. Add in his revenue sharing and luxury tax bills, and this season will cost Steinbrenner close to $100 million.

But George still maintains you have to spend money to make money, and Chuck Dolan proves him right in late March when he offers George $500 million for his team. Steinbrenner, who owns 60 percent of the franchise and controls its fate, releases a statement that boils down to one key sentence: "I don't ever intend to get out of the Yankees."

The Adidas case is also breaking his way. Sure, when MLB's decision is announced in April, Bud insists that George pay all the legal fees—about $500,000 once the two sides settle and the suit is dropped.

But Steinbrenner gets to keep his 10-year, $95 million deal, and Adidas will have a licensing and advertising agreement with MLB, adding more money to baseball's coffers.

"In the long run, George could be right—it could be very good for baseball," says baseball's COO Paul Beeston, who's moved into the Regency two floors below Steinbrenner. "He sometimes goes to the brink, but I disagree with people. I think he can be reasoned with."

With Opening Day at hand, Steinbrenner has every reason to feel good. His Yankees are the consensus team to beat and the value of the franchise has never been higher. He has a bright young general manager and, he has to admit, even his business executives are doing a good job. But when it suddenly comes crashing down—some of it literally—the Boss does what he always does: he looks for someone to blame.

The team is the first to stumble, starting out 0–3, including a 10–2 blowout in Anaheim in the season's second game. Every beat reporter is writing about 1985, when George fired Yogi Berra after a 6–10 start. "If I start worrying about that," Torre says, "I'll manage scared and distracted, and I can't do that." The Yankees get their first win, beating the A's 9–7, but when the Mariners crush his team 8–0 to open a three-game series, Torre is worried. He calls a team meeting and reaches out to Cone and Paul O'Neill.

"If you've got anything to say," he tells them, "say it now."

Cone loves playing for Torre, and he sees real concern etched on Joe's face, a look that says if his team doesn't turn things around soon, people could lose their jobs. Starting with the manager.

So Cone stands up in the clubhouse and talks about how devastated he was when they lost to the Mariners in '95, how he hates the Kingdome, and how angry he was last night to watch Seattle celebrate after each of its eight runs. "They're rubbing our noses in it," Cone says, his face getting flushed. "We need to get some payback now."

Cone and his teammates get their payback, taking the next two games and the series. The Yankees even their record with a win in their home opener, but the papers are still filled with stories that Steinbrenner is unhappy and might make a move. Not happening, says George. "As far as being impatient with my manager, no way," he says. "The same with the staff. It is not even in my psyche."

But it is in his psyche. He's worried about his team, and second-guessing his decision to make the untested Cashman his GM. "Stick, I'm not sure the kid can handle this job," Steinbrenner tells Gene Michael. "I need you to take over as general manager."

Michael lets the Boss vent, then calms him down. "George, I'm telling you, the kid can do this job," Michael says. "Just give Brian a chance. He'll be fine."

"Okay," Steinbrenner mutters, "but it's on you if this doesn't work."

Steinbrenner has something tangible to worry about before his team can play its next game. It's 3 p.m. on April 13, and the Yankees and Angels are ready to leave their clubhouses for batting practice when a loud boom reverberates around Yankee Stadium. The cause: an 18-inch long, 500-pound beam of concrete and steel came loose from the upper deck, crushing Seat 7 in Section 22 and punching a hole in the concrete right below it. Had the beam fallen 24 hours earlier, it would have come crashing down in the 7th inning of the A's-Yankees game.

"If someone were sitting there at the time that the beam came down, that person would now be dead," Mayor Rudy Giuliani says at a Stadium news conference. Steinbrenner, reached at his home in Tampa, says, "We'll overcome this one, but we've got to be sure it doesn't happen again. If that means a new stadium, we'll have to see."

Steinbrenner and Giuliani have been talking for several years about a new stadium to replace the 75-year-old landmark when the Yankees' lease runs out in 2002, and this can only strengthen George's hand. He wants out of the Bronx, blaming the sad state of the borough for the team's mediocre attendance. Everyone knows George's long-held wish is a new stadium on Manhattan's West Side. Talks that have been dormant are sure to heat up soon.

But there are more immediate concerns. Engineers will have to do a thorough inspection, which will take days, so the Yankees play their next game at the Mets' Shea Stadium, beating the Angels, 6–3. Steinbrenner calls Tigers owner Mike Illitch and persuades him to swap series dates, and the Yankees head to Detroit for the weekend. Meanwhile, talk radio and late-night shows are abuzz with suggestions that the Boss had the bolts loosened or even did it himself. Giuliani concedes the Yankees deserve a new stadium, then says a study commissioned by the city, state, and the team set the price of a West Side stadium at $1.06 billion.

Overlooked in all the turmoil: Torre and his players have turned things around. They take two of three in Detroit, then sweep three in Toronto. They return to the Stadium on April 24, and Steinbrenner is sitting in Seat 7, Section 22, to watch Darryl Strawberry hit his fifth home run and Cone beat the Tigers, 8–4. They win four of their next five, running their record to 17–6, and finish April atop the AL East for the first time this season.

What happens over the next four weeks tells Steinbrenner and every Yankees fan that this could be a special season. The Yankees win 20 of their first 25 games in May, and when Cone beats the Red Sox on May 29, the Yankees are 37–11, hold a 9½-game lead over second-place Boston, and look all but unbeatable.

The lineup is so deep newcomer Scott Brosius is hitting a team-high .346—batting ninth. Cone and David Wells are both 7–1, with the beefy Wells tossing a perfect game against the Twins on May 17. Rivera is now automatic, and Jeff Nelson and Mike Stanton form a terrific bridge to the star closer.

"The 1996 season was very special, and we have the chance to do that again," Rivera says. "And this year we have more talent."

Bud Selig can't help but chuckle as he walks out the door of the ballroom in Chicago's O'Hare Hilton. Neither can most of the men and the handful of women who asked Selig to leave the room so they could vote on whether to appoint him the ninth Commissioner of baseball. In 2,130 days as Acting Commissioner, Selig has rarely allowed a vote before knowing the outcome. And the outcome of this vote was decided a very long time ago.

It's July 9, exactly three weeks before Selig's 64th birthday, and as he walks up and down the hallway—Bud's a pacer, in good times and bad—he can't help but marvel that a kid from Milwaukee could become the most important man in baseball. It will feel good to finally make it official, to go from an owner serving a role to the man everyone will now call Mr. Commissioner. And to be paid accordingly—that will be satisfying, too.

The final drumbeat began in late February from an important place. "This search for a Commissioner is a charade—put the game in the hands of Selig and Beeston, and let's get on with it!" Steinbrenner told the *New York Times.* "Selig's a great consensus builder. I grow impatient with him at times, but he's the ideal guy."

Steinbrenner's clearly forgotten that Selig is the same man he blasted for mismanagement in the lawsuit he filed against baseball last May. Back then George wondered if Selig was listening to big market teams like his. And now? "Selig's the most impartial guy in the world when it comes to his team," Steinbrenner said.

A month later, Braves chairman Bill Bartholomay, the leader of the first Commissioner search-charade, weighed in. "I've known nine Commissioners, and he's the best we've had," said the 69-year-old Bartholomay.

Then it was Beeston who hinted that Selig was "finally" listening to the owners who keep begging him to take the job. "Maybe that's what will happen," he told MSG Network on Opening Day.

By June, Selig shared his intentions with so many people that *New York Times* baseball columnist Murray Chass reported it was already a done deal. "The search for a baseball Commissioner is over," wrote Chass, a frequent Selig critic. "It did not stray an inch from where it began."

And that result, said Selig's sparring partner Don Fehr, should not surprise anyone. Or change anything. "It was increasingly likely that the owners would ask him to take the job permanently," Fehr told reporters on June 27. "I don't think Selig being named Commissioner will change the way we conduct business. We now have an office to deal with on a daily basis. We won't treat this as a significant change."

It was two days later that Selig announced he'd hold the vote that's now taking place behind closed doors. And his timing could not be better. Baseball is so hot it's almost impossible for ESPN's *SportsCenter* to get to all the players turning heads and turnstiles: Roger Clemens notched his 3,000th strikeout of his 15-year career four days ago and is on his way to another Cy Young Award.

Cleveland's Manny Ramirez has 71 RBI and will finish with a career-high 145. Seattle's Alex Rodriguez will be only the third player to hit 40 home runs and steal 40 bases.

But no one has dazzled like Mark McGwire and Sammy Sosa,

whose mano a mano home run battle has practically everyone—
even non–baseball fans—checking St. Louis and Chicago box
scores. Sosa hit a record 20 home runs in June and has 33 for the
season. McGwire hit 11 by the end of April, 16 more in May, and has
a game-high 37. Both men—plus Ken Griffey—have Roger Maris
and his single-season home run record of 61 in their sights.

The Yankees are winning, often in spectacular fashion, and
while every other owner is loath to admit it, everyone makes more
money when the game's flagship franchise is flying high. And
these aren't the brawling Yankees of the Bronx Zoo, this is a team
filled with marketable players. Is there anyone more wholesome
than Derek Jeter?

Selig can boast that seven teams are on pace to go over the 3 million mark in attendance, and revenues will hit $2.5 billion—more
than double what they were when Selig took over in September of
'92. Rupert Murdoch paid a record $314 million for the Dodgers in
March, and last month Tom Hicks bought the Rangers for $250
million. Five new baseball-only stadiums have been built in the last
four years, with three more under way, all but one funded primar-
ily by local taxpayers.

By any measure, Selig's time as "Acting" Commissioner has been
a success. And no one's pushing Bud to move to New York now that
Beeston has settled in. Beeston fired Greg Murphy last fall (Selig
left that unpleasant task for him) and now he's ready to bring in Bob
DuPuy, Rob Manfred, and Sandy Alderson—all sharp executives
and Selig loyalists—to change the way the game is run. In the
months ahead Selig will announce plans to fold the two leagues'
business operations into one and call it Central Baseball, with everything and everyone reporting to the new Commissioner.

"Bud sets policy, and I implement it," Beeston tells everyone.

That's the same arrangement Bud has had with his daughter,
with whom he has run the Brewers for the past six years. And while
Selig will soon move out of County Stadium and into an office tower
downtown, their relationship will change in appearance only. Selig
is resigning from the Brewers Board and putting his 30 percent
share of the team in a trust. He's also giving up the president's
title—which will soon belong to Wendy—and his $450,000

Brewers salary, now that baseball will pay him $3 million—plus perks and bonuses—for each of the next five years.

Bud has always been the big-picture half of their partnership, Wendy has always handled the day-to-day, and that won't change. Bud has almost jealously guarded their relationship, never letting anyone come between them, and people who know them well understand that if one of them is in favor of something, so is the other.

Not a day goes by when father and daughter don't speak, and Bud doesn't have to ask to know it's already been a hectic year for his 38-year-old daughter. She's served as the team's chief operating officer, chief legal officer, and new stadium coordinator, all while pregnant with her first child, who was born on May 25.

Wendy's well regarded within the game, and she does have help close by. Her husband Laurel Prieb is the team's vice president of corporate affairs, and he's there for her at the ballpark and at home. And Bud trusts his good friend and general manager Sal Bando to take care of his team, despite the five straight losing seasons on Bando's watch. So does Wendy, who thinks of Bando as her uncle.

And now Selig's wait outside the ballroom is over. He walks back into the meeting room and his peers stand and clap. The applause lasts for several minutes, long enough for Selig's entire family—his wife and her parents, his three daughters and their husbands, his five granddaughters—to come in and take their places. Selig is then told what he already knows: he was elected unanimously. Now it's time to make his first address as The Commissioner.

He starts with a story about the late John Fetzer, the former Tigers owner he's talked about many times before. "John Fetzer was my mentor," Selig says, full of emotion. "He probably had more influence on me than any man other than my father. He taught me the basic lesson that so many in baseball never learn: the sport transcends all of us. He told me the only way you should ever decide anything is based on what's in the best interests of baseball."

Selig talks about ending the animosity that has plagued their relationship with the players and with each other. He thanks them all, his family included, for the support they've given him the past six years—"Has it really been that long?"—and tells them he wants to be judged—and paid—on how much the value of their franchises rises.

And he makes them a promise. "From this day forward," Selig says, "you'll have every ounce of energy in my body as we move the greatest game in the world along."

When their meeting ends, Selig and his family meet with reporters for a media conference that often feels like a celebration. "In the end, I think he knew it was the right thing to do," says Sue Selig, who's known for almost six years that this day would come. "This is a great day for our family, for baseball, and for the city of Milwaukee. It won't say 'Commissioner's Office, New York,' now. It'll say, 'Commissioner's Office, Milwaukee!'"

Selig addresses his working arrangement, saying he'll split time between Milwaukee and New York—though Beeston knows getting Bud to Manhattan will be a chore. He outlines how he'll work with Beeston ("I'll do more global things"), when he'll officially take office ("August 1"), and how tough it will be to leave the team he brought to Milwaukee 28 years ago ("Very tough, but it's time").

He's growing tired as the questions begin to repeat, and he's eager to end the questions and hug his wife, daughters, and all the grandkids. But there is one thing he wants on the record before he leaves the media.

The game still has a payroll-disparity problem, he says, and it's getting worse. His highest priority will be fixing a system in which the Orioles can afford a $70 million payroll and the Expos can afford only $9 million. He concedes their current revenue sharing plan helps, but he insists more help is needed for fans in every city to have "hope and faith" their teams can compete at the start of every season.

"If you remove hope and faith from two-thirds or three-quarters of your franchises," the new official Commissioner says, "you've hurt the game badly."

Chapter 18

SECRETS

August 17–November 27, 1998

THERE ARE TWO compelling narratives that transfix Americans during the long, hot summer of 1998. One is an endless government investigation turned sex scandal that has shaken the nation's faith in the man who runs the country. President Bill Clinton has done the unthinkable—he's carried on an illicit affair with a 22-year-old White House intern—and the country is bracing for his possible impeachment.

The other is the home run duel between Mark McGwire and Sammy Sosa, which has captured the imagination of a nation eagerly searching for an escape. And as the Clinton scandal grows tawdrier by the day, even Americans who never followed this sport look upon two ballplayers as saviors with every home run they hit.

On the night of August 17, Clinton sits behind a desk in his private residence in the White House. He stares straight into a television camera, the red light goes on, and the 42nd President of the United States tells the country about his dirty little secret.

"As you know, in a deposition in January, I was asked questions about my relationship with Monica Lewinsky," Clinton says, his voice breaking ever so slightly. "While my answers were legally accurate, I did not volunteer information.

"Indeed, I did have a relationship with Miss Lewinsky that was not appropriate. In fact, it was wrong. It constituted a critical lapse in judgment and a personal failure on my part for which I am solely and completely responsible....

"I know that my public comments and my silence about this matter gave a false impression. I misled people, including even my wife. I deeply regret that....It is time to...get on with our national life."

Like most Americans, Bud Selig is both disappointed and appalled as he watches the President's five-minute speech. He was a history major, as he likes to remind people, and he's never witnessed a spectacle like the one he's seen today. And more than most Americans, Selig is grateful McGwire and Sosa have come up big during the country's summer of need.

Baseball fans in parks across the land have treated the two players like royalty for almost two months now. Sosa is happy to play the supporting actor even as he matches his counterpart homer for homer, his engaging personality transforming the dour McGwire into a friendly giant. The six-foot-five, 245-pound McGwire has only recently grown into his role, and he appreciates Sosa being there to share the stage.

The schedule has put them on the same field in Chicago on August 19, just two days after Clinton's confession, and Americans are relieved to shift their attention to ivy-draped Wrigley Field. Both men enter the game with 47 home runs, on pace to match Roger Maris' record of 61. Their bats are silent in the first game, but the magic returns the next night. In the bottom of the 5th, Sosa sends the first pitch he sees deep into the seats down the left-field line for No. 48. McGwire pulls even with a solo home run three innings later, knotting the game, 6–6.

And that's where it stands in the top of the 10th when McGwire blasts No. 49, the difference in the Cardinals' 8–6 victory. Scores of writers from around the country crowd into an interview room moments later, where the two stars sit side by side, enjoying each other's company while answering the questions they've both heard so many times before.

At that same moment, another writer sits in Palo Alto, crafting his own take on the summer's feel-good story. Veteran Associated Press writer Steve Wilstein spent the better part of a month shadowing McGwire, Sosa, and Ken Griffey Jr., who is content to be the forgotten man in his peers' buddy movie despite 42 home runs of his own. Wilstein's story took an unanticipated turn when he called a cardiologist friend and asked about a bottle of pills he saw in McGwire's locker while he stood with a pack of writers waiting to do postgame interviews.

"What's Androstenedione?" Wilstein asked the doctor.

"A precursor to testosterone," the cardiologist told him. "And it can be really bad for the heart."

On August 20, McGwire hits No. 50 and No. 51 against the Mets, becoming the first player in baseball history to hit 50 or more home runs in three consecutive seasons. Wilstein's story comes out the following day.

"Sitting on the top shelf of Mark McGwire's locker, next to a can of Popeye spinach and packs of sugarless gum, is a brown bottle labeled Androstenedione," writes Wilstein. He explains that Andro is a legal supplement banned by the NFL, NCAA, and the Olympics for its steroid-like qualities and makes it clear that the 34-year-old McGwire has broken neither the law nor baseball's rules by using it.

But he also writes that Andro raises testosterone levels and is regarded outside baseball as cheating. "Androstenedione is no different than taking testosterone," Dr. John Lombardo, the NFL's adviser on steroids, told Wilstein. "It has anabolic qualities. Therefore it is an anabolic steroid."

The wire-service writer's story runs in media outlets across the country, and the first hint of McGwire's dirty little secret is revealed. But there will be no confessions, no televised requests for forgiveness. Not on this day or on any day soon.

This is one scandal no one wants to know about.

"McGwire is an adult who, as far as we know, is playing within the rules," writes Sports Illustrated's Jack McCallum, giving voice to the majority opinion. "To hold McGwire to a higher standard than his sport does is unfair."

The Boston Globe's Dan Shaughnessy, one of the nation's preeminent baseball writers, agrees. "Mark McGwire is stalking one of baseball's most cherished records, and suddenly he's engaged in a tabloid-driven controversy that's painting him as a cheater and a bad role model," Shaughnessy writes. "It's unfair."

And in a clear case of shooting the messenger, the Cardinals enlist the help of a local columnist, putting him in front of McGwire's locker and asking him to tell America what he sees. "To be able to decipher the label on this Andro bottle, you have to intentionally look, and look hard," St. Louis Post-Dispatch columnist Bernie Miklasz writes. "And that's out of bounds."

McGwire cannot agree more. He insists he hasn't done anything wrong and calls Wilstein a snoop. "Everything I've done is natural," says Big Mac. "Everybody that I know in the game of baseball uses the same stuff I use."

Any concerns Selig may have about public backlash disappear the next day in Pittsburgh when a sellout crowd greets McGwire with a standing ovation in his first at bat. McGwire rewards Pirates fans when he sends a ball deep into the right-center-field seats for home run No. 52. Another sellout crowd is on hand the next night—the Pirates' only two sellouts after Opening Day—and they get their own piece of history in the 8th inning when McGwire smashes No. 53.

Relieved that Wilstein's story has no legs, baseball and the union hold a joint press conference on August 26 to announce they've asked the two doctors who serve as their Health Advisory Board to look into the use of Andro and make recommendations. Their doctors already have a proposal: hire two Harvard researchers to study whether Andro has the anabolic properties Olympics officials and others claim it does, and whether it presents a danger to their players.

"No one can be faulted for staying entirely within the rules," says Fehr, who sits on the U.S. Olympic Committee. If Andro is a problem, he reasons, then Congress, which deregulated the supplement industry four years ago, should pass a law to prohibit its use. "We look forward to hearing from our medical representatives."

"The health of our players is of vital concern for all of us, and we want to assure they receive the most accurate medical and scientific information," Selig says. "I think what Mark McGwire has accomplished is so remarkable, he has handled it all so beautifully, and we want to do everything we can to enjoy a great moment in baseball history."

His first crisis as Commissioner safely behind him, Selig focuses on the historic home run race in earnest. He agrees to assign two detectives to protect McGwire when the Cardinals are on the road. Baseball designates four dozen baseballs for use once McGwire reaches 59, and works with the U.S. Treasury Department to mark the balls so they can be authenticated.

McGwire and Sosa both enter September with 55 home runs. McGwire blows by Hack Wilson's NL-record 56, clubbing four homers in two games against the Marlins. Sosa belts three in five days, the last coming September 5, when both players go deep on the same day for the 20th time this season. McGwire's homer, his 60th, comes against the Reds, whose manager received a voice mail not long ago from a fan pleading with him not to pitch around Mac, as Reds pitchers did 11 times in their previous six games.

"Please pitch to McGwire," the fan begged Jack McKeon. "This is what the country needs to help with the healing process and all the trouble that's going on in Washington. This will help cure the ills of the country."

The home run barrage brings all of baseball to St. Louis on September 7 for a two-game series with the Cubs. Selig arrives a day early and will commute back and forth from Milwaukee on his private jet. "There are times in life to celebrate," Selig tells the many reporters who have also arrived early. "This is a time in life to celebrate." And to help celebrate, he's invited the Maris family to sit in box seats behind first base for both games in St. Louis.

Sosa joins McGwire for a media conference before the first game and spends much of his time making jokes and giggling. Not long after, Mac steps in against Cubs pitcher Mike Morgan in the bottom of the 1st and smacks the third pitch he sees down the left-field line for No. 61, hit on his father's 61st birthday. McGwire rounds the bases, crosses home plate, points to his father John McGwire in the stands behind the backstop, and yells, "Happy birthday, Dad!"

Both McGwire and Sosa huddle with Baseball Hall of Fame director Jeff Idelson two hours before the next game, the last on the

Cardinals' home stand. McGwire promises to donate as much memorabilia as he can when he breaks the record. Then Idelson pulls out the bat Maris used to hit his 61st home run. McGwire rubs the barrel of the bat over his heart. "Roger," he says out loud, "you're with me."

Selig is sitting with Bob Costas and Stan Musial at 8:18 p.m. Central Time when McGwire steps in for the second time against Steve Trachsel. The Cubs right-hander tries to slip an 88 mph fastball past McGwire, but Mac is far too quick, and he rifles the ball straight down the left-field line. He races out of the batter's box thinking it's just a base hit, but the ball clears the fence by 10 feet, just inside the foul pole.

After 37 years, baseball has a new home run king.

A jubilant McGwire jumps up and down with Cardinals first base coach Dave McKay, then remembers to reach back and touch the bag. Every Cubs infielder congratulates him, and the entire Cardinals team mobs him at home plate. McGwire reaches through the crowd for his 10-year-old son Matthew, a Cardinals batboy, and hoists him high over his head.

McGwire is still hugging teammates when he sees Sosa, who's run in from right field to congratulate his friend, and McGwire gives him a bear hug, too. He runs over to the Maris family, seated at the far end of the Cardinals dugout, climbs the fence, and hugs both of Maris' daughters and each of the late Yankee's four sons. Rich and Randy Maris struggle to hold back tears.

It takes a full 11 minutes to restore order, and the rest of the Cardinals' 6–3 victory is an afterthought. A ceremony is held behind second base after the game to honor baseball's new home run record holder, and Selig is the first to speak. He hears a smattering of boos when he's introduced, but wins over the crowd when he calls the Cardinals "one of the proudest and most successful franchises in baseball history."

Then it's time to address McGwire, who is standing at the makeshift podium with tears in his eyes. "This is one of the most historic nights in baseball history," says Selig, who hands McGwire the first Commissioner's Historic Achievement Award, a 12-inch trophy with a sterling-silver base and a baseball mounted on top.

There's a signature on the ball, too.

It reads ALLAN H. SELIG.

The history major is now officially part of one of baseball's greatest nights.

McGwire thanks his teammates and friends, then tells the adoring crowd, "I wanted to do it for all of you—the best fans in the country." The Cardinals present McGwire with a red 1962 Corvette convertible, then drive him around the stadium so he can wave to the 43,688 fans who refuse to leave.

When McGwire retreats to the privacy of the clubhouse, he removes his uniform top, trousers, hat, and spikes and hands them to Don Marr, the president of the National Baseball Hall of Fame and Museum. Everything that McGwire used and wore this night is on its way to the Hall of Fame. One congratulatory phone call from a grateful President Clinton later, and McGwire's long night is reaching an end.

There's three weeks left in this season, and though the emotional peak has passed, the battle for the home run title is far from over. Sosa catches McGwire at 62, McGwire jumps back ahead, and when they each hit a home run on September 25, the two friends stand tied at 66. But that's the last homer Sosa will hit. McGwire hits a pair of home runs in each of his final two games, and baseball's home run record is set at 70.

Well before the final home run is struck, hundreds of people a day make the long trek to Cooperstown just to file past the cylinder holding the uniform and equipment McGwire used the night he broke Maris' record. It's only a fraction of the crowd Hall of Fame officials expect will flock to this picturesque town on the day McGwire takes his place alongside Babe Ruth, Ty Cobb, and all the other baseball greats whose plaques hang in baseball's Hall of Fame.

In all his 25 years as owner of the New York Yankees, George Steinbrenner has never had a team like the one he's watching this season.

It's not just that they are good, though that is certainly part of it. Since their 1–4 start, this team has put up numbers rarely seen. The team won its 100th game on September 4, the fastest any team has reached that mark in the 20th century. In the year of the home run, no Yankee has hit more than 30, but a record 10 players will reach double figures. They're No. 1 in scoring and pitching, Bernie Williams is the league's leading hitter (.339), and Mariano Rivera is the game's best closer.

And what once seemed impossible is now accepted: this team is every bit as intense about winning as its owner. When the Yankees lose a season-high four straight in late August, Joe Torre holds a team meeting, telling his players their sloppy play is unacceptable. They win the next game to run their record to 95–36 and their lead over second-place Boston to 16½ games.

It's an old-school team, just like its manager, who tells Yankees reporters he can't imagine his team hugging McGwire as the Cubs did after his record-breaking home run. Torre knows if a player fails to run hard to first, he doesn't have to say a word. Instead it's David Cone, Paul O'Neill, or Tino Martinez who gets up in the player's face, making sure he knows that isn't the way these Yankees play the game.

Yes, winning and doing it Steinbrenner's way certainly set this team apart. But what makes these Yankees so different is that they actually enjoy the company of their owner. Whereas other Yankees teams would dread the sight of George walking through the clubhouse, this one embraces him. Cone wields a sharp needle, and George laughs. Strawberry talks about his family, and George offers encouragement. Torre plays the ponies, and the Boss shares stories from his many years raising horses.

They all appreciate how eagerly Steinbrenner gets them whatever they need, whether he's buying the latest in training equipment or replacing a damaged piece of clothing, as he did in May when Brosius cut himself shaving and blood dripped all over his white dress shirt. Steinbrenner called and ordered a new shirt, which arrived at the Yankees clubhouse within the hour. George can talk all he wants about expecting his players to fear and respect him, but being accepted as a member of his own team is a dream come true.

He's even more sanguine about his young general manager, though he is not above calling Cashman during a Yankees game at the Stadium and asking why the batboys aren't running water out to the umpires on a hot day. He knows Cashman is learning on the job, and he appreciates how the young GM solicits input from Steinbrenner's advisers down in Tampa instead of railing against them (that will come much later). Most important, he respects Cashman for not being afraid to stand up to him.

Which is just what happened when George pushed hard to get Mariners ace Randy Johnson at the July 31 trade deadline. The 34-year-old Johnson will be a free agent at year's end and has worn out his welcome in Seattle, brawling with a teammate and pouting much of the season. Still, the thought of the six-foot-ten Johnson taking his blazing fastball to the Indians, who are very interested, and dominating his Yankees in the playoffs scared Steinbrenner to no end.

But Cashman wanted nothing to do with Seattle's problem child. A while back he noticed the Yankees never faced the left-hander when the Mariners made an East Coast swing, so he asked manager Lou Piniella why. Randy doesn't like to pitch in New York, Piniella said, so the manager always adjusted his rotation in order for Johnson to skip the Yankee Stadium crowd.

Cashman insisted the Yankees shouldn't empty their farm system for Johnson and told Steinbrenner what he heard from Piniella.

"I don't care," Steinbrenner said. "I want you to do this."

"Fine," Cashman said. "But I am going to tell everyone this was your fucking deal."

Steinbrenner paused. He still liked Johnson, but this was a ballsy move by Cashman, and he liked that, too. But most important, there's no way he wanted to be blamed if the trade was a bust.

"Okay, we'll do it your way," the Boss told Cashman. "But you better be right."

The Yankees beat Boston on September 9 to clinch the division, and at 102–41, the rest of the regular season is really about history. They win their 110th game on September 23, tying the 1927 Yankees for the best record in franchise history. They win the next two to break Cleveland's 34-year-old American League record for most victories, then win their last two to finish 114–48, two short of the Cubs' major league record set in 1906.

Yankees fans respond in droves. A crowd of 52,506 packs the 75-year-old Stadium to watch the Yankees beat the Orioles in the final game before the All-Star break, the fifth time the team's drawn more than 50,000 this season. That puts the team on pace to draw a franchise-record 2.83 million fans, giving Steinbrenner pause about leaving the Bronx.

"Do the 3 million, and then we'll talk about the Bronx after the season," says George. "That isn't getting me where I want to be, but maybe it would be worth talking about."

Three weeks later, the Yankees owner is feeling so flush he tells radio host Don Imus he's willing to put up some of his own money for a new stadium, no matter where it's built. "I wouldn't feel right just sitting back and saying, 'I want a new stadium,'" Steinbrenner says.

Then again, he might not have to. Talks about selling his team to Cablevision's Chuck Dolan grow more serious as the summer turns to fall. But major decisions like a new stadium and a new owner will wait until after the franchise's 24th World Series title is secured.

The Yankees draw Texas in the opening round, and New York pitchers hold the high-powered Rangers offense to one run in a 3–0 Yankees sweep. The team gets one piece of bad news the day before Game 3, and it is jarring: the stomach pain Strawberry's been feeling for two months is the result of a cancerous tumor in his colon. His surgery is set for October 3, two days later. Torre's voice cracks when he gives the team the news, leaving many players in tears.

"This is extremely upsetting to me," Steinbrenner says. "And it really shows that baseball is only a small part of life."

Cleveland, the team that ended the Yankees season so abruptly a year ago, is next. Steinbrenner's team takes the first game 7–2, and memories of last season's failure fade, only to reappear when Cleveland wins the next two games. The American League fines Steinbrenner after Game 2 when George calls Ted Hendry "one of the worst umpires in the league" for failing to call interference on a play at first base that leads to the Indians' go-ahead run in the 12th.

Steinbrenner is almost too silent after the Yankees lose Game 3 in Cleveland, sitting on a table in the trainer's room staring straight ahead, not speaking for almost 10 minutes. His team, so explosive all season, has scored just four runs in the last 29 innings. "We'll see what we're made of," the Boss says to no one in particular as he gets off the table and heads to the clubhouse exit. "I think we'll be fine."

He's more upbeat while walking through the clubhouse before Game 4. Don't get down, he tells one player after another. We'll beat this team. "New York is waiting for the World Series," he says before leaving the clubhouse, "not Cleveland." Hernandez rewards the Boss' confidence, throwing seven shutout innings in a 4–0 win, as does Wells, who wins the next game, 5–3. The Yanks wrap it up in front of the home crowd, beating the Indians 9–5 to earn a trip back to the World Series to face Ken Caminiti and the Padres.

The postgame locker room is packed when Steinbrenner emerges from Joe Torre's office, a cloud of smoke escaping along with him. He pushes his way to the center of the clubhouse, where Jeter spots him. "Hold on, someone is dry around here," says the shortstop, who slices through the crowd and empties a bottle of Champagne over George's head. "I got him," Jeter yells as he scoots away, while Steinbrenner stands and giggles.

"They're warriors," Steinbrenner shouts above the clamor. "I knew we would come back in this series. This is the way it should be. We should win."

The World Series is almost anticlimactic. The Padres are clearly no match for the game's best team, though George provides a few contentious moments. He micromanages preparations for Game 1, battling and losing to the Commissioner's office over who'll sing to open the game (Tony Bennett over Robert Merrill), the song ("America the Beautiful" over the national anthem), seat assignments for the Commissioner and the Maris family, and who'll throw out the first pitch (Sammy Sosa gets the nod over Yankees legends Whitey Ford and Phil Rizzuto).

A crowd of 56,712 and 1,100 members of the media watch the Yankees fall behind 5–2, then charge back when Chuck Knoblauch hits a three-run homer and Martinez blasts a grand slam in the 7th inning of a 9–6 win. They leave little doubt in Game 2, crushing the Padres 9–3. The Series then shifts to San Diego, where Steinbrenner complains about the state of the field at Qualcomm Stadium after an Eagles-Chargers game two days before Game 3. Brosius is the hero this time, hitting two homers to put the Yankees over the top, 5–4.

McGwire throws out the first pitch in Game 4 to a thunderous ovation before taking his seat in Selig's box. Mac gets another big hand in the 4th when he snags a foul ball heading straight at Sue Selig. "I want to thank you for everything baseball did for me this season," McGwire tells Selig as Pettitte and Kevin Brown match scoreless innings. "Are you kidding?" Selig says. "We're the ones who need to thank you."

The Yankees squeeze across a run in the 6th, then get two more in the 8th. Rivera pitches a scoreless 9th, and when Brosius throws out Mike Sweeney for the third out, the Yankees are once again World Champions.

The raucous Yankees clubhouse is called to silence when Selig and Steinbrenner climb onto the TV stage for the trophy presentation. The two men, who have battled, laughed, and cried over things big and small for most of the past quarter century, now stand face to face. And neither can hold back the tears, which fall freely down each man's cheeks.

Standing off to the side is Steinbrenner's younger son Hal. It's been a tough year between father and son — the arguments in their Tampa office getting a little sharper, Hal's stints away from the team growing even longer. But that's all pushed aside at this moment, and it's joy Hal feels as he watches his father embrace Selig. And a bit of wonderment, too, as he realizes it's the first time he's ever seen his father really cry.

Hal sees Yankees players have also taken note of his father's tears. And he can't help but think of the many meetings George has held these last few months to discuss selling his team, and wonders how much of that is what's playing with his father's emotions. Seeing his father up on the stage, his arm around Torre, then Brosius, the Series MVP, he wonders how many of these tears are for what George might be ready to lose instead of the championship trophy his team has just won.

*   *   *

Is this the year Steinbrenner will finally say yes?

That's what the Yankees owner's 16 limited partners are wondering when they meet with him in Cleveland on November 19. Many of the stories you've been hearing are true, Steinbrenner tells his partners. Cablevision owner Charles Dolan has made him another offer to buy their team, and this one is going to be hard to resist: $600 million, almost double the record $311 million Rupert Murdoch just paid for the Dodgers in March. And Murdoch's deal included real estate —the team's spring training complex in Vero Beach, Florida, and Dodger Stadium. Not only is there no land in this deal, but Dolan would also take over the torturous negotiations for a new stadium.

And perhaps the best part—at least for Steinbrenner—is also true: Cablevision would acquire the Yankees, but George would remain the team's managing partner, with final say over all personnel decisions as well as the team's payroll. What's more, Dolan is willing to put Steinbrenner in charge of Cablevision's other two sports teams—the Knicks and the Rangers—in a move that would turn George, now the most powerful man in baseball, into perhaps the most powerful man in all of sports.

Dolan's motivation for making the deal is clear. MSG's contract with the Yankees runs out in two years, and Dolan figures it makes more sense to buy the team than to spend almost as much for its invaluable television rights.

One of the limited partners is John Henry, who has to sell his 1 percent piece because he just agreed to buy what's left of Wayne Huizenga's Marlins. Florida finished dead last in the NL East and drew a meager 1,730,384 fans after Huizenga's fire sale. George likes Henry, but thinks the wealthy hedge fund manager's hopes of building a stadium are pure fantasy.

Steinbrenner is squabbling with some of the other small-stake owners over the terms of their partnership agreement and how much stock and cash each would walk away with in a deal with Dolan. But the limited partners are investors, not decision makers, so if George decides to sell all they can do is take the return on their percentages and go home.

Dolan, an old friend of Steinbrenner's dating back to their time together in Cleveland, is offering a $5 million salary to run all three teams, plus bonuses for postseason appearances and championship trophies. George is pushing for $10 million a year for the next 20 years.

But what he hears from Dolan four days later puts the deal in doubt. It seems James, the guitar-playing youngest of Dolan's three sons, is kicking up a storm. James oversees the Knicks and Rangers, and he has his heart set on running the Yankees should his father acquire baseball's most famous franchise. Giving up the Rangers and the Knicks instead is the last thing James is willing to do.

This is just the kind of trouble Hal and Steve Swindal, now perhaps George's most trusted adviser, have been warning about for months. "It's great that Chuck is your friend," they keep telling George. "But that doesn't mean running a team for him—if you'd really be running the team—isn't going to be more trouble than it's worth. This has disaster written all over it."

Both Hal and Swindal have been against this deal from the start. No, Hal told his father, that doesn't mean he wants to get more involved. He and Steve just don't think Dolan's offer for the most valuable franchise in sports is nearly good enough.

But it's more than that. "The Yankees are your life," Hal tells George. "What do you need the money for? None of us own yachts or spend a lot of money. You still drive an Oldsmobile! The Yankees are your passion. If you sell the team, what are you going to do?"

What is he going do to? That's the question nagging at George when he gets off the phone with Dolan the night of November 23. He has a team he loves and players who, for once, love playing for him. They've just won their second World Series in three years, and there's no reason to think they aren't capable of winning a few more. And the money is sure to be there when he puts the Yankees TV rights out to bid.

Or he could engage further with fabled investor—and new managing partner of the New Jersey Nets—Ray Chambers, who recently floated the idea of the Nets and Yankees joining forces to start their own sports network. You would be able to keep control of the team, Chambers told George at an introductory meeting at the swanky Metropolitan Club in Manhattan, while building equity in what will be a very valuable asset. Discussions between the two camps are ongoing, giving George more to think about as he makes his decision.

And now Dolan's son seems to be making the decision easier. Chuck is no longer talking about giving George the reins to all three teams, and it's growing less clear just how much control he'd have over the Yankees. Losing control of his team is simply unacceptable.

No, Steinbrenner decides, this won't be the year he sells his team after all.

Chapter 19

QUESTION OF BALANCE

January 26–July 14, 1999

Excuse me, Mr. Commissioner," says Lori Keck. "Where would you like this to go?"

Keck is standing in Bud Selig's office, holding a Brewers team photograph, one of the hundreds of pieces of Selig's baseball life he's collected over the last three decades. Selig's daughter Wendy calls her father a pack rat, and that has never been more evident than now, the final week of January 1999 and Selig's last in his cramped, dingy office in County Stadium.

Selig will have a new office and view next week, when he finally moves into his new digs, a spacious corner suite on the 20th floor of the Firstar Center, Wisconsin's tallest building at 42 stories. Instead of standing on a chair to peer out narrow windows and see parking lots, he can gaze through floor-to-ceiling windows that overlook the city on one side and the rising Miller Park on the other.

Selig's assistant has been packing for weeks—sorting out what goes downtown from what's earmarked for storage and eventual placement in a Brewers museum at Miller Park—and boxes are piled all around the 12-by-14-foot office Selig has called home for 32 years. Bud was all of 31 when he first took a seat behind the desk here in 1966 as he started his quest to replace the Braves, then starting their first season in Atlanta after 13 years in Milwaukee.

There was no cable TV back then, no cell phones or Internet. Computers were just about as big as his entire office. Neil Armstrong would walk on the moon, a doctor in South Africa would perform the world's first heart transplant, and a few hundred thousand kids would flock to Woodstock before another baseball team would once again call County Stadium home.

Two tickets to that first game—dated April 7, 1970—are still framed and hanging on one office wall. The Brewers, a collection of journeymen plucked in the expansion draft a year earlier, lost 12–0 that day. It was the first of 97 losses that season, but Selig hardly cared. He had a baseball team again, and this time he was in charge.

Selig's insisted on keeping every award, trophy, and picture he's been presented ever since. Money was always tight, forcing Keck to be creative when shopping for frames. She did make sure to buy a good one for the note sent from her former boss, Green Bay coach Vince Lombardi, which congratulates Bud for bringing a team back to Milwaukee. That frame still hasn't come down, with just days to go before they move.

Most of Bud's collection wound up on two inexpensive bookshelves. A rather plain-looking trophy sits in one of those cases, the trophy presented to Selig when his Brewers won the 1982 AL pennant, his team's only championship in 29 years. Pictures of Bud's parents are mixed in with those of Hank Aaron and Selig's other favorite players.

"What about this one?" Keck asks him, holding another team picture.

The phone rings, grabbing Bud's attention. "This is the Commissioner," says Selig, who started answering the phone this way as soon as he was elected last July. He's asked everyone to address him as Commissioner as well, now that he's no longer first among equals as chairman of the Executive Council.

As the final year of the millennium gets under way, Selig has an ambitious agenda and he's not wasting any time. He's preparing to eliminate the position of league president and fold the two leagues under his domain. It's a long-overdue move that will centralize baseball's business operations and, according to a Wharton School study, maximize its profits.

But the move is not without risk, at least for the short term. Selig's decision means saying good-bye to NL President Len Coleman, the game's highest-ranking African American. And the leading black players in the game have already criticized Selig for hiring Beeston and his three vice presidents without even interviewing a black candidate. Beeston had told Bob Watson about the baseball operations job in July of 1998, but Watson says he never heard back, and the job was later filled by A's general manager Sandy Alderson. Just a year after Selig punctuated the 50th anniversary of Jackie Robinson breaking baseball's color barrier by promising to promote greater diversity from top to bottom, not one African American made it to any of baseball's top five jobs.

"If the heads of baseball are not fair in that area, how can they expect the people underneath them to be fair?" Frank Robinson told the *New York Times* the same week Selig was moving into his new office. Similar complaints were lodged by Selig's friend Hank Aaron, Watson, Joe Morgan, and other prominent black voices in a game that was rapidly losing both black players and black fans.

Selig's explanation: he already had the best candidates for the positions in his inner circle. "We're not done yet," he told the *New York Times*, "and we're sensitive to the concerns that are raised." How Bud will address the concerns of the game's leading black voices remains unclear.

Something else hasn't changed, either: with the labor contract due to expire after the 2000 season, Selig is planning another run at George Steinbrenner's money. And this time with a new twist.

No longer able to plead poverty after the game's revenues jumped $700 million to $2.5 billion since the 1996 labor deal, Selig has a new battle cry: competitive balance. More than half the teams in baseball will start this season without "hope and faith" of competing, says the Commissioner. And he lays the blame for that dire situation solely on the ever-rising payrolls of the big revenue teams.

Forget that the current revenue sharing plan is expected to transfer $140 million from the top six teams to the bottom six this season. Or that revenue sharing won't be fully implemented until 2000, the same year Miller Park and three more new stadiums will debut. Or that nine teams drew at least 2.9 million fans last season, an MLB record.

Never mind that the Expos, Twins, and Royals all pocketed their revenue sharing checks instead of putting the money back into their team the way Steinbrenner does with his profits. Indeed, Montreal admitted it made a profit last season, when the Expos' $11 million revenue sharing check exceeded their payroll by $2 million.

And ignore the fact that all but six teams have reached the post-season since 1991, the best showing of any pro sport. Or that one of those six absentees just happens to be Selig's Brewers.

Fighting the appearance of talking out of both sides of his mouth, Selig told the media at the January 14 owners meeting that his sport was "in the midst of a marvelous renaissance" before adding, "But I can't stand here and tell you that we don't have a disparity problem. There are problems that need to be addressed."

His solution is classic Selig: at the same meeting, he announces the formation of the Blue Ribbon Panel on Baseball Economics, created to study baseball's payroll-disparity problem and offer recommendations to the Commissioner. To make sure he gets to the bottom of this problem, said Selig, he tapped people with "impeccable credentials" who could bring a "fresh approach."

And Selig's four choices indeed have impressive credentials.

But it's hard to see where the fresh ideas will come from.

George Mitchell, who will head up the study, has close ties to several owners. He will be joined by Yale President Richard Levin, who drafted MLB's first salary cap proposal in 1989, former Federal Reserve Chairman Paul Volcker, who represented the owners on baseball's first economic study committee in 1992, and Selig's friend George Will, who serves on the board of not one but two teams—the Orioles and Padres. Selig will chair the committee and appoint 13 other owners and team executives.

No one from the union will be included.

The Commissioner has laid down strict guidelines: the panel will only use economic data supplied by Major League Baseball—no independent research will be done, no outside data considered. And the panel will focus only on the seasons between 1995 and 1999, which just happen to be the seasons when teams with the deepest pockets—e.g., the Yankees—were better able to prosper after the self-inflicted losses related to the '94 strike.

"Mr. Commissioner," says Keck, walking back into Selig's office, "what about this one?" She's holding a tennis racket with a baseball-bat handle and trying hard not to laugh. It was a gift, one that took a playful swipe at the days when Selig actually had a hobby. "Oh, you can keep that one, Lori," Selig says, and now he's laughing, too.

Selig will be happy when this move is over and he and his staff of four—three administrative assistants and a security guard—settle into their new quarters come Monday. His old office won't lie vacant for even a day—his daughter and now Brewers President Wendy Selig-Prieb is already packed and ready to move in. But her stay will be short. Miller Park, the focus of much of Selig-Prieb's attention, is scheduled to be ready for Opening Day in 2000.

The Miller Park construction site draws a small crowd almost every day, especially when the men are scheduled to work on its one-of-a-kind fan-shaped roof. Selig has been a constant presence, and he was there 18 days ago when the first panel of the stadium's dome was hoisted up by the 467-foot crane dubbed Big Blue, itself so large it had to be assembled on the site.

The project manager postponed the lift of the 427-ton panel for 17 days, waiting for the wind to dip below 10 miles an hour. It was all of 8 degrees—but with no wind—at 9:30 a.m. on January 8 when Selig watched Big Blue lift the 260-foot-long, 100-foot-wide panel off the ground. It took three crews almost two hours to raise the panel 200 feet and slide it into place, where 30 ironworkers went about bolting and welding the roof to the stadium superstructure deep into the afternoon.

It would be hard to find a man in baseball more content than Bud Selig that day—or this day, either. So many of his dreams have come true. He is running his sport. His daughter is running his team. And the taxpayers are building him a stadium. Everything, it seems, is falling into place.

Brian Cashman is battling through traffic, intent on getting to the big organizational meeting at the Yankees' Tampa complex on time. It's February 17, the day before pitchers and catchers report for spring training, and Cashman doesn't want to give George Steinbrenner any more reasons to be angry with him. The Boss is mad enough already.

These should be the best of days for Cashman. At 31, he's the general manager of baseball's best team, one heavily favored to win its third championship in four years. Just two weeks ago he signed a three-year contract worth $1.1 million, a big raise from the one-year deal he requested after replacing Bob Watson last winter.

Steinbrenner declined to make the new contract public, then waited for Cashman to react, but the young GM didn't take the bait. He knows all about George's mind games, and he's determined not to let Steinbrenner torture him the way he tortured his previous 12 general managers. Cashman got to the top spot far sooner than he ever expected, and he's not going to let Steinbrenner's antics drive him away.

But there's no escaping George's anger right now, not after Cashman blew Derek Jeter's arbitration case. The Yankees' young star pointed to his .308 career batting average, his two championship rings in three years, and asked for a record $5 million for the coming season. Cashman countered at $3.2 million. Jeter's agent offered to settle at $4.1 million just hours before the case went to the arbitrator two days ago, but Cashman held firm.

"I'm going with your recommendation," Steinbrenner told him, "but you better be right."

Cashman learned he was wrong yesterday while preparing for Mariano Rivera's arbitration hearing, set for later today. The error cost Steinbrenner almost a million dollars. "You got hornswoggled," George roared at him over the phone. "You're on the fucking bubble."

It's clear Cashman missed the jump in the market—a jump largely driven by the Yankees—and now he's worried the arbitrator will favor Mariano's request for $4.25 million over the team's $3 million offer. Steinbrenner spends freely, but he detests getting beat at the bargaining table.

There will be holy hell to pay if he loses Rivera's case, too, Cashman thinks as he winds his way through Tampa's traffic. And George is still chewing on him for failing to reel in Roger Clemens, who's forcing his way out of Toronto. Steinbrenner dearly wants Clemens in a Yankees uniform after missing out two years ago, but months of conversations with Blue Jays GM Gord Ash have gone nowhere.

The reason is simple: every proposal from Ash starts with David Wells and ends with minor league star Alfonso Soriano, and that's not going to fly. Cashman is willing to deal Wells, even though the left-hander was a career-best 18–4 last season—including a perfect game—and Yankees fans love him. George likes him, too. But Cashman's heard the portly 35-year-old spent the offseason partying with actor Tom Arnold, and he's worried that Wells will come to camp fat and complacent.

But Cashman's not giving away Soriano, the team's top hitting prospect, not for a 36-year-old pitcher who can demand another trade—or a bigger contract—after this season. Not even one coming off back-to-back Cy Young Awards. Cashman's so tired of hearing about Clemens he never bothered to answer a voice mail from Ash yesterday. But Steinbrenner will want the latest news, so Cashman grabs his cell and punches in the Toronto GM's number.

"Make me an offer, Brian," Ash says when he hears Cashman's voice.

"No, Gord," Cashman says. "If you've got something in mind, then make me an offer."

Ash answers quickly. "I want Wells, Graeme Lloyd, and Homer Bush," he says. "Give me that, and you got Clemens."

Cashman can hardly believe what he's just heard.

Lloyd's a nice left-hander out of the bullpen. And Bush is a fine sub. Neither is essential.

This comes down to Wells for Clemens.

This is a no-brainer.

"Gord," says Cashman, no longer thinking about Rivera's arbitration, Tampa traffic, or much of anything else, "I'll get right back to you."

Steinbrenner isn't sure he really heard what his young general manager just told him. "Run that by me again," he says.

"If we give up Wells, Lloyd, and Bush, we get Roger Clemens," Cashman repeats.

"Tell them not to do anything until they hear from us," George says. "And get back here now!"

The Boss watched Clemens lead the AL in wins, strikeouts, and ERA in each of the last two seasons and dreamed what the burly right-hander would've meant to his Yankees. Indeed, some are calling Clemens—with his 233 wins, 3,153 strikeouts, 44 shutouts, and a record five Cy Young Awards—one of the three best pitchers of all time. Steinbrenner can already envision records falling in front of huge Yankee Stadium crowds. This will be bigger than signing Catfish Hunter, bigger than Dave Winfield, maybe even bigger than Reggie Jackson.

Hell, this could be the Yankees' biggest deal since acquiring another former Red Sox hurler—Babe Ruth.

Still, Steinbrenner wants the seven men now sitting in his Tampa office—Cashman, Torre, Gene Michael, and Tampa team Billy Connors, Mark Newman, Gordon Blakeley, and Lin Garrett—to put all concerns on the table. Everyone wonders about the fit: Clemens is larger than life, a surefire Hall of Famer whose every action commands attention. Would he upset the chemistry of a team that's achieved unrivaled success without relying on superstars?

And would his history be a problem? The Yankees were irate last season when Clemens hit Derek Jeter in the ribs—in a spring training game! And Torre was ejected for complaining when Clemens wasn't booted after he nailed Scott Brosius in the back last September. And how can a team that plays half its games in Yankee Stadium, with its hitter-friendly right-field porch, give up Wells, one of the game's best left-handed starters?

The men talk for hours, breaking at 7 p.m. to drive over to Malio's—Steinbrenner's favorite restaurant and meeting place—where they talk some more. By 9 p.m., Cashman tells Clemens' agent Randy Hendricks he can advise Roger that things are looking good. A few hours later, Steinbrenner asks for a decision. "I'm not going to vote—we'll do whatever you decide," he tells his men, leaving the door open for the blame to fall on someone else should things go wrong.

The decision comes quickly: all seven men want Clemens. Cashman looks at the clock, wanting to note the time of what he's sure will be the biggest deal of his career. It's 11:42 p.m. Then he calls Ash.

"You have a deal," says Cashman, who spends a sleepless night trying to figure out the best way to tell Wells he's been traded. And thinking about all the headlines Clemens will generate as a New York Yankee.

The next morning, an unshaven Wells, wearing his Yankees cap and a stunned look on his ashen face, sits across from Steinbrenner in the owner's office at Legends Field. Wells is still coming to terms with what Cashman and Torre told him an hour ago: he's out.

"Ah, Boss," says David Wells. "What did you do?"

Boomer and the Boss have a special relationship, and they are both trying to hold back tears now as they reminisce about the big things they did the last two seasons. "Best two years of my life," says Wells, who stands up and embraces George when there is nothing else left to say.

Yankees beat writers are used to covering major stories, and it's clear there's a big one today when the clubhouse doors open and they're instructed to gather in Torre's office. "We've traded David Wells for Roger Clemens," says Torre, who is just about beaming. A few minutes later Steinbrenner appears on the field and is instantly surrounded.

"We didn't buy a pennant with Clemens, we traded for him," the Boss says, at once defensive and defiant. He knows his fellow owners resent his success even as they continue to profit from it. He knows they're all pushing for a bigger cut of his revenues in the next contract. And he certainly knows Selig wants a bigger—and permanent—luxury tax to stop him from spending so much on his players. He just doesn't give a damn.

"I know I'm gonna hear it from other owners," Steinbrenner says. "But I can't operate by what other people think."

Steinbrenner gives everyone more to talk about seven days later when he announces he's signed a letter of intent with the New Jersey Nets to form a holding company called YankeeNets. The goal: to build a sports entertainment company that will maximize their combined television rights, sponsorship opportunities, and advertising deals.

The two sides—Steinbrenner and his Yankees partners and the Nets ownership group led by Ray Chambers and Lewis Katz—will each own 50 percent of the company and will share major decisions. They'll each own half of both teams but retain final say with their own franchises. The Nets partners will equalize the huge difference between the value of the Yankees ($600 million) and the Nets ($150 million) by giving George and his partners approximately $225 million. That means the Steinbrenner family, who owns 60 percent of the Yankees, will pocket a cool $133 million.

Steinbrenner's hopes for the new company are clear. YankeeNets will charge cable operators top dollar to carry its programming, which is projected to bring in $153 million in its first year. After rights fees for Yankees and Nets games are paid, the balance—an estimated $90 million at launch—will be split between Yankee-Nets and its investors. The partnership will also be able to shield some of the revenues on advertising deals, sponsorships, and sales of luxury boxes from MLB and NBA revenue sharing demands.

And the biggest payoff is yet to come. Instead of renting out both teams' TV rights, Steinbrenner and his partners will be building equity in a business that may one day be more valuable than the Yankees and Nets combined—by far. Analysts are already pegging the value of YankeeNets at almost a billion dollars.

Is it risky? Sure. No content company—and that's what sports teams are in today's information age—has ever tried anything this ambitious. Steinbrenner and his partners will have to build a television network from scratch, then persuade the very same cable operators they spurned to carry their programming at what is sure to be a hefty fee. That includes a very unhappy Chuck Dolan, who is already telling George this scheme won't work. But the Yankees are a trophy property. How can any cable company tell customers they won't be able to watch the perennial World Champions?

Ray Chambers has another goal. Since retiring in 1989 from Wesray Capital—where he and former Treasury Secretary William Simon pioneered the field of leveraged buyouts and became two of the richest men in America—Chambers has been a full-time philanthropist. His main focus: bringing his riot-torn hometown of Newark back to life.

Buying the Nets last October was an extension of his vision. Chambers is donating all his profits to Newark and four other impoverished New Jersey cities, and he hopes to complement the performing arts center he opened two years ago in downtown Newark with a sports arena for his new basketball team. He's already spent millions on this goal, and if putting a winning team on the court helps him reach that goal, he's willing to spend millions more.

George's new partners fly down to Tampa several times over the next few months to meet with him, his sons, Steve Swindal, Yankees COO Lonn Trost, and other advisers as the company takes shape. They have a long way to go before YankeeNets makes its first dollar—there are roles to define, staff to hire, and investors to recruit—and George has never been especially good at sharing decision making.

But then he's never parted with half his team before, either.

Sex sells.

And in 1999, no one sells sex better than blond temptress Heather Locklear, star of the Fox network's popular prime-time soap *Melrose Place*. So when Nike and the hip Wieden+Kennedy ad team lend Locklear's sultry smile to Major League Baseball, the grand old game finds something it's never had before: sex appeal.

The object of Heather's desire?

The long ball—what else?

By the spring of '99, even chicks dig the long ball. And with a rising number of players taking Andro—and others stepping up to stronger performance enhancers—there are more than enough long balls for everyone to dig.

The Nike commercial is baseball's big advertising splash for the spring. It opens with the game's biggest star, Mark McGwire, in the batting cage, walloping one ball after another into the faraway grandstand. And there's Locklear, pressed up against the cage in a tight gray T-shirt and red Cardinals cap, following every McGwire blast with a smile and a sigh.

Cut to the sidelines, where Atlanta's star pitchers Greg Maddux and Tom Glavine are throwing a baseball around without a fan in sight.

"How long are they going to worship this guy?" Glavine asks Maddux.

"Hey," Maddux shouts to the crowd around McGwire, "we have Cy Young winners over here!"

The two pitchers look at each other, then share an epiphany. So after first shopping for new Nikes (of course), they hit the gym hard.

Pumped up, the two pitchers step into the batting cage and rap out long ball after long ball. The hard knock of bat on ball draws a smiling Locklear into the picture, along with an alluring brunette.

"Hi, Tom," purrs Heather, giving Glavine her best come-hither smile.

The two men bump forearms.

"Chicks dig the long ball," Maddux tells Glavine.

But wait . . .

"Hey, have you guys seen Mark?" Locklear asks.

Nike's "Chicks Dig the Long Ball" ad debuts in April and is an instant hit, its punch line repeated by every *SportsCenter* anchor and local sportscaster whenever a home run is launched—which is early and often. On April 23, Cardinals third baseman Fernando Tatis sets a major league record by hitting two grand slams in a single inning against LA. On May 10, Red Sox shortstop Nomar Garciaparra blasts three home runs—two of them with the bases full—against Seattle. Ten days later, the Mets' Robin Ventura hits a grand slam in both ends of a doubleheader with Milwaukee.

And the big boys are again hitting homers in bunches. Ken Griffey Jr. hits 10 in a 19-game stretch in May. Sammy Sosa has a game-high 32 homers at the All-Star break, one of 14 players with 22 or more.

But the man the fans worship above all others is still McGwire, who is having another terrific season. The St. Louis superstar smacks 28 home runs in the first half of the season, putting him on pace for a record fourth straight 50-homer season. McGwire's every home run is national news, and any slump—like his April 19– May 3 home run drought—is a subject of grave concern.

Being baseball's poster boy is rewarding, but it also takes a toll. McGwire, now 35, has never been a star of this magnitude, and the demands—the endless stream of requests, the near-complete loss of privacy—begin to wear on him. He starts skipping batting practice without notice, leaving the thousands who arrive early to see his BP show with little to do but eat overpriced food and wait hours for the real game to begin.

He's snapping at the media. "Okay, I'm not the team spokesman," he barked at writers at Wrigley Field as they approached him after a game in early June. "There are other people we should be paying attention to."

McGwire's use of Andro is also a topic of much conversation. Early in the year, McGwire said he'd keep taking Andro until the government made it illegal or the Commissioner banned it, adding that he would no longer answer any questions on the subject. That includes any queries about the supplement company he's endorsing, the one advertising Andro as "the product behind McGwire's 70 home runs" and insisting their pills will "take your testosterone levels to new heights."

Most in the media defend McGwire's use of Andro, which makes little sense to Dr. Don Catlin, the longtime director of the world's biggest drug testing lab at UCLA. Catlin says he's embarrassed by the almost daily emails he receives from foreign colleagues asking why America hasn't banned the substance that other countries have outlawed for years. "Androstenedione is a steroid, there's no question about it," he says. "It shouldn't be available."

(It's also taken as a sign by a former Mets clubhouse man in

Long Island who is supplying steroids to a growing number of baseball players. Kirk Radomski figures that if baseball isn't concerned about Andro, which everyone in the business knows is an anabolic steroid in disguise, there's no reason to think the sport cares about the steroids he's mailing out on a regular basis.)

Baseball officials estimate that between 5 and 10 percent of players are using Andro now. The players think it's at least twice that many, and some of the savvy veterans wonder if McGwire and others are using Andro to mask the use of stronger performance enhancers.

That's part of what concerns Rangers pitcher Rick Helling, who thinks Don Fehr and other union leaders are underestimating the true scope of steroid use. "It's a bigger problem than you think," he told Fehr and his staff at the union's Executive Board meeting last December. "You don't see what the players see. There are guys feeling pressure to use drugs to keep their jobs. I think it's something we need to look into." Some of the 30-odd players at that meeting agreed, while some didn't, and Fehr instructed them all to talk to their teams this season and report back to the union.

It's San Diego superstar Tony Gwynn who once again puts the subject in perspective—and in the open. "We have discussions about this all the time—what if it's the last year of your contract and you feel you're not playing well?" Gwynn tells Jack Curry of the *New York Times* in July. "With the kind of money out there, could Andro or steroids make a difference in your play? And if you only take them one year to prolong your career, would it really be dangerous to your health?"

But none of these concerns makes much of an impression, not when almost every home run McGwire hits is considered historic. On June 8 he belted his 18th homer of the season and 475th of his career, which tied him with Hall of Famers Willie Stargell and Stan "The Man" Musial, now 78 and a beloved St. Louis legend. Next up: Yankees great Lou Gehrig at 493.

And McGwire memorabilia is already historic: in January, *Spawn* comic book creator Todd MacFarlane paid $3 million for Big Mac's 70th home run ball. It's the most ever paid for a piece of baseball history, far ahead of the $641,500 paid for the famous Honus

Wagner baseball card and the $451,541 just paid for the uniform the ailing Gehrig wore the day he proclaimed himself the luckiest man on the face of the earth.

And in this, the last baseball season of the 20th century, what better place to raise McGwire to legendary status than the 70th All-Star Game come July 13 in Boston's historic Fenway Park? In a brilliant marketing stroke, baseball decides to select an All-Century Team, voted on by fans from a list of 100 living and deceased legends. A full 41 of those legends will be introduced before the All-Star Game.

But first comes the Home Run Derby, now a prime-time fixture on ESPN, and the buzz inside Fenway is all about McGwire. Some Boston fans are content to stand outside the stadium, on Lansdowne Street behind left field, waiting to chase down McGwire blasts that fly over the Green Monster. One woman holds up a sign reading CHICKS DIG THE LONG BALL.

And McGwire delivers, swatting one long ball after another—a record 13 in the first round—almost all of them leaving the park. The most impressive: a 488-foot wallop that flies over the Monster and hits a billboard above faraway railroad tracks. McGwire's fellow All-Stars whoop it up as much as the fans, with many holding camcorders and recording every swing.

McGwire needs seven home runs to advance to the final round but can only muster three. "I probably tried a little too hard," he says. No one cares. Ken Griffey Jr. goes on to win the contest, but the fans—those at Fenway, those in uniform, and millions more watching at home—get what they were hoping to see.

If the Home Run Derby was all about selling baseball's present and future, the next night leans on the game's connection to its past. The evening opens with a video that borrows heavily from *Field of Dreams*, replete with the movie's sound track, its cornfield, and Kevin Costner at Fenway to narrate. "People will always come back to baseball," says Costner, in a veiled reference to the '94 strike that's now all but forgotten. "They call it America's pastime, but more appropriate, it's our present and future."

Fans and today's All-Stars applaud as 40 of the 100 All-Century nominees take the field. Willie Mays and Hank Aaron, Tom Seaver and Steve Carlton, triple crown winners Frank Robinson and Carl Yastrzemski, each dressed in a suit and wearing a baseball cap, stroll through the outfield to stand in an arc along the edge of Fenway's infield.

Costner introduces each All-Century nominee. These players, he says, "represent the most talent ever assembled on a baseball field." Roger Clemens is the second player Costner presents, and the Rocket draws a loud mixture of boos and cheers as he waves a hated Yankees cap. Catcher Carlton Fisk, another ex–Red Sox who finished his career elsewhere, is greeted warmly as he waves a Boston hat. Yastrzemski, beloved after playing 23 seasons in Boston, draws the loudest ovation.

And that leaves one more Boston favorite, a man who barely needs an introduction. "Ladies and gentlemen," the PA announcer says. "He wore the Red Sox uniform for 22 years. He wore the uniform of the United States Marines for $4\frac{1}{2}$ more. He was the last man to hit .400 in a season.

"Please welcome the greatest hitter that ever lived. No. 9, Hall of Famer, baseball legend... Ted Williams!"

Williams, a month shy of 81 and suffering from vision and mobility problems after a series of strokes, is driven into Fenway on a green golf cart. Teddy Ballgame retired in 1960 with a .344 career average, six batting titles, and a combative relationship with Boston fans. But on this night, he holds his right arm up high and waves his cap to the crowd—something he stubbornly refused to do as a player—and 34,187 adoring fans cheer and wave back.

The golf cart drives slowly down the right-field line, finally coming to rest 50 feet in front of home plate, where Williams will soon stand and throw the first pitch. But in an unscripted move, all the other players—legends and All-Stars alike—surround Teddy Ballgame for what amounts to a giant group hug. Player after player walks up to Williams, eager to shake his hand. Mike Piazza and Larry Walker have tears in their eyes. So does Joe Torre, who plants himself next to Williams' golf cart and doesn't leave. The Fox cameras catch Williams quickly wiping away the tears rolling down his face.

Suddenly, Williams grows agitated. "Where's McGwire?" he shouts. "Where's McGwire?" McGwire hustles through the crowd of players and squats next to Williams' cart as Ted starts talking. Then Williams starts pounding his hand on McGwire's shoulder.

"When you foul a ball off, do you smell smoke?" Williams asks McGwire.

"Ah, yeah, I do," says McGwire, clearly surprised by the question.

"I told Boggs and Mattingly that," Williams says. "They thought I was nuts."

The pregame celebration is running late, and the PA man twice asks the players to return to their dugouts. When the players finally relent, Tony Gwynn is there to steady Williams and help him locate Fisk, now squatting behind the plate. Williams tosses the ball on a fly to Fisk, who catches it, shakes the ball as if his team had just won the World Series, and rushes out to hug the legend while the crowd roars once again.

Taking this in from his seat next to the American League dugout is a beaming Bud Selig. Five days ago he celebrated his first year as Mr. Commissioner. Now he welcomes Ted Williams to the seat next to his, where he'll spend the next five innings talking to him about hitting and baseball history.

The AL goes on to win 4–1, but it's Williams' appearance that everyone will remember. Selig is thrilled that younger fans find his game sexy, thanks to Nike and McGwire. But the game's ability to connect one generation with the next—exactly as it's done tonight—is what makes baseball special.

There's no question sex sells. But in baseball, history sells even better.

It's going on 5 p.m. the next afternoon, and Selig is back in his Milwaukee office, finishing up another of the day's long string of phone calls. He's gamely trying to hold on to the excitement of the past two days, but it's not easy. Earlier today, the umpires' union announced that 57 of the game's 68 umps would walk off the job on September 2 to protest a growing list of grievances. Chief among their complaints: Selig's intention to move supervision of umpires to the Commissioner's office as part of his plan to centralize the game.

Umpires' union chief Richie Phillips prevented Selig's move earlier this season when he claimed changing supervisors would entitle his members to millions in severance pay. But their contract is up at season's end, and Selig has already lined up support to bring in replacement umpires.

Tomorrow he flies to Seattle, where he'll help the Mariners open their new $517 million stadium, the most expensive ever built. He'll also explain to city officials why the bulk of the yet-unpaid $100 million in cost overruns should be picked up by the taxpayers, not Nintendo, the $4.5 billion Japanese corporation that owns the Mariners. Taxpayers are wondering why the Mariners, who are contractually obligated to pay all overruns, should be allowed to dodge the bill—especially when they will keep every penny generated by the new stadium.

"If I had any brains, I'd get out of here and go home," he tells Lori Keck as he picks up a phone call. Moments later Keck sees another call come in. It's Selig's daughter. "Hi, Wendy," says Keck, whose mood changes quickly when she hears why Selig-Prieb is calling. "Okay, hold on," Keck says, who writes two words on a piece of paper:

WENDY. URGENT.

She rushes into Selig's office, turns on the television, then taps her boss on the shoulder and hands him the message. Selig picks up the call. "Dad," says his daughter, anxiety heavy in her voice. "It's really bad."

The picture on Selig's TV tells the story. What used to be the 467-foot crane called Big Blue is now a long piece of twisted metal draped over the crumbling side of the Brewers' new home, Miller Park. Large cement slabs litter the ground, and smaller pieces are still tumbling down the wreckage. Agitated voices and sirens puncture the background noise as the reporter on the scene delivers the details of the story.

At 5:15 p.m., Big Blue was lifting another 400-ton roof panel to the top of the stadium, 200 feet above, when the crane began to buckle. Soon the roof panel swung and crashed through the panels already in place before plowing through the right-field wall of the near-complete stadium. The crane came crashing through the wall next.

The crane operator shouted "Get out! Get everybody out of here!" as pieces of his rig began to snap before his eyes. But there was nowhere to go for the three men working up in another crane bucket when the giant collapsing arm of Big Blue severed their crane's line, sending them plummeting to their deaths. The reporter says high winds may have caused the crane to collapse.

Selig is stunned. Nothing prepares you for a moment like this, and his mind bounces between the tragedy unfolding before him and the job he still has to do. Selig is no engineer, but this looks bad. The cleanup alone will take months, and so much work has to be repeated. And if the accident was indeed caused by high winds, there will be plenty of questions asked about why the crane was even in operation.

Opening next spring—or anytime next season—is now in doubt. Insurance will cover most of the team's financial losses, but nothing can bring back the three men who lost their lives. Reporters are saying that police will search the crash site for any others who might have been injured or lost.

"I'll be there soon," he tells Wendy. He'll rush over to the stadium in a few minutes and stay as late as he can. But it's Wendy who will have to comfort the families tomorrow, deal with the Stadium Board, talk to the media, and answer all the hard questions.

Selig will still fly out to Seattle tomorrow, as planned. He is the Commissioner of baseball now, not just the owner of the Milwaukee Brewers. And he has a game to sell.

Chapter 20

RING FOR ROGER

July 31–October 29, 1999

I$_{T'S}$ $_{HARD}$ $_{TO}$ know who is more miserable on this sweltering final day of July at Fenway Park: the man standing on the pitcher's mound, sweating and swearing as another game slips through his fingers, or his friend and teammate sitting in the visitors dugout, wondering if this will be his last game in a Yankees uniform.

Both players are mysteries to George Steinbrenner, who is in Boston to take stock of Roger Clemens and Andy Pettitte, two pitchers who occupy very different places in his heart. The Boss idolizes Clemens, who's in the middle of his first start at Fenway in a Yankees uniform. Steinbrenner thought he struck gold when he swung a deal for Clemens in February. But the Rocket, five days shy of 37, has been a dud, entering today's game against his former team with a deceptive 9–4 record. More telling is his unsightly 4.67 ERA, the highest of his career and more than two runs higher than either of his last two seasons in Toronto.

Pettitte has performed even worse, losing eight of 15 decisions with a 5.65 ERA, making the 27-year-old pitcher the focus of trade rumors since June. The Boss has never been enamored with Pettitte, despite the left-hander's 74 victories in his four-plus seasons — the most among Yankees pitchers since '95 — and his vital role in the team's two World Series titles. He's also making $5.95 million and due for a raise when he goes to arbitration this winter. So it was no surprise when Steinbrenner ordered general manager Brian Cashman to put Pettitte on the market on July 17.

And when Pettitte was thrashed by the woeful White Sox three days ago—coughing up eight hits and three runs before Joe Torre lifted him just one out into the 4th—Steinbrenner was ready to cut the left-hander loose. At least 10 teams have been tracking Pettitte, and Cashman has a deal with the Phillies that will bring back two top prospects—pitcher Adam Eaton and center fielder Reggie Taylor—and a third prospect yet to be determined.

"I've been saying all along they've got to get Pettitte straightened out," Steinbrenner said the day after Andy's debacle in Chicago. Billy Connors, a key member of George's Tampa brain trust, has been pushing for a trade for weeks, insisting that minor leaguer Ed Yarnall is a better pitcher and is ready to step in. But Cashman and Torre have argued strongly against trading one of the team's core players.

"Once the season starts, it's up to Torre and Cashman," George told reporters before leaving for Boston. "We are all in this together—but the line falls on them."

Why Steinbrenner is upset about anything is a mystery to the defending champs, given their major league–best 62–39 record and their comfortable seven-game lead over Toronto in the AL East. David Cone gave George a perfect game against the Expos two weeks ago—the Yanks' second in two seasons—and more than 50,000 fans have flocked to the Stadium on 12 occasions, putting the Yankees on pace to draw 3 million fans for the first time in team history.

Even Yogi is back, ending his 14-year boycott—his payback after George fired him as manager just 16 games into the 1985 season. All it took was a check for $100,000 made out to the Yogi Berra Museum. The two men sat together on Opening Day, watching Hall of Famers Whitey Ford and Phil Rizzuto raise the Yankees' 24th World Series banner.

But the Boss hasn't spared the lash, and he again focuses much of his anger on Cashman. George has yet to forgive his young GM for losing arbitration cases to Derek Jeter and Mariano Rivera in February. (Never mind that Jeter is leading the league in hitting [.369] while leading the Yankees in home runs [19], RBI [72], and runs [88]. Or that Rivera is now the game's dominant closer, an All-Star whose entry into a game almost always signals a Yankees win.) He rarely misses an opportunity to berate his GM in public or private, even blaming him for Clemens' inability to equal his two Cy Young seasons. The Boss leaked a story that Cashman was excluded from an organizational meeting at the All-Star break, a story Cashman later knocked down. And on more than one occasion George has told reporters about player moves without telling his GM.

The Boss is also growing resentful of the credit Torre's getting for the team's success and of the time the manager spends doing sales pitches for Continental Airlines, Century 21 Real Estate, and the *New York Daily News*. But Torre is too popular to attack, so Steinbrenner has pounded on Cashman for Torre's transgressions, too.

If Cashman has ever wondered why Steinbrenner's sons choose to stay clear of their father, he knows full well now. And as Hank and Hal Steinbrenner understand all too well, the closer you get to George, the more abuse you suffer.

Nothing is good enough for George, especially after the magic of the 1998 season. Winning the World Series was once a goal for the Yankees; now it's a mandate, something the Boss reminds his team—especially his GM—almost every day.

No one has struggled to meet that challenge more than Clemens, who came to New York to win a championship but has found it difficult just to fit in. Despite his outsized persona and his macho preparation—the three-to-seven-mile runs between starts, the weight-lifting regime, the pregame neck-to-ankle hot-liniment rubdown, which requires a change of shirt between every inning— Clemens is shy and deferential almost to a fault on the days he's not pitching.

Yankees fans gave Clemens a long grace period, but they finally started booing the veteran two weeks ago, when the Braves tagged him for six runs and five walks in a 6–2 Atlanta win. They booed

him again last week, when he gave up a home run to Expos outfielder Shane Andrews, a .215 hitter, while slogging to a 7–4 win.

And today, Clemens is in danger of squandering a 5–2 lead in
the bottom of the 5th. He opens the inning with a walk to Trot
Nixon, who moves to second on a wild pitch. Clemens runs the
count full to leadoff hitter Jose Offerman, and Red Sox fans deri-
sively chant "Raaah-ger, Raaah-ger" as their former star gathers
himself on the mound.

Clemens goes into his stretch, delivers, and Offerman rockets
the ball through the middle for a single, scoring Nixon. The Fenway crowd erupts, and so does Steinbrenner, who clenches his jaw
and throws up his hands in his seat next to the Yankees dugout.
Boston GM Dan Duquette famously pronounced Clemens over the
hill when Roger left for Toronto. Now George is wondering if
Duquette's timing was off by a couple of years.

Clemens makes it through the 5th but leaves when Nomar Garciaparra singles to open the 6th. Garciaparra will score, closing the
book on Clemens, and the Red Sox push across a run in the 7th to
tie and another in the 9th to win.

Steinbrenner huddles after the game with Torre, who assures
him that things are just fine. Keeping Steinbrenner calm is maybe
the most important part of Torre's job, and his reassurances prevent the Boss from making bad decisions—like trading away Pettitte. A pack of reporters follows the Yankees owner into the players'
parking lot long after the game, throwing him questions about Clemens and Pettitte.

What did he think about Roger today?

"When I saw Roger with a 5–2 lead, I'm ready to say, 'The ballgame is over,'" he says. "But it didn't happen."

Will Pettitte still be a Yankee when the trade deadline ends at
midnight?

"The manager thinks we are all right, I'll tell you that," George
tells them. "And I have great confidence in my manager."

Just as long as his manager keeps winning championships.

Bud Selig turns on the TV and watches his 39-year-old daughter
step before the television cameras at County Stadium, where she'll

announce what they decided five days ago: the Brewers are firing their manager and general manager. It was a sad Commissioner who called GM Sal Bando with the news; after all, the former third baseman was Selig's first free agent hire back in 1977 and has worked for the team ever since. But six straight losing seasons— and 112 games into a seventh—are simply too many, even in Milwaukee. Now Bud watches Wendy talk about the team's fresh start and wishes it didn't have to be this way.

Bud has long dreamed of Wendy running his team, but this has not been an easy year. The crane accident was horrific. And the team isn't just losing games, it's still losing money—lots of money. With attendance slumping as badly as the team, the franchise stands to lose another $22 million, pushing their debt to $148.7 million.

Worse, the team's "fresh start" will take place in County Stadium, so the Seligs can forget that $30 million bump they expect when Miller Park opens its gates. Nor will the Seligs give their fans the competitive team they promised in exchange for building them a new stadium with public money. Whoever Selig-Prieb hires as the Brewers' next general manager will have a major rebuilding project on his hands.

No, the handoff to Wendy has not worked out as Selig had hoped, and he's certain he knows why: George Steinbrenner. Sure, George sent Wendy flowers and a nice note of encouragement the day she was officially named president of the Brewers. And he frequently comes to visit Bud and Sue when the Yankees play in Milwaukee, one of the few times Steinbrenner travels with his team. Bud and George have been in this game longer than any other owners, and their friendship continues to grow.

But what chance does Wendy have when George pays a handful of his players more than she pays their entire team? When Bud says the fans of more than half the teams in baseball no longer have "hope and faith" that their team can win, he's speaking from personal experience.

Of course, like most owners of losing teams, Selig refuses to consider that maybe he—and now his daughter—might not be very good at building a baseball team. Which would explain why he's calling the Reds—who at 66–46 are battling for the NL Central lead with a payroll almost $10 million less than Milwaukee's $43.4 million—an "aberration." The same goes for the A's, who have the game's fourth-lowest payroll ($24.8 million) and the AL's fifth-best record. Meanwhile, the Brewers are 52–60 and in fifth place, 15 games behind the first-place Astros.

No, Selig is certain it's the system that's at fault here, and his plan to fix the system remains the same: taking more of Steinbrenner's money. He also knows time is of the essence: Steinbrenner's partnership with the owners of the Nets to build their own cable network could create an even bigger gap between the Yankees and everyone else.

But first Selig travels to Cooperstown in mid-September for an owners meeting where he will consolidate his power. And what better place to make a historic change than this idyllic lakeside village in the foothills of New York's Adirondack Mountains that is home to the Hall of Fame. It was just two months ago when a record 50,000 fans made the annual pilgrimage to the holy land of the Church of Baseball, many traveling more than a thousand miles to witness Nolan Ryan, George Brett, and Robin Yount take their place among the game's greats.

More than 15,000 players have played major league baseball; before this day, only 178 have a plaque hanging in the two-story redbrick museum here on Main Street. It's the only sports hall of fame that truly matters, and most certainly the only one that serves as a moral barometer. That is why Pete Rose spent Induction Weekend selling his autograph on Main Street alongside the Hall of Famers but does not have a plaque inside the Hall. And it's why there's an exhibit called *In the Spirit of the Game*, dedicated to the people who gave back home run balls to Mark McGwire and Sammy Sosa.

It was Selig who introduced the three newest members on that hot July afternoon. Now he's returned to deliver big news: the owners are putting all American and National League operations under the Commissioner and eliminating the jobs of league president—roles that predate that of the Commissioner. It's a move that'll streamline the game's business operations, but a move that's being handled poorly.

Just how poorly is evident when Selig and outgoing NL President

Len Coleman meet with the media to explain the changes. "This is an historic moment that many have felt was long overdue," says Selig, who tells reporters that the decision was reached unanimously. Not so, says Coleman, sitting at Selig's side. "I voted against it," he says.

Coleman knew this day was coming more than a year ago, when a source close to Selig let the NL president know he was not in Bud's long-term plans. Truth be told, Selig instructed Bob DuPuy months ago to negotiate a settlement with both Coleman and AL President Gene Budig, who will stay on in the ill-defined role of vice president for educational and government affairs. Coleman will get the remaining $1.95 million on his contract and will become president of MLB Charities and a senior adviser to the Commissioner.

Some inside baseball believe Selig looked upon Coleman as a threat, given that Coleman was one of the few men interviewed for the Commissioner's job while Bud held the interim title. Others wondered how Selig could remove the lone African American voice in baseball's senior management team, for which he again will be roundly criticized.

No one stood in Selig's way on this decision, no matter what the fallout. But at least baseball no longer has the embarrassment of Marge Schott in its ownership ranks. Schott's 15-year tenure as majority owner of the Reds officially ended at this meeting when her sale to billionaire businessman Carl Lindner, who has been a limited partner, was unanimously approved.

The owners voted to table discussion of pending bids for the Royals and A's, saying they want to hear the Blue Ribbon Panel's report before making any decisions on small market teams. What they didn't talk about is the rising interest in contraction — the idea to eliminate as many as four teams to address revenue inequality between markets. Contraction would give the remaining teams a bigger slice of the revenue pie and, unless Selig objects, lower revenue sharing subsidies.

But while Coleman and Schott are the headlines at this meeting, Steinbrenner and the Yankees dominate the conversation behind closed doors, as they have at just about every meeting and conference call for years. And resentment is running especially high this season. No one cares that the Yankees' success is driving national TV ratings or selling tickets or moving merchandise—or that Steinbrenner's already paid $28 million in revenue sharing.

Steinbrenner's an economic bully, they all keep telling Selig. He's buying championships. He's bad for the sport. He's bad for the rest of us.

Selig could not agree with them more.

If the owners of baseball's other 29 teams already resent the Yankees' riches, what happens over the last two months of the season does little to change their minds. On September 11, the Yankees draw 55,422 for their game against the Red Sox, breaking the team's attendance record set a year ago, then draw another 56,028 the next day to surpass the 3 million mark for the first time in franchise history. They finish at 3.292 million, blowing past the city record 3.055 million fans the Mets drew in 1988.

Outgoing Mayor Rudy Giuliani is still working hard to get support for a new stadium in the Bronx, and now New York Congressman Charlie Rangel is seeking federal funding to improve the surrounding neighborhood. On September 18, the NBA approves the YankeeNets deal, a partnership some Wall Street analysts predict will generate $600 million in revenue in its first year, then grow from there.

In a season where the home run is again king—both McGwire (65) and Sosa (63) again surpass 60, and 11 other players hit at least 40—no Yankee hit more than 28. Still, the team finishes third in the AL in scoring and batting average. And for all the complaints about Steinbrenner's wild spending, the backbone of this team is homegrown. It's future first-ballot Hall of Famers Derek Jeter and Mariano Rivera who make the Yankees special.

This is the season Jeter establishes himself as one of the game's very best players, hitting .349 (second in the AL), belting 24 home runs, and driving in 102, all career highs. He now has 807 hits in his four-year career, a figure surpassed at the same stage by only Hank Aaron, Ty Cobb, and Pete Rose. His defense is once again superb, and his trademark jump throw from deep in the hole is a *SportsCenter* staple.

Rivera is the sport's biggest game changer. His control is impeccable and his cut fastball is the game's most devastating pitch. Rivera's 45 saves are the most in the majors, and he hasn't allowed a run—earned or unearned—since July 21, a stretch covering 28 games and 30.2 innings.

Defending batting champ Bernie Williams hits .342, trailing only Boston's Nomar Garciaparra (.357) and Jeter, and wins his third straight Gold Glove in center field. Jeter's best friend Jorge Posada wins the starting catcher's job from Joe Girardi and hits .285 after the All-Star break. And Pettitte shakes off his poor first half and anchors the pitching staff down the stretch, winning seven games with a tidy 3.46 ERA. But for Pettitte's brief stay in Houston in the mid-2000s, these five players are and will remain the heart of this franchise for most of the decade to come.

The Yankees brush aside the power-hitting Rangers in three games in the opening round of the postseason, then make quick work of the Red Sox, sending their archrivals home in five. The only bump in the road comes in Boston, where the Red Sox shell Clemens for five runs on five hits in just two innings of Game 3 at Fenway. Clemens starts the 3rd by allowing a hard single to Mike Stanley. And after he throws one ball to Brian Daubach, Torre pops out of the dugout, grabs each of Clemens' arms, and tells the pitcher he's pulling him now to save him for his next start.

Clearly rattled, Clemens strides off the field and quickly leaves the Yankees dugout. The crowd is chanting "Where's Roger?" while Cashman searches for the veteran pitcher, finding him in the visiting manager's office.

"Everything all right?" Cashman asks.

"Cash, I just want you to reconsider if you can please bring in Brian McNamee," Clemens blurts out. It was Cashman who rejected Clemens' request to hire McNamee when Roger came over to the Yankees. Cashman remembered McNamee from his time as the Yankees bullpen catcher in 1995 and thought he was trouble. But Clemens formed a strong bond with the trainer in Toronto and is desperate to bring him to New York.

"He knows how to train me," Clemens tells Cashman. "He's the one who can get me motivated."

"Okay, Roger," Cashman says. "I'll talk to George about it." Which Cashman does soon after the Red Sox finish thumping the Yankees, 13–1. "Do whatever he wants," the Boss says. McNamee will be back in a Yankees uniform come February.

The Yankees celebrate their third trip to the World Series in four years in Fenway's cramped visitors clubhouse after Orlando Hernandez's dominant start in Game 5. Players are posing for pictures and spraying Champagne while Steinbrenner holds court in the center of the room, repeatedly praising the team's heart. His young GM sips a beer while standing off to the side, gratified this team is as good as he thought it could be, and thinking about what a bastard the Boss has been all year. The Mariners have put out feelers to Cashman, but he has two years left on his contract and knows George would never let him go. Besides, he doesn't want to leave, no matter how badly Steinbrenner treats him. It's clear now that Cashman has a love-hate relationship with the man who's tormented him for months on end. He knows no other owner would have made him GM at 30, or given him the resources to build this powerful roster.

All things considered, Cashman believes the abuse is worth the reward—though often just barely.

The Braves beat the Mets the next day for the NL title, and instead of a Subway Series, talk centers on the meeting between the decade's two most dominant teams. The Braves have only one World Series title, but own eight division titles to the Yankees' three and finished the '90s with 925 wins, far ahead of New York's 851.

Once the World Series starts, though, there's little doubt which is the better team. The Yankees win the first two games in Atlanta handily, holding the Braves to seven hits and three runs while striking out 17. Trailing 5–1 in Game 3 at Yankee Stadium, Tino Martinez, Chuck Knoblauch, and Chad Curtis all hit home runs to send the game to extra innings, and Curtis hits another homer in the 10th for the win.

The only remaining suspense centers around Clemens and whether he can earn his first ring with a good performance in Game 4. It's not vintage Rocket, but Clemens turns in $7\frac{2}{3}$ strong innings. The Yanks tag John Smoltz for three runs in the 3rd and

Rivera sets down the heart of the Braves lineup in order for the final four outs. When Curtis squeezes Keith Lockhart's lazy fly ball in left, the Yankees have a 4–1 win and their 25th World Championship.

"I finally know what it feels like to be a Yankee," says Clemens just before a bottle of Champagne is emptied over his head.

"No one can ever say you didn't win a championship again," Steinbrenner tells Clemens, hugging the pitcher but somehow coming away without any of the bubbly soaking his blue blazer, white turtleneck, and gray slacks. George has rarely been as euphoric, hugging Bud Selig after the trophy presentation — "Great Commissioner!" he says — slapping his players on the back, making sure not to lose track of well-wishers Billy Crystal and Spike Lee.

Giuliani has already announced the city will honor the team with another parade down the Canyon of Heroes on October 29. By then, Steinbrenner expects to have a deal done with his friend Harvey Schiller, the head of Turner Sports, making Schiller the first chairman and CEO of YankeeNets. He's also talking to another friend, Rudy's Deputy Mayor Randy Levine, about becoming president of his team.

The Yankees have left little doubt that they are baseball's best team of the '90s. Now George has the chance to build something even bigger for the 21st century.

Chapter 21

HOPE AND FAITH

January 19–October 29, 2000

In June of 1976, Oakland A's owner Charles O. Finley sold off three stars—all on the same day—from the team that had won three consecutive World Series titles. He sent future Hall of Fame closer Rollie Fingers and All-Star outfielder Joe Rudi to the Red Sox for $1 million apiece, then sent 20-game winner Vida Blue to the Yankees for $1.5 million.

But Commissioner Bowie Kuhn stepped in and voided all three deals, invoking his "best interests of baseball" powers to stop Finley from dismantling the A's franchise. Kuhn's right to block the trades was later upheld by a federal judge.

In January of 1994, 16 months after ousting Fay Vincent, the owners gutted the "best interests" clause. It invested far too much power in one man, they explained. The Commissioner, after all, worked for them, not the other way around.

But now, just six years later, many of those same owners have had a change of heart. Today's game, they say, needs an all-powerful Commissioner—as long as his name is Bud Selig.

That's the big news coming out of the first owners meeting of 2000. And just to make sure everyone understands whose best interests they're talking about, they approve a resolution that permits Selig to take from the rich and give to the poor. The Robin Hood measure not only allows the Commissioner to take steps to ensure competitive balance, it *asks* him to do it.

Equally unusual: these powers will disappear when the current Commissioner leaves office.

"I'm not sure people understand how significant this is," Selig tells the media after the owners meeting at the Ritz-Carlton in Phoenix on January 19. So he explains. The new rule allows him to take the Yankees' share of the national television contract and give it to teams he deems financially troubled. And if anyone complains, another resolution gives him the authority to fine a team $2 million and an executive $500,000.

"It's an awesome responsibility," Selig says. "There's no question that the Commissioner's powers are greater than they've ever been, going back to 1921."

There is only one problem with Selig's awesome new powers: they are meaningless.

Selig can no sooner change the game's revenue sharing structure than he can order the Yankees to trade Derek Jeter and Mariano Rivera. Any change in revenue sharing must be approved by the players union because it has a direct effect on wages. It was the owners themselves who said so when they claimed revenue sharing and wages were "inextricably linked" seven years ago—a decision reinforced by Federal Judge Sonia Sotomayor.

So even as Royals owner David Glass proclaims this "a great day for baseball," the owners know it's all Kabuki theater. They also know the reason for this performance: their contract with the players expires at the end of the coming season. The goal of this show of strength is equally clear: intimidate their players and sway the fans.

What many owners at the Phoenix meeting do *not* know is Paul Beeston and Rob Manfred are holding secret talks with the union. And they're not going well. The union has already rejected the increase in revenue sharing that Selig has requested. And Don Fehr has also rejected Selig's request to make the luxury tax permanent.

But there is some real news coming out of Phoenix. The owners unanimously approve the sale of the Indians to Larry Dolan for a record $323 million. Outgoing owner Dick Jacobs bought the

Indians in 1986 for $35 million, realizing a nice $288 million gain. That's not lost on newer owners like Peter Angelos, who could reasonably expect to double the $173 million he paid for the Orioles just seven years ago if he chose to sell.

The owners officially amend their charter, eliminating the league offices and putting their powers under the Commissioner. And Selig persuades every owner to pool his Internet rights, with each team kicking in $1 million a year for four years for what will be called Baseball Advanced Media, or BAM. Many of these men have little understanding of the Internet in 2000. But they do understand projections that the Internet asset will mean millions for each team down the road.

A reporter asks Selig if he'll use his new powers to take the Yankees' share of the Internet profits and split it among the small market teams.

"I'm not going to get into the specific things I can and cannot do," Selig answers.

A wise choice.

Selig and Fehr do not agree on many things, but they do find common ground on what to do with the results of their joint study on Andro: nothing.

The study conducted by Joel S. Finkelstein and Benjamin Z. Leder of Massachusetts General Hospital found there was no change in testosterone levels—the key to building muscle—when test subjects took the recommended dose of 100 milligrams for seven days. However, subjects who were given a 300-milligram dose—an amount more likely to be taken by an athlete looking for a boost—did see a 34 percent increase in testosterone.

Andro's capability to build muscle is why the NFL, NCAA, and the U.S. Olympic Committee have all banned its use. But the supplement, made from a naturally occurring hormone the body uses to make testosterone, is legal in the United States. Fehr, himself a member of the U.S. Olympic Committee, is adamantly opposed to banning a product any other American is free to buy. And this is one time Selig is not interested in arguing the point.

On February 8, the two men issue a joint statement.

"We are pleased to have played a role in the contribution to better science that this study represents," Fehr says in the release. "The study suggests as a next step research into the possible relationship between the use of Androstenedione and athletic performance and we support those efforts, too."

The Commissioner is equally happy. "While we are pleased to have played a part in the advancement of science, we are also concerned about the effects of Androstenedione use," the statement quotes Selig as saying. "More research is needed and we support the efforts of Drs. Finkelstein and Leder."

The message to the sport's players could not be more clear: no one in charge is ready to power down the game of baseball just yet.

And when the 2000 season begins in April, it's clear that fans won't lack for their beloved long ball.

In the top of the 6th inning of a game on April 9, three Twins hit home runs over the course of four pitches from Royals pitchers. Two innings later the Royals hit three consecutive homers of their own. It's the first time in history two teams have hit back-to-back-to-back home runs in the same game.

April is all about the record book. On April 7, major leaguers smash 57 home runs in a single day. They finish the week with 262 home runs and the month with 931. All three home run totals are the highest in baseball history. The torrid start puts baseball on pace for 6,232 home runs, which would shatter the existing record of 5,528 — set last season.

The home run barrage continues into May, with players hitting two or more home runs in 63 games. One of three players to hit three in one game is 35-year-old shortstop Kevin Elster, who did not play at all last season. Elster entered the season with 74 home runs in his 12-year career, including 24 he hit for Texas in '96.

Everyone has his own pet theory for the continued increase in homers. Smaller parks. Diluted pitching after two waves of expansion teams. Corked bats. And the notion that the ball is juiced attracts enough believers that Selig sends VP Sandy Alderson with former ballplayer turned Rawlings rep Ted Sizemore to the Rawlings plant in Costa Rica to make sure the baseballs are up to spec.

An Associated Press writer comes up with a novel theory. The increase, he says, is due to an aesthetic change in the baseball. The balls used by Major League Baseball now carry the navy blue signature of the game's Commissioner instead of those of the deposed league presidents.

"I don't think we can take credit for it," Selig says, laughing.

But why all the fuss about home runs? "Clearly, the fans are not upset by the higher run totals," Selig says in mid-May. In fact, the Commissioner predicts another attendance record thanks to the jump in homers. "The fans seem to be enjoying it. We will continue to monitor the situation, but tampering with things at this stage would be pure overreaction.

"I can assure you that I am not spending any sleepless nights worrying about it."

The last time a team won three consecutive World Series titles, Yankees manager Joe Torre was a hard-hitting first baseman for the St. Louis Cardinals. He can still remember that 1974 season, when he marveled at the talent and focus of the Reggie-Catfish-Bando Oakland A's, who trounced a 102-win Dodgers team to complete their three-peat.

How different the world was back then. The A's won a best-of-five first-round series and then the World Series—seven victories in all—to earn their rings. Today, a team needs seven victories just to reach the World Series. In 1974, free agency—the bane of dynasties—was still two years away.

And while Charlie Finley was impetuous and mean-spirited, the A's owner was but a minor inconvenience compared to Torre's current boss, whose bluster masks his finely tuned ability to manipulate the media. And manipulating is what George Steinbrenner's been doing just about every day this season since Torre's team got off to a slow start in spring training.

Torre is dealing with George's latest move on the afternoon of June 14 as he holds his pregame meeting with reporters in his Yankee Stadium office. It's just 12 hours after his team suffered a 5–3 loss to the Red Sox, dropping them into a tie for first place with their archrivals. Many reporters standing in his office now were part of the media pack that tracked down George last night and asked the Boss what moves his two-time champions have to make to right the ship.

"Go talk to the manager and the general manager," the Boss said. "We better do something, don't you think?"

Torre hasn't seen the day's back pages yet, so he just stares straight ahead, his dark eyes set under his heavy brow, when several reporters relay Steinbrenner's challenge. *Geez, it's not even the fucking end of June, and these guys are pressing George's buttons on a daily basis.*

It's not as though Torre doesn't have enough on his plate. The team learned just one week into the season that pitching coach Mel Stottlemyre has life-threatening bone marrow cancer. Chuck Knoblauch can't seem to throw the ball to first base again, and David Cone, now 37, is 1–6 after 12 starts with a 6.49 ERA and might be through. Roger Clemens, today's starter, still hasn't found the form he showed in Toronto.

Steinbrenner also has a new favorite in recently hired Randy Levine, whose stated role is to grow the Yankees business and groom George's sons to take over — though Hank and Hal still have shown little interest in running their father's team. George has also made it clear to all that Levine is his eyes and ears in New York when the Boss is down in Tampa — which is most of the time — meaning Torre has one more person to worry about pleasing.

Then there's Brian McNamee, who's become a problem, just as Cashman feared. Cone jumped all over Mac the first day of spring training when he found Clemens' trainer leading pitchers in calisthenics instead of strength coach Jeff Mangold. That began a split between the pitchers who followed McNamee — in large part because of his relationship with Roger — and those who remained with Mangold.

But the manager knows what the writers are doing today. "You guys have it so easy with George," Torre says. "You go up to him, and you know you are going to get an answer, and you run with it."

Baseball rules mandate that managers keep their clubhouses open until 45 minutes before game time. But when batting practice is over an hour and 15 minutes before Clemens' first pitch against the Red Sox, the Yankees remain behind closed doors.

"Team meeting," the security guard tells the writers, who stand and wait for the doors to open. But even when one player after another slips in and out and admits there is no meeting, the door remains closed. Torre thinks his team needs a break. The writers will conduct no pregame interviews today.

Nor will they see much of Clemens, who is removed after the 1st inning with a groin strain, the same injury that plagued him last season. Torre is noticeably relieved when Rivera shuts down Boston in the 9th to save a 2–1 win. But the relief is short-lived as Torre watches the White Sox batter Andy Pettitte and three relievers, 12–3, the very next night.

Worse, he has to pull Knoblauch in the 7th after three more throwing errors. The second baseman dresses and leaves the Stadium with the game still in progress. The loss is the first of 10 in the next 13 games, a tumble that drops the Yankees to 37–35 and second place on June 28, three games behind Toronto.

Steinbrenner's response is predictable: an emergency meeting in Tampa, threats to every Yankees exec, and serious trade talks with the Cubs and Tigers. There's also a daily "Sosa Watch," even though Cashman considers Sammy a defensive liability and a hitter in decline.

Cashman deflects Steinbrenner until he can pull together a deal for the player the Yankees really need. The GM thinks the Indians' David Justice is the perfect fit, and on June 29 the Yankees send left fielder Rickey Ledee and two minor leaguers to be named to Cleveland for the veteran power hitter. Torre is thrilled. He inserts the patient Justice at DH behind cleanup hitter Bernie Williams and watches his team take off. The Yankees win 9 of their next 13 games, take sole possession of first on July 16, and never look back.

The Justice deal is notable for one other reason: the outfielder's $7 million salary pushes the Yankees' payroll past the $100 million mark, a baseball first and more than the combined payrolls of Minnesota, Florida, Kansas City, and Pittsburgh. Torre knows this infuriates those who complain that the Yankees buy their championships. Well, let them spend a few days in his shoes and see what they think.

Besides, the battle over money is between the Boss and Bud. Torre's job is to win ball games. And this year, that means the manager they once called Clueless Joe has a chance to win a third straight World Series and make baseball history.

The Blue Ribbon Panel report on baseball's economics was supposed to be finished by the beginning of this year. But each time it reached the Commissioner's desk, it was sent back with a simple message: the small market teams need more help.

The Brewers have a new general manager in Dean Taylor and a new manager in Davey Lopes—the game's ninth black manager—but the results are strikingly familiar. By the end of June, the team is 15 games under .500 and 15 games behind first-place St. Louis.

Not surprisingly, interest in Milwaukee is fading, with the Brewers failing to draw at least 10,000 fans nine times before the All-Star break. The low point is on May 22, when a major league–low 3,913 fans come out on a dreary Monday afternoon for a rescheduled doubleheader against the equally bad Astros—despite heavily discounted tickets. The financial losses continue to mount as well, with the team's debt now projected to reach $164 million by year's end.

But not every low-budget team is struggling. In fact, by the time the owners gather at the Waldorf Astoria in New York on July 14 for the release of the Blue Ribbon Report, it's Jerry Reinsdorf's White Sox—whose $31.7 million payroll ranks 26th—who have the game's best record at 55–33. Oakland, with the 24th-lowest payroll, has the third-best record in the AL, ahead of the Yankees and Blue Jays. And the Angels (18th) and Giants (17th) are both within striking distance in their divisions.

Even the Marlins, whose $20.3 million payroll is the game's second lowest, are 46–43 and closer to the top of their division than the big-spending Orioles.

Yet when Selig and the four independent members of the Blue Ribbon Panel—George Mitchell, Paul Volcker, Richard Levin, and

George Will—address the media gathered at the Waldorf, they seem convinced that the sky is falling.

"The 18-month study left absolutely no doubt that large and growing revenue and payroll disparities exist in Major League Baseball, causing chronic problems of competitive imbalance," Mitchell says. "The economic data clearly substantiate the widespread notion that the problems have become much worse and seem likely to remain severe unless Major League Baseball undertakes remedial actions proportional to the problem."

The Commissioner agrees. "We've never had a report like this," Selig says. "I was struck when I read it for the first time at the power of it."

It's also a farce. The report is based on financials provided solely by MLB—no outside input was permitted. It analyzes only the five seasons following MLB's costly decision to shut down the game, when big market teams with their deep pockets had a big advantage. And it assesses the success of the game's revenue sharing system a year *before* the system is even fully implemented.

Mitchell, Volcker, Will, and Levin unquestioningly accept baseball's assertion that only three teams—the Yankees, Indians, and Rockies—made a profit during the last five seasons. Even the Braves—who won their division in each season under review, opened a new stadium, and have their own television network—somehow managed to lose money. So did the Cubs, whose owners also have a superstation and play to a full house every game. Yet research done by *Forbes* indicates that both teams turned a profit—as did at least a dozen other franchises.

The four experts also accept MLB's claim that it lost $1 billion during these five seasons. By contrast, the financial magazine estimates a $400 million profit. Selig brushes off the story as shoddy journalism.

The panel's report offers several solutions to the problems they've uncovered, but only two really matter. One is a huge jump in revenue sharing—from the current 20 percent of local revenues to 50 percent. The other is a 50 percent luxury tax—renamed a "competitive balance" tax—on portions of payrolls above $84 million, a measure clearly targeted at the only team surpassing that threshold each of the past two seasons: the Yankees. Had the tax been in effect this year, it would've cost Steinbrenner at least $8 million.

Though the panel's recommendations are overreactions, the 87-page report is revealing in several ways:

It's the obvious blueprint for Selig's bargaining position for the next labor contract, which all but ensures the union will exercise its option to extend the current contract through 2001 and sets the stage for another acrimonious negotiation.

It's the first official recognition of "contraction," sending a loud message to the players about the growth of wages and to any city that refuses to build a taxpayer-financed stadium: give us what we want or we may fold your team.

It's a clear shot across the bow of the game's two biggest spenders, Steinbrenner and Peter Angelos. Either agree to higher revenue sharing and lower payrolls or we will put teams in the New York–New Jersey and Washington–Northern Virginia markets.

And it serves as Mitchell's debut as a staunch Selig ally. The highly respected former Senator has been renting out his credibility ever since leaving Congress in 1994. Among Mitchell's clients: RJR Nabisco, Philip Morris, and the three other tobacco companies negotiating with the attorneys general of 40 states to reach a settlement after lying to Americans for decades about the dangers of cigarettes; the Chocolate Manufacturers Association, which needed the former Senator to lobby Congress after the industry was caught using child slave labor in Africa; and General Electric, which is trying to avoid paying to clean up the Hudson River after dumping poisonous waste into the famous waterway for years.

Mitchell is the voice presenting the Blue Ribbon Report. If baseball follows the report's findings, the Senator says, it will rescue the game from financial ruin and give every team "hope and faith" of reaching the postseason. Some teams may have to relocate, he says, but the panel's remedies will eliminate any need for contraction.

Selig knows the mention of contraction will grab the attention of Congress. That's why baseball's lobbyists at the influential Washington law firm BakerHostetler are currently putting the report in binders and delivering it to every member of Congress.

Baseball will go on to spend almost $4.5 million lobbying Congress over the next four years, more than the NFL, NBA, and NHL combined.

One of the lobbyists is Lucy J. Calautti, wife of Senator Kent Conrad (D-ND) and former chief of staff for North Dakota's Byron Dorgan, the ranking Democrat on the Senate commerce committee. Both politicians are keenly interested in the baseball team that plays in neighboring Minnesota, which is a prime candidate for contraction. It won't be long before members of Congress are also talking about baseball's "competitive balance problem."

Don Fehr is dismissive when the media asks for his response. "We always get some report like this before a negotiation," he says.

Steinbrenner, the only owner not present at the Waldorf, goes one step further: he refuses to answer media calls. The Yankees paid $22 million in revenue sharing last season and expect to pay another $25 million or more this season. The Blue Ribbon plan would more than double that bill—before the competitive balance tax. *What the hell do reporters expect him to say?*

Steinbrenner has other fights on his hands at the moment. While Selig is taking aim at his bank account, Cablevision's Chuck Dolan is doing all he can to prevent YankeeNets from partnering with mega-talent-agency IMG to build a regional sports network around the Yankees and Nets. Cablevision's owner insists the IMG deal violates the clause in his contract with the Yankees that allows him to match any offer for the team's television rights. State Supreme Court Justice Barry Cozier soon rules in Cablevision's favor.

Dolan continues to tell Steinbrenner his grand scheme to build a regional sports network will never work, especially since George keeps complaining to him about his YankeeNets partners. And George is listening to his old friend. Truth is, the differing philosophies and big egos on both sides of YankeeNets have clashed from the start. Even things as simple as the logo on the company stationery and who sits where on the team bus for the Yankees' ticker-tape parades have been subjects of tense, high-level debates.

But it's the decision to purchase the New Jersey Devils that creates a deep rift between Steinbrenner and Chambers, the two anchors of this partnership. Chambers wants the team as part of his plan to build a new sports arena in Newark, while Steinbrenner argues loudly that it's a bad investment. When the deal closes on August 22, YankeeNets puts up only $40 million, with Chambers and Lewis Katz paying the balance of the $176 million purchase price. And there will be no cash calls made on YankeeNets, either. The terms grate on Chambers, giving Katz—a sworn George adversary—more ammunition to use against Steinbrenner.

Dolan steps on another Yankees-IMG deal in the fall, matching IMG's $52 million offer for the team's 2001 television rights. But the deal contains a clause that would end Cablevision's right to match any offer, and Dolan heads back to court seeking to reinstate his advantage. This time Cozier tells both sides to work out their differences or he'll hear the case in court come spring.

With freedom from Dolan within its grasp, YankeeNets hires star lawyer David Boies. The two sides come close to a joint venture, with YankeeNets buying half of Cablevision-owned Fox Sports New York in exchange for a long-term rights deal. But Dolan pulls out after a handshake deal, leaving many on the YankeeNets side thinking it was all a ploy to delay the search for investors and shake up Steinbrenner, who is already worried about meeting payroll if Boies wins YankeeNets its freedom.

No one else shares George's concern—Chambers comes from the investment world and is confident they'll have their pick of investors. And Boies lays down an edict: do not talk to anyone at Cablevision—especially Chuck Dolan—until this is settled. "They're all very crafty guys," Boies says.

The partnership is paying Boies, one of the country's foremost litigators, $1,000 an hour for his work, so it would seem logical to follow the lawyer's instructions. Thing is, George Steinbrenner has never been especially good at following orders, even from someone as smart as David Boies. He has Dolan on speed dial, and that can only mean trouble for the future of YankeeNets.

Joe Torre knows these are not the record-setting Yankees of 1998—or even the Yankees of last season—who fly out to Oakland the first week of October in their quest for a place in history. His earlier teams rolled over opponents in the regular season, then won all but three postseason games, going eight for eight in the World Series. This team has 87 wins, the fewest of any playoff team, including the youthful, low-budget A's, who won 91 games and the AL West.

To be sure, any team with the Jeter-Rivera-Pettitte-Posada core is going to contend. But it was David Justice who made the difference between making the playoffs and going home early. The veteran supplied the power Cashman wanted without Sosa's drama, hitting 16 home runs and driving in 49 to spark a 45–23 run. And Clemens was a different pitcher when he returned from the disabled list, going 9–0 with a 2.19 ERA during the streak that lifted the Yanks atop the AL East, nine games ahead of Boston.

Cashman also made several strategic moves, including picking up outfielder Glenallen Hill, who hit 10 home runs in his first 51 at bats, and Cincinnati's All-Star pitcher Denny Neagle, who stabilized a rotation weakened by injuries. In all, the Yankees added $20 million in salary once the season started, more than the $17.5 million Twins owner Carl Pohlad is paying his entire team.

But this is still an aging team that has its share of holes in its $112 million roster. David Cone, whom the Boss brought back for $12 million on Cashman's recommendation, pitched so poorly he was almost left off the postseason roster. Tino Martinez and Scott Brosius combined for only 32 home runs. Ten different players have played left field.

New York staggered into the postseason, dropping 13 of its last 18 games, many by wide margins. Fittingly, they were losing to the Orioles, 13–2, on September 29 when a Boston loss flashed on the Stadium scoreboard. The AL East title was theirs, but the Yankees hardly knew what to do with the Champagne in their clubhouse after their fifth straight loss.

Only three teams in the past 50 years had losing records in September and went on to win the World Series. The last: the A's in 1974, when they completed their run of three straight titles. The Yankees will follow Oakland's path, but it isn't easy. Jason Giambi and the A's push them to five games. They need six games to escape Alex Rodriguez and the Mariners. The World Series matchup with the Mets is every Yankee's worst nightmare. Really, what player wants to be anywhere near the Boss if the team were to lose the title to the Mets?

For the fans and media, this five-game Series will be remembered for the Roger Clemens–Mike Piazza confrontation. In July, Clemens beaned Piazza while trying to brush him back, a play the media—and Piazza—hyped for weeks. Their rematch in Game 2 receives enormous attention, revving the always emotional Clemens well into his red zone.

Clemens opens with two strikeouts, and then the much-hyped Game 2 confrontation begins. Piazza swings at the Rocket's second pitch and shatters his bat, sending a large, jagged piece bouncing toward the mound. Piazza jogs to first and an overamped Clemens grabs the broken bat and flings it toward the Yankees dugout. He misses Piazza by a foot, which empties both dugouts and touches off a heated debate about the Rocket's intentions, his aim, and his sanity.

When order is restored, Clemens hurls eight shutout innings before leaving with a 6–0 lead. The Yankees survive a Mets rally for a 6–5 win and a 2–0 Series lead. The Mets climb back into the Series with a win in Game 3, but it's Clemens v. Piazza that dominates conversation for days.

Yet for many Yankees, this October will be remembered for Cone's final pitch as their teammate. It comes in the 5th inning of Game 4, with Neagle clinging to a 3–2 lead with two out and none on. In steps Piazza, who'd crushed a two-run homer in the 3rd. Out of the dugout pops Torre, signaling for Cone.

Torre has a special place in his heart for Cone, who's patrolled Joe's clubhouse from Day One. Coney's a winner, too—until this season, when his fastball rarely broke 90 and he could no longer locate his breaking pitches. The result: 11 losses in the first 12 games and an ugly 4–14 season.

Still, Torre considered starting Cone in Game 4 at Shea. But Cone advised his manager he couldn't go deep into a game anymore. "I can help you in relief," he told Torre before the game. And now is his chance. "There's two outs," Torre tells him. "We need one more."

Cone works Piazza to a 1–2 count. His next pitch is a fastball—"no better than 86, but just up and in enough," he says—and Piazza pops up to second. Cone leaves the game when Torre pinch-hits for him in the top of the 6th.

"Thank you," he tells Torre.

One game later, Rivera is again on the mound for the season's final out, throwing up his arms in celebration of the Yankees' 26th World Series title and the three-peat. The team joins Finley's A's, the 1949–53 Yankees (five straight), and the 1936–39 Yankees (four) as the only teams to win as many as three consecutive titles. This time these Yankees know exactly what to do with the Champagne waiting in their clubhouse.

An emotional Steinbrenner stands in a corner of the packed clubhouse moments later, dripping with the bubbly Jeter once again poured over his head. "This was a great one to win," the 70-year-old owner says. "This team showed me as much heart as any team I've ever had."

George chokes on the last few words, then his chin drops to his chest as he weeps. It's a few moments before he looks up again. "We've been down a tough trail," he says. "Okay?"

Steinbrenner's more composed a few days later, when he picks up the phone and calls Rivera. The two men have grown close over the past few years, a relationship Rivera both treasures and keeps private. The star and the owner had made a wager before the season began. If the Yankees repeated, Steinbrenner would pay the airfare back to Panama for Rivera, his wife Clara, and their three young sons. If the team fell short, Rivera would buy George dinner anywhere the Boss wanted.

"Well, I'm ready to pay up," says Steinbrenner when Rivera answers the call. Five first-class tickets arrive a day later. The Boss knows how much Clara hates to fly and hopes the extra expense makes the experience a little more bearable.

As for making things a little more bearable for Selig and baseball's other owners? That's another story entirely.

Chapter 22

DOLLARS AND NO SENSE

December 19, 2000

Bud Selig is lying in bed in his room at Sinai Samaritan Medical Center, careful to prop up his bandaged left leg. He's just had surgery yesterday morning to repair the broken kneecap he suffered in a nasty spill on his icy driveway. It's December 19, and he's lost count of the number of times his wife has told him this is exactly why he should leave Milwaukee for their winter home in Scottsdale, just as she does. But Bud hates leaving Milwaukee, no matter what the season.

He turns on the TV to watch yet another cable news show on the story America is still talking about. Just one week ago five Supreme Court justices stopped the recount of votes in Florida, a decision that made George W. Bush the President-elect of the United States. Half the country is overjoyed, the other remains in shock.

It is still hard for Selig to believe. After all, this is the same George Bush who not long ago was pulling practical jokes at quarterly owners meetings. He still remembers Bush's passion when he told Bud how much he wanted to be Commissioner after Fay Vincent was fired. That same man will soon be the next leader of the free world.

But as stunning as the news is, Bush's tainted victory isn't the only thing on Selig's mind. He's still trying to digest the latest spending spree by Bush's former colleagues at the Winter Meetings in Dallas. By then, Steinbrenner had already given Roger Clemens a two-year, $30.9 million extension and signed Orioles free agent pitcher Mike Mussina to a six-year, $88.5 million deal. The four-year, $68 million extension Carlos Delgado signed with Toronto in October made the Blue Jays first baseman the highest-paid player in the game. But not for long. Colorado owner Jerry McMorris—who sat on the Blue Ribbon Panel!—set the stage when he handed Denny Neagle a five-year, $51.5 million deal on December 4. Five days later the Rockies owner signed pitcher Mike Hampton to a staggering eight-year, $123.8 million contract.

On December 11, Texas owner Tom Hicks—another Blue Ribbon Panel member—walked up to the podium at the Wyndham Anatole hotel and announced that he'd signed Alex Rodriguez to a 10-year, $252 million deal. The contract—the highest in *all* of sports—is $2 million more than Hicks paid for the Rangers, their stadium, and the surrounding land. Just a few hours later, the Red Sox give Manny Ramirez $160 million over eight years to play in Boston.

Selig issued the usual gloom-and-doom pronouncements about the state of the game, but he knows full well there is always a spending binge every time baseball signs a new national TV deal. And the deal he signed with Fox on September 27 was a big one: $2.5 billion for six years, $1.9 billion more than the previous contract. And that's before ESPN kicks in $175 million in 2003, then $200 million in both 2004 and 2005.

But Selig—who received a $1 million bonus for the Fox deal—has made it clear he wants this kind of spending on players to stop. And he'll be carrying the Blue Ribbon Panel's revenue sharing and competitive balance tax proposals into next year's labor talks to make sure of it. He already took his narrative out for a trial run in November, when Senator Mike DeWine (R-OH) held a hearing on the perils of competitive imbalance in baseball.

Selig told DeWine that he's "never witnessed the type of despair" baseball owners exhibit today, testifying that at least 16 teams start the season without any hope of reaching the postseason. George Mitchell solemnly agreed. "Before the patient dies, remedial action should be taken," Mitchell testified. Senator DeWine, a Reds season-ticket holder, was quickly convinced.

"The evidence is overwhelming that baseball has entered an era that is very, very dangerous," DeWine said.

The Commissioner failed to identify which of the 16 teams lacked hope this past season, which was wise, because teams with the 14th, 17th, 24th, and 26th ranked payrolls all made the playoffs. And two of those teams—the White Sox and the Giants—had the best records in their leagues.

Selig also took great care to avoid any mention of contraction, an idea more and more owners are embracing as the year draws to a close. In October, Selig told the owners he'd instructed Paul Beeston and Bob DuPuy to study the ramifications of shutting down two or more franchises. Expos President David Samson flipped out, demanding to know whether his troubled franchise was a target. (The short answer: yes.) By then, everyone understood Samson's stepfather Jeff Loria, who's alienated the fans, media, and politicians in Montreal, bought the team a year ago with the idea of moving it to Washington.

But that's not going to happen. The Washington market is far too valuable as leverage for owners threatening to move if their cities won't build them a new stadium. And if baseball moves back to Washington, it will be as an expansion team, so everyone gets a piece of the action.

It's no coincidence that every team on the contraction list but the Angels—both Florida teams, the A's, Twins, and Expos—are fighting stadium battles with their local politicians. Patience with these cities is running low among owners, who see a bigger cut of the national pie if two or more teams are eliminated. Problem is, while most owners favor contraction, none want to give up their team. Not even Pohlad, who's issued more threats to his hometown than any owner on baseball's hit list.

Selig isn't enamored with the idea, either. He's not eager to be remembered as the Commissioner who shrunk the game, though if that's the consensus, he'll fall in line. Beeston and DuPuy have already spoken with the owners of the targeted teams, including a midsummer meeting with John Henry when they sat on his

160-foot yacht and discussed teams he might buy should they fold the Marlins. Selig would love to see Henry, a billionaire hedge fund manager, bring his small market sensibilities to the big market Red Sox.

Beeston has also told Don Fehr the owners would increase rosters to compensate for lost jobs, and he's certain he can convince the union leader not to stand in their way. But Selig is not so sure. Especially since the union exercised its option in August to extend the current contract through 2001, giving Steinbrenner and the other large market teams another year to keep spending big.

This also gives everyone one more year to load up on steroids, just as Selig is finally ready to start weaning the game off performance-enhancing drugs. The Commissioner, who ignored the Andro study in February and chuckled with the media about fallen home run records last spring, is no longer laughing. Too many records have been broken, too many aging players are performing as they did in their primes—if not better—and too many reporters have stopped being cheerleaders and started asking tough questions.

In April, *ESPN the Magazine*'s Jeff Bradley wrote about the time his brother Scott, then a backup catcher trying to hang on toward the end of his nine-year major league career, was told by a former player that steroids were the answer. No, Jeff Bradley wrote, he's never seen a player shooting up. But how could the veteran writer not wonder who was using steroids after sitting with players during BP and listening to them play a guessing game they call "who's on 'roids?"

By the All-Star break, reporters began wondering how Mark McGwire could hit 30 home runs in only 221 at bats—one every 7.37 official plate appearances—while hobbling on an arthritic right knee, a telltale sign of steroid use. Talk show callers were questioning the growth spurt of 35-year-old Barry Bonds, who's on his way to a career-high 49 home runs in just 480 at bats.

We need a plan to get us to the next contract, Selig told his labor chief, Rob Manfred. And it wasn't long before baseball decided to conduct random testing in the minor leagues—where the union has no jurisdiction—starting in 2001. Manfred let the union know baseball wanted the same thing for the majors in their next contract.

"We are clearly interested in getting some sort of steroid testing program in place," Manfred told the New York Times in a revealing story published on October 11. The Times spoke with more than 25 major league players, coaches, and trainers, and the consensus was clear: baseball had a steroid problem.

"Players nowadays feel if it looks like it can help you, they'll try it," said Marlins outfielder Cliff Floyd, who told the newspaper he figured steroid use in baseball ran as high as 40 percent. "I came up with that number from talking to a lot of players. That's how the game is and that's probably how it's going to be for a long time."

It's going to be hard to put the genie back in the bottle, and that's what makes a player like Alex Rodriguez so attractive. He is as powerful as Bonds and Sosa but still graceful and lithe, able to glide across the infield to make all the plays at shortstop, with a rocket for an arm.

Simply put, it's hard to take your eyes off A-Rod when the star player takes the field. He's young, handsome, and just so talented. He won a batting title at age 21, when he hit .358. He went 40–40 two years later—only the third player in history to hit those magic numbers—when he hit 42 home runs and stole 46 bases. Now 25, Rodriguez already has 189 home runs and 595 RBI—49 more homers and 101 more RBI than Hank Aaron at the same age. If Alex stays healthy, he could wind up owning the game's record book.

But why, Selig asked Hicks, did the Rangers owner have to put a target on A-Rod's back with that obscene contract? Didn't he understand that Alex will now be expected to get a hit every time the winning run is on base, or make the special play in the field whenever the game is on the line?

The reason is simple: Hicks, who built a personal fortune of $750 million as a leveraged-buyout artist, sees A-Rod as a brand—the Natural. To Hicks, Alex Rodriguez isn't just a baseball player, he's the key to turning the Texas Rangers into a sports and entertainment giant able to compete with the Dallas Cowboys on both the local and national stage.

And that makes it hard for Selig to argue with Hicks. He's going to push like hell to make sure there are no more contracts like the one Hicks just handed his young superstar. And Selig won't sign another labor deal that doesn't include random testing for steroids. But just like the Rangers owner, the Commissioner of baseball thinks it's good business to build his game around Alex Rodriguez for years to come.

PART IV

POWER PLAY
(2001–2003)

Chapter 23

MILLER TIME

March 30–September 10, 2001

THE AUDIENCE APPLAUDS as President George W. Bush strides confidently to the podium in the wood-paneled East Room of the White House. Dressed in a light blue suit, crisp white shirt, and pale blue tie, Bush is smiling, and there's an undeniable twinkle in his eye. And why not? Standing on risers behind him are 42 of the greatest baseball players and managers who ever lived. Yes, he's now the 43rd President of the United States, but being around baseball stars still makes George Bush feel like a kid.

"Laura and I are delighted to welcome you all to the People's House," Bush tells his guests. "This is an exciting day for my administration and all the baseball fans that live here in Washington."

It's been a busy first two months in Washington for the young President. Shrugging off his contentious election, Bush has aggressively pursued his agenda, sending an education bill favoring charter schools to Congress on just his sixth day in office. He quickly reversed Clinton's executive order on the environment, removing caps on carbon emissions and opening the Arctic National Wildlife Refuge for drilling. And he's worked tirelessly to pass a mammoth $1.6-trillion tax cut that skews heavily toward the rich. Though this isn't the compassionate conservatism Bush promised on the campaign trail, at least half the country is smitten by his forceful and carefully crafted persona.

But today is March 30, and Opening Day is just two days away. What better time to enjoy the perks of being President? Hank Aaron, Reggie Jackson, and Sandy Koufax are standing behind him now, applauding. So are Duke Snider, Nolan Ryan, Carl Yastrzemski, and 36 more Hall of Famers. How cool is that?

But the person the President acknowledges first is not in the Hall of Fame. At least not yet.

"I first want to thank the Commissioner for coming," says Bush, looking directly at the man from Milwaukee seated in the front row. "Mr. Commissioner, it's good to see you again, sir. You're doing a great job in shepherding our National Pastime through some pretty tough times."

Commissioner Bud Selig smiles broadly and nods to the President. It's been a busy three months for Selig, too. He laid out his bargaining plan at the mid-January owners meeting in Phoenix, with the aggressive moves on George Steinbrenner's money and high player salaries coming straight out of the Blue Ribbon Report. The owners even approved one of Selig's pet ideas—a draft that would allow teams with losing records to take players from the teams at the top.

The current labor contract expires in October, and Selig does not expect the union to play past August without a new agreement for fear of another lockout next spring. Paul Beeston is still his lead negotiator, but Selig has let everyone know who makes the decisions. "This time the owners will be speaking with one voice," he's said on many occasions. "Mine."

Clarified roles aside, there are serious doubts that Selig can reach a new labor deal without a work stoppage. And the President has already told baseball not to look to Washington for help. "I hope there's not a strike," Bush said a few days before his inauguration. "But it's going to be up to the participants. They shouldn't be looking to me."

Selig would prefer a settlement without Washington's help or the need for contraction. The idea of eliminating several teams is still popular with many owners, though no one—with the possible exception of his good friend Carl Pohlad—is willing to give up his club. Certainly not Montreal's Jeff Loria, who is now threatening to sue if Selig tries to shutter his franchise.

Still, the Commissioner recognizes the threat of contraction gives him leverage with both the union and cities still reluctant to build new stadiums. And that's why baseball VP Bob DuPuy dutifully continues to collect information on likely candidates for elimination.

But this is far from Selig's mind now as he listens to Bush ad-lib his way through a 15-minute speech. "There are some familiar faces here, but none more beloved than Yogi Berra," Bush says. "Some in the press corps here even think he might be my speechwriter."

Bush chuckles along with the crowd, then rambles through one story after another as only a real fan can, recalling everything from his first game at the Polo Grounds to his own baseball card collection.

"It is such an honor for us to welcome you here," he says. "Thank you for coming, and I hope you enjoy the lunch as much as I know I'm going to."

It is hard to tell who delights in shaking hands and taking pictures more, Bush or the players. While Selig is enjoying himself, the Commissioner is on a tight schedule. He leaves immediately after the luncheon and is sitting in his Miller Park suite just a few hours later, watching the White Sox–Brewers exhibition in the stadium's trial run. He feels a mixture of relief and pride when it's apparent the new building will pass its first test.

He's on a plane the next day to Puerto Rico, where he watches the widow of Roberto Clemente throw out the first pitch Sunday night before Toronto plays Texas in the season opener. Then he's back home Thursday night with Hank Aaron to honor Warren Spahn as the first inductee in the new Milwaukee Braves Hall of Fame.

And now it's April 6, Opening Night at Miller Park. Selig is standing with his wife Sue, Wendy, and Wendy's husband Laurel Prieb in a loading bay under the stadium. They watch as a team of black SUVs rolls to a stop. The door to one opens, and out jumps the President, who spies his welcoming party and walks right over.

"Hey," says Bush, lifting up his pants leg. "What do you think of these cowboy boots?"

The First Lady and National Security Advisor Condoleezza Rice have also made the trip. So has former Wisconsin Governor Tommy Thompson, now Secretary of Health and Human Services, along with Transportation Secretary Norm Mineta. But Bush has little interest in his traveling party. The President is eager to meet the Cincinnati and Milwaukee players, and Secret Service agents surround the President and the Commissioner as they walk through the catacombs to the clubhouses.

Bush enters the Reds clubhouse first and is greeted with an awkward silence. "Do we just stand here and stare at each other?" he asks, and the players suddenly flock to the President's side, many snapping pictures with disposable cameras. Bush greets each player with "Nice to meetcha" and ends their brief chats with a slap on the player's shoulder.

The Brewers are far looser when Bush strolls in. "You're looking great," the President tells Rod Carew, draping an arm around the Brewers hitting coach. "Now, this guy played a lot of ball games," he says loudly while shaking hands with 38-year-old Tony Fernandez. Most players are ready with new baseballs and Sharpies to get Bush's signature.

Bush tells the Brewers he still hasn't decided what pitch he'll throw when he takes the mound. "Split finger," he says at one point, flexing his right shoulder, then demonstrating the proper grip. "But I may go with some breaking stuff, know what I'm saying? Big breaking curve stuff."

The 15 minutes allotted for this visit pass quickly, and the President and the Commissioner are then escorted to the Brewers dugout, where Selig dons a white MLB jacket and Bush pulls on a blue warm-up jacket with BREWERS emblazed across the chest. Selig walks out of the dugout first, receives an appreciative ovation from the sellout crowd of 42,024, and throws a looping strike to Brewers manager Davey Lopes.

It's the President's turn next, and Bush gets a nice reception in a state he lost by 5,708 votes in November. He winds up and throws a pitch that bounces six feet in front of the plate and wide. Lopes snares the errant toss while Bush holds his pose for several seconds. Maybe the splitter wasn't the best idea.

Bush leaves the mound as Selig steps up to a microphone to address his fans. "After all of these years and all the struggles, it's hard for me to articulate how I feel today," Selig says. "I want to say to all of you tonight, there are many people who played a role in building this magnificent ballpark, but none greater than all of you."

Once the game begins, Bush trades stories and one-liners with Selig while they watch the Reds take an early lead with Miller Park's first home run in the top of the 4th. The Brewers surge back with three runs in the bottom of the inning, but it's soon time for the President to leave, and Bud and Sue walk Bush and the First Lady back to their waiting car. "I just can't believe it," Sue Selig says when it's her turn to bid Bush good-bye.

"What?" Bush asks. "You can't believe that I am here or that I am President?"

"I can't believe you are the President," Sue answers. According to Gallup, 47 percent of Americans share her disbelief.

Selig is back in his suite when Milwaukee first baseman Richie Sexson slams a solo home run in the bottom of the 8th to give the Brewers a 5–4 win, their first of the season. And it's clear the $414 million Miller Park, with its one-of-a-kind retractable roof, 70 luxury suites, and fan-friendly sight lines, is a winner, too. The Brewers are now projecting a $50 million increase in revenues, $20 million more than original estimates.

Still, the Commissioner knows that a new stadium can only help a franchise so much, especially when you're trying to pay down $164 million of debt. Cable television money dominates the game now, and the Brewers' $4.6 million television and radio deal is just about the lowest in the game. The big market teams rake in 10 times as much — or more.

With contract talks just now heating up, Selig is looking for a much bigger cut of the television pie. His friend in the White House has good reason to be worried about this baseball season.

* * *

"I think we should take the $70 million offer for the Yankees rights fee and extend our relationship with MSG for 2002," says George Steinbrenner, his voice rising. "It's going to take time to build a network and we need the money now—we have a big payroll, a lot of bills, and no guarantee we'll find investors."

Steinbrenner pauses while the others sitting in the conference room of the New York law firm LeBoeuf, Lamb, Greene & MacRae listen closely. YankeeNets Board members Ray Chambers, Finn Wentworth, Tom Murphy, George's son-in-law Steve Swindal, and their lawyer David Boies have heard George air these concerns before, and their looks of disapproval do little to push Steinbrenner off his chosen course.

"I don't share the bitterness towards Chuck Dolan and Cablevision that many of you have," George says. "I trust Chuck. He's a friend, and I don't feel good about leaving him. Hopefully, our lawyers can negotiate a deal for 2002 quickly, but it would not trouble me if we had to go an additional year."

This is the same message Steinbrenner put in a March 17 memo to his YankeeNets partners, chairman Harvey Schiller, and Boies just after Dolan sent them a one-paragraph letter offering $70 million to air Yankees games in the 2002 season. George is worried, and for good reason. The Yankees have a $110 million payroll, the highest in baseball history, and once again are at best a break-even operation. The Nets are losing millions. And YankeeNets is burning through money, hiring a management staff—Schiller alone is earning $2 million a year—building out a network infrastructure, and paying $1 million a month in legal fees while trying to break free of Cablevision.

It's April 17, the second day of arbitration hearings before U.S. District Judge Frederick Lacey, who was appointed by a state judge to arbitrate the nine-month Cablevision-YankeeNets dispute. At issue: Dolan's contention that a clause in Cablevision's recently expired contract with the Yankees provides the cable giant the right to match any offer for the team's television rights. In perpetuity. A ruling in Dolan's favor would kill any chance of YankeeNets starting its own regional sports network.

The first day of arbitration brought questions from Lacey and a surprise from (and for) Steinbrenner: sequestered in a room with several of his partners, Steinbrenner revealed an all-stock offer from Dolan to buy the Yankees outright. Chuck claims the deal is worth $1.2 billion, Steinbrenner reported. But when Chambers pushed for details, it turned out that Dolan valued the Cablevision stock north of $100 a share. The stock closed at $67 on April 16, down $14.94 since the start of the year and heading south. (Indeed, it would slump to $47.45 by year's end.) The offer was misleading — at best — and George turned silent.

But now there's a real deal on the table: Dolan has agreed to give YankeeNets its freedom for $30 million, payable in three installments. What the partners won't have is carriage on Cablevision, which represents almost 40 percent of the Yankees' 8 million customer base. "Your network will never run on my system," Dolan tells Steinbrenner, and George knows his friend is not bluffing.

No carriage on Cablevision. No investors. Another $30 million spent that they don't have. "Look, I don't see what we lose by waiting another year," Steinbrenner says.

Chambers thinks Steinbrenner could not be more wrong. An analysis by Morgan Stanley, the investment bank hired by YankeeNets to guide them through this process, projects a loss of $63 million of equity for every year the project is delayed. Turning down their freedom may also lead to a class-action suit from their current investors. And Chambers' contacts in the investment world have expressed strong interest in financing their network — now called Project Ultra — once YankeeNets breaks free of Cablevision.

"George," Chambers says, "I assure you that if we break away from Cablevision we'll have the money you need for the Yankees payroll. We can't be afraid of success."

"Why would you guarantee that to me?" Steinbrenner asks.

"Because I think the upside potential for all the partners is so much greater than if we were to stay with Cablevision," Chambers replies.

Just then, the phone rings. Lewis Katz, who missed today's arbitration hearing to meet with Comcast President Brian Roberts, is on the line from Philadelphia. And when Katz comes on the speakerphone, there is panic in his voice. "Roberts says there is something going on with this deal," Katz says. "I don't know what it is, but I don't think we should pay the $30 million."

And that's when Tom Murphy has heard enough. Normally a quiet, reserved presence, Murphy bangs his fist on the table. "What the hell is going on?" Murphy says. "This is what you guys have been litigating about for the last two years. This is what you want. You want your independence.

"Take the damn deal!"

For a moment, no one knows quite what to say. Everyone present—including George—has the highest regard for the 75-year-old Murphy, who spent most of his 42-year career building Capital Cities Communications from a small broadcasting company into a multibillion-dollar media corporation encompassing both television and newspaper chains. In 1985, he engineered a merger with ABC, turning the struggling broadcaster back into a powerhouse. Murphy retired in 1996, a month after selling Capital Cities/ABC to Disney for $19 billion.

Chambers knows he doesn't have to say anything more. He looks over at Steinbrenner, and George nods. "Okay," George finally says. "Let's make the deal."

Judge Lacey tells the YankeeNets partners they have 60 days to reach a final decision, but the course is set before they leave the building. Within weeks, Chambers and YankeeNets President Wentworth are talking to several of the top private equity firms on Wall Street, with Steve Rattner's Quadrangle Group emerging as their favorite. In typical YankeeNets dysfunction, the Yankees are entertaining offers from Goldman Sachs, and it's soon obvious that both firms are prepared to invest hundreds of millions in this venture, putting the value of the new network north of $800 million.

What's less obvious is how they plan to convince Dolan to put their network on his cable system.

Selig and Don Fehr agreed early this year to keep negotiations out of the media, and the 23 meetings between MLB's Beeston and Rob Manfred and the union's Michael Weiner and Steve Fehr have remained under the radar. The story, though, remains the same: the small market teams want more revenue sharing—50 percent is their starting point—and lower salaries. The union has reservations about the former and firmly opposes the latter. They also want no part of the luxury tax plan. Talk about testing for steroids is on the agenda, but it has not yet made it to the bargaining table.

In late June, Beeston flies to Milwaukee to give the Commissioner details of a union proposal the president of baseball finds encouraging. But Manfred has quietly told Selig the union's proposal is nowhere near the 50 percent in revenue sharing and the 50 percent luxury tax the Commissioner is after, so Selig makes Beeston wait five days before hearing him out. Beeston has barely finished his pitch when Selig says he's pulling the plug on all contract talks with no indication of when he wants to start them again.

While contract negotiations break down—once again putting the game's future in doubt—it's another season for big moments, milestones, and surprises in the game Selig oversees. And another season of disappointment for his hometown team.

Barry Bonds sets a record pace for home runs early, and hits his 50th home run—and 544th of his career—on August 11, the earliest a player has reached that mark. "It's something my godfather [Willie Mays] said I should have done years ago. I finally accomplished it, and he can leave me alone for a while," says the ever-gracious Bonds, who at 37 is also the oldest player to hit 50 homers.

Diamondbacks pitcher Randy Johnson—also 37 years old—blanks the Pirates on August 13 for his 16th win. Johnson's 10 strikeouts give him 277, putting the six-foot-ten left-hander on track for a record fourth straight 300-strikeout season.

Alex Rodriguez, the game's best shortstop, shows a touch of class at the All-Star Game in Seattle when he walks onto the field and switches positions with Cal Ripken, who was voted the starter at third in his final season. It gives Ripken a record 15 All-Star starts at shortstop, and the Orioles icon hits a home run and is named MVP in the American League's 4–1 win.

The Mariners are 63–24 at the break, on pace to eclipse the Yankees' three-year-old record for wins. The bargain-basement Twins, on everyone's list for contraction, are 55–32, the league's second-best record.

Selig's Brewers get off to a good start in their sparkling new home and end May four games over .500. But they've suffered a wave of injuries, none worse than Jeffrey Hammonds' sore right shoulder. The center fielder was Wendy's and GM Dean Taylor's big move in the offseason, signing him to a three-year, $21 million deal. Hammonds goes on the DL in mid-June and will have season-ending surgery a month later.

If this were New York, Steinbrenner would tell Brian Cashman to find a suitable replacement. But it's Milwaukee, and Selig's daughter tells the media that the team cannot afford to replace its highest-paid player. The Brewers go into a tailspin by late June and never recover, sending them to their ninth straight losing season. This is not the team Selig promised in exchange for his new stadium.

A host of new stars debuts in 2001, none better than Seattle's Ichiro Suzuki. The Japanese import goes 9 for 14 in a three-game mid-August series in Boston to raise his average to .344. (Ichiro will finish with a game-high 242 hits, the most in 79 years.)

St. Louis fans welcome rookie Albert Pujols, who hits his 29th home run on August 20 and is batting .333, while they say good-bye to Mark McGwire. Steroids have helped Big Mac belt 21 home runs in just 223 at bats, but he's hitting .197 in what turns out to be his injury-marred farewell. (After hinting at retirement all season, McGwire will make it official on November 11.)

Steroids are also helping Rodriguez, who is hitting .322 with 37 home runs and 107 RBI when the Yankees come to Texas for a four-game series in late August. In past seasons, Jeter and A-Rod have stayed at each other's homes when their two teams meet. But those sleepovers—and their close friendship—ended in March when Rodriguez told *Esquire* magazine, "Jeter's been blessed with great talent around him. He's never had to lead. You go into New York, you wanna stop Bernie and O'Neill. You never say, 'Don't let Derek beat you.'" Jeter, as distrustful privately as he is pleasant publicly, rarely gives people a second chance and quickly slammed the door on Rodriguez.

The dustup with Jeter is the first real blemish on A-Rod's résumé.

It won't be the last.

It's been a typical season in the Bronx: the Yankees are in first place and Steinbrenner is unhappy. The Boss held the usual emergency brain-trust meetings in Tampa while the team was stuck in second place in mid-June and rumors swirled of his displeasure with Torre. But the team started winning games in bunches by the end of the month, regaining first place for good on July 3, and peace was restored.

Clemens, now 39, has finally turned into the pitcher Steinbrenner thought he signed two years ago, winning 19 of his first 20 decisions in dominant fashion. He beat his former teams in his last two starts, striking out 10 Red Sox hitters in a 3–1 win, then holding the Blue Jays to two runs over 7.1 innings on September 5—the 15th time he allows two or less runs this season and lowering his ERA to 3.44. The five Blue Jays who go down on strikes give the Rocket 191 strikeouts in 196.1 innings—against 60 walks and 183 hits—which all but wraps up Clemens' sixth Cy Young Award.

The 4–3 win over Toronto pushes the Yankees' lead over second-place Boston to 9½ games with 22 to play, and only one real question remains: can Clemens go a record 20–1 when he faces the Red Sox in the final game of the season between the two rivals? A sell-out crowd is in the Stadium on September 10 to find out, but the game is rained out before Clemens throws his first pitch. History will have to wait another day.

The Yankees do make history of a different kind later that night. Though the dysfunction and distrust that plagues YankeeNets continues to grow—things get so tense that CEO Harvey Schiller is asked to draw up a code of conduct for partnership meetings—a deal for a regional sports network is finally struck. Goldman Sachs and Quadrangle will each invest $150 million and split 40 percent of the new network, which values the venture at $850 million.

Industry veteran Leo Hindery, who has close ties to the Dolans, kicks in $20 million and will come aboard to run what will soon be called the Yankees Entertainment and Sports—YES—Network.

Steve Swindal and Ray Chambers' son-in-law Michael Gilfillan will take over as cochairs of YankeeNets, replacing the soon-to-depart Schiller.

On September 10, executives and lawyers for all sides are at the law offices of Irwin Kishner at Herrick, Feinstein in midtown Manhattan when Steinbrenner makes one last call from his suite at the Regency, asking yet again if Goldman and Quadrangle will make good on their deal. Assured there is little to worry about, George gives his approval. At a few minutes shy of 1 a.m., all the documents are signed and the deal is done.

The details of this groundbreaking deal will be spelled out in a front-page story in the *New York Times* the following day. It's a story almost no one will read.

Bud Selig and George W. Bush (L) congratulate Brewers star Robin Yount on his 3,000th hit on September 9, 1992, after Selig was named Acting Commissioner. *(AP Photo/Dave Schlabowske)*

No one is happier when George Steinbrenner rides back into baseball in March 1993 than the media. *(Bill Frakes/Sports Illustrated/Getty Images)*

Selig trudges to the podium at County Stadium on September 14 to announce the end to the 1994 baseball season. *(Milwaukee Journal Sentinel)*

Bill Clinton and union chief Don Fehr exchange ideas at the White House before the President's unsuccessful attempt to end baseball's labor conflict on February 7, 1995. *(Courtesy William J. Clinton Presidential Library)*

Mark McGwire's steroid-fueled chase for home run No. 62 climaxes with this swing on September 8, 1998, wiping out the memory of the lost 1994 season. *(AP Photo/John Gaps III)*

George Steinbrenner and Joe Torre choke up after the Yankees sweep the Padres in the 1998 World Series, the team's record 125th win of the year. *(Bob Rosato/ Getty Images)*

Starting in 1999, Selig conducts baseball's business from a spacious suite overlooking Lake Michigan in Milwaukee. *(Darren Hauck/New York Times/Redux Pictures)*

A familiar sight: Mariano Rivera celebrates the final out of the 2000 World Series against the Mets, the Yankees' fourth title in five years. *(Chang W. Lee/New York Times/Redux Pictures)*

Terrorist threats don't stop President George W. Bush from saluting fans before the third game of the 2001 World Series in an emotional Yankee Stadium. *(Courtesy New York Yankees)*

Bud Selig and Wendy Selig-Prieb have a lot to say during the 2002 All-Star Game at Miller Park, which ends in a controversial tie. *(AP Photo/Morry Gash)*

Derek Jeter (L) turns his back on Alex Rodriguez when his former best friend joins the Yankees in 2004. *(Ezra Shaw/ Getty Images)*

After four seasons without a title, George Steinbrenner has plenty to say to Joe Torre (L) and Brian Cashman (R) in spring training of 2005. *(New York Daily News/Getty Images)*

(L-R) Bud Selig, Rob Manfred, and Don Fehr are sworn in before Congress on March 17, 2005, to answer questions about the use of performance-enhancing drugs in baseball. *(Simon Bruty/Getty Images)*

Barry Bonds becomes the all-time home run leader with this swing on August 7, 2007. *(Robert Beck/ Getty Images)*

George Mitchell points a finger at the game's players when he issues his report on the use of performance-enhancing drugs in baseball on December 13, 2007. *(Chuck Solomon/ Getty Images)*

Hal Steinbrenner dedicates the team's 27th championship to his father after the Yankees defeat the Phillies on November 4, 2009, to win the World Series. *(Nick Laham/ Getty Images)*

The players turn to Don Fehr's plainspoken deputy Michael Weiner when Fehr retires as union chief at the end of 2009. *(AP Photo/ Richard Drew)*

Mariano Rivera lays roses on home plate before the first game at Yankee Stadium after the death of George Steinbrenner in July 2010. *(AP Photo/Frank Franklin II)*

Rob Manfred (L) and Bud Selig meet the media on August 14, 2014, soon after the owners elect Manfred to succeed Selig as Commissioner. *(H. Darr Beiser/USA Today Sports/Reuters)*

Chapter 24

MORE THAN A GAME

September 11–November 6, 2001

BRIAN CASHMAN IS speeding down I-95 on this crisp, sunny September morning, unsure of what the world will look like once he reaches Yankee Stadium. One minute he's staring into a mirror at his home in Westchester, knotting the tie he was going to wear for a luncheon today honoring George Steinbrenner. The next minute his wife Mary is telling him a plane just flew into one of the Twin Towers.

Nothing is making any sense. Certainly not what he's hearing on his car radio.

At 8:46 a.m. an American Airlines 767 slammed into the World Trade Center's north tower, the radio announcer says.

At 9:03 a.m., a United Airlines 767 flew into the south tower.

At 9:31 a.m., President George Bush calls both strikes an "apparent terrorist attack on our country."

At 9:37 a.m., an American Airlines 757 jetliner crashes into the Pentagon.

At 10:03 a.m., a United Airlines 757 crashed in a field outside Shanksville, Pennsylvania.

Like every American on the morning of September 11, Cashman struggles to comprehend the scope of what is unfolding. He can see the giant plumes of black smoke rising from the World Trade Center as he pulls off the highway exit in the Bronx for Yankee Stadium. And by the time he races up to his office and turns on his TV, things are even worse. So much worse.

The television cameras follow small, dark objects, one after another, as they fall down the side of the burning north tower. They're office workers who were trapped in the floors above the inferno, men and women who've chosen to fall 100 stories to their death rather than be burned alive. Orange flames flare out of the giant dark holes in the top floors of each tower, just the edges of the fires that rage within.

Then the south tower comes crashing down. Thousands of office workers and first responders can be seen scrambling to escape the huge white clouds that billow down the streets of lower Manhattan. The chaos intensifies when the north tower collapses 39 minutes later, and all anyone watching can do is wonder how many people got out before the fall. And hope their family members and friends were among the lucky ones.

Cashman is still close to Tim Coughlin, his former roommate of three years. The 29-year-old son of football coach Tom Coughlin works as a bond trader for Morgan Stanley on the 60th floor of the south tower. Like so many New Yorkers with family and friends who have jobs at the World Trade Center, Cashman calls his ex-roommate's cell, but none of his calls get through. It will be almost 24 hours before he learns that a Port Authority police officer directed Coughlin to a safe route out under the south tower, just minutes before it came crashing down. The female officer never left her post.

Cashman's eyes are still riveted to the television screen as he starts dialing his players, trying to locate those who live in the city first. The GM gets Derek Jeter, who says he's talked with Tino Martinez and Gerald Williams. "We're all fine," Jeter says. Cashman finds Torre, who is also calling players. He reaches Rick Cerrone, the team's communications director, and asks him to tell the media today's game is postponed.

Tomorrow's game? Who knows what tomorrow will bring.

Cashman gets a call through to Steinbrenner at the Regency and isn't surprised when it's Randy Levine who picks up. The Yankees president, who lives on Manhattan's Upper East Side, was supposed to fly out to Milwaukee for an owners meeting late this morning. But the only planes flying now are the F-16 fighter jets circling the city.

"Guess you didn't make it to the owners meeting in Milwaukee," Cashman says.

"No—Buddy canceled it," Levine says. "Can you believe what's happening?"

"How's the Boss?" Cashman says.

"Like everyone, he's trying to figure out what just happened," Levine says. "We talked to Giuliani and told him the Yankees will do anything he needs us to do. He told us to stand by. He'll let us know when he needs us. This is just crazy."

Cashman goes back to calling to his players. He leaves a message for Chuck Knoblauch and another for Roger Clemens, who's already in a rental car with his wife, driving home to Texas. Clemens lives in the shadow of the Trade Center and was awakened by a call from a friend to alert him to what was happening. He rushed to the roof of his building in time to see both towers tumble down. He'll make his first stop in Tennessee, where he gets word that the mother of one of his close friends was on one of the hijacked planes.

Cashman finds White Sox GM Kenny Williams, whose team is in town for a three-game series with the Yankees. Williams has tried to find a way out of the city for hours without success. "You can stay in my house," Cashman tells Williams, who declines. He's lined up a bus to get the team out first thing tomorrow morning, and he doesn't want to risk even a minute's delay.

Not an hour passes before a young staffer tells Cashman that the Stadium is being evacuated. "Bomb threats," he tells the GM. Of course. What better target than America's most famous Stadium? Cashman hurriedly gathers his papers, takes a look around his office—who knows when it will be safe to return?—and rushes to his car. As he pulls out of the team's parking lot, he sees a handful of Stadium workers milling about and looking lost.

"What are you waiting for?" Cashman shouts from his window.

"Are you gonna wait and see if this place comes down, too? Just shut it down and go home!"

Bomb threats are called in all around the nation, and federal and state authorities are shutting down landmarks, banking centers, and skyscrapers. That includes Milwaukee's 42-story Firstar Center, home to Firstar Bank, the Foley & Lardner law firm, the private equity firm Baird Capital, and the Commissioner's office. Bud Selig has set up shop across the street at the stately Pfister Hotel, huddling with owners when he is not trying to get through to the White House.

Selig had scheduled a special owners meeting today and tomorrow to discuss contraction, but those plans were quickly scrapped. John Ellis and others with the Mariners organization jumped in a car as soon as the news hit and are driving back to Seattle. Braves executive Stan Kasten is driving back to Atlanta. The six or seven owners who made it to Milwaukee and stayed have given Selig their ideas about when baseball should get back on the field.

Selig hears from Karl Rove, who tells him the administration is weighing security concerns against a strong desire to get America back to what's normal. Like playing baseball. But how do you play baseball when no one is sure how many bodies lie beneath the rubble in New York City? A decision about tomorrow's games will have to wait until tomorrow.

It's a tired Commissioner who comes to the phone to talk to the *New York Times* late in the afternoon of a day that already feels endless. "I'm going to have to use my judgment," Selig tells the paper. "We are a social institution that needs to be not only responsible but hopefully helpful as we move forward. I don't have a timetable.

"Right now I'm in shock."

The shock is not going to wear off anytime soon.

The daily bomb threats will continue for weeks as many Americans—and every New Yorker—wait for the next attack, which they are sure is coming. Selig is one of many business and government leaders tasked with figuring out how this new world works, how they're supposed to balance security and sensitivity with dollars and cents.

On Wednesday morning, the Commissioner cancels the next day's games, then comes back that afternoon and cancels games for Friday, too. A day later he announces play will resume Monday, with the six days of missed games tacked on to the end of the season. The Mets will open in Pittsburgh instead of New York, giving the city an extra four days to tighten security, get a final count on the dead and missing, and finish grieving. If that's possible.

"I really don't think it's the right time to play baseball," says Jeter, who lives near the United Nations on Manhattan's East Side.

By midweek, Shea Stadium's huge parking lots are transformed into staging areas, with food, clothes, and equipment arriving by the crateful as hundreds of volunteers load them onto trucks bound for lower Manhattan. Todd Zeile and John Franco are among the many Mets doing the heavy lifting. So is their manager, Bobby Valentine, who lost a close friend in the south tower and can't seem to leave this stadium. About half the team is out visiting area hospitals. Shea's suites become sleeping quarters for firemen who have flooded into New York from all around the country. Rescue workers sleep in cots set up in the stadium's hallways and tunnels.

Both baseball and the players union give $5 million to the newly created MLB-MLBPA Disaster Relief Fund. Steinbrenner pledges $1 million to a fund for the families of police officers and firefighters killed in the towers' collapse and offers the Stadium to rescue workers to shower and sleep. The mayor wants to hold a prayer service at the Stadium. "Of course," George says.

Giuliani calls Steinbrenner on Friday with another request. "We need help with morale," the mayor tells his friend. It's still too dangerous at Ground Zero, Giuliani says, but could Steinbrenner ask some of his players to visit a few key places on Saturday?

"The Javits Center, St. Vincent's Hospital, and the Armory," Giuliani says.

"Done," says Steinbrenner.

Others in the Yankees organization aren't as sure. They've all been waiting to do something—anything—to help, and visiting volunteers at a convention center and injured rescue workers at a hospital is perfect. But the Armory is where parents, wives, husbands, and so many children are waiting to hear if the DNA samples they carried with them match any of the remains found at Ground Zero.

"Is that really appropriate?" Cashman wonders. This same day Giuliani announces the city still has 52 unidentified bodies and 408 unidentified body parts. The list of missing stands at 4,717. Do family members really want the Yankees attracting attention on one side of the room if they get word about their loved ones on the other?

Giuliani tells Steinbrenner and Levine not to worry. "You'll help," he says. "Trust me."

It's a bright and sunny Saturday morning when a handful of Yankees players, coaches, and executives arrives at the Stadium. They look up at the snipers on rooftops bordering the Stadium, poised to provide extra security. This is the Yankees' new life. They all gather at the pitcher's mound, kneel, and say their prayers. A short workout follows, then they load into a couple of vans and head to Manhattan.

They talk to volunteer workers from all corners of the country at the Javits Center, and everyone is now a Yankees fan. Then it's time for the two-mile ride over to the Armory on Lexington Avenue.

Cashman, Torre, and Levine are on the trip. So are coaches Willie Randolph, Lee Mazzilli, and Don Zimmer, and Yankees PR man Rick Cerrone. Jeter, Knoblauch, Bernie Williams, Scott Brosius, Mariano Rivera, and Paul O'Neill are all there, too.

No one moves when they park at the Armory. Out the windows they can see the fence surrounding the Armory covered with photos, each one a husband or wife, a son or daughter who is still missing. *Damn, we're just a baseball team. Of what use can we possibly be to these poor people?*

Someone from the mayor's office boards one of the vans. "We've told them you were here," he says. "They really want you to come in."

The group slowly enters the building, where they stop again, not sure what to say or do. A family member recognizes the Yankees contingent and waves for them to come inside, and many of the grieving walk over to greet them. Several pull out pictures of their loved ones wearing Yankees hats and pinstriped jerseys.

Others remain in a daze, staring at their visitors. Bernie Williams walks over to a woman, devastation etched on her face, tears welling in her eyes. "I don't know what to say," Bernie tells her softly. "But you look like you need a hug." The two embrace, and both of them cry.

Torre meets a woman who says she was a student of Joe's sister Marguerite, a nun at a Catholic school in Queens. A young boy, whose family is inquiring about his father, comes over to O'Neill, whose left foot is encased in a protective walking boot for the stress fracture he suffered eight days ago. The two talk for several minutes before parting, and O'Neill limps over to Cerrone.

"He wanted to know how I felt," he tells Cerrone. "Can you believe that?"

When it's time to leave, many of the Yankees embrace those who must now return to reality. "Thanks for coming, we won't forget this," they are told repeatedly. No, they weren't intruders. Instead, they provided a few moments of welcome relief and a reminder that life will not always be as hard as it is today. The Yankees are emotionally drained but also uplifted by the knowledge that they could help people whose suffering is unimaginable.

It's a day they won't soon forget, either.

This is what the new normal looks like:

Hundreds of police officers—more in major cities—patrol outside and inside every baseball stadium and are joined by National Guard troops with rifles strapped across their backs. Bomb-sniffing dogs check the stands, tunnels, and locker rooms before games. Fans are told to leave coolers and backpacks home. Small bags and purses are allowed—but will be searched—and fans should not be alarmed if they're patted down at the gates. Even players have to show identification before they're granted entry.

Once everyone makes it inside, the games are part pledge of allegiance, part revival meeting, part celebration of America. Selig asks for a pregame moment of silence and instructs teams to play "God Bless America" instead of "Take Me Out to the Ball Game" at the 7th-inning stretch until further notice. He orders 400,000 small American flags to be handed out to fans for each team's first game back, and an American flag patch is sewn into the back of every player's cap and the neckline of his jersey.

Monday night's games are filled with emotion. At Coors Field, Diamondbacks and Rockies players solemnly unfurl a giant American flag across the outfield. At Fenway Park fans lock arms and sing "New York, New York" during the 7th-inning stretch. Spontaneous chants of "U-S-A! U-S-A!" break out during games across the nation.

The Commissioner's flags do not arrive in Pittsburgh in time for Monday night's game with the Mets, so Pirates officials hand out I LOVE NY pins to everyone who comes to the hastily scheduled game. Players line both sidelines for the moment of silence; the Mets wear hats honoring police, firemen, and rescue workers and have "9-11-01" stitched into their right sleeves.

Pittsburgh fans also open their wallets, donating almost $100,000 during the game for a relief fund for the hundreds working at Ground Zero. The Mets win, 4–1, with the decision going to Brooklyn-born reliever John Franco. "For three hours, I hope we gave some pleasure to the guys who have been working," says Franco, who now lives in Staten Island, home to many of the firemen and policemen lost on September 11. "We're not playing just for ourselves, we're playing for the whole city of New York."

The Yankees return to play one night later in Chicago, where the atmosphere is again filled with emotion. White Sox fans give standing ovations to Yankees players as they come out for batting practice, and signs embracing New York—CHICAGO LUVS NY... NEW YORK, CHICAGO WEEPS WITH YOU... WE ARE ALL YANKEES—are held or hung in every corner of Comiskey Park. Both teams stand along the baselines and applaud policemen and firemen as they take positions ringing the infield. Officers solemnly hand candles to managers Joe Torre and Jerry Manuel.

"We love you, New York!" bellows one fan, breaking the pregame silence.

New York belts three homers and beats Chicago, 11–3. One night later, Roger Clemens makes history, pitching six strong innings in the Yankees' 6–3 win to become the first pitcher to go 20–1. Clemens stands at the clubhouse door waiting for his teammates after the game, hand extended in thanks, but most Yankees hug the Rocket instead. Roger is smiling when he meets with reporters a few minutes later, but talks much more about firemen and policemen than fastballs and strikeouts.

"It doesn't have the same feeling it would've had a couple of weeks ago," Clemens says.

That same day, Paul Beeston calls Don Fehr and tells him contraction is off the table for next season. Fehr isn't surprised. Americans were slow to embrace baseball after it shut down during the best of times, but now they're turning to the game to reflect and recover in the worst of times. How can they shut down any city's baseball team after this?

New York is still in mourning—and on edge—when the Braves arrive to play the Mets on September 21. It's the first sporting event in the city since September 11, and talks of chemical and biological attacks circulate daily. Smoke still rises from fires burning below the rubble at Ground Zero, where hundreds of rescue workers continue to search the 16 acres of broken concrete and melted girders.

Giuliani's confidence and determination have buoyed New Yorkers, and the mayor receives a thunderous ovation when he joins the Braves and Mets on the field at Shea Stadium later that night for pregame ceremonies. Diana Ross, dressed in black with a red, white, and blue ribbon over her heart, sings "God Bless America," and the crowd of 41,235 cheers loudly when policemen, firemen, and rescue workers are introduced. The camera finds one fan holding a sign with just the right message: ONCE BITTER RIVALS, NOW UNITED!

Indeed, the spirit of national unity seems to have sapped the usual acrimony from tonight's game. "If I looked at the game objectively," the Braves' Chipper Jones says, "I'd be rooting for the Mets."

The Mets are again wearing the hats of the NYPD and FDNY. Manager Bobby Valentine and every player will wear these hats for the rest of the season. They also donate a night's pay to a rescue workers' relief fund, an amount in excess of $450,000.

Many of the players will talk of being in a daze when the game finally begins, no one more than Mets catcher Mike Piazza, whose apartment is five miles from where the Twin Towers stood just 10 days ago. Piazza lets a perfect throw home bounce off his glove in the 4th inning for the game's first run, and the Braves hold a 2–1 lead when the catcher steps to the plate with one out and one on in the bottom of the 8th. He watches Steve Karsay's first pitch sail down the middle of the plate untouched.

Piazza takes four slow steps back from the plate, trying hard to focus, then digs back in. Karsay throws another fastball, and this time Piazza swings and launches a majestic fly ball far over the left-center-field fence. The stands are literally shaking, fans hugging, jumping, and shouting, as Piazza rounds the bases. Never has a home run meant less about a game and more about a people than this one right now.

The game ends minutes later, and the fans listen to Ray Charles' recording of "America the Beautiful" while the PA man reads the stats of the home team's 3–2 win. The stands remain full, as if leaving will bring everyone back to reality, and renewed chants of "U-S-A! U-S-A!" follow one after another.

It's a sentiment that continues at games everywhere as Americans struggle to find the balance between everyday life and new terror threats. The Yankees clinch another AL East title on September 25. One day later Diane Sawyer asks her *Good Morning America* audience, "Should you buy a gas mask?" in response to terror warnings. Sammy Sosa hits his 59th home run on September 27 and carries an American flag high over his head as he rounds the bases at Wrigley Field. Alex Rodriguez, the first shortstop to hit 50 homers, hits his 52nd and last of the season on October 4, the same day anthrax is discovered in the Florida offices of the tabloid newspapers *National Enquirer* and *Star.*

Bonds continues his chase of Mark McGwire's home run mark, but most Americans are more focused on President Bush's deliberations over when to take the country to war. The Giants star breaks McGwire's record on October 5, hitting Nos. 71 and 72 in a Friday night game in San Francisco when much of the nation is asleep. He will finish with 73. Selig is not in attendance, choosing instead to be at Tony Gwynn's last game in San Diego. Neither is Bonds' father, who was in Connecticut for a charity golf event.

(Despite the constant swirl of steroid rumors that engulfed Bonds all year long, the 37-year-old will be rewarded with a five-year, $90 million contract in January.)

The Yankees play their last four games in Tampa, where Centcom—United States Central Command—is meeting at Mac-Dill Air Force Base to finalize plans for an invasion of Afghanistan. The Yankees lose the first three games to the Rays, but it's not the final game of the season, on October 7, that has Steinbrenner's attention. Like the rest of the nation, he's far more concerned with the announcement his friend George Bush makes that afternoon.

"On my orders," the President says while sitting stiffly at his desk in the White House Treaty Room, "the United States military has begun strikes against Al Qaeda terrorist training camps and military installations of the Taliban regime in Afghanistan.

"More than two weeks ago, I gave Taliban leaders a series of clear and specific demands. None of these demands were met. And now, the Taliban will pay a price."

For the next four weeks, Americans will alternate between watching news footage of bombs falling on Kabul and following postseason baseball. Like most Americans, Steinbrenner figures this war will last no longer than the seven months Bush's father took to drive Saddam Hussein out of Kuwait 10 years ago. And like most Americans, Steinbrenner could not be more wrong.

Only two teams in baseball history have ever won as many as four consecutive World Series. Joe McCarthy's Yankees did it at the end of Lou Gehrig's career and the beginning of Joe DiMaggio's in 1936–39. Casey Stengel's Yankees won five straight in 1949–53, when DiMaggio was handing off to Mickey Mantle. It was often said that rooting for those Yankees teams was like rooting for U.S. Steel. Or, as iconic Chicago columnist Mike Royko once wrote, "Hating the Yankees is as American as pizza pie and cheating on your income tax."

But no one hates George Steinbrenner's Yankees—not this year, not with the nation at war against the terrorists who attacked this team's home city. To most Americans, this isn't a baseball team trying to win its fourth straight World Series. No, these Yankees are the nation's touchstone to a city still sorting through the rubble and mourning its dead. For once, rooting for the Yankees feels like the right thing to do.

Sadly, it doesn't look like this new feeling will last very long. Oakland comes into Yankee Stadium to open the postseason and wins two tight, well-played games. No team has ever come back to win a best-of-five division series after losing the first two games at home. And these A's, a power-laden team blessed with strong starting pitching and a star closer, beat the Yankees in six of nine regular-season games—all six wins coming in Oakland.

Just when it appears all may well be lost, it's Jeter who pumps life back into his team, this time with a defensive play for the ages. It comes in Game 3, with the Yankees clinging to a 1–0 lead in the bottom of the 7th. Oakland's Jeremy Giambi is on first after a two-out single. Terrence Long slams a double into the right-field corner, and when Shane Spencer's throw sails over the heads of two cutoff men, Giambi has a clear path to home plate with the tying run.

Then suddenly there's Jeter, flashing across the diamond, gloving Spencer's errant throw on the dead run as he crosses the first baseline, then flipping the ball backhand to Jorge Posada. Giambi is so stunned to see Posada with the ball that he never slides, and the Yankees catcher tags the A's outfielder a split second before Giambi's foot hits home plate.

Properly inspired, Rivera closes out the game, then watches his teammates pound the A's 9–2 the next day. Mo's back on the mound for the final two innings of Game 5, striking out the last two A's hitters to complete the comeback.

"These kids have been through so much emotion in this city," says Steinbrenner, whose players meet with rescue workers and family members of those lost on September 11 before every home game. "Then to come up with this for the city is great."

Steinbrenner's team brushes aside Seattle—winners of a record-tying 116 regular-season games—in five games, and much of America is pulling for the Yankees to win a World Series title for the people of New York. Standing in the way are the Arizona Diamondbacks, a team just four years old and already a major concern for the game's Commissioner. If Selig is worried about Steinbrenner spending too much of his money chasing after players, he may be even more worried about Arizona's Jerry Colangelo signing players with money he *doesn't* have.

Colangelo has spent more on Curt Schilling, Randy Johnson, Matt Williams, and his other stars than his team brings in—by far. The Diamondbacks are $48 million in the red after just three seasons, and if 10 players—including the entire five-man rotation—had not agreed to defer large chunks of their salaries back in February, the team would not have been able to meet its payroll. It's this kind of recklessness Selig is determined to stop with the next contract.

But Colangelo's deficit spending looks awfully shrewd when first Schilling and then Johnson dominates New York, holding the Yankees to one run and six hits as the Diamondbacks sweep the first two games in Arizona. Johnson, the player Cashman talked Steinbrenner out of acquiring, is especially masterful in Game 2, allowing just three hits and striking out every Yankees starter at least once in a 4–0 shutout.

The Series shifts to New York and a packed Yankee Stadium. Both teams have known for days that President Bush was making his third trip to this stricken city on October 30 to throw out the first pitch in Game 3, so everyone understands emotions will be running high. And when Attorney General John Ashcroft announces a day before the game that there's credible evidence of another terrorist attack coming within the week, all of New York is on high alert.

Mayor Giuliani assigns 1,200 police officers to the game, the Secret Service again positions snipers on rooftops ringing the Stadium, and bomb-sniffing dogs search everywhere from grandstand seats to each locker in both clubhouses. The Stadium opens more than three hours early so fans can get through the airport-style metal detectors that have been installed at every gate. No one enters without identification.

When the Diamondbacks bus arrives at 5 p.m., each player—no matter how recognizable—is stopped at the entrance and searched with a metal-detecting wand before he can enter. Every Yankee goes through the same drill.

Air Force One touches down at Kennedy Airport, and the President's helicopter flies by the Empire State Building, illuminated in red, white, and blue, before landing adjacent to Yankee Stadium in Macombs Dam Park at 7:25 p.m. Bush is escorted through secured tunnels in the bowels of the Stadium and into the umpires' room, where he autographs baseballs while a Secret Service man is outfitted with umpire gear. The agent will be on the field with Bush.

An aide finds a batting cage, and Bush is practicing his pitching motion while wearing his bulletproof vest when Derek Jeter walks over to meet the President. "Hey, Mr. President, how are you doing?" Jeter says as the two men shake hands.

"Good," Bush answers. "Good luck tonight."

"I hear you're throwing out the first pitch," says Jeter. "Are you going to throw the ball from the mound or in front of the mound?"

"I think I'll throw it from the base of the mound."

"I wouldn't do that if I was you, Mr. President," says Jeter, his black game bat in hand. "You better throw it from the mound or they'll boo you. This is Yankee Stadium."

"Well, okay, I'll throw it from the mound."

The two men shake hands again, and Jeter begins to walk away, then he stops and looks over his shoulder. "Don't bounce it, Mr. President," he says. "They'll boo you."

Moments later, the President emerges from the Yankees dugout wearing a blue pullover with the letters FDNY stitched across the back, and 55,820 fans erupt in thunderous applause. The ovation grows louder as Bush climbs the mound and louder still when the President lifts his right arm high in the night air and gives a thumbs-up sign to the crowd.

Bush then winds up and throws a strike to Yankees catcher Todd Greene. "U-S-A" chants echo through the Stadium as the President strides off the field, waving to the crowd. He passes a sign that captures the crowd's emotions — USA FEARS NOBODY. PLAY BALL — stops to shake hands with Giuliani and Senator John McCain, sitting beside the Yankees dugout, then disappears down the dugout steps.

It is a huge moment and a huge night. It is America standing tall against its enemies, and doing so by playing a game of baseball.

Bush is ushered to Steinbrenner's box, where he spends the first three innings with the Yankees owner, Selig, and New York Governor George Pataki before returning to Washington. Clemens delivers an overpowering performance, giving up one run and striking out nine before handing a 2–1 lead to Rivera in the 8th. Mo strikes out four of the six batters he faces, securing the win and pulling the Yankees back into the Series.

If Game 3 was all about emotion, the next two games are nothing short of magic. With the Yankees trailing by two with two out in the 9th, Tino Martinez belts a two-run homer off Arizona's ace reliever, 22-year-old Byung-Hyun Kim. An inning later, Jeter tags Kim for a game-winning home run to even the Series. The Yankees are down to their final out again the next night, trailing 2–0, when Scott Brosius takes Kim deep for another game-tying home run. Rookie Alfonso Soriano rifles a game-winning single in the 12th, and the Yankees are now the team of destiny.

The Series returns to Arizona, where the Diamondbacks beat up on Andy Pettitte—who's unaware he is tipping his pitches—and crush the Yankees, 15–2, setting up a climactic Game 7. But there is another game going on behind the scenes. With the current contract expiring at midnight, November 7, labor negotiations restarted when the Series was in New York. And Selig, looking to gain the upper hand, had a surprise for Fehr.

The owners are once again considering contraction.

Fehr is stunned. Even floating the idea is a public relations disaster. He barely has time to think through the implications of Selig's possible maneuver when Beeston tells him contraction is officially on the table minutes before Game 7. This time Fehr erupts.

"You fucking guys don't know what the fuck you're doing," Fehr shouts. "This is crazy."

The deciding game is a taut affair. The Diamondbacks push a run across against Clemens in the 6th, and the Yankees answer with a run off Schilling in the 7th. And when Alfonso Soriano hits a solo home run in the 8th, Torre calls on Rivera for a two-inning save to nail down the team's fourth straight World Series title, the 27th in Yankees history. Rivera strikes out the side in the 8th but allows a leadoff single in the 9th, then throws a ball slickened by wet grass into center field on a sac bunt, putting runners on first and second with no outs.

Jay Bell bunts back to Rivera, who throws to third to nail the lead runner, then watches in disappointment when Brosius fails to throw to first to double up the slow-running Bell. When Tony Womack hits a broken-bat double down the right-field line, Game 7 is tied.

Rivera hits the next batter, and Torre pulls the infield in against Luis Gonzalez, Arizona's 57-homer cleanup man. Gonzalez swings at an 0–1 pitch that breaks his bat and bloops the ball over the drawn-in infield. It lands no more than a foot onto the grass in left-center field, but it's more than enough to score Bell with the winning run.

The Diamondbacks, not the Yankees, are the World Champions.

The Yankees season ends with a cracked bat and a furious George Steinbrenner, who is waiting for his team in the visitors locker room. Fox put up a stage when it appeared the Yankees would win, shaking the superstitious owner to the core. Enraged by his team's loss, he stands at the door to the locker room, arms folded across his chest, glaring at each Yankee as they walk into the room. Rivera enters, meets Steinbrenner's angry stare, then quickly looks away and finds his locker. Standing next to George, cringing and embarrassed, is his 31-year-old son Hal, who wishes he could walk away and hide.

After the last Yankee has walked through the clubhouse door, Steinbrenner seeks out Brian Cashman. He has a message for his young general manager. "We've done it your way," the Boss tells Cashman. "Now it's my turn." He'll give the GM and Torre new contracts this month, but he'll make their lives miserable, too. No longer the team of destiny, the Yankees are headed back to the kind of dysfunction only the Boss can create.

Steinbrenner's reaction aside, the Diamondbacks' 9th-inning rally off the game's premier closer is a fitting end to the most dramatic World Series anyone can remember. For two weeks, the Yankees and Diamondbacks enthralled a nation still worrying about terrorist strikes, anthrax, and a reeling economy. The social institution of baseball has delivered, providing Americans with a blanket of comfort and a path back to normalcy.

Just as Bud Selig hoped it would.

And yet two days later, the Commissioner tells America the social institution of baseball is closing the doors on two of its teams.

"No modern American sport has done this, but it makes no sense for Major League Baseball to be in markets that generate insufficient local revenues," Selig announces after the owners vote 28–2 to approve contraction. "The teams to be contracted have a long record of failing to operate a viable major league franchise."

Fehr is in his Manhattan office when Selig delivers the news. After all these years, very little the Commissioner does surprises him. The game's labor contract expires tomorrow at midnight, but its rules still apply the next day when Fehr files a grievance, contending that contraction violates baseball's basic agreement with its players.

Selig refuses to announce the two teams slated for elimination, and Fehr is pretty sure he knows why. The Expos are a given; Montreal drew all of 642,745 fans this season. And sources tell Fehr that Twins owner Carl Pohlad has agreed to take the money—closer to $150 million than the $250 million the media reports—and run. But it's virtually impossible to eliminate two teams in time for the 2002 season: the grievance is sure to go to arbitration, which will take months, MLB's already sent out a schedule for all 30 teams, and in September the Twins signed a contract that locks them into playing in the Metrodome for another year.

Fehr sees this announcement for what it is: a threat to get a new stadium in Minnesota and a hammer to get concessions from the union at the bargaining table.

That Selig would make this bluff now is a bit tough to stomach. It's not the first time he's thrown the entire sport under the bus to get his way—this is, after all, the man who canceled the World Series in pursuit of a salary cap—but the timing borders on despicable. It's been a long, tense six weeks living and working in New York, which continues to look, feel, and even smell like a war zone. It's unsettling to look down 5th Avenue, still shrouded in dust, and not see the Twin Towers.

The Yankees postseason had given New Yorkers something to rally around, just as the World Series had shown the nation—and the world—that Americans could get on with their lives. Selig is right, baseball is more than a game, and Fehr is almost offended by the insensitivity of the Commissioner's decision.

He sits down at his computer and types out a new press release.

"Over this last season, and especially over the last several weeks, we have been reminded vividly of the special place baseball holds in America," Fehr writes. "This makes it all the more unfortunate that the clubs would choose this moment to dash the hopes of so many of its fans."

Chapter 25

BUD'S BLUFF

November 7–December 23, 2001

THE REACTION TO Selig's contraction announcement is swift and overwhelmingly negative. Fans are outraged and blister the Commissioner in radio talk shows across the nation. The media excoriates Selig, and many of the leading columnists and television anchors call for his resignation. "I honestly believe that we can get this done by the end of November," an unperturbed Selig tells baseball's own MLB.com.

Which is nonsense. But Selig has decided a bargaining chip is a bargaining chip, no matter how much bad publicity it draws.

The union files a grievance that is certain to go to arbitration, rendering Selig's November timeline moot. A Minnesota judge grants a temporary injunction against any action by MLB in response to the Minneapolis Stadium Board's claim that the Twins have to honor the one-year contract extension they quietly signed on September 26. The contract gives the Twins the stadium rent free but requires them to play the full season unless they are unable to because of a "strike, an act of God, a natural casualty, or a court order." Yet another giveaway that Selig's threat for contraction in 2002 is a bluff.

But that doesn't mean it can't happen a year later. And that's one reason why Florida Attorney General Bob Butterworth subpoenas documents from the Commissioner, the Marlins, and the Devil Rays to learn whether the two Florida teams are on Selig's hit list. "Why are they always hiding behind closed doors?" Butterworth complains. "They act like they are electing a pope."

And Congress, sensing headlines, is immediately up in arms. Senator Paul Wellstone (D-MN) and Representative John Conyers (D-MI) reprise their old standby, both introducing legislation to revoke baseball's antitrust exemption while announcing they'll call Selig in for hearings. "I am angry," Wellstone says. "This decision to eliminate these teams is a betrayal by owners who have put their own profits before loyalty to fans."

Selig is undeterred. The plan to take care of all his ownership issues has been in place for months, voted on and approved at an Executive Council meeting not long after September 11. The owners know—or should know—that contraction for the 2002 season is impossible, but there is significant support for folding two teams in 2003 unless they get big increases in revenue sharing and the luxury tax in the next contract. Baseball will buy the Expos from Jeff Loria for $120 million, run the team for at least the coming season, then either fold or move it to another market, where it'll be sold for a handsome profit.

Selig silences Loria's threats to sue with an interest-free loan— and other perks—so he can buy John Henry's Marlins for $150 million. Henry, the billionaire commodities trader, is negotiating with Disney to buy the Angels. If the Angels deal falls through—Disney chief Michael Eisner keeps changing his mind about selling— Henry will jump into the bidding for the Red Sox. Selig thinks having an owner with small market experience in a major market would help solve the game's spending problems, and the Commissioner made it clear he'll do whatever it takes to keep Henry in the game.

But the Contraction Show must go on for the rest of 2002. In Minnesota, Pohlad's son Jim sends a letter to employees—which is leaked to the media—to let them know the awful truth. "When we are posed the question, 'Why should the Minnesota Twins not be contracted?'" Pohlad writes, "we are unable to find a plausible answer."

Selig tells the people of Minnesota they should "take a good look in the mirror" when assigning blame if they lose the Twins. His reason? A city and state that won't build a new stadium don't deserve a major league team.

But it's curious to see who is considered deserving in baseball and who is not. Selig spends four weeks telling anyone who will listen that baseball lost $518 million in 2001—despite a record $3.5 billion in revenues—with only five teams turning a profit. Yet on November 27, baseball's owners unanimously vote to grant Selig a three-year contract extension and a big raise—20 months early—meaning the man from Milwaukee will be Commissioner at least through 2006, when he will earn $14.5 million, plus bonuses, a security detail, use of a private plane, and other perks.

There are hard feelings all around when Selig and Beeston secretly meet with Don and Steve Fehr in Milwaukee on December 3 to restart contract talks. Selig is unhappy about having to go to Washington in three days for a hearing to justify contraction. Don Fehr wonders what happened to Beeston's promise, made on September 19, that contraction was off the table. Beeston tells the Fehrs that he spoke in the emotional aftermath of September 11 and should not have been taken seriously.

"You wiped out all the positive feelings we got from the World Series," Fehr tells Selig. "And you made it harder to negotiate."

"I think we can recapture those good feelings," Beeston says. "And I think it's possible to get a quick deal."

On cue, Selig lays out his new plan. A two-year agreement with teams evenly sharing 50 percent of local revenue—more than double the current level—and a permanent 50 percent tax on all payrolls of $98 million and above. A draft of international players, who are now free agents able to sign with any team, and a limit on the amount of debt a team can carry, a clear attempt to rein in deficit-spending teams like the World Champion Diamondbacks.

Accept this deal, Selig says, and we won't contract until 2003.

Don Fehr stares directly at Selig. Fehr's default look is one of disdain, and that is especially true when he's in Selig's presence. How poorly can small market teams be faring if Selig's own team had the highest operating profits this past season? MLB's own numbers show that Miller Park pushed the Brewers into baseball's middle class—indeed, their $16.1 million in operating profits this season ranked first in the game, ahead of the Mariners ($15.5 million) and the Yankees ($14.3 million).

Fehr's response is quick and pointed. This is a big step backwards, he tells the Commissioner. The players don't like the luxury tax, and the increase in revenue sharing would leave rich teams like the Yankees with far less money to spend on players. And Bud's offer to delay contraction? "That promise has little value," Fehr says. "It looks like contraction can't happen until 2003 anyway."

The union leader looks over at Beeston, who is clearly uncomfortable. Fehr knows Paul has fallen out of favor, and he's seen how that script plays out. He watched Selig throw Dick Ravitch, his handpicked labor negotiator, under the bus during the ruinous 1994 talks. Hell, Bud threw the whole sport under the bus that year, canceling the end of the season—and the World Series with it—in the owners' relentless pursuit of a salary cap.

He saw how Selig let Randy Levine twist in the wind in '96 after Fehr and Levine had ironed out a deal. And he knows Beeston is a short-timer now, too. Selig's latest proposal is a big step back from Fehr's talks with Beeston over the last two years—it's even worse than the Blue Ribbon plan—and the union leader can only guess whom Bud will put at the bargaining table next.

"I'm tired of dealing with a puppet," he tells Selig. "Let us know when you want to get serious about these negotiations."

It's December 6, and the Commissioner is sitting in front of the House Judiciary Committee, sharing a table with pro wrestler turned Minnesota Governor Jesse Ventura, Twins President Jerry Bell, and union special counsel Steve Fehr. John Conyers, the longtime Michigan Democrat, requested this hearing to ask why baseball should keep its antitrust exemption and remain a monopoly if it has to shut down two teams in order to turn a profit.

"I come here very interested in what I hear will be some tremendous accounting theories the Commissioner will put forward about how tough things are," says Conyers, whose slowly spoken opening statement drips with sarcasm. "God knows I support the underdog. Let's root for the little guy, like the *owners* who are hemorrhaging."

Selig is the first on the panel to speak. He repeats his well-rehearsed talking points: the half a billion dollars in losses he insists the owners have suffered this past season, their $3 billion overall deficit, the need to shut down two teams—instead of relocating them—in order for the game to survive. His staff has prepared charts and graphs to aid Selig's presentation. "It has become clear," Selig says, pointing to a big chart hanging from an easel at the front of the room, "that there are clubs that generate so little in local revenue that they have no chance of achieving long-term competitive and financial stability."

The hearing is chaired by Jim Sensenbrenner of Wisconsin, who counts Major League Baseball as one of his campaign contributors. The chairman grants Selig an extra 10 minutes for his opening statement— "because it is so complex," Sensenbrenner tells a surprised Conyers—and it's not the last time he will come to the Commissioner's aid today. Selig will stall, dissemble, and take a few body blows, but in the end, baseball's antitrust exemption will remain intact. It always does.

Ventura speaks next, and he's both direct and blunt. "This is asinine—these people did not get wealthy by being stupid," says Ventura. The governor has repeatedly rejected requests for a new stadium from Carl Pohlad, second only to Ted Turner as the richest man in baseball, who turned a profit this year by pocketing his revenue sharing checks and paring the Twins' payroll down to a game-low $24.1 million. Ventura says he won't change his mind, especially with his state facing a $2 billion deficit—but he knows what would happen if he did.

"I bet if we build a new stadium," he says, "there would be no problem keeping a team in Minnesota."

Conyers asks Selig why the financial statements baseball has provided are so short on details, lacking even the salaries given to owners and their families. He also knows the financials MLB gives the union, as per their bargaining agreement, are both confidential and far more thorough. Baseball has already threatened to sue the union should it try to share those statements with Congress, leaving Conyers puzzled.

"The summary information you've turned over to us is meaning-less," Conyers says. "In essence, you've told us, 'We lose money, but we can't trust you with the details.' Would you reconsider to provide this committee with some real records about each team—the sala-ries, consulting fees paid to club owners, their family members?"

> SELIG: Our figures are audited three different ways. The Play-ers Association gets all the numbers. The Blue Ribbon Panel got the audited statements—
> CONYERS: Don't you know the union can't give those state-ments to anybody? You just sent a letter, your lawyers, that you'd sue Fehr if he released—
> SELIG: Congressman Conyers, you have the audited financial statement for six years. You have all the information that Messrs. Volcker, Will, and—
> CONYERS: Staff keeps whispering in my ear, "We don't have the numbers, we don't have the numbers."
> SELIG: I'd like to know, since they've been audited three differ-ent ways, what information are you looking for?
> CONYERS: Didn't you hear me?
> SENSENBRENNER: The time of the gentleman has expired.

A few minutes later, Mel Watt (D-NC) picks up where Conyers was cut off.

> WATT: How does contracting the number of teams fix your problems?
> SELIG: It's one of the things that when we've looked at it, it's one of the things that helps fix the system.
> WATT: How?
> SELIG: How?
> WATT: Have you given us the same records that you've given to the union?
> FEHR: Can I get in on this?
> WATT: Yes, Mr. Fehr.
> FEHR: I believe you have received a fraction of what the players have received.

WATT: So the question is, could we get the same information you've given the players over the last five years?

SELIG: The only thing I'm told that we haven't given you, uh, you have all the same information now that the Blue Ribbon committee had.

WATT: Well, the problem is the Blue Ribbon committee guy [George Mitchell] is now trying to buy into baseball.

Republican Jim Ramstad, who represents a handful of Minneapolis suburbs, poses a question that Selig hoped to avoid. "Let me ask you, Commissioner Selig. Your counsel has not yet selected the teams for contraction, is that correct?"

SELIG: No, I have not selected the teams along with the clubs.

RAMSTAD: The two teams have not yet been selected?

SELIG: That is correct.

But it's California Democrat Maxine Waters whose five minutes of questioning truly puts Selig back on his heels.

"We don't have a lot of time," Waters says and directs her first question to Fehr. "Do you have information from the Commissioner that has not been given to us?"

"I believe we have a lot of information you don't have," says Fehr, who poses a question of his own. "Can we be released from our confidentiality agreement with baseball to give you what you want?"

Waters reads a letter dated November 30 sent to the union and signed by baseball Vice President Robert Manfred. Break the confidentiality agreement, Manfred writes, and we'll pursue immediate legal action.

"Do you feel you cannot answer our questions or you'll be sued by the Commissioner?" Waters asks Fehr.

Yes, he answers.

Waters turns to Selig. "Will you give us the information that the union has?"

Selig offers Waters a puzzled look. "We have given, as I've said before... No American sport has ever given this kind of—"

Waters cuts Selig off in midsentence. "Mr. Commissioner, will you give us the information you have given to the union?"

No, Selig says. "It's confidential."

"Will you permit *the union* to give us this information?" Waters asks.

"You'll have to talk to our lawyers, but they have a confidentiality agreement," Selig says.

Waters allows Fehr to interrupt. Half of what baseball claims it lost comes from four rich teams, Fehr says, all recently purchased by media conglomerates: the Dodgers, Braves, Blue Jays, and Rangers.

"Would you like an explanation for how they can take such losses?" he asks Waters.

"We'd like an explanation," says Waters, turning to Selig. "The federal government is asking you for information," Waters says. "You are not going to give us this information, and you will sue the players if they give it to us. Is that what you are saying to us?"

"No, I don't believe I am," Selig answers.

"What, then, are you saying?"

"I am saying that we have given you all the financials that all of us work with and—"

"Mr. Selig, let me remind you that you are under oath," Waters says sharply, waving a finger at Selig. "I'm going to rephrase my question."

But Sensenbrenner gets there first. "The gentle lady's time has expired," he says. It is the fourth time the chairman has cut off a questioner asking why the union has information this committee does not. The hearing will go on for several hours, but this question is never answered. Nor will the committee subpoena the documents in question.

The information the union has will never see the light of day.

Selig leaves Washington a bit bloodied, but as the year draws to a close, he has almost everything lined up to his liking.

The threat of contraction remains intact, putting pressure on Minnesota politicians to fund a new stadium for his friend Carl Pohlad and tying up the union with a mountain of paperwork. It's also slowing down the free agent market as general managers wait to see if stars like Montreal's Vladimir Guerrero and Minnesota's Johan Santana are going to shake free.

Montreal owner Jeff Loria has been shipped down to Florida, given his sweetheart deal, and finally silenced. Suitors are already lining up to bid on the Expos should Selig decide to move the team to Washington. Meanwhile, the Commissioner will be part owner of a second team, and there'll be no pretense of putting the team in a blind trust, as he did in Milwaukee. Selig will personally name the new president, general manager, and manager of the Expos.

Things continue going Selig's way when, on December 18, a federal judge blocks the Florida attorney general's investigation into contraction. The judge's stated reason: the game's antitrust exemption allows Selig to keep baseball's plans secret. Florida's AG was right—baseball conducts its affairs with the secrecy of a papal election.

And on December 20, Selig gets the news he's been waiting for: Red Sox CEO John Harrington announces the bidding for the iconic franchise has been won by John Henry. The price: a record $700 million, which includes an 80 percent stake in NESN, the all-important cable TV station that carries Red Sox games. Henry's group also includes Tom Werner, who was a big Selig supporter when he ran the small market Padres in the mid-'90s; Werner's San Diego CEO, Larry Lucchino; and George Mitchell, the voice of the Blue Ribbon Panel. All four men will arrive in Boston favoring increased revenue sharing. (At least for now.)

There is immediate pushback to the new Red Sox ownership and its many ties to Selig. Massachusetts Attorney General Tom Reilly, whose job includes overseeing charities that benefit from trusts—like the Yawkey Trust, which controls the Red Sox—says he's launching an investigation into the sale. At issue: why higher bids from New York lawyer Miles Prentice ($790 million) and Cablevision's Chuck Dolan ($720 million) were overlooked. Congressman William Delahunt (D-MA) is wondering the same thing and wants another congressional hearing into baseball's antitrust exemption.

The rabid Boston media quickly accuses the Commissioner of

tipping the scale in favor of Henry, who joined the bidding just four weeks ago after giving up on Eisner and the Angels. "The record will show that when it came time to step up, Harrington caved to Commissioner Bud Selig and the Lords of the Sport," writes *Boston Globe* columnist Dan Shaughnessy, echoing the sentiments of most in the media and Red Sox Nation. "So now we have this band of carpetbaggers, taking charge of our most cherished institution."

Selig does his best to sound indignant. "Frankly I am insulted by the suggestion that we did anything improper," Selig says. "I never instructed John Harrington or any of the bidders to do anything for anyone."

Of course, Selig never had to say anything. He simply had to make it known that baseball would never approve Chuck Dolan or Miles Prentice. Dolan's brother Larry owns the Indians, and few owners wanted to have brothers—or another cable baron—in the game. And there were questions about how much debt Prentice was using to finance his bid. No one wanted another Arizona situation.

But most everyone in ownership favors Henry. Especially Selig, who has listened to the soon-to-be-former Marlins owner beg him to do something about the disparity between rich teams and everyone else in baseball. An ownership with small market sensibilities in a major market is a dream come true. If only Selig could convince Steinbrenner to see things the same way, the end of 2001 would be all but perfect.

But there's little chance of getting George to listen. Only a few days earlier the Yankees signed Jason Giambi, Oakland's best player, to a seven-year, $120 million deal. Giambi hit 38 home runs and drove in 120 runs last season, when he hit .342. And at 30, the big first baseman is still in his prime.

There was no way the small market A's could match the Yankees' offer, though many in Oakland wondered why the A's refused to give Giambi a no-trade clause last spring when he was ready to accept their six-year, $91 million offer. But the money, not Oakland's decision, is Selig's focus. Giambi's deal pushes the Yankees' payroll past $125 million, easily the highest in baseball.

Yet Steinbrenner keeps calling, asking Bud why he's after so much of the Yankees' money. And then George goes off and breaks the bank. Again.

All Bud can tell him is the same thing he's just told Twins fans. Look in the mirror.

Chapter 26

TROUBLE AHEAD

January 17–July 7, 2002

The first month of 2002 is not a time of great optimism in America, and the mood will only grow worse as the year wears on. More troops are shipped out to fight in Afghanistan, the FBI still doesn't know who is sending anthrax-laced letters, and the CIA warns of more terror attacks on U.S. soil. Unemployment, a mere 3.8 percent on Opening Day last April, is now 5.5 percent and rising. Ford fires 35,000 workers—its biggest layoff in two decades—and Houston-based energy giant Enron collapses in an accounting scandal. After a brief comeback, the stock market will hit a four-year low by July.

It's with all this in mind that Don Fehr looks out at baseball's owners and team executives in an airy conference room at the Arizona Biltmore hotel. Fehr is sitting at a table with his brother Steve, Gene Orza, and three players, all here at the behest of Bud Selig. "Many of the owners have never met you," the Commissioner told Fehr. "It can only help us find a way to make a deal."

It's Thursday, January 17, more than three months since baseball's labor contract expired, and not much has changed since November 6, when Selig announced his plan to eliminate two teams. With pitchers and catchers due to report in four weeks, Selig hasn't moved off the proposal Fehr rejected in December.

Fehr doesn't think today's meeting will accomplish much, though anything that might help prevent a ninth straight stoppage of play is worth trying. Especially since there won't be Cal Ripken, Mac and Sammy, and a Yankees three-peat to bail them out this time around. But what, Fehr wonders, can he possibly tell these owners that will help?

That Selig never gave MLB President Paul Beeston authorization to make a deal?

That Selig's plan for contraction has once again turned the game's players against the Commissioner?

That Selig's intransigence means another strike is all but inevitable?

This is precisely what Fehr told the players at the union's Executive Board meeting last month. "Expect the worst," he advised them, even though the business of baseball has never been better. Just yesterday, the owners officially and unanimously approved the sale of the Red Sox and its cable network for $700 million—more than double the previous record price for a franchise, set just two years ago. John Henry and his partners were so eager to close the deal they agreed to give $30 million to local charities so Massachusetts Attorney General Tom Reilly would stop asking why two higher offers were turned down.

Fehr decides it's best just to clear the air.

"Negotiations on a new contract have always been contentious," Fehr tells the owners. "We tried to avoid that by having secret talks with Paul Beeston and Rob Manfred, but Bud Selig halted those talks without so much as an explanation."

Fehr looks to the back of the room, where Selig is pacing, as Bud usually does when others are speaking, and then over at Beeston, the only baseball official sitting at the table with him and his staff. He knows Selig will soon replace Beeston. Selig never cared much for Beeston's friendly relationship with the union, and Beeston has long since tired of trying to get a straight answer from the Commissioner.

"We never received a counterproposal," Fehr says. "Then you sprang contraction on the players after telling us you would not contract in 2002. That's not the way we should do business."

Still, Fehr tells them, the union is willing to overlook all this "in the interest of making a deal peacefully."

He can almost hear all their eyes rolling.

Fehr can't resist tweaking the Commissioner, so he walks his audience through the litany of bad press baseball has received since the end of the World Series. The fierce backlash over contraction. The news of a loan Pohlad made to Selig in 1995 that violated baseball's rules. Calls for Selig to resign from Congressman John Conyers and politicians in Minnesota and Florida.

"We certainly hope," Fehr says, "that this period will be brought to an end."

When Fehr is done lecturing, Selig opens the floor for questions. And that's when San Diego's John Moores shows just how much tension remains between the owners and the union leader.

"Do you believe us when we tell you about the losses we have suffered?" the Padres owner asks, looking toward the three players—Tony Clark, Mark Loretta, and Rich Aurilia—sitting with Fehr.

Fehr begins to answer, but Moores instantly cuts him off.

"I want to hear what the players have to say," Moores says tersely.

Selig jumps in quickly. "John," he says, "they can answer your question however they want."

Honestly, says Fehr, it's hard to take your claims seriously when so much of your losses are accounting maneuvers. All three players nod in agreement, and more eyes roll. Only a few more questions are asked before Selig signals the session is about to end. "We are ready to make a deal," Fehr says. "We just ask that you think about things from our point of view as well as your own."

The meeting adjourns. Fehr and Selig meet the media separately, and any illusion of cooperation instantly disappears. Fehr is asked if the players will pledge not to strike. No, he says, "but a strike is considered a last resort." Selig's proposal to increase revenue sharing to 50 percent from 20 percent is simply too high, he says, and the demand for a permanent luxury tax is a real reach. "Players aren't luxuries," Fehr says.

Selig tells reporters he has no plans to lock out players when spring training opens next month, but he won't take that option off the table, either. "You never rule anything out forever." And contraction, he insists, is still in the picture.

But Selig tips his hand, saying that relocation is coming in the near future, with Washington the prime candidate. Translation: baseball will take possession of the Expos as soon as Henry and Montreal owner Jeff Loria agree on a price for the Marlins. The team will play this season in Montreal, then move to Washington in 2003—Selig's promise to Baltimore owner Peter Angelos to stay out of the D.C. market be damned.

Everything falls in place for Selig in the next few weeks. On February 4, the Minnesota Supreme Court saves Selig from the embarrassment of calling off contraction when it rules the Twins must play the 2002 season in the Metrodome. "While the clubs would have preferred to contract for 2002," Selig says with a straight face, "events outside of our direct control have required us to move the date of contraction to 2003."

The owners approve the sale of the Marlins to Loria and make baseball's purchase of the Expos official on February 12. That allows Selig to make a public relations splash by naming Omar Minaya the team's GM—the game's first Hispanic general manager—and Frank Robinson the new manager.

With the decks clear, contract talks are set to resume the first week of March with a slightly different look. Rob Manfred, long Selig's back-channel conduit to labor talks, is now Bud's lead negotiator. Bob DuPuy, who officially replaces the ousted Beeston on March 3 as president and COO, also has a seat at the table.

Negotiations open on March 4 and are civil at first, but things turn personal just one day later. A rumor circulating for weeks finally makes its way into the national media: sources say the players are considering a boycott of this season's All-Star Game if a new labor agreement is not reached by the break.

The site of the game: Milwaukee.
The goal of the story: embarrass the Commissioner.
The tone of the 2002 labor talks has just been set.

George Steinbrenner strides into the crowded conference room at Legends Field, where a meeting of the Board of YankeeNets and several of its investors is about to start. There is a lengthy agenda for the three-year-old company, but it's an item that's not on the list that's got everyone's attention. It's almost noon on March 19, the official launch day for the Yankees Entertainment and Sports Network, and all eyes are soon riveted on the televisions placed around the room.

The screens turn Yankees blue, a countdown appears, and the final 10 seconds tick off before yielding to the familiar stentorian voice of Yankees PA announcer Bob Sheppard. "Your attention, please, ladies and gentlemen," says the man who's introduced every Yankees lineup for the past 50 years. "You're watching the YES Network, the home of champions."

As former CNN sports anchor Fred Hickman talks about one YES program after another, Steinbrenner knows exactly what he's watching: a way to truly maximize the value of the Yankees.

"George," YES CEO Leo Hindery says after Hickman's 30-minute introduction is done and the Board meeting is set to begin. "This network is going to be around for a long time."

Hindery and his new staff got YES up and running from scratch in just six months, but there were plenty of hurdles. The first came almost immediately, when Quadrangle, one of the two private equity firms financing the network, was unable to raise the funds it needed after the attacks of September 11 and pulled out seven days after the deal was announced. Goldman Sachs stepped up and put another $150 million into the deal, cementing their relationship with the Steinbrenners and the Yankees.

The biggest obstacle was and remains Chuck Dolan, who has been true to his word. Cablevision's 3 million customers are not watching today's broadcast, and they won't see a single game this season. Dolan is refusing to pay the steep price YES is getting from the other cable companies in the metro area—$2 per subscriber per month—and he's steadfastly refused to make the Yankees part of Cablevision's basic package. Every Board member here today knows the battle with George's friend from Cleveland will be won or lost in court, so there is still much work to do.

The war with Dolan will be costly—more than $70 million in lost revenue alone—but Steinbrenner now has a television network, which means the Yankees are no longer just a baseball team. They're a reality TV show, and putting a star-driven championship team on the field has never been more important, no matter what restrictions Selig tries to put on them.

It's a very different team that YES will showcase in this, the Yankees' 100th season. Gone are Paul O'Neill, Tino Martinez, Scott Brosius, and Chuck Knoblauch, departing with 14 World Series rings among them. In their place are free agents Robin Ventura and Rondell White, rookie Nick Johnson, and the marquee attraction, Jason Giambi.

The Yankees were so eager to get Giambi's big bat for the middle of their lineup that they were willing to overlook his almost daily misadventures at first base. Giambi has an average glove, limited range, and a scattershot arm. Yankees fans—and infielders—used to the Gold Glove of Don Mattingly and the dependable defense of Martinez are in for a shock.

The Yankees were also willing to grant a request made by Giambi's agent: remove any mention of the word *steroids* from his contract. The Yankees now insert steroids language into every contract, a response to widespread suspicion about the use of the performance-enhancing drugs. The team granted Giambi's request, confident the contract still contained language about the use of illegal drugs that could void the deal should Jason be found using steroids. And there's little reason to think their decision will ever be made public.

The team will be stunned when it learns neither assumption is true.

Steinbrenner finally met the big first baseman on the first full day of workouts last month. He walked over to Giambi at the batting cage, hugged the man he will pay $120 million over the next seven years, and gave him some simple advice. "Just be yourself," he told

Giambi, who had to trim his hair and shave his scraggly beard to conform to Steinbrenner's rules.

"Thanks for making a dream come true," said Giambi, who cried when looking over at his father, John, during his New York media conference back in December. Father and son are lifelong Yankees fans; Giambi chose the No. 25 because the two numbers add up to seven, the number worn by his father's idol, Mickey Mantle.

If Giambi simply matches his average production of the past three seasons—38 home runs, 114 RBI, a .330 batting average, and .458 on-base percentage—Steinbrenner will have few worries about the Yankees offense. And the only apparent problem with his pitching staff for the coming season is having six veteran starters for their five-man rotation. The Boss, who entertained writers in spring training with tall tales of his "semiretirement," personally re-signed David Wells at year's end, soon after Brian Cashman signed Sterling Hitchcock to join Roger Clemens, Mike Mussina, Andy Pettitte, and Orlando Hernandez.

Steinbrenner got plenty of flak for once again undermining his GM, but his decision looks smart two weeks into the season when Pettitte injures his elbow trying to put something extra on a fastball and winds up on the disabled list. Pettitte has battled elbow trouble since '96, his second season as a Yankee, and he's learned how to pitch in pain. But this time it's different. The pain is too great, and two weeks on the DL turns to four, with no end in sight.

The Yankees send him to Dr. James Andrews, who assures Pettitte there is no structural damage and advises rest and continued rehab in Tampa. But Pettitte isn't sure that's enough and sends for Brian McNamee, whom Cashman fired at the end of last season for recruiting players to use him as a personal trainer. Clemens hired McNamee to train him this offseason, often inviting Pettitte to join him in the workouts, and now Andy has a special request.

"Dude, I'm hurt pretty bad," he tells McNamee. "You said human growth hormone can heal tissue fast. I think I want to try it."

"Andy, are you sure?" McNamee asks.

"Yeah, I mean, I'm making a lot of money," Pettitte says. "I need to get back."

Pettitte gets four shots of HGH from McNamee over the next two days. But his pain persists, and it will be mid-June before he rejoins the Yankees.

While Pettitte mends, Giambi starts slowly and finds out just how demanding Yankees fans can be. He hears the boos in the home opener—his fourth game as a Yankee—when he grounds into a double play with two runners on base. The boos get louder when he strikes out in his next two at bats, and a few chants of "Tino, Tino" are mixed in when he hits a dribbler in front of the plate. A fly out in the 8th inning of a 4–0 Yankees win leaves Giambi at 2 for 16 and still looking for his first RBI.

An old friend gives Giambi a call later that night with a little advice. "Hey, just relax," says Mark McGwire, who retired last November after two injury-filled seasons. "You're too good a player. Just go about your game."

Giambi is still using Deca-Durabolin, the same powerful steroid he used in Oakland, and his bat clicks into gear in May. Giambi hits his fifth home run of the young season in a 9–2 win over the A's on May 2, Torre's 600th win with the Yankees. He blasts a grand slam through the driving rain in the 14th inning at the Stadium on May 17, wiping out a three-run Twins lead to give the Yankees a wild 13–12 win. On May 27, Giambi hits a pair of home runs in a 10–6 win over the White Sox.

In 28 games in May, Giambi bats .340, with 10 doubles, 24 RBI, and 10 home runs. This is the big bopper Steinbrenner expected. And the Yankees are winning—they're 36–19 by month's end, two behind Boston in the AL East—and their 87 home runs put them on pace to break the team's record of 240, set 41 years ago.

"It's nice to have that weapon," Torre says. "You get behind and, 'Boom.' It's something we haven't had in the last several years. But I still don't want to rely on that."

Maybe not. But Torre's boss isn't complaining. Home runs make for good television, and Steinbrenner and his YankeeNets partners now have a network to think about, too.

Ken Caminiti shifts in his seat as the reporter from *Sports Illustrated* reviews the ground rules for their interview one more time.

Caminiti's known Tom Verducci for a number of years, and when the *SI* baseball writer called a few days back and asked if he'd be willing to talk about steroid use in baseball, Caminiti wasn't surprised. It's only a matter of time before someone talks openly about the worst-kept secret in baseball, he figured. Might as well be him.

It's early April, the first spring Caminiti hasn't been on a major league baseball field in 15 years, and life without baseball has not been easy. Hell, life *with* baseball was never easy for him, either. The Braves released him on November 6. Eight days later Houston police opened the door to his room at a Ramada Limited hotel, smelled crack cocaine burning, and arrested Caminiti and two younger men. All three were charged with possession of the drug.

He pleaded guilty as charged on March 21, and State District Judge Bill Harmon told Caminiti he was getting a big break: three years' probation, with orders to attend weekly therapy sessions and continue the 12-step Alcoholics Anonymous program he'd already started. "You've committed your last offense," Harmon told the 38-year-old. "You've had your last drink. You've had your last controlled substance."

And now Caminiti's in his house in Houston, ready to talk about one of the controlled substances he took while playing baseball. He's already told Verducci he won't talk about other players. But he will speak on the record about what he did and why he did it.

"Okay," says Verducci, holding out his digital recorder. "If you're ready, I'll turn this on and we can get started."

"Sure," says Caminiti, and he begins telling Verducci about his use of steroids. About how he started injecting the drug in 1996, the year he won his MVP with the Padres, and how he never stopped. About coming to spring training "as big as an ox" in '98, the season he led San Diego to the World Series. About how the drug changed him and how it's changed the game.

"At first I felt like a cheater," he says. "But I looked around, and everybody was doing it. Back then you had to go and find it in Mexico or someplace. Now it's everywhere."

Caminiti talks about how steroids made him feel stronger and faster and how the drug gave him confidence and focus. How he could swing with almost no effort and "crush the ball 450 feet." About how he doesn't believe an asterisk should be placed beside his name and the 239 home runs he hit. "I've made a ton of mistakes," Caminiti says. "I don't think using steroids is one of them."

What would he tell younger players? "I can't say, 'Don't do it,' not when the guy next to you is as big as a house and he's going to take your job."

How many players are using steroids now? "It's no secret what's going on in baseball—at least half the guys are using steroids. The guys who want to protect themselves by lying have that right. But I've got nothing to hide."

The two men talk straight through the afternoon. Caminiti talks about the price he paid, the torn tendons and pulled muscles that came from getting too big too fast. He talks about his estranged wife, too. The only good thing about being out of baseball, he says, is he can make the 45-minute drive to Nancy's house and see their three daughters more often.

Verducci tells him *Sports Illustrated* has been working on this story for almost three months and that dozens of players, team executives, and trainers have talked about what they've seen. "You've got guys in their late 30s, almost 40, throwing the ball 96 to 99, and they never threw that hard before," Texas pitcher Kenny Rogers told *SI*. "I'm sorry, that's not natural evolution." Says Arizona's Curt Schilling, "I know plenty of guys now are mixing steroids with human growth hormone. Those guys are pretty obvious."

But Rogers and Schilling don't name any users. No one does. And Caminiti is the only player willing to admit he used performance-enhancing drugs.

"This is going to be pretty big, isn't it?" Caminiti says.

"Yes, it is," Verducci answers.

"I don't have anything to hide," Caminiti replies.

Caminiti is right—the story is big, and the reaction to his words is swift and predictable.

Fans who rushed to fill stadiums and watch their heroes crush batting practice homers now complain about a record book rendered meaningless and wonder which performances they can trust. Writers who just four seasons ago gushed over McGwire's

19-inch biceps now point fingers at oversized players and speculate about which ones are cheating.

Senator John McCain, who voted to deregulate the supplement industry eight years ago—which resulted in amphetamine- and steroid-laced products popping up on health food store shelves everywhere—quickly calls for hearings. And owners who profited so handsomely from the steroid-fueled game—including the one sitting in the Commissioner's office—bang the table for testing after hiding behind the union's privacy concerns for most of a decade.

Caminiti quickly tries to walk back his estimate of the number of players using steroids, but it is too late. Reporters now start almost every interview by asking if a player is one out of every two major leaguers using steroids. Jose Canseco upped the ante just days after the *SI* story, confirming that he had also used steroids. The former MVP claims in mid-May that 85 percent of the game's players were users, too, and promises to tell all in a book he plans to write.

Selig was worried about a scandal even before Caminiti came clean and had asked Manfred to put a testing proposal on the table in March. This was something management did not do in 1996, despite the Commissioner's subsequent—and increasingly frequent—claims to the contrary. Manfred's proposal bans steroids and Andro, and requires three random tests a year for all major league players. Repeat offenders would be disciplined, but results would be kept confidential.

The union still opposed testing but knew it had to respond to Manfred's proposal. And that's when Gene Orza started talking to Don Fehr about survey testing—where players would be tested but not identified—to determine what percentage of players were really taking performance-enhancing drugs (PEDs). All results would be kept private, but if an agreed-upon percentage of players tested positive in 2003, it would trigger random testing with penalties.

Now, with management pushing hard for testing and chatter about steroids at an all-time high, the union schedules a meeting with every team to get the players' views. Nothing has divided players more than the subject of testing, even players who want no part of PEDs. Much of their concern revolves around trust: Will the owners keep the results confidential? Will they use positive tests to get rid of players they no longer want and look the other way with their stars? Who will conduct the tests? Will there be an appeals process? And can they be sure the government will never take possession of the results?

Fehr has taken plenty of criticism for his steadfast stand against drug testing, but this issue is far more complicated than most people are willing to admit, inside the game and out. How can you tell players to stop taking legal supplements, even though you know some of them may contain illegal substances? How many veterans have heard GMs tell them to "get bigger" because the game relies on home runs now, not singles and doubles? What do you tell the many Hispanic players who grew up using steroids — which are legal in their countries — when they return home to play winter ball?

These and other issues are on Fehr's mind when he flies to Washington on June 18 to appear with Manfred before a Senate Commerce subcommittee overseeing baseball. McCain uses his opening statement to say he is greatly concerned about baseball, but he's "more concerned about the effect this recent spate of publicity has on young athletes all over America." Manfred calls steroid use "a high-priority item for us" and says MLB has been waiting three months for the union to respond to its drug testing proposal.

Subcommittee chairman Byron Dorgan (D-ND) says he doesn't want to see baseball become a game in which players are forced to "engage in the use of performance-enhancing drugs in order to make it." Fehr says all talk of testing comes down to one word: privacy. "The Players Association has always believed that one should not invade the privacy of an individual without cause related to conduct," he says, "merely because of his status as a baseball player."

Both Manfred and Fehr ask Congress to look into the problems it caused by deregulating the supplement industry. "With all due respect," Fehr says, "if children are using substances like Androstenedione, it is in large part because 11-year-olds can walk into stores and buy them. Congress can do something about that.

"It doesn't answer the question of what you do in baseball. But I respectfully suggest it's a much bigger question."

Fehr's suggestion does little to pacify McCain, who wonders if ballplayers realize the credibility of their sport is at stake. "Players read the newspapers, they watch television," Fehr answers. "They understand the significance that this particular controversy has."

Senator Peter Fitzgerald (R-IL) is more pointed. "Do members of your union understand if they oppose mandatory drug testing they could be inviting congressional action and that it would probably be more draconian than a voluntary program amongst the players and owners?"

Yes, Fehr says, they do. "I can assure you that as the players debate and discuss this among themselves, the views of everyone will be taken into consideration," he says.

Fehr leaves Washington without committing to drug testing, but he realizes once team meetings resume that the mood of the players has changed. Even players who remain opposed to testing realize public pressure—and the politicians—will not disappear without a drug testing agreement. On July 7, USA Today runs a CNN/Gallup/USA Today poll showing 86 percent of baseball fans think players should be tested for steroids and 80 percent think steroids were a factor in many of the records that have recently fallen.

That same day, USA Today releases another poll showing 79 percent of major league players favor independent testing for steroids. "I don't have a problem with getting tested because I have nothing to hide," Derek Jeter tells the newspaper. "Steroids are a big issue. If anything like a home run or any injury happens, people say it's steroids. That's not fair."

Not every player agrees with Jeter, including Yankees player rep Mike Stanton. "It is not as easy as saying yes or no; there's legal stuff," Stanton says. But Fehr and Orza have heard enough. They'll run Orza's survey idea past the players on the Executive Board later this month, and if the Board doesn't have strong objections, Fehr will put it on the bargaining table in early August.

The plan is not perfect, but it's one the union leaders can live with. At worst, it gives steroid users time to get off the stuff. But both men fail to anticipate just how many players take the game one season at a time. Steroids are making some of them rich and keeping many others in the game. If these players fail their tests, the only consequence might be random drug testing next season. They'll deal with that if and when the time comes.

Besides, most players are confident the union will be there to protect them. It always has, and there is no reason to believe that will change.

Chapter 27

NEW DEALS

July 5–August 30, 2002

It's the first of five days of All-Star festivities in Milwaukee, and Bud Selig, the man most responsible for this grand show coming to his hometown, is once again playing the gracious host. Selig kicks it all off on Friday, July 5, personally welcoming the first wave of fans to MLB's FanFest, where fans young and old can face life-size images of Roger Clemens and Mark McGwire in state-of-the-art batting and pitching cages, take a seat in a replica MLB dugout, and, of course, get free autographs from current Brewers and star old-timers like Rollie Fingers, Fergie Jenkins, and Rusty Staub.

The ESPN star-making machine showcases the game's home run hitters in the popular home run derby Monday night before the All-Star Game. Jason Giambi belts 24 balls into the Miller Park grandstands to beat Sammy Sosa by six. Barry Bonds, the game's foremost home run hitter, manages just two, then laughs about it with Selig while sitting at the Commissioner's table at the All-Star banquet a few hours later.

But no one is laughing the next night—least of all Bud—when an entertaining and well-played All-Star Game is tied 7–7 in the middle of the 11th inning and both teams are out of pitchers and players. The camera zooms in on the perplexed Commissioner as he talks nervously with managers Joe Torre and Bob Brenly from his box near the NL dugout. Finally, Selig throws up his hands and tells the umpiring crew the game is over even if the NL fails to score in the bottom of the inning.

The sellout crowd of 41,871 erupts as soon as the public address announcer relays Selig's decision. With tickets priced at $175 and $125, it's hard to blame them. Forgotten are Torii Hunter's spectacular catch to rob Bonds of a home run in the 1st inning and the monster shot Barry hit off the facing of the second deck for a two-run homer in the 3rd. Instead, a visibly distressed Selig endures a half inning of continual boos and chants of "Let Them Play," and more than a few calls of "Bud Must Go!"

Selig's crowning-achievement-turned-nightmare ends when Giants catcher Benito Santiago looks at a called third strike for the final out, leaving the Marlins' Mike Lowell stranded at second. It's the first time the Midsummer Classic has ended in a tie since 1961, back when baseball played two All-Star Games a year. "Clearly, this is not the ending I had hoped for," the embarrassed Commissioner says a few moments later. "I can't articulate how tough it is."

The writers can. Ken Daley of the *Dallas Morning News* calls the tie "the most serious black eye for his staggering sport since Selig canceled the 1994 World Series." Dwight Perry of the *Seattle Times* asks, "Is it just us, or has baseball's Bud Selig Era just been one never-ending Bad Hair Day?" The *New York Post*'s Tom Keegan writes, "It went on forever and solved nothing, following the same path as labor strife during Bud's tumultuous reign as baseball's Commissioner."

But the action that really matters took place earlier that day. That's when four men—the union's Michael Weiner and Steve Fehr, MLB's Bob DuPuy and Rob Manfred—met at the Milwaukee law office of Foley & Lardner. The Gang of Four talked for 40 minutes with one goal in mind: jump-starting contract talks, which have been stalled amid the usual accusations of bad faith from both sides.

All four quickly agreed that the shutdown everyone is now predicting would be nothing short of disastrous. How can baseball tell America it can't figure out how to share revenues of more than

$3.5 billion when the country is mired in a recession, unemployment is rising, and the stock market is cratering? And no one wants to think about pictures of empty stadiums on the first anniversary of September 11.

They all understood both sides have a lot to lose. The owners are projecting $3.6 billion in revenue and 68 million in attendance. The players hit a record-high $2.4 million average salary this season. Baseball would be forced to give Fox a $500 million refund if another postseason is lost. And a recent poll showed baseball a strong No. 2 in the hearts and minds of sports fans, a long way from its fifth-place ranking—right behind women's figure skating—after the shutdown in '94.

Are they really going to put all that at risk again?

Yes, there are areas of great disagreement. The union thinks Selig's revenue sharing demands would depress salaries and discourage big market teams from working to increase revenues—why take risks when you'd only keep about half the reward? They question changing from a split revenue sharing pool to a straight pool, which benefits baseball's middle class instead of teams with the least revenue. Weiner and Fehr made it clear that the players are still opposed to contraction. And there's no way the union will ever agree to Selig's request for a $100 million fund to use as he sees fit. Distrust of this Commissioner still runs deep—very deep.

DuPuy and Manfred were adamant that the owners need to tax the highest payrolls. Sure, call it a Yankees tax, but they have to rein in the big spenders—especially Steinbrenner, who pays backups more than some teams pay their stars. They want an international draft to keep George from driving up the price of foreign talent. They want to establish a ratio of assets to debt—a debt service rule—so no team can follow the Diamondbacks' example and borrow so heavily they have to beg players to defer salaries just to make payroll.

And the Commissioner's men make it clear that a drug testing agreement is a must—Selig is no longer willing to risk a scandal on his watch. (Little did any of them know that an anonymous IRS agent in San Francisco is already working hard to turn steroid use into the biggest scandal the game's ever seen.)

DuPuy, Manfred, Weiner, and Fehr all know the clock is ticking, even though the union decided against setting a strike date at their

Executive Board meeting yesterday in Chicago. The Gang of Four left Foley & Lardner agreeing on only two things: they would keep the lines of communication open and they'd keep their talks out of the press. It wasn't much, but at least they could report back to Selig and Don Fehr that negotiations have started again.

Selig gets out of a limousine in front of baseball's Park Avenue headquarters, rushes past a man yelling obscenities at him, and takes the elevator up to his office on the 31st floor. It's August 28, and there is reason to believe that a new collective bargaining agreement with the players might be at hand. It's also less than 48 hours before the union's strike date, set two weeks ago, and history is not on their side. The time has come for the Commissioner to leave Milwaukee and be where the action is.

Selig has no intention of sitting down at the bargaining table himself. Like Don Fehr, Selig has allowed the Gang of Four to do the heavy lifting, signing off if and when he's satisfied with the results. And the results have been positive, even if the process has often been two steps forward, one step back.

A pair of major breakthroughs came in early August, when the two sides agreed on Gene Orza's survey testing proposal and then came to an understanding on a debt service rule. Both sides gave ground on revenue sharing, but talks stalled over the luxury tax, and on August 16 the union finally set a strike date: August 30, the Friday of Labor Day weekend, traditionally one of baseball's biggest gates of the season.

Once more, a season of record-setting performances was put in jeopardy, leaving baseball fans—from teenage girls in Jeter jerseys to the man in the Oval Office—in an uproar. "The baseball owners and baseball players must understand if there is a work stoppage, a lot of fans are going to be furious," President Bush said when the strike date was announced. "And I'm one of them."

The Gang of Four almost cleared the luxury tax hurdle when the union proposed a fundamental change. If the tax is really about reining in big spenders rather than holding down salaries, Weiner said, lower the tax rate but allow it to increase each time a team crosses the threshold. Management agreed. But progress again stalled when Don Fehr sent a letter to agents—leaked to the *New York Times*—claiming the owners' proposal would greatly increase both the Yankees' and Mets' revenue sharing and tax bill. The plan, Fehr wrote, is "tantamount to a salary cap."

George Steinbrenner is more than aware of the damage Selig's plan will do to his bottom line, and the two old friends have been arguing over the Commissioner's proposals for most of the season. The Boss, whose payroll is now a record $135 million, has already hired star lawyer David Boies and threatened Bud with a lawsuit if Selig doesn't scale back his demands. Yankees President Randy Levine has been all but living at MLB headquarters, pounding away at Selig's lieutenants for a deal that would treat George's team more kindly, an outcome that seems increasingly unlikely.

The Gang of Four continued to narrow the differences in the days following Fehr's letter. But on August 24, Fehr attended a bargaining session at MLB and told management negotiators—now including Peter Angelos and Cubs CEO Andy MacPhail—that the players wanted to phase in revenue sharing. The meeting devolved into a shouting match, and Manfred shared his frustration in a conference call with the media.

"We could not have been more disappointed," Manfred said. "I don't think the proposal they made will help us. I don't think Don getting angry helped us, and I must admit I don't think these conference calls are going to help us."

The next morning Steve Fehr received a call on his cell phone. "Okay," Manfred said, "where do we go from here?"

And now it's almost 6 p.m. on August 28, and Manfred and DuPuy are briefing Selig on where negotiations stand. The union has accepted the luxury tax. Management has agreed to phasing in revenue sharing. But the two sides remain apart on the numbers, including the percentage of players who must fail the drug test in order for penalty testing to kick in. "The same issues still exist," Selig tells reporters when he leaves MLB offices late Wednesday night. "I think today's meetings have been very constructive. But I can't say we're any closer on those issues."

The next day is a marathon of meetings, conference calls, and rumors as the Gang of Four works to beat the clock. Manfred and

DuPuy say they are willing to lower the owners' revenue sharing number, and Weiner and Steve Fehr say they can live without the last year of the five-year deal being tax-free. An agreement is reached on drug testing: if 5 percent of the players test positive for steroids next year, drug testing with penalties will start in 2004.

Selig holds a series of calls to update the owners. Don Fehr is five blocks away at union headquarters with the Braves' Tom Glavine and B. J. Surhoff, debriefing his brother and Weiner, then updating player reps around the country by phone. But both Atlanta players, like everyone else in baseball, are still wondering whether they will be playing tomorrow.

In Washington, Bush says he won't get involved but asks players and owners to think about what a strike would do to America's national spirit. And Senator Arlen Specter says Congress will again hold hearings on revoking baseball's antitrust exemption if the players go out on strike.

Steinbrenner and Levine take turns calling Selig to air their concerns. The Yankees are playing in Toronto, where a sign saying SAVE BASEBALL. CONTRACT THE YANKEES hangs from the upper deck. "They're blaming the Yankees because other people don't make money. That doesn't make sense to me," Torre says before the game. His shortstop agrees. "We have an owner who wants the best team on the field to win," Jeter says. "You can't fault him for that."

Both sides hold late-night conference calls. The payroll figure at which the tax would kick in remains the key issue. It's past midnight when Selig leaves to catch some sleep at his hotel while the Gang of Four practices shuttle diplomacy. They meet at MLB at 1:30 a.m., with tax levels still the biggest of several sticking points. At 4:30 a.m. Manfred and DuPuy leave for a meeting at the union, taking a freight elevator to a rear exit to avoid the four dozen or so reporters waiting in a light drizzle for a decision.

Weiner and Steve Fehr are back at MLB at 6 a.m. to hear another management offer. The session lasts 30 minutes, and as Fehr pulls on his backpack over the same yellow shirt he's worn for two days and begins his walk back to the union, a new thought occurs to him: unless something goes wildly off track at the last minute, there is not enough left in dispute to justify a work stoppage. A deal, Fehr realizes, is inevitable.

Not everyone back at union headquarters agrees. Both Don Fehr and Gene Orza are toying with the idea of going out for the weekend. The small market teams pushing the hardest line are in no position to take a financial hit, they reason, and a short break in play could lead to a better deal. But Glavine makes it clear the players have no desire to strike, especially with the two sides so close. Instead, it's time to make two important calls.

"We're coming over," Weiner says when Manfred answers his phone. "Don and Gene will be with us. Glavine and Surhoff are coming, too."

The next call is to Red Sox player rep Tony Clark, a rising star in the union who has told his teammates to gather at Fenway Park rather than meet at the airport for their flight to Cleveland, where they're scheduled to play at 7:05 p.m. It's almost 7:30 a.m. when Steve Fehr calls Clark with news that an agreement is all but done. "Stay near a phone," he says.

Selig has returned by the time of Weiner's call, and Manfred and DuPuy walk to his office with the news. "It's over," DuPuy says. "They cannot come over here with Don and the players, with all the reporters downstairs, to tell us anything other than they are accepting the deal."

It's just past 9 a.m. when the union contingent arrives. DuPuy and Manfred show the delegation into a big conference room, where Angelos and MacPhail await, then ask the Fehr brothers and Weiner to join them in Selig's office down the hall.

"It's good to see you again, Don," Selig says from behind his desk.

"Glad we are here before the deadline," Fehr says.

Everyone takes a seat, and there is a quick review of where negotiations stand. The deal is oh-so-close, with a few details on tax thresholds, free agent compensation, and the minimum wage still unresolved.

"We have made a lot of progress," Selig says. "There are only a few things left to get done. Let's get this deal done today and finally avoid a work stoppage."

"We agree," Don Fehr says.

And with that all but Selig rise and walk down to the conference room to work out the final details. Each time a decision is reached, DuPuy and Manfred get up, walk back down the hall, and run it past Selig.

The three men had discussed refusing to make any changes before the union arrived, but they also realized there was no reason to draw a hard line, not with a deal so close. An hour later, Manfred and DuPuy take one last proposal to Selig. "Is this it?" Selig asks. Yes, his two lieutenants tell him.

"Well, let's bring everyone in."

There is a palpable sense of relief as both bargaining teams assemble in Selig's office.

"I am delighted that we have reached an agreement before the deadline," Selig says.

"I'm happy we were able to get this done," Don Fehr says. "And relieved."

There are few pats on the back and much work still to be done. A joint media conference is set a few blocks away, at the InterContinental Hotel. Selig wants to start calling the owners in his inner circle. Fehr will be talking to player reps.

Weiner walks out and calls Clark in Boston. "It's done," Weiner tells the veteran, and at 11:30 a.m. the Red Sox are aboard a bus and on the way to Logan Airport for their flight to Cleveland. Not a single inning of a single game will be missed for the first time since—well, since forever.

At 1 p.m., Fehr and Selig stand side by side at a podium, banners for MLB and the union hanging behind them. Their crisp dark suits, dress shirts, and ties—red print for Selig, gold print for Fehr—can't mask each man's fatigue as the televised media conference begins.

"I think a lot of people never believed they would live long enough to see these two parties come together, make a very meaningful deal, and do it without one day of a work stoppage," Selig says. When Selig strains to hear a reporter's question, Fehr leans over and whispers the question in Bud's ear. It's the closest the two men have been in years.

"The thing that makes me the happiest is we can now once again turn our complete attention to the field," Selig says.

"All streaks come to an end," says Fehr, "and this is one that was overdue."

By any measure, the deal is a win for the owners—especially those in small markets. There's a substantial increase in revenue sharing—from 20 percent to 34 percent of local revenue—which will be phased in and reach $258 million when fully implemented in the third year of the four-year deal. Fehr says the union accepted a permanent competitive balance tax that will increase from 17.5 percent to a maximum 40 percent depending on the number of consecutive times a team crosses the graduated thresholds.

Contraction is off the table until the deal runs out on December 19, 2006, but the union has agreed not to stand in the owners' way if they choose to contract two teams in 2007. Teams will have three years to comply with a new debt service rule, and the minimum salary increases to $300,000.

And drug testing is now part of baseball. Every player will be tested at least once in 2003, with management allowed to randomly test up to 240 players a second time. All results will be anonymous. If 5 percent of players fail the test, penalty testing will start in 2004. If 2.5 percent or less test positive for two consecutive years, testing will end.

"I think the deal is sensitive to the concerns I've raised over the years," Selig says. "Both sides feel comfortable with what's been done here. I certainly do."

The team hit hardest: Steinbrenner's Yankees, who will pay an estimated $50–$55 million in revenue sharing and taxes in 2003. To no one's surprise, Steinbrenner is the only owner who votes against the deal. The Boss is still considering a lawsuit against baseball.

The big winner: Selig's Brewers, who'll receive a $16.3 million payday under the new revenue sharing plan. It's the biggest win in years for Milwaukee. The Brewers' response: cut the payroll by $10 million.

Chapter 28

RENOVATIONS

September 25–December 29, 2002

Wᴇɴᴅʏ Sᴇʟɪɢ-Pʀɪᴇʙ ʟᴏᴏᴋs once more at the mirror she's pulled from her purse, pushes back her dark brown hair, and takes a deep breath. This moment has been coming for months, ever since she told her father she wanted to step down as the president and CEO of his baseball team. The announcement was set for tomorrow, September 26, three days before this awful season will mercifully end.

She had planned to walk out and meet the media, smile, and introduce local hero Ulice Payne as the new president of the Brewers. And in her final act as president, she was going to introduce former Texas GM Doug Melvin as the new general manager, the man who'll team with Payne to usher in a new era for Milwaukee baseball.

That was her plan. But all that changed earlier today, when she learned someone had leaked the news to the *Milwaukee Journal Sentinel*. A radio host with a drive time talk show also had the news. So she finally told Dean Taylor that his three-year run as Brewers GM was over this morning. And now she's taking one more deep breath before facing the cameras and reporters in the hastily called media conference this late September evening at Miller Park.

Just one more botched play in a season Wendy would just as soon forget.

First it was firing manager Davey Lopes after 15 games—12 of them losses. Then slugger Geoff Jenkins went down for the season in mid-June when he slid awkwardly into third base and blew out the ligaments in his right ankle. Interim manager Jerry Royster's embarrassing on-the-field argument with closer Mike DeJean punctuated July.

Outfielder Alex Sanchez was disciplined for laughing in the outfield in late August, only to break his leg while sliding into second base on September 1. They benched Jose Hernandez eight times in the final two weeks of the season so the veteran shortstop would finish with 188 strikeouts, one short of the single-season strikeout record.

No Brewers regular will hit .300 or 30 home runs or score 100 runs. No starting pitcher will win more games than he's lost or have an ERA lower than 4.10. No reliever will save as many as 30 games. Almost a million fewer fans showed up at Miller Park this season than in its debut a year ago, far short of the 3 million Selig-Prieb expected would come out and support her team.

This is not the way Wendy wanted to leave. But then, there have not been many seasons to remember since she took over for her father 10 years ago this month. The Brewers are 413–558 on Selig-Prieb's watch. This year's team is 55–102, its 10th straight losing season, and no matter what happens in the last five games, it will go down as the worst team in the franchise's 33-year history.

Wendy promised to give the fans a winning team if they gave the Brewers a stadium, a promise she failed to keep—and the backlash has been harsh. She's been blistered on talk radio and scolded in the pages of the town's newspaper. She's withdrawn so much the media is making comparisons to the late reclusive billionaire Howard Hughes.

It is time to leave, even if her legacy is in tatters. Her father has his share of critics, no question, but Bud will always be remembered as the man who brought a baseball team back to Milwaukee. Even though his daughter ran a mom-and-pop shop in the big money era of Steinbrenner and built a world-class stadium, she'll always be remembered as the Selig who turned the team to dust.

Bud was disappointed with her decision, but he understood. And he likes Ulice Payne very much—he has ever since the former Marquette basketball player worked so hard on the Stadium Board to make sure the taxpayers gave Selig his new ballpark. Payne is a true insider, a member of a handful of local boards and managing director of the Milwaukee office of Foley & Lardner, the influential law firm Bud and baseball have used for decades. And now the Commissioner can boast about hiring the first black president in Major League Baseball, too.

Besides, the money that will flow to the Brewers thanks to the new labor agreement will help pay down the debt—now $131 million, down $40 million from 2001—so Selig and his daughter can finally sell their team. Not yet, but soon. Wendy loves the Brewers, has loved them since she was a little girl. Now 42, she's dedicated her entire adult life to this team. But really, how much longer can the Commissioner own the controlling share of one of the game's 30 teams?

Her husband Laurel pokes his head into her office. "Ready?" he asks. "The press is all waiting in the media room."

The newspaper cameras click away, and Selig-Prieb ends her tenure with an explanation and an apology. She's staying on in the newly created role of Chairman of the Board and will concentrate on the team's charitable efforts and "issues related to Major League Baseball." But she's through with the team's day-to-day operations. That now belongs to the six-foot-six man with a five-year contract sitting by her side.

"He's the boss," Wendy says with a tilt of her head to Payne.

She has one last thing to tell the fans. "I want to personally apologize to our fans for the failings of this season," Selig-Prieb says. "The season has been tremendously disappointing, painful, and at times embarrassing. We can talk about reasons and offer excuses, but the season met no one's expectations."

The rest of the conference is a blur. Incoming GM Doug Melvin talks calmly about challenging the team's scouts to find the next comeback player of the year and the 19th-round draft pick who turns into a gem. Melvin's strength is judging talent, and his Rangers won three division titles in seven years before Tom Hicks bought the team and turned it over to Alex Rodriguez. Melvin understands how to build a winner, and knows the first thing he has to change.

"We have to start thinking that we do have a chance," says Melvin, who doesn't realize he's just taken an indirect shot at Wendy and her father and their years of moaning about seasons doomed from the start. "You can't get into a negative mind-set and say we don't have a chance. I'd like to start today and change that attitude."

There is no shortage of irony when Payne tells reporters his models for success are the A's and the Twins, two teams the Commissioner thought about shutting down. He acknowledges his lack of baseball experience, says he has great confidence in Melvin— whom he's just met—and admits he "doesn't have all of the answers" but vows to find them.

"I'm going to take this challenge quite seriously," he says.

When asked about being the first African American president of a major league team, Payne says he feels good but insists he'd rather be remembered for his performance. He says the new labor agreement gives the Brewers a better chance to compete and claims he's ready to "take the bitter with the sweet."

The team's new president also concedes he had reservations about leaving his job at Foley & Lardner to run the team still under the rather large shadow of the game's Commissioner. "But I've been assured that I have full authority to make changes," Payne says.

He'll soon learn those assurances come with exceptions.

While the Brewers close out the season with more losses and changes—Milwaukee fires interim manager Jerry Royster after the team lost four of its final five games—several teams the Commissioner labeled aberrations joyously prepare for postseason play. Counting the wild-card Angels, who'll take on the Yankees in the opening round, three teams from Selig's contraction derby reach the playoffs. The A's reeled off a 20-game winning streak—only the 1916 Giants (26) and 1935 Cubs (21) had longer runs—and tied the Yankees with a game-high 103 wins.

Oakland's first-round opponent: Pohlad's Twins, who ran away with the AL Central with the fourth-lowest-paid roster in baseball, one step above Oakland.

"We have different teams in the playoffs, and that's good—I'm delighted," the Commissioner says on the eve of the playoffs. "But does that take away from what we've been saying? No."

Maybe that's because Steinbrenner's Yankees are once again the odds-on favorite to win another World Series title. New York is Milwaukee's polar opposite, selling a team-record 3.5 million tickets and winning its fifth straight AL East title. Giambi paid big dividends, belting 41 home runs, driving in 122, and hitting .314. Soriano led the AL with 209 hits and fell one home run short of 40–40 in a lineup that scored a game-high 897 runs. David Wells won 19 games in his return to New York, and a rejuvenated Andy Pettitte—with a little help from HGH—was the Yankees' best pitcher down the stretch, winning 11 of 13 decisions.

Steinbrenner's $135 million collection of stars has a combined 543 games of playoff experience. The scrappy Angels have two—a pair of appearances by pitcher Kevin Appier with Oakland in 2000. All goes according to form when Giambi, Bernie Williams, Derek Jeter, and Rondell White hit home runs to power New York to an 8–5 win in Game 1.

But after the Yankees blow an 8th-inning lead and lose Game 2, both the momentum and the series shift to Anaheim. The Angels wipe out a five-run deficit and win Game 3 to push the Yankees to the brink. And when Anaheim scores eight times on 10 hits in the 5th inning of Game 4, New York's season is all but over. The Yankees endure chants of "Go Home Yankees" from Angels fans, who watch their team roll to a 9–5 victory and the first postseason series win in the franchise's 42-year history.

It's the first time Steinbrenner's team has gone home before reaching the World Series since 1997, and it's easy to see why: the Angels hit .376—the highest in division-series history—while the Yankees stranded 44 runners in scoring position. The final ERA for the staff Joe Torre calls the best he's ever managed: 8.21.

Year One of doing it George's way is anything but a success. Steinbrenner immediately schedules an organizational meeting at his Tampa headquarters, but he can't wait even a day to vent his frustration. It's almost midnight when the Boss picks up the phone in his hotel suite and calls Yankees President Randy Levine.

"Get your fucking ass over to the Regency," Steinbrenner tells Levine.

"Why?" Levine asks.

"Just get here," Steinbrenner says.

Levine gets dressed, tells his wife he has to see his boss, grabs a cab, and a few minutes later walks into the Regency. He calls Steinbrenner. "I'm here," Levine says.

"Wait for me in the lobby," George says.

Forty minutes later the elevator door opens. Steinbrenner emerges, spies Levine, and walks over to his team president.

"Your fucking team sucks. Now get the fuck out of here," says Steinbrenner, who heads back to the elevator before Levine can even reply.

The Angels dispatch the surprising Twins in five games to advance to the World Series. Waiting for them are the Giants and the game's best hitter. A year after setting the home run record, Barry Bonds hit a career-high .370, best in the game. He slammed 46 home runs in only 403 official at bats—opponents walked him an astonishing 198 times—a performance that boosted the sales of ZMA, the supplement he endorses for a former Bay Area musician-turned-entrepreneur named Victor Conte.

The two West Coast teams wage an extraordinary Series, mixing blowouts with games decided by a single run. The Angels emerge as the unlikely champions after seven games, but Bonds is by far the biggest story. The Giants superstar hits .471 with four home runs in 17 at bats—the Angels walk him 13 times—erasing a career of mediocre postseason performances. The only negative is persistent speculation over whether Bonds is using steroids.

"They're testing us next year," says a defiant Bonds. "That will answer all your questions."

But a federal agent in Bonds' backyard has already decided not to wait that long.

* * *

Anyone wondering how George Steinbrenner will respond to the new labor agreement and its "Yankees tax" will find out soon enough. While Selig tells interested groups in Portland and Washington, D.C., to prepare bids to purchase the Expos, Steinbrenner sends a clear message to his adversaries.

On December 19, Steinbrenner hands a three-year, $21 million contract to 28-year-old Japanese star Hideki Matsui. "This year, I hit 50 home runs with 107 RBI, and my batting average was .334," Matsui wrote in a letter he sent to all 30 teams. "I hope your team will be interested to offer me a contract." Many were, but Steinbrenner made sure Godzilla—Matsui's nickname in his home country—wound up in pinstripes after first signing a partnership agreement with Matsui's team, the Yomiuri Giants, the premier franchise in Japan.

On Christmas Eve, the Yankees announce they've signed star Cuban pitcher Jose Contreras to a four-year, $32 million contract. Steinbrenner has already picked up Pettitte's $11.5 million option for next season. And when he finally signs off on a one-year, $10.1 million deal to bring back Clemens—who is seven wins shy of 300 and announces he'll enter the Hall of Fame wearing a Yankees cap—George's payroll will swell to $166 million, a full $40 million higher than it was at the start of last season.

"The Evil Empire extends its tentacles even into Latin America," says Red Sox President Larry Lucchino, whose new general manager, 28-year-old Theo Epstein, was no match for George in the battle over Contreras.

Steinbrenner also wants to let everyone know who he holds accountable for his team's first-round failure and who he blames for the labor deal he's convinced unfairly punishes his team. This time he chooses the *New York Daily News* as his messenger, and the paper sends reporter Wayne Coffey down to Tampa to interview the Boss for a package of stories that will run at year's end, commemorating Steinbrenner's purchase of the Yankees exactly 30 years ago to the week.

The two men sit in a spotless blue-carpeted conference room overlooking Legends Field. Pictures of Mickey Mantle and Joe

DiMaggio hang on the wall behind George, who tells Coffey he wants to "sound the bugle" on Torre and his coaching staff. He's never had a better friend as a manager than Torre, Steinbrenner says, and he's glad Torre has become a local icon and "a surefire Hall of Famer."

But Torre was fired as manager three times before coming to New York, George reminds Coffey, who can't help but notice how much it grates on the Yankees owner that Torre receives so much credit for the Yankees' success. "I will not see him drop back into the way he was before," Steinbrenner says. "He's come this far because of an organization—and he's got to remember that."

And George wants Jeter to remember that baseball comes first. "He wasn't totally focused last year," says the Boss. "When I read in the paper that he's out until 3 a.m. in New York City going to a birthday party, I won't lie—that doesn't sit well with me."

Steinbrenner says he's more mellow now and insists the "young elephants"—son-in-law Steve Swindal and his sons Hal and Hank—are going to run the business one day. He thinks his battle with Cablevision will affect the entire television industry. And he defends signing Matsui and Contreras while warning Boston owner John Henry not to trust Lucchino: "He talks out of both sides of his mouth."

But George saves his sharpest words for the man in Milwaukee and his new labor deal. "I'm a Bud Selig man," says Steinbrenner, and Coffey can hear the "but" even before George utters another word. "But you work your butt off to build up your team, and then you are faced with an additional penalty?"

George pauses, letting his words sink in. "I consider Selig a good friend. But while I'm loyal to Bud Selig, the biggest beneficiary in this whole plan is the Milwaukee Brewers. That doesn't seem quite right.

"Sometimes I don't know how he sleeps at night."

Chapter 29

TIPPING POINT

February 5–July 7, 2003

As America enters 2003, there are few more respected figures in the country than Colin Powell. Raised in the tough neighborhoods of the South Bronx, Powell rose through the ranks of the military to become a four-star general, then Chairman of the Joint Chiefs of Staff, and now President Bush's Secretary of State, the first African American to hold that office. What better man to sell the President's case for the invasion of Iraq?

"We know that Saddam Hussein is determined to keep his weapons of mass destruction; he's determined to make more," Powell tells the U.N. Security Council on February 5. "Leaving him in possession of weapons of mass destruction for a few more months or years is not an option."

Nary a dissenting voice is heard in Congress or the national media, but as baseball players are reporting to spring training, several hundred thousand protesters line the streets surrounding the U.N. on the icy morning of February 15. An estimated 6–10 million people elsewhere in America and around the globe join in protest, begging their governments not to march into war in the Middle East.

Unmoved, President Bush sends military forces into Iraq on

March 19. The administration is far too preoccupied with "Shock and Awe" to pay any attention to an IRS agent investigating a supplement company with ties to baseball's biggest star. That will soon change.

Baseball offers the country little relief with a tragic start to the spring. Orioles pitcher Steve Bechler collapses on the mound during an afternoon workout, is rushed to the hospital, and dies of heatstroke early the next day. The 23-year-old Bechler was overweight and on a crash diet when he died, but an autopsy also reveals a high dose of Ephedra, an amphetamine-like supplement used to boost energy and cut weight.

While still available over the counter, Ephedra products have been linked to 88 deaths and 1,500 reported health problems, including heart attacks, strokes, and seizures. Ephedra products are banned in the NFL and the Olympics, but not in baseball. They rang up $1.3 billion in sales in 2002.

Commissioner Bud Selig reacts quickly, banning Ephedra in the minor leagues, and his daughter prohibits its use in the Brewers clubhouse. Don Fehr sends out a memo cautioning players "to be extremely reluctant to use any products containing Ephedra." But Selig and Fehr know amphetamine use has been widely accepted for generations. Players may now steer clear of Ephedra, but no one is ready to give up their greenies.

The future of steroid use rests on random testing of players on each team's 40-man roster—1,198 players in all—which begins the first day of March. Players can be tested at any time from spring training up to the second-to-last week of the season, and if 60 players test positive, penalties will kick in for the next two seasons.

All goes smoothly the first week, when testers show up at the camps of the Yankees, Mets, Giants, and Angels. But tension surfaces on March 11, when two testers arrive at Tucson Electric Park before a Mariners–White Sox game and 16 Chicago players refuse to take their tests. Tom Gordon, the unofficial spokesman for the group of 16, tells player rep Kelly Wunsch these players are boycotting the test so they'd be counted as positive, thus greatly increasing the chances of tougher testing next season.

"We need a level playing field," says Gordon. "We need a comprehensive steroid policy for the good of baseball, and it seems the union does not want that."

While the two testers wait next to urinals in the clubhouse bathroom, the players are at their lockers arguing loudly. Too many players are still using steroids, say many of those refusing to take their tests. Other users have switched to HGH, they claim, which can't be detected in urine. "We're tired of having to decide between using drugs or losing our jobs," several players say.

Catcher Sandy Alomar Jr. speaks up, saying it's every player's responsibility to take the test. "That's what we agreed on," insists the 14-year veteran and son of a former major leaguer.

Wunsch has heard enough by the time he takes a call from Gene Orza, the union's point man on steroid testing. "I'm not sure how the Players Association will react, but you are breaking ranks with your fellow players," Orza tells Wunsch. Orza is sure some of those boycotting want tougher testing. But he's just as sure that others are balking because they have something to hide and are worried the results won't remain confidential.

"We made an agreement, and all players should abide by it in good faith," Orza says.

Wunsch returns to the clubhouse, relays Orza's words, and looks at his teammates. "Let's take the test," he says. The energy behind the boycott ebbs, and each player chosen for testing walks into the bathroom and is given a testing kit. Several will later tell the media off the record that they felt coerced by the union.

Though there are rumors of dissension over testing in other camps, there are no more public rebellions. But there are hard feelings, especially among the union's player leadership. "If guys felt they wanted something stronger, then they didn't speak up at the meetings," says Braves star Tom Glavine, the National League player rep. "We met with every club. Every player on every team had an opportunity to voice their opinion."

Neither Selig nor Fehr offers any comment, citing the program's confidentiality clause. Keeping the results confidential was the most crucial aspect of getting this agreement, even for the players who were in favor of testing. And when testing for the rest of spring training is completed without incident, both men are confident that whatever the outcome, the confidentiality of the program will remain intact.

They will learn otherwise just six months later.

"Joe, what the hell are you going to do about Wells?"

George Steinbrenner's question hangs in the air, and everyone sitting in the fourth-floor conference room at Legends Field waits for Joe Torre's answer. In a book David Wells coauthored, the Yankees pitcher claims 25–40 percent of major league ballplayers are using steroids and the game is awash in amphetamines. But that's not what's bothering George about excerpts from *Perfect I'm Not* being read all around the country.

Wells' real crime: the veteran says he was half drunk the day he pitched his perfect game in 1998, after partying all night with the cast of *Saturday Night Live*. Wells also says Mets slugger Mike Piazza should have shoved his broken bat up Roger Clemens' butt in the 2000 World Series. Then there's the picture of the rotund Wells standing naked, backside to the camera, in a field of sheep. Wells has embarrassed the Yankees, and there is no worse sin in Steinbrenner's world than bringing dishonor to the pinstripes. George has always liked Wells, but the Boss can't excuse this transgression. And now he wants to know what his manager plans to do about it.

"I'm not going to tell him anything," Torre tells Steinbrenner. "This has nothing to do with me. If you have something to say to him, you say it to him."

The others Yankees execs sitting around the conference table— Brian Cashman, COO Lonn Trost, assistant GM Jean Afterman— try hard not to groan. Randy Levine, listening in from New York by speakerphone, has to try even harder. Not only is George killing him about Wells every day, but Selig's been bitching to Levine about the pitcher's claims of widespread use of drugs. There's never been any love lost between Levine and Torre, and right now it's all the Yankees president can do to hold his tongue.

George has been pushing hard since the Yankees' collapse against the Angels last fall, and everyone here knows this isn't the time to push back. None of them are sure just when winning it all went from the team's goal to the Boss' obsession, when anything less than a World Series title signified failure. But they all know it now.

And everyone else in the organization knows it, too. It's not hard to sense that at 72, Steinbrenner feels his time to oversee another big run is growing short. Or that George thinks everyone is letting him down—again. The Yankees still don't have a deal with Cablevision, keeping the fledging YES Network in the red. His Yankee-Nets partners told him they'd get Cablevision owner Chuck Dolan to bend, damn it, but his old friend from Cleveland just rejected yet another agreement in February.

George still doesn't see the urgency he expects from Torre, and that better change this season. But it's Cashman—as always—who takes the brunt of Steinbrenner's frustrations. George has whacked him on everything from the grand slam and two wild pitches Contreras gave up in the 1st inning of his Yankees debut to the Red Sox signing the Twins' 26-year-old platoon first baseman David Ortiz. "I like him—we should have signed him," George told Cashman, who knows Steinbrenner's interest in Ortiz began only after the Red Sox signed him.

Then there's Derek Jeter. If Wells is George's prodigal son, Jeter is far and away his favorite, but the 28-year-old shortstop is still seething over George's dig at his lifestyle last December. "He made a reference to one birthday party, and now I'm like Dennis Rodman," Jeter said soon after camp opened. "I don't think that's fair. My priorities are straight."

Steinbrenner still isn't sure. "He always gives 100 percent," George tells reporters, "but I need 110 percent."

And George has no idea about the looming problem with Jason Giambi. His big first baseman spent two weeks last fall on an All-Star tour in Japan, where he met Greg Anderson, who introduced him to designer steroids from the Bay Area supplement company Balco. Take these, said the man who trains Barry Bonds, and you won't have any worries about baseball's new drug test. Giambi followed Anderson's instructions, never imagining how quickly he'd regret his decision.

But that will be next spring's problem. Right now Steinbrenner is focused on the growing headache Wells' book has become. HarperCollins, the book's publisher, is moving up the release to March 14 to take advantage of the buzz it's already generated. If Torre doesn't know what to do with Wells, George will figure it out for him.

"I want you to make him the 11th pitcher on the staff," says the Boss, and everyone around the table cringes. Wells won 19 games last season, more than any other Yankees pitcher and tied for seventh best in the league.

"I can't do that," Torre says. "I don't like the son of a bitch all that much, but he can still win games."

"Well," George says, "when are you going to have a talk with him about all this?"

"George, I've told you, that's not my job."

Levine is still on the line and can keep quiet no longer.

"Just do it, Joe!" Levine says.

"Shut the fuck up, Randy," Torre snaps.

"Don't tell me to shut the fuck up," Levine says. "Just do what you're told!"

Cashman, who's served as Torre's shield for years, jumps in. "Okay, I'll take care of this," says the GM, who is close with Wells. "It's on me."

Cashman takes two days to read the book and another two days to talk to Boomer and his agent. They agree on a fine of $100,000—over the union's protests—and Wells publicly apologizes to his owner, his teammates, and the fans.

The rest of training camp doesn't go much better. Mariano Rivera injures a groin muscle and will start the season on the DL. The team posts an uninspiring 16–13 exhibition-season record, belying its status as favorites to return to the World Series. Steinbrenner refuses to speak to Wells, who further upsets his boss by not showing up for a *Sports Illustrated* cover shoot with George and the team's five other starting pitchers.

And with the season just two days away, the Yankees are still not on Cablevision, and that battle rages on. Dolan continues to tell Steinbrenner he'll carry YES, just not on the basic tier, where every one of Cablevision's 2.9 million customers pay for it—whether they watch the channel or not. Dolan wants YES to earn its money as a pay channel, just like HBO, which would significantly cut the network's profits.

But the issue is bigger than that, and Dolan knows it. Every other provider has a clause in its contract allowing it to shift YES from basic, where it now resides, to a pay tier if any other provider secured such a deal. A mass move to a pay tier would effectively cripple the YES business model, if not its very survival.

Dolan's plan blew up when Leo Hindery, the CEO of YES, convinced New Jersey's lawmakers that Cablevision was violating antitrust laws by putting the network on a pay tier while other sports networks ran on basic. That put YES on Cablevision's basic tier in the Garden State and opened the door for the same move in New York. Everyone at YES thought New York Mayor Mike Bloomberg had brokered a deal two weeks ago, but it suddenly fell apart in the last few days. Yet another strategy and bargaining session is set for later this afternoon—this one with New York's aggressive Attorney General Eliot Spitzer—which is not the way Steinbrenner wants to spend the final day of spring training.

Maybe that's why the Boss decides to embarrass his general manager again. A few hours before the Yankees play the Phillies in their final exhibition game—after which they'll break camp and fly to Toronto for the season opener—Steinbrenner tells Cashman to personally collect the keys for rental cars used by every player and coach this spring.

This is a job for an intern, not a GM, but Cashman's been down this road before. He knows fear and humiliation are George's chosen methods of motivation.

"Absolutely not," Cashman says. "I am not going to do it."

"What do you mean you won't do it?" Steinbrenner says.

"That's a waste of my time," Cashman says, "and it's a waste of the money you're paying me."

"Well," says George, "then your assistant has to stay here for a week to help make sure every minor leaguer gets to the right team."

Not long after the Yankees beat the Phils 4–3, Steinbrenner, Levine, Trost, and outside counsel David Boies begin a marathon bargaining session to get YES on Cablevision, with Spitzer pushing hard on both sides. Negotiations stretch until 2 a.m., then resume after a five-hour break. A deal is finally reached a few hours later that satisfies neither side but serves as a stopgap they can both live with. About 1.1 million Cablevision subscribers who already pay for the MSG and Fox Sports New York networks will receive YES for free, while the company's remaining 1.8 million customers will have to pay $1.95 per month if they choose to watch the 2003 Yankees.

And the kicker: if a negotiated settlement can't be reached by next season, the dispute will go to binding arbitration.

The deal comes just weeks before YankeeNets CFO Keith Hightower reports that the network will finally break even in the first quarter of 2003 — even without carriage on Cablevision. Just about every penny of profit YES earns from Cablevision will go straight to the bottom line, but everyone connected to YankeeNets knows their partnership is over. Four years of constant infighting over issues large and small have taken a serious toll, and talks to end this relationship are only months away.

But at exactly 6:47 p.m. the first YES broadcast appears on Cablevision, and — for the moment — all the partners are happy.

Drug testing is no longer the biggest thing on Selig's mind when the season finally opens. Alex Rodriguez goes yard against Anaheim on April 2, making him the youngest player — at 27 years and 249 days — to reach 300 home runs. But Rodriguez is unhappy playing for the cellar-dwelling Rangers, and Bud is worried news that the game's best player wants out of Texas will soon make the rounds.

Two days later Sammy Sosa hits his 500th career homer, making him the 18th player to join that select club. On the same day, Barry Bonds blasts the 615th home run of his career off the Brewers' Todd Ritchie in Milwaukee's home opener. Only Hank Aaron, Babe Ruth, and Willie Mays have hit more.

But Selig is not thinking much about home runs, either. The Commissioner is preoccupied with the fates of the two teams in which he holds ownership stakes, especially the one in Milwaukee, where he's convinced that Ulice Payne—the man he armed with a five-year contract to change the team's fortunes—is making a mess of things.

Selig and Wendy Selig-Prieb have lost faith in the man they hired barely six months ago. Their unhappiness surfaced early, when Payne purged the organization of many of Selig's longtime employees, from high-ranking executives to the man who put together the team's media guides. Their unhappiness grew as they became concerned Payne was not grasping the realities of running a baseball team in a small market.

Of course, Payne has concerns of his own. He inherited a team with but one true star—Richie Sexson—a weak pitching staff, and a bunch of bad contracts, most notably the three-year, $21.75 million deal they gave oft-injured Jeffrey Hammonds. (Hammonds will be released in June.) Their season-ticket base has fallen below 8,000 from 11,000 a year ago, when the team lost almost $10 million. There's little chance Payne will allow GM Doug Melvin to improve the team if it means increasing their $40.6 million payroll, the third lowest in the game.

Selig is never one to keep what he's thinking to himself, and when Payne heard the whispers that Bud was displeased with his work—one rumor has the Commissioner assigning someone from MLB to assess the Brewers president's work—he demanded a chance to clear the air. The meeting takes place on April 6 at Miller Park, right before the Giants complete a three-game sweep of the Brewers. In calm, measured terms, Bud and Wendy share their concerns, deny that either has badmouthed him, and tell Payne they're still rooting for him to succeed.

"No one wants to make this work more than I do," says Selig-Prieb.

But Payne might be missing the real endgame: the Seligs are getting the team ready for sale. Selig's conflict of interest has long ago grown awkward, no matter how many times he reminds people that his stake in the Brewers is in a blind trust.

Of course, selling the team even a few years ago was nearly

impossible: too many losing seasons left the Brewers too far under water. The chance for a sale improved after Selig used revenue sharing checks to pay down the debt and got the taxpayers to build a domed stadium, which some analysts say could double Selig's asking price.

It's hard to dispute that paying down such a large debt is bad business. Or that keeping payroll low while restocking the farm system isn't a smart way to build a winner. But neither measure fulfills Selig's promise to give the fans a winning team—immediately—once Miller Park opened.

And this team has little hope of winning. It finally gets its first victory in the season's seventh game, a 5–3 win in Pittsburgh, but loses eight of the last 11 games in April to end the season's first month in last place in the NL Central, where they are destined to finish the season.

By May 11, the Brewers are 13–24, and attendance is flatlining: they're averaging 15,891 fans a game, down 30 percent from a year ago. With these kinds of results, Payne confronts his critics head-on. "My club is in the bottom of our division in a new ballpark, we lost 200 games the last two years, and we lost 900,000 fans," he tells the media. "Everyone's questioning the pace of change, but the fans here are paying for the park."

Things are going far better with Selig's other ownership interest. Frank Robinson has the Expos playing sharp, heads-up baseball. He has two legitimate stars in outfielder Vlad Guerrero and second baseman Jose Vidro, and a group of good young role players. He has two stud starters—Livan Hernandez and Javier Vazquez—and a bullpen full of live young arms. The Expos finish April 17–10, tied with the Braves for first in the NL East.

Things are going even better on the business side. No, not in the short term. The Expos still aren't drawing—everyone in Montreal knows this team is leaving. They're even playing 22 "home" games in Puerto Rico this season. But Selig is playing for the future. Jerry Reinsdorf heads up a relocation committee that's been talking to groups in Washington, D.C., Northern Virginia, and Portland since the beginning of the year. And the two men have a plan for earning back far more than the $120 million MLB paid for the franchise in

2002: any city hoping to land the Expos must build a stadium—no strings attached—before Selig even begins listening to people who want to bid on the team.

The plan surfaced when the first group from Washington made its presentation to Reinsdorf's committee at MLB's offices on Park Avenue back in January. DC Deputy Mayor Eric Price laid out his plan, proudly telling Reinsdorf the financially strapped city was prepared to pay two-thirds of the estimated $300 million needed to build a stadium.

"Is that the number you had in mind?" DC Sports and Entertainment Commission Executive Director Bobby Goldwater asked Reinsdorf.

"Yes," Reinsdorf answered. "Except we were thinking of a different split. We were thinking of three-thirds, no-third."

Everyone in the group chuckled, and Reinsdorf smiled, too. But he was serious. And the news did little to diminish interest. Indeed, seven groups will soon make offers for the team.

The heated competition for the Expos is part of the news Selig delivers to the dozen sports editors who are meeting with the commissioners of pro sports in New York in late April. He also shrugs off suggestions that Baltimore owner Peter Angelos would oppose putting a team in Washington. "We had discussions, but he has never exerted any pressure on what we should do on the matter," Selig says.

Short of suing Major League Baseball—something expressly forbidden by MLB's constitution—there is little pressure Angelos can bring to bear, no matter how often he complains. It's true MLB told him it would not rule out returning a team to Washington—only 38 miles down the road from Camden Yards—when Angelos was bidding on the Orioles in 1992. But it's also true that Selig promised Angelos several times that he would never go against Peter's wishes.

But that's not how Selig sees it. If the city of Washington makes the best pitch—and that's what Reinsdorf is telling him to expect—then Selig will make sure his friend in Baltimore is duly compensated. And to Bud's way of thinking, making Angelos a terrific deal is a promise kept.

Selig has one more bit of news for the sports editors: he plans to retire when his current contract runs out on December 31, 2006. "There comes a time in life when you want to do something different," says Selig. "When I got the extension [in 2001], I told everyone that was it for me.

"I don't think I'll change my mind."

Reporters who regularly cover the Yankees stopped trying to make sense of the owner's actions long ago. Just ask the questions, write the news, and let the headlines roll.

So no one's surprised when George Steinbrenner spends much of the spring berating Jason Giambi for brooding when the Boss should have been thanking his first baseman for playing through patellar tendinitis in his left knee, a tender right hamstring, and a staph infection in both eyes. Giambi, struggling to keep his average above .200, didn't think he could sit with Derek Jeter already out for the first six weeks with a dislocated shoulder. Especially when Giambi's own backup, Nick Johnson, went on the DL with a broken hand.

Nor did any reporters think it unusual for the Boss to berate Brian Cashman when the team suffered a 3–12 slump in May after cleanup hitter Bernie Williams was hobbled by a torn meniscus for a month. Williams underwent arthroscopic surgery on May 21 and will be out until early July. Cashman received a plane ticket to Tampa for an in-person temper tantrum with Steinbrenner.

There are the usual swipes at Andy Pettitte—whom George continues to consider soft—for losing four of five in May. And plenty of harsh words for young Jeff Weaver, who seems to have forgotten how to pitch since Cashman brought him to New York in a much-heralded trade last summer.

But even the media veterans—and many in the Yankees organization—are puzzled when George calls a 4 p.m. media conference before his team's June 3 game at Cincinnati's Great American Ball Park. George has an important announcement he says just can't wait. Derek Jeter—the player George dressed down for his lifestyle this winter and feuded with this spring—is now the 11th captain in Yankees history.

"He's earned it—he's going to be the most important Yankee

captain ever," Steinbrenner says from Tampa while Jeter sits in the Reds media room, a blue-and-white Yankees banner draped over a red wall behind him. Jeter gamely defends the time and place for George's announcement.

"An honor is an honor regardless of where you get it; it just doesn't make a difference," says Jeter, who joins the ranks of Babe Ruth, Lou Gehrig, and Don Mattingly as Yankee captain. "It goes without saying that this is an honor that is not thrown around lightly by this organization."

Nor is it an honor often used as a tool to embarrass the team's manager, especially by an owner who worships at the altar of Yankees Tradition. But Steinbrenner is already insisting "it would be sick media stuff" to take today's event as a shot at Torre. "We needed a spark," George says. "I felt the need for leadership." But isn't that Torre's job?

Steinbrenner never told his manager about this decision, leaving that chore to Cashman. "I know this will make Joe very happy," says Steinbrenner, who knows better. Torre has often said his team doesn't need a captain, and he hasn't had one since he arrived eight years and four World Series titles ago.

But that's of little concern to Steinbrenner, who is still annoyed that Torre isn't pushing his players harder. It's also no secret that George believes Torre and his coaches don't work hard enough, especially for what he's paying them. And few things anger Steinbrenner more than people who don't earn their keep.

Still, why now? His team has just won four of its last six and sits in first place, 1½ games ahead of Boston. Despite their many injuries, the Yankees are 33–23, the second-best record in the AL. And they'll be back home in six days.

Why send Cashman when his wife is expected to give birth to their second child any day? And if this is so vital, why are Steve Swindal and Hal Steinbrenner here while George sits in Tampa? "That's a good question," says Hal.

There's no sign of the spark George expected—the Yankees lose today, then drop four of the next seven—but there's too much talent on this team to keep losing. Powered by the pitching of Pettitte and Rivera and hot hitting by Jeter and a healthier Giambi, the

Yankees put together a 16–2 run and soon sit three games ahead of the Red Sox entering a big game against their archrivals on July 7.

Steinbrenner nervously paces the Stadium's auxiliary press box as a classic duel between Mike Mussina and Boston's Pedro Martinez unfolds. He sweats when Mussina yields a 1st-inning run, complains when Pedro hits Jeter in the Yankees' first at bat, cheers when his team ties it up in the 7th.

And he cries when Boston boots newcomer Curtis Pride's soft grounder in the 9th, allowing the winning run to score.

Reporters rush to Steinbrenner, who does little to hide the tears streaming down from behind his oversized sunglasses.

"I'm just proud of the way Mussina pitched," Steinbrenner says.

And the tears?

"You know, I'm getting older," says the Boss, who turned 73 three days ago. "As you get older, this starts happening more."

Chapter 30

LOOKING FOR ANSWERS

September 3–October 29, 2003

A LANKY SIX FOOT SEVEN, with a clean-shaven head and piercing brown eyes, Jeff Novitzky is hard to miss—unless the Internal Revenue Service special agent is rummaging through a Dumpster in the dead of night, which Novitzky has been doing just about every week since August of 2002. Each time, he meticulously sorts through plastic bags, vials, and torn packages inside the garbage bin behind the Bay Area Laboratory Co-Operative—Balco—a nutritional supplement company in an industrial park hard by the San Francisco airport. When he spies anything of interest, he carefully places it in a bag of his own. When done, he climbs back out and drives home to make sense of it all.

The early findings of his "Dumpster diving"—his information-gathering specialty—were intriguing enough to convince Novitzky's superiors to pursue what appeared to be a small hub for steroid distribution. IRS agents are often key to drug investigations, using their knowledge of the financial system to crack open cases when dealers attempt to launder their drug money. Steroids, though, have rarely made the cut among law enforcement agencies working to stem the decades-long surge of heroin, cocaine, and crystal meth trafficking.

But Novitzky's case has special appeal. Many of Balco's clients are high-profile athletes, mostly track-and-field stars who run under the banner of the company's flagship product, ZMA. Others play for the baseball team 20 miles up the road in San Francisco, including the athlete whose trainer's SUV—license plate W8 GURU—is often found parked at Balco. Novitzky isn't the only one who suspects that Barry Bonds owes his late-career power surge to steroids, but he's the only one who has a handful of narcotics agents working with him to prove it.

Novitzky has followed Bonds just about his entire life. The two grew up about seven miles apart, Novitzky the son of a high school basketball coach in blue-collar Burlingame, Bonds the son of a star baseball player who lived up the San Francisco peninsula in upscale San Carlos. It was clear early on that Bonds, four years Novitzky's senior, was destined for greatness, starring in baseball, football, and basketball. Bonds also earned a widespread reputation as a boastful player who often taunted his opponents.

Novitzky starred in basketball and track at Mills High School, clearing seven feet in the high jump and graduating in 1986, the same year Bonds broke in with the Pittsburgh Pirates and led all NL rookies with 16 home runs and 36 stolen bases. Novitzky tried and failed to make Lute Olson's University of Arizona basketball team, then came home to play backup forward and teammate to his big brother at San Jose State. He graduated with an accounting degree, took a job with the IRS' criminal division in San Jose, and settled into a quiet, comfortable life with his wife and three daughters.

At 31, he was a special agent—top salary $145,000—earning a reputation as someone who paid attention to detail and knew how to close a case. And he continued to follow Bonds, who joined the Giants in 1993 and by decade's end was being mentioned as one of baseball's all-time greats.

By then, Novitzky was hearing whispers in local coaching circles that Balco owner Victor Conte was dealing performance-enhancing drugs to elite athletes. The agent grew curious when a bulked-up Bonds, the biggest of Conte's ZMA endorsers, hit 34 home runs despite missing 60 games with an elbow injury in 1999. In 2000,

Novitzky joined the Burlingame gym Bonds used, located right around the corner from Balco, where he observed the 35-year-old star working out with Greg Anderson. When Bonds hit a career-high 49 home runs that season, Novitzky strongly suspected the player was using steroids. When Bonds hit a record 73 a year later, he was all but sure.

And now, after a year of collecting evidence, Novitzky has a warrant to search the company he suspects is supplying Bonds and other elite athletes with steroids. At 12:20 p.m. on September 3, Novitzky arrives at Balco with 24 agents from the IRS, the FDA, and the San Mateo County narcotics squad. A dozen agents wearing protective vests, their 9mm handguns drawn, follow him inside, where Novitzky tells Conte and the two others who work there — Jim and Joyce Valente — that he has a warrant to search the premises.

Five hours later, Novitzky has boxes of vials containing performance-enhancing drugs, including one Conte calls the Clear — a liquid with anabolic properties — and another he calls the Cream, a balm containing testosterone. Both engineered to be undetectable by baseball's new drug testing program. Novitzky also leaves with several boxes of documents, including medical records for a handful of professional athletes.

Next stop: Greg Anderson's condo, where Novitzky and two agents find vials and containers of steroids and human growth hormone and more than 100 syringes. The agents also seize $63,920 from a safe and a drawer in Anderson's kitchen, some of the cash in envelopes with the first names of known athletes written on them.

Of particular interest are documents that appeared to be calendars, listing dates and names of steroids and other performance-enhancing drugs. Several are labeled JASON GIAMBI. Others carry the initials B.B.

The quiet life of Jeff Novitzky is over. The troubles for Barry Bonds, Jason Giambi, and Major League Baseball have just begun.

The Yankees hold off one last Red Sox run in early September, clinch their sixth straight AL East title on September 23, and finish

101–61, tied with Atlanta for the game's best record. By all measures, it is a truly successful season. Jeter hits .324, just missing his first batting title. Leadoff hitter Alfonso Soriano steals 35 bases, belts 38 home runs, and drives in 91. And catcher Jorge Posada hits 30 homers with 101 RBI and will finish third to Alex Rodriguez in MVP voting.

Andy Pettitte wins 21 games, Mike Mussina and Clemens both win 17, and Jose Contreras looks like a future ace after replacing Jeff Weaver in the rotation in late August. Mariano Rivera collects 40 saves, and his 1.66 ERA is a career best.

Despite spending the entire summer in first place, there is little joy for the Yankees. George Steinbrenner's season-long rants—second-guessing Joe Torre and demeaning his coaches, questioning the heart of his players and berating Brian Cashman—have drained the spirit if not the life from this team. "It hasn't been fun," a weary Torre admits.

Steinbrenner is still cracking the whip as the postseason begins, but there are two subjects that remain off-limits. The Boss is silent about his bitter dissatisfaction with his YankeeNets partners (who are equally dissatisfied with him). The truth is, he was never comfortable giving up half the Yankees—despite retaining control and getting the big payday and half the Nets in return—and divorce papers will be drawn up before the year is out.

More immediately, he remains quiet about Giambi's relationship with Balco, which grows more troubling by the day. Like every owner in baseball, Steinbrenner has been advised by MLB not to comment, so he's handed the problem to team President Randy Levine.

And it's Levine who gets the call when federal agents appear at the Stadium a few hours before the Yankees and Twins take the field for Game 1 of the ALDS. They're there to serve Giambi with a subpoena to appear before the grand jury looking into the Balco case in San Francisco. It's a clear attempt to attract publicity, but Levine finds a friendly ear at the Justice Department, where he worked during the Reagan administration, and the agents are turned away. Giambi will be served a day later at his Manhattan apartment.

Steinbrenner is more concerned with what happens on the field that day, and he is immediately disappointed. The Boss fumes as Bernie Williams misplays a ball in center field, Soriano throws the ball away at second, and Giambi—who struck out a career-high 140 times this season—strikes out twice more in a dreadful 3–1 loss. "I am not a good loser," Steinbrenner says, "and I am upset."

When the Twins pull even with the Yankees in the 5th inning of Game 2, the Boss unleashes a stream of invective at Cashman, and the general manager replies in kind. Things quickly escalate, and the shouting reaches its zenith when Steinbrenner throws down a challenge.

"You want out, fine!" he yells. "You can go take a job with the Mets if you think that will make you happy."

Word of the confrontation reaches reporters soon after the Yankees beat the Twins, 4–1. And when Steinbrenner hears them buzzing about Cashman and the open general manager's job across town, he sends out Levine to control the damage and let everyone know the Mets do not have permission to speak with his GM. "On behalf of the Yankees and George Steinbrenner, no permission was granted," Levine says. "Brian Cashman is our GM."

The Yankees sweep the next two games to dispose of the Twins, but Steinbrenner goes after Cashman again after the Yankees drop Game 1 of the ALCS against Boston, 5–2. Still steamed hours after David Ortiz hit a two-run homer—his seventh against the Yankees this season—George confronts his GM. "I told you we should have signed Ortiz!" he says. "Why didn't you listen?" This time Cashman, who's heard the Ortiz line many times before, walks away bemused.

The rest of the ALCS is a tense, taut affair that goes the distance, punctuated by a brawl in Game 3, superb pitching, and clutch hitting. It's the series that announces Boston as New York's equal, and the final game is a classic, its outcome determined by a pivotal mistake and an unlikely hero.

Five outs from the World Series, with a 5–3 lead before an anxious Yankee Stadium crowd, Red Sox manager Grady Little decides to let tiring ace Pedro Martinez close out the 8th. It's a decision that would cost Little his job. Martinez, who's already thrown 115 pitches, promptly gives up consecutive doubles to Matsui and Posada, the second tying the game.

Rivera and knuckleballer Tim Wakefield match scoreless innings to keep the game tied. At 16 minutes past midnight, Yankees third baseman Aaron Boone steps into the batter's box to open the bottom of the 11th. The Fox announcers are still bantering when Boone swings at Wakefield's first offering and connects. The ball sails through the crisp October night and smacks off the facade of the left-field mezzanine, sending the Yankees to their 39th World Series and whipping the Stadium into a frenzied celebration.

The wild-card Marlins are the Yankees' unlikely opponents in a World Series that feels like a letdown. Not to Steinbrenner, though— not when it's the big stage, and certainly not against a team in his adopted home state.

But little goes as planned. The teams split the first two games in New York, and it's clear the veteran Yankees are having trouble handling the Marlins' aggressive brand of baseball. Once in Miami, there is little to celebrate. Steinbrenner comes down with the flu and rarely leaves his rented yacht. Worse, news that Giambi and Barry Bonds will appear before the Balco grand jury finally breaks, and it dominates the off-day run-up to Game 3.

"To be honest with you, I don't know what this is about," says Giambi, who does know that he stopped taking Balco's steroids after the All-Star Game out of concern they were wrecking his knee. "I didn't do anything wrong."

The Commissioner jumps to Giambi's defense. "The people have not been charged with anything," says Selig. "We've got to be careful. It's unfair to jump to any conclusions about Barry Bonds and Jason Giambi."

Mussina pitches brilliantly to win Game 3, but the Yankees lose Game 4 when Weaver gives up a home run to Alex Gonzalez leading off the 12th. Giambi asks out of Game 5 with his bum knee, David Wells can't make it past the 1st inning, and Steinbrenner's team falls, 6–4, forcing a return to New York with no margin for error.

Steinbrenner is in better health but terrible spirits when he arrives at Yankee Stadium for Game 6. Will your team show up tonight? reporters shout as George strides toward the owner's gate. "Well, we better," he says. Pettitte is terrific, allowing just two runs on six hits in seven innings before yielding to Rivera. But the Marlins' Josh Beckett is even better, scattering five hits while shutting down the Yankees.

The Marlins big right-hander is so dominating that with one out in the 8th and his team down, 2–0, Steinbrenner decides the game is over and seeks out his general manager. "Meeting in Tampa Monday," Steinbrenner says. "And it's not going to be pleasant."

Beckett ends the 8th with a double play, then retires New York in order in the 9th, and it's the Marlins who celebrate as another Yankees season ends without a championship. An hour and a half later, Marlins owner Jeff Loria runs an ecstatic lap around the bases while outside the Stadium reporters swarm Steinbrenner as he bolts to his limo.

"Will Joe Torre be back next year?" several reporters yell.

"I've said many times, yes," barks Steinbrenner.

"What about Cashman?"

"I'm very satisfied with Joe," repeats the Boss as he ducks into the limo and drives off, leaving the question hanging in the air.

The entire Yankees front office contingent flies down to Tampa early Monday afternoon, and this time Joe Torre is included. Swindal, growing more comfortable in the role of George's unflappable adviser, convinces the Boss that the manager's input is valuable, so there is Torre at Steinbrenner's regular table at Malio's on Tuesday night, and he's ready to speak his mind.

"I will not endure another season like this one," Torre says. He understands who's in charge, he tells the Boss, but the second-guessing has to stop. "I don't want to be here just because I have a contract," says Torre, who has one year left on his three-year, $15.2 million deal. "It's important that ownership trusts me."

Steinbrenner nods and says he understands. But it's soon apparent that he just can't make this big of a change. Steinbrenner is in the lobby of the Yankees complex the next morning when a low-level staffer walks in at 9:02 a.m. George fires him on the spot for being two minutes late. After all-day meetings to map offseason strategy, George is persuaded to rehire the young staffer.

Not all George's impulsive mistakes will be so easily fixed.

Chapter 31

TESTING POSITIVE

November 11–December 28, 2003

Gene Orza looks over at Rob Manfred, curious as to why baseball's Vice President for Labor is suddenly pecking away at his BlackBerry. It's November 11, and the two men are sitting with a handful of Yankees and union officials in a Hyatt hotel conference room in Tampa for the second day of Bubba Trammell's arbitration hearing. The Yankees stopped paying Trammell when the outfielder walked out at midseason, a decision Trammell claims he made for medical reasons. But Orza is sure whatever is holding Manfred's attention now has little to do with what the doctor on the stand is saying.

Moments later Manfred hands Orza a slip of paper. He's just received an email from Comprehensive Drug Testing (CDT), the company running baseball's drug testing program. The results are in, Manfred wrote. As per the labor agreement, no names were given, just the number of positive results, and Manfred's already done the math. CDT says 104 players tested positive, more than enough to surpass the 5 percent threshold needed to trigger random testing next season.

There's a small smile on Manfred's face. From his perspective, this is about as good as it could get: the number of positive results is high enough to get the testing program the Commissioner wanted but low enough to prevent the perception that baseball has a drug epidemic on its hands.

The two men meet in the hallway when arbitrator Shyam Das calls a break.

"When do you want to announce?" Manfred says.

"Stop," replies Orza. "You know we have to do more than just read the results."

Orza and Manfred inform their superiors and soon begin the process of validating the test results. Orza is convinced that many players are still taking Andro and other steroid-laced supplements even though the union gave each player a list of legal products that would turn up positive for steroids. The question is whether there will be enough of these positives and other questionable results to push the total below 60, the number needed to trigger penalty testing.

For two days the union man and his MLB counterpart work with their own experts and those from Quest Diagnostics, the lab that conducted the urine tests. Manfred agrees to reject eight positives, leaving 96 on his list. Orza insists the number is 83, though that is still far above the threshold. He's not surprised, just disappointed. Orza figured there were players taking steroids, though far fewer than Ken Caminiti or Jose Canseco claimed. He just thought the players would kick the habit once testing began.

Clearly, he was wrong.

The news is announced in a conference call on November 13. Bud Selig, who's in Milwaukee working to put out a very different kind of fire, releases a statement. "Hopefully, this will, over time, allow us to completely eradicate the use of performance enhancement substances in baseball," the Commissioner says.

A now conciliatory Manfred tries to put a good face on the results of baseball's first drug test. "A positive rate of 5 percent is hardly the sign that you have rampant use of anything," he says. "From our perspective, it's still a problem. We'd like it to be at zero."

A player failing next season's random testing will receive treatment, education about the drug he abused, and will be subject to more testing. On a second positive, a player will be publicly identified and face a 15-day suspension or a $10,000 fine. The penalties escalate until a fifth positive merits a one-year suspension— unpaid, like all suspensions—or a $100,000 fine.

"Plainly, many of the widely publicized claims regarding steroid use in the sport turn out to have been grossly uninformed, as do the suggestions that the agreement with the clubs was designed to avoid a penalty-based testing regimen," Orza says on the conference call.

Orza drafts a memo to the 1,198 players tested, explaining what's taken place and what it all means, then mails it out the following day. The drug agreement makes it clear that both MLB and the union will supervise the timely destruction of the players' test results held at CDT in Long Beach, California, and the urine samples at Quest's Las Vegas facility, though no exact time frame is specified. It's a busy time of the offseason for Orza and Manfred, with free agency under way, salary arbitration looming, and both sides preparing for their Winter Meetings. Somehow they'll have to squeeze in a trip out to Long Beach and Las Vegas.

But on November 19, Manfred makes a call to Orza that changes everyone's plans. "The government just served us with a subpoena at our office for the test results of the 11 players connected to Balco," says Manfred.

The feds make a mistake—the evidence they seek is not at the Commissioner's office but in drug testing labs in two other states. But Manfred and Orza know they have a new problem on their hands. Phone calls fly between the two all day. They share many of the same concerns. This subpoena may well shatter the promise of confidentiality—the major concern even for players who supported testing—especially in light of how eager the government was to serve a grand jury subpoena to Giambi in the spotlight of the postseason.

The loss of privacy for these 11 players could end the drug testing program in its infancy. It's one thing to ask players to give urine samples to their employers under the guarantee of confidentiality. It's quite another for the government to gain possession of them. No one knows what the feds plan to do with these tests, but it's hard to see anything good coming from this.

Then there's the matter of their contractual obligation to destroy the test samples. Both sides contact outside counsel with experience in criminal law: MLB again turns to Morgan, Lewis, and the union talks with the San Francisco firm Keker & Van Nest, who've had success dealing with the U.S. Attorney's office overseeing the Balco investigation.

The answer Selig and Fehr hear from their advisers is just what they'd been told to expect: once the subpoena is served, everything requested is considered evidence in a criminal investigation and cannot be touched. And that goes for the results and samples of all 1,198 players tested, not just the 11 connected to Balco.

By now, everyone knows it's only a matter of time before the investigators turn up at the right places with new subpoenas. And they're all aware of the worst-case scenario: a subpoena for the test results and samples for all 1,198 players.

But it won't be long before Selig and Fehr discover things can get even worse. Much worse.

Bud Selig walks into his corner office, sits down behind his cluttered desk, then turns and stares out his window at the cold, dark waters of Lake Michigan. The news of the government subpoena yesterday was not good, no question about it. But right now, it's hard for Selig to see how things could get any worse than they are here in Milwaukee.

Simply put, the last two weeks have been a living hell: just about everyone in his hometown — damn, his entire home state — seems to have turned against him and Wendy. The reason: Brewers President Ulice Payne broke ranks two weeks ago and confirmed reports that the team plans to slash its payroll and trade away its best player. The news set off a firestorm that shows no sign of abating.

At least Payne's messy divorce from the Brewers is almost complete. All that remains is the final wording of the nondisclosure clause in his separation papers. Payne has already done enough damage with just one story, and there's no reason to let him say anything more.

It all started late on Friday, November 7, when Selig was stunned by a call from a reporter asking him to respond to sources claiming the Brewers are planning big budget cuts—claims, he told Selig, that Payne already confirmed. It was not hard to figure out that Payne was the probable source. Damn, Bud knew Ulice was unhappy—he'd heard all about the memo Payne sent to the Board on October 23 strongly questioning the proposed budget cuts. And he was pretty sure Ulice knew of Selig's unhappiness with him.

But he never thought the former Foley & Lardner law partner would take his complaints public.

"I can't comment on the team's finances or budget," Selig told the reporter, though he did point out that the Brewers were just one of 15 teams cutting payroll this offseason. Of course, he didn't mention the planned cuts would reduce the Brewers' payroll to $30 million, the second-lowest in the game. Two days later, the story appeared on the *Milwaukee Journal Sentinel*'s front page under a headline that made Selig cringe. CUTS MAY IMPERIL BREWERS ON FIELD, it read. SHRINKING PAYROLL WILL MAKE IT TOUGH TO REVIVE.

The details were ugly, and Payne's comments made it all that much worse. He confirmed that the Brewers Board approved slashing the payroll by a full 25 percent. And that the reduction meant the team would trade Richie Sexson, their best and—at $8.6 million a year—most expensive player. It may also mean the exit of Geoff Jenkins, the team's only other All-Star, who will earn $8.25 million in 2004.

In return, the Brewers want low-paid prospects with—they hope—big upsides. The Brewers, the newspaper wrote, were starting over. Again. "We don't envision a significant ramp-up until our young prospects are here and we're able to fill around them," Payne explained. "There was no talk of significant payroll increases in the foreseeable future."

But didn't the Brewers promise a competitive team if the taxpayers financed Miller Park? "All I can say is the Brewers ramped up their payroll when Miller Park opened," Payne told the paper. "But the wins didn't go up and attendance went down. In essence, the plan failed. So now there is a new plan."

Does he worry that Brewers fans will feel betrayed? After all, the team raised average ticket prices 54.6 percent when Miller Park opened and, under this new plan, will have cut its payroll

40 percent over the past two seasons. "I hear from the public and the fans on a regular basis," Payne said. "That's my main concern."

Selig could only manage a sad laugh. After this story, Payne's only concern is the best deal his lawyer can cut for the remaining four years of his five-year guaranteed contract.

The first two days following the *Journal Sentinel*'s story were eerily quiet. The Brewers issued a brief statement on November 11, insisting everyone in management—including Payne—signed off on next season's budget and telling fans, "We are more optimistic about the future of our club than ever before." And that's when the backlash finally hit—with a vengeance.

The fans flooded the talk shows with phone calls and left hundreds of posts on the *Journal Sentinel* website. Their message was clear:

They want Ulice to stay. And they want Bud and Wendy to go.

"You can't win with the current ownership," wrote a former season-ticket holder. "Ulice was a breath of fresh air. To lose him is to dump on the customers one more time." Said another Miller Park regular, "It is now obvious that the owners no longer care to compete, they just want my money. I feel like I have been kicked in the gut."

The politicians turned out in full force as well. Former Governor and current Health and Human Services Secretary Tommy Thompson weighed in from Washington. "The taxpayers stepped up, built the stadium, and kept Wisconsin a major league state," he said. "Yet the Brewers have not upgraded the quality of their team." Milwaukee County executive Scott Walker said he feared the cost-cutting and Payne's expected exit would put the team in a tailspin and announced he'd ask the county attorney to find ways to pressure the Brewers to change course.

"The Seligs just scammed the living dickens out of the people of this state," said State Senator Mike Ellis, a longtime Selig foe. And Assembly Speaker John Gard called for Wisconsin's independent Legislative Audit Bureau to examine the Brewers' books. "The taxpayers of this state have made a multimillion-dollar investment in this team and taken the club's decisions on faith," Gard said. "This week's revelations of a 'fire sale' have shaken this faith, and it is time for us to look at the books and review how the team is managing its finances."

The media insisted the Commissioner is still calling the shots for the Brewers while labeling both Selig and his daughter incapable of building a decent team. They sang Payne's praises, mourned his likely departure, and told the Seligs it was time to leave. "This team needs an exorcism," bellowed the city's leading radio host Charlie Sykes, just one of many who called for the Seligs to sell the team.

Selig hovered over the storm in silence—at least publicly—leaving it to his daughter to battle back. Four days after Payne's revelations, Selig-Prieb finally sat down with the *Journal Sentinel* reporters. She slammed those who claimed the Commissioner is still running the team. "He absolutely is my father, we can agree on that," she said. "But does he influence my thinking? No, he doesn't."

Is there any chance her father will decide to sell the team? "No," she said. "Not at all."

The uproar intensified the very next day, when the *Journal Sentinel* revealed the details of a report given to prospective investors in July, outlining the team's plans to cut the budget for every season through 2006. Whatever hold the Seligs once had on their fans was officially gone.

And now Selig is at his desk while his team's lawyers negotiate the final details of Payne's departure: almost $3 million to buy out the remaining four years on his contract plus his options to buy into the team. And an airtight nondisclosure clause. The two sides reach an agreement later this day, and both the Brewers and Payne take the high road when it is announced on November 21.

"On behalf of the Board, the club, and its management, we thank Ulice for his service and wish him the best in the future," the Brewers' statement reads.

"As I leave my position today as president of the Milwaukee Brewers, I do so with a sense of pride in what the team has accomplished," Payne writes in a statement of his own.

The Brewers announce a search for Payne's replacement, but much will happen before it even gets started. Sexson is traded on

December 1, the centerpiece of a nine-player deal that brings back rookie pitcher Chris Capuano and journeyman shortstop Craig Counsell from Arizona. The Seligs agree to share a portion of the team's books with three of the city's leading businessmen, but government officials push for and will eventually get a state audit of the Brewers' finances.

"We're looking for somebody who combines credibility and integrity but has demonstrated management skills," says John Canning, the Brewers Board member in charge of the search for a new team president. "We're going to be deliberate. There is no timetable."

Which is just fine with Selig, who has another search in mind: he's about to start looking for the next owner of the Milwaukee Brewers.

George Steinbrenner, looking a little pale and more than a little sad, is walking by himself into the Church of the Palms in Sarasota. It's Saturday, December 27, 10 days since his good friend Otto Graham died from an aneurysm, and Steinbrenner is joining Graham's wife, three children, and about 100 other relatives and friends for a memorial service to say their good-byes.

George grew up idolizing Graham, a Hall of Fame quarterback who led the Browns to three titles when George was a teenager in Cleveland. "He's a god in Cleveland," Steinbrenner would often say about the man almost nine years his senior who would become a close friend. The two men played golf together, laughed and shared stories at banquets, and always made sure to support each other's charity events.

Steinbrenner looked up to Graham, and he was saddened—and a bit terrified—when Graham was diagnosed with early stages of Alzheimer's disease in 2001, the same affliction that robbed George's father of his mind and dignity before his death in 1983. Steinbrenner knew Graham was in poor health, so he wasn't surprised on December 17 when Otto's wife Beverly called from her husband's room at Sarasota Memorial Hospital.

It's bad, she told him before holding the phone up to Graham's ear. You hang in there, George told his friend, who was too weak to speak. But Steinbrenner could hear his friend breathing, and Beverly told him that Otto's heart rate jumped while he was listening. A few hours later, Graham was gone.

Steinbrenner knows his friend's death is a wake-up call, a sign to slow down and enjoy life before it's too late. He's 73, and he's already attended too many funerals these last few years. But George has never run faster, and he's hard-pressed to see how that's going to change any time soon.

After all, he's finally ready to build a new stadium—and foot the $800 million bill. Randy Levine and Steve Swindal better be right that deducting the loan payments for the construction costs will save him a third of his revenue sharing bill, which is costing him $40 million this year. And he just got his luxury tax bill: $11.8 million. *Damn Bud Selig!*

Steinbrenner's more than pleased that the YankeeNets partnership will soon end—the lawyers started working on that on December 8—but he'll have to wait until the spring to know if an arbitrator will force Cablevision to carry his YES Network on its basic tier. *Damn Chuck Dolan!*

And how's he supposed to slow down when he's still at war with Brian Cashman? The two have been at odds all year but never more so than this month, when George signed veteran outfielders Gary Sheffield (35) and Kenny Lofton (36) without involving his general manager, who was close to a deal with 28-year-old All-Star right fielder Vladimir Guerrero. Steinbrenner's happy with Cashman's deals for Kevin Brown and Javier Vazquez to replace Clemens, who just retired, and Andy Pettitte, who just signed with Houston. And he thinks signing Tom Gordon to set up Mariano Rivera is smart. *But how the hell did Cash lose Curt Schilling to the Red Sox?*

No, the Boss is not happy with his general manager, even if he just extended his contract. Sure, he told Cashman in July to forget about his $1.15 million option for 2005, and said it again during their shouting match in Game 2 of the ALDS. But that was before he heard about the *New York Post* story on December 14, the one reporting that Cashman was telling people he was looking forward to getting out from under Steinbrenner the minute his contract ran out at the end of next season.

A day later, Steinbrenner instructed his public relations man Howard Rubenstein to tell the media he was picking up Cashman's option for 2005. Cashman was in his backyard building a snowman with his two young kids when the *Post*'s George King called him. "You have any comment about Steinbrenner picking up your option?" King asked him. "Well, the *New York Post* is officially the one telling me, because I know nothing about it," Cashman answered. "So I have no comment."

So no, Steinbrenner hasn't cut back this month. If anything, he's put more pressure on everyone, including—especially—himself. But Steinbrenner pushes all this out of his mind as he walks into the crowded church. The service is touching, and now there's a slide show. George is standing when they show slides of him with Otto, a lump forming in his throat.

Graham's daughter Sandy is just starting to talk when George feels light-headed and begins to sway. He staggers a step or two, gropes for a chair, misses, and falls forward, his head slamming the chair with a loud thud before he lands facedown on the carpeted floor.

The room instantly turns to chaos, with people yelling, others calling 911, and most everyone crowding around Steinbrenner. A nurse and paramedic attending the service push their way to George, who is ghostly white and unconscious as they loosen his shirt and tie and prop up his legs. It's almost two minutes before George opens his eyes, and the color returns to his face as he slowly realizes he must have passed out.

"I'm okay, I'm okay," he says when paramedics from Sarasota Memorial arrive and help him onto a gurney. He's embarrassed as he's wheeled out to a waiting ambulance while everyone applauds. He's given intravenous fluids and an electrocardiogram in the ambulance and is in a chatty mood when he arrives at the emergency room. "Thanks for the service," he tells the medics. "It was very good."

Steinbrenner spends the day taking medical tests, telling family and friends crowding into his room that he feels great, and taking calls. "You all right?" asks Randy Levine when he finally gets through the hospital switchboard. "Well, I'm not dead yet," George jokes. "I'm fine, I'm fine. It was just hot."

But the family is concerned. George has never liked doctors and rarely visits one, and his knees are badly in need of repair, but his constitution has always been every bit as steely as his will. That's why they were all surprised when he took ill at the World Series, getting so sick he lost his balance and fell. And now this.

Steinbrenner's unhappy when he's told he has to stay the night at the hospital, and unhappier still when told he will not be discharged until early evening the following day. He spends the day watching football, instructing Rubenstein on what to tell the media, and talking to Dr. Andrew Boyer, his personal physician, who traveled up from Tampa to oversee care of his longtime patient.

Boyer crafts his own statement for the media. "George Steinbrenner recovered in a few minutes and he's been doing well ever since," it reads. "He has had a very extensive cardiac and neurological workup. He's feeling well, and his general health is excellent."

Boyer is told there are about a dozen reporters camped in front of the hospital, some who arrived before dawn. Several are sitting in lawn chairs when Steinbrenner's doctor walks out to speak with them.

"He's doing great," Boyer says. "All the tests were normal."

You've said Steinbrenner has never experienced anything like this before, says one reporter. Can you tell us what may have caused him to collapse?

"Sometimes in a stressful situation," Boyer says, "you just pass out."

Given all the stress Steinbrenner will face come the New Year, it's anyone's guess if—or when—this could happen again.

PART V

REVISIONIST HISTORY (2004–2007)

Chapter 32

GOVERNMENT INTERVENTION

January 16–September 29, 2004

Bud Selig is walking the neatly groomed grounds of Gainey Ranch, the upscale community in Scottsdale where he and Sue keep their winter home. It's early evening, and he's wearing what he always wears on his walks: a blazer over a white shirt, dark slacks, and black dress loafers.

The Commissioner loves this time of year in Arizona. It's January 16, just a few weeks before pitchers and catchers report for spring training. He's been coming to spring training in Arizona ever since his father helped him scrape together $300,000 to purchase a tiny stake in a baseball team 35 years ago. Buying into a team that trained in Arizona was a nice little bonus. There's something about the warm, dry air here that invigorated him then, and invigorates him even more now that he's 69.

But spring training is not what's on Bud's mind tonight. Just a few hours ago his daughter Wendy stood before the assembled media at Miller Park and announced that the Selig Era will end as soon as a buyer is found for their team. If all goes as planned, this spring training will be Selig's last as owner and managing partner of the Milwaukee Brewers.

It's time — probably long past time. And this announcement

should make it that much easier for his surrogates to get him a contract extension, an effort that began soon after Selig announced his intention to walk away when his current deal expired at the end of 2006.

Selig's held on to the Brewers for the same two reasons that drive so many of his baseball decisions: money and Wendy. In 2001, the Brewers' debt was $171 million—as much as, if not more than, the team was worth. Cash calls, payroll cuts, and growing revenue checks have whittled the debt down to a more manageable $110 million. Industry analysts figure the franchise and its one-third stake in Miller Park is worth between $180 million and $200 million. Selig is hoping for closer to $220 million.

But this decision is as much about Wendy as it is about money—maybe more. Bud always wanted to give his daughter the chance to run his team, but the experience has not worked out the way they'd hoped. She's been hammered for everything that has gone wrong these last 11 years while rarely—if ever—receiving credit when things go right. It's Wendy who oversaw the construction of their jewel of a ballpark and then negotiated the 30-year lease that will keep the franchise in Milwaukee long after her father sells the team. And she'll leave a farm system that ranks as one of the game's very best.

But the Brewers haven't had a winning season after Wendy took over in September of 1992, and attendance is back to pre–Miller Park levels. Hiring Dean Taylor as general manager was a mistake, and signing injury-prone Jeffrey Hammonds to the richest free agent deal in team history was a disaster. None of this did anything to shake the notion that Wendy got where she was solely because her father owned the team or that her father was still making many of the team decisions. And now too many fans are calling his budget-cutting daughter a liar—or worse.

Yes, the time is definitely right to sell the team, just as it's the right time to finally move the Expos out of Montreal and sell them, too, ending Selig's other conflict of interest. He told the owners two days ago that a decision should be reached by the All-Star break, though most already assume—correctly—that the Expos will soon call Washington, D.C., home.

And Selig is oh so close to getting everyone to sign off on Frank McCourt's purchase of the Dodgers from Rupert Murdoch, even though the Boston parking lot mogul appears to be seriously under-capitalized. But Murdoch wants out, McCourt is the only one willing to meet the $430 million asking price, and Bud wants to keep Rupert happy. Given Murdoch's reach—Fox will pay MLB $416.7 million per year to broadcast their games through 2006, and his regional sports networks are paying 19 teams for their TV rights—it's easy to see why.

All this would make tonight's walk a pleasure but for that damned IRS agent and the Balco prosecutors out in San Francisco who appear determined to make Selig—and everyone else in baseball—utterly miserable. While Wendy was delivering her news today in Milwaukee, federal agents were serving the subpoena that Selig and Don Fehr have been waiting for since last November, one that confirmed their worst fears. No longer content to chase after Bonds and the other 10 players connected to Balco, the government is asking for every test result and urine sample taken in 2003, all 1,438 of them.

Which means the 104 players who tested positive are now in jeopardy. The window into the secret world that will define the rest of Selig's career—and Fehr's as well—has just been pushed wide open.

Union and MLB lawyers are still formulating a legal strategy to combat the new subpoena when the President takes them all by surprise on January 20, highlighting steroid abuse in his State of the Union address. In a speech that repeatedly raises the specter of terror attacks, the President calls out athletes using steroids right between calls to increase testing for illicit drugs in high schools and double the funding of abstinence programs to combat sexually transmitted diseases among teenagers.

"Athletics play such an important role in our society, but unfortunately, some in professional sports are not setting much of an example," the President says. "So tonight I call on team owners, union representatives, coaches, and players to take the lead, to send the right signal, to get tough, and to get rid of steroids now."

Three weeks later, Attorney General John Ashcroft announces a 42-count indictment of Bonds' trainer Greg Anderson and three other Balco defendants before TV cameras from the steps of the Justice Department. The government drives the point home again on February 17, releasing documents showing baseball is at the heart of the Balco investigation. And on March 1, the first of a steady stream of leaks appears in the *San Francisco Chronicle*, which reports the government has information that shows Anderson gave Balco's designer steroids to Bonds, Jason Giambi, Gary Sheffield, and three other baseball players.

It's no surprise when John McCain summons Selig and Fehr to Washington for another hearing on March 10. The Senator is at his self-righteous best, accusing both men of "aiding and abetting cheaters" and issuing one threat after another. "Your failure to commit to addressing this issue straight on and immediately," he thunders, "will motivate this committee to search for legislative remedies."

Fehr, looking pale and wan from gallbladder surgery he had two weeks ago, pushes right back. He reminds McCain that union members should not be required to forfeit their Fourth Amendment right to privacy because they play major league baseball. He insists the sport's nascent drug testing program is working and tells McCain the government should clean up *its* act and get steroid precursor supplements like Andro off the market—a door, Fehr reminds McCain, Congress opened when it deregulated supplements in 1994.

Selig can't help but wonder about Fehr's tactics. If only the union leader had listened when Bud wanted to install testing with punitive measures as early as 2001, the season he started drug testing in the minor leagues. Instead, Fehr insisted on survey testing first, then a treatment-based approach—rehab, fines, identities of users kept secret—if and when the random testing threshold was crossed. Maybe if Fehr had listened then, they wouldn't be sitting in Washington now.

But here they are, and Bud has his own strategy: throw the union under the bus. Yes, he tells McCain, he's ready to institute random testing year-round. Yes, he thinks players should be suspended for the first violation. And yes, he knows why they don't have either policy in place.

"We obviously accepted less than we wanted," Selig testifies about the drug agreement with the union in baseball's 2002 contract. "In my judgment as the Commissioner, we had pushed the MLBPA as far as it would go without a strike. The clubs, whatever their conviction, were profoundly concerned about the impact of another strike."

Selig leaves Washington and quickly issues another gag order, this one forbidding any baseball official from discussing steroids. He keeps the pressure on Fehr by having stories leaked that he's thinking about using his "best interests of baseball" powers to unilaterally impose a new testing program. Baseball's lawyers know that any change in the drug agreement has to be collectively bargained, but these stories are good politics.

The real bargaining is going on between the union and the Balco prosecutors over the government's subpoena of the 2003 drug tests. At the government's request, the union's Gene Orza writes a white paper outlining the MLBPA's position, stressing the confidentiality guarantee in baseball's collective bargaining agreement, and raising concerns about violating the privacy rights of players not connected to Balco. The government ignores it.

In February, the union and Comprehensive Drug Testing had assured the government in writing that it would protect the subpoenaed records until the two sides resolve the dispute on their own, or until it is decided by the courts. The head of the Justice Department's Criminal Division wrote to CDT's legal counsel advising him the government accepted this assurance. A month later, the government served another subpoena for the 11 players with ties to Balco but did not retract the subpoena for all the records.

This is where things stand on April 7. With no compromise reached, the union files a motion in the federal court for the Northern District of California to quash both of the government's subpoenas for the 2003 tests. The next day, lead investigator Jeff Novitzky gets in his car and drives 394 miles to Long Beach, where he asks a judge for a warrant to search CDT for the records of the 10 players tied to Balco. (One player was found not to have any ties to Balco.)

The key to Novitzky's request: his stated concern that CDT could conceal, alter, or destroy these records.

Novitzky fails to tell the judge about CDT's written guarantee to protect the records he is seeking. Nor does he mention the hearing scheduled to consider the union's motion to dismiss the subpoenas for these records. Based on what he knows—and doesn't know—the judge grants the search warrant for the tests of the 10 ballplayers connected to Balco. He also instructs Novitzky to return to CDT any data he might find that does not involve these specifically named men.

Novitzky then leads 11 armed agents into the CDT office and serves the warrant. After several calls between CDT's counsel and government lawyers, the company's CEO hands Novitzky a list of test results for the 10 players named in the warrant. Not good enough, says Novitzky, who wants the computer expert on his team to search the entire CDT computer system. Before long, the agent is clicking through directories and making copies on disks.

When he is done, the government has possession of 11 disks containing the 2003 drug tests for every Major League Baseball player as well as results for a few NFL and NHL teams, several athletic events, and a handful of private businesses. In all, Novitzky walks out with more than 4,100 files—2,911 of which have nothing to do with Major League Baseball—completely ignoring the order of the judge who issued the search warrant.

The union and CDT file a flurry of motions to get back the seized files while the government asks for search warrants to get information they already have in their possession. And after promising to keep confidential the names of the 104 players who tested positive, the government attaches a list of their names to several of its motions, needlessly risking the privacy of the players involved.

One of those lists is sent to the union, another to MLB. It is the first time anyone at the union or MLB sees the names of the players who failed their drug tests, and several of the names stun them: Alex Rodriguez. David Ortiz. Manny Ramirez. Sammy Sosa. And more. This is no longer just about Bonds and Giambi. Orza and Manfred soon begin talks about suspending drug tests for the players on the government list until each player can be told he is a potential target of a government investigation.

No one at the union or MLB ever dreamed that a federal agent would seize their confidential drug testing results—there is simply no precedent for such an act. It is the first indication that the government's investigation is more about punishing baseball players than stopping the distribution of steroids—and it won't be the last.

George Steinbrenner stands on the tarmac of the private-plane runway at Tampa Airport as the chartered jet carrying his son Hal, Brian Cashman, Joe Torre, and communications director Rick Cerrone taxis to a stop. The four men are flying in from New York, where they joined the welcoming party for Alex Rodriguez at Yankee Stadium on their newest superstar's first day in pinstripes. Now the jet's passenger door swings open, and as the four men climb down the portable stairway, the team's 73-year-old owner greets each one with a big smile and warm words.

"You men really did a great job today, a great job," says Steinbrenner, his blue Windbreaker zipped tight in the cool early evening air. "I'm really proud of all of you. Really proud."

None of these men can fully believe their good fortune. Wasn't it only one month ago when incumbent third baseman Aaron Boone blew out the ACL of his left knee playing basketball, leaving Cashman desperate for a replacement with spring training looming? Was it a stroke of luck or fate that put Cashman and Rodriguez side by side on the dais of the Baseball Writers banquet in New York nine days later, where an idea was born?

Cashman knew Alex was still desperate to leave Texas after a trade sending him to Boston fell through, but he wasn't sure if the Gold Glove shortstop was desperate enough to shift to third base. The longer Cashman chatted with the league's MVP, who talked at length of his unhappiness playing for the hapless Rangers, the more probable the idea appeared. Dozens of phone calls shrouded in secrecy followed, with few besides Cashman, Texas GM John Hart, and Rodriguez in the loop.

And by the time Cashman was prepared to go to George with the deal, almost three weeks later, Alex was ready to change positions, Hart was ready to take Alfonso Soriano in return, and Rangers owner Tom Hicks was willing to pay $67 million of the $179 million balance remaining for the last seven years of Rodriguez's contract.

Steinbrenner didn't need much convincing, even if adding Rodriguez would push the Yankees' 2004 payroll past $180 million—though he wanted to make sure Jeter understood his shortstop job was safe. Both George and Cashman told the team's captain there would be no quarterback controversy on this team. And when Selig reluctantly blessed the deal on February 16—"I will not allow cash transfers of this magnitude to become the norm," Selig promises, "but given the quality of the talent moving in both directions, I have decided to approve the transaction"—the Yankees had done what the Red Sox could not: land the game's top player.

George sent his son Hal to New York for the announcement—as big as any in Yankees history—while he watched the media conference on YES at the Yankees' minor league complex. And now he's happy that everyone is back home safe.

"Your rental cars are right over there," says Steinbrenner, who had the staff bring the cars to the airport rather than making the travelers taxi over to Legends Field, as everyone else usually does. The four men can only say thanks, raise an eyebrow at this small display of kindness, and wonder how long the Boss' good humor will last.

George will still have temper tantrums, and he'll still bluster at staff meetings. But it's a different George Steinbrenner who presides over matters big and small this spring training. That becomes abundantly clear when he stops in Joe Torre's office a few days into camp. Their relationship throughout 2003 had been frosty, and the two men had not spoken since season's end. But George's mood is noticeably different when he asks his lame-duck manager what he wants to do after this season.

"I'd like to manage a little longer," Torre says.

"Good," Steinbrenner says. "Steve [Swindal] will talk it over with you."

A day after regulars report, George is in his customized golf cart—Yankees blue, GMS plates—driving around camp slowly enough to good-naturedly answer a host of reporters' questions.

How is his health?

"I'm fine—you all think I'm going to die," he says. "Everybody's coming up to me—'Sign this baseball.' You want one of the last autographs."

Does he think Jason Giambi—who reported to camp 20 pounds lighter than last season—or Gary Sheffield has taken steroids?

"No. They know how I feel about it, and I think they feel the same way."

Is there tension between Rodriguez and Jeter? "You people need to let this drop. I don't *think* it's a nonissue—I *know* it's a nonissue."

Why is he using a golf cart to get around?

"I'm slowing down, and I have bad knees," he says, smiling. "Okay, boys, that's it for today. I have work to do."

George loves having Don Mattingly back in uniform as the team's hitting coach, and he's pleased Joe Girardi is Torre's new bench coach, replacing Don Zimmer, who he detests. Writers churn out "happy George" stories, and not even five straight losses in spring training games—which a year ago would have meant a slew of midnight meetings—can alter his mood.

"I'm not bothered," Steinbrenner says. "I think Joe knows where we are."

He's thrilled when the YankeeNets partnership officially ends on March 23, meaning he can buy back shares in the Yankees. On the same day, an arbitrator rules that Cablevision must carry YES on its basic tier through 2009, a decision that almost doubles his team's audience and substantially improves his bottom line.

But privately, he's beginning to worry. There are days when it's more than his bad knees and the weariness of age that trouble Steinbrenner. Days when he's not sure of his decisions; when he tries but can't remember what he did a few hours ago, the name of a friend, or the right word for what he wants to say. Worse are the moments when he can't control his emotions, when the tears well up, then spill out and run down his cheeks.

Aren't these the things that were happening to his friend Otto at the end? None of these things happen every day, but they're happening often enough, and George doesn't know why or when they will occur.

Like Opening Day at Yankee Stadium. It's an hour or so before pregame ceremonies when Cerrone drives Steinbrenner in a golf cart toward a makeshift set in left-center field for interviews with sportscaster Warner Wolf and news anchors Dana Tyler and Ernie Anastos of WCBS. The Boss is in a fine mood, despite his team losing two of their first four games in Tampa. Hey, if you can't get excited about Opening Day at Yankee Stadium, he says, when can you get excited?

West Point cadets are already lined up in the outfield, where they will unfurl a huge American flag for the national anthem. Steinbrenner waves to fans chanting "Thank you, George" as he takes his place on the set next to Wolf, who he's known for years. Steinbrenner is wearing large dark glasses, and it's soon apparent he is fighting back tears.

"George, first of all, is your health okay?" Wolf asks. "You're looking good."

"I'm okay," says Steinbrenner, whose voice cracks and lips quiver as he tries to go on. Dana Tyler pats him softly on the shoulder to comfort him.

"I just feel pretty emotional about this team and its players," George tells her, "and I hope they feel the same way."

Steinbrenner tells Wolf that Bud Selig is doing a great job. "I just wish he wouldn't take so much money from me," he says. He gets through a few more questions before mentioning that he received a phone call from Roger Clemens yesterday.

"What did he say to you?" Anastos asks.

"He said, 'I just want to thank you... for making me... a Yankee," says Steinbrenner, sobbing. "I said... 'You were a great player.'"

Hours later, after the Yankees beat the White Sox, 3–1, George is beaming when he meets with the media. "I'm having a great time," he says, his voice strong and steady.

The next day the Yankees announce that Steinbrenner has given Torre a three-year, $19.2 million contract extension, keeping the 63-year-old manager a Yankee through 2007. But the news does little to spark the team, which loses nine of its next 14 games. Six of the losses were to Boston—including three straight at the Stadium— but there are no words of panic coming out of Tampa.

"I have a great manager in Joe Torre and general manager in

Brian Cashman, and have confidence in both of them," Steinbrenner says in a statement issued by Howard Rubenstein.

It's during this stretch when Rubenstein, who has all but supplanted the Boss as the public voice of the Yankees, introduces George to Juliet Macur, a young reporter from the *New York Times* assigned to write a profile of Steinbrenner. After grilling Macur on her background—Where did she grow up? What did her parents do? Where did she go to school?—he tells Macur to set up an appointment with his secretary.

A week later Macur walks into a conference room overlooking Legends Field in Tampa with Steinbrenner, who pulls out a chair for her at the conference table. "Can I get you anything?" he asks. "Lunch? Coffee?"

Macur arrives expecting the tyrant she's grown up reading about. Instead she discovers a man who is open about his flaws, full of regrets, and surprisingly vulnerable.

He tells Macur he is afraid to die, asking her several times how much longer he'll live. "To 75?" George asks. "To 80?"

He talks about all the funerals he attends—"You see your friends die, you think about dying yourself." He tells her about his regrets over his temper tantrums—"Guess that will be my legacy"—and the calls he still gets from reporters. "All they're looking for is controversy," George says. "I don't like that. They twist my words."

He forgets the name of his longtime secretary Judith, calling her Rita, his mother's name. He tells Macur he stays at the Carlyle when he's in New York, though he's lived in the same suite at the Regency for decades. And he admits it's now a struggle to control his emotions. "Well, I don't cry all the time," says George, who cries three times in the two-hour session. Macur has to choke back her own tears several times, too.

He tells her he loved his father but that Henry Steinbrenner was a hard, unrelenting man who always focused on his son's failures. "I'll never forget what my father said after he heard I bought the Yankees," he tells Macur. "'Well, the kid finally did something right.'" The "kid" was 42 years old.

It's a story George has told often, but it's several moments before he can continue. And when he does, he speaks with regret about verbally abusing his own four children, especially his two sons. It's not lost on him that he has become the father he so resented.

When the interview is done, George walks Macur to the door and surprises her with a huge bear hug. "You're nice," he says.

Steinbrenner's team breaks out of its early slump, and by the time Jeter's average breaks .200, on May 11, they've won 10 of 13 games. Rodriguez, Jorge Posada, and Hideki Matsui's bats are red hot for the entire month, and the team moves past the Red Sox and into first place in the AL East on June 1, where they'll stay the rest of the season.

Things are back to normal in the Bronx.

Everywhere but the owner's box.

Alex Rodriguez swings and rifles the ball into right-center field, the deepest part of Houston's Minute Maid Park, driving in David Ortiz before he pulls into third with a stand-up triple. A-Rod's RBI pushes the AL's lead to 7–1 in the top of the 4th inning of the 2004 All-Star Game, all but ensuring a win and World Series home-field advantage.

Bud Selig takes this all in from his box next to the NL dugout, where he's waiting to be introduced to the crowd of 41,886 at the end of this inning. Selig would like the score to be a little closer, but it's hard not to be caught up in the excitement at this stunning retractable-roof stadium, which the taxpayers of Houston built for his friend Drayton McLane, the billionaire owner of the Astros.

How can he not be enthralled by the action he's already seen in this All-Star Game? After almost 10 years of record-breaking performances, the love affair the Commissioner and fans have with the long ball has never been stronger. This game is but a reflection of what they've been enjoying all season.

In Boston, Ortiz (22 home runs, 76 RBI) and teammate Manny Ramirez (26–77–.342) are keeping the Red Sox on the heels of the Yankees. The Boston duo's doppelgangers reside in St. Louis, where Scott Rolen (18–77–.342) and Albert Pujols (21–57–.304) have powered the Cards to a league-best 55 wins. The Phillies' Jim

Thome has 27 homers, top among the seven All-Stars with at least 20. Indeed, there have been so many off-the-charts offensive performances that it's easy to overlook 39-year-old Randy Johnson's perfect game back in May.

But there is no overlooking Barry Bonds, who at two weeks shy of 40 is still the most feared hitter in the game. His numbers at the break—23-48-.365—can't tell the whole story, because most teams have just about stopped pitching to him. He's already been intentionally walked 71 times—26 more intentional walks than any player not named Barry Bonds has ever received in an entire season. He's averaging a home run every 8.3 at bats, has struck out just 19 times, and his on-base percentage is an unworldly .628.

If the constant stream of anonymous sources linking Bonds to steroids is bothering him, it certainly doesn't show. Nor is it bothering the fans. The Giants are averaging 40,200 fans a game at home—96.8 percent of SBC Park—and 36,943 on the road, trailing only the Yankees and the Cubs.

Business is good everywhere outside Montreal, where the Expos are playing their last season in Canada. Every Red Sox and Cubs game was sold out by the third week of April. The Yankees are the leader of nine teams on pace to draw more than 3 million fans. Another 11 teams will draw at least 2 million—including the Brewers.

But no one is having a more rewarding season than the game's Commissioner. By late June, four well-heeled bidders emerged for his Brewers, and the franchise that plays in the game's smallest market is certain to fetch at least $200 million. Later in July he'll have the best seat in the house when Paul Molitor, the last true bright spot for the team in Milwaukee, is inducted into the Hall of Fame. And the Expos should bring in at least twice what the Brewers are expected to get when Selig puts them on the market this fall. No one is questioning the Commissioner's decision to buy the team now.

Selig is also threading the needle on the steroid controversy remarkably well, building his cover story even as the tale continues to grow. While the union works feverishly to get back the 2003 drug tests illegally seized by the feds, Selig has been telling

Congress that he's all for tougher testing and bigger penalties. And we'd *have* a tougher program if only the union would get out of the way, Selig keeps repeating.

But the union has legitimate concerns. The government shattered baseball's promise of confidentiality to its players when Novitzky raided CDT. In response, MLB and the union quietly decided to upgrade the program's security, which delayed testing for all players until July 8—a decision they did not announce, leaving players to wonder when they would be tested. Union lawyers are working on how and when they will notify the players who tested positive in 2003 that the government is holding their drug tests.

But now Bonds has just popped up to end the National League's three-run rally in the 4th, and it's time for Selig to walk out to the TV camera set up along the first baseline. Waiting for him is Roger Clemens with his wife Debbie and their four sons. Roger wants to be surrounded by family when Selig presents him with the Commissioner's Historic Achievement Award in front of the hometown fans.

"Roger, your 21-year Hall of Fame career has been highlighted by many awards, honors, and remarkable performances," says Selig, his words echoing throughout Minute Maid Park. "Your name will always be mentioned with the greatest pitchers in the history of this game."

Selig pauses to let Roger enjoy the huge roar from the fans.

"Roger, you've done a lot for so many, and all of us are very proud of you," Selig says. He hands the Rocket a silver-and-gold trophy, then reaches up and puts his right arm around Clemens' thick neck for a heartfelt hug.

The chase for records and milestones resumes when the season starts again two days later. Clemens wins his last six decisions, lifting his record to 18–4 and pitching the Astros into the playoffs. He'll become the oldest player to win the Cy Young Award, winning it a record seventh time. Greg Maddux collects his 300th win on August 7, and Ichiro Suzuki gets his 200th hit on August 26. He'll finish with 262 to break George Sisler's 83-year-old record for hits in a season. Sammy Sosa hits his 574th career home run—seventh on the all-time list—in the Cubs' last game of the season.

The Dodgers' free-agent-to-be Adrian Beltre surprises everyone by smacking 26 second-half homers, more than the career-high 23 he hit all last season.

But no one closes the season quite like Barry and Bud. On September 17, Bonds takes San Diego's Jake Peavy deep for home run No. 700. A week later, two employers from Quest Diagnostics show up at SBC Park to administer Barry's drug test. "I'm glad this is finally happening," Bonds says. "They'll get the results, and it will clear my name." A few hours later, Bonds hits the second pitch he sees off Dodgers starter Odalis Perez for his 44th home run.

Bonds finishes the season with 45 home runs—leaving him 11 shy of the Babe—and hits .362 to win his second batting title in three seasons. He sets records for walks (232), intentional walks (120), and on-base percentage (.609). It will surprise no one when he's named MVP for the fourth straight season and seventh time overall, something no one in baseball has ever done.

Watching—and worrying—over the game's best hitter is the Commissioner, who is still campaigning for tougher drug testing in mid-August, when the owners make a big announcement: they've persuaded Selig to stay past 2006. All it took was a three-year extension averaging $18 million a year plus continued use of a private plane and other perks.

"We no longer have the internal bickering among owners— that's the thing I'm most proud of," says Selig, who has watched revenues grow to $4.1 billion, more than three times what they were when he took over 12 years ago. "I must admit that when I look at it today, you almost have to pinch yourself."

Selig has that same feeling a month later, when the Brewers announce that Mark Attanasio, an investment firm owner from LA, will soon become the next owner of the Brewers. Attanasio arrived late to the bidding but walked away the winner when he agreed to pay $223 million for the Commissioner's team— $43 million more than Arte Moreno paid for the Angels just one year ago. At that price, Selig will make a tidy profit from his 28.6 percent stake in the Brewers.

And just a few days later he ties up another loose end: the Expos are moving to Washington. "This was a team that had to be moved," Selig says in a teleconference from his Park Avenue office. "We knew it had to relocate. This was a team we were anxious to get rid of."

A big contract extension, the sale of the Brewers, relocating the Expos — Selig has checked off almost everything on his to-do list for 2004. All that remains: a plan to insulate himself from the taint of steroids.

Chapter 33

CURSES

Mid-September–Late December, 2004

ALEX RODRIGUEZ AND Gene Orza are having lunch at a restaurant in midtown Manhattan on a bright mid-September day. They make an odd couple: one's the sculpted, six-foot-three, 225-pound third baseman wearing wraparound sunglasses and a practiced look of nonchalance, the other's the short and rumpled union leader with reading glasses, a quick wit, and a mischievous smile. The two have known each other since 1993, when Orza, the union's contract compliance officer, found a way out of the bad deal Alex signed soon after Seattle drafted him No. 1 overall.

Rodriguez, then barely 18 and the son of a single mother, was grateful for Orza's help, and the two men have grown friendly over the years. They had a spat last December, when Orza sat with Alex and his wife Cynthia at MLBPA headquarters and explained why the union was blocking a deal that would send the Rangers short-stop to Boston. The Red Sox would only make the trade if A-Rod took a $28 million pay cut—terms Rodriguez was ready to accept— but the union refused to permit such an arrangement.

"It's a precedent that will affect every other player," Orza told Rodriguez, who bolted from the room. Alex soon got over it, espe-cially when he became a Yankee a few months later.

But this is not a social call, Orza tells his young friend as soon as they order—not this time. There's a problem with his 2003 drug test, and he wants Rodriguez to listen carefully.

"The government is in possession of documentation from which it might conclude that you have tested positive for steroids," Orza says. It's the same message Orza's delivered to David Ortiz, David Segui, and others on the list of 104 players who tested positive in 2003, a list that has been split between him, Michael Weiner, and Steve Fehr. "Understand that I am not telling you that you have tested positive for steroids, because I don't know. But I cannot guarantee what the government thinks."

But Rodriguez can. He knows he took testosterone and Primobolan last season, just as he had in each of the two seasons before that. He had wondered if his name was on the list when he received the memo about the government seizure back in April, but he's been able to push the thought out of his mind.

Besides, there have been plenty of distractions in his first season playing for George Steinbrenner, though thankfully, the Boss has not really been one of them. Everyone around here whispers that Steinbrenner hasn't been the same since he collapsed at Otto Graham's funeral, even if he still pounds on Cashman after every loss. Either way, Rodriguez hasn't been a target, even when he expected to be. Rodriguez heard nothing from the Boss after July 24, when he and Red Sox catcher Jason Varitek got into a shoving match that led to a brawl and cost Alex a four-game suspension. Nothing's been said about his season-long trouble hitting with men in scoring position (he only recently pushed above .200). And not a word about the cold war Jeter is still waging against him. Alex has praised Derek all season—"He's the heartbeat of this team," Rodriguez has said time and again—but his ex-friend is well known for holding a grudge, and this one is airtight. Their teammates have been forced to choose sides, and that's hardly been a contest, leaving Alex on an island all his own.

But what will Steinbrenner say about the news Orza just delivered if it ever becomes public?

Orza assures Rodriguez only a handful of people involved with the drug testing program have seen the list. Don Fehr hasn't seen it, and neither has Bud Selig—both by choice, just as the program was designed. No owner has seen it, either. But that could change, depending on what the government does. Prosecutors have already defied orders from two federal judges to return the list, so it's hard to know what will happen next.

"You will want to consult with counsel and consider your options," Orza tells Rodriguez. "You might not want to give urine anymore if you think it is going to be seized by the government."

I haven't been tested this year, Rodriguez says.

You'll be tested sometime in the next two weeks, Orza tells him, stating what should be obvious. There are little more than two weeks left in the regular season, and the drug agreement clearly states that every player will be tested before the season ends. "Talk to your lawyer before you decide what you want to do," Orza says.

It is not a productive two weeks for Rodriguez, who—like every other player contacted by the union—decides to take his drug test. He hits .245 and strikes out 14 times in 14 games. But he plays for a winner now, and Rodriguez finally gets to celebrate on September 30, when Bernie Williams slugs a walk-off two-run homer to beat AL Central champ Minnesota, 6–4, clinching the Yankees' ninth straight AL East title.

Big thing are expected after the Yankees win a league-best 101 games, hit a team-record 242 home runs, and draw 3.8 million fans, another team record. And all goes well for the first seven games of the postseason. Rodriguez rediscovers his stroke in the ALDS against the Twins, hitting .421 and scoring the series-clinching run on a wild pitch in Game 4. And he and his teammates are brilliant in the first three games against Boston in the ALCS—all New York victories, including a 19–8 rout in Game 3 at Fenway that prompted several Red Sox to congratulate the Yankees on their 40th AL pennant.

But everything changes in the 9th inning of Game 4. Mariano Rivera is protecting a 4–3 lead when he walks leadoff hitter Kevin Millar. Boston manager Terry Francona inserts pinch runner Dave Roberts, who promptly steals second. Bill Mueller follows with a line-drive single, driving in Roberts as Rivera swings his right arm in disgust. Three innings later, David Ortiz hits a two-run home run, and Boston has its first win of the series.

The Red Sox come from behind again in Game 5 and win on an RBI single by Ortiz in the 14th. Boston momentum shifts to New York panic when the Red Sox cruise to a 4–2 win in Game 6 to even the series. And when Kevin Brown opens Game 7 by giving up a two-run homer to Ortiz in the 1st, then Javier Vazquez gives up a grand slam to Johnny Damon an inning later, the Yankees' epic collapse is all but complete.

Steinbrenner watches all this from his box, and he is still there watching the postgame show when he turns to Cashman. It's been a long, strange season. They traded for the best player in baseball and spent close to $200 million in payroll, which will cost them $30 million in luxury taxes on top of their $60 million revenue sharing bill. In baseball history, 25 teams have taken a 3–0 lead in postseason series, and every one of them advanced to the World Series. Until now.

A year ago, Steinbrenner threatened Cashman's job on a regular basis, humiliated him by holding him out of the Winter Meetings, then exercised the GM's option for 2005 out of spite, never bothering to tell Brian himself. But now, an hour after the biggest collapse in baseball history, he has a different message.

"Your job is safe," George tells Cashman. "Be prepared to get after it this winter."

There will be no interviews, either. Rubenstein puts together the last media release of the season and hands it to his boss, who gives his approval. Minutes later Rubenstein dutifully delivers it to the media.

"I congratulate the Boston Red Sox on their great victory, and I want to thank our loyal fans for their enormous support," the statement said. "Of course I am disappointed, because I wanted a championship for them and for our city. You can be assured we will get to work and produce a great team next year."

The Curse officially ends on October 27, when four Red Sox pitchers shut down the Cardinals, 3–0, to complete a four-game World Series sweep. After 86 years of near misses, broken dreams, and endless heartache, the Red Sox are World Champions for the first time since a young left-hander pitched Boston's favorite team to the title in 1918. One year later that pitcher—Babe Ruth—was traded to the New York Yankees, the deal the Red Sox and their fans have been cursing ever since.

"It's an overwhelming sense of joy and relief," says Boston majority owner John Henry, who just three years ago was the owner of the small market Florida Marlins. Now he's standing in the middle of the Red Sox clubhouse, watching the players he paid $127 million this season—a payroll second only to the Yankees—douse each other with Champagne. "It's vindication for all the frustration," Henry says. "All the waiting has finally paid off."

But as historic as this postseason has been, it can't drown out the sport's steroids story. On October 10, Gary Sheffield told *Sports Illustrated* he did not know the substances he received and used from Balco were steroids. On October 16, the *San Francisco Chronicle* reported that it has a tape of Bonds' trainer Greg Anderson telling a friend that Bonds took an undetectable steroid and that Anderson expected to be tipped off about the date of Barry's 2003 drug test. Two weeks later, the government revealed documents in which Balco executive Jack Valente says he gave Bonds steroids. Valente will dispute the claim, but no one will listen.

There's plenty of drama behind the scenes, too. While Selig continues to push Fehr to adopt MLB's minor league drug policy and its year-round random testing, two federal district court judges instruct the government to return the 2003 test results. Judge Florence-Marie Cooper is the third judge to so order, finding in mid-September that "the government callously disregarded the affected players' constitutional rights." In an earlier decision, Judge James Mahan asked if the Fourth Amendment, which protects citizens against illegal search and seizure, "had been repealed" and instructed the government not to inspect the data it seized before returning it.

The government ignores Cooper's order, as it had the previous two. Federal agent Jeff Novitzky continues to review all the data seized from CDT while the prosecutors in charge of the investigation appeal each decision to the United States Court of Appeals for the Ninth Circuit. The chase after the 104 players who tested positive in 2003 continues.

The story goes quiet in November, when the country reelects President Bush, who promises to privatize Social Security and continue his war on terror. As is customary, many cabinet members resign, including Attorney General John Ashcroft, who had taken a strong personal interest in the steroids investigation. Bush replaces Ashcroft with White House Counsel Alberto Gonzales, who will soon make a key decision that complicates life for Mark McGwire.

But the year ends as it began: with Giambi, Bonds, and Balco in the crosshairs. In the first few days of December, the *San Francisco Chronicle* runs excerpts of last year's secret grand jury testimony from Jason Giambi and Bonds that are leaked to the paper by Jack Valente's defense attorney. The newspaper puts out Giambi's story first. The Yankees first baseman, who has repeatedly denied ever using performance-enhancing drugs, provides the grand jury with a detailed account of steroid injections and human growth hormone use.

Told he would be granted immunity from prosecution if he told the truth but would face perjury charges if he lied—the same deal offered every player who came before the grand jury—Giambi testified that Greg Anderson gave him what the trainer called the Clear and the Cream. The first is a steroid in liquid form, the other a balm containing steroids.

"Did Mr. Anderson provide you with actual injectable testosterone?" Assistant U.S. Attorney Jeff Nedrow asked Giambi.

"Yes," Giambi said.

Referring to an alleged steroids calendar from January of 2003, Nedrow asked, "And this injectable T, or testosterone, is basically a steroid, correct?"

"Yes," Giambi said.

"And did he talk to you about the fact that it was a steroid at the time?" Nedrow asked.

"Yeah, I mean, I...I don't know if we got into a conversation about it," Giambi said. "But we both knew about it, yes."

The *Chronicle* posts the story on the morning of December 2, and it's only a matter of hours before Yankees President Randy Levine is meeting with MLB Vice President Rob Manfred. The two former colleagues speak for an hour, and the conversation boils down to one thing: the $84.5 million left on Giambi's contract.

"Can we void the last four years of his deal?" Levine asks.

"No," Manfred says. "The union will fight it, and they will win."

The same question dominates talk radio in New York, which is all Giambi all day long. The tabloids have a field day. BOOT THE BUM, screams the *New York Post* front page, labeling Giambi THE LYIN' KING.

DAMNED YANKEE, shouts the *Daily News*.

It's Selig's worst nightmare: a big star on the game's most famous team unmasked as a cheat. But he barely has time to remind baseball officials that they are barred from discussing steroids before the *Chronicle* comes back with the Bonds story the very next day.

The home run king's testimony is less straightforward than Giambi's but no less damning. At several points Bonds admits to "unknowingly" taking substances that are now known to be designer steroids. Yes, he told the grand jury, Anderson gave him the Clear and the Cream. No, he testified, he did not know what either product contained. Nor did he question his longtime trainer.

"When he said it was flaxseed oil, I just said, 'Whatever,'" Bonds testified. "It was in the ballpark...in front of everybody. I mean, all the reporters, my teammates...they all saw it. I didn't hide it."

"Were there any effects from those two items that made you think, 'Gee, he didn't tell me it was a steroid?'" Nedrow asked Bonds.

"If it's a steroid, it ain't working," said Bonds, who insisted that Anderson would never give him an illegal substance without telling him. We're friends, Bonds testified, and Anderson "wouldn't jeopardize our friendship."

The two stories hit hard. President Bush issues a statement urging baseball to deal with the use of steroids and all other illegal performance-enhancing substances immediately. McCain threatens to introduce his own drug testing legislation if baseball does not replace its current program with "one as stringent" as the one used by the minor leagues. "I'll give them to January," McCain says.

This time Fehr isn't arguing. It's clear now that the current program, with its single test and no penalties for first-time offenders, was a mistake, especially with the twin fires of Balco and CDT threatening to torch the game's credibility. The program did not do enough to discourage steroid use, nor did it convince anyone that the players and their union were serious about cleaning up the game.

Now two of the game's biggest stars have been outed as steroid users, even as the union and their lawyers continue the battle to recover the test results still in the hands of the government. On December 10, Federal Judge Susan Illston, who is also presiding over the Balco case, issues yet another order for the government to return baseball's tests. The prosecutors again appeal, putting the fate of players in the hands of the Court of Appeals for the Ninth Circuit—as well as the growing number of lawyers, clerks, and other people who have seen the list of positive results.

If the union loses, scores of players face subpoenas and the same risk of perjury that ensnared Bonds and Giambi. Fehr and the union lawyers spend much of their annual Executive Board meeting in December explaining the legal ramifications of the CDT case, and it doesn't take long for all in attendance to understand the need to re-open the drug agreement with MLB.

Selig's men push hard, and a new agreement is all but completed before they break for Christmas. In addition to tests in spring training, the tentative agreement stipulates there will now be unannounced, year-round random testing for all players, including those who don't spend the offseason in the United States.

Most important, the identities of first-time offenders will be revealed. The plan also calls for a 10-game suspension for the first positive test, 30 games for the second, and 60 games for the third—all without pay.

A good year for baseball—a very profitable year—is ending badly. But both Selig and Fehr are hopeful that their new agreement will finally get the game's drug problem under control.

Nothing could be further from the truth.

Chapter 34

SELIG'S CHOICE

February 9–May 17, 2005

RANDY LEVINE STARES hard at Jason Giambi and asks the one question on the mind of everyone sitting in the Yankees president's Manhattan law office.

"Did you take steroids?"

Brian Cashman, assistant GM Jean Afterman, and Giambi's agent Arn Tellem all shift in their seats, waiting for the player to respond. It's a simple question, but the answer is far more complicated than Giambi ever imagined.

It's February 9, two months since the nation read all about Giambi telling a grand jury how he would stick a testosterone-loaded syringe in his ass, how he'd pinch the skin around his belly button and inject HGH, and how he loaded up on designer steroids from Balco. But now he has a new worry. Some details of a book written by his former teammate Jose Canseco trickled out three days ago in the *New York Daily News*, and they put Giambi right in the crosshairs.

It was Mark McGwire who introduced Giambi to steroids, says Canseco in *Juiced*. According to the former Oakland star, his two teammates would head into a bathroom stall in the team's clubhouse and inject each other with anabolic steroids while he shot up in the stall right next to them. Giambi was so hooked, Canseco wrote, that everyone knew the Yankees first baseman was the biggest juicer in the game.

The only saving grace for the Yankees is that Canseco took dead aim at even bigger game: the book focuses far more on McGwire and even accuses the sitting President of the United States of participating in the scandal. Giambi knows much of what Canseco wrote is true, but Canseco's sordid reputation and his high praise of the powers of steroids has kept this story from catching fire.

But that's about to change.

Giambi knows Levine has already tried to void the remaining $84.5 million on his contract and that he wouldn't have done it without George Steinbrenner's blessing. Giambi called George two weeks ago, promising he was still the player the Boss thought he signed in the winter of 2001—not the one who's hit .216 since the 2003 All-Star Game. What he didn't say was his poor play coincided with his decision to stop taking steroids.

Jason knows everyone now sitting in Levine's office remembers Tellem instructing the Yankees to strike any reference to steroids from their contract if they wanted to sign him. It was one of about 20 things Tellem asked the Yankees to change, but it's the only thing people will hear if the story ever gets out. The Yankees can always say there were other clauses covering the use of illegal drugs, so striking any mention of steroids was no big deal— though the request was clearly a red flag.

Giambi, now 34, has done two-a-days all offseason, honing his baseball skills by day and lifting weights every night. Team doctors have pronounced him fully recovered from last summer's treatment to remove the benign tumor in his pituitary gland. The Yankees signed Tino Martinez to play first, so he's going to be the team's designated hitter. Which he hates. But he knows the days of dictating terms are over.

He also knows the Yankees have him on a short leash. And so do the Balco prosecutors, who already threatened to send him to jail if he didn't tell the truth about his steroid use to the grand jury. What if they call him back in after Jose's book is published? What if they ask about McGwire?

Giambi's lawyers keep reminding him that no one knows what the government is going to do. That's why they've advised Jason to remain silent if anyone but the government asks about steroids. Anything he says can—and most certainly will—come back to haunt him.

"Jason," Levine repeats, "did you take steroids?"

The seconds pass like hours before Giambi finally speaks.

"I just can't answer that," he says.

Levine isn't surprised.

"You can't fuck around with any of this stuff anymore," Levine says. "We're monitoring you."

And so is the media. Giambi hasn't said a word since the grand jury story broke, and the interview requests have piled up. It's going to be a feeding frenzy in spring training, Levine tells him. "You have to do something up here first," the Yankees president says.

A day later Giambi faces the media in the Yankee Stadium conference room, with Joe Torre sitting on a folding chair to his right, Tellem at his left. Both Torre and Tellem are dressed in dark suits and ties, their heads hung low, eyes cast at the floor. Giambi wears a dark T-shirt under a black blazer and fixes his gaze on each reporter who asks him a question.

No, Giambi tells the first reporter, he has not read the *Chronicle* story on his testimony yet. That said, "I feel I let down the fans, I feel I let down the media, I feel I let down the Yankees, and not only the Yankees, but my teammates," Giambi says, turning to look Torre in the eye.

He apologizes repeatedly, though for what he does not say. "I accept full responsibility," he says, "and I'm sorry."

What about the stories Canseco wrote about you? "I find it delusional," Giambi says. "It's sad that Josey is that desperate to make a dime."

How do you think the fans will treat you? "Everybody makes mistakes," he says. "I hope people will give me a second chance."

Will they ever get to hear your whole story?

"I know the fans might want more," Giambi says as the 30-minute session draws to a close. "Because of all the legal matters, I can't get into specifics. Someday, hopefully, I will."

No one is more interested in how the New York media responds to Giambi's comments about Canseco than Bud Selig. The Commissioner knows full well that one of his main tasks this season — perhaps his biggest task — will be controlling the steroids narrative. And Canseco's book may now present the biggest challenge.

Everyone knew Canseco was writing a book, and everyone knew Jose was convinced he was blacklisted when he could not find a job at the end of his career. But no one thought he would break the code of silence that every player, from star to scrub, has always honored. "After batting practice or right before the game, Mark and I would duck into a stall in the men's room, load up our syringes and inject ourselves," Canseco wrote about his former Bash Brother. "I was the godfather of the steroid revolution in baseball, but McGwire was right there with me as a living, thriving example of what steroids could do to make you a better ballplayer."

Canseco didn't break the code — he shattered it. The book moved from Oakland and McGwire to Texas, where Canseco claimed he tutored Ivan Rodriguez, Juan Gonzalez, and Rafael Palmeiro on the benefits of steroids. "I personally injected each of those three guys," Canseco wrote. "Many times."

And the team's famous general managing partner, the one who loved to walk through the clubhouse and pal around with the players? President George W. Bush "had to have been aware" of rampant use on his team, Canseco wrote.

Selig's plan for Canseco was simple: have his surrogates shoot the messenger. "I'd be surprised if there was any significant follow-up," Vice President for Baseball Operations Sandy Alderson — Canseco's former GM in Oakland — tells the media. "It's hard to understand why anyone would make these allegations — to sell a book?"

At first pass, the strategy appears sound. Selig considers Canseco a malcontent and a freak, a view shared by many in the media who remember Jose more for allowing a fly ball to bounce off his head — and over the right-field fence — in Cleveland in 1993 than as the first player to hit 40 home runs and steal 40 bases when they voted him MVP in 1988. Most writers simply don't take him seriously.

But Selig and his aides have trouble getting their stories straight.

On February 6, former A's manager Tony La Russa tells the *New York Daily News* that Canseco openly joked about using steroids. A week later, Selig says Sandy Alderson—La Russa's former boss—insists neither he nor La Russa knew anything about Canseco's steroid use.

"They deny it vehemently, and I don't blame them," says Selig, oblivious to La Russa's earlier statements. "Sandy would have no reason to lie to me."

The following week brings more problems. On February 12, Bonds' mistress Kimberly Bell tells *Fox News* that Barry told her he started using steroids in 2000. Two days later, Canseco's tell-all hits bookstore shelves—it's already a bestseller from advance sales alone. On February 15, news of Giambi's stricken steroid clause appears in the *New York Times*.

That same day, the *Daily News* reports that an FBI agent told MLB Canseco and other A's showed up as steroid users during an agency investigation in 1994. The information, says agent Greg Stejkal, was ignored. Alderson denies that baseball ever heard from the FBI, a statement MLB will have to retract several years later.

Canseco makes two appearances on *60 Minutes*, the first on February 13, the next three days later on *60 Minutes Wednesday*. Each time he repeats his most damning allegations to Mike Wallace. Did management know all this was going on? asks an incredulous Wallace. "The owners knew it," Canseco says. "The Players Association knew it."

Both Fehr and Selig decline to appear on either show. Fehr provides a statement focused on the new drug testing plan while Selig sends Alderson to make his case. "I'm not here to suggest there wasn't a sense that something was going on in the case of some individuals," Alderson tells Wallace. "But the notion that as an institution baseball was aware of a problem is just not true."

But your manager says he knew about Canseco, Wallace says.

"That's news to me," Alderson answers.

"Why didn't he tell you?" Wallace asks.

"You'll have to ask him," Alderson says.

The question is never asked. Baseball is not the only institution engaged in willful ignorance.

While the Commissioner is calling reporters to complain about their coverage of this story, there are complications happening behind the scenes. Federal agent Jeff Novitzky is in Baltimore talking to an FBI informant who says he has ties to a ballplayer using steroids—Orioles outfielder Larry Bigbie. The only thing the informant knows about Bigbie's steroids dealer is that he lives in New York, but it's enough to keep Novitzky interested.

Congressman Henry Waxman knows nothing about Novitzky's tip either, but Selig's refusal to look into Canseco's claims grabbed the California Democrat's attention. Nothing still garners headlines like baseball, and he'll make the case that steroid use in baseball is a public health crisis. And the only way to address this crisis is to haul a handful of baseball stars before the House Committee on Oversight and Government Reform and grill them while the TV cameras roll.

Never mind that this very committee refused to hold hearings into torture at Iraq's Abu Ghraib prison. Or failed to investigate the leak of undercover agent Valerie Plame's name. Or never looked into how the Bush administration could send troops to war in Afghanistan and Iraq without proper armor. Steroids in baseball is an issue everyone in Congress—on both sides of the aisle—can rally around.

Quoting from *Field of Dreams* in a letter to committee chairman Tom Davis (R-VA), Waxman says it's high time the committee looked into how baseball is handling its problem with performance-enhancing drugs. They need to do this, Waxman writes, for the good of the kids who look up to baseball players. So while the country wages two wars and millions of American workers struggle with shrinking wages and rising health care costs, the powerful House Oversight Committee decides that getting to the bottom of baseball's steroid problem is a matter of utmost importance.

Bud Selig is in his suite at the Ritz-Carlton in downtown Washington, D.C., running through his lines. It's March 16, and his senior staff is prepping him for tomorrow's House committee hearing on steroids in baseball. They're serving up the questions he should expect, polishing the talking points he will repeat. Selig is a born politician, but he does his best work in back rooms or on the telephone, not in front of television cameras with opponents looking to score points.

And Selig knows that scoring points is all tomorrow is really about. He was surprised earlier this month when Tom Davis and Henry Waxman sent "invitations" to him and Don Fehr to appear before their committee, along with Mark McGwire, Jason Giambi, Rafael Palmeiro, Sammy Sosa, Jose Canseco, Curt Schilling, and Frank Thomas. And he was angered when the two congressmen sent out subpoenas when most of their invitations were turned down.

But Selig was amazed by what he heard when baseball's Washington lawyer Stan Brand asked Waxman and Davis what they were really after. We want more hearings, they told Brand, and a long list of documents. We also want tougher penalties for players who test positive for performance-enhancing drugs.

And we want baseball to conduct an internal investigation.

An investigation?

Selig wonders how the congressmen can be serious when there are two active and aggressive government investigations already under way. The government still has all of baseball's 2003 drug tests, despite court orders to return them to the union. Hell, prosecutors have already sent out Barry Bonds' urine to be retested for Balco's designer steroids.

So while the tug-of-war over the 2003 tests is being litigated in the Court of Appeals for the Ninth Circuit in California, Davis and Waxman want baseball to expose even more of its players to possible prosecution by conducting an internal investigation. *Are they fucking kidding?*

Selig doesn't even understand why he's in Washington at all. He and Fehr already strengthened baseball's drug testing program, just as John McCain instructed them to do last March and again in December. Under the new agreement announced just this past January, a player is now identified and suspended 10 games on his first violation. In addition, players will be tested year-round, and there is no limit on the number of tests baseball can request. So why is Congress holding a hearing *before* this new program even gets started? And after Selig just announced that only between

1 and 2 percent of players tested positive last season under the old program?

But Davis and Waxman have latched on to Bud's ankle and aren't letting go. So it's up to Bob DuPuy, Rob Manfred, and the others in Selig's suite tonight to make sure the Commissioner looks good tomorrow.

Everyone on the committee's witness list is in town with the exception of Giambi, who got a pass when the Justice Department stepped in and determined the Yankees star's testimony could hurt their criminal investigation into Balco. There's no way the Balco prosecutors are going to let anything jeopardize their case.

The parents of three young baseball players who committed suicide are in town, too, and two of them are ready to testify that steroids played a key role—*the* key role—in the death of their sons. One father is the cousin of former Dodgers star pitcher Burt Hooton. Davis and Waxman aren't satisfied with blaming baseball players for the rise in steroid use among teenagers. They want Americans to know that Mark McGwire and Sammy Sosa and Rafael Palmeiro have blood on their hands, too.

Selig wonders if McGwire has finally made up his mind about testifying tomorrow. Selig is fond of Mark, and he doesn't want to believe that any of the things Canseco wrote about him are remotely true. What the Commissioner doesn't know is that McGwire spent three hours in Davis' office today, offering to admit he used steroids if Davis can get him full immunity. The Virginia Republican is a big baseball fan and wanted to help McGwire, so he put in a call to Attorney General Alberto Gonzales asking him to grant Mark's request.

Davis was almost giddy talking baseball with the home run champ while waiting for the AG to get back to him. But when Gonzales did call back, the news was what Davis expected. The attorney general refused to grant McGwire immunity, even though it would have allowed Davis' committee to get exactly what it wanted: a confession from one of baseball's biggest stars.

Davis could see McGwire was crushed. Mark is 41 years old and now leads a quiet life with his second wife Stephanie and their two young sons in their house on a golf course in Irvine, California.

Canseco's already pulled back the curtain on the home run champ's secrets. McGwire wants to unburden himself, but doing so without immunity could lead him into a courtroom. So McGwire will follow his lawyer's advice and refuse to talk about his past, even if that appears to validate what his former teammate has written.

Selig feels confident he knows his lines when he walks into the Rayburn House Office Building the next morning. One of the committee aides puts the Commissioner and his staff in an office where they can watch the day's first panel on TV as they testify. "This is not a witch hunt," Davis says as he brings the room to order. "We're not asking for witnesses to name names. Furthermore, today's hearing will not be the end of our inquiry."

It's not long before Davis swears in Dr. Denise Garibaldi. Selig stares at the TV screen as the psychologist from suburban San Francisco tells the committee that her son Rob grew up "idolizing Bonds and the Bash Brothers" and was good enough to be drafted by the Yankees in the 41st round out of high school in 1999 and earn a scholarship to USC. But scouts kept telling her five-foot-eleven, 125-pound son that he was too small to make it big, so Rob drove to Mexico soon after graduating from high school and bought his first cycle of steroids. He got bigger—eventually reaching 165 pounds—and starred at Santa Rosa Junior College and then USC. But he struggled academically, began taking medication for depression and a learning disability while still on steroids, and eventually lost his USC scholarship. At 24, he shot and killed himself one block from his home.

"There's no doubt in our minds that steroids killed our son," Garibaldi says. "In his mind he did what baseball heroes like Canseco had done."

Next is Don Hooton, whose 17-year-old son Taylor, a baseball star in Texas, also turned to steroids when a JV coach told him he had to get bigger if he wanted to reach the pros. He, too, took his own life, and Hooton places the blame squarely on the large shoulders of major leaguers.

"Let me tell you that the national jury of young people have already judged your actions and concluded that many of you are guilty of using illegal performance-enhancing drugs," Hooton says. "But instead of convicting you, they have decided to follow your lead.

"In tens of thousands of homes across America, our 16- and 17-year-old children are injecting themselves with anabolic steroids. Just like you big leaguers do."

Davis clears the wood-paneled hearing room for a short break. When he gavels the hearing back in session, it's standing room only, with a long row of photographers lining one wall. Selig and Fehr sit in the first row behind the table where their players will testify, with the three sets of parents sitting another row back. One million households are tuned in to see what will happen next.

The players slowly walk in and take their seats. They all refused to be sworn in with Canseco, so each raises his right hand and takes the oath separately. Canseco is the first to speak, and he advises the committee he cannot tell them much because he, too, was denied immunity. He's worried what he might say will adversely affect his ongoing legal problems.

But Canseco says he stands by what he wrote, and he does have a few words he'd like to get on the record. "If Congress does nothing about this issue, it will go on forever," the self-proclaimed steroid pioneer says.

Sosa's advisers grilled him in advance about his steroid use and are reluctant to have him answer questions outside his native Spanish, so veteran D.C. lawyer Jim Sharp has already told the committee he will speak for his client. Reading from Sosa's sworn statement, Sharp says the player did nothing to break the law in America or his native Dominican Republic. "To be clear," reads Sharp, "I have never taken illegal performance-enhancing drugs."

Rafael Palmeiro delivers a short but memorable opening statement. Looking up from his prepared text and jabbing his left index finger toward the committee, he emphatically delivers his message. "I have never used steroids, period," says Palmeiro, his dark eyes ablaze. "I do not know how to say it any more clearly than that."

But it's McGwire who everyone in the packed hearing room is here to see. He's smaller than most fans remember, at least by 40 pounds, and as he reads his prepared statement through a pair of reading glasses, he chokes back tears. He expresses his sympathy to the parents who lost their sons, but tells the committee that answering questions about steroids puts players in an untenable position.

"If a player answers no, he simply will not be believed," McGwire says. "If he answers yes, he risks public scorn and endless government investigations. My lawyers advised me that I cannot answer these questions without jeopardizing my friends, my family, or myself. I intend to follow their advice."

McGwire's credibility is almost gone. His reputation is about to go next. Missouri Democrat William Lacy Clay: "Can we look at children with a straight face and tell them that great players like you played the game with honesty and integrity?"

McGwire: I am not going to talk about my past.

Clay: In addition to Andro, which was legal at the time that you used it, what other supplements did you use?

McGwire: I am not here to talk about the past.

New York Republican John Sweeney: Were you ever counseled that precursors or designer steroids might have the same impact?

McGwire: I'm not here to talk about the past.

Maryland Democrat Elijah Cummings: Are you taking the Fifth?

Tom Davis: The gentleman made it clear...

McGwire: I'm not here to discuss the past. I'm here to be positive about this subject.

North Carolina Republican Pat McHenry: You said you would like to be a spokesman on this issue. What is your message?

McGwire: My message is that steroids are bad. Don't do them.

McHenry: How do you know they're bad?

McGwire: Pardon?

McHenry: Would you say you have known people that have taken steroids and have seen ill effects, or would your message be that you have seen the direct effects of steroids?

McGwire: I have accepted my attorney's advice not to comment on this issue.

McGwire never strays from his lawyer's advice, sounding guiltier with each refusal to discuss his past. Gone is the hero Senator Ted Kennedy once lauded as the home run king of working families in America. In his place is a man who all but admits his career was built on a foundation of lies. If Davis and his committee think public humiliation can deter teenagers bent on using steroids, McGwire has been the perfect witness.

Selig and Fehr are the headliners when Davis calls the last panel later this evening, and though the committee members take turns battering both men, the session with the game's decision makers lacks the tension and emotion of the previous two.

Selig testifies that he barely heard mention of steroids in his sport until reading about the bottle of Andro found in McGwire's locker in 1998, no matter how many committee members show him examples that prove otherwise. Yes, Selig concedes, he wishes he knew in 1995 what he knows now, but no one should question his commitment on this issue. "Baseball had no drug program at all until I took over," he says. "None, zero."

Selig insists the new drug testing program will work if they only give it a chance, but says he is ready to institute even tougher penalties. The reason he hasn't done that already? The union. But he's not blaming the players, at least not tonight. "Baseball will not rest and will continue to be vigilant on the issue of performance-enhancing substances as we move toward my stated goal of zero tolerance," Selig says.

Fehr methodically answers questions for the dwindling number of committee members in the room. He understands this hearing for what it is. If this committee was serious about cutting off teenagers' access to steroids and other dangerous drugs, it would regulate the sale of supplements, a practice Congress ended in 1994. But the $21 billion supplement industry is now too strong, and going after the makers of products like Ephedra is not going to get these committee members on ESPN or the nightly news.

One lawmaker after another asks Fehr why players should get more than one chance when they break the law. He calmly reminds them of the "well ingrained notion of progressive discipline in collective bargaining agreements in this country." Cummings thunders that people in his district who are caught with drugs are thrown in jail, not given the five chances Fehr's union members receive in their new agreement.

"My personal view is that our job with violations of substance use is not to destroy careers. Our job is to stop it," says Fehr.

The daylong hearing has stretched past its 11th hour when the committee's chairman brings the proceedings to a close. For now. "We are going to watch this closely," Davis tells Fehr and Selig. "We represent people from vastly different districts, but tonight, we speak with one voice, conservative and liberal, Democrats and Republicans. This is not the end of our investigation into steroids."

It doesn't take Selig long to react to the game's new landscape. He's soon back in Washington, quietly meeting with the congressmen who are eager for the Commissioner to investigate steroid use in his sport. Selig knows how this game is played, so he listens, nods, and expresses interest, all the while hoping Congress will eventually lose interest and move on.

But Selig shifts his approach when several committees begin pulling together bills to mandate Olympics-style drug testing for all professional sports—legislation no one in Washington thinks has a prayer of passing. Rather than honoring the agreement he signed with the players just three months earlier, the Commissioner sends Fehr a letter on April 25, outlining a far more stringent drug testing program: a 50-day suspension for the first drug violation, 100 days for the second, and a lifetime ban for the third. He also wants to test for amphetamines.

"I am asking you now to demonstrate once again to America that our relationship has improved to the point that we can quickly and effectively deal with matters affecting the interest of our sport," Selig writes.

Any improvement in this relationship evaporates when Fehr balks and then Selig squeezes harder, giving a copy of the letter to the *New York Times*. The newspaper runs the story on May 1, one day before Twins reliever Juan Rincon becomes the fifth player this season to be suspended after failing his drug test. This time Fehr replies, sending a letter of his own that he shares with MLB.com.

"As you have acknowledged, the Joint Drug Agreement is, in fact, working well, as indicated by the very low number of positives from 2004, before the new provisions were agreed to for this year," writes Fehr, who says he's open to a discussion, but not through the media. "Accordingly," he concludes, "I will not here otherwise respond to your letter."

Fehr's response neither surprises nor moves Selig, whose proposal is unanimously passed by the owners on May 11. Six days later Selig and Fehr are back in Washington for a hearing called by Cliff Stearns, the chairman of the House Energy and Commerce Subcommittee for Consumer Affairs. And this time the focus is not on baseball alone. Stearns has brought in the commissioners from all four major sports to discuss his proposal for an Olympics-style two-year ban for first-time drug offenders.

"Anything that impugns our integrity we must deal with and deal with quickly, with harsher penalties," says Selig, who tells the committee that his latest proposal to the players will rid baseball of performance-enhancing drugs. But if his best attempts fail? "I would not resist federal legislation if Congress continues to believe that a uniform standard is necessary," he says.

Selig has been on the losing end of every major battle he's waged against Fehr. He was crushed when the owners colluded against free agency. He was blamed for canceling a season and then the World Series in his misguided attempt to secure a salary cap. He was scolded by a federal judge for using replacement players.

But now Congress has handed him a club to use against his longtime adversary, and he fully intends to use it. As often as he can.

Chapter 35

TRANSFER OF POWER

Mid-March–December 14, 2005

GEORGE STEINBRENNER IS sitting in a large leather chair in the Legends Field locker room, fielding the questions YES Network host Michael Kay is soft-tossing his way. Dressed in a blue dress shirt and gray blazer, he looks much like the George of old, save for the white hair. But the constant fidgeting with his glasses, the disoriented, uncomfortable look in his eyes, and his short, robotic answers to Kay's questions tell a different story:

"What were you thinking when Billy Martin and Reggie Jackson went at each other on national TV?" asks Kay, referencing one of the most storied episodes in Steinbrenner's tenure.

"I didn't like that at all," says George.

"Were you watching on TV?"

"I was watching on TV."

"Was it hard?"

"It was a very hard moment."

Steinbrenner tapes this episode of the YES Network's *Center-Stage* interview show on a sunny March afternoon, and by the time it airs in late May, it's must-watch programming not only for Yankees fans but for beat writers and media critics looking for clues to explain George's continued absences. The man who once courted the media and hungered for headlines is rarely seen in public. And when he does appear, it's with a security detail to keep the media at bay. These days, there are more questions about Steinbrenner than answers.

Make no mistake, Steinbrenner can still summon up his old self. He gets a head start on payback for his team's collapse in last fall's ALCS when the Yankees are in Fenway for Boston's home opener on April 11. In a classic Boss move, he orders YES not to show the Red Sox receiving their World Series rings during the pregame show.

When his heavy investment in the starting rotation—Jaret Wright (three years, $21 million), Carl Pavano (four years, $39.95 million), and 41-year-old personal favorite Randy Johnson (three years, $48 million)—is an early-season flop, Steinbrenner is quick to blame pitching coach Mel Stottlemyre, unsettling his manager in the process. "There's a lot of tension," Joe Torre says. "On a scale of 1 to 10, it's probably at an 8."

And when Jason Giambi starts poorly—hitting .195 with 29 strikeouts in 27 games—Steinbrenner orders Torre and Brian Cashman to tell their designated hitter to work out his problems in the minors. Giambi exercises his right as a veteran and declines, ratcheting the tension closer to a 10.

Steinbrenner's *CenterStage* interview airs on May 22, the day after a loss to the Mets drops the Yankees to 22–21. He has a few good moments, like when he offers a tale about Lou Piniella protesting the Boss-mandated haircuts. "Lou once told me, 'Mr. Steinbrenner, Jesus had long hair,'" George tells Michael Kay. "I said, 'Yeah, but look out there, Lou. See that swimming pool? Jesus could walk across that swimming pool. You do that and you can wear your hair any damn way you want.'"

But the lasting image is of a man nearing 75 in declining health, an image at odds with the clips of the swaggering Boss interspersed throughout the program. In one telling moment toward the end of the show, Kay asks Steinbrenner whom he'd want with him in a foxhole.

George looks at Kay and chokes up. "My father," he says softly. "He would know what to tell me to do."

The interview will draw the highest rating in the series' history. And it will never air again.

It's a somewhat more confident Steinbrenner who strides into the Stadium Club at Yankee Stadium for an important event three weeks later. This June 15 afternoon is one of the increasingly rare times the Boss is the center of attention as elected officials, reporters, and team executives crowd into the wood-paneled room.

After almost 20 years of threats, blueprints, and public debates, Steinbrenner is ready to announce plans for a new ballpark. The new stadium—to be built right next door—will be a replica of the old one, except with more restaurants and shops, and three times as many luxury suites. The Yankees will pay an estimated $800 million in construction costs (the final bill will rise in excess of $1.5 billion) under a public/private plan that draws plenty of protests from those opposing subsidies for sports stadiums.

Under the PILOT program (payment in lieu of taxes)—typically used to fund projects like hospitals, airports, and bridges but increasingly being used for stadiums—the Yankees will cover tax-exempt bonds issued by the city. The tax-exempt status of the bonds will lower the borrowing cost—saving the Yankees tens of millions—and the team will pay no rent or property taxes for the stadium it will own and operate. And the city and state are kicking in about $200 million for land, parking lots, and infrastructure costs (a bill that will double by 2008).

Also helping the team's bottom line: a clause in baseball's last labor deal allowing teams to deduct construction costs for new stadiums from their revenue sharing payments, reducing George's bill by about a third.

Governor George Pataki and New York City Mayor Mike Bloomberg are among the luminaries in attendance, and both men will soon walk up to the lectern to deliver their remarks and take any questions. But it's George's turn first.

In a pinstriped shirt tucked under a tie and blue blazer, a World Series ring on each hand, George steps briefly into the spotlight. He talks about what a thrill it is to build a new park and how great it is to stay in the Bronx. "We want to do something here for the people who support the team," he says. Then he thanks Randy Levine, COO Lonn Trost, and Steve Swindal for the hard work that made this day a reality.

When he gets to Swindal, he adds an unexpected twist.

"One day," Steinbrenner says, "Steve is the man who will take over for me."

Swindal is momentarily stunned. *Did George really just say I am going to run the Yankees someday?* Sure, Steve has gotten his fair share of battlefield promotions during his 22 years in the Steinbrenner family. There was the Coca-Cola bottling plant in the Bahamas George told him to run, and when that deal fell through the Boss made him the boss of the tugboat company in Tampa. A few months later, Steinbrenner tells him he's going to run a racetrack he just bought in Chicago.

So it's not the first time George has told him about a big job without any advance notice. And it's not as though the subject hasn't been discussed. Swindal and Hal Steinbrenner have already talked over why it makes sense for Steve to step up when George is ready to step down. They both know Hank doesn't want to run the business end of the Yankees. And Hal wants to stay in Florida to watch his three young daughters grow up before they go off to Culver Academies in Indiana, where all the Steinbrenner children go; by now, Steve's two children are both away at the school.

Swindal's already the general partner who travels from Tampa to New York several times a month to oversee the family business. It was Swindal who was cochairman of YankeeNets, and it is Swindal who is now chairman of Yankee Global Enterprises, the holding company for the team, its stake in YES, and other extensions of the Yankees brand. And he's grown more involved with the team since George had him negotiate Torre's extension last spring.

Everyone can see that Steve understands his father-in-law. Always deferential to George, Swindal represents the family at ownership meetings and sits on MLB committees. He's seen how hard George pushes himself, as if there were someone standing over his shoulder, still waiting for him to prove himself. Swindal knows he has George's ear—as much as anyone can—and he's taken plenty of the Boss' abuse, too.

Swindal's also seen how George dotes on his grandchildren and how much better he is with Hal away from the office than he is when he drags his younger son into team meetings. He remembers George thanking him for teaching Hal—14 years Steve's junior and like a little brother—how to hunt and fish. And he'll never forget a drive home with George one day, soon after he began working at American Ship, when his father-in-law turned to him and said, "Steve, the only thing I'll ever ask of you is to take care of my family." He promised George he would, and he's done his best to keep that promise.

It's with all this swirling in his mind that Swindal leaves the room as the press event winds down. He is almost out the door when veteran Associated Press reporter Ron Blum stops him.

"Sounds like you're the chosen one, Steve," says Blum.

Swindal smiles and shakes his head. "Don't read too much into that, Ron," he says. "I'm not."

Steinbrenner is still in good spirits later that night when he watches his team beat the Pirates, 7–5, at the Stadium to even their record at 32–32. But things change two weeks later, when he summons Levine, Cashman, and Gene Michael to Tampa for emergency meetings on the morning of Monday, June 27. The Boss wants to know why he's paying $200 million for a team that just lost three of four games to last-place Tampa and is stuck in third place in the AL East.

Steinbrenner, Swindal, and the team executives spend hours discussing trades, evaluating the farm system, and reviewing picks from the recently concluded draft. But when the New York contingent heads back to the Bronx on Wednesday morning, no major changes are made. The only news comes in an email response to questions about George's future from the Associated Press.

Steinbrenner, through Rubenstein, says he won't speculate on when he plans to step down. But he knows who will take over when he does.

"Steve Swindal," he says, "will be my successor."

It's the afternoon of July 12, time for Bud Selig's annual conversation with the nation's baseball writers at the All-Star Game. The Commissioner looks around the media room at Detroit's Comerica

Park, recognizing many of the writers who show up at this midseason game year after year. Selig has always enjoyed the give-and-take with baseball writers, something he had far more time for when he was running a team and not the entire sport.

Selig especially enjoys sharing a good story, and the first half of this season has given him more than enough tales to go around. The White Sox are the surprise team in the American League, reaching the break at a game-best 57–27. The Nationals are an even bigger surprise, leading the NL East at 52–36, drawing big crowds, and driving up the franchise's asking price.

Cubs first baseman Derrek Lee is this season's feel-good story, making his first All-Star lineup at age 29 by hitting a game-high .378—102 points above his career average. Young Marlins left-hander Dontrelle Willis is 13–4 and has people talking baseball in Florida. Ageless Roger Clemens, who'll turn 43 in three weeks, dominates NL hitters, striking out 112 in 122 innings with a 1.48 ERA.

Business is brisk, too. "We passed the 40 million mark in attendance Sunday, which is absolutely stunning," says Selig, who predicts that revenues will surpass $4 billion—more than triple the haul when he took office. Even the Brewers are on pace to finish in the black.

"The game has never been healthier or more popular," declares the Commissioner.

But then comes the question he dreads. "Are you worried," a reporter asks, "that you will be remembered as the Commissioner who turned a blind eye to steroids?"

Selig's face flashes with anger. He knows his legacy is at stake, and two weeks shy of 71, he prizes nothing more dearly. Selig waits a moment, regains his composure, then delivers the message he'll repeat over and over again until he convinces himself it's true: he had no idea what was happening in his own game.

"In the '90s, I went from camp to camp and talked to every manager, general manager, even owners in some cases. And not one person ever came to me about steroids," he says, citing conversations with general managers Billy Beane, Brian Cashman, and John Schuerholz. One man he doesn't mention is former Padres GM Randy Smith, who spoke publicly about steroids in 1995.

"This sanctimonious, 'Well, he should have known...' It's easy to look back and rewrite history."

Then he wraps his arm around a media he knows is still embarrassed about the story it missed, too. "You all were in the locker rooms every day. What did you see?" Selig asks. "I'm not being critical of you guys; I was there with you. People can say that we knew, but I'd like to know on what basis. There certainly is no medical evidence. There was no testing."

There is testing this season, and six players have been caught cheating since the new program started five months ago. "The system is working," says Selig, who thinks revealing a player's name on the first positive test is the reason for that success. He called public disclosure "the greatest deterrent of all" back in January, when the current plan was announced. "It surprises me more people do not understand that," he said that day.

But that was then. Now he understands the current testing program isn't going to stop questions like the one he just heard about his legacy, no matter how many players are caught cheating. Nor is it going to stop calls for more action from John McCain and every other congressional representative looking to garner an easy headline at Selig's expense.

The success of the new drug testing system is no longer enough. Now, Selig tells the media, we need harsher punishments—much harsher. And that's why it's imperative the union accept the "three strikes and you're out" policy he proposed in April: 50 games for the first positive test, 100 for the second, a lifetime ban for the third. This plan, the Commissioner says, is the only way fans—the ones flocking to his parks—will believe baseball is serious about ending the use of steroids.

"There is an integrity issue involved," he says. "And I believe the integrity issue transcends whether this program is working or not."

Fehr is in Detroit, too, and will have his own sit-down with writers. But the union leader understands the game Selig is playing. He knows he's really negotiating with Congress, not Bud, and that Selig's pivot is all about public relations. And he knows when he talks about protecting player rights it sounds like lawyer talk for protecting cheats.

With its back to the wall, the union is close to an agreement to increase the number of tests and begin screening for amphetamines. The major sticking point is the length of suspensions. Fehr keeps telling Bud's negotiators that they're trying to stop steroid use, not ruin careers. But Selig's men aren't buying it.

Neither is their boss. If Fehr wants to go back to Washington for another day of ridicule before Congress, that's his decision; Selig wants no part of that. Besides, these grandstanding lawmakers have allowed Selig to stake out the high ground, and there is no way he's giving up that advantage.

Especially after August 1, when baseball announces that Rafael Palmeiro has tested positive for steroids.

It's hard to know what's worse—the memory of March 17, when the 20-year veteran jabbed a finger toward the House Reform Committee and declared he'd never touched steroids, or the standing ovation he received in Seattle on July 15, when Palmeiro rapped a double for his 3,000th hit, joining Hall of Famers Hank Aaron, Willie Mays, and Eddie Murray as the only players to have hit 500 or more home runs (Rafael has 566) and 3,000 hits.

Palmeiro was privately looking over his shoulder that night in Seattle while celebrating his achievement. He'd tested positive for Winstrol, a high-powered anabolic steroid, back in May. He appealed, telling arbitrator Shyam Das that a contaminated B_{12} shot he received from teammate Miguel Tejada must have led to the positive result. Das was unconvinced and issued his decision two weeks after Palmeiro's big hit.

Fehr insists that catching a high-profile player like Palmeiro "should serve to dispel doubts about our determination to rid baseball of illegal steroids or the effectiveness of our testing program." But no one is listening. Not even support from his former boss—"Rafael Palmeiro is a friend—he testified in public and I believe him," President Bush says during an interview with the Knight Ridder news service—slows the frenzy that follows.

Jose Canseco's claim that he injected Palmeiro with steroids suddenly sounds credible. Rumors fly that baseball intentionally withheld the news until after Palmeiro got his 3,000th hit. Selig and Fehr have to release a joint statement saying they're not withholding results of other stars who have failed their tests. There are more calls for increased testing.

Selig continues to rebuff all union proposals that fall short of his 50–100–life standard, while the baseball season reaches a climax on and off the field. Albert Pujols is the first player to hit 30 or more home runs in his first five seasons, finishing an MVP season with 41 homers and 117 RBI. Clemens posts a game-best 1.87 ERA—the lowest of his career—leading Houston to a wild-card berth. Barry Bonds returns on September 14 and hits five home runs before season's end, giving him 708 home runs—within easy striking distance of the Babe—and a realistic shot at Hank Aaron's record 755.

Barry's return is of great interest to ESPN and John McCain for two wholly different reasons. On September 14, ESPN announced a $2.36 billion, eight-year deal with baseball starting next season, bringing MLB's total revenue from cable and radio rights to an average $397 million a season—double what it received in its last package. And the network is already developing its plans for Bonds' march into history.

On that same day, Senate Republicans vote down a proposal by Senator Hillary Clinton for "an independent, bipartisan panel to investigate" the government's failures following Hurricane Katrina. A day later, McCain announces he'll hold yet another hearing into steroids and pro sports. The Senator instructs the commissioners of the four major pro sports to come before his Committee on Commerce, Science, and Transportation on September 28 to discuss legislation mandating Olympics-style testing and penalties in professional sports.

Two days before the hearing, Fehr outlines his latest proposal in a letter to Selig. The union accepts all but the penalty aspect of the Commissioner's plan, instead proposing 20 games for the first violation and 75 for the second instead of 50 and 100, with a lifetime ban for a third violation subject to an appeal. "It appears the 50-game initial penalty is principally a response to criticisms which had been made of our current program," writes Fehr, who also gives the letter to the media. "But we are still required to adopt, and defend, reasonable, fair and appropriate agreements."

Selig is not moved. Nor are the five Hall of Famers Selig brings to the hearing. The appearance of the baseball legends is great theater, and McCain is so delighted that he asks the five players — Hank Aaron, Lou Brock, Phil Niekro, Robin Roberts, and Ryne Sandberg — to speak first. He interrupts Aaron to ask the big question: What does Hank think baseball should do about the records set by players using steroids?

Aaron defers to Selig. "I want to applaud the Commissioner," says Aaron, sitting next to Selig. "And I also just want to make sure that we clean up baseball." Says Brock, "The stiffer the penalty, the greater the message is sent."

Selig, now being advised by former Bush White House press secretary Ari Fleischer, reiterates his determination "to clean up baseball" and is roundly praised by the committee. If an agreement with the union can't be reached, he says, he'd accept the committee's proposed two-year suspension for a player's first drug violation.

Fehr takes a different tack. He reminds the committee that the players and the Commissioner agree on almost everything. Punishment, he says, is where they draw an important line. "Penalties should be designed for effective deterrence, not for punishment for its own sake," Fehr says. "The penalties the clubs are asking for, and the ones provided in the bills being discussed today, do not meet that standard."

And that's when McCain explodes.

"Don't you get it?" he all but shouts at Fehr. "How many more Rafael Palmeiros are there going to be? It's not complicated. All sports fans understand it.

"I suggest you act and you act soon."

Yes, Fehr gets it.

And he gets what he has to do, too.

Fireworks are still gleaming in the sky above Angel Stadium of Anaheim, celebrating the home team's Game 5 win over the Yankees in the ALDS, when a group of reporters approaches a somber Brian Cashman in the visitor clubhouse. They settle into a semicircle around the general manager and start peppering him with questions about the loss, the end of the season, and the 38-year-old's future. One particular question gives him pause.

"Did it creep into your mind that this could be the last Yankee season you are involved in?"

Cashman gets out a few words, but his voice cracks, and he can feel tears starting to well up in his eyes. He covers his quivering lips and takes a slow, deep breath as he fights to regain his composure.

There are too many conflicting emotions coursing through his mind. It's been almost 20 years since he started working for this team as a 19-year-old intern in the Tampa office, and he's sure he's just watched his last game as GM of the Yankees. It's hard to believe he's lived his entire adult life in this upside-down world. He's never had a family vacation. He never goes anywhere without first making sure he's reachable by phone.

How many times has Steinbrenner forced him to fly down to Tampa for a talk they could have easily had over the phone? How many public embarrassments has he suffered over the years, like the time George banned him from walking on the grass behind the batting cage so he couldn't talk to any of the beat reporters?

Still, he could take all that if he knew he had George's trust, if he could make decisions the way every other GM does instead of competing with Steinbrenner's shadow operation in Tampa. Even though they rode a strong second half to their eighth straight AL East title, these Yankees—stocked with too many designated hitters, not enough good fielders, and the oldest pitching staff in franchise history—were never Cashman's idea of a perfect team.

But how could he build a well-balanced team when there's a table full of advisers 1,100 miles away planting ideas in the Boss' head? Ideas mentioned during a night out at Malio's or while attending a hockey game or at any number of daily meetings too often turn into set-in-stone decisions before he ever has a chance to object. Yet he's the one George holds accountable.

That's what has made Steinbrenner's near-daily complaints so difficult for Cashman to stomach. And that's why Cashman put off all talk of a new contract until after the season. George may have receded from the public eye, but he's still a constant presence in his general manager's ear.

Cashman knows he wouldn't have to deal with all this in Washington or Philadelphia or Arizona, three franchises waiting to see if Brian walks when his contract is up on October 31 before filling their GM positions. He knows he owes so much to Steinbrenner, who took a risk on a 30-year-old kid. But after eight years of dysfunction, he just doesn't think he can do this anymore.

Cashman exhales and tries to answer the question again. He opens his mouth to speak, but now the tears are rolling down his cheeks and he can't make them stop. Embarrassed, he wipes his eyes and gets up to leave the clubhouse. The reporters hear a mumbled apology and something about addressing the question tomorrow.

Cashman isn't the only one wondering about his future. Torre has been the Yankees manager for 10 years, and even though the game's highest-paid manager has two years and $13.2 million left on his contract, he isn't sure coming back is worth the trouble. Like Cashman, he's tired of the bullshit—the attacks on his coaches, the repeated warnings that his job is in danger, the constant second-guessing—that is part and parcel of his job.

If he's going to be in pinstripes next year, Torre wants to talk to the Boss first. So on October 17 he flies to Tampa, meets George in the owner's office at Legends Field, and tries to clear the air.

"I didn't have a very good time," Torre says.

"None of us did," Steinbrenner replies.

Torre says he did not appreciate Steinbrenner funneling tough questions through postgame interviews on YES. George complains he barely heard from Torre all season. The two men both say they'll try to do better.

"Joe," George says. "We want you back."

"Boss, that's what I wanted to hear," says Torre, who has one more thing to tell the owner. "I'd be disappointed if Brian left."

So would Steinbrenner, who is surprised when Steve Swindal and Randy Levine tell him that Cashman is serious about leaving. The young GM met with both men soon after the Angels series and broke down again, telling them he just couldn't take another year of organizational chaos. Give us a written plan, they told him, so Cashman put together a long memo, complete with job descriptions and lines of reporting, with everyone in baseball operations reporting to the GM. Levine and Swindal thanked him, tweaked the plan, and gave it to George.

"Boss, Brian is going to leave if you don't change the way we operate," says Swindal, who's been softly pushing Steinbrenner to give Cashman full control for months.

The GM is sitting in his office the week after Torre announces his return when his phone rings. He already knows who's calling.

"Why are you leaving me?" asks Steinbrenner, sounding wounded. Cashman knows the Boss is a master manipulator and digs in.

"Boss, we've spoken this whole year; you know how I feel," Cashman says. "You don't trust me, and you're going to have to find someone that you can believe in."

When Steinbrenner doesn't cut him off, Cashman keeps pushing.

"You're a military man, you know there has to be a chain of command. But we don't have one. And it's killing us. There are storm clouds all around us—it's going to be like it was in the '80s all over again. And I can't be a part of it.

"You need to have a strong person that you respect. I think I can do it, but you don't believe it. Until you do, I can't work here."

To Cashman's surprise—and relief—Steinbrenner relents.

"I want you to stay," George tells him. "I want you to implement everything you are talking about. I will stay out of your way."

Cashman's already come to terms with leaving the Yankees organization, but he's not sure how he can leave the man who's responsible for everything he is, everything he's been able to accomplish. The Boss says he'll give him what he wants. How can he say no?

"Okay, George," Cashman says. "If you can give me that, I'll stay."

Steinbrenner quickly appoints Swindal to negotiate Cashman's new contract, and they reach an agreement on a three-year, $5.5 million deal on October 27. They make the announcement at the Stadium the next day, and while Cashman plays the company man, he's firm in his new role.

"I am the general manager," he tells the press. "And everybody within the baseball operations department reports to me."

Cashman soon turns his attention back to preparing for the new season. After all, he'll be running their offseason organizational meetings in a few days. And for the first time in recent memory, those meetings will be in New York instead of Tampa.

Roger Clemens trudges off the mound after striking out Chicago's Scott Podsednik to end the second inning in Game 1 of the World Series. He ducks into the Astros dugout and limps through the tunnel that leads to the team's locker room. The Rocket's thrown 54 pitches, allowed three runs and four hits, and the elastic sleeve he's wearing on his left thigh is doing little to ease the pain of his strained left hamstring. This is not how he envisioned ending his eighth World Series start.

Astros trainers pull down the sleeve to see if there's any way they can help Clemens, but too much fluid has already built up in his leg. His night is over, leaving fans back in Houston to wonder if Clemens' 22-year career is over, too. And when the White Sox complete a four-game sweep on October 26 to win their first title in 88 years, speculation over Clemens' retirement grows stronger.

The Astros paid Clemens $18 million this season and allowed him to stay home in Houston on days he wasn't pitching on the road. But despite his strong season, management has been non-committal about asking back a pitcher who's pushing 44 for a third season in Texas. Clemens put off retirement talk until after the season, but he's made no secret of wanting to spend more time with his wife and four sons. If Roger retires—and stays retired—the clock will begin ticking on the five years before the best pitcher of his generation enters the Hall of Fame.

A few days later, another longtime baseball man mulling retirement sits in a conference room in New York City, where he's talking strategy with the man who will follow him as executive director of the Players Association. Don Fehr has already told Michael Weiner the 2006 labor negotiation is almost sure to be his last. But he doesn't want to saddle Weiner with what has now become a multifront battle on steroids. There's no end in sight to the government's interest in Barry Bonds—the two men at the heart of the Balco case, Victor Conte (four months) and Bonds' trainer Greg Anderson (three months), will soon start their prison sentences—and who knows what headaches will result from the book two *San Francisco Chronicle* reporters are writing about the ongoing Balco investigation.

Most important, the legal team Fehr's hired is still working hard to regain possession of the 2003 drug tests seized by the government. Fehr hasn't seen the list of players who tested positive, but he knows the release of the names of several of those players would be big news. Weiner, the union's well-liked, 43-year-old general counsel, shouldn't have to face this. He deserves a fresh start.

Right now, Fehr's listening to the results of Weiner's last discussion with MLB's Bob DuPuy and Rob Manfred on a new drug testing program. The two sides have already agreed to hire an independent administrator for testing, increase the number of tests, and add testing for amphetamines. Fehr made one more attempt at lowering the penalties for testing positive, proposing 40 games for the first violation.

The Commissioner turned it down, Weiner says. Again. "Bud says he doesn't think that will make Congress go away," Weiner tells Fehr.

Fehr could complain about Selig, curse out the man who chose to cater to Congress instead of standing up for the game's players— but to what end? This fight has always been with a Congress playing the politics of distraction. Economists have been issuing warnings about a housing bubble that is sure to burst. And the day before the World Series ended, America suffered its 2,000th casualty in Iraq, a war Congress blindly approved and continues to fund. Cracking down on baseball is a perfect way to change the national conversation. Selig got a gift, pure and simple—an easy way to burnish his reputation by coming down hard on the players who helped make him rich.

Fehr has his concerns about Congress, too. He's sure he'd file a lawsuit if Congress forced its own drug testing plan on baseball, insisting the Fourth Amendment prevents the government from dictating medical decisions to a private business. But given how conservative the courts have become under years of Republican administrations, there's no guarantee the union would win that fight. And even if it did, there's good reason to worry about retribution. Republicans control the White House, the Senate, and the

House and have been openly hostile to labor for decades. Who knows what trouble a lawsuit would bring?

So with great reluctance, Fehr tells Weiner to let MLB know they have the deal they've wanted since April. And on November 15, Weiner and baseball Vice President Rob Manfred travel to Washington to explain their proposal to Tom Davis and get the House Government Reform Committee chairman's blessing. Davis, little known outside the Beltway until Mark McGwire made his March 17 hearing unforgettable, now has a national audience when he announces that baseball has met his standards.

"There's been a cloud over the game I love," Davis says. "I think this stops the rush of legislation as it regards baseball at this time. What we did is the right thing. We were vindicated by the result."

John McCain signs off on the deal. So does Jim Bunning, who cosponsored McCain's bill—but not before issuing a warning. "I and my colleagues will be watching very closely," the Kentucky Senator says. "And if things unravel, we still have tough legislation we can move through Congress."

Selig is euphoric. Congress is praising him, he got the terms he wanted, and he is certain no one can say he turned a blind eye to steroids ever again. The fact that the union suddenly looks weak is a bonus he'll savor for months.

"This not only is a historic day in baseball but a very meaningful one," Selig tells reporters. "I think what we did today was not only clearly good for the sport, but clearly good for the health of its players and the health of people all over this country.

"I believe this policy will eradicate steroid use in baseball."

Fehr can only shake his head at Selig's words. Eradicate steroid use? When has punishment ever succeeded as a deterrent in America's failed war on drugs? Chemists like Patrick Arnold, who now faces three felony charges for his role in developing and distributing the undetectable steroid for Balco, are always one step ahead of the drug testers. What will Selig do next if players continue to be caught taking performance-enhancing drugs?

Those, however, are concerns for another day. There are still more than enough problems to take care of now. Indeed, the very same day the new drug agreement is announced, a lawyer for the union is in a federal court in San Francisco, arguing that the government should obey lower-court orders to turn over the 2003 drug tests.

But the union leader is unaware that another crisis is looming. The tip federal agent Jeff Novitzky received from an FBI informant last February has led him to Kirk Radomski, a former Mets clubhouse man who is supplying steroids and HGH to dozens of major league players. At 6 a.m. on December 14, Novitzky knocks on the door of the drug dealer's colonial-style house in Manorville, New York, 70 miles east of Manhattan.

Radomski answers, and his life instantly changes. For the next six hours, 50 federal agents pull apart Radomski's house and walk out with 18 boxes filled with vials of steroids, HGH, thousands of needles, and a cache of documents including credit card and bank statements, tax returns, address books, and mailing receipts.

When the last box is removed, Novitzky drives Radomski to a diner five miles away, where they meet Assistant U.S. Attorney Matt Parrella, the lead prosecutor on the Balco investigation.

"Everything stops now," Parrella tells him. "If you sell to one more player and we find out about it, you'll go to jail. You're going to work with us."

Radomski understands he has no choice but to cooperate.

And suddenly, a very different clock starts ticking for Roger Clemens.

Chapter 36

CALLING MR. MITCHELL

Mid-March–June 6, 2006

It has to be about more than just Barry Bonds."

Bud Selig looks over at the courtly gentleman sitting to his right, the one who's just brought the conversation in the room to a halt: George Mitchell. It's the third week of March, and the two old friends are in the 31st-floor conference room next to the Commissioner's office at Major League Baseball headquarters. Selig asked Mitchell to meet with him and his inner circle in New York to discuss leading an investigation into steroid use by the game's most visible player.

But the Senator, it seems, thinks Selig needs to aim higher.

"It really can't be a Barry issue, it has to be the whole sport," Mitchell tells Selig and his team. "No investigation will be successful unless you expand it. It's the only way it will have any credibility."

Selig thought he'd put baseball's steroids problem behind him when he nailed Don Fehr to the wall last fall, forcing the union leader to accept the toughest testing program in pro sports. Fehr was *so damned determined to protect the players* that Bud is convinced the public now understands that he's the one dedicated to cleaning up the sport.

But that all changed three weeks ago, when *Sports Illustrated* ran an excerpt from a book called *Game of Shadows.* "The Truth," as the magazine humbly billed the story, traces Bonds' alleged use of steroids all the way back to 1998. Stories about Bonds and steroids are nothing new: the government's still pushing for a perjury charge over the Giants star's 2003 grand jury testimony. And Selig has already been asking baseball's lawyers if he can suspend Barry should the player be indicted.

This, however, is different. *Game of Shadows* is a tawdry tale of popping pills and backside injections, angry mood swings and ugly outbreaks of acne, petty jealousies and racial tension. Many of the headlines come from Bonds' former mistress Kimberly Bell, who speaks in great detail about the downside of the drugs she says Barry uses: the threats he left on her answering machine, tapes of which she put in a drawer for safekeeping. The bones in his skull that grew too large. The testicles that got too small. The periodic bouts of sexual dysfunction.

The upside, however, is undeniable: The home run record in 2001. The 136 home runs in the three seasons after that, leaving Bonds just 53 short of overtaking Hank Aaron as baseball's all-time home run king. His first batting title when he hit .370 in 2002 at age 38. As team doctors told Selig back in 2000, there's a reason why players are taking these drugs — they work.

The salacious stories left Selig disgusted. "It's even worse than I thought," he told friends. It left him frustrated, too, because this is what everyone around baseball is talking about. Not about the record attendance and revenues posted on Selig's watch a year ago, records sure to be broken again this year. Or the multiple bidders who are eagerly vying for the once-moribund Nationals franchise. Or the arrival of stars like Ryan Howard and Justin Morneau, CC Sabathia and Cliff Lee — and all the other attractive young players who have the TV networks offering record contracts to broadcast Selig's game.

No, all anyone is talking about now is Bonds and the dirty little secrets revealed in *Game of Shadows.* Especially down in Washington. It was only a matter of days after "The Truth" hit the newsstands that Selig started getting calls from his old friends in

Congress, who told the Commissioner that if he didn't do something about Barry Bonds, they would do it for him.

And that's why Selig is sitting in this conference room today with his three top lieutenants—Bob DuPuy, Rob Manfred, and Frank Coonelly—and outside counsel Tom Carlucci, listening to Mitchell outline how they should address their latest steroids crisis. And it's why Selig is promising Mitchell a free hand to do whatever it takes to get the job done.

"Anything you need to do, you do," Selig tells the 72-year-old Senator. "George, if you take this job, we're not going to tie your hands in any way. You will have carte blanche."

No one in the room is arguing with Selig—that debate has already been waged and lost. DuPuy, Manfred, and others close to Selig advised him to ride this one out. An investigation was sure to unhinge the players union after it accepted not one but two revisions to the drug testing program in the last 14 months. Their new program is plenty tough. With negotiations for a new contract set to begin in just a few weeks, the timing of this investigation could not be worse.

More than a few of the game's owners are sure to be displeased, too, they told Selig. What owner hasn't looked the other way at some point over the last decade when their GM signed a player they had every reason to believe was using steroids? And it would be hard to find many owners who want to pay Mitchell millions just to clean up the Commissioner's legacy and do nothing for their bottom line. They don't mind vouching for Bud, but shelling out big bucks to do so isn't anyone's idea of a good investment.

Selig keeps saying this investigation will give them closure on steroids, but no one really buys that. Not with the government still holding on to the 2003 drug tests. Not with prosecutors still chasing after Bonds. And not with the rewards of using steroids still outweighing the risks for their players.

But Selig ended those discussions the way he always does when he grows weary of listening. "Nobody elected you the ninth Commissioner of baseball," he told them. And this Commissioner has so many chits built up that he doesn't have to ask the owners for permission to launch an investigation.

Bonds has never been one of the Commissioner's favorites. Selig admired Mark McGwire, inviting him to sit in his box for the 1998 World Series and throw out the first pitch in Game 4. And he adored Sammy Sosa, twice going to Sammy's birthday party at the player's home in the Dominican Republic. But he's always been wary of Bonds, who assured Selig a year ago that all the stories about him and steroids were untrue.

Selig told Bonds he'd be tougher on him if he lied, and he meant it. So soon after reading the *SI* story, Selig called the San Francisco–based Carlucci, who'd been closely monitoring the case at Bud's behest for more than a year. Put a plan together to investigate the Giants star and a team of lawyers to carry it out, Selig told him.

At a meeting in New York a week later, Carlucci told Selig the investigation needed a big name to sell it. George Mitchell, Selig quickly decided, was his first and best choice.

"I'll call him," Selig said. "I'm sure I can get him to do it."

Mitchell had just walked out of a hotel room on his way to chair a Disney stockholders' meeting when Selig called with his latest request. "You know I've never said no to anything you've ever asked from me," Mitchell told him. "But if I do it, I'll need complete independence."

Selig said of course, Mitchell agreed to meet in New York, and now the Commissioner and his staff are talking with the Senator, assuring him once again that he'll have free rein if he accepts the job. "George," Selig says, "you can follow the evidence wherever it goes."

Selig tells Mitchell he'll have access to owners, management, and anyone working for Major League Baseball—from managers and coaches to trainers and clubhouse attendants. The players are another story. Mitchell won't have subpoena power, and everyone in the room knows that getting the union to cooperate is all but hopeless, especially with the Balco prosecutors just itching to investigate anyone with a connection to steroids.

But Mitchell is on good terms with Fehr, whom he asked to help straighten out the bid-rigging scandal for the Salt Lake City Olympics when he ran that investigation. "Maybe I can persuade Don it's in his best interests to cooperate so we can get this all behind us," offers Mitchell, who said he'd reach out to Fehr. "I'm hopeful."

The Senator raises the subject of his conflicts of interest: he's chairman of Disney, which owns MLB's broadcast partner ESPN, and he sits on the Board of the Boston Red Sox. And he's been Bud's friend for years. Selig dismisses each concern. Who's going to question the man his peers voted the most ethical person in Congress?

Mitchell says his contacts with Congress are still strong, especially with Henry Waxman, the man most interested in chasing after every steroids story. Carlucci says he'll introduce Mitchell to Kevin Ryan, the U.S. Attorney in San Francisco overseeing the Balco inquiry, and to Matt Parrella, the prosecutor running the investigation itself.

There are still a lot of questions to work out. Will they reveal names if they learn of players using drugs? That will be Mitchell's call, though no one in the room doubts his decision will be yes. Will guilty players be disciplined? That one's up to Bud. Can Mitchell promise to keep whatever he's told confidential? Only inside baseball—the government can still subpoena whatever it wants.

Selig asks Mitchell if he's sure he has time to take this on. Yes, Mitchell tells him, but he'll want to bring in another lawyer from his firm DLA Piper to work with Carlucci and his team. "Whatever you need," the Commissioner tells him.

Mitchell says he'd like a day to think it over, but Selig is hardly surprised when his friend calls back and accepts. News of the investigation is already beginning to leak by the time the media is called to baseball's office on March 30 to hear all the details.

Selig and Mitchell sit side by side at the center of the dais, both in dark blue blazers and starched white shirts. The Commissioner opens, telling the crowded room that he's asked the Senator to get to the bottom of baseball's drug problem once and for all. *Game of Shadows* was a tipping point, says Selig, and now it's time for action.

"When it comes to the integrity of this game, baseball must confront its problems head-on," Selig says solemnly. "An impartial, thorough review is called for."

And the person best equipped to handle this task is the man

sitting to his right, the former federal prosecutor and judge, the man who brokered peace in Northern Ireland. Any perceived conflicts of interest are immaterial where the Senator is concerned, Selig says. "Senator Mitchell's leadership of this investigation ensures that it will be both thorough and fair," the Commissioner says. "He's the best qualified guy."

Selig says that Carlucci and Jeffrey Collins, another lawyer from baseball's outside law firm Foley & Lardner, will assist Mitchell. They will focus on the time period after August of 2002, when baseball initiated its first drug testing program. But if the Senator finds reason to expand the investigation, "he has my permission to follow the evidence wherever it may lead," Selig says, squinting into the TV cameras. "He has my full support."

Selig says Mitchell has no timetable. Everyone in Major League Baseball will be required to cooperate with the investigation, and he hopes the players will do the right thing and cooperate, too.

And the Commissioner wants to make one more thing clear before they take questions. It concerns the statement they were all handed when they walked in, the one from the Commissioner's office that says Selig asked the union to put a drug policy in place in 1994 but the union turned him down. "I find the revisionist history that's gone on in some places to be remarkable," Selig says.

None of the reporters ask Selig why he's on record stating he'd never heard of steroids until the Andro story broke in 1998 or why he told Bob Nightengale that he was not aware of any steroid problems when the reporter asked him about PEDs back in 1995. But they do have other questions about the scope of Mitchell's investigation.

Will everything Mitchell learns be made public?

"That's the point of the investigation," Selig says.

Does that include naming players?

"Yes," he says.

Are there any limits on what Mitchell can do?

"The Commissioner has given me complete and unhindered authority to conduct this investigation in any way possible," says Mitchell.

Will the Commissioner discipline any players who Mitchell finds guilty?

"I want to see what he finds," answers Selig, saying he wants to keep his options open. "That will be the time to make those kinds of judgments."

Despite a string of appearances during spring training that hinted at a renewed vitality, George Steinbrenner is noticeably silent as baseball's highest-paid team—New York's payroll is $195 million after signing Johnny Damon away from Boston for $52 million over four years—gets off to a sluggish start. The Yankees lose 10 of their first 22 games, though it's clear Brian Cashman's put together a fearsome lineup. Damon and Jeter are perfect set-up men for 37-year-old Gary Sheffield and 35-year-old Jason Giambi, who have both shrugged off concerns about age and steroids use. And the Yankees have uncovered another gem in second-year infielder Robinson Cano, who's batting ninth and hitting .316.

The team clicks when Alex Rodriguez finally starts hitting. The Yankees third baseman sparkles in May, lifting the team to a first-place tie with Boston at 31–20. It's a good spring across town, too, as second-year manager Willie Randolph has his Mets in first place in the NL East behind young stars Jose Reyes and David Wright, the power hitting of Carlos Beltran, and veteran Tom Glavine anchoring the pitching staff. But no one can match Albert Pujols, who enters June with 25 home runs in 51 games, leading the Cardinals to an NL-best 34–19 record.

Selig is also having a good spring. On May 3, the Commissioner announces the sale of the Nationals to 80-year-old real estate developer Ted Lerner. The purchase price: $450 million, vindicating Selig's much-ridiculed decision to buy the Expos for $120 million four years earlier. "This has been a long journey," Selig says, "but I think history will prove it maybe was time well spent."

Indeed, the sale price is so good that Selig convinces the owners to take the balance of baseball's haul—more than $200 million after each team gets back its original investment and expenses—and put it in an investment fund. "The owners will only spend it on players," Selig tells Bob DuPuy. A major reason Lerner went so high for the perennial loser: baseball pushed the cash-strapped

D.C. government to ante up $610 million for a new stadium, which will open in 2008.

"There's no question that the Nationals will spend the money to be competitive," Selig says.

Selig is also pleased that close friend Carl Pohlad's 11-year wait for a new stadium is finally over. On May 26, Minnesota Governor Tim Pawlenty signs a bill to build a new 39,504-seat open-air stadium for the Twins. Lawmakers insist on one provision: the Twins cannot move or be contracted in the next 30 years. But there's one provision they can and will ignore: a requirement to hold a referendum on any new sales tax. The result: Minnesota taxpayers are on the hook for $392 million to provide a new home for the billionaire's team.

But despite the steady flow of good news, the Barry Bonds problem continues to gnaw at Selig. The union has quietly made it clear that it will contest any attempt to suspend Bonds should the government indict him on any or all of the charges — perjury, obstruction, tax evasion—they're rumored to be pursuing. Selig makes headlines in late April when he announces that baseball has no plans to commemorate Bonds when he hits home run No. 715 to pass the Babe.

"Don't read anything into it," Selig says. "Now, should Barry break Hank Aaron's record, that's a different story."

For once, the Commissioner has public opinion behind him: in a recent Associated Press poll, 65 percent of those surveyed judge baseball's treatment of Bonds to be fair. Even the Babe's 88-year-old adopted daughter Julia Ruth Stevens agrees. When contacted by the Milwaukee media, Stevens says she thinks Bonds' pursuit of Ruth is tainted, though she did admit to having a soft spot for the star-crossed slugger after watching a recent episode of his ESPN reality show.

"Honestly, I had nothing but sympathy for the guy," Stevens says. "He's got so much on his plate right now. Largely, it's of his own doing. But when he tears up and everything, you can't help but feel badly for him."

Others are not as kind. Bonds is booed unmercifully everywhere the Giants play. In San Diego, one fan throws an oversized plastic needle onto the field. An Astros fan arrives dressed as a syringe. Houston pitcher Russ Springer throws at Bonds several times and is cheered when he's ejected after finally hitting Barry with a pitch. Websites pop up across the country, imploring teams to walk Bonds to stop him from passing Ruth.

A large contingent of national writers are following Bonds when he arrives in Milwaukee for a two-game series on May 3, one day after hitting No. 712. Selig, whose office is 3.2 miles from Miller Park, declines to attend either game.

It's another two weeks before Bonds finally passes Ruth. It's the 4th inning of a sun-splashed afternoon game at San Francisco's AT&T Park when Bonds steps in against Colorado's Byung-Hyun Kim with a runner on first and no outs. He runs the count full, then unloads on a 90 mph fastball, sending it sailing halfway up the center-field bleachers, 445 feet away.

The sellout crowd of 42,935 stands and cheers as Bonds circles the bases. Selig made no plans to celebrate Barry, but the Giants did. Banners unfurl from the light towers on either side of the scoreboard in center field, one showing Bonds swinging a bat, the other depicting Aaron swinging above the No. 755. Bonds takes two curtain calls, and when he jogs out to left field for the next inning, another banner unfurls, this one picturing Bonds, Hank Aaron, and Willie Mays along with the No. 715.

Champagne toasts flow in the postgame locker room despite the 6–3 Giants loss. "This is the best group of guys I've ever played with in my entire life," says Bonds, who is in the last year of his contract.

But how much longer he'll remain in a Giants uniform is as uncertain as the outcome of the grand jury's deliberations. Most legal experts predict Bonds will be indicted before the current grand jury term ends in July. Will Selig decide to suspend him and dare the union to lodge an unpopular protest? Will the Giants, who have been supportive throughout their star's problems, want to endure another trying season—even if the home run record is within Barry's grasp?

Or will Bonds simply decide he's had enough, no matter how this season ends? That's one question, Bonds tells reporters, he's leaving for another day. He's averaged 45 home runs each season from 2002 to 2004 before missing all but 14 games in 2005 with three knee surgeries, and he's now 41 home runs from passing Aaron. At his current pace, Barry will end this season with 23 home runs, a mere 18 from holding the most cherished record in all of sports.

"If you play long enough," Bonds says, "anything can happen."
That's exactly what Bud Selig is afraid of.

"Be my eyes and ears."
That's what Selig told Tom Carlucci soon after George Mitchell told the veteran lawyer he was no longer part of his team. The dismissal stung, though Carlucci had to concede Mitchell made the right call. How could Selig call this an independent investigation if he used lawyers from Foley & Lardner, baseball's longtime outside counsel—and Selig's personal law firm?

That was months ago. He quickly accepted Selig's offer to be MLB's liaison to the Senator's investigation, and now he's the man in the middle, explaining to each of baseball's 30 teams what Mitchell and his lawyers are doing, what Mitchell needs, and why he needs it.

And he's also the one telling Mitchell that all baseball teams are not created equal, that small market teams don't always have the staff and expertise to promptly hand over the blizzard of documents and emails Mitchell is demanding. And it's Carlucci who has the unenviable task of making sure that the man who brought peace to Northern Ireland doesn't overstep his bounds.

The problems start almost immediately. In April, Mitchell bypasses the union and sends letters directly to a handful of players, requesting their medical records, drug test results, and contact information. It's a clear violation of baseball's collective bargaining agreement just as baseball management is opening negotiations on a new labor deal with the players. Carlucci tactfully reminds the Senator that he and his team—his lawyers actually do most of the interviews—have to follow all the game's rules.

The union is less tactful. On May 5, union general counsel Michael Weiner sends out an email to all players and their agents.

Weiner writes that Mitchell has already ignored the players' statutory rights, and the union's top lawyer strongly urges them to reach out to the union if they are contacted by the Senator or his staff. "The scope of the investigation to date is plainly inconsistent with the provisions of the Basic Agreement," Weiner tells them.

There's also an early dustup about legal representation. Mitchell is adamant that MLB employees — everyone from team presidents to clubhouse attendants — sit for interviews without a lawyer, a demand that prompts howls of protest. Carlucci brokers a compromise: teams can provide in-house counsel or hire an outside lawyer to represent their employees. Still, Mitchell issues a warning: anyone showing up with a personal lawyer will be referred to Selig for discipline.

Then there's what many are quietly calling Mitchell's "eye test." When you're sitting in the dugout and watching batting practice, Mitchell and his team ask managers and coaches, who do you *suspect* of using steroids? The same question is put to general managers, trainers, scouts — anyone who comes into regular contact with players. The tactic stuns team lawyers, who complain bitterly about this line of questioning on the weekly conference call Carlucci sets up as a clearinghouse for complaints.

Carlucci is surprised as well. It's his job to sit in on these interviews, making sure MLB employees understand they are obligated to answer questions posed by Mitchell and his lawyers. But how can he tell baseball people to speculate on what players are doing if they don't have the facts to back it up? "Did I see players get bigger and stronger?" a coach would say. "Yes. But I'm not going to speculate on why when I never saw or heard anything."

But Mitchell refuses to back down. The Commissioner gave him carte blanche, the Senator reminds his critics. And if Selig has any objections, he isn't making them known.

Mitchell's also surprised when he discovers that a number of teams are opposed to his investigation — strongly opposed. That can only mean one thing: Selig never shared with Mitchell what he'd heard on the conference call with ownership soon after he decided to conduct this investigation.

"What's the point?" Selig was asked repeatedly. "Why are we

killing our own product?" Let Congress investigate, owners and team executives told him as they rattled off one objection after the next. We're going to shell out millions of dollars. We're turning our managers and coaches into snitches. We're poisoning the well with the union.

Nonsense, Selig told them. "This has to be done," he replied. "It will bring us closure."

Few were buying Selig's explanation. Fewer were happy about his decision. But no one's willing to say out loud what some think Mitchell's investigation is really about: cleaning up Bud Selig's legacy.

Which is about the best thing the union will call it. Almost every union official sees Mitchell's investigation as nothing short of an act of betrayal by the Commissioner. The 2003 survey testing already revealed that the game had a drug habit. Enough stars were already identified as users — Giambi, Palmeiro, Canseco, Caminiti, and more — to prove that the problem wasn't confined to a few isolated cases. And the union already opened the collective bargaining agreement twice to upgrade the game's drug testing program, now the most stringent in all of sports.

The union wonders what adding a few more names to the list of users could possibly accomplish. You can be against steroids but in favor of fairness, union officials tell reporters. And what is fair about relitigating the past when both sides have already admitted they made mistakes and have taken big steps to correct them?

No one knows what the government plans to do with the 2003 tests they refuse to relinquish. And no one knows what will happen to any information a player hands over to Mitchell. The Senator is promising to keep everything confidential, but both Selig and Mitchell have said the public will be told everything Mitchell uncovers. That doesn't square up. And the union knows there's nothing Mitchell can do to prevent government prosecutors from seizing anything he learns. Maybe Mitchell will play fair, but the government's already proven it will break the rules if and when it sees fit. Even a first-year law student knows the union would fail to perform its basic fiduciary responsibility unless it advised players to seek counsel before deciding to meet with Mitchell.

Trouble with the players was expected. But Mitchell is not getting anywhere interviewing club employees, and he tells Selig that much of what he and his three lawyers doing most of the fieldwork are hearing is "transparently false." Frustrated, he asks the Commissioner to discipline anyone failing to cooperate with stiff fines and, in the worst cases, the loss of their jobs.

Mitchell's ire grows on June 6, when the *Arizona Republic* uncovers an affidavit for a search warrant for the home of veteran Diamondbacks pitcher Jason Grimsley. Filed by Balco investigator Jeff Novitzky, the affidavit is a stunner: Grimsley admits using steroids to help him recover from an injury while with the Yankees. He says he switched to using growth hormone once drug testing started, and has popped amphetamines most of his career.

"Everybody had greenies," Grimsley told investigators. "That's like aspirin."

Grimsley identified a handful of players taking steroids and the trainers who were their suppliers, though all names were redacted. Referred to but not named is Kirk Radomski, Grimsley's supplier and the man who turned the pitcher over to Novitzky.

Since the raid on his house in December, Radomski has recorded dozens of conversations with his clients for the feds. He's mailed out packages and handed over the FedEx receipts with return addresses, along with the checks the athletes used to pay for the steroids and human growth hormone. His last call was to Grimsley. Once news got out that the pitcher was busted, all Radomski's clients understood that his operation had been busted, too.

The 15-year veteran said amphetamine use was so rampant before being included in testing this season that there were two pots of coffee in clubhouses throughout baseball, one marked "unleaded," the other "leaded" to indicate it was laced with amphetamines. Latin American players, Grimsley said, were the major source of that drug.

Mitchell is left wondering how those he and his lawyers have interviewed could know nothing about any of this when Grimsley's affidavit, now all over the Internet, described a sport still rife with drug users.

After three months, Carlucci worries that Mitchell is growing tired of finding nothing but closed doors. The Senator's overtures to Fehr have been unsuccessful, and no players have come forward. Mitchell approached Kimberly Bell, but the government told him all witnesses in the Bonds case are off-limits until further notice. And even if Bonds is indicted, it will be months—maybe a year—until the trial is over and the witnesses are free to talk.

Mitchell's best hope might be a long shot: a study of blood tests from players' spring training physicals that, in the hands of the right person, could be used to identify trends in things like cholesterol levels that would indicate the presence of anabolic steroids. The right person would be Dr. James J. Heckman, an economist and Nobel laureate at the University of Chicago, known for his work on "latent variable analysis," the process he would use to determine the level of steroid use in baseball over the last several years.

The study would have to be "deidentified"—stripped of all information that would identify any players. Mitchell has asked Carlucci to shepherd this one through, and the lawyer knows it won't be easy. There are HIPAA laws to navigate and different medical privacy laws in just about every state. A meeting has been set for late July to discuss the idea with the union, which has already raised objections. Several team lawyers have objections, too.

Carlucci thinks back to the initial meeting with Mitchell. They all knew this investigation wasn't going to be easy—that Mitchell would have to rely on his powers of persuasion. And yes, the Senator is being paid handsomely for his efforts. But right now, it's hard to see how Mitchell will turn his investigation into a success.

Chapter 37

LAST STAND

July 4–October 31, 2006

W HY DO YOU keep fighting for Joe?" Randy Levine asks. "He'd never fight for you."

Brian Cashman lets the question hang there, unanswered, as the two men gather their thoughts after the brutal tongue-lashing they've just received from George Steinbrenner. The Boss has faded from public view. His sore knees have slowed him down. And there are as many bad days—when he struggles with his memory and finds himself disoriented—as good. But there's no question he's still capable of erupting, and this is the worst outburst the two Yankees executives have experienced in quite some time.

George's frustration started to roil when a loss to the Mets three days ago pushed the Yankees to a season-high four games behind Boston in the AL East. And as the runs piled on during today's humiliating 19–1 loss to the Indians in George's hometown—and on July 4, his 76th birthday—Cashman knew what was coming. So he wasn't at all surprised when Levine conferenced him in to the phone call with their boss.

"What the hell is going on with this team of yours?" Steinbrenner shouted from Tampa. "I'm spending $200 million, and what is Torre giving me? Nothing!"

Cashman tried to tell George that it wasn't entirely Joe's fault—both Gary Sheffield and Hideki Matsui have been out since late May with wrist surgeries. Their young star Robbie Cano went down with a hamstring injury two weeks ago. But that was a mistake.

"Shut the hell up, Cashman!" Steinbrenner said. "The whole team is letting me down, do you hear me? Just tell Torre he better fix this!" And he hung up the phone. Calls from Steinbrenner often end abruptly, and now Cashman is on the line listening to Levine. "You have to call Joe in Cleveland," Levine says. "Tell him George just put down the gauntlet."

Cashman knows both Steinbrenner and Levine truly dislike Torre; they've disliked the manager for years. Steinbrenner never forgave Torre for writing a book after winning it all in '96, the one in which Joe claimed he kept quiet about the extent of George's behind-the-scenes meddling. Cashman had to laugh about that. Steinbrenner, burned badly by the media and fan reaction when he fired Buck Showalter in '95, long ago shifted his attacks to his GM—first Bob Watson and now Cashman. Torre is on scholarship, Cashman often jokes—he has no idea the hell other Yankees managers endured.

The GM knows Steinbrenner and Levine think Torre is in it for himself, and it's getting harder and harder to defend Joe. Even Cashman, Torre's longtime ally, has to admit that success and money have changed the Yankees skipper. Torre came to the Yankees close to bankruptcy. Now he's in the middle of a three-year, $19.2 million deal through 2007—the highest for a manager in baseball history—and has his pick of endorsement opportunities.

"Father Joe," whose door was always open for his players in the early years, is now "Joe, Inc.," who entertains business partners in the manager's office. And Cashman worries that Torre seems to have time only for the players who won titles for him, a feeling that is splitting his clubhouse. Many disillusioned new Yankees have asked Cashman if this is the same Torre they've heard players rave about in years gone by.

"We're on the clock here, Joe," he's told Torre several times the last few seasons. "George is spending all this money, and he's sick and tired of losing. Those championships we won don't count anymore." Joe just smiles, pats Brian on the back, and tells the GM he worries too much. But scholarships last only so long—especially when you haven't won a title in five years—and the owner is apologizing to fans for that failure at the end of every season.

The once-tight relationship between Cashman and Torre is beginning to fray, too. Cashman still thinks Torre went around him to get Ron Guidry as pitching coach last November. Torre wanted Guidry to replace Mel Stottlemyre. Cashman told Joe he had nothing against Guidry, but the former Yankees star had never coached on any level. Yet when George asked Torre who he wanted, Joe said Guidry, and Steinbrenner made the deal.

When Cashman assigned an intern to track pitch counts in spring training, Torre accused him of spying. Cashman has begged Torre to stop burning out one relief pitcher after another—Steve Karsay, Paul Quantrill, Tom Gordon, and Tanyon Sturtze have all broke down from overuse. And now it looks like Torre will break Scott Proctor, the hard-throwing young reliever who's already on pace to throw more than 100 innings this season.

But Torre's not listening, and he's bristling over the changes Cashman's made this year. Cashman has eliminated the overlap George built into the system, redefined roles, and added a department for quantitative analysis—10-men deep—pulling the Yankees into baseball's modern age of statistics.

In Torre's case, he was pulled in kicking and screaming. Cashman has given him sheets charting hitters' tendencies, and Joe's ignored them. He's provided the manager with detailed studies on matchups, and Torre reminds him there's a heartbeat in this game. Cashman tells him less talented teams are beating the Yankees by paying attention to these numbers, and Torre says he'll always manage with his gut.

Torre's gut just might cost him his job one of these days, Cashman thinks as he punches his manager's number into his cell phone. Maybe this time, hopes Cashman, he'll listen. But the Yankees GM is not counting on it.

Torre holds a team meeting before the next game—"Nothing more than making sure that we're ready to play," he says—and the

Yankees respond by battering the Indians, 11–3. The win kicks off an 18–6 roll that wipes out the Red Sox lead and lifts the Yankees into first place on August 3, one game ahead of Boston. It's second-year players Chien-Ming Wang (5–0, 1.64 ERA) and Melky Cabrera (.319, 12 RBI, 12 runs) who deliver much-needed energy and production. And Cashman makes a big move at the trade deadline, getting Philadelphia's Bobby Abreu—a .301 lifetime hitter—for three prospects.

But it's Derek Jeter who truly ignites this run. The 32-year-old captain hits .396 and knocks in 20 runs in what is rapidly becoming a career year. Jeter puts together 13 multihit games, raising his season average to .354. All of which is in stark contrast to the one Yankee who is not producing: Alex Rodriguez.

Rodriguez is mired in a slump that is now entering its third month. Since his strong play in May, last year's AL MVP has hit just .265 with nine home runs, striking out 52 times in 53 games. Alex is slumping in the field, too, with every ground ball hit his way a potential adventure. In one gruesome game against the Mariners on July 17, Rodriguez threw the ball away three times, pushing his season total to 16 errors—one more than the previous two seasons combined. He also struck out with the bases loaded after Seattle intentionally walked Giambi ahead of him. Though the Yankees won, 4–2, the 53,444 fans jeered Rodriguez at every opportunity, now a regular feature of his life at the Stadium.

Even away from the Stadium, there are few safe havens for the star-crossed Yankee. Rodriguez was spotted in Central Park with his wife and two young daughters the morning of the Mariners game, and media critics wondered if he was too tired to play that night. The tabloids are using him for headline fodder—E-ROD and K-ROD are the mainstays. "Why Do We Hate This Guy?" asks ESPN .com. Talk show hosts and their callers plead for the Yankees to trade him.

"Alex isn't going anywhere," Cashman repeats publicly. Privately, he pushes Torre to urge Jeter to show public support for the man Derek once considered his close friend. Cashman knows most Yankees are leery of paying attention to Alex for fear of offending Jeter, who's made his disdain for Alex all too clear. It's for the good of the team, Cashman tells Torre, but the Yankees manager won't buy in.

Neither does Jeter. "My job as a player is not to tell the fans what to do," he tells reporters when questioned about the fans' treatment of Rodriguez.

Noticeably absent from the debate is Steinbrenner, whose appearances at the Stadium are increasingly rare. New York newspapers are now assigning reporters to stake out the owner's entrance before and after games, but when Steinbrenner shows up on July 15, security guards keep the media 30 yards away, enforcing the team's new policy for protecting the Yankees owner.

The next sighting is on August 16, the brutally hot afternoon the Yankees break ground for the new stadium. Looking pale, his face a bit puffy, Steinbrenner needs help to climb up the makeshift podium in a parking lot of the old Stadium, and speaks for all of 25 seconds. "It's a pleasure to give it to you people," says Steinbrenner, who repeats the phrase "you people" three times. "Enjoy the new stadium."

Steinbrenner is hustled to his car after the 90-minute ceremony, leaving team officials to answer questions about their vanishing leader. "Believe me, he's still the Boss," Cashman says. "He just doesn't relish publicity the way he used to," public relations guru Howard Rubenstein explains. "He's a great chairman," Levine says, "and like all the great ones, he's learned to delegate day-to-day operations."

It's Yankees communications director Jason Zillo, tasked with answering questions about Steinbrenner day in and day out, who puts it best. "We don't feel it's our owner's responsibility to answer questions after every home game that he attends," Zillo says.

Rodriguez's bat finally comes alive in September—A-Rod hits .345 with seven homers and 20 RBI in his first 17 games of the month—and the Yankees officially clinch the AL East on September 20. The team is sitting in the visitors clubhouse after a 3–2 loss to Toronto, watching the Twins put down the Red Sox on a big-screen TV. Corks pop and Champagne and beer flow as the Yankees celebrate their ninth straight AL East title.

In 13 days, they'll face the Tigers at the Stadium in the ALDS, and the pressure will mount once again. Everyone celebrating in the clubhouse tonight understands that another first-round exit will not sit well with the Boss.

"We need to make this postseason a lot longer than it's been for us," says Torre, who may finally be listening to Cashman. "Hopefully, we're poised to do something special."

The cascade of boos from the 33,989 fans in Miller Park rains down on Barry Bonds the moment he is announced. The aging Giants star ambles to the plate and responds with a sly smile as he digs in against Brewers left-hander Chris Capuano. He's heard a lot worse this season.

He's also on a tear. What Bonds does tonight is the only meaningful thing in this September 23 game between two losing teams playing out the string. Last night, Bonds hit a 403-foot home run off Brewers right-hander Chris Spurling, tying Hank Aaron for the most home runs by a National League hitter. Now he has the chance to break one of Hank's records in the same town Aaron started and ended his playing career.

Capuano, who surrendered a line-drive single to Bonds in the 1st, enjoys a 6–1 lead in the bottom of the 3rd. The tall, left-handed finesse pitcher misses with his first pitch to Bonds. His next offering is a fastball that tails back over the middle of the plate. Bonds jumps on it with that short, powerful stroke, sending the ball sailing to right-center field. Brewers outfielders Brady Clark and Corey Hart can only watch as Bonds' drive just clears the fence.

The 734th home run of Bonds' career momentarily silences the crowd as the new National League home run king circles the bases. The fans resume booing Bonds in each of his three remaining trips to the plate in the Brewers' 10–8 win. There is no visit—or even phone call—from the Commissioner, who watches the game on TV at his home 14 miles away, the same place he's been for the first two games of this series. Major League Baseball makes no mention of the feat.

What Bonds' 26th and last home run of the 2006 season elicits instead is a list of questions.

Will Bonds return next season to chase Aaron's all-time home run record of 755, now just 21 homers away?

Will he do it in a Giants uniform?

Will he be under indictment for perjury, obstruction of justice, tax evasion—or all three?

Some or all of these questions seemed moot as recently as late July, when the feds appeared on the verge of indicting Bonds and the 42-year-old looked close to retirement. But Barry's trainer Greg Anderson chose jail time over testifying against his childhood friend, U.S. Attorney Kevin Ryan got cold feet, and the government convened a new grand jury instead of issuing an indictment.

Anderson, the only person other than Bonds who can say whether the player knowingly took steroids, left jail after 15 days, when the first grand jury looking into perjury and obstruction charges against Bonds ended its term. But he went back in on August 28 after refusing to testify before the new grand jury. And there he remains, sitting in his 8-by-12-foot cell, as tight-lipped as ever about what Bonds did or did not do.

It was about that time that Bonds' play changed for the better. On August 20, the Giants star was hitting just .235 with 16 home runs and 51 RBI. In the fifth and final year of his $90 million contract, with bone chips floating in his left elbow, Bonds talked more about retirement than chasing records. And the Giants made little effort to discourage him.

But tonight's home run was his 10th in his last 27 games. Playing once more like a seven-time MVP, Bonds is hitting .400 in his last 106 plate appearances, with 26 RBI, 21 walks, and 22 runs scored.

"There's a pretty big difference in what he looked like the first time we played," says Brewers manager Ned Yost, who last saw Barry in mid-July. "He's healthy now, he feels better, and it shows." And now both Bonds and the Giants are talking about spending at least one more season together.

How much longer the feds and Senator Mitchell will spend chasing after Bonds—and what they will find—is still anyone's guess.

George Steinbrenner is angry. He went to sleep angry after the Tigers eliminated his Yankees from the playoffs in four games, he

woke up angry, and he's still angry as he listens to Howard Rubenstein read back the statement he released earlier this morning. It's
been 90 minutes since Rubenstein sent out the Yankees owner's
promise to make changes, big changes, for next season. Now
George wants his public relations man to make a change in his
promise.

Read it back again, he tells Rubenstein.

"I am deeply disappointed at our being eliminated so early in the
playoffs. This result is not acceptable to me nor to our great and
loyal Yankee fans," Rubenstein says over the phone. "I want to congratulate the Detroit Tigers organization and wish them well. Rest
assured, we will go back to work immediately and try to right this
sad failure and provide a championship for the Yankees, as is our
goal every year."

"Change that to *absolutely* not acceptable," Steinbrenner says.

"George—"

"Howard, just do it!"

Rubenstein is unfazed, as he always is when talking his volatile
client off the ledge. "George, the writers have been calling all morning about the *Daily News* story," Rubenstein says. "They say Torre
was stunned when he heard about it. I told them no decision has
been made and you have nothing more to say."

"Good. Send out this statement again."

Steinbrenner hangs up and mulls over the turmoil of the last 24
hours. The *Daily News* ran with the story he leaked to them last
night. The headline OUTTA HERE! in great big block letters screams
off the Sunday edition's front page over a picture of Joe Torre.
Inside, the story says George is about to fire his manager and hire
former Yankees player and manager Lou Piniella, one of his longtime favorites.

Torre's stunned. How the hell can he be stunned?

George is tired of hearing what a great job Torre did juggling his
lineup when Matsui and Sheffield went down this season. And he's
tired of hearing about the nine straight AL East titles. He pays
Torre more than any other manager—*far more*—to win World
Series titles, not division titles. Didn't he spend $200 million to
give Torre the best collection of players in the game? Didn't he tell

Torre he had to win this year, not get beat—*get embarrassed!*—by a team that pays its players less than half of what he pays his team? Detroit's payroll is $82 million, equal to what he pays Derek Jeter, Jason Giambi, Alex Rodriguez, and Mike Mussina combined.

Torre's great strength has always been dealing with his players, but Steinbrenner wonders if that's still true. Why hasn't he done anything about the Jeter-Rodriguez rift? Why did his problems with A-Rod show up in a *Sports Illustrated* story written by the coauthor of Torre's book? And why did he bat Rodriguez eighth in Game 4? Rodriguez is as fragile as he is talented, and batting him "double cleanup"—as Torre so flippantly put it—was a surefire way to break his confidence right when the Yankees needed him most.

George has been annoyed about Joe's distractions for months. His deals to endorse products like Bigelow tea. His racehorse. His charitable foundations. *Hell, Joe, do those on your own time.* Torre is supposed to be thinking of one thing during the baseball season, and one thing only: George's team.

About the only thing going Steinbrenner's way is the lack of media interest in his health. At least for the moment. And this is the best George has felt in months, even if his knees are really killing him. The doctors keep saying he should get his knees cleaned out or maybe even replaced, but George doesn't believe much in doctors. Never has. He's three months past his 76th birthday, and his aversion to doctors just isn't going to change.

Besides, it's not his knees that worry him. He's not going to see any doctors about those other problems, either, especially since right now he has no need for help. It's been a while since his hands have trembled. Or since he's cried for no reason—except when he sees his son Hal's little girls. That always seems to bring him to tears these days.

His memory is still fading in and out, but he's concentrating on the good days and trying to ignore the bad. And on this day, Steinbrenner knows exactly what he wants to talk about with his lieutenants: Joe Torre. He's ready to get rid of the manager, even with a year left on his contract. He's never liked Torre's laid back methods, and even if they worked before, they're not working now. So when

Swindal, Levine, Cashman, and Lonn Trost all check in for their conference call this Sunday afternoon, George asks the only question that matters:

"Tell me why I shouldn't fire my manager."

Swindal speaks first. He feels strongly that Torre has earned the chance to finish out his contract, the one Steve negotiated for him four years ago, and not because they would have to pay Joe the final $7 million whether they keep him or not. He's done a good job, Swindal says—the team won 97 games despite all their injuries and an aging pitching rotation. "I vote for bringing him back," says Swindal.

Trost quickly agrees, and Cashman speaks next. The young general manager has his own issues with Torre. The manager has to stop abusing his relievers. He has to stop favoring the old guard, even if it's unintentional. And he has to repair his relationship with Rodriguez. But the GM and manager have been successful together too long and worked through too many problems for Cashman to think these things can't be fixed.

"I don't think we should fire Joe," Cashman says. "We had a bad series. It happens. I don't think getting rid of Torre will solve any of our problems. I think it will only make things worse.

"Are we better than we have performed? Yes. Does Torre have flaws? Yes. But we are still making the playoffs every year, and Joe is popular. We're stepping on our dick if we fire him. This run's not over yet."

Steinbrenner asks Levine what he thinks, though the Boss already knows. His team president and Torre have battled almost from the day the former New York City deputy mayor arrived in 2000. Steinbrenner expects Levine to be his eyes and ears when he's home in Tampa, which is most of the time now. But Torre considers Levine a well-paid spy.

Levine thinks Torre has lost his focus and his team. But he's not going to fight the group. Not this time. "Boss, I think you know how I feel," Levine says. "But if everybody else thinks Torre should come back, then I'll go along."

Cashman and Swindal call Torre on Monday, urging him to call Steinbrenner and tell him how much he wants to come back. Torre agrees. "Boss, all I ever wanted to do was make you proud," Torre tells Steinbrenner later that day. "If you think in your heart you have to make a change, then you should do it. But I'd like to stay and finish the job."

The Boss told his manager he had not yet made his decision, and Torre still doesn't know his fate when he walks into his office at the Stadium on Tuesday around noon. The Yankees have called a media conference for 1 p.m. to discuss their manager's future. His scholarship has officially ended, just as Cashman warned him it would. It's one thing for George to tell the press your job is in jeopardy, it's another when he really means it. And this time he does.

Sitting with Torre is his friend Arthur Sando, a veteran PR man. If he's fired, Torre wants Sando to set up his own press conference—out of the Stadium, of course—so Joe can tell his side of the story. The phone rings in Torre's office a few minutes before 1 p.m. It's Cashman, calling from the Yankees offices upstairs. Also on the line are Swindal and Levine—and George. "Joe," Cashman says, "Mr. Steinbrenner would like to speak with you."

"Joe, we want you to manage the team," Steinbrenner says. He waits a few moments to let his words sink in. "But I want you to understand that I will be holding you accountable. Cut out the distractions. Be the manager. I expect you to win this year—it's about time. And I don't expect to hear any excuses."

It's a relieved though somewhat miffed Torre who sits at the podium in the Yankees media room a few minutes later, wearing a dark blazer, blue shirt, and red tie, answering questions from the New York reporters. Steinbrenner has hardly given him a vote of confidence. That's a point George makes abundantly clear in the release his PR staff hands out as the reporters file in.

"I spoke to Joe Torre today and I told him, 'You're back for the year,'" the statement reads. "'I expect a great deal from you and the entire team. I have high expectations and I want to see enthusiasm, a fighting spirit and a team that works together. The responsibility is yours, Joe, and all of the Yankees.'

"Yes, I am deeply disappointed about our loss this year. We have to do better. And I deeply want a championship."

"It's about time." Torre bristles at the words. The team hadn't won

a World Series in 18 years before Torre got there, and he gave Steinbrenner four championships in five years. No one had done that in
53 years. His teams have made the playoffs every one of the last 11
seasons. Only Atlanta's Bobby Cox can say the same thing.

Even if George isn't the raging tyrant he once was, Torre is finally
discovering what life under Steinbrenner was like for Billy Martin,
Lou Piniella, and all the other managers who came before him. But
he will be the manager for at least one more year. So he alternately
smiles and grimaces as reporters ask their questions, each one a
variation on the same theme: How does it feel to be—what? Publicly humiliated?

"You can't pick and choose the parts you like about working for
George Steinbrenner," Torre says. "You have to understand the
whole package. He requires a lot, we know that. When you work
here, you have to understand that every year may be your last
year."

Torre pauses, then continues. "He gave me his support," the
Yankees manager says. "I'm just pleased I'm able to stay on and do
this."

Five.

That is the number of times Don Fehr has shared a podium with
Bud Selig to announce a new labor deal for baseball.

It's also the number of times he's listened to Selig use the word
historic to describe the nature of their agreement, the fifth coming
right now before the nation's baseball media in a crowded Busch
Stadium conference room. It's the afternoon of October 24, and
Fehr is sitting next to Selig in the middle of a dais 10-men strong,
with baseball players, union officials, and MLB officials at each
man's side. In a few hours, the Tigers will play the Cardinals in
Game 3 of the World Series, which is tied at a game apiece.

But first, the Commissioner of baseball has a few things he
wants to say about the new six-year labor deal the owners have just
reached with the game's players.

"This is an historic agreement for a number of reasons," says
Selig. He leans into the microphone in front of him and ticks off
his talking points. "First, it is the longest labor contract in baseball

history. Second, we reached the agreement nearly two months before the deadline. And third, by the end of this contract, baseball will have gone 16 years without a strike or lockout."

Five times Selig and Fehr have announced a deal together. There was always some unfinished business with the previous four deals — something more Selig wanted, something less Fehr wanted to give him. Something that would form the battlefield for the next labor war.

But there was every reason to believe this fifth time was going to be different for one simple reason: the economics of the game appear to be working for both sides. The players have free agency and salary arbitration and are generally happy with the system. The owners have revenue sharing and a competitive balance tax, and all but the one owner based in the Bronx are generally happy with their arrangement. There should be no issue out there to serve as a battleground going forward.

And there wouldn't be if Selig had let their drug agreement do its job, stood up to the headline seekers in D.C., and not hired George Mitchell. The union has little doubt about where the blame is going to fall in Mr. Mitchell's investigation.

In fact, Selig and the Senator have started publicly condemning the players for refusing to cooperate in the investigation and accusing the union of telling them not to talk. After the union twice opened the basic agreement to toughen the drug testing program last year, Fehr and his colleagues see the Commissioner's decision to launch the Mitchell investigation as a betrayal of everything the two sides have accomplished through collective bargaining in 20 years.

Hell, with Mitchell looming behind the scenes, it's just short of a miracle that this deal was done peacefully — or at all.

Fehr stares out at the several hundred reporters crammed into the conference room while Selig congratulates both sides on what they've done. Fehr finds the familiar faces — Murray Chass of the *New York Times*, Bernie Miklasz of the *St. Louis Post-Dispatch*, Peter Gammons, now working with ESPN, and a few other veterans who have been here before when there were far fewer smiles and a lot more gritted teeth.

There are many faces Fehr barely recognizes and even more that he doesn't know at all. Heck, many of these reporters here today were barely out of grade school when he and Selig announced their first agreement together, the shotgun marriage then-Commissioner Peter Ueberroth pushed them into after a two-day strike back in 1985.

Fehr never intended to be in this job this long, but here he sits, coming to terms with Bud Selig for the fifth time. It's the second time without a work stoppage and the first time without the threat of a strike or lockout.

And, he's all but certain, it's the final time with Don Fehr as the executive director of the Players Association.

That was part of his message last Saturday night at MLB headquarters in New York, the one he delivered after it was apparent that a deal was at hand. Selig had been in a day earlier to give a pep talk and then fly back to Milwaukee. Late Saturday night, Fehr, his brother Steve, Michael Weiner, and a few union lawyers were finally just sitting back and relaxing. So, too, were Bob DuPuy and Rob Manfred, baseball's top negotiators, and their small team of lawyers.

After so many ugly battles and so many angry words in previous negotiations, they all agreed this deal was reached in a professional fashion. It was a moment to savor, especially for the man who had been at it the longest.

"This will be probably be — may well be — my final negotiation," he told the group that night. "In all the years I've been involved with these negotiations, I never thought I'd be able to say there is cooperation between players and management and an environment that allows the game to grow.

"But after all these years, I can finally say that. I am very proud of that."

Both sides have reason to be proud. Revenues this season will reach $5.6 billion, a 56 percent increase from the beginning of the current contract in 2002. Attendance will surpass 76 million, setting a record for a third straight season. The new television contracts with Fox and TBS, combined with the one-year-old deal with ESPN, are going to bring in $5.5 billion over seven years, another record haul. Baseball's website is booming, and more regional sports networks are coming online every season.

The players' average salary is now $2.87 million, an all-time high. For comparison, this year's $327,000 minimum salary is slightly more than the average player's salary in 1984. By any measure, the business of baseball has never been better. "You always have a better relationship when both sides are making money," Tigers manager Jim Leyland told reporters in the interview room moments before the contract was announced. "When you're putting money in a lot of pockets — and in our case it's a lot of money — it tends to make people feel real good."

Indeed, both sides felt so good that they weren't looking for anything more than minor revisions. The new deal retains the revenue sharing and competitive balance tax rules that were established in the 2002 agreement with only slight changes in thresholds and rates. There are no changes in the drug testing program, and no team will be contracted during the life of the agreement.

There was one thing Fehr wanted that had little to do with money: a big turnout of players at bargaining meetings. He got that, too. Nearly 100 players participated in at least one bargaining session, and many more took part in conference calls and team meetings. It was important for management to see the players at the table, to understand they were engaged and invested in the process. And he wanted to make sure the players understood that, too.

For as proud as Fehr is to have reached a productive working relationship that has ushered in a new Golden Age, as Selig loves to say, and as relieved as he is that this agreement means the game will enjoy 16 seasons without a work stoppage, he still knows it is dangerous for the players to let down their guard as long as the man sitting to his left remains the Commissioner of baseball.

Selig is done talking now, and it's Fehr's turn to speak. He's not going to bring up Mitchell, though he knows the reporters here want him to address that subject. But those are words best saved for another day.

"I share the Commissioner's view that our game has experienced enormous growth," says Fehr, who predicts the new agreement will keep the boom going. "We were able to conclude this new agreement because the two parties brought to the table a respect for the positions and needs of the other. As a result, the discussions were workmanlike and pragmatic, and, while difficult on some issues, the talks were conducted in a mutual attempt to get the job done."

If only Fehr could say the same about Selig and his friend's ongoing investigation.

George Steinbrenner feels very much at home on the picturesque Chapel Hill campus of the University of North Carolina. This is where his daughter Jennifer went to college, graduating in 1981, five years behind the man she would marry, Steve Swindal. Steinbrenner brought his Yankees here for exhibition games three times while Jenny was an undergrad. And just this spring, George wrote a check for $1 million to help renovate the baseball stadium. When completed, the stadium entryway will be called the Steinbrenner Family Courtyard.

On the pleasantly warm afternoon of Sunday, October 29, George Steinbrenner and his wife Joan are settling into their seats alongside Jenny and Steve in the campus' historic Playmakers Theatre, home to the school's musical theater troupe. They all flew in earlier today to watch Haley Swindal play the starring role of Sally Bowles in the troupe's production of *Cabaret*.

Haley, the oldest of George's 13 grandchildren, is a junior and a talented singer and actress. Steinbrenner is enjoying his granddaughter's portrayal of the scantily clad cabaret singer when he begins to feel ill. By the time the second act ends, he is ghostly pale, his eyes are closed, and he is fading in and out of consciousness. Someone in the audience calls the school's public safety office as director Benjamin Rumer clears the theater. Steinbrenner is alert but complaining of chest pains as the paramedics wheel him to the ambulance and speed off to the university hospital.

You suffered a series of small transient ischemic attacks, the doctors tell him. They give the family the same news, with a bit more detail. Although it's not a stroke, the doctor explains, a TIA is a blockage of blood to the brain that can bring on stroke-like symptoms. If the blockages break up quickly, there is no damage to any brain tissue. If.

"I'm fine," Steinbrenner tells everyone. He insists that Haley not miss the second performance of the play later that night. The doctors run tests to make sure Steinbrenner is stable and suggest that he remain in the hospital a few days. "Forget it!" says George, who is already telling his family to make plans to leave in the morning.

Steinbrenner is resting back in Tampa by the time the *Daily Tar Heel,* the university's student newspaper, reports the story two days later. "It looked like he had fainted," a student sitting two rows behind Steinbrenner told the paper, which reports that the Yankees owner suffered chest pains. The story soon hits the wires, and Rubenstein is ready with a statement.

"George Steinbrenner is well and raising hell today," Rubenstein wrote. "George felt ill during the performance, which was held in a Revolutionary War auditorium with no air-conditioning and the windows closed tight—it was very hot."

Rubenstein also takes all calls for the Yankees owner. No, he tells New York reporters, Steinbrenner did not suffer chest pains. Yes, George is already back to work. "I talked to him yesterday and again today," Rubenstein says. "He's in great spirits, and we're all very pleased."

The Yankees have a lot of decisions to make this offseason: Should they pick up the options on 37-year-olds Sheffield and Mussina? Do they make an offer to Andy Pettitte, now a free agent? Is Melky Cabrera their everyday center fielder? George is indeed involved and back at his desk at the team's Himes Complex in Tampa, though only for a few hours each day.

He's gone to see his personal doctor but refuses to share anything he's learned with Swindal, his sons, or any of his senior staff. Nobody is surprised: George has always kept his health concerns to himself.

But it won't be long before questions about George's health won't have to be asked. The answers will be there for all to see.

Chapter 38

A CHANGE IN PLANS

March 28–May 6, 2007

G EORGE STEINBRENNER TURNS away from his dinner in the Legends Field cafeteria and puts his arm around his daughter Jessica. Her four kids take a break from horsing around to crowd around their mother and Bumpa, as they call George. Felix Lopez, Jessica's husband, stands up and pulls out a cell phone so he can snap a picture of the happy moment. For one of the few times this spring, the Steinbrenners are smiling.

It's March 28, and George is still recovering from the mini stroke he suffered last October. It's been slow going. He still comes to the office for a few hours most days, but he's far from the one-man show of old. His memory is foggier than ever, and his ailing knees make it hard to get around. But he's happy to be here today with his family to watch the Yankees play the Astros.

Tonight's game should be one-sided—his team's starting lineup boasts a collective 34 All-Star appearances to the Astros' two—but his Yankees have only managed one win in their last six games and George is annoyed. He's come to accept that these March games don't count, but George has never gotten used to losing.

Not that he has seen many of those losses in person, and his absence from camp has been duly noted by the Yankees beat writers. He hasn't spoken to the media since a brief session the day camp opened, so his presence today in the cafeteria is drawing everyone's attention. George scowls when he sees the reporters approaching, but few can pass up the chance to ask him the one question that is on everyone's mind.

"George, who is going to run the team now that Steve is gone?" one of them asks.

The grandchildren pay the reporters no heed and have already resumed scampering around the table. George merely shakes his head and waves the writers away. Not long afterward, Yankees interns are distributing a statement from the Boss issued by Steinbrenner's PR man Howard Rubenstein back in New York.

"I'm the boss," it reads. "I continue to be the boss, I have no intention of retiring, and my family runs the Yankees with me.

"When I'm ready to say something, I'll say something. I don't really appreciate being mobbed and people screaming at me."

This is the second statement the writers have received from Rubenstein's office today. The first is what prompted the reporter's question and officially changed the Yankees landscape: after weeks of media speculation, Jennifer Steinbrenner and Steve Swindal announced they have filed for divorce. The Yankees hierarchy has just been turned on its head.

"Although their marriage is dissolving, they remain friends and maintain a strong mutual respect," the statement read. "They are devoted to their two children and will make them their shared focus."

With today's announcement, the chairman of Yankee Global Enterprises, the same man George publicly anointed his successor two years ago, will soon be on the outside looking in. George liked and respected Steve — hell, he still does — and the Boss had grown comfortable with Swindal as the voice of the family in the daily operation of the Yankees. But this is a family business, and if Swindal is no longer family, there's no way he can continue to run Steinbrenner's empire.

George knew that Jenny and Steve's marriage had been strained, but all existing problems were exacerbated on February 15, when Steve was arrested for driving under the influence of alcohol. When a police officer pulled him over for speeding, Swindal claimed he was on his way to a marina to spend the night on his boat. He failed a field sobriety test and spent five hours in a Largo, Florida, jail before being released on $250 bail. He pleaded not guilty on March 15, and a pretrial hearing is set for April 5.

Swindal had tried to keep their marriage together, but when Jenny filed divorce papers yesterday, it made an already difficult spring that much worse. The family still has the wagons circled around George, whose health has become their overriding priority. And they just recently learned that Hal Steinbrenner and his wife Christina are separating, too. The couple has three daughters, all under age 10, and appeared happy. No one saw this coming.

And now, this very private family is figuring out their new roles on a very public stage. There's little question that Hal, the MBA in the family, will assume the duties of Swindal, his mentor and surrogate big brother, no matter how uncomfortable that might be. Less certain is the role of Hank, who turns 50 in five days and moved back to Tampa from the Steinbrenner horse farm in Ocala to join the family effort to care for his dad. Jenny is talking about wanting to play a role now as well. And Jessica's husband Felix is a team vice president without a real portfolio. Swindal and Lopez do not have a good relationship, so Felix will be looking for a bigger role when Steve is gone.

But Steve is not gone yet. He has shown up for work every day since his arrest on the advice of his lawyer. Indeed, he's already made plans to attend Opening Day at the Stadium, five days from now. No one really expects George to tell Steve to leave, so someone is going to have to broker a deal to settle Swindal's contract and his small stake in the team. And no one is ready to do that.

Selig and the owners are watching the Yankees situation with understandable interest. There is little concern about the day-to-day operation: they all have confidence in Yankees President Randy Levine and COO Lonn Trost to keep the team's expanding business on track, and in Brian Cashman to do the same with the team on the field. But more than a few owners are wondering if the Steinbrenner family might sell the team and who might be interested in buying the sport's premier franchise.

All of this is happening as the Yankees empire continues to expand. The Yankees drew a team-record 4.25 million fans last season, the second straight season above the magic 4 million mark. Revenue from luxury-box sales is up 202 percent in the past eight years, and the new stadium, set to open in 2009, will have three times more suites than their current home.

The Yankees are in early talks with Dallas Cowboys owner Jerry Jones to start a hospitality company and run concessions at the new stadium and others around the country, which would add a projected $30 million in revenue from Year One. And the YES Network is succeeding beyond expectations, generating more than $300 million in revenue last season. Everything the Yankees businessmen touch, it seems, is turning to gold.

It's a tougher road for Cashman, who is trying to win it all—that mandate remains unchanged—with a team in transition. The young GM is determined to reduce the team's bloated payroll and just dumped Gary Sheffield and Randy Johnson—two players he never wanted—in trades for a slew of pitching prospects.

He brought back Andy Pettitte on a one-year, $16 million deal, but Bernie Williams won't be on the Yankees roster for the first time in 16 years. Cashman and the coaching staff did not see a place for Bernie, who can no longer play center field or hit well enough to play full-time and lacks the requisite skills to be a productive sub. The soft-spoken Williams rejected Cashman's nonroster invitation to spring training and has faded from the scene quietly.

Cashman still hasn't found a way to repair a clubhouse fractured along several fault lines, none worse than the ever-widening gulf between Torre and Alex Rodriguez. The superstar third baseman, who can opt out of his contract at season's end, hasn't forgotten the embarrassment of batting "double cleanup" in last season's ALDS fiasco. And the rift between Rodriguez and Derek Jeter is finally official after Alex, who has spent the past three seasons insisting things with his old friend were just fine, told reporters on the second day of camp, "You don't ask about Derek anymore, and I promise I'll stop lying to you."

The Yankees want to keep Rodriguez, but Cashman has already said he won't extend the third baseman's contract, which has $91 million and three years remaining after this season. Would the Yankees really let Rodriguez walk if he plays out his option? That's a question that can't be answered until the Steinbrenners decide who is going to run George's team.

The answer to the succession question emerges before the first month of the season is complete. George and a host of Steinbrenners— his four children, Felix, and three grandkids—are in the owner's box in the Bronx for the Yankees home opener against the Tampa Bay Devil Rays on April 2. George wears oversized sunglasses— now a trademark—despite the gray day. They all stand and clap when the widow and son of Cory Lidle—the Yankees pitcher who died in a small plane crash in Manhattan last fall—throw out the first pitch alongside Jason Giambi, Lidle's high school teammate.

Steve Swindal is watching from the suite reserved for limited partners, and though he doesn't visit the owner's box or see his in-laws during the game, he insists everything is normal. "It's business as usual," he tells reporters. "I am here."

Swindal continues to show up for work at Legends Field upon his return to Tampa while his marriage winds down. But it's been awkward for everyone, and in late April Swindal walks down the hall and into Hal's office, where he finds both Steinbrenner brothers. He takes a seat in front of Hal's desk and looks squarely at the young man he's watched grow up.

"What do you think?" Swindal asks. "I've been with you guys for a long time."

Hal looks at his two big brothers. He knows his quiet life as a hotel developer is over. He and Hank have agreed to be partners running the team—Hank handling the baseball side, Hal making the business decisions—but MLB's bylaws require one man to be the control person. Everyone's content to defer to George's wish to remain general managing partner, but deep down, Hal knows the responsibility will eventually fall to him.

And he knows what he has to say now, no matter how much it hurts.

"Steve, you can't expect to stay here if you're not married to my sister," Hal says. "It's just not realistic."

Hank nods in agreement. Steve starts to speak, but there's really nothing left to say. It won't be long before the team announces that negotiations to buy out Swindal's contract are almost complete.

George Steinbrenner leans forward as Derek Jeter picks up a grounder off the bat of Seattle's Willie Bloomquist and runs over to tag the second base bag and end the top of the 7th inning. It's May 6, and George is watching the game on TV at home in Tampa, waiting for the surprise announcement he knows is coming. Soon Yankee Stadium PA announcer Bob Sheppard asks fans to direct their attention to the owner's box behind home plate.

Standing in the open window, dressed sharply in a pinstriped suit, wearing a World Series ring on one hand and holding a Yankees microphone in the other, is Roger Clemens. Fans look to the right-field video screen, recognize the Rocket, and start cheering.

"Thank y'all," Clemens says. "Well, they came and got me out of Texas. I can tell you it's a privilege to be back. I'll be talking to y'all real soon."

The outfield dot-matrix screen declares ROGER CLEMENS IS NOW A YANKEE, and the crowd rises to its feet and roars its approval.

George is happy, too. His team sure as hell needs the spark Clemens could provide. Despite a spectacular April from Alex Rodriguez—14 home runs, 34 RBI, a .355 average—the Yankees entered today's play two games under .500 and 5½ games behind the AL East–leading Red Sox. This is not what the Boss expected when he told Joe Torre he could manage his team for another season.

The Yankees' big weakness: a shaky and injury-prone starting rotation. Cashman began floating the idea of bringing back the 44-year-old Rocket a few weeks ago. He and Clemens' agent Randy Hendricks worked out a prorated one-year, $28 million contract on May 4, and it was the GM's idea for Roger to announce his return live at the Stadium. It's an exciting, memorable moment, but it's also bittersweet. In years gone by, George would have been stand-ing right there with Roger, soaking up the attention and adulation.

And only a few months ago, Steve Swindal would have been in the loop, too. Now Steve is gone, and George's health continues to fade.

At least Clemens is back in pinstripes. And after all that's gone wrong, the Yankees are counting on that to be a good thing.

Chapter 39

MITCHELL GETS HIS MAN

April 9–November 16, 2007

Bud Selig's public relations war on drugs is operating at full speed as his 15th Opening Day as Commissioner nears. His goal is simple: make sure the public understands that management—especially the Commissioner—had no knowledge whatsoever of major league players using performance-enhancing drugs.

And that means staying as far away from Barry Bonds as he can, a strategy that quickly turns the San Francisco star's pursuit of Hank Aaron's record into a national morality play. Bonds entered the season 22 home runs shy of breaking the game's most coveted record. Should the Commissioner validate Bonds' accomplishment by attending the record-setting game? Or should he shun the man who may soon stand accused of lying to a grand jury about using steroids?

It's a question Selig is asked at every public appearance. And it's a question he continues to answer—with great solemnity—as he does at the Diamondbacks home opener on April 9: "I have not made my decision yet," Selig tells reporters. "I will do whatever I think is in the best interests of baseball."

This is why he asked George Mitchell to investigate steroid use in baseball, he reminds the media as often as he can. Hiring Mitchell has been a win-win for Selig from Day One, no matter how much the Senator has struggled without the players' cooperation. Mitchell seemed genuinely surprised that he could not persuade Don Fehr to cooperate with his investigation. Selig knows Fehr well enough not to be surprised, but he also understands the box in which he's so shrewdly placed his longtime adversary.

Every time Mitchell complains that the union refuses to cooperate with him — which the Senator has done often — it makes Fehr look like he and his players have something to hide. And every time Fehr and his staff publicly complain about the questions asked by Mitchell, it looks like they're protecting players who cheat.

Case in point: the union blasted Mitchell for writing letters to Bonds and several other players connected with Balco, requesting they allow their teams to turn over their personal medical records. Mitchell also asked these players to sign waivers that would allow teams to send him past, present, and future records. "Nothing is more important than the integrity of the game of baseball," Mitchell wrote in letters that went out on February 1.

Fehr was furious with Mitchell's request. The union has already advised the players not to give up their Constitutional rights — some things *are* more important than baseball — when Gary Sheffield's response to Mitchell's letter appears in *USA Today*. "This is all about getting Bonds," Sheffield told the newspaper on February 26. "If this was legitimate and they did it the right way, it would be different. But this is a witch hunt. They're just trying to collect a lot of stuff that doesn't make any sense and throw the shit against the wall."

Fehr was furious with Mitchell's request. The Senator and the union have already clashed over what Mitchell and his lawyers are allowed to do under the basic agreement. They drew up a separate agreement to make sure there were no gray areas. These new requests, Fehr thought, clearly crossed the line. And in a letter that found its way into the *New York Times,* union general counsel Michael Weiner told Mitchell: "We feel your actions have left us no choice but to advise the players you have written to not to respond to your letter at this time."

But the nation's baseball writers were seeing developments like this the same way the Commissioner was: the union was protecting cheaters. Fehr almost always had the upper hand when the playing field was the country's labor courts. But this is the court of public opinion, and for once Selig is trouncing the union leader.

About the only downside for Selig are the complaints from owners who are unhappy with Mitchell's lawyers asking for reams of documents and email files. But Selig will take that trade-off. Besides, all he has to do is remind them what Mitchell said at the owners meeting in January: work with him or expect another trip to Washington for more hearings before the Senator's old friends in Congress.

Mitchell continues to alternately cajole and threaten the union, but Fehr and the players won't budge. With nowhere else to turn, Mitchell's only remaining option is the medical records analysis proposed by James J. Heckman, PhD, at the University of Chicago. Heckman says he can strip the records of player identities, then produce data that will show the percentage of players using steroids on a yearly basis. The union initially agreed to cooperate, but as the season gets under way a handful of teams and the union are having second thoughts, leaving Mitchell empty handed.

But most if not all of the Senator's problems disappear when Balco lead prosecutor Matt Parrella calls Mitchell in mid-April. We've caught someone who has dealt steroids to dozens of major league players, and now he's working for us, he tells the Senator. Let's talk about how we can work on this together.

Parrella doesn't reveal the dealer's name to Mitchell until just before Kirk Radomski pleads guilty to distributing steroids and money laundering in the U.S. District Court of Northern California on April 27. And then the whole world learns about the one-time Mets clubhouse man, now 37, who admits to selling testosterone to dozens of players all across the major leagues. Parrella says Radomski, whose crimes carry a sentence of up to 25 years in prison and $500,000 in fines, has already testified before a grand jury and has agreed to cooperate with Mitchell's investigation in exchange for leniency.

Selig is delighted, and it's clear the Senator is confident he now has what he needs. On May 4, Mitchell tells the media he's asked a number of active players to come in and speak with him, sparking speculation that these are Radomski's customers. Parrella tells reporters he is providing Mitchell information "on an item-by-item basis," and Mitchell tells the New York Times that his investigation is now entering its final phase.

"We expect to meet soon with the players whose interviews we have requested," says Mitchell, who reminds everyone that the Commissioner has agreed to make all the Senator's findings public. With everything now falling into place, Selig issues a gag order, telling all 30 clubs to stop saying anything about Mitchell's investigation.

Mitchell first meets the man who will bail him out in New York on June 7 at the DLA Piper offices on 6th Avenue, right across from Radio City Music Hall. "Just tell me the truth and tell me what happened, even if it is the smallest thing," Mitchell tells Radomski. "If I ask a question and you don't remember or are not sure, don't say anything. I just want the truth."

Radomski looks around the crowded 29th-floor conference room. Parrella and Novitzky are there, along with two other federal agents. They all remind Radomski that if he lies to Mitchell, his deal for a more lenient sentence is off. Mitchell has his staff there, too: Charlie Scheeler, who'll write most of Mitchell's report, and two more DLA Piper lawyers. It's an awful lot of suits for a small-time drug dealer from Long Island.

"I'll tell you the truth," Radomski tells Mitchell. "I just don't want to look like some drug peddler or pusher."

And then comes Radomski's story: dealing steroids to stars such as Lenny Dykstra—his first client—Todd Hundley, and Mo Vaughn and to role players such as Larry Bigbie, David Segui, and Adam Piatt. He shows Mitchell phone records, post office receipts, canceled checks, and his address book, containing the names of dozens of major leaguers. Mitchell gives him a list of every major league player and asks him to identify all his customers. It's not long before the Senator is sure his report has the necessary bite.

Radomski tells Mitchell he only met with a handful of his clients face-to-face in New York—that most of his deals were done over the phone. Yes, he's given instructions on how to use these drugs.

But save for one journeyman pitcher, he never witnessed any player take the drugs he sold them.

Nor did Radomski know what one of his steady customers did with the steroids and human growth hormone he sold him. But that customer is Brian McNamee, the trainer for Roger Clemens and Andy Pettitte. And he's given Radomski plenty of hints about who the drugs are for.

There's another big crowd in the DLA Piper conference room when McNamee walks in with his lawyer on July 9. He, too, has cut a deal with the feds, who remind McNamee that any false statements to Mitchell will result in criminal prosecution. And soon McNamee is telling Mitchell about the times he injected Clemens with Winstrol, a potent steroid, when they were together in Toronto. And again when McNamee joined the Yankees in 2000.

While McNamee is telling his story to Mitchell, the union is filing a motion to keep all the information in Radomski's affidavit secret. The motion will fall on deaf ears. And four days later, Mitchell sends a letter to the union requesting a meeting with Clemens, a request that is forwarded to Clemens' agent.

The Rocket once pitched for the team of Mitchell's dreams. Now he's the answer to the Senator's prayers.

It's an unusually chilly late-July night in Milwaukee, though the roof is open in the 4th inning at Miller Park when Bud Selig and his security guards walk into the press box. A sellout crowd is on hand to watch the first-place Brewers play the Giants. Many in the crowd are here to see Barry Bonds, who is now three home runs away from breaking Hank Aaron's record of 755.

Selig isn't one for organized press briefings, so he gathers up the media for an impromptu session. He pokes fun at several of the regulars as he leads them to the media cafeteria, a few yards down the hall.

"Beautiful night, a ball game in my home town, and I thought I'd come to the game tonight and probably Saturday and Sunday," the Commissioner tells them. "It's part of my routine that I generally come in to see all of you, and I didn't want it to seem like I was ducking you. That's frankly why I'm here."

But it's not the media the Commissioner has been ducking. Selig continued his season-long cat-and-mouse game with Bonds at the All-Star Game in San Francisco a week ago. Not once in the three-day event did Selig take the time to visit the hometown hero, who was voted to his 14th All-Star team with a late rush in the final week of voting. And at his annual midseason luncheon with the baseball media he emphatically knocked down a report that he had decided to follow Bonds in his pursuit of Aaron's record after the All-Star Game.

"I have made no decision on the Barry Bonds situation. None. Zero," Selig said gruffly. "I'll do what I believe is in the best interest of the sport."

But now Bud speaks in an unusually soft tone, telling reporters Aaron's record is a deeply personal matter to him. He says he won't comment on reports that Bonds had asked him to reach out to Aaron, who has said publicly he wants nothing to do with Bonds' run at his record.

"I will let Hank speak for himself," the Commissioner says.

And if Bonds breaks the record this weekend in Milwaukee?

"Whatever happens happens," he says.

He says he has no plans to meet with Bonds while the star is in town—the two men have not spoken in almost three years—and will decide Sunday if he'll travel to San Francisco to follow Bonds if Aaron's record remains unbroken. "One has to use what I think would be called common sense," Selig says.

He shrugs when asked if he'll consider the record legitimate. "We won't get into it, let's see if he does it," he says. "Whatever else happens, I'm not passing judgment."

The Miller Park crowd serenades Bonds with boos when he steps into the batter's box at 7:12 p.m. with runners on first and second and one out. He grounds out, starting an 0-for-4 night. He's booed loudly every trip to the plate.

Bonds is in the starting lineup the next day for a nationally televised game and answers questions for 17 minutes before the game. He's asked about the news that the Balco grand jury's term has just been extended. "I'm not concerned," he says defiantly. "Do I look concerned?" A reporter asks Bonds how he would feel if Selig were not in attendance when he breaks Aaron's record. "We haven't talked in a while, but I have respect for Bud," Bonds says. "Bud has always been kind to me."

Bonds goes 0 for 2 with two walks, sits out Sunday's game, and leaves town for a seven-game home stand in San Francisco. Selig at first decides to stay behind, then has a change of heart and flies to San Francisco late Tuesday afternoon. But not before releasing a statement to explain his thinking.

"Out of respect for the tradition of this game, the magnitude of the record and the fact that all citizens in this country are innocent until proven guilty," Selig's statement reads, "I will attend Barry Bonds' next games to observe his potential tying and breaking of the home run record, subject to my commitments to the Hall of Fame this weekend.

"I will make an additional statement when the record is tied."

Bonds celebrates his 43rd birthday while Selig is in the air traveling, but he has little else to cheer about until Selig leaves for Cooperstown on July 27. After going 22 of 23 days without a homer, Bonds hits No. 754—a solo shot to deep left-center field—in the 1st inning off Marlins rookie Rick van den Hurk. By then, Selig is beginning the three-day celebration of Cal Ripken Jr.'s and Tony Gwynn's induction into the Hall of Fame. Only Ripken obliquely references Bonds' march on baseball history, calling the induction "a way to step back from the controversy. Maybe we'll be back to reality tomorrow."

Selig is back on the Bonds watch in Los Angeles, then moves on to San Diego with Barry still one home run behind Aaron. The Commissioner has thought long and hard about what he should do when Barry ties and surpasses his good friend's record. Should he stand and applaud? Should he stand and keep his hands at his side? Should he express his displeasure and remain in his seat?

He finally has to make a decision at 7:29 p.m. on August 4, when Bonds rockets a pitch into the left-field stands off Clay Hensley, who two years earlier failed a steroids test while still in the minor leagues. Bonds circles the bases, jumps on home plate, and hugs his son Nikolai while teammates surround him in celebration.

The 42,497 fans react in mixed fashion: Many boo, many others cheer. Some hold up Bonds jerseys. A few fans hold up signs depicting an asterisk.

Selig takes it all in from his seat in Padres owner John Moores' box. The ESPN camera finds Selig moments after the record-tying homer, standing with hands thrust in his pockets, a scowl on his face. There will be no Commissioner's visit to the press box this night, no postgame trip to the Giants locker room, only a written statement handed to reporters in the 9th inning:

"No matter what anybody thinks of the controversy surrounding the event, Mr. Bonds' achievement is noteworthy and remarkable."

Bonds shrugs off the Commissioner's statement in a cheerful media conference following the game, won by the Padres, 3–2, in 12 innings. "He's welcome to come talk with me anytime," says Bonds. He's glad this home run is behind him — "The hard part is over now," he says — and thanks the folks in San Diego. "I really appreciate the way San Diego handled it and the way their fans handled it," Bonds says. "It's been a fun ride."

Bonds announces he's sending the batting helmet he wore tonight to Cooperstown, and he'll do the same with the one he'll wear when he breaks the record. But that won't come tomorrow. Bonds says he's sitting out the final game against the Padres and will return to the lineup Monday when the Giants start another home stand against the Nationals. "It's like saying to my own family, I'm coming home," Bonds says.

Selig will not be going to San Francisco. Instead he'll be flying to New York to prepare for his sit-down with George Mitchell on August 8 to discuss what he knows about drug use in baseball. "It was scheduled a long time ago," says Selig, promising that someone from his office will pinch-hit for him at the Giants game.

The scene in the Giants' AT&T Park locker room the night of August 7 is like most that have come before it: an edgy media circulating among Bonds' teammates, asking questions about the man sitting off by himself, an invisible wall keeping out all but a chosen few. One of those allowed inside is ESPN baseball editor Claire Smith, who's known Bonds since his days with the Pirates.

Neither considers the other a friend, but they recognize their shared experience: Bonds is one of the few African American stars left in the game, Smith is one of the first black reporters to cover the sport.

Smith walks over to Bonds, who looks up from his easy chair in front of his locker and smiles. Barry is surprisingly relaxed and open, and the two talk about their families and mutual friends. Traces of bemusement and bitterness surface in Bonds when the conversation turns to the media circus that surrounds him. "They call me a liar and an idiot, then want to come and talk to me every day," he tells her several times.

Bonds is even more conflicted when their talk shifts to the Commissioner. "He never spoke to me the night I tied the record," Bonds says.

"Yes, I know," Smith replies.

"He's not here tonight, is he?" Bonds asks. "I swear, I really don't give a damn."

Bonds says nothing more about Selig.

"You know Frank and Jimmie Lee are here," says Smith, referring to baseball Vice Presidents Frank Robinson and Jimmie Lee Solomon, the two highest-ranking African Americans in the game. Smith approached both men earlier that night, asking if they would congratulate Barry if he broke the record this game. Both glared, then adamantly insisted they would.

The conversation turns to Aaron, who long ago distanced himself from Bonds and the home run chase. The two men have known each other for years, and not long ago they had discussed plans along with Willie Mays for a joint marketing campaign. But Bonds knows why things have changed.

"Hank's in a tough spot," Barry says. "I don't blame him. I understand."

Smith thanks Bonds for his time and walks away, chats with a few ESPN staffers, and rushes off to a production meeting. This is going to be a busy night. She catches up with Barry once more before the game, stopping him just as he's about to take the field for batting practice. The Giants have played a video tribute to Bonds after each homer in the run-up to No. 756. Muhammad Ali did one.

So did Mays and Robinson, who hit 1,246 home runs between them.

Who'll speak on the big night?

"It's gotta be Hank, right?" Smith asks Bonds.

"I can't tell you," answers Barry, a smile lighting up his face. "But I think you can figure it out."

The wait ends in the bottom of the 5th, when Bonds blasts a high-arcing shot 435 feet into the right-center-field seats off Nationals right-hander Mike Bacsik. A party for 43,154 fans erupts, with fireworks, water cannons, and streamers everywhere. Bonds' teammates are there as he crosses the plate. So are his family members. Mays, Barry's relentless defender, leaves his box seat to join his godson on the field. Then everyone looks to the scoreboard.

The man congratulating Barry on the big screen is Hank Aaron.

"I move over and offer my best wishes to Barry and his family on this historical achievement," Hank says in a tape made a month earlier. "My hope today, as it was on that April evening in 1974, is that the achievement of this record will inspire others to chase their own dreams."

Giants manager Bruce Bochy sends Barry out to left field, then immediately pulls him so the crowd can give their star a thunderous standing ovation. Bonds jogs into the dugout and down the tunnel, followed closely by Robinson and Solomon. All three men duck into the clubhouse, where Solomon hands Bonds a phone. Selig is on the other end.

"Congratulations, Barry," Selig says. "You've endured a lot. I have a lot of respect for you."

Their conversation is brief. So is the Commissioner's statement, released by MLB moments later.

"While the issues which have swirled around this record will continue to work themselves toward resolution, today is a day for congratulations on a truly remarkable achievement," it reads.

Bonds enters the postgame press conference wearing jeans, a black T-shirt, a black hat, and a huge smile. He gives special thanks to Aaron and his message—"It meant everything to me, absolutely everything"—says home run No. 755 was the tough one, then defends what he's just accomplished.

"This record is not tainted at all—period," he says. "You guys can say whatever you want."

The next day, President Bush tells his secretary to find Barry Bonds and put him on the line. He wants to congratulate the man the Justice Department is still chasing down. "You've always been a great hitter, and you broke a great record," the President tells Bonds.

It's one day later when Aaron tells the *Atlanta Journal-Constitution* he may talk to Bonds about the record someday. "To be honest," Aaron says, "I'm as happy for him as anybody."

With the record broken, talk in San Francisco shifts to whether the last-place Giants will ask Barry back for another season. That speculation ends September 21, when the Giants announce they will sever ties with their superstar after 15 years at season's end. "I would have loved nothing more than to retire as a Giant," says Bonds, who plays one last game in San Francisco four days later. He finishes with 28 home runs, a game-high 132 walks, and—65 hits shy of 3,000—a strong desire to keep playing. The home run record now stands at 762.

"There is more baseball in me," Bonds says. "My quest for a World Series ring continues."

It's the Red Sox who win their second World Series ring in four years, with Selig once again handing the championship trophy to owner John Henry, the man he handed the franchise to five years ago. Boston's four-game sweep of Colorado caps a stunning season for Selig and MLB, which reached a record 79.5 million in attendance and surpassed $6 billion in revenue.

But the good vibes end on November 15, when the Commissioner gets word that Bonds has been charged with four counts of perjury and one count of obstruction of justice. Reporters call Selig when the news breaks, asking if he's decided to suspend Bonds. The Commissioner ducks the question—just barely.

"While everyone in America is considered innocent until proven guilty," Selig says, "I take this indictment very seriously and will follow its progress closely."

The following day *New York Times* baseball columnist Murray Chass captures what most of baseball is thinking. With the game's home run king now facing up to 30 months in jail if proven guilty, baseball eagerly turns its attention to the player most likely to break Bonds' record.

"Major League Baseball officials suddenly have a new rooting interest," Chass writes. "His name is Alex Rodriguez."

Chapter 40

QUESTIONS AND ANSWERS

November 14, 2007–January 17, 2008

I've heard that you guys hate me," Alex Rodriguez says. "Is that true?"

It's all Hal Steinbrenner can do to keep from rolling his eyes and shouting back his own question: *Are you fucking kidding me?*

No wonder baseball players so often drove his father into a fury. Has Alex been paying *any* attention to what's been going on around here? Does he know George is terribly ill? Does he know that two divorces have shaken our family to its core? That everyone in our family is still figuring out their roles? That we're in the middle of building a stadium that's now going to run us $1.2 billion and we've just replaced a Hall of Fame manager?

In a year full of questions—big, complicated questions—this is by far the dumbest question anyone has asked Hal Steinbrenner.

"Alex," Hal says calmly, "how can I hate you? I don't even know you."

Steinbrenner and his brother Hank are sitting in the living room of his Tampa home with Rodriguez and his wife Cynthia. Yankees President Randy Levine and general manager Brian Cashman are there, too. George Steinbrenner is not. It's November 14, and 17 days have passed since Rodriguez opted out of his contract with the Yankees—a poorly handled decision that the player soon regretted.

Rodriguez didn't just opt out of the remaining three years of his historic 10-year, $252 million contract—he did it a full 10 days before his contract was up. Worse, his agent made the announcement as the Red Sox were completing a World Series sweep of the Rockies, giving the announcement maximum exposure. And Alex did it without answering any of the phone messages that Hal and his brother left for him, messages requesting they sit down and discuss a lucrative contract extension.

"Scott fucked this up," Alex says, blaming his agent Scott Boras, who was not invited to today's summit. "I'm so sorry, he wasn't authorized to do it."

"Do you really want to be a Yankee?" Hank asks. "I just hope you appreciate what being a Yankee means."

"I do," Rodriguez answers.

Hal listens while his brother exacts a bit of revenge for the past three weeks of nonsense. A soap opera starring the team's best player—the game's best player—is about the last thing he needed. Hal knows Bud Selig and the owners are wondering if he really wants the job of running the sport's most important franchise. So are many of the team's limited partners, who've been planting anonymous questions about him and Hank in the New York tabloids.

Hal is still wondering if he wants this life, too. He treasures his privacy as much as his father craved the spotlight. And being the man in charge of the New York Yankees is not a private life.

But once his sister Jenny divorced Steve Swindal, thereby kicking the acting head of the Yankees out of the family, Hal felt compelled to step into the void. He soon flew to New York and asked Levine and Lonn Trost for a crash course on everything from the team's burgeoning payroll to the cost overruns of the new stadium. On September 28, he was officially named Swindal's replacement as the chairman of Yankee Global Enterprises, the holding company that controls the Yankees and YES Network.

His personal life has been equally—if not more—tumultuous. His marriage of 12 years officially ended in September, and running back and forth to New York hasn't made it any easier to see his three young daughters. And it broke his heart when Steve, an important presence in his life for as long as he can remember, left in disgrace. Now it's his big sister Jenny who has an office and a new job at Legends Field.

But the biggest challenge is George, who for most of Hal's 37 years was nothing less than a great white shark, chewing up everything and everyone in his path, including his four children. He was especially tough on Hank, 12 years Hal's senior, riding him so hard at Yankees meetings that he just stopped showing up. Hal knew his father's health was declining, but with Steve handling the business and Jenny and Jessica tending to his father's needs, he'd been able to look past the bad days and concentrate on the good ones.

George's collapse at UNC last fall made his failing health impossible to ignore, and the family met with a neurologist this past June to learn exactly what was wrong. George was suffering from something similar to Alzheimer's, the neurologist told them. But instead of a steady decline, George's condition would level off, drop after another episode, then level off again.

And the episode at UNC hit George hard. "The condition is here to stay," the doctor said. "And it's going to get worse."

Even so, George made it clear he did not want to give up being the managing general partner, and no one argued the point. Not now. They all watched their team struggle last season, then lose in the first round for the third straight year. The Boss called Levine, Cashman, and Lonn Trost down to his home on October 16 to meet with him and his sons to decide Torre's future—and it felt like nothing had changed.

George didn't want to bring Torre back, but Cashman fought hard—again—to keep the 67-year-old manager. The GM conceded he had some problems with Joe, but the core of this team is still loyal to Torre. And the stability he brings to the table will be invaluable should the Yankees get hit hard by the Mitchell Report—which seems likely, given the number of players the Senator's lawyers wanted to talk to.

In the end, they agreed to offer Torre a one-year, $5 million deal, with a $1 million bonus for every playoff round the Yankees reach. Yes, it was a $1.4 million cut in base salary, but Torre would still be the highest-paid manager in the game and have a chance to earn another $3 million if he took the team to the World Series. "It's a fair deal," George said. That was good enough for Hal.

Torre walked into George's office at Legends Field the next day and sat down across from Hal, Hank, Levine, and Trost. George, subdued and hidden behind oversized sunglasses, sat behind his desk. Cashman, Torre's biggest supporter, sat behind the manager. At George's request, Levine laid out the details of the contract.

Then it was Hal's turn to talk. He knew what they had in Joe, the stability he brought, how good a manager he was, how much the fans loved him. Hell, Hal loved him. But he and Hank were just starting to figure out how this was going to work, and they wanted the freedom to have one season with Joe before deciding what comes next. "Joe," Hal says, "we'd like you to come back, and we think this is a good offer. And it's our final offer."

"I can't accept this deal without a second year," Torre said.

There was little else for anyone to say. And as Torre rose to leave, Hal told him they would find a place for him if he wanted to stay. "Our door is always open," Hal said. "You can work for the YES Network or elsewhere in the organization."

Torre just shook his head, walked over to George, and extended his hand. "Good luck, Joe," George said. "Thank you, Boss," Torre said.

Torre shook hands with everyone else in the room, then walked out the door 10 minutes after he walked in, ending a 12-year partnership that produced four World Series championships, 12 straight playoff berths, 1,173 victories, and a reserved spot in an alcove in the Hall of Fame. Two weeks later Torre was introduced as the new manager of the Los Angeles Dodgers. His contract: $13 million for three years.

Hal's a great believer in delegating—unlike his father, who gave his executives responsibility but held on to all the authority—so it was Cashman who ran the rigorous interview process in the search for Torre's replacement. Hal and Hank spoke to all three candidates—Don Mattingly, Joe Girardi, and Tony Pena—but it was Cashman who made the final recommendation. Mattingly was the favorite—especially with George—but Cashman favored Girardi. The Steinbrenner brothers agreed.

And Alex Rodriguez had opted out in the middle of the manager search. The Yankees had tried to talk extension during the season, but A-Rod and Boras turned a deaf ear. Hal and Hank told both men that if Alex left, their relationship was over. Hank, who by now is falling in love with the media spotlight, called a *New York Times* writer the minute he heard the news, catching Tyler Kepner as he was walking into the boisterous Boston locker room.

"It's a shame, but we are all in agreement: myself, my dad, my brother, all the baseball people," he told Kepner. "If you don't want to be a Yankee and paid what you're being paid, we don't want you. That's the bottom line."

While Hank continued to lambaste Rodriguez, Cashman started putting together a deal with St. Louis for Scott Rolen, and Alex began to realize he'd made a mistake. No one was stepping up to pay him the $350 million Boras was asking, so he called a friend at Goldman Sachs, who called Goldman's Yankees connection Gerry Cardinale, who called Randy Levine. A few dozen phone calls later, the outlines of a 10-year, $275 million contract were in place and a meeting was scheduled in Hal's living room.

"I just want to make sure there are no hard feelings," says Alex, after pledging allegiance to the Yankees yet again.

"Alex, if we didn't like you, you wouldn't be sitting in my house," Hal says.

Hal knows his brother and Levine want Alex's bat in their lineup, and while he'll swallow hard over Rodriguez's price tag, Hal understands this is about more than Alex's Gold Glove, his home run bat, and the third MVP trophy he is about to win. The 32-year-old superstar stands a good chance of chasing down Bonds' home run record, which would be pure gold for YES and the new stadium. Analysts are already predicting Alex could add $450 million to the Yankees' bottom line over the life of the 10-year deal. Re-signing A-Rod is a no-brainer.

The rest of Hal's offseason falls into place as well. Cashman re-signs Posada two days before the A-Rod meeting, reluctantly giving him a fourth year after Hank Steinbrenner told the media the team was open to the idea. He also locks up Mariano Rivera with a three-year, $45 million deal on November 19 and brings Andy Pettitte back with a one-year deal for $16 million.

The union and Selig both approve the marketing deals in Rodriguez's contract, and now the only thing Hal and Hank are still waiting on is a decision from Clemens about returning for another season. While the Rocket deliberates, the Yankees set December 13 for the conference call to announce all the details of A-Rod's new contract. Little do they know Clemens will be the bigger story that day—and not for the reason they had hoped.

Bob DuPuy has read enough. Baseball's chief operating officer walks away from the conference table, pulls his cell phone from his pocket, and punches in the number for his impatient boss in Milwaukee. It is December 11, two days before the release of George Mitchell's report on steroids in baseball. DuPuy and three other baseball executives are getting an early read at Mitchell's midtown Manhattan office, and he knows Selig is sitting by his phone, waiting to find out if he's going to get what he paid for.

"He names 89 players," DuPuy tells Selig. "And there's one player that's going to make news: Roger Clemens."

"Well, that's disappointing," says Selig.

"I think Clemens is probably going to fight this," DuPuy says. "His legacy, the Cy Youngs. I think there is a chance of some formal litigation."

Selig listens intently. Clemens is clearly going to be the major headline of Mitchell's report, and the Commissioner agrees with DuPuy that Roger is likely to fight his former trainer's allegations. And fight hard.

"Let me know what George says about it," Selig says. "Stay in touch."

DuPuy turns back to the task of reading through Mitchell's 409-page report. He's there with Rob Manfred, MLB's Vice President for Labor; Frank Coonelly, another of baseball's top lawyers; and Tom Carlucci, the Foley & Lardner lawyer who served as the teams' liaison to Mitchell. The Senator welcomed them a few hours ago, handed out his report, and told them to feel free to ask any questions.

But the baseball men understand they're not here to edit or shape Mitchell's report. Sure, Mitchell will listen to their concerns. But this is about making sure the Senator's report doesn't run afoul of any agreements between the Commissioner's office and the Players Association. And nothing more.

An hour or so later Mitchell walks back into the conference room with Charlie Scheeler and John Clarke, two DLA Piper lawyers who conducted many of the interviews these past 20 months. It's been a long haul for the 74-year-old Mitchell, who announced in August that he had prostate cancer. The prognosis is good, the doctors told Mitchell, and he'll start treatment in a few weeks.

Genial and self-assured, Mitchell smiles as he takes a seat and turns to the MLB lawyers. "Any questions?" he says. DuPuy and Carlucci both ask if he is completely comfortable with Brian McNamee's credibility, given how tough the report is on Clemens. They have some doubts.

"Yes, I understand this will be a significant disclosure. We thought it through, and I am confident McNamee is telling the truth," says Mitchell, who reminds them that McNamee's deal to avoid prosecution hinges on whether he is honest with Mitchell. "He was very motivated to be truthful," the Senator says.

The lawyers for both sides talk through the 20 recommendations in Mitchell's report, spend a little time discussing how the media conferences will be handled, then thank Mitchell for his work.

They all walk the six blocks back to MLB headquarters, where DuPuy enters his office and starts writing a memo he'll soon email over to Selig. The phone rings almost immediately. It's Selig, who wants to know what else they learned about the report. DuPuy runs through all the important points, but both men know only two words really matter.

Roger Clemens.

*   *   *

There is one thing Mitchell wants to make clear when he unveils his report to the media two days later in the crowded ballroom of Manhattan's Grand Hyatt hotel: "From my experience in Northern Ireland, I learned that letting go of the past and looking to the future is a very hard but necessary step to dealing with an ongoing problem," he says during his hour-long press conference. "That's what baseball now needs."

Mitchell's desire to look forward may have something to do with the contents of his tome. Though he names 89 current and former players, much of what he reports is rehashed versions of books, media reports, and baseball's own list of suspended players. Jose Canseco, whose tell-all book *Juiced* is referenced often, is cited 105 times. Barry Bonds, who pleaded not guilty to four counts of perjury and one count of obstruction of justice in federal court last Friday, is mentioned 103 times without breaking any new ground. Mark McGwire, Rafael Palmeiro, and Jason Giambi are also mentioned prominently. If nothing else, Mitchell and his staff proved to be good readers.

The exception is the material provided by Kirk Radomski and Brian McNamee, two men dropped into Mitchell's lap by federal prosecutors who are now on a mission to clean up baseball (and, potentially, advance their careers in the process). Almost two-thirds of the players in Mitchell's report were provided by the two admitted drug dealers, who agreed to name names in order to stay out of jail. Mitchell concedes that Radomski only "observed" or "participated" in the drug use of one of the 53 players he names. But the former Mets clubhouse man did provide dozens of FedEx receipts, canceled checks, and thank you notes, all of which are reprinted on more than 30 pages of the report.

But nothing in Radomski's paper trail leads to the report's star attraction. That material all came from the mouth of McNamee, who recounted Roger Clemens' alleged doping in great detail. The former trainer claimed that he "injected Clemens in the buttocks four to six times with testosterone" in one of 82 references to Clemens' alleged drug use.

"According to McNamee, from the time that McNamee injected

Clemens with Winstrol through the end of the 1998 season, Clemens' performance showed remarkable improvement," the report says on page 170. "During this period of improved performance, Clemens told McNamee that the steroids 'had a pretty good effect' on him."

McNamee also claims he supplied drugs to Chuck Knoblauch and Clemens' close friend Andy Pettitte. None of McNamee's accusations are corroborated by other sources—not even by Radomski, who admitted McNamee never told him Clemens used drugs. "It was implied," Mitchell quotes Radomski as saying on page 174.

Mitchell has dodged questions about whether his report would name names for months, despite promising complete transparency in March of 2006, when the investigation was announced. The government had the option to withhold the name of any player in Mitchell's report, and it declined. Among those left in the dark about what to expect were Fehr and his lawyers, who weren't granted the same advance notice as the Commissioner's office, despite their repeated requests.

According to Mitchell, the decision to identify players was his and his alone. "After considering that issue very carefully, I concluded that it is appropriate and necessary," he tells the media. "Otherwise I would not have done what I was asked to do."

But just what Mitchell did is unclear. If adding another big name to the list of players who stand accused of using steroids was the goal, Mitchell's report is a success. If the goal was to define the scope of the problem, even the man upon whose testimony most of the report rests says Mitchell barely scratched the surface. "The bad thing about the Mitchell Report is there are so many other names out there that they missed," Radomski would soon tell ESPN.

Mitchell is willing to declare that everyone in the game shares the blame for "baseball's Steroids Era," though barely anyone in management is mentioned by name and any discussion about agents and steroids never makes an appearance. Also left out are the many teams that operate baseball academies in Latin America, where steroids can be purchased legally and street agents —called buscones—peddle them to kids eager for an escape from the region's pervasive poverty.

He singles out the players and their union for being uncooperative—though after lambasting them for 20 months, Mitchell now says their decision to remain silent is "understandable"—and mildly scolds the Commissioner and the game's owners. He proposes 20 recommendations to improve the sport's drug testing program, including the establishment of an investigations department within MLB.

And then Mitchell anoints Selig judge and jury. "I urge the Commissioner to forgo imposing discipline on any players named in this report," Mitchell says, "except in those cases where he determines that the conduct is so serious that discipline is necessary to maintain the integrity of the game."

Left unsaid is who will pass judgment on the Commissioner, owners, and front office officials who allowed players to use steroids despite warnings from team doctors and trainers—and who greatly profited from their use. Mitchell takes one final question before leaving the podium. What does the Senator say to critics who believe he was compromised by his role as a director of the Red Sox, who emerge from his report unscathed?

"My request now is as it was in Northern Ireland," Mitchell says. "Judge me by my work."

Two hours later Bud Selig addresses the media at the Waldorf Astoria. By then, Mitchell's report is posted on baseball's website, complete with an executive summary, a full list of players broken out as a separate story, and praise for the Senator's work from Congress. "This is a good day for integrity in sports," Representatives Henry Waxman and Tom Davis say in a joint release, which also includes a request for Mitchell, Selig, and Don Fehr to appear before their committee to discuss the findings.

As Selig approaches the lectern, he can't help but believe this report will do exactly what he said it would: bring closure to the so-called Steroids Era. He's just flown in from Milwaukee and he's been prepped for this appearance by Ari Fleischer. Now he's ready to accept the accolades befitting the only Commissioner with the nerve—as Mitchell has religiously repeated—to conduct an independent study into his sport's drug use.

"This is a call to action," the Commissioner says, "and I will act."

Selig pledges to institute all Mitchell's recommendations that do not require union approval and to meet with Fehr soon to discuss how to implement the rest. "There is nothing in his recommendations that I could even begin to disagree with," Selig says.

A reporter asks him what surprised him most about the players named in the report. "In the name of candor, I have not read the entire report," Selig says. "But from what I have been briefed, I'm satisfied that he achieved what I asked him to do."

But that isn't completely true. Selig's a bit miffed that his friend took the hammer out of his hands, asking him not to punish any of the players in the report. Selig has not taken punishment off the table—exactly what Fehr warned players about as they considered speaking with Mitchell—and besides, if anyone is going to look magnanimous, it should be Bud, not the man he hired. "Senator Mitchell acknowledges the ultimate decisions on discipline rest with the Commissioner, and he is correct," Selig says. "If warranted, those decisions will be made swiftly."

More important, Selig's upset that the report did not completely exonerate him. He's happy to have Mitchell and his reputation on MLB's side, and Clemens is sure to attract most of the attention. But the Commissioner didn't pay the Senator upwards of $20 million (everyone's best guess, since Selig won't even show the bill to the owners) for Mitchell to leave a shred of doubt that Bud's hands are clean.

And the next question hits that point straight on. "Mitchell said everyone was at fault," says a reporter from the *American Lawyer*. "Do you agree you were at fault?"

Selig scrunches his face in a pose familiar to all in attendance, and waits a few moments before answering.

"You know," he says slowly, "hindsight is wonderful, and I have great respect for Senator Mitchell. And I understand he feels that way. But there are a lot of people in baseball who clearly feel differently. Our program is clearly working, and what we need to do now is look forward."

At 6 p.m., Fehr starts his press conference at the InterContinental Hotel. He admits the steroid problem was bigger than he understood, and he expects to have more to say once he's had a chance to fully review the report. The union thought Mitchell's decision not to give them a copy of the report until one hour before it was released was petty and unprofessional—and in keeping with the way the Senator conducted his investigation throughout.

"We did request a meaningful opportunity to review his lengthy report prior to today," says Fehr, who met with Mitchell nine times over the past 20 months. "We thought it would have made sense. But that request was denied by both Senator Mitchell and the Commissioner's office."

Fehr reminds everyone that the players have repeatedly agreed to tougher and tougher testing during the last several years. He promises the union will adopt a valid urine test for HGH when one becomes available. And he says he's open to amending the drug program but suggests it might make sense to see if the agreement works before changing it yet again.

Fehr is neither combative nor testy, a departure from his usual tone when he's forced to explain himself to the press. But while he doesn't comment directly about the inclusion of Clemens in this report, Fehr's warning to "consider the nature of the evidence presented and the reliability of its source" is a clear slap at Mitchell's reliance on McNamee and Radomski. And he's alarmed about the damage he feels the report has already done.

"Many players are named," Fehr says. "Their reputations have been adversely affected, probably forever, even if it turns out down the road that they should not have been."

Fehr's meeting with the media is winding down when a reporter asks for his take on the overall impact of Mitchell's work. Fehr has never considered Mitchell to be anything more than what he really is: a lawyer hired to do an internal investigation. A high-profile lawyer, no doubt, and highly paid for sure. But companies conduct internal investigations all the time. Rarely are their findings made public, and Fehr's hard-pressed to remember another case in which the federal government swooped in and supplied key witnesses.

"I hope I will conclude—down the road and after whatever happens happens—that it was not detrimental," he says. "I'll let you know when I'm in a position to make that judgment. I'm not today."

* * *

Clemens and Pettitte are not surprised when they hear the news coming out of New York. It was about a week ago when McNamee sent a series of panicked text messages to Pettitte, telling the pitcher he was sorry—so, so sorry—that he told the feds about the drugs and injections he'd given Andy and Roger—and that the prosecutors then made him tell everything to Mitchell.

The two pitchers, who have trained with McNamee for the last several years, have different reactions. Clemens' lawyer Rusty Hardin issues a statement soon after Mitchell's report is released. "Roger has been repeatedly tested for these substances and he has never tested positive," Hardin says in a statement. "He has not been charged with anything, and yet he is being tried in the court of public opinion with no recourse. That is totally wrong."

Pettitte takes a different approach. He makes no public statement. Instead, the next day he calls Brian Cashman, who puts him on a conference call with George Steinbrenner and Randy Levine. Pettitte admits that what Mitchell wrote about him is true and tearfully apologizes to the Boss.

"I'm sorry, I feel so terrible," the pitcher says, his Texas drawl breaking. "I was just trying to get healthy and get back to the team. I didn't know it was illegal, but I should have known better."

"You're doing the right thing, Andy," George says.

Levine and Cashman echo George. They commend Pettitte for taking responsibility, promise their support, and advise him to go public with his admission. Andy releases a statement on December 15, admitting that he used HGH for two days while rehabbing an elbow injury in 2002. "If what I did was an error in judgment on my part, I apologize," Pettitte says in his statement. "I accept responsibility for those two days."

The buzz surrounding the Mitchell Report continues for days, thanks in part to Jose Canseco—somehow now a voice of reason on steroid issues—who calls the document incomplete and immediately starts the guessing game about players who were not named. "There are definitely a lot of players missing," Canseco tells the Fox Business channel. Prodded to name specific players, he singles out Alex Rodriguez. "I could not believe his name was not in the report," he says.

An interview with Rodriguez airs on *60 Minutes* on December

16. The show's producers originally told Alex they wanted to do a story around his latest record-setting contract, but with steroids dominating the news, Katie Couric asks him point-blank if he ever used PEDs.

"No," Rodriguez replies. "I've never felt overmatched on the baseball field. I've always been in a very strong, dominant position."

What Couric does not ask Rodriguez is if he has ever applied for a little-known exemption for the use of banned drugs—a Therapeutic Use Exemption—included in the Joint Drug Agreement. Under this provision, a player can apply to the program's independent administrator for permission to use a banned substance if he can show medical cause. The request is not made public, and is forwarded to the point men for the drug program at MLB and the union only after a determination is made, and must remain confidential.

Rodriguez applied for such an exemption this past February, when he asked Dr. Bryan W. Smith, the program administrator, for permission to use testosterone. Smith reviewed A-Rod's medical condition, found evidence of a testosterone deficiency, and granted an exemption. Rodriguez got the news two days before reporting for spring training. Only the union's Gene Orza and MLB's Rob Manfred (and presumably their assistants) were told that Rodriguez and one other player were given permission to use testosterone, and another 109 players received medical clearance to use other banned substances, mostly some form of amphetamine to treat attention deficit disorders.

As she wraps up her questions about the steroid controversy, Couric asks Rodriguez what he thinks about Mitchell naming 22 Yankees in the report—the most of any team in baseball. "These are guys that I play with, they're my teammates," Rodriguez tells Couric. "If anything comes of this, I will be extremely disappointed. And it will be a huge black eye on the game of baseball."

Clemens is the next Yankee—now former Yankee—to appear on *60 Minutes*, and on January 6 he repeatedly tells Mike Wallace that he has no idea why McNamee is telling all these lies about him. Clemens' legal team mounts a defense that is a direct attack on McNamee's rather suspect credibility, complete with a defamation suit and a secretly taped conversation between the trainer and the star pitcher. For his troubles, Clemens is invited to speak before Waxman's Reform and Oversight Committee.

But first Waxman and his committee want to hear from Mitchell, Selig, and Fehr, and the three men travel to Washington for another nationally televised hearing on January 15. Mitchell is first to testify, and he spends two hours explaining his investigation. His former colleagues treat him with respect and deference, stopping often to praise the report. The only rough patch: repeated questions about the reliability of Brian McNamee.

I believe him, Mitchell says. "He had an overwhelming incentive to tell the truth."

Selig and Fehr face only a slightly tougher time. Selig finally does what he should have done when all this started: he accepts blame. "I accept responsibility for everything that happens in our sport," says Selig. There are those in the game who wonder what might have been had Selig taken responsibility when all the trouble started and pledged to clean up his game. Would Congress have intervened? Would a Mitchell Report have been necessary? But they would never dare say that to their boss.

Fehr also accepts blame. "In retrospect, action could have and should have been taken sooner," says the union leader. "As an institution, the Players Association bears some responsibility for that. So do I."

Properly chastised, both baseball men are sent off with praise by the committee members. "I'm impressed and pleased with both of the gentlemen representing baseball and what they said," Waxman says when he meets with the media. Davis, who chaired the 2005 hearings, agrees. Then he adds, "If we don't see them again, that's fine with me."

Two days later, baseball's owners make an announcement of their own. They, too, are pleased with Selig. Though the Commissioner has barely started the second season of a three-year deal, they announce they are extending Selig's contract through 2012. What they don't announce is that Selig's compensation could surpass $30 million in the final year of his deal.

The Commissioner and the game's owners may be tired of being the subject of all these congressional hearings, but no one's ever said steroids was bad for business.

PART VI

LEGACY
(2008–2010)

Chapter 41

THE MORE THINGS CHANGE

February 18–December 23, 2008

It's February 18, and the scene Hal Steinbrenner is watching with his brother and father on the TV in George's office is the same one unfolding a few hundred yards away on Legends Field. Just 20 minutes earlier, Andy Pettitte had been standing in this room, repeatedly telling George, "I'm so sorry, I'm so sorry," while the Boss kept saying, "Don't worry, don't worry." When George had heard enough, he called the pitcher closer to him. "We love you," George told him. "You're part of the family. Give me a hug."

Now Pettitte is sitting at a table facing reporters and cameras, flanked on either side by manager Joe Girardi and general manager Brian Cashman. The presence of Derek Jeter, Jorge Posada, and Mariano Rivera sitting off to one side is a reminder of just how much Pettitte means to the Yankees. And the presence of Andy's two high-priced lawyers is a reminder of just how entangled Pettitte is in Roger Clemens' battle with George Mitchell and Congress.

"I am sorry," Pettitte tells reporters about the revelations that he has used HGH. "I know in my heart why I did things. I know that God knows that. I'm going to be able to sleep a lot better."

Andy hadn't quite listened to the Yankees brain trust last December when they told him to confess all his sins. He said a lot more under oath two weeks ago, telling congressional lawyers that he'd taken HGH a second time, in 2004, when he went on the DL with the Astros. Then came the bombshell: Pettitte testified that Clemens told him in 1999 or 2000 that he used HGH. Andy is now a key witness in the case against his good friend Roger.

Pettitte was excused from yet another hearing called by Congressmen Henry Waxman and Tom Davis, this one starring Clemens and Brian McNamee, the man who claimed he injected both pitchers with steroids. The televised hearing did little to improve the image of Clemens or Congress. Clemens angrily insisted McNamee was lying. He more calmly said his friend Andy "misremembered" their talks. Democrats on the committee called Clemens a liar and a cheat, while the Republicans called McNamee a drug dealer who could not be trusted.

The partisan bickering was laughable, but the outcome for Clemens was not: there will be a perjury investigation into his testimony that will eventually lead to an indictment and a trial.

All this is context for Pettitte today as he finishes his prepared statement and says he's ready to take questions. Andy's answers are mostly brief and hollow, his eyes in a fixed stare. He only used drugs to recover from an injury and help his team, he insists, never to gain a competitive advantage. He has no idea how things will work out between him and Roger—who, he says, taught him more about pitching than he could have ever imagined. And all he knows is that McNamee is telling the truth about him.

"I hope the friendship with Roger will still be there," he says. "I love him like a brother."

The press conference runs just short of an hour. Pettitte gets up to leave, hugs Jeter, Posada, and Mo, then walks off, saying he has to get back to work. Watching from his father's office, Hal Steinbrenner has reason to hope that Pettitte's "Aw, shucks" confession will put this problem behind them and allow the Yankees to concentrate on baseball.

If only he could feel as hopeful about the power-sharing arrangement with his big brother Hank. It was just last fall when George's two sons agreed that Hank would oversee the baseball end of the family business while Hal watched over the team's finances.

George was pleased that his older son was finally showing an interest in his team, and Hal was happy with an organizational chart listing them as cochairmen.

This can work, Hal kept telling himself. Then came the fight over Johan Santana, who the Twins were offering up for prospects last winter. Cashman and his scouts thought Santana had lost something: their charts showed the left-hander had stopped throwing his slider around midseason. Instead, the GM wanted to rely on the organization's top pitching prospects—Phil Hughes, Ian Kennedy, and Joba Chamberlain—for the coming season.

Hank wanted to rip a page from his father's playbook and trade their prospects for the two-time Cy Young Award winner. Sorry, said Hal, Santana didn't fit into the team's budget. And yes, the Yankees would now operate on a budget, albeit a large one. Hal is not his father.

Hank is not his father, either, but he's tried to imitate him, making veiled threats and expressing his displeasure in the media. "If we miss the playoffs by the end of this year, I don't know how patient I'll be," he said in late January when the Yankees passed on Santana. "But it won't be against the players. It will be a matter of maybe certain people in the organization could have done something else."

The rhetoric was ratcheted up after the Mets swooped in and dealt for the Twins ace. "It's a fact that myself and my dad wanted Santana," Hank said two days before Pettitte's apology. "Obviously I could have done it if I wanted to."

A day later, he was back at it. "If Santana could have made the difference for us and the young pitchers aren't ready, people have to be held accountable," he told *Newsday*.

Pettitte's arrival puts Hank's headlines on hold, but only for the moment. It's clear the older Steinbrenner brother has his father's thirst for the back page. But while George understood how to manipulate the media, it's the reporters who are manipulating Hank. And before long, they're mocking him, too. By the time February is out, they're calling the 51-year-old Steinbrenner Baby Boss—or worse—in their stories. Yet Hank can't stop answering every call and returning the ones he misses.

The real Boss is all but invisible to the media and the fans until March 27, the final day of camp. That's when they find George sitting in a golf cart in front of the Yankees dugout before the final exhibition game. Every Yankees player stands on the dugout steps, looking out at the tarp-covered scoreboard in left-center field. Hal and Hank Steinbrenner pull at cords and the tarp falls away, revealing the stadium's new name: GEORGE M. STEINBRENNER FIELD.

"This is a great thing," Steinbrenner says to reporters standing nearby before circling the field in his golf cart to a standing ovation. "It makes me proud."

Steinbrenner's daughters Jennifer and Jessica also take part in the pregame ceremonies. His wife Joan throws the first pitch as her 77-year-old husband is ushered up to his box, where two guards keep fans and reporters away.

After the game, Hank and Hal meet with the media. Reports swirled in the offseason that the team was on the market, while others had the YES Network, now generating revenues of almost $400 million a year, also up for sale. Both brothers stress there is nothing to either story. "There are no plans to sell," says Hal. "That's not going to change."

As the reporters leave, one hangs back and asks Hank about Jose Canseco's latest book, *Vindicated*. The former player has written that Rodriguez has used steroids. "In this age of drug paranoia, everybody's going to say that everybody hitting the ball over the fence is on 'roids," Hank says. "There is such a thing as a natural, and Alex is a natural. It's that simple."

Rodriguez has a solid start to the season, hitting .308 through the first 20 games, but the team goes 10–10. The trouble: poor pitching, especially from two of the young pitchers Cashman refused to part with for Santana. Hughes is 0–3, allowing 16 earned runs in $16\frac{1}{3}$ innings, while Ian Kennedy is 0–2, giving up 15 earned runs in 14 innings. Overall, the starting rotation is 7–9 with a 5.33 ERA.

All of which puts the spotlight on hard-throwing Joba Chamberlain, who is 1–0 with a 1.42 ERA while coming out of the bullpen. Cashman's plan is to ease the 22-year-old Chamberlain into the starting rotation, but by April 20, Hank Steinbrenner has seen enough. "I want him as a starter, and so does everyone else, and we need him there now," Steinbrenner tells reporters from Tampa. "You don't have a guy with a 100 mph fastball and keep him as a setup guy. You have to be an idiot to do that."

Publicly, the "idiot" behind the decision takes it all in stride. "I think Hank and everybody are all on the same page," Cashman says. "These are things we discuss internally all the time, and we'll continue to do so. It's as simple as that."

But privately Cashman, who's enjoyed two seasons of autonomy, is grinding his teeth, much as he did all spring training. And that has the younger Steinbrenner brother concerned. Cashman's in the final year of his contract, and there'll be plenty of suitors if he wants to leave. The two men have already talked over a game plan to get the Yankees back to the World Series, and Hal would hate to lose Cashman, especially now. But Brian has already announced he won't make that decision until the season's end.

The concern now is that Hank might make that decision an easy one.

The Yankees' slow start turns into a season of mediocre results, and on August 27 Hank Steinbrenner is huffing and puffing his way across the players' parking lot, steamed by the loss he just witnessed in only his second visit to Yankee Stadium all year. And this one really hurt. The 11–3 thrashing at the hands of the Red Sox all but ended any lingering hopes the Yankees had of reaching the postseason, leaving them 10½ games behind surprise AL East leader Tampa Bay and seven games out of a wild-card berth.

"They sucked," Steinbrenner spits out as he searches for his car.

All signs are pointing toward the end of the Yankees' string of 13 consecutive postseason appearances. As transition seasons go, this one has been all about bumps and bruises, many of them inflicted by the man who's just passed judgment on his father's team.

The season's biggest gamble—putting the ball in the hands of the team's young pitchers—blew up, thanks largely to injuries and incompetence. Kennedy, judged the 26th-best prospect in all of baseball entering this season, was demoted in early May after going 0–2 with an 8.37 ERA. He returned for three mediocre starts later in May, went on the DL for 33 days with a shoulder strain, then joined Triple-A Scranton. He came back for one start in early August, was shelled, then sent back down for good. Hughes was 0–4 with a 6.62 ERA before going on the DL with a fractured rib in late April. Only Chamberlain has thrived, pitching well first as a reliever and then as a starter, but he went down on August 6 with tendinitis.

Injuries ravaged the Yankees, which should not have been a complete surprise, since this team—average age 30.95—is the second oldest in the game. Jorge Posada, who just turned 36, had surgery to repair his right shoulder in late July; he played 51 games. Hideki Matsui (34) played only 93 games, Johnny Damon (34) and Alex Rodriguez (32) both spent weeks at a time on the DL, and No. 1 starter Chien-Ming Wang never returned from an ankle injury he suffered in mid-June.

But Cashman deserves credit for plugging the holes without giving up prospects or busting the budget. And while some pined for Joe Torre, Joe Girardi's done a fine job keeping a flawed team in contention the entire season. Especially with Hank Steinbrenner's season-long habit of saying the wrong thing at the worst possible time.

Perhaps Hank's most egregious stumble came after the Yankees dropped seven of 10 on a crucial road trip earlier this month and he told reporters the team will come back and win it all next year. When the team returned home on August 15, Hal met with Derek Jeter, Cashman, and Girardi in the manager's office. His message: management has not given up on this season.

But while no one is ready to quit, the only date that really matters anymore is September 21, when the Yankees will take the field for the last time in the House That Ruth Built. And when that day arrives, signaling the end of 85 years at the iconic Stadium, the atmosphere is thick with emotion. The gates open seven hours early so fans—54,610 strong, lifting the season total to a Yankees-record 4.3 million—can enjoy one last walk around the warning track before the pregame festivities get under way.

Soon past Yankees greats take the field at their old positions, with the sons of Mickey Mantle and Roger Maris representing their fathers. Bernie Williams, happily returning to the Yankees fold for the first time since his messy divorce from the team in 2007, jogs out to a standing ovation. Willie Randolph rubs some infield dirt on his uniform, visibly savoring being back in pinstripes three months after being canned by the Mets. The perfect game batteries—Don Larsen and Yogi Berra, David Cone and Girardi, and David Wells and Posada—meet on the mound for the snapshot of a lifetime.

Current Yankees walk around with digital cameras, recording the ceremonies. Highlights of big moments and big stars play on the scoreboard screen. (Noticeably absent: any clips of Roger Clemens.) Babe Ruth's daughter Julia Ruth Stevens, whose father hit the first home run at the Stadium in 1923, throws out the first pitch, and the final game at the Stadium begins.

Pettitte pitches into the 6th inning, and catcher Jose Molina hits a home run in the 4th inning—the last homer at the Stadium—to put the Yankees ahead for good. Mariano Rivera induces Orioles second baseman Brian Roberts into a ground out to end the game, and when first baseman Cody Ransom hands Rivera the ball, the legendary closer dedicates it to the team's owner.

"Mr. George, he gave me the opportunity and he gave me the chance," Rivera tells reporters. "The least I can do is give the ball to him."

George is back in Tampa, soaking in the many kind words being said about him while at home with his wife Joan and Hank. "He decided a couple of days ago to stay with my mom and watch the game at home, and he's watching now as we speak," Hal Steinbrenner says into the TV camera. "Tonight's about this facility over 85 wonderful years. As excited as I am to go to a new facility, I have mixed emotions. But this was an amazing night."

The Yankees are officially eliminated from the postseason two nights later, and the season ends as it began—with Hank spouting off. This time it's all about the Yankees having a better record than Joe Torre's Dodgers, who will win the NL West to reach the postseason. "The biggest problem is the divisional setup in major league baseball," he wrote in a piece for the *Sporting News*. "I didn't like it in the 1970s, and I hate it now. It isn't fair."

* * *

The Commissioner of baseball reads Hank Steinbrenner's *Sporting News* column with dismay and makes a mental note to mention his displeasure to Randy Levine. He's on the phone often with the Yankees president, one of the few men he knows George truly trusts, as he watches and waits for the Steinbrenner sons to sort out how to run their father's team.

Damn, he misses George. He misses the healthy George Steinbrenner, not the man he last saw at the All-Star Game at Yankee Stadium in mid-July. Selig clapped along with the rest of the crowd during the pregame ceremony when George—flanked by Hal, Jennifer, and son-in-law Felix Lopez—rode around the outfield in a golf cart, at times waving to the fans. But it was clear to everyone watching that the person hidden behind the large sunglasses was not the Boss they remembered, the man who ran roughshod over managers, players, and the rest of baseball for so many years. No, it didn't take an old friend to realize that George was disoriented and uncomfortable.

At ride's end, the golf cart pulled up to the pitcher's mound, where Yogi Berra, Goose Gossage, and Reggie Jackson walked one at a time over to George. All three had legendary battles with their boss, but each kissed him on the cheek as tears slid down from behind Steinbrenner's dark glasses.

It's a moment Selig will never forget. Just four years younger than his ailing friend, the Commissioner knows he has much to be thankful for. Especially this 2008 season, when so many other things have gone right.

Selig is still reaping rewards from the Mitchell Report, which—despite its obvious flaws—continues to be widely praised. Back on April 12, Selig signed off on yet another new drug testing program with the union, agreeing not to punish any players Mitchell exposed as cheats in exchange for incorporating most of the Senator's 20 recommendations. The key provisions: doubling the number of offseason tests and putting operation of the program into the hands of an independent administrator.

Selig had already implemented recommendations that did not

require union approval. He was especially eager to establish an investigative unit, which now allows him to ferret out suspected users who don't fail their tests. He hails the new drug testing program as the toughest in all of sports, confident he'll now be remembered as the man who cleaned up baseball.

Selig was relieved that he no longer had to answer questions about Barry Bonds. Barry can still hit — probably better than half the DHs in the American League — but no team was interested in signing the 43-year-old home run king, even after his agent lowered the asking price to the game's $390,000 minimum. The union is looking into filing collusion charges, but it's going to be hard to make a good case for a player who's currently facing charges of lying to a grand jury about his alleged use of steroids.

There are only two questions about Bonds left to be answered: Can his lawyers keep him out of jail? And will the baseball writers vote him into the Hall of Fame when he appears on the ballot in five years? Bonds is far from the only superstar of his generation left wondering if his road to Cooperstown is now blocked.

Selig's delighted to see the team in Tampa finally come of age. The Rays, behind strong pitching and rookie sensation Evan Longoria, are this season's surprise team, clinching the AL East on September 26 and finishing with 97 wins. It's the first winning record in the franchise's 11-year history.

It's been a noteworthy season for the Commissioner's former team, too. The Brewers have played winning baseball since May, and despite an early September slump that cost manager Ned Yost his job, the team is poised to overtake the Mets for the NL wild-card berth in the final game of the season on September 28.

There's little mystery to why the Brewers are in this position: it's the pitching of CC Sabathia, the six-foot-seven power pitcher GM Doug Melvin grabbed at July's trade deadline — a move Bud could only have dreamed about making when he owned this team. Sure, Milwaukee finally has an offense to be reckoned with — the power tandem of Ryan Braun (36 homers) and Prince Fielder (34) is one of the game's best — and they're surrounded by a bevy of quality role players. But it's Sabathia — a free agent at season's end — who's carried this team. The big left-hander has won 10 of 12 decisions for Milwaukee, including six complete games, and heads into today's crucial finale against the Cubs with a minuscule 1.78 ERA.

Sabathia is pitching on three days' rest for the third straight start, and he's locked in a 1–1 duel in the bottom of the 8th when Braun slugs a two-run homer for a 3–1 Brewers lead. Sabathia finishes what he starts again, getting a double-play grounder to close out the game. Miller Park stays full for another 30 minutes, all eyes glued to the out-of-town scoreboard in left field to see if the Marlins can beat the Mets and send the Brewers to the postseason for the first time since 1982.

The Marlins take a 4–2 lead in the 8th on a pair of solo homers. The Mets threaten but don't score in the bottom of the 8th, then go down quietly in the 9th. And when Ryan Church flies out to end the Mets season, Miller Park erupts into tearful celebration. Streamers and confetti pour down from the rafters, fireworks shoot up from behind the outfield walls, and Sabathia stands atop the Brewers dugout spraying fans with Champagne.

The Brewers drop Game 1 of the division series against the Phillies, and Sabathia has little left for Game 2, leaving in the 4th inning of a 5–2 loss. But nobody in baseball is happier than Selig when the series shifts to Milwaukee. The man who dedicated several years of his life to securing taxpayer funding for the $414 million ballpark will finally see a playoff game at Miller Park. The Commissioner's enthusiasm spills over as he does a victory lap through the spacious press box before Game 3.

"I keep telling people I'm neutral, and I'm supposed to be, but I was thrilled when I walked in here," Bud says. "It's a wonderful day for Milwaukee, for Wisconsin, and a very emotional day for a lot of people."

The Brewers win Game 3, giving Selig a chance to take center stage the next day before the home crowd. The last note of the national anthem is still echoing when the Miller Park PA announcer calls out Selig for the ceremonial first pitch. The Milwaukee crowd is on its feet, the clapping and cheering magnified by the banging of thousands of Thunderstix as the 74-year-old Commissioner walks to the base of the pitcher's mound.

Dressed in dark slacks and a blue sweater under a shiny white MLB jacket, Selig settles into his stance. His throw makes it over the plate, and he thrusts his hands over his head as the applause crescendos again. He high-fives Brewers owner Mark Attanasio, walks off the field, and disappears into the home dugout.

The Brewers season ends three hours later when they fall 6–2 to the Phillies, who go on to beat the Rays in a World Series overshadowed by a historic presidential election and a full-blown economic collapse. Selig braces for a tough offseason, with teams already worried about selling season tickets, luxury boxes, and advertising when 500,000 Americans have lost their jobs over the last two months. Several teams have told him they plan to cut back their payrolls, but Attanasio has made it clear he plans on offering big money to sign Sabathia.

Unfortunately for the Brewers owner, the Yankees have made the same decision.

Hal Steinbrenner climbs into his black Cadillac SUV and drives slowly down the driveway of his parents' South Tampa mansion. It's been a long day at the end of a long November week for George Steinbrenner's younger son. He's been talking about this day with Randy Levine for the last few months—the day he would get his father's blessing to assume George's role as the managing general partner of the New York Yankees.

And today was that day. The power-sharing arrangement with Hank, an attempt to keep his older brother involved, was creating confusion about the present and uncertainty about the future. One day it was a bondholder wondering who was in charge, the next day one of their bankers was asking the same question. Some of the team's limited partners— the ones who did not know Hal well or didn't know him at all—were puzzled over who made the big decisions, too.

The New York media was doing its part, making sure the question about who's in charge was asked on a regular basis. It's been 20 months since Hal took control of his father's team, and he'd been more than content to do his job and remain quietly in the background. But even longtime employees were concerned about what the future held.

Hal quieted the concerns of one of those employees two months ago. "Things are going to calm down soon," he told Brian Cashman. The general manager's contract was up at the end of October, and Seattle and Washington were among several teams sure to take a run at him. Hank talked of resurrecting his father's Tampa front office to "advise" Cashman in mid-September, an idea Hal killed immediately.

"I'd like you to stay," Hal told Cashman. Yes, Hank and the rest of the family will all be involved, but everyone's role will soon be clear. "And I think you'll be happy with the results. I think we can do great things together." Cashman bought in, signing a three-year contract for $6 million on October 1.

Yes, the time has come to make perfectly clear—to everyone—just who is running the Yankees. That's what Hal and Randy decided the team's president would tell his parents. "Everybody is a little concerned right now," Levine told George and Joan earlier this week. "It's not like it was 10 years ago. We have banks, we have bondholders on the Stadium, we have rating agencies, and these people are a little nervous, and it's beginning to hurt the business.

"I really feel this is the time we need to make this change so everybody can see that things are under control."

George agreed. Then Levine sat down with each of Hal's siblings, explaining what all this meant. Baseball requires one control person for each team, and their father was now ready to relinquish that position. Hal has been attending league meetings for the past two years, participating in baseball matters, looking out for the Yankees' interests. That's a big part of this job.

But it's more than that—much more. This isn't the business their father once ran, Levine told them. It's the one he envisioned years ago. Today's Yankees are the centerpiece of a growing entertainment company, one with its own lucrative cable network, sponsorships, and Legends Hospitality, a concessions and merchandising partnership with the Dallas Cowboys and Goldman Sachs. Announced just a few weeks ago on October 20, Legends will supply concessions—high-end and standard fare—for both the Yankees and Cowboys, with an eye toward expanding to other teams in every major sport.

If anyone has an objection to Hal's becoming the control person, Levine told Hank, Jenny, and Jessica, this is the time to speak up. No objections, they all told him. We support our younger brother. Joan felt the same way, and George could not have been more pleased when Levine reported back. Hal was his choice as well, he told the Yankees president, but he wanted to hear from everyone first. "Help him the same way you've helped me," the Boss told Levine.

All this is swirling in Hal's mind as he winds his way home. George still comes to the office a couple of days each week, and Hal keeps him abreast of major developments and seeks his advice on big decisions. But there is no question that this team is Hal's responsibility now. And the youngest member of the Steinbrenner family already has some big plans.

"Are you going to spend money chasing free agents the way your father did?"

That's the only real question put to Hal Steinbrenner in his short meeting with baseball's ownership committee at MLB's quarterly meeting in New York City on November 19.

"I'm here to be a good partner," Steinbrenner says. "I respect what my father has done, but I'm a different person. The Yankees are going to be a good partner in the industry, and we hope to grow the industry along with everyone else. I'm looking forward to participating."

A day later, the owners unanimously approve Steinbrenner as the Yankees' new general managing partner. "I realize it's a great responsibility," Steinbrenner tells reporters when the meeting adjourns. "My dad is a tough act to follow. But he's been slowing down for the last couple of years. I have been intimately involved with all aspects of the company. My duties aren't really going to change, and my work isn't really going to change much."

That same day, Mike Mussina announces his retirement. With Jason Giambi, Carl Pavano, and Bobby Abreu already gone, the

Yankees have now shaved $88.5 million off last season's $209 million payroll. But not for long.

Despite an economy in free fall—533,000 Americans lose their jobs this month, the most since 1974, and everyone understands this is just the beginning of a very bad run—the Yankees are ready to start spending. Hal Steinbrenner may differ in style from his father, but he understands he needs a playoff team to fill his new stadium and hold his TV audience. And he also knows there might not be all that much time left for his father to see another World Series flag raised at Yankee Stadium.

CC Sabathia is the Yankees' top priority, and they already offered the left-hander $140 million for six years on November 14, the first day teams were allowed to negotiate with free agents. But Sabathia has reservations: he's heard the team's clubhouse chemistry is terrible. "That's one of the reasons we're ready to write you a big check," Cashman tells him. "People gravitate to your personality. We want you to help fix that."

Jeter is one of several Yankees who call Sabathia to allay his fears, and on December 11, the big man signs a seven-year, $161 million deal, a record high for a pitcher. The Brewers, who offered $100 million for five years, didn't have a chance. Two days later the Yankees add A. J. Burnett, signing the 31-year-old right-hander to a five-year, $82.5 million contract. The hard-throwing but injury-prone Burnett went 18–10 for Toronto last season, setting career highs in strikeouts (231) and innings (221). A big plus: A.J. is 20–5 with a 3.29 ERA in the tough AL East.

"I'm not going to say money wasn't an issue—of course it was," says Burnett, whose two young children bring pinstriped teddy bears to his introductory media conference. "But I have a chance to win five years in a row. Whether you admit you love them or hate them, everybody wants to be a Yankee."

Cashman wants to make one more move: signing switch-hitting, Gold Glove first baseman Mark Teixeira, who hit .308 with 33 homers and 121 RBI last season with the Braves and Angels. But both Hal and Hank keep telling him no, even though their chief rival—the two-time World Champion Red Sox—are the favorites to land the 28-year-old power hitter. Cashman keeps asking, and when a deal between Teixeira and Boston falls apart in late December, he pushes to use the money set aside to re-sign Andy Pettitte to help make the numbers work.

The GM's persistence pays off, and on December 23, Cashman announces he's signed Teixeira for $180 million over eight years.

The signing brings the team's spending spree to $423.5 million. The Yankees now have the four highest contracts in baseball— A-Rod, Jeter, Sabathia, and Teixeira—at a cost of slightly more than $800 million.

Teixeira's deal comes just one day after the Yankees receive a $26.9 million luxury tax bill, underscoring the obvious: this tax isn't going to stop the Steinbrenners from spending whatever it takes to win. "At the rate the Yankees are going, I'm not sure anyone can compete with them," Brewers owner Mark Attanasio tells Bloomberg News. "Frankly, the sport might need a salary cap."

And once again, history repeats itself. The Yankees sign the game's top free agents. The owner in Milwaukee calls for a salary cap. Some things just never change, no matter who is in charge.

Chapter 42

MOVING ON

December 18, 2008–November 30, 2009

DON FEHR RECEIVES a bit of good news as 2008 draws to a close. Earlier in the year, a three-judge panel of the United States Court of Appeals for the Ninth Circuit in San Francisco declared the government's seizure of Major League Baseball's 2003 drug tests was legal, reversing earlier rulings by three different federal judges. On December 18, the same court decides to vacate the 2–1 decision and start the proceedings from the beginning before the full court.

The list isn't back in the union's hands yet, but the ruling still prevents the government from pursuing the players involved.

What the judges can't prevent are leaks, despite putting all the evidence under seal. And the first name that comes out is a big one: Alex Rodriguez. On February 7, *Sports Illustrated* cites four anonymous sources who claim the Yankees star failed his 2003 drug test, setting off a firestorm that pits Selig against Fehr once again.

Rodriguez admits his guilt two days later in an interview on ESPN with Peter Gammons, claiming he only used steroids for the three seasons—2001–2003—he played in Texas. "I did take a banned substance, and for that I am very sorry," says Rodriguez, whose voice wavers often during his 30-minute confession. "I'm guilty for a lot of things. I'm guilty for being negligent, naive, not asking all the right questions. And to be quite honest, I don't know exactly what substance I was guilty of using."

He's also guilty of having a poor memory, one that improves slightly eight days later when he makes another confession on the first day of spring training at Yankees camp. *Sports Illustrated*'s story on February 7 reported that Rodriguez took testosterone and Primobolan, an anabolic steroid. Sitting at a table with manager Joe Girardi and GM Brian Cashman, Rodriguez tells the 200 reporters in attendance that he and an unnamed cousin bought a drug he called "boli" in the Dominican Republic and injected it for an energy boost.

"I was immature, and I was stupid," he says. "For a week here, I kept looking for people to blame, and I keep looking at myself."

Soon after the *Sports Illustrated* story, the *New York Times* writes that unnamed baseball officials are angry that Gene Orza, the union's chief operating officer, and the union itself did not destroy the 2003 test results once they had been tabulated. The story is nonsense. Selig and his lieutenants know baseball's joint drug agreement called for both parties to oversee the destruction of the 2003 tests. They also know the government issued its subpoena just six days after both sides received the results, leaving little time to get the work done.

But Selig is once again forcing Fehr to play defense. Fehr explains to the media that the results were in the process of being destroyed when the government issued its first subpoena. "Once you find out that a subpoena has been issued, you obviously cannot destroy anything that is involved in an active investigation," Fehr says. "So we didn't."

No one is listening to Fehr, who is quickly losing the public relations battle—again. Selig lets Fehr try to explain himself for three days before issuing his first statement. "While Alex deserves credit for publicly confronting the issue, there is no valid excuse for using such substances, and those who use them have shamed the game," Selig says.

Ten days later, Selig is once again rewriting history. "Starting in 1995, I tried to institute a steroid policy," Selig tells *Newsday*, forgetting he's long been on record saying he never heard a word about steroids until Andro was discovered in Mark McGwire's locker in 1998. And what stopped Selig in 1995? "We were fought by the union every step of the way," he says.

Chicago owner Jerry Reinsdorf agrees, telling MLB.com that Fehr is responsible for the entire Steroids Era. Other baseball owners and officials pile on. So does the media, which alternately criticizes Fehr for not destroying the test results that proved players took steroids, and blames him for protecting players who took performance-enhancing drugs. Fehr can only laugh at the hypocrisy. But then again, after all these years, he's come to expect little else.

Fehr's real regret, one he'll never share with the media, is that he was too slow to recognize how steroid use was dividing the players. The strength of the union had always been Fehr's ability to keep it united, find a consensus, and formulate a winning strategy. That didn't happen here, leaving the players vulnerable to a Commissioner, a band of federal agents, and a number of congressmen looking to exploit the issue for personal gain.

And so the leaks continue to trickle out. On May 8, Manny Ramirez, who pumped life into a listless Dodgers team when he was traded to LA a year ago, is suspended for 50 games for testing positive in spring training for a banned female fertility drug often taken by steroid users to restore testosterone production. The 36-year-old Ramirez, who is hitting .348 with six home runs and 20 RBI for the first-place Dodgers, will forfeit $7.7 million of his $25 million salary.

The 11-judge panel in California is still deliberating whether the government violated Fourth Amendment protections against illegal search and seizure in its CDT raid when the New York Times reports on June 16 that another anonymous source claims Sammy Sosa is also one of the players on the list of 104 who tested positive in 2003. If the court again rules in favor of the government, the union expects it will be open season on another 100 or more players. Meanwhile, they have no idea how to stop the leaks.

The union chief has been thinking seriously of stepping down for more than a year, grooming Michael Weiner to take over in time to lead negotiations when the current labor deal expires in the fall of 2011. He's told a handful of people close to him that he's decided to retire at the end of the year, and now word is getting out. Fehr knows many will believe the rash of steroids scandals finally drove him from the game, but he long ago learned there was little he could do about what people say and think about him.

On the morning of June 22, he assembles his staff in the union's main conference room. Sitting to Fehr's right at the top of the long table is 92-year-old Marvin Miller, the union's first executive director and still its godfather. "A lot of people know I've been thinking of retiring for some time, and I think that leaving at the end of this year would be the right time," Fehr says. "I will turn the reins over to Michael at the next Executive Board meeting."

With that, Michael Weiner takes the seat to Fehr's left. Dressed in his usual jeans and Chuck Taylor sneakers, Weiner keeps things simple. "I'm honored by the appointment and thrilled at the opportunity," he says.

There's a brief silence before Orza speaks up. "As the senior staff member let me simply say on behalf of all of us..." and then he starts to clap. The rest of the staff joins in, and Fehr's good-bye announcement ends as the applause dies down.

Fehr holds a short conference call with the union reps of the 30 teams, then publicly announces his decision on a conference call with reporters a few hours later. He'll be 61 next month, and after 26 years as the union's executive director—32 years at the union in all—it is simply time to go. "After a while, it all wears you down," Fehr tells his listeners. "I think it will be good for everybody."

He calls it an honor to follow Miller, expresses complete confidence in Weiner, and says he leaves his post with no regrets. And that includes what he calls "the Barbara Walters question"—how it feels to leave with so many players' reputations tainted by steroids scandals.

"We made an agreement that the results should be kept confidential, and we think it should have been adhered to," Fehr says. "Nobody ought to be violating those court orders, and if the reports are true that lawyers are leaking these results, that's really troublesome.

"We were often criticized because of our attention to privacy and other issues related to this matter. But it was the right thing to do."

And he also knows it should never have gotten this far.

Bud Selig is upbeat as baseball reaches the All-Star Game in St. Louis. The reports of drug use by Rodriguez, Ramirez, and Sosa were obstacles, but the public now seems immune to the steroid revelations. Wall Street bankers and hedge fund managers have replaced baseball players in the media crosshairs, and while the country's economy crumbles, baseball's website and TV network are thriving and the game's attendance is holding firm.

There's no question Americans are hurting and anxious, and with good reason. On March 6, the Labor Department announced that 651,000 Americans lost their jobs over the preceding month, the first month of President Barack Obama's term. Another 663,000 jobs were wiped out before Opening Day. On June 1, General Motors, once the nation's leading company, filed for bankruptcy.

Once again, it appears Selig is right about his sport's role in America: a nation worried about losing homes, jobs, and health care turns to baseball for comfort. As if to drive the point home, President Obama agrees to come to St. Louis and throw out the first pitch for the All-Star Game, the first President to take the mound at the Midsummer Classic since Gerald Ford in 1976.

The game arrives at the break having delivered another round of milestones and terrific performances to take America's mind off its troubles. Gary Sheffield, now a Met, hits his 500th home run on April 17 against the Brewers, his first team. Ivan Rodriguez, now with the Astros, surpasses Hall of Famer Carlton Fisk when he catches his record 2,227th game on June 16.

Two certain Hall of Famers have stunning first halves. Albert Pujols became the seventh player to hit 30 home runs before July when he hits a pair of homers on June 30. The Cardinals first baseman reaches the break hitting .332 with 32 home runs and 87 RBI. Twins catcher Joe Mauer, a .317 career hitter in his first five seasons, is hitting a major league leading .373. Both Pujols and Mauer will be named MVP at season's end.

Derek Jeter gets his 2,600th hit on June 2, pulling within range of Lou Gehrig's Yankees record 2,721, which Jeter will surpass in mid-September. The new Yankee Stadium, despite early criticisms for high ticket prices and an overabundance of home runs, fills up often to watch a team that starts slow but goes 13–5 to reach the break at 51–37, three games behind Boston in the AL East.

The Red Sox are now second baseman Dustin Pedroia's team, and the reigning MVP is hitting .303 with 65 runs scored and 40 RBI. The Red Sox play before their 514th straight sellout at Fenway Park in the final game of the first half, and are one of nine teams on pace to draw at least 3 million fans.

Obama pops out of the National League dugout wearing jeans and a black White Sox jacket. He stops to talk to Cardinals Hall of Famers Stan Musial and Bob Gibson, then strolls to the mound to a huge ovation. The left-hander delivers a soft toss to Albert Pujols, who scoops up the pitch before it has a chance to bounce in front of the plate.

The game is a tight affair, with the Tigers' Curtis Granderson tripling in the 8th inning and scoring on a sac fly to give the AL a 4–3 lead. Mariano Rivera nails down the game in the 9th for a record fourth career All-Star save, giving the AL its 13th straight All-Star Game without a loss and home-field advantage in the World Series.

It's a delighted Commissioner who proclaims the four-day All-Star celebration an unqualified success. At his annual address to the baseball writers earlier in the day, he boasted of the game's triumphs despite the country's economic turmoil.

"Overall, I must tell you, the popularity of this sport comes through in a more meaningful way this year than perhaps any other," says Selig. Baseball's attendance is down just 5 percent from midseason a year ago. "If you take the two New York ballparks with less capacity, we're probably down about 3.8 to 4 percent. To be where we are, given what's going on in the economy and the world, is absolutely remarkable. This could be our greatest season."

But priorities are priorities, and before Selig ends his talk, he issues a warning to fans of last year's surprise team: the defending

AL champion Rays may have to leave Tampa, the Commissioner says, if the city doesn't build them a new stadium, no matter how deep the current recession may be. "They need to change their stadium situation," Selig says. "I think that is clear."

At just after 7 p.m. on October 28, a black minivan with tinted windows pulls into the bowels of the new Yankee Stadium. A throng of security guards rushes to the vehicle as George Steinbrenner is helped into a wheelchair. He looks up and sees a familiar face. "Hey, Cash," he says to general manager Brian Cashman.

The two men move toward an elevator, which takes them upstairs to Steinbrenner's box. In a few minutes, George's team will take the field against the defending-champion Phillies. After six years, the Yankees are back in the World Series.

Despite the early season distractions, it's been a bounce-back year in the Bronx. Rodriguez recovered from hip surgery, ignored the "A-Roid" taunts, and hit 30 homers with 100 RBI in 124 games. Robinson Cano blossomed, hitting .320 with 25 homers and 85 RBI. Jeter hit .334 and stole 30 bases, and ageless Mariano Rivera—a year shy of 40—saved 44 games.

The three big newcomers paid big dividends: Sabathia and Burnett combine for 32 wins while Teixeira wins a Gold Glove at first and hits a league-leading 39 home runs. New York sets a team record with 244 homers—the best in the majors—and leads the game in scoring (915 runs) and wins (103).

It's been a big season for the bottom line, too. The Yankees drew 3.7 million to their smaller but more luxurious new park, contributing $397 million to revenues that easily clear half a billion dollars. They are once again the only team to pay the luxury tax—the $25 million payment brings their seven-year total to $174 million, 92 percent of what baseball has collected since instituting the tax in 1997. The team kicks in another $70 million in revenue sharing this season. But it's clear they can afford it.

Steinbrenner is in his box when Bud Selig comes to pay his friend a visit. It's also been a big year for Bud, who earned $18 million and change. Only 10 players will take home more than the game's Commissioner in 2009.

Steinbrenner watches his team fall to the Phillies, 6–1, then returns the following night to see the Yankees even the Series, with home runs from Hideki Matsui and Teixeira powering a 3–1 win. The family wants Steinbrenner to be part of all this, but they go to great lengths to shield him from the fans and media. They are worried about putting too much stress on George, who finds traveling difficult and gets disoriented in unfamiliar places like the new Yankee Stadium. This will be the last game he'll attend.

His team takes two of three in Philadelphia, and George is home in Tampa in front of the TV with his wife and a few friends when the Yankees return to the Bronx, one victory away from their 27th title. The grounds crew is wearing T-shirts with WIN IT FOR THE BOSS printed across the front as the fans fill the Stadium. The drama ends early when Matsui drives in six runs in the first five innings. Not long after that, Rivera records the final out of a 7–3 victory, and his teammates pour out onto the field in celebration for the first time in nine years.

An image of the championship trophy glistens on the massive scoreboard in center field along with the words BOSS, THIS IS FOR YOU. As always, Frank Sinatra's "New York, New York" blares over the sound system as the fans celebrate. The Commissioner is soon standing on a makeshift stage in the middle of the infield along with the Steinbrenner family and Yankees team officials and players.

"I want to take this opportunity to congratulate the World Champion New York Yankees," Selig says to raucous applause. Standing opposite Selig is Hal Steinbrenner, who can't help but think that this moment—standing on this stage, about to say hi to his father back in Tampa—completes the transition that began almost three years ago.

"I want to congratulate the Steinbrenner family for a job really well done," Selig says. "And to my friend George—I wish you were here. This one's for you."

Selig hands Hal the gold and silver World Series trophy, Steinbrenner raises it over his head, and the cheers from the crowd swell again. Hal thanks the fans for their support, then turns his attention to Tampa. "Dad, I know you are at home watching with Mom," he says. "This one is for you."

Girardi, Matsui, and Pettitte all answer a few questions from the Fox announcer. And when the last interview ends, Hal and Hank Steinbrenner, Randy Levine, Lonn Trost, and Brian Cashman crowd into Girardi's office to call George. Hal is holding the phone, congratulating his father and trying hard to hear George's reply over the noise. He thinks he hears his father say he's proud of him, but George's voice is shaking and it's clear he's crying. This time, though, the tears are from happiness.

Emotions are bubbling over in the Yankees locker room, too. Rodriguez is the center of attention, and he is clearly enjoying his moment of redemption. His botched confessions in February and his history of miserable postseason play have been washed away by four weeks of sterling performances. He singled and scored two runs tonight to finish the postseason hitting .365 with six home runs and 18 RBI. He scored 15 runs in 15 games and had a .500 on-base percentage. "This feels even better than you can imagine," he's telling everyone who comes his way.

The team's general manager is both satisfied and relieved. He worked hard to persuade CC Sabathia to come to New York and even harder to convince Hal Steinbrenner to stretch the team's budget to sign Teixeira when the first baseman's deal with the Red Sox fell through. He feels vindicated for standing firmly behind Girardi after his team missed the playoffs last season.

And maybe, just maybe, this will help him get over the bitterness he felt after Joe Torre wrote that Cashman betrayed him in the manager's failed contract talks with the Yankees in 2007. "Don't ever fucking talk to me again," Cashman texted his former friend and ally in January after reading the book Torre coauthored.

Matsui is surrounded by reporters from Japan and America, all wanting to know if he thinks he's just played his last game as a Yankee. (He did.) But right now he is enjoying being named the World Series MVP. There was little doubt who the hottest hitter was in this Series. Matsui had six hits in his final nine at bats, finishing the six games hitting .615 with three home runs and eight RBI.

Taking in the Champagne-soaked celebrations from his corner of the locker room is Mariano Rivera. He was disappointed earlier in the day when Hal Steinbrenner told him that George was not at the game. Now he's quietly sharing his feelings with a handful of reporters. "I wish Mr. Steinbrenner was here so I could give him a big hug," Rivera says. "He's the driving force behind all of this. And he's definitely a part of me."

Rivera was a 26-year-old set-up man when he won his first World Series ring in 1996, three years after the end of Steinbrenner's now-forgotten second suspension. He looks around and sees Jeter, who hit .407 in this Series, then Pettitte, who won the clinching game all three times this postseason. These two veterans are the only other players who were on the field that October night 13 years ago.

Tonight marks the fifth time the three men have celebrated winning a championship together. And it's the first time without George walking over, extending his hand, and congratulating them.

Somehow it doesn't feel quite the same.

Don Fehr walks down the palm-tree-lined entrance of the palatial Hyatt Regency at Gainey Ranch, the end of the 10-minute walk from his parents' home here in Scottsdale, Arizona, and finds his younger brother Steve. It's November 30, Steve's 58th birthday. It's also Don Fehr's last day as the executive director of the Major League Baseball Players Association, and the two brothers walk into the conference room for what will be the final MLBPA meeting in Don's long and successful career.

It's the union's annual Executive Board meeting, and as he has done every year since taking over as executive director, Fehr kicks off the three-day event with his take on the state of the game. And the news is good: revenues, attendance, and salaries are still rising. The union's licensing program and pension fund are thriving. As always, the union staff is monitoring the free agent market to make sure the owners play by the rules. Yes, they've had labor peace for 14 years, but that doesn't mean they can let down their guard, he tells the player reps from the game's 30 teams.

Never let down your guard.

His final address done, Fehr reaches into his pocket, pulls out a gavel, and hands it to Michael Weiner, the man he trained to take his place. Fehr settles into his seat as Weiner takes charge of his first meeting. After 32 years—25 as union chief—Don Fehr's work in baseball is done.

He returns one night later for a dinner in his honor. His going-away present of sorts was determined a few months ago when Weiner hired a compensation firm to determine what Fehr would have earned had he not capped his salary at $1 million in the contract he signed in 1992. The figure: $11 million.

A cadre of retired players has flown in for Fehr's farewell dinner. Stars Dave Winfield, Dave Stewart, and Don Baylor. The rank and file: Phil Garner, Brett Butler, B. J. Surhoff, Scott Sanderson, and Buck Martinez. These are many of the men who worked shoulder to shoulder with Fehr through the lockouts and the strikes, who were there when the average player salary was $289,000, who know what it's taken to push it to the $3.24 million the players enjoy today.

They were delighted to hear him called the game's most powerful man when he proved the owners guilty of collusion—a $280 million win for the scores of players affected—beat back management's push for a salary cap, and fought off contraction. They understood what it took to hold together a group of players far more diverse and wealthy than the union led by Marvin Miller, players who never knew life without the Players Association to protect them.

And they're still wincing about the large share of the blame he's taking for the game's struggle with performance-enhancing drugs. Maybe Fehr would have moved faster if he'd had a partner at MLB who wasn't as consumed with his legacy. Maybe he would have made the same mistakes. Or maybe, as one of their union brothers who couldn't make it tonight said recently, he was just doing his job.

"I think the players who did it and the players who didn't say anything share the blame," said David Cone, who worked closely with Fehr and pitched during the rise of the Steroids Era. "We hired Don to protect our rights. That's what he did."

One by one, the players come to the podium to tell their stories about Fehr. Baylor, a member of the committee that chose Fehr to succeed one-year flop Ken Moffett in 1983, talks about how hard Fehr worked to prove himself to a wary group of players. Garner gets everyone laughing about Fehr's terrible golf game and how many tissues and inhalers the union chief would use the longer their labor wars would last.

But it's Winfield who gets to everyone—especially Fehr. "I count being in the union as one of the things I cherish most in life," says the Hall of Famer, who spent 10 long seasons in New York. "I needed it perhaps more than any of my fellow players because of what George Steinbrenner put me through. I don't know if I could have survived that time without the assistance and support of the union. And Donald was always there for me."

Winfield looks over at Fehr, who's waging an unsuccessful battle to hold back tears. Fehr's guard is finally down, and like everyone there save Fehr's wife Stephanie and brother Steve, it's a side of the union chief Winfield has never seen. "I can't speak to what other unions did, but this union took care of business," Winfield says. "And Don was a big reason for that."

It's finally Fehr's turn to speak, and it's not long until his voice catches and his eyes grow moist. Everyone in the room understands the heavy emotional and physical toll 25 years of constant vigilance has taken on him. He's been a wartime leader—did he really have a choice?—and that meant never, ever being able to let down his guard.

Until now.

Chapter 43

ROAD TO COOPERSTOWN

January 11–August 24, 2010

MARK MCGWIRE FIDGETS nervously in a large chair inside a makeshift studio in Newport Coast, a small town in Southern California. It's early in the evening of January 11, but he's already had a very long day. McGwire started this second Monday of the New Year with a round of phone calls to admit what everyone had long assumed was true: he used steroids while he was hitting all those home runs.

And now he's sitting across from Bob Costas, who's shuffling his notes just as a producer signals the start of their live interview on MLB's television network.

"At the time you were doing steroids," Costas says in his opening question, "did you feel as if you were cheating?"

McGwire stares straight ahead, blinks once, and answers. "As I look back now, I can see how people can think that," he says. "But as far as my God-given talent, I don't see it."

It is not an easy interview for McGwire, who a week earlier learned only 23.7 percent of the baseball writers voting for the Hall of Fame had put him on their ballots, well short of the 75 percent needed for entry to Cooperstown. He's never been comfortable speaking to reporters, and this is one interview he has been dread-ing for years. But once he decided to accept Tony La Russa's offer to become the Cardinals hitting coach, this interview was inevitable.

So Big Mac sits across from Costas and repeatedly admits his sins, chokes back tears more than once, then turns defiant as the questioning goes on. "I was given a gift to hit home runs," he tells Costas, insisting his 583 homers—tied for eighth with Alex Rodriguez on baseball's all-time list—were a result of studying pitchers and learning how to shorten his swing. "The only reason I took steroids was for health purposes."

Costas talks about McGwire's call earlier today to Roger Maris' widow Pat—"I felt I needed to do that," McGwire says—and points out that the family considers Maris the true home run record holder.

"They have every right to," McGwire says. "I can't turn back the clock. All I can say is I'm sorry and I totally regret everything I've done."

"Do you view your achievements now as authentic?" Costas asks.

"I'd have to think so," McGwire says.

Almost the moment the 49-minute interview is done, the media and fans rip McGwire for saying steroids didn't help him hit home runs and demand that he apologize. Again. Largely overlooked is McGwire's revelation that he was ready to admit he used steroids when he testified before Congress in 2005. The government had refused to give him immunity—which former Congressman Tom Davis quickly confirms—and his lawyers advised him against any confessions.

Lost, too, is McGwire's contention that Bud Selig and Tony La Russa knew nothing about his steroid use until he told them the very morning of his announcement. Digging into Selig and La Russa's knowledge of steroids has never been high on the agenda of the baseball media, and the subject is quickly dropped. It's always been easier to blame Don Fehr.

La Russa is one of the Commissioner's favorites, and by the fall of 2009 he was ready to bring McGwire back into the fold. Cardinals owner Bill DeWitt called Selig to gauge his reaction. The Commissioner told DeWitt he would not stand in McGwire's way.

That's all DeWitt needed to hear. The Cardinals—the lone team

in baseball without an African American player on its roster—
fired hitting coach Hal McRae, the lone African American on its
coaching staff, to make way for McGwire. The move was announced
on October 26, the same day La Russa signed on to manage the
Cardinals for his 15th season. McRae, whose batters hit .263 for
the NL Central division champs—tied for fourth-best in the
league—is the only change La Russa makes to his coaching staff.

"I don't know how many years I have left to manage, and I
wanted to take this opportunity to invite a guy who I think has a
very special talent," La Russa said about McGwire, who played
almost his entire career under Tony, including the last four and a
half seasons, when he hit 220 home runs.

Selig was equally enthusiastic last October, telling reporters he
was "delighted" to have Mark back in baseball. "I have no misgiv-
ings about this at all," he said that day. "Mark McGwire is a very,
very fine man, and the Cardinals are to be applauded."

Earlier this morning, Selig and McGwire spoke by phone.
McGwire apologized for using steroids and thanked the Commissioner for his support. McGwire, never one for long talks, kept the
conversation short. Selig decides to let the former star do all the
talking today, choosing to release a prepared statement hailing
McGwire's admission as yet another example of Bud's success in
cleaning up the game.

"I'm pleased that Mark has confronted his use of performance-
enhancing substances as a player," Selig says in a statement. "The
so-called Steroids Era—a reference that is resented by the many
players who played in that era and never touched the substances—
is clearly a thing of the past, and Mark's admission today is another
step in the right direction."

The Players Association is pleased that Selig, for once, is not
demonizing a player when talking about steroids. But as the first
year under new Executive Director Michael Weiner unfolds, no one
at the union is letting down his guard.

They are bemused when the 14-man committee to "improve
baseball on the field"—created by Selig in the waning days of
2009—holds its first meeting a few days after McGwire's announce-

ment and tosses around ideas like realignment and eliminating the designated hitter. Selig chairs the group, which also includes 13 current and former members of baseball management. Tony La Russa is there, as is unofficial Bud biographer and apologist George Will.

There is no one under the age of 42 on the committee, and no one who's played the game in the 21st century. More telling: there are no current players or union officials. Given that anything of substance decided by the Gang of 14 has to be cleared by the union — which has fought off several attempts to eliminate the DH through the years — it's a glaring omission. Selig loves to boast about 16 years of labor peace, but no one at the union — including its new executive director — trusts the Commissioner any more than they did when he was colluding on salaries, trying to impose a salary cap, and canceling a baseball season.

Of greater concern is Selig's continued quest to scrub his legacy of all ties to "the so-called Steroids Era," as the Commissioner often calls the seasons of record-setting home runs. Union veterans are worried that Selig will try to test Weiner, much as he tested Fehr with collusion in Fehr's early years — and the issue of performance-enhancing drugs is a logical testing ground.

One challenge comes in March, when an unnamed baseball official tells the *New York Times* that Selig is considering using blood tests for human growth hormone in the minor leagues. It is widely suspected that a number of baseball players have switched from steroids to HGH, which cannot be detected by urine tests. The story follows news that an English rugby player failed a blood test for HGH, the first positive result in the six years the test has been in use.

The union knows Selig is determined to get a test for HGH before 2012, the year he says he will leave office. And the Commissioner seizes another opportunity to put the union in a public relations trap two weeks later, when boxers preparing for a match agree to blood testing. "We are currently exploring the feasibility of conducting blood testing for HGH in the minor leagues as soon as possible," baseball VP Rob Manfred says in a statement, adding that the Commissioner's office has begun "a dialogue with the union on blood testing."

The union has steadfastly opposed blood testing, citing privacy and reliability concerns. But where Fehr would have come out swinging, Weiner won't be cornered. "We look forward to further discussions as we jointly explore how we might strengthen our program as it relates to HGH," says Weiner, fully aware that a reliable blood test is nowhere on the horizon.

The transition from Fehr to Weiner has gone smoothly, as everyone at the union expected. The 48-year-old Harvard law grad has run the day-to-day operations of the union for much of the last decade, and the players are comfortable with his laid back personality and his ability to explain complex issues in an easy-to-grasp manner.

It's already been a busy first year. In January, Weiner reached an agreement with Manfred to jointly monitor the way the Marlins spend their revenue sharing proceeds. Florida's had the lowest payroll in three of the last four seasons, and in 2006 the Marlins spent $15 million on player salaries—half of what the team received through revenue sharing.

And on April 6, Weiner announces the union is looking into concerns among agents and players of collusion after a slow winter in the free agent market. "We have concerns about the operation of this year's market, and we're investigating those concerns," Weiner says.

Revenue sharing and players' salaries will both be on the table when Weiner and Manfred begin negotiations for a new contract sometime before the end of the year. Testing for HGH is certain to be on the table as well. Weiner doesn't think Selig is working to box him in ahead of labor talks, but others at the union are not as sure. They know these are Selig's legacy years and fully understand what that means.

There's no denying George Steinbrenner is ill. He can no longer get around without a wheelchair, and he can rarely stand up without the help of aides. But tonight is a good night. Tonight, seven days past his 80th birthday, George is enjoying dinner at his mansion in the leafy, older section of Tampa, smiling, talking, even laughing.

One night later George is rushed to St. Joseph's Hospital. His heart is failing, say the doctors. Jenny and Jessica, who have been watching over George almost every day, are comforting their mother Joan. Hank and Jessica's husband Felix are pacing. Hal has one eye on his father, the other on his three young daughters. There's not much to do now but watch the nurses walk in and out of George's hospital room, glance at his monitors, and make sure the oxygen mask over his mouth and nose is secure but comfortable.

It's 3 a.m., George seems stable, and Jenny turns to her weary kid brother. "Why don't you take the kids home?" she says to Hal. "We'll call if anything changes here."

Hal collects his sleepy girls and walks out of St. Joseph's and into the early morning darkness of July 13. He drives home, opens the door, and his phone rings. It's Felix. "You better come back here quick," he says.

There's a blood clot near George's heart, and the doctors are deciding what to do. Alarms are going off, a sound you never want to hear in a hospital. Now the nurses are clearing the room, getting ready for the doctors to put George under so they can try to save his life. But they can't. At 6:30 a.m., George Steinbrenner is pronounced dead.

Word travels fast. Mariano Rivera is in Bermuda with his wife Clara, where he is hoping to recharge for the second half of the season. Rivera, who skipped the All-Star Game in Anaheim with a slight muscle pull in his abdomen, is walking through the hotel lobby on the morning of July 13 when a fan stops him. "Did you hear that George Steinbrenner was rushed to the hospital this morning?" the man says.

Rivera stares at the man for a moment, blinks back the first of his tears, and reaches for his phone. He knew this day was close when he saw his friend in Tampa the first weekend of the season. George made it to the final game of the Yankees' series with the Rays, and he always made it a point to see Mariano before leaving the stadium.

Steinbrenner was sitting in a wheelchair, his nurse at his side, as the team filed out of the clubhouse. Rivera, who'd saved the

Yankees' 4–3 win an hour earlier, walked over to the team's 80-year-old owner and hugged him gently.

"I love you, Boss," said Rivera, surprised at how frail his friend felt.

"I love you, too," George said. "Keep doing good. How you feeling?"

"How you feeling, Boss, how are things?"

"I'm good. Keep doing good—you have to do good."

Now Rivera is on the phone, waiting for Yankees traveling secretary Ben Tuliebitz to answer his call.

"Ben, it's Mo. Is it true?"

"I'm afraid it is," Tuliebitz says. "George died of a heart attack this morning at 6:30. There was nothing they could do. I'm sorry, Mo."

Randy Levine is in Lake Placid. Yankees executives were never allowed to take vacations during the All-Star break under George, who always thought he could pick up ground while the other teams relaxed. Hal has different rules, and the Yankees president is in the resort city with his wife when his cell phone rings. "George died this morning," Hal tells Levine. "I'm so sorry," Levine says.

"Thank you. Can you please make the calls?" Hal asks.

Levine looks at his BlackBerry. It's not quite 7 a.m. Saddened to lose both a boss and a friend, Levine and his wife pack up and head back to New York to start making arrangements. On the drive he calls out to Anaheim, where he wakes up Bud Selig. "George passed away this morning," Levine says.

It's been a painful few weeks for Selig. Just five days earlier his brother Jerry died after a long battle with cancer. Bud still worries about his own experience with skin cancer over the past five years. And his wife Sue's brother died from cancer five weeks ago. Now George is gone. Selig knew his friend was suffering, knew George's illness had robbed him of the vitality that made him appear bigger than life. At least now George's suffering was over.

Selig and Levine talk several times throughout the day, exchanging information and making plans. Bud will ask for a moment of silence for George tonight after the All-Star lineups are announced. The flags of America, Canada, and California will fly at half-mast, and a video tribute will be shown on the stadium screen. The

Yankees will hold a pregame ceremony when the team returns to New York in three days. In a few hours, Bud will do an interview with Bob Costas for baseball's network and website.

"He owned the team in the biggest market, I owned the team in the smallest market—we never should have been friends," Selig tells Costas. The Commissioner looks tired and sad; it's been a long few hours. "But we were friends. Good friends."

"Does George Steinbrenner belong in the Hall of Fame?" Costas asks.

"Look, George was going to do what was best for the Yankees, but there is no question about it, he had a great impact on the game," Bud answers, the words coming quickly now. "He was great for the game, great. I don't mind, I don't mind telling you...well, Bob, I'm going to miss him."

No one in baseball knew both sides of Steinbrenner better than Selig, who is visibly shaken through most of the first 10 minutes of his annual talk with the national media. All of it is spent reminiscing about George. "He never gave me a problem, not one time," Selig says. "We may have disagreed on some things, but in the end he'd always say, 'Do what you want.' And bam, he'd slam the phone down. That was the end of the conversation."

Major League Baseball pulls together a media conference for the Yankees in Anaheim before batting practice, one for Andy Pettitte, Alex Rodriguez, and Joe Girardi and a separate one for Derek Jeter. "He expected a lot and he demanded a lot," Pettitte says. "He raised, I believe, the level of not only the Yankees organization but the bar around baseball for other teams to try to keep up and compete."

Jeter has too many stories to tell. The note the Boss sent explaining what he expected from the kid the Yankees drafted with the sixth pick in '92. The time, early in his career, when George yelled at Derek for getting doubled off third base on a line drive. The call after he named Jeter captain seven years ago.

"It's tough, because he's more than just an owner to me," says Jeter. "He's a friend of mine. He will be deeply missed."

Jeter last saw his friend at the home opener, when he and Girardi gave George his World Series ring. "I teased him and told him he had to take off his Ohio State ring and replace it with the Yankee ring," says Derek, who had planned to visit with George in Tampa over the next two days.

Much is written about George over the next several days—about the outsized personality, the serial firings, the free agent signings. How he turned a $10 million investment into an empire worth billions, one that will escape estate taxes thanks to Congress' failure to close a loophole in the tax code for 2010. How he donated millions to help people—supporting the pediatric emergency center at St. Joseph's Hospital, providing scholarships for the children of slain Tampa police officers, quietly paying for the funeral of a local high school football player who was shot and killed.

The sharp edges are nearly forgotten now, the mistreatment of employees and his two suspensions mentioned only in passing. A gleaming new stadium and a lucrative TV network stand as twin monuments to his vision. The free agent contracts surpassing $100 million stand as a testament to how much he helped reshape the game. He passes as a man respected by most and loved by many, though just how well he understood this in his final years is, sadly, in question.

Steinbrenner's family is preparing for the private funeral in Tampa three nights later when the memorial ceremony for George is held in the Bronx. New Yorkers recognize a part of their identity has moved on, and all eyes are on Yankee Stadium on this warm July night. Players and coaches from the Tampa Bay Rays stand along the third baseline. Mariano Rivera and the Yankees straddle the first baseline. Mo stands closest to home plate, two red roses wrapped in blue ribbon pressed to his chest.

An army bugler plays taps as Rivera walks forward slowly and places the flowers on home plate. Mo told a few teammates before the game that it still didn't feel real. Now it finally does.

"Good-bye, Boss," he whispers. "I'll miss you."

Cooperstown. It represents a piece of anyone who's ever taken part in the game of baseball. But only the lucky ones get to live here.

Andre Dawson has been waiting for this moment for nine years, and there were many days when he figured it would never come.

He played major league ball hard and well for 21 years, made eight All-Star teams, and won an MVP. Everyone considered the Hawk a star, though not everyone was sure Andre was a Hall of Famer. But here he is on a warm, humid Sunday in late July, sitting in a tall director's chair on an outdoor stage in Cooperstown beside the Commissioner of baseball. Dawson is ready to take his place in history.

Induction Weekend is all about history. Dawson was never the game's most important player, but his career and Selig's are inextricably linked. It was Dawson who produced the signature moment of the Selig-led collusion plan, handing the Cubs a blank contract in March of 1987 when the power-hitting Gold Glove outfielder found no takers for his services. Chicago gave him a one-year, $500,000 deal—half of what he'd made a season earlier—and he rewarded the Cubs with 49 homers, 137 RBI, and an MVP award.

It is Dawson's first team, the Expos, that Selig bought and sold in the contraction scheme. And it's Dawson's generation that Selig now holds up as the last to play baseball without the taint of drugs. That's something both Dawson and Selig know is untrue. But history has a way of changing in Cooperstown.

Selig arrived in town one day after mandating that all minor leaguers have their blood tested for HGH in 2011, the same flawed test that was floated for the major leagues this spring only to be dismissed by most experts as little more than a PR tool. The timing is no coincidence. It will be a combination of Hall of Fame players and team executives who will decide if Selig enters the Hall, and performance-enhancing drugs will be his litmus test.

Selig, his staff, and the rest of baseball's royal family are headquartered at The Otesaga, the historic 101-year-old hotel that stretches for 700 feet along the shore of Otsego Lake. The majority of living Hall of Famers travel here every Induction Weekend, and this year is no exception. Hank Aaron, Bob Gibson, and Tom Seaver are among the 47 who made the trip. They're all fiercely proud of their exclusive club; more than 17,000 men have played in the major leagues, and only 203 are enshrined in Cooperstown. It's good to be among peers every summer for a fun—and profitable—weekend.

Hundreds of fans packed the quaint little town Saturday afternoon, all hoping to catch sight of baseball's legends. It's not difficult. By late morning, dozens of Hall of Famers and a handful of familiar stars are sitting behind tables in makeshift booths up and down Main Street, autographing bats, balls, hats, and pictures, all for a price. Frank Robinson rushed past two familiar reporters to take his seat, sign his name, and collect $75 for each signature. Reggie Jackson signed for $100. Pitcher Jim Bunning, who will leave the U.S. Senate at the end of the year, charged only $50.

Many of the same fans watched as their heroes were driven down Main Street in antique cars later that evening. The parade ended at the Hall, where an invitation-only cocktail party awaited. Round tables were set up for the players in the alcoves of the main hall, where their plaques hang. A long row of serving tables divided the room, which soon filled with MLB officials, a few from the union, and the men and women who decide which players reach Cooperstown and which don't—the game's writers.

Selig entered late, preceded by two security guards, who floated through the crowd ahead of him. He chatted up Bob Nightengale of *USA Today* and Phil Rogers of the *Chicago Tribune,* two of the game's most influential writers. Bud slowly worked his way around the room, greeting the ex-players warmly, one hand on each man's shoulder, shaking hands, leaning in to listen and talk. No one is a bigger fan of these men than Selig.

The next afternoon, all 47 Hall of Famers are seated behind Selig and their club's newest member, who are now both watching the video of Dawson playing on a screen to the right of the stage. There's the majestic swing that produced 438 home runs. There's Dawson chasing down a fly ball in Wrigley Field, then throwing out a runner trying to tag up and score.

Each play is described in admiring tones by a narrator, who also tells the 20,000 fans looking up at the stage that Dawson's blank contract offer to the Cubs in 1987 "was the mark of a true team player." There is no explanation of why the Expos and Cubs were the only teams to offer Dawson a contract. The word *collusion* is never spoken. Cooperstown may be all about history, but not everything makes the cut.

Dawson, long considered one of the game's class acts, is gracious when he steps up to speak. He thanks the fans of the Expos, fans who made the three-hour drive across the border to honor him. Baseball may have forgotten Montreal, but these fans remember why and boo Selig each time his name is mentioned.

Andre expresses his affection for Chicago, where he won his MVP award. He talks movingly about his childhood, about how baseball gave him a life he never thought he'd live. He talks about how his wife iced his aching knees, about the path laid down by black players who came before him, and the honor of sharing a field with so many great athletes. He thanks the writers for always treating him fairly.

Dawson is about 10 minutes in when his mood shifts. There are people who've made mistakes and damaged the game, he says, mistakes "that have taken a toll on all of us." Dawson never says the word *steroids*, but there is little question about the point he wants to make. "Individuals have chosen the wrong road," he says. "Others still have a chance to choose theirs. Do not be lured to the dark side."

Dawson pauses, then continues for another 40 minutes, telling stories, praising the game he loves, thanking family and friends. Before he's done, Dawson jokes about several of the men sitting behind him. He draws the biggest response for his tale about pitcher Goose Gossage.

"Goose is the only player I know who could drink a case of beer on the flight between Chicago and St. Louis," Dawson says, stopping for effect. "And still pitch lights out the next day."

The crowd laughs. So does Selig and every player on the stage.

Left out of Dawson's talk of drug use in baseball—approved and unapproved substances—is the game's love affair with amphetamines that dates back at least to the times of Willie Mays and Mickey Mantle. Indeed, Gossage—who has spoken out loudly about shutting the doors to Cooperstown to all steroid users—has openly discussed using amphetamines to overcome the haze of alcohol, sometimes simply to stay awake in the bullpen. Baseball banned amphetamine use in 2006, but more than 100 players a season receive a medical exemption to continue using the drug.

Yes, Cooperstown is all about history. But sometimes it depends on who writes the script.

It's been a tough summer for fans of the Milwaukee Brewers. Their team lost nine straight in May, has had a winning record for just two days, and entered the last week of August sitting 12½ games behind the NL Central–leading Reds. Any real talk about the Brewers now revolves around the idea of trading star first baseman Prince Fielder, who'll be a free agent at the end of next season.

It hasn't been a good year for a lot of people in Milwaukee. The city ranks third in the nation in jobs lost, trailing only Detroit and Las Vegas. The local employment picture is so bleak that it takes a month just to get an interview at the HIRE Center, a job bank in Milwaukee. With its tax base shrinking, the city recently reported that the sales tax used to finance Miller Park, due to be retired in two years, will be extended indefinitely. Some estimate the stadium's true cost at almost $1 billion.

None of this is on the minds of the 250 invited guests sitting under a tent in front of Miller Park on the sunny afternoon of August 24. It's a celebrity gathering: Hall of Famers Hank Aaron, Frank Robinson, and Ernie Banks sit up front with Jackie Robinson's widow, Rachel. Joe and Frank Torre are here, too. White Sox owner Jerry Reinsdorf sits near Randy Levine, Paul Beeston, Bill Bartholomay, and scores of other baseball executives. There's columnist George Will and former Wisconsin football coach Barry Alvarez.

All are here to witness the unveiling of a seven-foot bronze statue of the man who saved baseball in Milwaukee.

"Bud Selig is responsible for everything we have here today, including this magnificent stadium," master of ceremonies Bob Uecker tells the guests with a grand sweep of his left arm.

· Uecker, natty in his olive-green suit, white shirt, and yellow tie, stands at the podium on a large stage with the Milwaukee Symphony Orchestra playing softly behind him. To his left sit Senator Herb Kohl and Brewers owner Mark Attanasio and his wife Debbie. To Uecker's right is a giant blue curtain, behind which stands the statue of Selig commissioned by Attanasio last fall.

"I was with Bud on many occasions up at the State Capitol when things weren't going well with getting a new stadium," Uecker continues. "Some of the things that were written and said about Bud were really bad, unbelievable stuff. But he never wavered. And he won. And that is why we honor him here today.

"So it is with great pleasure that I introduce my friend Allan H. 'Bud' Selig."

Selig and his wife Sue walk through a side entrance on cue, shake a few hands, and take their seats on the stage for a program honoring baseball's Commissioner. All Bud's children are here, including Wendy and husband Laurel. The couple flew in from Phoenix with 12-year-old Natalie, who is missing her first two days of seventh grade at the request of her grandfather. Selig wanted all five of his granddaughters here for his big day. "She can't miss this," Bud told Wendy.

Many of the game's owners have made the trip to Milwaukee as well. There's Marlins owner Jeff Loria, whose team was caught pocketing revenue sharing money by the union back in May. One day earlier, documents leaked to the website Deadspin showed Miami cleared $50 million in profits over the last two seasons — upsetting news for the Florida legislators who are building a new stadium with taxpayer funds. Loria consistently told Florida leaders he could not afford to build the stadium or even help finance it. John Henry and other big market owners have already been telling Selig they want to scale back revenue sharing in the next labor deal, and this news is only going to give Bud more headaches.

There's Dodgers owner Frank McCourt, handpicked by Selig in 2004 to replace Rupert Murdoch in Los Angeles. McCourt's nasty season-long divorce from wife and Dodgers President Jamie has embarrassed Bud and baseball, revealing the couple borrowed against the franchise's escalating value to finance a lifestyle that includes five homes, private jets, and luxury spas. Many in baseball questioned whether the highly leveraged McCourts could afford the team and wondered why Bud ignored the game's debt rules when he ushered them in. Now Selig is sending word through friends that it may be time for the McCourts to sell their team, no matter how the divorce case is settled.

Most of the New York office is here, too, including Bob DuPuy, who knows his days as Selig's No. 2 man are all but over. No one knows how to read Selig better than DuPuy, who started working for Bud as his personal lawyer in 1988. First it's the phone calls that don't get returned, then the assignments that used to come your way but now go to others. It's been like this for months, and DuPuy knows why. When Bud claimed he'd retire after his latest three-year extension in 2008—"This is clearly it," he said about the deal that would take him through 2012. "I say this without equivocation"—several owners suggested Selig name DuPuy his successor.

DuPuy urged these owners not to take the idea to Bud, and with good reason: Selig all but threw the owners out of his office when they made the suggestion. And now there are people—some of them under this tent today—who've convinced Bud the whole idea came from DuPuy. After 20 years of loyal service, he's lost Selig's ear, a disappointment he's finding hard to fathom. But DuPuy has read the signs well. On September 28, baseball will announce his resignation.

Many of the men who played for Bud's Brewers are here, and each player walks to the stage wearing his old jersey as the orchestra plays the theme song to *Field of Dreams*. Robin Yount talks about how Selig treated his players more like family than employees. And how the Brewers hated to look up in the stands when things were going poorly because Bud would be sitting there "with his face buried in his hands."

Attanasio tells everyone there'd be no baseball in many small cities if not for Selig, "one of the greatest men baseball has ever known." Senator Kohl jokes about the older pitcher Selig snuck into the title game to beat Kohl's team back when they were both sixth graders in Milwaukee. "And that's the man who protects the integrity of this game!" Kohl says.

Hank Aaron is last to speak. Aaron and Selig have been friends for more than 40 years—"through good times and tough times, through laughs and tears," Hank says. They don't always agree. When Selig announced he wanted to return the home run title to Aaron earlier this year, Hank said no, the record belongs to Bonds.

But there is real affection between the two men, and the crowd listens intently as Aaron declares Selig the greatest Commissioner in the history of Major League Baseball. "He is an American hero, a baseball hero, and a civic icon and visionary," Aaron says. "Bud Selig is my hero."

The two men embrace, and now it's time to unveil the statue that will stand between those of Aaron and Yount. The two best players to wear Milwaukee uniforms meet at the right side of the stage and pull on long ropes as the orchestra comes to life again, playing the theme to *The Natural*.

Slowly the curtain pulls back, revealing the seven-foot bronze statue of Selig as a younger man. The likeness is remarkable, with the bespectacled man's left hand pushed into a pocket, the other arm extended forward, a baseball sitting in the palm of his right hand. The crowd stands and applauds as the ceremony comes to a close.

"It was tough for me today, I was really emotional," Selig tells the media in a post-ceremony session he shares with Attanasio, Aaron, and Yount. "This is one of those really unique times when a kid had a dream and it came true."

There is just one more part of the dream left to realize, and that should happen in due time. Though one can debate the merits of saddling his hometown with a billion-dollar bill for a baseball stadium, it's doubtful there would be a team in baseball's smallest market without Selig's persistence and powers of persuasion. For that, today's statue is well deserved.

But this is only part of Selig's legacy. It's the owners now surrounding Selig, hands outstretched to congratulate him, who represent Selig's biggest impact on this game. It's been his ability to find common ground between big market owners like Tom Ricketts of the Cubs and small market owners like David Glass of the Royals, old hands like Tigers owner Mike Illitch and newcomers like Nationals majority owner Ted Lerner, that ended the internal divisions that held back baseball for so many years.

Yes, Bud's small market obsession made life more difficult for the Yankees and teams in other major markets — Boston, Chicago, Los Angeles — to thrive, the key to capturing a national audience in every sport. There's a fine line between achieving competitive balance and discouraging innovation, and Selig often erred on the side of holding back the big boys who typically drive the game.

And yes, Selig's refusal to look upon Don Fehr as a partner instead of an adversary was destructive, most notably when he threw away the goodwill baseball earned after September 11. Worse is his insistence that the players take full blame for baseball's steroid crisis, a decision that wiped out a generation of stars—a growing problem in a sport where players compete against history as well as today's opponents on a daily basis.

But there's no denying that baseball has prospered greatly under Selig's leadership. Those who focus only on his shortcomings, or insist that the tech boom made baseball's surge in revenues inevitable, forget the dark days when the big market owners' refusal to share revenues with their small market brethren threatened to cripple the sport. Selig's ability to forge consensus season after season, labor deal after labor deal—and the prosperity that followed—deserves to be honored with a $15\frac{1}{2}$ by $10\frac{3}{4}$ inch bronze and wooden plaque in Cooperstown.

Hanging right alongside plaques for George Steinbrenner and Don Fehr.

Epilogue

THE VERY PRIVATE Steinbrenner family says their public good-bye to the Boss in a grand affair at Yankee Stadium on September 20. Bud and Sue Selig escort Joan Steinbrenner onto the field, where she joins her four children — Hal, Hank, Jenny, and Jessica — to watch a four-minute video that receives a warm reception from the 47,437 fans in Steinbrenner's $1.5-plus billion Stadium. "When you put the pinstripes on, you're not just putting on a baseball uniform" is George's opening line played over a montage of his career. "You're wearing tradition."

Moments later, Joan is riding in a golf cart with Yogi Berra, part of a procession out to Monument Park, the open-air museum in center field. Don Mattingly and Joe Torre are part of it all, too, making their first appearances here since leaving after the 2007 season. Alex Rodriguez and manager Joe Girardi lead the entire Yankees team to the stairs and platform at the outfield fence.

The family takes their place between the commemorative stones for Joe DiMaggio and Mickey Mantle, facing a white banner with the Yankees top-hat logo at its center. Both Steinbrenner daughters fight back tears as Joan steps forward and pulls down the white curtain, unveiling a plaque featuring George's likeness carved in bronze and his legacy written beside it.

"A true visionary who changed the game of baseball forever," the tribute reads, noting the seven World Series titles and 11 pennants won in his 37 years running the Yankees. "He was considered the most influential owner in all of sports."

The plaque is huge — seven feet wide, five feet high, and 760 pounds, even without its marble base — and immediately sparks a mini controversy. No one questions George's place among the game's giants, but in the days that follow, fans and reporters wonder why Steinbrenner warrants a memorial twice as large as those for DiMaggio, Mantle, Babe Ruth, and Lou Gehrig. If nothing else, it makes for a lively debate while the defending champions settle for second place behind the Rays and the wild-card slot, sweep the Twins in the ALDS, then fall short of the World Series in a six-game ALCS loss to Texas.

But the critics miss the point. The size of George's monument is not just about the Babe and the Iron Horse, or Joe D. and the Mick, beloved Yankees all. The giant plaque is about how the family will remember George and the impact he had on each of their lives. By that measure, Monument Park's newest tribute may even be a bit too small.

No one understands this better than Hal Steinbrenner, now firmly entrenched as George's successor. Early on, George's younger son showed he understood his role when he cornered the free agent market and won a championship for his fading father in 2009. But a very different test lies immediately ahead: easing the team's aging icons—responsible for five championships and rehabilitating George's image—into retirement while still winning titles.

It won't be easy. Jorge Posada's catching skills, never great, have declined significantly, so the 39-year-old vet will unhappily join a crowd at DH in 2011. Mariano Rivera is still superb at 40, but Derek Jeter is 36 and hit .270—47 points below his career average—while 38-year-old Andy Pettitte missed 57 games in 2010 with a groin injury that wouldn't heal. All but Posada are free agents, and Steinbrenner, who's staring at a $200-plus million payroll, wants to re-sign each one. But for how much? For how many years? And in what roles?

The young Yankees boss gets off to a bumpy start on November 2, when he ends a rare radio interview by saying negotiations with Jeter "could get messy." And they do. The two sides squabble over money—Hal wants to cut Jeter's pay, Derek wants a raise for all he's accomplished—and a month-long war of words between Jeter's agent Casey Close and Steinbrenner's GM Brian Cashman fills the tabloids.

In the end, Steinbrenner signs off on a three-year, $51 million deal—a slight cut from the average $18.9 million Jeter had earned the past 10 years—with the player's option for a final year at

$8 million. He then tells Jeter and Cashman to patch things up. But Jeter, who still holds a grudge as well as he lines singles to right, has different ideas. "This turned into a big public thing," he says. "That is something I was not happy about. I let my feelings be known."

Things get uglier with Jeter's best friend Posada, who's hitting .165 as the full-time DH on May 14 when manager Joe Girardi pencils him in to bat ninth against Boston. Posada tells Girardi he can't play, unleashing frustration on both sides. Cashman goes on Fox's national broadcast and blasts his veteran, and Posada lashes back to reporters after the game. The tabloids feast for a week, then move on, and Posada says good-bye with little fanfare in a media conference on January 24, 2012.

Steinbrenner does a better job with Pettitte and Rivera come the 2013 season. Pettitte, who retired in 2011 only to return for the last two seasons, bows out in a quiet meeting with reporters. Rivera, who appeared in nine games in 2012 before tearing up his right knee shagging fly balls in batting practice, is honored at every stop during the Yankees season. The Twins give him a rocking chair made from bats they broke trying to hit his cutter. The Dodgers give him a fishing rod—Rivera's father was a fisherman—and the A's hand him a surfboard. All three teams pledge $10,000 to the Mariano Rivera Foundation. So does Toronto.

Yankee Stadium is decked out with stars past and present on September 22 for an emotional Mariano Rivera Day. Among the many gifts: Yankees President Randy Levine hands Mo a $100,000 check for Rivera's foundation; Hal and his wife Christina hand him a beautiful Waterford crystal replica of his glove. Rivera thanks his teammates, his family, and his fans when it's his time to speak. He singles out only one Yankee.

"The man I wish was here is George Steinbrenner," Mo says. "I love him so much, and I do miss him."

There are no postseason games for these 83–77 Yankees, though no one can blame Rivera. At 43, he saved 44 games, won six, and posted a 2.11 ERA. When David Robertson, Mo's heir, records the final out of the season, Rivera's countdown to Cooperstown officially begins.

In between the send-offs, Steinbrenner sells a piece of the YES Network in a deal so big it can only make Bud Selig shudder. On November 20, 2012, the Yankees sell 9 percent of their 34 percent stake to Fox, which also buys 40 percent from Goldman Sachs and the network's other major shareholders. The deal values YES at $3.4 billion—almost double what the team is worth. Fox also spent heavily to keep Steinbrenner's Yankees on YES for 30 years: a $500 million bonus and yearly payments that start at $85 million and surpass $300 million in the final seasons of the deal.

The Yankees, who've paid upwards of a combined $1.5 billion in revenue sharing, which started in '96, and luxury taxes, which were phased in beginning a year later, lobbied for relief when a new labor contract was negotiated in November of 2011. No deal, said Selig, who instead offered up an inducement for Steinbrenner to cut his spending. Any big market team with a payroll under the luxury tax threshold of $189 million by 2014—read: the Yankees—would get a revenue sharing check they would not otherwise receive.

Given the tax savings—the Yankees have paid 92 percent of all luxury taxes collected, including $18.9 million in 2012—Selig thought he'd given Hal a strong incentive to cut payroll. And for two years, getting below $189 million was Steinbrenner's public mantra. Indeed, he passed on superstars Josh Hamilton and Albert Pujols and ignored Cuban star Yasiel Puig when each hit the market.

But missing the playoffs in 2013 translated into the team's lowest attendance—3.3 million—since opening the new Stadium. More alarming, YES lost a third of its viewers. So Steinbrenner reversed course, signing free agents Jacoby Ellsbury, Brian McCann, and Carlos Beltran for almost $300 million combined. He gave $12 million to Jeter, back for one final season after missing a year recovering from a broken ankle.

Then he wooed Japanese superstar Masahiro Tanaka to New York, handing the 25-year-old pitcher a seven-year, $155 million deal. Even with the loss of All-Star Robinson Cano, who left when Steinbrenner refused to match Seattle's 10-year, $240 million offer, the Yankees entered 2014 with a $203 million payroll. So much for reining in this Steinbrenner.

There was no repeat of the 2009 magic, however—no 28th

World Series title, not even a berth in the expanded postseason. Instead, injuries sideline four-fifths of the rotation for most of the year, including the impressive Tanaka (13–5, 141 strikeouts, and only 21 walks in 136.1 innings, a 2.77 ERA), who missed 74 days with a partially torn ligament in his right arm. Several key players lost big chunks of time, others just looked old or tired as the team struggled to score more than three runs a game.

Indeed, the only highlights are callbacks to the past. The Yankees give first Tino Martinez then Paul O'Neill their own plaques in Monument Park. And they retire Joe Torre's No. 6 on August 23 — four weeks after the former manager failed to thank George Steinbrenner in his Hall of Fame induction speech.

Then the big day: September 7, when the Yankees honor Jeter. The ceremony unfolds much like those before it: old Yankees stars reappear, this time joined by Derek's good friend Cal Ripken and his fellow Nike pitchman Michael Jordan. Highlights dance on the video screen, a reminder for the 48,110 fans what their favorite son looked like before age and injury reduced him to the average player he's been all season. Hal and Christina lead a group of Steinbrenner grandchildren out of the dugout to present Jeter with a Waterford crystal trophy etched with Jeter's final season logo.

Steinbrenner watches Jeter single in the 1st, one of only four hits in a 2–0 loss to the Royals that pushes his team closer to postseason elimination. The official end comes 17 days later, marking the first time the Yankees failed to reach the postseason in consecutive seasons since George returned from Fay Vincent's suspension in 1993. Jeter runs out to shortstop at Yankee Stadium for the last time one night later, fighting back tears all game before smacking a walk-off RBI single in the bottom of the 9th for a 6–5 win.

On September 28 in Boston, Jeter plays his last game, leaving to a standing ovation after an RBI infield single in the 3rd inning. His final numbers — 3,465 hits (No. 6 on the all-time list), 260 home runs, 358 stolen bases, a .310 average, and five World Series titles — will soon be engraved on a plaque in Cooperstown.

And now the last member of the Yankees dynasty is gone, a fading memory for all who don't understand how important Jeter's team was to repairing the damage done to baseball by the self-inflicted wound that was the 1994 season. The money is there for Hal Steinbrenner to rebuild his team, but 2014 showed it takes more than money to build a champion.

Will Hal get as lucky as George and find a Jeter, a Rivera, a Bernie Williams, and more, all at the same time? Does he have the same drive his father had to win year after year? Will delegating more power to Yankees President Randy Levine and GM Brian Cashman prove as successful—and entertaining—as the Boss' one-man show?

Selig and the game's owners were loath to admit how much they needed George after 1994. As Selig prepares to leave the stage, baseball might soon discover it needs George Steinbrenner now more than ever.

Don Fehr never could sit still. So it is no surprise that he agrees to lend a hand, free of charge, when the woebegone NHL Players Association comes calling at the end of 2009, soon after Fehr left baseball. Nor is it surprising that Fehr says yes when the hockey players ask him to be their leader in December of 2010. With Commissioner Gary Bettman once again looking for big concessions when their labor deal expires after another season, the NHL players need a fighter. At 62, Fehr still wakes up ready to brawl.

The battle commences at 12:01 a.m. on September 16, 2012, when Bettman makes good on his promise to lock out the players after two months of fruitless talks. For Fehr, it's déjà vu all over again. The owners, who got a salary cap after a lockout wiped out the entire 2004–5 season, insist they need a bigger piece of the revenue pie and an end to salary arbitration if all their teams are to survive. The players insist the big money teams should share more of the game's $3.3 billon in revenue with their small market partners.

Both sides know the drill—there's been a lockout in each of Bettman's three labor negotiations since he became Commissioner in 1993—and as the shutdown enters the late fall, the owners start going after Fehr. The American labor leader doesn't care about hockey, the owners say, all he's interested in is money for the players. Fehr is lying to the players about our offers, they charge, the union man simply can't be trusted.

Others know better. "The players are behind Don Fehr 100 per-cent," says one NHL agent, echoing what most on the players' side think. "He's breathed life into the union."

And Fehr still knows how to keep his players united. Every player is welcome at negotiating sessions, and Fehr makes sure the union picks up the tab for their flights and accommodations. One day it's superstar Sidney Crosby sitting at the bargaining table; another day it's enforcer Kevin Westgarth. Any player who can't make it to meetings can use the union's mobile app to check on negotiations.

But there's something different about Fehr in these negotiations, too. Always caustic and combative with Selig and baseball's negoti-ators, Fehr stays calm after even his toughest sessions with Bett-man. He brushes off owners' attacks without a response. Maybe it's the change of venue. Or perhaps it's the sad news he hears in August—Michael Weiner has an inoperable brain tumor—or Marvin Miller's death in November at age 95, after a three-month battle with liver cancer.

Whatever the reasons, Fehr also decides not to battle the hockey media, in marked contrast to his final years in baseball, when things were so strained many reporters stopped calling him even on the biggest stories. Instead, it's a relaxed and patient union leader who explains the players' position and answers every ques-tion as the lockout pushes into the New Year.

And it's a tired but satisfied Fehr who stands with Bettman at 6 a.m. on January 6, announcing that an outline for a deal had been reached. "Hopefully, within just a very few days, the fans can get back to watching people who are skating," Fehr says, "and not the two of us."

Fehr receives good reviews for holding the line on revenue shar-ing and salary arbitration, and limiting the concessions made by his players. But his masterful performance also underscores the bitter way he left baseball, angry and dismayed that he could not prevent an overaggressive government investigation from violating the rights of more than 100 men. Nor stop an overzealous Com-missioner who cared more about repairing his reputation than ruining those of dozens of players.

Fehr always defined his job as protecting the players from the worst instincts and actions of management, something he did almost without fail for 26 years until he fell short at the end. Even though the U.S. Appeals Court in California ultimately vindicated him—on September 13, 2010, it instructed the government to return the 2003 drug test results it illegally seized—Fehr knows now he was slow to react to the impact steroids were having on the game. And slow to engage the players to get to the heart of the problem. Had he reacted sooner, would fewer players have had their careers tainted—in some cases destroyed—by performance-enhancing drugs?

Perhaps. But then, how different could things have been with a partner he never felt he could trust?

It's only 11 months later when Fehr walks toward a mound of dirt at windswept Cedar Park Cemetery in northern New Jersey, takes hold of the long wooden handle of a spade, and shovels dirt onto the coffin of Michael Weiner. On this sunny but cold November 24, 2013, Fehr performs what Jewish tradition considers the final kindness for his friend and protégé: escorting him from this world into the next. He stares into Weiner's grave for a moment, puts the spade back in its place, and walks away so dozens of others at the grave site can do the same.

Just an hour earlier Fehr was listening to Weiner's wife Diane Margolin address the hundreds of mourners packed into the sanctuary, aisles, and lobby of Robert Schoem's Menorah Chapel. Bud Selig and Rob Manfred sat in the third row. Alex Rodriguez stood in a hallway. Others, many wearing Weiner's trademark Chuck Taylor sneakers, sat on the floor. Her husband, Diane said, did not fear death. "He led a thoughtful life, one in concert with his beliefs and values," Michael's wife of 28 years said. "He had no regrets."

Fehr recognized something special in Weiner early, bringing him into the union two years after Michael graduated from Harvard Law School. Before long it wasn't hard to see Weiner as a kinder, gentler version of the man who hired him, though no less passionate about protecting the rights of his players. Fehr understood Weiner had the common touch he lacked and wisely used him to communicate with players and ease tensions with their opponents in management.

And when it was time to say good-bye in December of 2009, Fehr was confident he'd left his players well protected. But now, less than four years later, Weiner is gone, felled at 51 by the cancer discovered just 16 months ago.

A week and a half later, Tony Clark is elected the MLBPA's new executive director, becoming the first player ever to lead the union. Fehr also spotted Clark early, recognizing Tony's commanding presence and ability to communicate well before the big first baseman called it quits in 2009. As a player, the six-foot-eight Clark was a journeyman performer for six teams in 15 seasons. As a leader, Clark is a natural.

Fehr knows Clark has the respect and trust of the players. But he's concerned, as are other veterans of baseball's union movement. With the current agreement expiring on December 1, 2016, word is already circulating that several owners want to test Clark. Talk of a salary cap has even resurfaced. Clark doesn't have the deep bench Fehr had—few on the staff Weiner was still building have any experience with a strike or lockout in baseball. And just one player will start the 2015 season having played through a work stoppage: Alex Rodriguez.

Fehr has never forgotten how Selig and the owners persuaded him to give back a year of salary arbitration in his first negotiation. Nor has he forgotten the next three seasons marred by collusion, a lockout in 1990, then the '94 shutdown. Selig—an instigator in all these—says he's retiring, but Fehr's heard all that before.

Besides, Chicago's Jerry Reinsdorf, Kansas City's David Glass, and their allies—anti-union men all—aren't going anywhere. And Selig's trusted soldier Rob Manfred is all but certain to be the next Commissioner. Some things, Fehr knows, will never change. No matter who sits in his old office.

Bud Selig is fidgeting in a chair in the middle of his Milwaukee office while technicians from *60 Minutes* check the lights and adjust the microphone on the lapel of his blue blazer. It's a few weeks after November 21, 2013, the day baseball arbitrator Fredric Horowitz completed hearings on Alex Rodriguez's appeal of Selig's record-setting 211-game suspension for taking performance-enhancing drugs. It's a charge the Yankees third baseman continues to deny. Horowitz is expected to announce his decision in early January, and Selig is so confident the arbitrator will uphold most if not all of the punishment he meted out on August 5, he's ready to get an early start on his victory lap with CBS' Scott Pelley.

"In my judgment, his actions were beyond comprehension," Selig says when Pelley starts asking questions, "and I'm somebody who's now been in the game over 50 years."

"You had never seen anything like it," Pelley repeats, no question mark intended.

"I hadn't, no.

"And so you decided to make an example of him," Pelley said.

"I wouldn't call it an example," the Commissioner answers. "I think the penalty fit what I saw as the evidence. Put all the drug things on one side and then all the things he did to impede our investigation. I think 211 games was a very fair penalty."

To fully understand Selig's rationale, you have to understand what else Selig tells Pelley. "This was a battle to save the game," Selig says. "And I was determined not to lose to Rodriguez."

So determined that his No. 2 man Rob Manfred had to talk him down from banning the 38-year-old broken-down star—A-Rod's played only 221 of 434 games the last three seasons, hitting 34 home runs, driving in 119, and batting .274—for life. That was all the negotiating Selig was willing to do, so he turned a deaf ear when Union Executive Director Michael Weiner suggested 100 games, a penalty that would have cost Rodriguez at least $16 million in lost salary.

Would Rodriguez have stood down if Selig and Weiner had arrived at an agreement? We'll never know.

We do know what happened next: an unsurprising, ugly, and unnecessary war of words and deeds. No one outside the three-ring circus surrounding A-Rod suggests Rodriguez—or any of the other 13 players caught using drugs supplied by the anti-aging clinic Biogenesis—should go unpunished. Or that A-Rod's penalty should not be severe. But no one is clamoring for Alex's head, either; not the fans who have grown used to the idea of baseball stars cheating, not the baseball media, not even the opportunists in Congress.

Taking the high road might have cut this steroid scandal short while still making a strong anti-drug statement. But the Commissioner—who has complete discretion to mete out punishment for those caught cheating by his investigative unit rather than a failed drug test—saw only the opportunity to burnish his legacy. And he went overboard. The result: a near-daily steroid narrative that overshadowed the game's pennant races, postseason, and offseason.

Selig, who on September 23 reaffirmed his decision to retire, effective January 24, 2015, likes to frame everything in historical context. What history will show is the ninth Commissioner of baseball bungled the final act of his 22-year career.

It all started in late 2012 when a disgruntled employee at a South Florida anti-aging clinic named Biogenesis stole a boatload of client records and several of clinic owner Tony Bosch's personal notebooks. Porter Fischer, upset that Bosch refused to repay a $4,000 loan, made numerous copies of the stolen files, one of which he gave to a free weekly newspaper. The *Miami New Times'* story, published January 29, 2013, named Rodriguez as well as All-Stars Bartolo Colón, Nelson Cruz, and Melky Cabrera and other stars as Biogenesis clients and users of illegal drugs.

A battle for evidence between Selig and Rodriguez immediately followed, and representatives for both sides began blowing down doors in the seedy underbelly of Florida's multibillion-dollar anti-aging industry. Also in play: the loyalty and cooperation of Bosch, who was already under investigation by the DEA for dealing drugs to minors, businessmen, and elite athletes, and by Florida's Department of Health for impersonating a doctor.

Neither side covered itself in glory. According to Bosch, Alex started paying Bosch's mounting legal fees, suggested he leave the country, and spent hundreds of thousands of dollars buying up Bosch's stolen records. Rodriguez called baseball's investigation a witch hunt, stormed out of his own grievance hearing when he learned Selig wouldn't be compelled to testify, and repeatedly denied taking illegal PEDs—something he would cop to in late January of 2014 in exchange for immunity from federal prosecution.

Rob Manfred oversaw an investigative team that numbered as many as 30 former policemen and federal agents—including a former head of the Secret Service. They offered Fischer $125,000, and then a $1,000-a-week consulting job in exchange for his trove of files—Fischer turned down both—then paid an ex-con calling himself "Bobby from Boca" $125,000 in cash for Biogenesis files containing evidence of drug use by Rodriguez and others. The head of baseball's Department of Investigations, the man who handed "Bobby" $125,000 in cash at a South Florida diner, also had a sexual relationship with a potential witness, a nurse at Biogenesis.

Most important, Manfred filed a lawsuit against Bosch and his inner circle, claiming they interfered with baseball's drug program by supplying drugs to players, actions MLB said cost the sport millions and injured its reputation. The suit, which many legal experts said lacked merit and would never have made it to trial, armed baseball's agents with subpoena power and put Bosch—a coke addict already tens of thousands of dollars behind in child support payments to two ex-wives—in a financial vise. In March of 2013, Bosch flipped in exchange for baseball dropping its suit, promising to indemnify him from civil suits by any players, and paying his legal bills—which would climb past $1 million.

MLB also signed off on a bodyguard at $2,400 a day for a full year—total cost: $876,000—when Bosch claimed he feared Rodriguez would try to injure or kill him for talking to MLB. All this to add an extra 50–100 games to a suspension of a man whose importance to the game has long since faded.

Many of these details were repeated in the nation's media and Horowitz's hearing room right up until the arbitrator handed down his ruling. On January 11, Horowitz announced he had trimmed A-Rod's punishment to 162 games, effectively banning Rodriguez for the 2014 season—the remainder of Selig's time as Commissioner. One night later, *60 Minutes* airs its double segment, "The Case of Alex Rodriguez."

Pelley tells viewers that the Commissioner's "unprecedented investigation was aimed at protecting the clean players." But the centerpiece of Pelley's report is Bosch, who CBS portrays as a star, at one point showing him on a boat, the wind blowing through his hair with the Miami skyline as the backdrop. The drug dealer describes the night he drew A-Rod's blood in a nightclub bathroom stall. He ticks off the drugs he claims to have given Rodriguez—"testosterone, insulin growth factor one, human growth hormone"—while boasting about his expertise. He says he told Alex to turn in only the urine from "midstream" to avoid detection. (Rodriguez has never failed multiple drug tests since 2004.)

Finally, Bosch tells Pelley that revealing all this about A-Rod has put his life in danger. It's a charge *60 Minutes* chose not to substantiate.

Pelley also interviews Manfred, asking baseball's chief operating officer how he could trust Bosch's testimony after spending so much money to get him to talk. Manfred points to the corroborating evidence Bosch supplied, then adds, "Mr. Bosch's credibility on this issue, whatever his motivations, whatever we did for him, was established by his willingness to come in, raise his right hand, and testify." Yes, baseball set the bar very high.

What Pelley doesn't ask Selig or Manfred is why the Boca Raton police department says baseball ignored a request from a detective in the Florida Department of Health not to buy evidence because it was stolen. (Baseball insists it was never told.) Or why they didn't report the evidence they bought until a Boca Raton detective asked about it eight months later. And Pelley doesn't ask either man to respond to Bosch's claim that steroid use in baseball is still rampant, and beating its drug test is a "cakewalk."

Instead, Pelley closes his show with this point: "Bud Selig has announced his retirement as Commissioner of baseball," he says. "Part of his legacy is the establishment of the toughest anti-doping rules in all of American pro sports."

Reaction to Selig and Manfred's performance and the *60 Minutes* report is swift and scathing. The union releases a statement an hour before the piece airs: "It's unfortunate that Major League Baseball apparently lacks faith in the integrity of the arbitrator's decision and our Joint Drug Agreement, [and] could not resist the temptation to publicly pile-on against Alex Rodriguez." Yahoo asks if Selig "opened up his Milwaukee home to Bosch to keep him out of harm's way from A-Rod's alleged hit men." NBC columnist Joe

Posnanski labels the whole show "ugliness," adding, "The only winner in the whole mess seems to be the drugs themselves, which apparently work miracles and, if used right, are undetectable."

Selig's response? "We did what we had to do."

But the reaction shouldn't have surprised Selig. Just how badly his overreach on Rodriguez's suspension backfired was broadcast loud and clear by ESPN a few months earlier. In mid-September, the sports network released a poll of self-described baseball fans, conducted from August 20 to 22 by the prominent sports polling firm Turnkey. The question: Who is the current face of baseball?

The answer?

Not Miguel Cabrera, on his way to his second straight MVP.

Not Mike Trout, the Angels' young Mickey-Mantle-in-waiting.

Not even veteran Yankees icon Derek Jeter.

No, the fans' choice as the face of baseball?

Alex Rodriguez.

It's a weary Bud Selig who looks out at the group of owners who've been intensely debating the last meaningful decision of his career: the man who'll become the next Commissioner of baseball. It's August 14, and they've been going at it in this ballroom in Baltimore's Hyatt Regency for hours—far longer than Bud had hoped or expected.

Selig doesn't mind that the voting went a round or two. Hell, it should be difficult to choose a successor to someone who's been as successful as he's been. But under baseball's rules, Red Sox co-owner Tom Werner, the opposition's choice to run against Rob Manfred, has already been defeated and is off the ballot. Now it's just an up-and-down vote on Bud's handpicked successor, and those opposed—led by his close friend Jerry Reinsdorf—are trying to run out the clock, hoping to adjourn without a decision so they can put up another candidate against Manfred at a later date.

Selig is at the head of the room, tapping the mic to get everyone's attention. He's never been surer of his decision to retire as he is right now. It takes far too much energy to corral these masters of the universe, a task he's performed well for more than two decades. He's just turned 80, and he's attended far too many funerals and delivered far too many eulogies the last few years. There are better ways to spend the rest of his days than twisting arms and making promises.

But he refuses to leave Baltimore today without getting this one last wish.

"It's been a long day and everyone is tired, but we are not going to leave here until we select a Commissioner," Selig tells them. "If we did, everyone would say we were dysfunctional, and they would be right. That would hurt the game, and I will not let that happen."

He's known this day was coming since early spring, when he finally convinced the owners this would be his last season. And that's when he told them he wanted Manfred, his loyal soldier for the past 20 years, to be the game's 10th Commissioner.

He also knew Reinsdorf did not approve of his choice, and would put up a fight. Hell, Jerry's reminded Bud he didn't consider the 55-year-old Manfred to be CEO material in almost every one of their daily talks for months. Reinsdorf let Manfred know, too, calling him in early spring. "We need a visionary leader, not a labor lawyer," the White Sox owner told baseball's chief operating officer.

It's not the first time Bud and Jerry have disagreed about an important baseball decision, but the media was so thick with stories of their "feud" that Selig put out a statement six days ago. "Reports of personal animosity between Jerry Reinsdorf and me — or any other alleged disputes between owners regarding the process or the candidates — are unfounded and unproductive," his statement read. The next day he issued a gag order.

But what really upset Selig — really wounded him — was the heart of Reinsdorf's campaign against Manfred: Rob would be an extension of Bud's closed-door policy, Jerry told the owners; he'd make decisions in secret, cut side deals, and leave many of them out of the loop, just as Bud did. Only Bud didn't see it that way.

So Selig hit the phones as he'd always done. Reinsdorf made it a bit more difficult when he persuaded Werner, one of Bud's favorites, to pursue the Commissioner's job. And when Selig saw Reinsdorf's man gaining support, he pushed the meeting up from November. Selig was sure he had 20 of the 23 votes he needed to put his man in office. Now he had two days to procure the final three votes.

It didn't take long for this meeting to become both a referendum on Selig's tenure and a peek at what life is going to be like without him. No one doubts that keeping this gang of owners united instead of at each other's throats went a long way toward unlocking the game's potential. Selig leaves office with revenues hitting a record $9 billion this season—up from $1.2 billion when he took charge in 1992—with five franchises now valued at $1 billion or more.

(Selig wisely requested that his compensation be linked to the rise or fall of franchise values. That's why Bud, who enjoyed a nice upper-middle-class life before becoming Commissioner, will walk away with an estimated net worth in excess of $200 million. And that's not counting the $35–$40 million he will collect over the next five years, the first two of which—and possibly more—he will serve as Commissioner Emeritus. There are some in ownership who are concerned by Selig's role and have let Manfred know how important it is that he be seen as independent.)

But now there is open talk that the big market teams want a big rollback in the $400 million of revenue sharing each season. And the labor hawks are back. Indeed, the big rumor making the rounds here has Reinsdorf, Toronto's Paul Beeston, Cincinnati's Bob Castellini, Anaheim's Arte Moreno, and Arizona's Ken Kendrick making a blood oath to come out of the 2016 labor negotiations with a salary cap. If true, they only need three more votes to block any labor deal they don't like.

Other concerns were aired, too, problems that Bud—and the owners—have ignored in the final years of the Selig Era. Strip away today's big paydays and you find a sport supported by an aging, predominantly white audience accustomed to the game's leisurely pace—a pace MLB's research shows does not appeal to the younger generation. What happens in the not-so-distant future when the Baby Boomers move on? Will the younger generation reverse course and take their place?

Or will they follow the lead of Amazon CEO Jeff Bezos, who 11 days after this meeting will announce he's paying $970 million in cash for Twitch, a three-year-old Internet company that's become the go-to site to play and watch others play video games? Viewership for the World Series has exceeded 16.6 million homes only once in the past six seasons—when the Yankees won it all in 2009. In 2013, the League of Legends World Championship—the video gamers' title series—was staged in a sold-out Staples Center and watched online by 32 million viewers, an audience four times larger than the one that logged in the previous year.

The core audience for electronic gaming: 18- to 34-year-old males, the group most prized by the nation's advertisers. It's also the group that's been deserting Major League Baseball's ballparks and broadcasts for much of the last decade.

It's these trends that served as cover for the 10 owners—Reinsdorf, Beeston, Castellini, Kendrick, Moreno, Boston's John Henry, Milwaukee's Mark Attanasio, Tampa's Stu Sternberg, Washington's Ted Lerner, and Oakland's Lew Wolff—who cast their secret ballot for Werner when voting started today at 1:30 p.m. They all pointed to the television producer's string of hit shows (*The Cosby Show, That '70s Show*) as proof he is a man of vision. But Werner got only nine votes on the next ballot, one shy of the minimum to remain in contention, leaving Manfred just two short of what he needed to win.

Manfred got 22 on the third ballot but only 20 on the next, sending the room into chaos and Selig into action, twisting arms, cutting deals, and telling everyone to prepare for a long night. Selig and Manfred allies like Yankees President Randy Levine whip the vote back to 22–8, and when Washington's Lerner switches to Manfred on ballot No. 6, it's all over. Selig asks for and receives a symbolic 30–0 vote before the Commissioner and the Commissioner-elect leave to meet the media.

"There is no question that I would not be standing here today if not for Bud," says Manfred, who shares the podium with his mentor. "I hope that I will perform as the 10th Commissioner in a way that will add to his great legacy."

"There is no doubt in my mind he has the training, the temperament, the experience to be a very successful Commissioner," Selig says, "and I have justifiably very high expectations."

Soon after he's offered up his last observation, Selig is in a car heading to the airport for his flight back to Milwaukee. He'll be on the road again in five days, flying out to Oakland as part of his campaign to visit every team before season's end. It will be a low-key event. He'll meet with the front office people, schmooze the print and Internet folks, and sit down for interviews with the A's radio and TV teams.

He'll dodge any and all questions about the A's proposed move to San Jose, a hot-button issue here that he's been "studying" for six years; it's Rob Manfred's problem now.

He will tell them his proudest achievement is baseball's 18 years of labor peace. He'll remind them there was no way he could have known about steroids. He'll insist—again—that the players' strike is what cut short the '94 season; he simply had no choice. And he'll tell them it was his push for revenue sharing that has given fans of small market teams like theirs what they all deserve: hope and faith that their team can compete at the start of every season.

He'll look back on all that has happened during his 22 years in charge and proudly state he's leaving the game with no regrets. "And that's unusual," he'll say, "because I'm very tough on myself." But most important, he's there for the same reason he's promised to make it to every major league city: to give them all a chance to say good-bye to the ninth Commissioner of baseball.

They'll never see another one like him.

ACKNOWLEDGMENTS

This book traces back to the spring of 1956, when my father David, an ardent Yankees fan, put his four-year-old son in a pinstripe uniform and taught him how to hit a baseball behind their apartment building in Bayside, Queens. Thus began my love affair with baseball and the discovery of the generational bond between father and son that makes this sport so special. And, of course, my dream of one day playing center field in Yankee Stadium. The dream faded in my early teens; my passion for the sport—and the bond with my father—only grew.

I met an equal in my love of the game when Claire Smith joined the sports staff of the *Hartford Courant* in 1982, which started a friendship that has never waned. I learned much about seeing athletes as real people with real lives and real problems while working with Claire, who was breaking down barriers as the first African American woman to cover the Yankees and Major League Baseball in the '80s. After we went in different directions in 1990, it was with great excitement that we decided to work together on this book. Sadly, Claire had to leave our project a little more than one year in, but her spirit and her values are present on every page.

Many others shaped this book, no one more than David Black, who showed me what being a good agent is all about. It was David who convinced me I could make the leap from magazine writer to author. He listened when I needed an ear, picked me up when I was down, and kicked my rear when it was time to focus. No writer has ever had a better advocate, or a better friend.

My younger son Steven was my first researcher, back when this book was more concept than story. I'll never forget the very long Sunday we spent together, moving storyboards around a table until the moment we stepped back and realized we finally had the arc of this very complicated tale. Steven left after a year to start a success-ful career of his own, but his ideas flow throughout this book.

Andy Werle graduated from Wesleyan in the spring of 2012 and signed on for a nine-month gig as my researcher to earn some money while waiting for his bandmates to graduate so he could begin his music career. Two and a half years later, Andy's impor-tance to this book cannot be overstated. Researcher, copyeditor, writer, interviewer, chief sounding board—he filled all these roles with more skill and dedication than I had any right to expect. Andy rode shotgun on this book, and it was a great comfort to know he always had my back. He is off now to start his own career, too, and I will miss him dearly.

Andy was also responsible for bringing in Henry Robertson, who did the same excellent research work down the stretch as Mike Kelly, one of my former journalism students at Stony Brook University, did early on to help get this book off the ground. Thank you both.

At Little, Brown, I owe thanks to Michael Pietsch, who green-lighted this project, and Reagan Arthur, who saw it through. I owe much to executive editor John Parsley, whose judgment and experi-ence in book publishing was invaluable to this first-time author. John's enthusiasm for this book never wavered, no matter how many times I asked for—and was granted—more time to get it right. I am grateful for his patience, his suggestions, and his ele-gant idea for the name of our book.

Thanks to the rest of the Little, Brown team who worked so hard to make this book as good as it could be: Sarah Murphy, Malin von Euler-Hogan, Barbara Clark, Barb Jatkola, Ruth Cross, and Jeffrey Gantz. Special thanks to Karen Landry, whose good nature, lilting laugh, and steady hand kept me calm and focused while we closed the book.

I am deeply in debt to my older son David, who read the first drafts of every part of this book as they were completed and pro-vided detailed critiques of what worked and—more important—what didn't. And many thanks to Lisa Jacobs, whose suggestions on the early drafts were essential, and to Barry Geisler for his time, talent, and critiques of the final draft.

When I realized it was foolish to think I could transcribe what turned out to be many hundreds of hours of interviews, my sister

Enid Skahill stepped in and performed miracles, turning around transcripts quickly and accurately—no small feat given how often I wander into tangents. But more than transcribe, Enid developed a feel for the people I interviewed and offered valuable insights into their character. I am in her debt.

The same is true for Maisie Todd, who juggled my photo needs with raising her two-year-old daughter, all while pregnant with her second child. My colleague and friend from our days together at *ESPN the Magazine,* Maisie is responsible for the wonderful pictures you see in this book. All I had to do was say yes.

One of the great treats of writing this book was traveling to all corners of this country. No city was more captivating than San Francisco or more welcoming than Milwaukee, where my friend and *Journal Sentinel* editor in chief Marty Kaiser and his staff's terrific coverage of Bud Selig, Milwaukee, and all things Brewers enriched this story in ways I could not have imagined. Marty stepped down as editor of his hometown paper at the end of February 2015 in search of a new adventure; I wish him well and remind him to enjoy the journey.

I could not have made it through these past five years without the friendship, encouragement, and good humor of every one of these people: Jeff Pessah, Phil Jacobs, Shirley Cohen, Dennis Skahill, Shay, Kathleen Carre, Kody Gurfein, Steve Glickman, Dave and Karen Rosenthal, Mike Cohen, Jung-hwa Lee, Shareeda Allen, Kris Fitzpatrick, Adrienne Lotson, Aimee Chamernik, Barbara Selvin, and Dave Dircks. Thank you all for keeping me sane.

And finally, this book would never have been written if not for my wife Suzi, who five years ago told me the same thing she's told me so many times in our 37 years together: go chase your dream. But this time was different: she would have to support us while I learned how to be an author. And to ensure my success, she listened to my endless stream of stories, propped me up when I was pulled down with doubt, endured so many of the book's characters all but taking up residence in our home, and discovered her own talents when I disappeared to report and write for long stretches of time. I have no idea how to repay her, to make up for all she's sacrificed and given me, but I will spend the rest of my days trying.

NOTES AND SOURCES

The Game is the result of hundreds of hours of interviews with more than 150 people conducted during a five-year span. The sources come from a wide spectrum of organizations, including Major League Baseball, the Major League Baseball Players Association, the New York Yankees, the Milwaukee Brewers, and several government, law enforcement, and business agencies. Many sources agreed to multiple interviews, some numbering well more than a dozen sessions, as well as lengthy email communications. Below is a list of some of the sources.

The book is written as a narrative, relying on events and anecdotes to tell the story of the last 20 years of baseball. To re-create these scenes, I drew on interviews with those involved or with direct knowledge of these events and reconstructed dialogue based on the recollection of my sources. I also relied on notes taken in meetings, congressional transcripts, court documents, videos, and work by other reporters, as cited in these notes.

Sources

Jean Afterman, Dom Amore, Michael Attanasio, Sal Bando, Don Baylor, Jeff Bradley, Steve Buckley, Gerry Cardinale, Brian Cashman, Rick Cerrone, Ray Chambers, Tony Clark, Roger Clemens, Len Coleman, David Cone, Victor Conte, Bob DuPuy, Doug Glanville, Tom Glavine, Paul Haagen, Rusty Hardin, Tom Haudricourt, Rick Helling, Orel Hershiser, Jeff Idelson, Marty Kaiser, Lori Keck, Randy Levine, Rob Manfred, Don Mattingly, Doug Melvin, Gene Michael, Marvin Miller, George Mitchell, Dave Montgomery, Bruce Murphy, Tom Murphy, Bob Nightengale, John Norquist, Gene Orza, Steve Phillips, Laurel Prieb, Willie Randolph, Dick Ravitch, Tom Reich, Jerry Reinsdorf, Lauren Rich, Mariano Rivera, Rick Schlesinger, Bud Selig, Wendy Selig-Prieb, Buck Showalter, Dan Silverman, Claire Smith, Jeff Smulyan, Martha Stansell-Gamm, David Sussman, Steve Swindal, Lonn Trost, Bobby Valentine, Fay Vincent, Don Walker, Bob Watson, Michael Weiner, Finn Wentworth, Kenny Williams, Dave Winfield

Books

Assael, Shaun. *Steroid Nation: Juiced Home Run Totals, Anti-aging Miracles, and a Hercules in Every High School: The Secret History of America's True Drug Addiction.* New York: ESPN, 2007.

Boies, David. *Courting Justice: From NY Yankees v. Major League Baseball to Bush v. Gore, 1997–2000.* New York: Hyperion, 2004.

Bryant, Howard. *Juicing the Game: Drugs, Power, and the Fight for the Soul of Major League Baseball.* New York: Viking, 2005.

Canseco, Jose. *Juiced: Wild Times, Rampant 'Roids, Smash Hits, and How Baseball Got Big.* New York: Regan, 2005.

———. *Vindicated: Big Names, Big Liars, and the Battle to Save Baseball.* New York: Simon Spotlight Entertainment, 2008.

Elfrink, Tim, and Gus Garcia-Roberts. *Blood Sport: Alex Rodriguez, Biogenesis, and the Quest to End Baseball's Steroid Era.* New York: Dutton Adult, 2014.

Fainaru-Wada, Mark, and Lance Williams. *Game of Shadows: Barry Bonds, BALCO, and the Steroids Scandal That Rocked Professional Sports.* New York: Gotham, 2006.

Felix, Antonia. *Sonia Sotomayor: The True American Dream.* New York: Berkley, 2010.

Glanville, Doug. *The Game from Where I Stand: A Ballplayer's Inside View.* New York: Times, 2010.

Golenbock, Peter. *George: The Poor Little Rich Boy Who Built the Yankee Empire.* Hoboken, NJ: Wiley, 2009.

Gould, William B. *Labored Relations: Law, Politics, and the NLRB—A Memoir.* Cambridge, MA: MIT, 2000.

Helyar, John. *Lords of the Realm: The Real History of Baseball.* New York: Villard, 1994.

Jennings, Kenneth M. *Swings and Misses: Moribund Labor Relations in Professional Baseball.* Westport, CT: Praeger, 1997.

Lewis, Michael. *Moneyball: The Art of Winning an Unfair Game.* New York: W. W. Norton, 2003.

Madden, Bill. *Steinbrenner: The Last Lion of Baseball.* New York: Harper, 2010.

Miller, Marvin. *A Whole Different Ball Game: The Inside Story of the Baseball Revolution.* Chicago: I. R. Dee, 2004.

Minutaglio, Bill. *First Son: George W. Bush and the Bush Family Dynasty.* New York: Times, 1999.

Mnookin, Seth. *Feeding the Monster: How Money, Smarts, and Nerve Took a Team to the Top.* New York: Simon & Schuster, 2006.

Pearlman, Jeff. *Love Me, Hate Me: Barry Bonds and the Making of an Antihero.* New York: HarperCollins, 2006.

———. *The Rocket That Fell to Earth: Roger Clemens and the Rage for Baseball Immortality.* New York: HarperCollins, 2009.

Radomski, Kirk. *Bases Loaded: The Inside Story of the Steroid Era in Baseball by the Central Figure in the Mitchell Report.* New York: Hudson Street, 2009.

Simon, Ron. *The Game behind the Game: Negotiating in the Big Leagues.* Stillwater, MN: Voyageur, 1993.

Thompson, Teri, Nathaniel Vinton, Michael O'Keefe, and Christian Red. *American Icon: The Fall of Roger Clemens and the Rise of Steroids in America's Pastime.* New York: Alfred A. Knopf, 2009.

Torre, Joe, and Tom Verducci. *Chasing the Dream: My Lifelong Journey to the World Series: An Autobiography.* New York: Bantam, 1997.

———. *The Yankee Years.* New York: Doubleday, 2009.

Vincent, Fay. *The Last Commissioner: A Baseball Valentine.* New York: Simon & Schuster, 2002.

White, Bill, and Gordon Dillow. *Uppity: My Untold Story about the Games People Play.* New York: Grand Central, 2011.

Zimbalist, Andrew S. *Baseball and Billions: A Probing Look inside the Big Business of Our National Pastime.* New York: Basic, 1992.
———. *In the Best Interests of Baseball? The Revolutionary Reign of Bud Selig.* Hoboken, NJ: Wiley, 2006.

Journals

Damiani, Bettina, and Dan Steinberg. "Loot, Loot, Loot for the Home Team: How the Proposal to Subsidize a New Yankee Stadium Would Leave Residents and Taxpayers Behind." *Good Jobs New York*, February 2006.
Fallone, Edward A. "Reflections on the Accident at Miller Park and the Prosecution of Work-Related Fatalities in Wisconsin." *Marquette Sports Law Review* 12, no. 1 (2001): 105.
Green, Andrew L. T. "Spreading the Blame: Examining the Relationship between DSHEA and the Baseball Steroid Scandal." *Boston University Law Review* 90, no. 1 (2010): 399.
Kucheryavaya, Maria. "New York City Strikes Out: The Financing of Yankee Stadium." *Columbia Economics Review*, spring 2011.
Leder, Benjamin Z., Christopher Longcope, Don H. Catlin, Brian Ahrens, David A. Schoenfeld, and Joel S. Finkelstein. "Oral Androstenedione Administration and Serum Testosterone Concentrations in Young Men." *JAMA: The Journal of the American Medical Association* 283, no. 6 (2000): 779.
Martens, Kevin E. "Fair or Foul? The Survival of Small-Market Teams in Major League Baseball." *Marquette Sports Law Review* 4, no. 2 (1996): 323.
McCann, Michael. "Dietary Supplement Labeling: Cognitive Biases, Market Manipulation and Consumer Choice." *American Journal of Law and Medicine* 31 (2005): 215.
Staudohar, Paul D. "The Baseball Strike of 1994–95." *Monthly Labor Review*, March 1997, 21.

Newspapers and Magazines

Achievement.org. "George Mitchell Interview." June 7, 2002.
Amore, Dom. "At Last, Giambi Putting It Together." *Hartford Courant*, July 7, 2005.
Anderson, Dave. "Jeter Made Difference for Yankees." *New York Times*, September 26, 1996.
———. "Look Who's on Yanks' Payroll." *New York Times*, March 2, 1994.
———. "Will Reggie Join Yogi's Boycott?" *New York Times*, October 8, 1996.
———. "A Yankee Celebration of Fine 1996 Vintage." *New York Times*, October 19, 1996.
Antonen, Mel. "Baseball Players Want Drug Testing." *USA Today*, July 7, 2007.
Araton, Harvey. "Being Boss Has Its Emotional Moments." *New York Times*, February 21, 1999.
———. "Team of the Moment, Team of the Century; Clemens Leads the Yankees to Their Third Title in Four Seasons." *New York Times*, October 28, 1999.
Armas, Genaro C. "Umpires Decide to Strike Back." Associated Press, *Milwaukee Journal Sentinel*, July 15, 1999.

Assael, Shaun, and Peter Keating. "Who Knew?" *ESPN the Magazine*, November 9, 2005.

Associated Press. "Baseball to Examine Supplements." August 26, 1998.

———. "Bonds Hits No. 715 to Pass Babe Ruth." ESPN.com, May 28, 2006.

———. "Bud Selig Gets a Standing Ovation for This Strike." *USA Today*, October 5, 2008.

———. "Canseco: Steroid Use by Players at 85%." *Los Angeles Times*, May 18, 2002.

———. "Clinton Praises Ripken as True American Hero." *Spartanburg Herald-Tribune*, September 7, 1996.

———. "Committee to Look at Replay, Playoffs." ESPN.com, January 13, 2010.

———. "Franco's Win for New York—and New York." ESPN.com, September 17, 2001.

———. "McGwire Ball Buyer Revealed." *Los Angeles Times*, February 9, 1999.

———. "Players Visit with Workers, Family Members." ESPN.com, September 16, 2001.

———. "Poll: Fans Doubt Baseball's Steroid Policy, Bonds." ESPN.com, April 25, 2006.

———. "Smaller but Angrier Crowds See Openers." *Los Angeles Times*, April 27, 1995.

———. "Three-Homer Seventh Overwhelms White Sox." ESPN.com, September 18, 2001.

———. "Vincent's Turmoil Stalls Credit Deal." *Milwaukee Journal*, August 27, 1992.

———. "Yanks, Nets, Devils Separate from Company." ESPN.com, March 23, 2004.

Associated Press and *Milwaukee Journal Sentinel*. "Stunned Selig Cancels Games." *Seattle Times*, September 12, 2001.

Aukofer, Frank. "Selig Testifies on Anti-trust." *Milwaukee Journal*, December 10, 1992.

Austin American-Statesman. "It's Come to This: A Replacement Trade." March 3, 1995.

Bagli, Charles V. "Sale Might Let Steinbrenner Run 3 Teams, Officials Say." *New York Times*, September 17, 1998.

———. "As Stadiums Rise, So Do Costs to Taxpayers." *New York Times*, November 4, 2008.

Bauman, Michael. "Cheers and Jeers for Molitor: That's Wisconsin." *Milwaukee Journal*, June 27, 1993.

———. "Is This a Sign of Bleak Times?" *Milwaukee Journal*, December 8, 1992.

———. "Selig: This May Be 'Our Greatest Season.'" MLB.com, July 14, 2009.

———. "Selig's Tears Tell a Story." *Milwaukee Journal*, September 10, 1992.

Begley, Ian. "He Was Friend, Mentor and...the Boss." *ESPN New York*, July 17, 2010.

Berardino, Mike. "Security Striking for Presidential Pitch." *Sun Sentinel*, October 31, 2001.

Berghaus, Bob. "Bad Vibes: Hamilton Admits Small Market Woes Are Concern." *Milwaukee Journal*, June 4, 1993.

————. "Ball Shifts Back to Owners' Court." *Milwaukee Journal,* September 9, 1994.

————. "Baseball Enters Abyss of Uncertainty, Selig Calls Off the 1994 Season." *Milwaukee Journal,* September 13, 1994.

————. "Brewers Players Believe Replacements in '95 a Possibility." *Milwaukee Journal,* September 15, 1994.

————. "Fehr Tactics." *Milwaukee Journal,* March 6, 1993.

————. "Final Seconds Ticking Down on Molitor Era." *Milwaukee Journal,* December 7, 1992.

————. "For the First Time since 1904, World Series Wouldn't Be Played." *Milwaukee Journal,* September 13, 1994.

————. "Goodbye Milwaukee, Hello Toronto." *Milwaukee Journal,* December 8, 1992.

————. "Molitor May Be Offered Less Than He Got in '92." *Milwaukee Journal,* November 20, 1992.

————. "Molitor Ponders Pact; Brewers Look to Be Fair with 'Creative' Deal." *Milwaukee Journal,* November 30, 1992.

————. "Molitor's Likely to Leave; Veteran Rejects Second Offer." *Milwaukee Sentinel,* December 7, 1992.

————. "Molitor Talks about Owners Summit, Strike." *Milwaukee Journal,* August 8, 1993.

————. "Now Molitor, Brewers Face Season of Decisions." *Milwaukee Journal,* October 4, 1992.

————. "Owners Explore Playoff Expansion." *Milwaukee Journal,* March 5, 1993.

————. "Owners Make Some Progress in Negotiations for Revenue Sharing Deal." *Milwaukee Journal,* January 18, 1994.

————. "Owners Sense Urgency, Optimism at Talks." *Milwaukee Journal,* August 11, 1993.

————. "Revenue Plan a Victory for Selig to Savor." *Milwaukee Journal,* January 19, 1994.

————. "Selig an Easy Choice, Other Owners Declare." *Milwaukee Journal,* September 10, 1992.

————. "Selig Says Loan Not Out of Ordinary." *Milwaukee Journal,* June 14, 1992.

————. "Selig Stands Firmly behind Owners' Plan." *Milwaukee Journal,* June 15, 1994.

————. "Selig Will Stay On as Interim Commissioner." *Milwaukee Journal,* January 20, 1994.

————. "Showdown Near as Owners Make Proposal." *Milwaukee Journal,* June 14, 1994.

————. "Steinbrenner Backs Selig as End Nears." *Milwaukee Journal,* September 13, 1994.

————. "They're Out; The Name of the Game Now Is Strike and Run." *Milwaukee Journal,* August 12, 1994.

————. "Union Battle Is Next Round." *Milwaukee Journal,* January 19, 1994.

Bergquist, Lee. "Stadium Options Discussed; Committee Talks of Public Funds." *Milwaukee Sentinel,* June 30, 1992.

Berkow, Ira. "Baseball Owners as Comedians." *New York Times,* December 15, 1992.

————. "Mattingly's Elusive Dream." *New York Times,* July 29, 1994.

————. "No Matter What's Said, Reinsdorf Can Be Found in Eye of Storm." *New York Times,* December 15, 1992.

Bice, Daniel. "Thompson Slams Norquist on Fuel Fee." *Milwaukee Sentinel,* August 21, 1993.

Binole, Gina. "Nike's Digging the Long Ball Delivered by W&K Campaign." *Portland Business Journal,* May 16, 1999.

Birger, Jon, and Tim Arango. "The Yankees Face Life after George." *Fortune,* August 3, 2007.

Bloom, Barry. "Bonds Indicted on Federal Charges." MLB.com, November 16, 2007.

————. "Mandatory Steroid Testing to Begin." MLB.com, November 13, 2003.

Blum, Ronald. "Commissioner's Office Likely Will Not Pursue Canseco Allegations." Associated Press, February 11, 2005.

————. "Murphy Fired." Associated Press, October 17, 1997.

Bodley, Hal. "'Boss' Has Firm Grip on Helm." *USA Today,* March 18, 1998.

————. "Medical Examiner: Ephedra a Factor in Bechler Death." *USA Today,* March 13, 2003.

————. "MLB Union Proposes 20-Game Ban for Positive Steroid Test." *USA Today,* September 26, 2005.

————. "Selig to Control Baseball Internet Revenue." *USA Today,* January 21, 2000.

Bondy, Filip. "Bombers' Old Identity Now Going, Going, Gone." *New York Daily News,* May 27, 2002.

Borden, Sam. "Joe Must Go...Back to Work; Boss Holds Fire, Demands Ire." *New York Daily News,* October 11, 2006.

Borowski, Greg J. "Bush Lives Out Kid's Dream." *Milwaukee Journal Sentinel,* April 7, 2001.

Borowski, Greg J., et al. "Ballpark Disaster—Big Blue Crane Collapses—3 Killed—Strong Winds Cited as a Possible Cause." *Milwaukee Journal Sentinel,* July 15, 1999.

Boswell, Thomas. "Fans Allow Yankees Leeway on Strike Zone." *Washington Post,* April 27, 1995.

————. "History, Fans Embrace Ripken in 2,131st Game." *Washington Post,* September 7, 1995.

Botte, Pete, et al. "Finale Has Boss 'Very Emotional.'" *New York Daily News,* September 22, 2008.

Bowdoin Alumni Magazine. "George Mitchell: Down East Majority Leader." Summer 2003.

Bowles, Peter. "America's Ordeal; City Gets First $2B in U.S. Aid." *Newsday,* September 22, 2001.

Bradley, Jeff. "Gen XXL." *ESPN the Magazine,* April 3, 2000.

Brown, Maury. "Interview: Fay Vincent." BusinessofBaseball.com, November 8, 2005.

Browne, Ian. "Fehr Wants Time to Review Report." MLB.com, December 13, 2007.

Bryce, Robert. "Stealing Home." *Texas Observer,* May 9, 1997.

Burke, Kerry, and Tracy Connor. "The Boss Collapses; Steinbrenner Stricken during Fla. Memorial." *New York Daily News,* December 28, 2003.

Chass, Murray. "Back to Business: Baseball Votes to Drop 2 Teams." *New York Times*, November 7, 2001.

———. "Baseball Adversaries Go to Bat and Strike Out." *New York Times*, August 25, 1994.

———. "Baseball Is Considering a New Round of Expansion." *New York Times*, December 7, 1993.

———. "Baseball Owners Implement a Cap on Players' Pay." *New York Times*, December 23, 1994.

———. "Baseball Owners Lean toward Lockout." *New York Times*, September 11, 1992.

———. "Baseball Owners Quit Fight; Opening Day Is Set for April 26." *New York Times*, April 3, 1995.

———. "Baseball Owners Vote to Reopen Labor Talks." *New York Times*, December 8, 1992.

———. "Baseball Players and Owners Appear Close to New Deal." *New York Times*, August 11, 1996.

———. "Baseball's Labor Talks Are Going Nowhere." *New York Times*, November 16, 2001.

———. "Baseball's Owners Reject Players' Bid to Tax Rich Clubs." *New York Times*, September 10, 1994.

———. "Baseball's Owners: Wait till Next Week." *New York Times*, December 16, 1994.

———. "Baseball Squabbles, Even on President's Driveway." *New York Times*, October 15, 1994.

———. "Beam May Be the Leverage." *New York Times*, April 14, 1998.

———. "Blame the Expansion for Homer Explosion." *New York Times*, September 19, 1993.

———. "Bonds and the Giants Come to an Agreement." *New York Times*, December 9, 1992.

———. "Bonds Charges Deepen Baseball's Shame." *New York Times*, November 16, 2007.

———. "Brushback Pitch: Owners to Kill Pension Payment." *New York Times*, August 3, 1994.

———. "Call It Baseball or Call It Business, It's Still Booming." *New York Times*, August 8, 1993.

———. "Ceremony, Circus Act and Even Some Fans Greet Game's Return." *New York Times*, April 27, 1995.

———. "Choice of Commissioner Moves to Back Burner." *New York Times*, March 4, 1993.

———. "Contract Omission Says It All." *New York Times*, February 11, 2005.

———. "DuPuy to Replace Beeston at No. 2." *New York Times*, March 6, 2002.

———. "Dykstra Is Like a Modern Miracle." *New York Times*, October 1, 1993.

———. "Everybody Is Shut Out at the White House Talks." *New York Times*, February 8, 1995.

———. "Grandfather Martinez Is Set to Throw Some Strikes for Atlanta." *New York Times*, February 22, 1998.

———. "A 'Hands Off' Owner Completes 20 Years." *New York Times*, January 3, 1993.

———. "In a 'Dear Bud' Letter, CBS Opposes Lockout." *New York Times*, October 30, 1992.

———. "Injunction Hearing Set; Clubs Offer New Plan." *New York Times*, March 28, 1995.

———. "It's a Table for 6 Owners." *New York Times*, April 24, 1993.

———. "The Labor Deal Hinges on the Word from Selig." *New York Times*, October 26, 1996.

———. "League Presidents Out as Baseball Centralizes." *New York Times*, September 16, 1999.

———. "Let's Share, Ravitch Tells Baseball's Owners." *New York Times*, December 1, 1992.

———. "Letter from Fehr Showed He Had Hope for Talks." *New York Times*, June 1, 2002.

———. "Management Touts Togetherness Theme." *New York Times*, July 20, 1994.

———. "Mattingly Wins $1.975 Million in Arbitration." *New York Times*, February 18, 1987.

———. "Mitchell Seeks to Put Teeth into Inquiry." *New York Times*, June 22, 2006.

———. "Molitor Gets Chance This Time Around." *New York Times*, August 3, 1993.

———. "Mr. Break-It and Mr. Fix-It." *New York Times*, January 4, 1998.

———. "Negotiating Teams Move to Night Round of Talks." *New York Times*, March 2, 1995.

———. "Negotiating Tone Helped Lead to Deal." *New York Times*, September 1, 2002.

———. "A New Owners' Meeting Gets Off to a Slow Start." *New York Times*, January 18, 1994.

———. "No Commissioner, and Perhaps No Penalty for Schott." *New York Times*, November 22, 1992.

———. "No Lockout? No Strike? No Way to Really Tell until the Labor Talks Begin." *New York Times*, January 10, 1993.

———. "No Runs, No Hits, No Errors: Baseball Goes on Strike." *New York Times*, August 12, 1994.

———. "No Strike, but Maybe No Added Playoffs." *New York Times*, August 18, 1993.

———. "Now What? Baseball's Labor Deal Is Rejected." *New York Times*, November 7, 1996.

———. "No Yankee Jacket Required: Is Showalter In or Out?" *New York Times*, October 27, 1995.

———. "Oh, Strike That: Talks Put Off until Further Notice." *New York Times*, August 26, 1994.

———. "On Baseball; Congress Nudges Union in Selig's New Lineup." *New York Times*, November 16, 2005.

———. "One Year Later, Stoicism and Words of Concern from Vincent." *New York Times*, September 5, 1993.

———. "Owner against Owner: It Could Be 9 Innings in Court." *New York Times*, September 5, 1992.

———. "Owners Adopt Revenue Plan, but It's Tied to Salary Cap." *New York Times*, January 19, 1994.

———. "Owners and Players Stand Still; Clock Runs." *New York Times*, July 19, 1994.

———. "Owners Approve Playoff Format." *New York Times*, June 18, 1993.

———. "Owners Approve Realignment of Divisions." *New York Times*, September 10, 1993.

———. "Owners Chose Their Course." *New York Times*, February 12, 1995.

———. "Owners Circle Bases without Ever Scoring." *New York Times*, September 7, 1993.

———. "Owners Favor Realignment, More Playoffs." *New York Times*, March 5, 1993.

———. "Owners Give New Powers Only to Selig." *New York Times*, January 23, 2000.

———. "Owners Link Salaries to Revenue Sharing." *New York Times*, February 18, 1993.

———. "Owners' New Voice Is Peddling Same Line." *New York Times*, November 12, 1994.

———. "Owners Pass Cap Plan to Present to the Players." *New York Times*, June 9, 1994.

———. "Owners' Plan Has Payoff for Cardinals." *New York Times*, November 25, 1994.

———. "Owners Scrap Salary Cap to Create a Ray of Hope." *New York Times*, February 5, 1995.

———. "Owners Take Steps to Prevent a Strike." *New York Times*, August 13, 1993.

———. "Owners Terminate Season, without the World Series." *New York Times*, September 15, 1994.

———. "Owners Unveil Salary Cap Proposal to a Chilly Reception from Players." *New York Times*, June 15, 1994.

———. "Owners Vote to Use Replacements as Talks Go On." *New York Times*, March 31, 1995.

———. "Plan Would Give Boost to Middle-Class Teams." *New York Times*, July 15, 2000.

———. "Players Association Sets Strike Date of August 12." *New York Times*, July 29, 1994.

———. "Players Must Wait for Owners to Settle Their Differences; Union Finds Itself Left in the Dark." *New York Times*, July 12, 1993.

———. "Players Offer Ideas on Sharing Owners' Wealth." *New York Times*, August 13, 1994.

———. "Players Union Chief Talks to Owners." *New York Times*, January 18, 2002.

———. "Players Union Delays Vote on a Strike Date." *New York Times*, June 17, 1994.

———. "Players Union Proposes Tests for Illegal Steroids." *New York Times*, August 8, 2002.

———. "A Question of Pace: Is Selig's Too Slow?" *New York Times*, August 29, 1996.

————. "Reluctant Baseball Owners Approve Pact with Players." *New York Times*, November 27, 1996.

————. "Replacement Players May Play Ball Next Year." *New York Times*, November 30, 1994.

————. "Revenue-Sharing Ball Is in the Owners' Court." *New York Times*, August 10, 1993.

————. "Salary Cap Taken Off Immediate Agenda." *New York Times*, December 1, 1994.

————. "Selig, Contradicting Negotiators, Says There Is No Deal." *New York Times*, October 27, 1996.

————. "Selig Has Become Target of Some Players' Anger." *New York Times*, March 5, 2002.

————. "Selig, in a Sense of Mourning, Cancels Baseball Games." *New York Times*, September 12, 2001.

————. "Selig Names Panel to Study Payrolls." *New York Times*, January 14, 1999.

————. "Selig's Daughter Resigns as Brewers' Chief." *New York Times*, September 26, 2002.

————. "Selig Set to Drop 'Acting' from Commissioner." *New York Times*, June 18, 1998.

————. "Selig's Threat: Settle Soon, or Wait till Next Year," *New York Times*, September 3, 1994.

————. "Selig Still Doesn't Want to Be the Commissioner." *New York Times*, October 29, 1993.

————. "Six to Eight Are on List for New Commissioner." *New York Times*, September 8, 1993.

————. "Steinbrenner Angers Executive Council." *New York Times*, May 8, 1997.

————. "Steinbrenner Banned as Executive Council Member." *New York Times*, May 14, 1997.

————. "Steinbrenner Discussed Selling a Piece of Yankees." *New York Times*, March 20, 1998.

————. "Steinbrenner Solvent, Baseball Says." *New York Times*, November 6, 1993.

————. "Stormy Times Bringing Bright Spots for Yanks." *New York Times*, September 15, 1993.

————. "Take Away the 'Acting' Label: Selig Is Baseball's Commissioner." *New York Times*, July 10, 1998.

————. "Talks Are Feverish with Strike Due Tomorrow." *New York Times*, August 29, 2002.

————. "Talk-Show Diplomacy Won't Settle the Issue." *New York Times*, August 2, 1994.

————. "Those Tumultuous Winter Meetings Conclude under a Cloud." *New York Times*, December 10, 1992.

————. "Threat of a Bloc Veto Hangs over Meetings." *New York Times*, January 16, 1994.

————. "Threat of Congress Shadows Mitchell's Steroids Inquiry." *New York Times*, March 2, 2007.

————. "A Title Is Diminished but the Salary Soars." *New York Times*, February 15, 1994.

———. "Tougher Adversaries Might Face the Union." *New York Times*, March 5, 1995.

———. "Two Sides Firmly Apart with Deadline in Sight." *New York Times*, August 28, 2002.

———. "Uneasy Are the Men Who Sign Those Lineup Cards; Tigers Give Anderson a Leave of Absence." *New York Times*, February 18, 1995.

———. "Union May Be Attaching Strings to Playoff Plans." *New York Times*, August 18, 1993.

———. "Union Talks of Solidarity, and of Return." *New York Times*, February 17, 1995.

———. "Unruly Fans Disrupt Tigers' Home Opener." *New York Times*, May 3, 1995.

———. "Vincent, Bowing to Owners' Will, Resigns as Baseball Commissioner." *New York Times*, September 8, 1992.

———. "What's $32 Million More? Yanks Sign Contreras." *New York Times*, December 25, 2002.

———. "When It Comes to Members of Minorities, How Soon Baseball Forgets." *New York Times*, January 24, 1999.

———. "The White Sox Take a Stand on Steroid Tests." *New York Times*, March 12, 2003.

———. "Will a Realignment Be Good for the Game?" *New York Times*, October 21, 1993.

———. "Yanks' Tab with New Rules: $77 Million." *New York Times*, December 7, 1996.

Chass, Murray, and Charles V. Bagli. "Steinbrenner Is Said to Be Close to Sale of Yankees to Cablevision." *New York Times*, November 21, 1998.

Christian, Carol. "Former Astros Player Caminiti Pleads Guilty to Drug Charge." *Houston Chronicle*, March 22, 2002.

Clines, Frank. "Small-Market Played Role in Departure, Molitor Says." *Milwaukee Journal*, June 26, 1993.

Coffey, Wayne. "Boss Looks Back, Warns Jeter and Joe in Exclusive Sit-Down with News." *New York Daily News*, December 29, 2002.

Conason, Joe. "Fortune's Child: George W. Bush and His $15 Million from a Shady Baseball Deal." *Harper's Magazine*, February 2000.

Cook, Ron. "Slam Dance." *Pittsburgh Post-Gazette*, June 9, 1996.

Culpepper, Chuck. "George Has Curious Reply." *Newsday*, October 26, 2003.

Curry, Jack. "All the Magic Is Gone from the Yankees' Numbers." *New York Times*, September 14, 1994.

———. "Baseball Backs Stiffer Penalties for Steroid Use." *New York Times*, November 16, 2005.

———. "Bonds Hits No. 756 to Break Aaron's Record." *New York Times*, August 8, 2007.

———. "Call of the Wild Card: The Yankees Clinch Playoff Berth." *New York Times*, October 2, 1995.

———. "Cashman Stays Silent about Future." *New York Times*, October 28, 1999.

———. "Cone Makes Up His Mind: 3 Years in Pinstripes." *New York Times*, December 22, 1995.

———. "Day 2 a Time for Quiet Discussion." *New York Times*, March 3, 1993.

———. "Enter the Once and Future King." *New York Times*, February 25, 1993.

———. "Everyone's in Gear, Including Steinbrenner." *New York Times*, February 25, 2004.

———. "Extra Practice Pays as Bonds Ties Aaron's Mark." *New York Times*, August 5, 2007.

———. "The Fall of a Baseball Autumn; The Ballplayers' Strike Seems to Have Been Inevitable." *New York Times*, September 20, 1994.

———. "House Invites 7 Players to Drug-Policy Hearing." *New York Times*, March 4, 2005.

———. "If the Ax Falls, Watson Will Not Run for Cover." *New York Times*, September 12, 1996.

———. "In a Surprise, the Brewers Say the Team Is for Sale." *New York Times*, January 17, 2004.

———. "It's Winter, but Steinbrenner Is Warming Up." *New York Times*, December 11, 1992.

———. "Joyful Molitor Is the Blue Jay with the Red Eyes." *New York Times*, October 25, 1993.

———. "Just Like That, It's Monday in Park with George." *New York Times*, March 2, 1993.

———. "League Championship Series; There's Not Much to Say after a Stunning Defeat." *New York Times*, October 10, 1998.

———. "Listen Hard: Steinbrenner Is as Silent as Yankee Stadium." *New York Times*, September 14, 1994.

———. "Manager Showalter Meets the Meddler." *New York Times*, February 14, 1993.

———. "Mattingly Ponders His Future." *New York Times*, August 11, 1994.

———. "Mattingly Slips a Rung on Yank Ladder." *New York Times*, April 14, 1993.

———. "Mattingly Won't Play Blame Game." *New York Times*, September 26, 1993.

———. "McGwire Stopped His Use of Andro Four Months Ago." *New York Times*, August 6, 1999.

———. "Michael Is Taking 'the Return' in Stride." *New York Times*, February 28, 1993.

———. "Midseason Report; So Far, Nothing Has Slowed the Yanks." *New York Times*, July 9, 1996.

———. "The Owner Gives Torre a Vote of Confidence." *New York Times*, September 19, 1996.

———. "Owners Link Salaries to Revenue Sharing." *New York Times*, February 18, 1993.

———. "Owners Looking Hard at Revenue Sharing." *New York Times*, August 12, 1993.

———. "A Return to Glory." *New York Times*, October 27, 1996.

———. "Selig Seeks Harder Line on Drugs in Baseball." *New York Times*, May 1, 2005.

———. "Steinbrenner Criticized for Signing Strawberry." *New York Times*, June 21, 1995.

——. "Steinbrenner's Tears of Rage and Joy." *New York Times*, July 8, 2003.

——. "Steroid Investigation Begins, but Not without Some Concerns." *New York Times*, March 31, 2006.

——. "Subway Series; Teary Steinbrenner Soaks Up the Excitement." *New York Times*, October 27, 2000.

——. "Tearful Giambi Is Proud to Put On the Pinstripes." *New York Times*, December 14, 2001.

——. "Today's Forecast: Hurricane George." *New York Times*, March 1, 1993.

——. "Torre Remains Placid amid Swirl of Rumors." *New York Times*, June 15, 2000.

——. "2 Balks Follow Jackson's Address." *New York Times*, January 13, 1993.

——. "Watson Hopes 80 Hours Is Enough." *New York Times*, April 29, 1997.

——. "Winning Wounded: Mattingly and Williams on D.L." *New York Times*, April 14, 1993.

——. "Yankees and Wells Hope Fine Ends Story." *New York Times*, March 10, 2003.

——. "Yankees Clinch and Paint Town in Pinstripes." *New York Times*, September 26, 1996.

——. "Yankees Concerned as Cone Still Feels Numbness." *New York Times*, May 7, 1996.

——. "Yankees Finally Get It Right and Land a Lefty." *New York Times*, December 11, 1992.

——. "Yankees in Crisis at Top? Of Course." *New York Times*, December 17, 1992.

——. "Yankees Trade Roberto Kelly to Reds for O'Neill." *New York Times*, November 4, 1992.

——. "Yankees Welcome Their Nemesis." *New York Times*, February 19, 1999.

——. "Yanks' New Strategy Has Tampa Imprint." *New York Times*, December 13, 1992.

——. "Yanks Pull the Switch: Mattingly Bats Fifth." *New York Times*, July 21, 1994.

——. "Yanks Spirit Watson Away from Astros for G.M." *New York Times*, October 24, 1995.

——. "Yet Another Era Begins as the Yankees Hire Torre." *New York Times*, November 3, 1995.

——. "A Youthful but Yankee-Wise Leader." *New York Times*, February 4, 1998.

Curry, Jack, and Jere Longman. "Results of Steroid Testing Spur Baseball to Set Tougher Rules." *New York Times*, November 14, 2003.

Curry, Jack, and Tyler Kepner. "The Month of May Has Been Difficult for the Boss." *New York Times*, May 28, 2003.

Daley, Ken. "No-Win Situation; Selig Reluctantly Calls Game after Teams Run Out of Players." *Dallas Morning News*, July 10, 2002.

D'Amato, Gary. "Stayin' Alive: Brewers Muster Their Mojo for Miller Park's Postseason Debut." *Milwaukee Journal Sentinel*, October 5, 2008.

Darcy, Kieran. "The Man Who Would Be King." ESPN.com, June 6, 2008.

Davidoff, Ken. "Boss Names Jeter Captain." *Newsday*, June 4, 2003.

Daykin, Tom, and Daniel Bice. "Retractable Domed Stadium to Be Proposed for Downtown." *Milwaukee Sentinel*, January 5, 1994.

Daykin, Tom, and Rick Romel. "Brewers Want Stadium with Convertible Roof." *Milwaukee Sentinel*, February 26, 1994.

———. "A Stadium Downtown." *Milwaukee Sentinel*, February 7, 1994.

De Krestor, Leela. "Yank 'Heir' $queeze Play." *New York Post*, April 25, 2007.

Diamos, Jason. "Yankees and Jeter Reach Agreement." *New York Times*, March 11, 1997.

DiComo, Anthony. "Selig: Report Is a 'Call to Action.'" MLB.com, December 13, 2007.

Eder, Steve. "Biogenesis Founder Surrenders to D.E.A. Agents." *New York Times*, August 5, 2014.

Edes, Gordon. "Foul Called on Dykstra." *Fort Lauderdale Sun Sentinel*, February 17, 1995.

———. "Marlins' Barger Dies at Owners' Meetings." *Fort Lauderdale Sun Sentinel*, December 10, 1992.

———. "MLB Finally Gets Picture on TV Deal." *Fort Lauderdale Sun Sentinel*, November 12, 1995.

———. "Selig Says He Never Saw Signs of Steroids." *Boston Globe*, July 13, 2005.

Elfrink, Tim. "A Florida Clinic Supplies Drugs to Sports' Biggest Names." *Miami New Times*, January 31, 2014.

———. "Florida Investigator: I Warned Major League Baseball Not to Buy Stolen Records." *Miami New Times*, October 14, 2014.

Fainaru, Steve. "Expos for Sale: Team Becomes Pawn of Selig." *Washington Post*, June 28, 2004.

———. "Selig Plays Hardball on Stadium Deals." *Washington Post*, June 27, 2004.

Fainaru-Wada, Mark. "Dreams, Steroids, Death—A Ballplayer's Downfall." *San Francisco Chronicle*, December 19, 2004.

Fainaru-Wada, Mark, and Lance Williams. "Bonds Got Steroids, Feds Were Told." *San Francisco Chronicle*, March 1, 2004.

———. "Bonds Used Steroids in 2003, Trainer Says on Secret Recording." *San Francisco Chronicle*, October 16, 2004.

———. "Giambi Admitted Taking Steroids." *San Francisco Chronicle*, December 2, 2004.

———. "Investigator Urges Bonds to Aid Probe of Steroids." *San Francisco Chronicle*, February 26, 2006.

———. "The Truth: Barry Bonds and Steroids." *Sports Illustrated*, March 13, 2006.

———. "What Bonds Told BALCO Grand Jury." *San Francisco Chronicle*, December 2, 2004.

Fauber, John. "Secrecy Surrounds Brewer Finances." *Milwaukee Journal*, April 3, 1994.

Feinsand, Mark. "Hank, Bosox Bomb Yanks. New Boss Fumes over Stink." *New York Daily News*, August 28, 2008.

———. "Notes: Boss Says Cashman Responsible." MLB.com, July 5, 2006.

Fish, Mike. "FBI Knew of McGwire's Steroid Use." ESPN.com, January 11, 2010.

———. "Radomski's Legacy: The Man Who Made the Mitchell Report Sing." ESPN.com, February 12, 2008.

Flaherty, Tom. "The Problem Solver." *Milwaukee Journal*, September 27, 1993.

———. "A Special Friendship." *Milwaukee Journal*, February 11, 1994.

———. "Toronto's Star, Now." *Milwaukee Journal*, September 26, 1993.

Footer, Alyson. "Clemens, Pettitte React to Report." MLB.com, December 13, 2007.

Freeman, Mike, and Buster Olney. "New Drug Tests in Baseball Stir Debate among Players." *New York Times*, April 22, 2003.

Frey, Jennifer. "Mets vs. Yanks: Guy Named Bubba at 2d, Guy Named Sisk on the Mound." *New York Times*, March 5, 1995.

Garcia-Roberts, Gus. "MLB's A-Rod Inquiry: Investigators Were Told Documents Were Stolen, but Bought Records Anyway, Officials Say." *Newsday*, May 11, 2014.

Gardner, Charles F. "Brewers 10, Giants 8: Wild and Crazy Crew Surges, Falls Back, Then Rallies." *Milwaukee Journal Sentinel*, September 24, 2006.

Gilbert, Craig. "The House That Bud Built." *Milwaukee Journal*, March 6, 1994.

———. "Many Factors Led to Lottery's Landslide Loss." *Milwaukee Journal Sentinel*, April 6, 1995.

———. "Why Brewers Tossed a Changeup." *Milwaukee Journal Sentinel*, January 15, 1995.

Glauber, Bill. "Toast of the Town." *Milwaukee Journal Sentinel*, September 29, 2008.

Grant, Peter. "Off Field Paydays Torre, Valentine Capitalize on Teams' Success." *New York Daily News*, October 19, 1999.

———. "Yankees' Push for TV Profits Sparks Clash of Power Players." *Wall Street Journal*, June 12, 2003.

Hack, Damon. "Fans Balance Flag-Waving with Pennant-Racing." *Newsday*, September 22, 2001.

Hallissy, Erin. "Lawmakers Enter Fray on Drug Use in Baseball." *San Francisco Chronicle*, December 6, 2004.

Handley, Daniel P, Jr. "Ballpark Figure: Selig Envisions New Stadium." *Milwaukee Journal*, April 13, 1993.

———. "Baseball's Future Rides on Talks." *Milwaukee Journal*, August 8, 1993.

———. "Baseball's Power Broker." *Milwaukee Journal*, September 29, 1992.

———. "Ending Clouds the Day." *Milwaukee Journal*, September 10, 1992.

———. "Jackson Group Plans Protest against Brewers." *Milwaukee Journal*, April 9, 1993.

———. "Loss Said to Be at Least $5 Million." *Milwaukee Journal*, October 9, 1992.

———. "Norquist Says Brewers Need More Help to Build Stadium." *Milwaukee Journal*, August 13, 1993.

———. "Revenue Wrangling: Owners Still Working on a Deal." *Milwaukee Journal*, August 25, 1993.

———. "Selig-Prieb Steps Up to the Plate." *Milwaukee Journal*, August 10, 1993.

———. "Speak Up Now, Norquist Says." *Milwaukee Journal*, May 12, 1993.

———. "Still Brewing: Revenue-Sharing Plan Renews Talk of Stadium." *Milwaukee Journal*, January 20, 1994.

———. "We Don't Want to Go, Selig Asserts." *Milwaukee Journal*, June 3, 1992.

———. "Will a Strike Halt the Season?" *Milwaukee Journal*, April 3, 1994.

Harris, Craig, Joseph A. Reaves, and Nick Piecoro. "D-Back Admits Steroid Use." *Arizona Republic*, June 7, 2006.

Harris, Elliott. "Media Friendly? Mighty Selig Has Struck Out." *Chicago Sun-Times,* July 11, 2002.

Hartford Courant. "Reaches a High; the Art of the Deal." *Newsday,* September 1, 2002.

Haudricourt, Tom. "August 12 Baseball Strike Date Set, Players Vow to Fight 'Long as It Takes.'" *Milwaukee Sentinel,* July 29, 1994.

———. "Baseball Official Set to Quit over Power Loss." *Milwaukee Journal Sentinel,* September 11, 1999.

———. "Baseball Owners Impose Salary Cap." *Milwaukee Journal Sentinel,* December 23, 1994.

———. "Baseball Revenue Plan 1 Vote Shy." *Milwaukee Sentinel,* January 7, 1994.

———. "Baseball's Future Rides on Talks." *Milwaukee Sentinel,* August 8, 1993.

———. "Baseball Stalemate Seems Likely No Talks Held; Start of '95 Season in Question." *Milwaukee Sentinel,* September 13, 1994.

———. "Big-Market Group Bolts, Has Caucus." *Milwaukee Sentinel,* August 12, 1993.

———. "Brewers Putting Up $90 Million." *Milwaukee Journal Sentinel,* August 20, 1995.

———. "Brewers Won't Limit Search for New Duo." *Milwaukee Journal Sentinel,* August 13, 1999.

———. "Canseco an Unsavory Messenger, but His Story Rings True." *Milwaukee Journal Sentinel,* February 13, 2005.

———. "Designated Hero: He's Just the Ticket." *Milwaukee Sentinel,* June 22, 1993.

———. "Despite Labor Strife, Selig Bears No Permanent Scars." *Milwaukee Journal Sentinel,* June 28, 1998.

———. "Fan Appreciation—Rally Brings Cheers for Selig, Petak, Jeers for Norquist." *Milwaukee Journal Sentinel,* June 23, 1996.

———. "Fehr Is Hoping Talks Pick Up." *Milwaukee Sentinel,* March 28, 1994.

———. "Fehr Scolds Selig for Reneging." *Milwaukee Journal Sentinel,* November 12, 1996.

———. "History Moving On Up—Commissioner Selig Clearing Out of Cramped Office." *Milwaukee Journal Sentinel,* January 27, 1999.

———. "In Seattle, Selig's Heart Remains in Milwaukee." *Milwaukee Journal Sentinel,* July 16, 1999.

———. "An Intentional Walk into the Sunset—Selig's Dark Cloud Will Finally Lift." *Milwaukee Journal Sentinel,* January 17, 2004.

———. "Journal Sentinel Q & A—Selig Cites 'Machiavellian Behavior.'" *Milwaukee Journal Sentinel,* June 17, 1996.

———. "Keeping Score—Baseball Setting a Record Pace for Runs." *Milwaukee Journal Sentinel,* May 10, 2000.

———. "Labor Conflict Hits Baseball, Critical Meetings Set for Kohler." *Milwaukee Sentinel,* July 31, 1993.

———. "Molitor Follows Brewers' Saga." *Milwaukee Sentinel,* May 24, 1993.

———. "Molitor Never Gave Price Tag." *Milwaukee Sentinel,* May 25, 1993.

———. "Molitor's Emotional Year Ends with Title." *Milwaukee Sentinel,* October 25, 1993.

———. "Molitors Leaving Milwaukee Area." *Milwaukee Sentinel,* January 11, 1993.

————. "Next Few Days Vital in Impasse, Clock Ticking toward Cancellation." *Milwaukee Sentinel*, September 10, 1994.

————. "Owners Back Selig's Competitive Balance Draft." *Milwaukee Journal Sentinel*, January 18, 2001.

————. "Owners Leave Sport in the Dark; Baseball Meetings Accomplish Little." *Milwaukee Sentinel*, August 12, 1993.

————. "Owners OK Revenue Sharing." *Milwaukee Sentinel*, January 19, 1994.

————. "Owners Select Selig to Take Temporary Leadership." *Milwaukee Sentinel*, September 10, 1992.

————. "Rising Salaries Highlight Rifts." *Milwaukee Sentinel*, March 9, 1992.

————. "Rookie Baseball Owners Escalate Salary Wars." *Milwaukee Sentinel*, December 14, 1992.

————. "Selig Doesn't Want Top Job." *Milwaukee Sentinel*, December 10, 1992.

————. "Selig Feeling Sense of Pride." *Milwaukee Journal Sentinel*, March 25, 2001.

————. "Selig Holds Meeting to Discuss Stalemate." *Milwaukee Sentinel*, August 5, 1994.

————. "Selig Joins Bonds Watch—He's in San Francisco to See Homer Pursuit." *Milwaukee Journal Sentinel*, July 25, 2007.

————. "Selig Plans to Catch Series with Bonds." *Milwaukee Journal Sentinel*, July 21, 2007.

————. "Selig Says Career Would Be 'Failure' If Team Left." *Milwaukee Sentinel*, January 17, 1994.

————. "Selig Scoffs at Miller's Comments, Acting Commissioner Denies Union-Busting Charge." *Milwaukee Sentinel*, August 16, 1994.

————. "Selig's Love of Game Praised at Statue's Unveiling." *Milwaukee Journal Sentinel*, August 24, 2010.

————. "Selig Takes Last Stand, Leaves Custard Behind." *Milwaukee Sentinel*, September 15, 1994.

————. "Selig Vows Action, Calls Vote 'Significant.'" *Milwaukee Journal Sentinel*, January 21, 2000.

————. "Selig Will Get Involved When Time Is Right." *Milwaukee Sentinel*, August 27, 1994.

————. "Selig Will Stay On as Interim Commissioner." *Milwaukee Sentinel*, January 20, 1994.

————. "Union-Busting Accusation Disputed." *Milwaukee Sentinel*, September 3, 1994.

————. "With Cancellation Looming, Owners Scattered." *Milwaukee Sentinel*, September 12, 1994.

Haudricourt, Tom, and Don Walker. "Cuts May Imperil Brewers on Field." *Milwaukee Journal Sentinel*, November 9, 2003.

————. "Legislators Want to Audit Brewers." *Milwaukee Journal Sentinel*, November 13, 2003.

————. "Payne Buyout Complete." *Milwaukee Journal Sentinel*, November 22, 2003.

————. "Payne May Be Done at Brewers." *Milwaukee Journal Sentinel*, November 12, 2003.

Heath, Thomas. "Baseball Urged to Let Teams Relocate." *Washington Post*, July 15, 2000.

Hellmich, Nanci. "FDA Awaits Ephedra Report after Baseball Player's Death." *USA Today*, February 20, 2003.

Helyar, John. "Can Baseball Get Sponsors Back in the Ballgame?" *Wall Street Journal*, November 15, 1996.

Herzog, Bob. "Mets Take a Turn Pitching In." *Newsday*, September 17, 2001.

Heyman, Jon. "Angry Steinbrenner Speaks Up." *Newsday*, September 14, 1993.

———. "Boss Risks Losing Winner Cashman." *Newsday*, October 10, 2003.

———. "Can Tigers 'Surpass' '62 Mets?" *Newsday*, May 4, 2003.

———. "A Difficult Job Is Done Well." *Newsday*, September 19, 2001.

———. "Jason Not Just Bulky but Balky." *Newsday*, October 21, 2003.

———. "MLB Investigation Upsets Union." *Newsday*, May 5, 2006.

———. "When Joe Got in Boss' Face." *Newsday*, February 20, 2004.

Hoch, Bryan. "Clemens Announces Return to Yanks." MLB.com, May 6, 2007.

Hofmann, Dale. "Opening Onslaught Is a Good Start." *Milwaukee Journal Sentinel*, April 27, 1995.

———. "Selig Keeps Owners Together in Battle." *Milwaukee Sentinel*, September 15, 1994.

———. "Selig-Prieb Takes Issue with Brewers' Critics." *Newsday*, November 14, 2003.

———. "Vincent Voted Down, Commissioner Says He's Not Quitting." *Milwaukee Sentinel*, September 4, 1992.

———. "Well-Liked Selig Is Baseball's Ultimate Power Broker." *Milwaukee Sentinel*, September 24, 1992.

Holtzman, Jerome. "Owners Doubt That Levine Is the Real Deal." *Chicago Tribune*, October 30, 1996.

Horgan, Sean. "Schott Takes Some of Blame." *Hartford Courant*, December 10, 1992.

Howard, Johnette. "Looks Like George Has Lost His Fastball." *Newsday*, May 25, 2005.

Hummel, Rick. "50–50: Elite Group of Two; McGwire, Ruth Linked Forever in Baseball Lore." *St. Louis Post-Dispatch*, September 11, 1997.

Hunt, Michael. "Barry's Visit Brings Anything but Fun." In My Opinion. *Milwaukee Journal Sentinel*, July 21, 2007.

———. "Molitor Return Earns Loud, Long Greeting." *Milwaukee Sentinel*, June 26, 1993.

Idelson, Jeff. "First Class for the Bat; Its Bearer Tags Along." *New York Times*, September 23, 2013.

Jaffe, Harry. "How DC Got Baseball Back." *Washingtonian*, April 2005.

Jehl, Douglas. "President Will Call on Congress to Impose Baseball Arbitration." *New York Times*, February 8, 1995.

Jenkins, Bruce. "Day Dark—Our Pastime in Ruins." *San Francisco Chronicle*, September 15, 1994.

Jones, Richard P., and Joe Williams. "Brewers Seek More Public Aid." *Milwaukee Journal Sentinel*, February 17, 1996.

Jordan, Pat. "Whaddya Mean No Man Is an Island?" *Los Angeles Times Magazine*, February 26, 1995.

Justice, Richard. "Baseball Studies Andro; No Plans to Issue Ban." *Washington Post*, February 9, 2000.

————. "McGwire Surpasses Maris with 62nd Home Run." *Washington Post*, September 8, 1998.

Kaplan, David. "The Most Hated Man in Baseball." *Newsweek*, August 5, 1990.

Keegan, Tom. "Final Outcome Par for Selig's Course." *New York Daily News*, July 10, 2002.

Kepner, Tyler. "The Astros' Plans Still Include Clemens." *New York Times*, October 24, 2005.

————. "A Careful Apology from Giambi." *New York Times*, February 11, 2005.

————. "Giambi Leads Newcomers into Camp." *New York Times*, February 20, 2002.

————. "Hank Steinbrenner on A-Rod: 'He Doesn't Want to Be a Yankee.'" NYTimes.com, October 29, 2007.

————. "His Final Victory Is a Yankees Empire Restored." *New York Times*, July 13, 2010.

————. "A Long Goodbye to an 85-Year Run." *New York Times*, September 21, 2008.

————. "Matsui and the Yankees Agree to a Deal." *New York Times*, December 20, 2002.

————. "McGwire Admits That He Used Steroids." *New York Times*, January 11, 2010.

————. "No Word from Steinbrenner Yet on His Manager." *New York Times*, October 9, 2006.

————. "Sightings of Steinbrenner Are Plentiful and Playful." *New York Times*, February 23, 2006.

————. "Steinbrenner Appoints Jeter Captain of the Yankees." *New York Times*, June 4, 2003.

————. "Steinbrenner Son Elected Chairman of Yankees." *New York Times*, September 29, 2007.

————. "Swindal Divorce Shakes Up Yankee Hierarchy." *New York Times*, March 29, 2007.

————. "Time for Reflection and Dissection in Yankees' World." *New York Times*, October 12, 2005.

————. "Torre Says No to Yankees' Offer and Ends 12-Year Era." *New York Times*, October 19, 2007.

————. "Torre Tells His Boss to Stop Meddling." *New York Times*, November 1, 2003.

————. "The Trials of Jason Giambi." *New York Times*, January 31, 2005.

————. "Wells's Book Has Teammates Amused and Torre Concerned." *New York Times*, March 1, 2003.

————. "Yankees Are Working on a Settlement with Swindal." *New York Times*, May 17, 2007.

————. "Yanks' Cashman Preparing for Next Year." *New York Times*, October 22, 2004.

Kepner, Tyler, and Jack Curry. "Yankees' Swindal Is Arrested in Florida." *New York Times*, February 16, 2007.

Kepner, Tyler, and Maria Newman. "Yankees Manager Torre to Return Next Season." *New York Times*, October 10, 2006.

Kernan, Kevin. "Big Mac to Jason: Easy Does It." *New York Post*, April 7, 2002.

————. "The Boss' Big Day—George Gets Own Field of Dreams." *New York Post*, March 28, 2008.

Kifner, John. "Spring Rite for the Yankees: Complaining about the Stadium." *New York Times*, June 9, 1994.

King, George. "Boss Sticks It to Brian; Blocks GM's Departure by Picking Up Option." *New York Post*, December 15, 2003.

————. "Cashman to Shea? Livid Boss Told GM He Can Cross Town." *New York Post*, October 11, 2003.

————. "Deal All but Done—Rodriguez's Megapact Could Top $300M with Revenue Sharing." *New York Post*, November 16, 2007.

————. "The Fenway Flop Boss Fumes after Clemens Blows Lead." *New York Post*, August 1, 1999.

————. "George Taps In-Law as Successor." *New York Post*, June 29, 2005.

————. "Hal Won't Stick Fork in Yankees." *New York Post*, August 22, 2008.

————. "Neverending Torre—Joe Has His Eyes on 2005." *New York Post*, February 19, 2004.

————. "Yanks Make It 'E'-Z for Twins; Sloppy Defense Puts Bombers in 1–0 Hole." *New York Post*, October 1, 2003.

Konigsberg, Bill. "Jose Canseco Barred from Attending News Conference on Mitchell Report." *USA Today*, December 14, 2007.

Kristof, Nicholas. "Road to Politics Ran through a Texas Ballpark." *New York Times*, September 24, 2000.

Lamke, Kenneth R. "Bye-Bye Brewers? Selig Says He, Other Baseball Owners Will Decide." *Milwaukee Journal Sentinel*, June 15, 1996.

————. "Loan Offered to Keep Baseball in City, Joyce Says Team Is 'Common Cause, Connection among Us.'" *Milwaukee Journal Sentinel*, June 30, 1996.

————. "Miller Park Workers Raise the Roof." *Milwaukee Journal Sentinel*, January 9, 1999.

————. "Petak's Loss Doesn't Bolster Prospects for Stadium Deal, Officials Say." *Milwaukee Journal Sentinel*, June 5, 1996.

————. "Stadium Plan Is a Hit." *Milwaukee Journal Sentinel*, June 27, 1996.

Lapointe, Joe. "Owners and Union Complete 5-Year Deal." *New York Times*, October 24, 2006.

————. "World Champs; Soaked in Victory, Steinbrenner Savors It All Again." *New York Times*, October 28, 1999.

Lebowitz, Larry. "Marlins Won't Be Sold Short." *Orlando Sentinel*, November 7, 1997.

Leung, Rebecca. "MLB Swings Back at Steroid Claims." CBSNews.com, February 15, 2005.

Lidz, Frank. "Baseball after the Boss." *Portfolio*, August 2, 2007.

Lilly, Brandon. "Steinbrenner Sheds Tears with His Opening Say." *New York Times*, April 9, 2004.

Lindlaw, Scott. "Bush Throws Out First Pitch before Game 3." Associated Press, October 31, 2001.

Lockwood, Wayne. "Hall of Shame Awaits If Selig Calls." *San Diego Union-Tribune*, September 13, 1994.

Lupica, Mike. "Tribute to a Hero in Jackie's Memory, No. 42 Lives Forever." *New York Daily News*, April 16, 1997.

Macur, Juliet. "Emotional Steinbrenner Aims to Put All His Houses in Order." *New York Times*, May 2, 2004.

———. "Guilty Plea Widens Baseball's Steroids Scandal." *New York Times*, April 28, 2007.

———. "Voices: From Fearsome to Softy in One Interview." *New York Times*, July 13, 2010.

Macur, Juliet, and David E. Sanger. "Baseball's Steroid Panel Asks Active Players to Appear." *New York Times*, May 5, 2007.

Madden, Bill. "Boss: We'll Win It Next Year." *New York Daily News*, October 7, 1997.

———. "Embattled MLB Union Chief Donald Fehr Steps Down, Owed a Debt of Gratitude." *New York Daily News*, June 23, 2009.

———. "A Permanent End for Some." *New York Daily News*, October 9, 1995.

Mahler, Jonathan. "Oedipus Bronx." *Play Magazine (New York Times)*, March 2, 2008.

Marchand, Andrew. "Bobby Stays to Do His Part." *New York Post*, September 17, 2001.

Martin, Douglas. "George Steinbrenner: He's Back. And He's Still the Boss." *New York Times*, October 25, 1992.

Martino, Sam, and Lori Skaliltzky. "Boos Greet Selig, Stadium Plan." *Milwaukee Journal Sentinel*, September 7, 1995.

Maske, Mark. "With Timeless Grace, Ripken Becomes a Legend." *Washington Post*, September 7, 1995.

McCarron, Anthony. "Yanks Welcome Andy, Steinbrenners Say All Forgiven." *New York Daily News*, February 19, 2008.

McConnell, Jackie. "Tug Line Winning Corporate War at Sea." *Tampa Bay Business Journal*, September 16, 1996.

McKinley, James C. "Giuliani and Rangel Strike a Deal on U.S. Aid." *New York Times*, April 2, 1994.

———. "Guessing the Score: Open Secret—A Special Report; Steroid Suspicions Abound in Major League Dugouts." *New York Times*, October 11, 2000.

———. "Woman in the News; Strike-Zone Arbitrator—Sonia Sotomayor." *New York Times*, April 1, 1995.

Mencimer, Stephanie. "Scorin' with Orrin: How the Gentleman from Utah Made It Easier for Kids to Buy Steroids, Speed, and Spanish Fly." *Washington Monthly*, September 2001.

Miklasz, Bernie. "Andro Isn't What Powers McGwire." *St. Louis Post-Dispatch*, August 26, 1998.

———. "Everyone Seems Pumped Up about McGwire and Andro." *St. Louis Post-Dispatch*, August 29, 1998.

———. "McGwire's Heart Measures Up; Fans Had Big Role in Making Deal Work." *St. Louis Post-Dispatch*, September 17, 1997.

Miller, Scott. "Mariano Rivera: Birth of the Cutter Was 'Gift from God.'" CBSSports.com, July 14, 2013.

Milton, Steve. "Mission Accomplished; Owners Gameplan Is to Bust Baseball's Union." *Hamilton Spectator*, September 15, 1994.

Milwaukee Journal. "The Book on Molitor: Agent Details Cocaine Use, Tough Talks." September 28, 1993.

———. "We'll Know in a Week Whether Baseball Will Resume." September 3, 1994.

Milwaukee Journal Sentinel. "Fans Stand, Cheer for Selig." June 15, 1996.

Moran, Malcolm. "Mobbed in Milwaukee: Yount Gets No. 3,000." *New York Times,* September 10, 1992.

————. "Yank Numbers: Double Plays, First Place." *New York Times,* August 14, 1993.

————. "Yount Stirs Crowd but He's One Hit Away." *New York Times,* September 9, 1992.

Murphy, Bruce. "The Embarrassing Failure of Miller Park." *Murphy's Law.* UrbanMilwaukee.com, April 16, 2002.

————. "The Eternal Stadium Tax." *Murphy's Law.* UrbanMilwaukee.com, July 27, 2012.

————. "Our Billion Dollar Baby." *Milwaukee Magazine,* February 2001.

————. "Storm Warnings." *Milwaukee Magazine,* December 1996.

Neel, Eric. "Why Do We Hate This Guy? The Softest Superstar." *ESPN the Magazine,* August 7, 2006.

Nelson, James. "Pitch for New Stadium May Lose Speed." *Milwaukee Sentinel,* September 15, 1994.

Newhan, Ross. "Baseball Negotiations Have Nowhere to Go." *Los Angeles Times,* February 9, 1995.

————. "Baseball Owners Open Door to Talks." *Los Angeles Times,* December 8, 1992.

————. "Head of Players Union Calls Negotiator for Owners a 'Hatchet Man.'" *Los Angeles Times,* August 23, 1994.

————. "NLRB Votes to Seek Injunction against Owners." *Los Angeles Times,* March 27, 1995.

————. "Owners to Open Talks on Revenue." *Los Angeles Times,* August 11, 1993.

————. "Owners Want Vincent Out of Baseball." *Los Angeles Times,* September 4, 1992.

————. "Pitchers Hit the Showers in April." *Los Angeles Times,* May 5, 1996.

————. "Ravitch and Some Owners Oppose the Hiring of a Commissioner until the Player Talks Are Completed." *Los Angeles Times,* February 17, 1993.

————. "Selig Gets Big Show of Support." *Los Angeles Times,* November 28, 2001.

New York Times. "President Urges Sides to Continue Talks." August 17, 2002.

New York Times Editorial Board. "The Case against Iraq." *New York Times,* February 6, 2003.

Nichols, Mike, and Kenneth R. Lamke. "Council Approves Stadium Loan." *Milwaukee Journal Sentinel,* July 31, 1996.

Nightengale, Bob. "Bonds Not Concerned about Possible Indictment." *USA Today,* July 22, 2007.

————. "The Game behind the Game, Negotiating in the Big Leagues." *Los Angeles Times,* July 24, 1993.

————. "Sheffield Unfazed by Probe." *USA Today,* February 26, 2007.

————. "Steroids Become an Issue." *Los Angeles Times,* July 15, 1995.

O'Connor, Ian. "Joe Is in Why of the Storm—Taking Job a Torre-ble Mistake." *New York Daily News,* November 3, 1995.

O'Keeffe, Michael. "Long Road for Selig, MLB." *New York Daily News,* November 8, 2001.

————. "MLB, Union Deny Rumors of Positive Tests." *New York Daily News*, August 11, 2005.

Olney, Buster. "After Three Errors, Knoblauch Walks Out." *New York Times*, June 16, 2000.

————. "Clemens Bends, and Yanks Strangely Wilt." *New York Times*, August 1, 1999.

————. "Cone and the Yankees Are Back in Business." *New York Times*, April 25, 1998.

————. "How the Boss Changed His Stripes." *New York Times*, September 27, 1998.

————. "League Championships; After They Rejoice, Yankees Have Ample Time to Regroup." *New York Times*, October 20, 1999.

————. "League Championship Series; Revived Red Sox Batter Clemens as Martinez Silences Yanks." *New York Times*, October 17, 1999.

————. "League Championship Series; Yanks Get One Day to Revel and Rest." *New York Times*, October 15, 1998.

————. "Pettitte's Head, It Appears, Is on the Trading Block." *New York Times*, July 30, 1999.

————. "President Warms Up, Then Throws Strike." *New York Times*, October 31, 2001.

————. "Spring Training—Yankees; Praise for Irabu." *New York Times*, March 14, 1998.

————. "With No. 110, Torre's Team Matches '27 Yanks." *New York Times*, September 24, 1998.

————. "Yankees Subtract a Star but Add a Legend." *New York Times*, February 19, 1999.

Olson, Drew. "Baseball Owners Reject Labor Deal." *Milwaukee Journal Sentinel*, November 7, 1996.

————. "Happy Holidays? Not for Baseball." *Milwaukee Journal Sentinel*, December 23, 1994.

Pearlman, Jeff. "Escape from New York." *American Way*, March 15, 2009.

Penn, Nate. "The Godfather, Part II." *GQ*, February 19, 2008.

Pennington, Bill, and Jack Curry. "Andro Hangs in a Quiet Limbo." *New York Times*, July 11, 1999.

Pierce, Charles P. "Does George Mitchell Have the Juice?" *Boston Globe Magazine*, October 8, 2006.

Pugmire, Lance. "Clemens Named in Drug Affidavit." *Los Angeles Times*, October 1, 2006.

————. "Fingering 'Nails.'" *Los Angeles Times*, April 24, 2005.

Purdy, Matthew. "Resentment Zone; Officials' Courtship of Yankees Stirs Anger in the Bronx." *New York Times*, May 2, 1994.

Quinn, T. J. "Players Step Up but Keep Bats on Shoulder." *New York Daily News*, July 9, 2002.

Raab, Scott. "Alex Rodriguez: Jackpot!" *Esquire*, April 2001.

Raissman, Bob. "George Is Now a Shell of a Boss." *New York Daily News*, May 24, 2005.

————. "60 Minutes to Credibility, Canseco Has Bud Blushing." *New York Daily News*, February 18, 2005.

Rinard, Amy. "Brewers Might Need Subsidies in Future, Report Says." *Milwaukee Journal Sentinel*, June 15, 1996.

———. "$50 Million Loan to Team Is Not a Sure Thing." *Milwaukee Journal Sentinel*, August 24, 1995.

———. "Stadium Plan Keeps Team Here 30 Years." *Milwaukee Journal Sentinel*, August 20, 1995.

Rinard, Amy, and Steven Walters. "The Final Pitch Backers Scramble before Today's Vote." *Milwaukee Journal Sentinel*, September 27, 1995.

———. "Senate's Wild Night Yields a 'Yes' Vote." *Milwaukee Journal Sentinel*, October 7, 1996.

Roberts, Selena. "Sources Tell SI Alex Rodriguez Tested Positive for Steroids in 2003." *Sports Illustrated*, February 7, 2009.

Romel, Richard. "3-day Event to Honor Yount Will Boost Game Attendance." *Milwaukee Sentinel*, May 27, 1994.

Rush, George, Joanna Molloy, Marcus Baram, and K. C. Baker. "Boss' Son-in-Law Makes Pitch for Alimony." *New York Daily News*, July 7, 1998.

Samoray, Jeff. "Mac at the Corner: Home-Run Icon's Rare Visit to Tiger Stadium Carries Clout." *Detroit News*, June 4, 1999.

Sandomir, Richard. "At Hall of Fame, Day Dedicated to Two Icons." *New York Times*, July 30, 2007.

———. "Baseball Breaks with Its Television Past." *New York Times*, May 9, 1993.

———. "Bronx Is Up as Yankees Unveil Stadium Plan." *New York Times*, June 16, 2005.

———. "Cablevision and YES Reach an Agreement." *New York Times*, April 1, 2003.

———. "Calling All Yankee Fans: 'I'm Boss and I'm Baaack.'" *New York Times*, March 1, 1993.

———. "Chicago (Not in Standings) Now in First." *New York Times*, August 25, 1992.

———. "Congress Keeps Pressure on Leagues." *New York Times*, May 19, 2005.

———. "Decision Said to Favor YES." *New York Times*, March 24, 2004.

———. "Everyone Agrees: Steinbrenner's Plaque Is Big." *New York Times*, September 21, 2010.

———. "In a First, Steinbrenner Offers to Help Pay for a New Stadium." *New York Times*, July 29, 1998.

———. "In His Book, Canseco Says Giambi Overused Steroids." *New York Times*, February 12, 2005.

———. "Lucrative YankeeNets Deal Nears Completion." *New York Times*, August 8, 2001.

———. "Purchase of Devils Is Made Final." *New York Times*, August 23, 2000.

———. "Selig Defends Contraction to Congress." *New York Times*, December 6, 2001.

———. "Selling Americans Their Own Pastime." *New York Times*, June 12, 1996.

———. "Steinbrenner Is Back with His Old Pitches." *New York Times*, February 28, 1993.

———. "Stepping on Major Toes with a Big Adidas Deal." *New York Times*, March 4, 1997.

———. "They're the YankeeNets: A Marriage Made for the Tube." *New York Times*, February 26, 1999.

———. "YankeeNets Getting Own Cable Network." *New York Times*, September 11, 2001.

———. "Yankees and Adidas Agree On a Big Sponsorship Deal." *New York Times*, March 3, 1997.

———. "Yankees Could Start Own Network after Agreeing to Deal with MSG." *New York Times*, April 25, 2001.

———. "Yankees Have Plenty of Clout in Television Rights." *New York Times*, August 8, 2000.

Sandomir, Richard, and Michael S. Schmidt. "Steinbrenner Is Doing Well after Hospital Stay." *New York Times*, November 1, 2006.

———. "Steinbrenner Retreats from the Spotlight." *New York Times*, August 17, 2006.

Schmidt, Michael S. "Baseball Lords Vexed by Plan for a New King." *New York Times*, May 22, 2014.

———. "Baseball Promotes Selig's Deputy." *New York Times*, August 14, 2014.

———. "New Boss Wants to See Chamberlain Start (Now)." *New York Times*, April 21, 2008.

———. "New Tool Could Help in Testing for H.G.H." *New York Times*, March 28, 2010.

———. "On Hand for Opener, Swindal Is on Outside Looking In." *New York Times*, April 3, 2007.

———. "Ortiz and Ramirez Said to Be on '03 Doping List." *New York Times*, July 30, 2009.

———. "Result for Rodriguez Revives Testing Controversy." *New York Times*, February 9, 2009.

Schmuck, Peter. "Owners to Face Charges of Unfair Labor Practices." *Baltimore Sun*, December 15, 1994.

Schoenfield, David. "Still 30 Teams: Contraction Timeline." ESPN.com, February 5, 2002.

Schulman, Henry. "MLB: No Plan to Honor 715." *San Francisco Chronicle*, April 28, 2006.

Schultze, Steve. "State Stands Ready to Help, but Brewers Haven't Asked." *Milwaukee Journal*, May 13, 1993.

Seidel, Jeff. "Congress Reacts to Mitchell Report." MLB.com, December 13, 2007.

Sexton, Joe. "Royals Make Cone Game's Highest-Paid Pitcher." *New York Times*, December 9, 1992.

———. "Steinbrenner Offers a Blast of His Own." *New York Times*, August 23, 1988.

Shaughnessy, Dan. "All-Star Eve Is a Home Run Party: In and Out of Fenway, Fans Celebrate." *Boston Globe*, July 13, 1999.

———. "Sold Towne Team." *Boston Globe*, December 21, 2001.

Shea, John, with Mark Fainaru-Wada. "Giambi Told to Testify in Lab Probe." *San Francisco Chronicle*, October 20, 2003.

Sheehy, Gail. "The Accidental Candidate." *Vanity Fair*, October 2000.

Sheinin, Dave. "Mitchell to Head Steroid Investigation." *Washington Post*, March 31, 2006.

Sherman, Joel. "Bombers Waited till Price Was Right." *New York Post*, February 19, 1999.

———. "Boss Socked by One-Two Punch Fed-Up; Cashman Tells Pals He's Gone after Season." *New York Post*, December 14, 2003.

———. "Boss Takes More Jabs at Yankees; Torre and Jeter Not off Hook." *New York Post*, February 21, 2003.

———. "Inside the Complex Trade That Brought A-Rod to the Yanks." *New York Post*, February 15, 2014.

———. "Sad End for Cashman?" *New York Post*, October 11, 2005.

———. "This Move Smells like a Cap'n Crunch." *New York Post*, June 4, 2003.

———. "Truly Amazin' Spirit Shines On." *New York Post*, September 22, 2001.

Shpigel, Ben. "Yankees, Past and Present, Pay Tribute to Steinbrenner." *New York Times*, September 20, 2010.

Smith, Claire. "Baseball, Apple Pie and Politics." *New York Times*, November 17, 1993.

———. "Baseball Bans Cincinnati Owner for a Year over Racial Remarks." *New York Times*, February 4, 1993.

———. "Baseball Is Searching for Direction." *New York Times*, November 25, 1992.

———. "Bush Backs His Man Completely." *New York Times*, September 6, 1992.

———. "Coming Eventually: A New Commissioner." *New York Times*, December 19, 1992.

———. "Fehr Awaits 2 Words: Delay Ball." *New York Times*, September 11, 1992.

———. "For the Boss, a Change for the Better." *New York Times*, August 8, 1996.

———. "In Baseball, Reinsdorf Smiles Alone." *New York Times*, November 21, 1996.

———. "McGwire Wears His Heart on 19-Inch Biceps." *New York Times*, December 27, 1997.

———. "Owners Circle Bases without Ever Scoring." *New York Times*, September 7, 1993.

———. "Owners Offer a Tax System or Stricter Cap." *New York Times*, November 18, 1994.

———. "Owners Take Sides as Vincent Dispute Heats Up." *New York Times*, June 11, 1992.

———. "Payments, Not Games, Are Latest Issue." *New York Times*, September 7, 1994.

———. "Perhaps a New Era, but Note the Asterisk." *New York Times*, January 19, 1994.

———. "Players' Labor Motto: Expect the Worst." *New York Times*, March 3, 1994.

———. "Pleading the Ballplayers' Cause." *New York Times*, August 11, 1994.

———. "The Power and the Glory; Mark McGwire Cracks Home Runs and Creates Expectations." *New York Times*, May 7, 1998.

———. "Sock of Ages: McGwire Homer Is a Laser Shot into Hall of Fame." *Philadelphia Inquirer*, September 9, 1998.

———. "That Moldy Song from the 1970's Isn't Disco." *New York Times*, June 5, 1995.

————. "Vincent Will Not Go without a Struggle." *New York Times*, September 4, 1992.

————. "White House Takes Cut at Ending Baseball Strike." *New York Times*, October 14, 1994.

Souhan, Jim. "Selig Offers Little Hope for Twins." *Minneapolis Star Tribune*, November 16, 2001.

Sporting Goods Intelligence. "Adidas-Yankee Deal Sparks 'Anarchy' in Baseball." March 1997.

Sports Business Daily. "YES Debuts amid Glitches; Is Cablevision Flap a 'Test Case'?" March 20, 2002.

Steinbrenner, Hank. "Hank Steinbrenner: Clean Up Baseball's Mess." *Sporting News*, September 24, 2008.

Stone, Larry. "Man about Cooperstown: Molitor Takes His Place with Game's Best." *Seattle Times*, July 25, 2004.

Street, Jim. "Squeeze Play: M's Junk Training Table Goodies." *Seattle Post-Intelligencer*, March 10, 1995.

Strupp, Joe. "'S.F. Chronicle' BALCO Reporters to Write Book." *Editor & Publisher*, March 30, 2005.

TotalProSports.com. "Ex-Phillie Darren Daulton Is the Self Proclaimed Drug-Lord of Sports." June 20, 2009.

Van Dyck, Dave. "Red Sox Making It a Race." *Chicago Sun-Times*, September 1, 1996.

————. "Schott Says She's Sorry—But Few Hear." *Chicago Sun-Times*, December 10, 1992.

Van Voorhis, Scott. "Foul Ball? AG Questions Low-Bid Sox Deal." *Boston Herald*, December 22, 2001.

Vecsey, George. "Players May Have Fehr's Olympic Ambition to Thank for Ephedra Warning." *New York Times*, March 9, 2003.

————. "Yankee Boss Reaches Crossroads in the Bronx." *New York Times*, October 28, 1996.

Verducci, Tom. "Totally Juiced: Confessions of a Former MVP." *Sports Illustrated*, June 3, 2002.

Waldstein, David. "Hitched to an Aging Star: Anatomy of a Deal, and Doubts." *New York Times*, March 30, 2013.

Walker, Ben. "Schott May Be Making Deal with Baseball." Associated Press, December 9, 1992.

————. "Tragedy Marks End of Winter Meetings." Associated Press, December 10, 1992.

Walker, Don. "Between the Seams: Selig out of Fay-vor." *Milwaukee Journal Sentinel*, September 19, 2002.

————. "A Grand Opening—Big Bash, Big Blast Make Winners of Brewers." *Milwaukee Journal Sentinel*, April 7, 2001.

————. "Halted but Not Deterred." *Milwaukee Journal Sentinel*, February 6, 2002.

————. "New Brewmasters—Payne Possesses Strong Blend." *Milwaukee Journal Sentinel*, September 26, 2002.

————. "Pitch by Players Foul to Owners." *Milwaukee Journal Sentinel*, August 25, 2002.

———. "Selig Plans His Final At-Bat." *Milwaukee Journal Sentinel,* April 25, 2003.

———. "Sen. Mitchell Warns MLB Owners." *Milwaukee Journal Sentinel,* January 18, 2007.

Walker, Don, and Drew Olson. "Brewers Shuffle." *Milwaukee Journal Sentinel,* September 26, 2002.

Walters, Steven. "Delays, Surprise Pinch-Hitter Deliver Come-from-Behind Win." *Milwaukee Journal Sentinel,* October 7, 1995.

Washburn, Gary. "Palmeiro Suspended 10 Days by MLB." MLB.com, August 1, 2005.

Washington Post Editorial Board. "Irrefutable." *Washington Post,* February 6, 2003.

Weisberg, Jacob. "Liberal Tobacco Whores." *Slate,* August 10, 1997.

Wharton, David, and Helene Elliot. "Sheffield Says He Used BALCO Steroid Cream." *Los Angeles Times,* October 6, 2004.

Wilson, Duff. "Lawmakers Intensify Their Fight over Steroids." *New York Times,* March 11, 2005.

Wilstein, Steve. "Drug OK in Baseball, Not Olympics." Associated Press, August 21, 1998.

———. "Jeter Answers the Boss." Associated Press, February 13, 2003.

———. "Supplement, McGwire Linked throughout the 'Net." Associated Press, December 9, 1998.

Wise, Mike. "Owner Keeping Hands Off." *New York Times,* July 26, 1994.

———. "Steinbrenner Trying to Make 'Economic Sense' of It All." *New York Times,* August 12, 1994.

Wittenmyer, Gordon. "Pohlads Consider Twins Hopeless." *St. Paul Pioneer Press,* November 10, 2001.

Wojciechowski, Gene. "Boss Absent, but Not at All Forgotten." ESPN.com, November 4, 2009.

Wolfley, Bob. "Brewers' Broadcast Take Mere Pittance." *Milwaukee Journal Sentinel,* April 8, 2001.

Ziegler, Mark. "Fatal Errors." *San Diego Union-Tribune,* October 31, 2004.

Zipay, Steve. "It's George, by George: Yankees, Winning, Losing." *Newsday,* May 19, 2005.

Documents

Major League Baseball (MLB)

1994 MLB Collective Bargaining Agreement.

2002 MLB Collective Bargaining Agreement.

2006 MLB Collective Bargaining Agreement.

2011 MLB Collective Bargaining Agreement.

2005 MLB Joint Drug Prevention and Treatment Program (two updates in 2005).

2008 MLB Joint Drug Prevention and Treatment Program Update.

Levin, Richard C., George J. Mitchell, Paul A. Volcker, and George F. Will. *Report of the Independent Members of the Commissioner's Blue Ribbon Panel on Baseball Economics.* MLB.com. July 2000.

Mitchell, George J. DLA Piper US LLP. *Report to the Commissioner of Baseball of an Independent Investigation into the Illegal Use of Steroids and Other Performance Enhancing Substances by Players in Major League Baseball.* December 13, 2007.

Statements and Press Releases

MLB Statement on 2003 Survey Test Results. MLB.com, November 13, 2003.

Government Reform Committee Statement on Issuance of Subpoenas to Major League Baseball Executives and Players. March 9, 2005.

Rubenstein, Howard J. Statement on George Steinbrenner's Hospitalization. "Yankee Boss Gets Right Back to Work." *New York Times,* November 1, 2006.

Commissioner's Statement on Mitchell Report. MLB.com, December 13, 2007.

MLB Statement regarding *Sports Illustrated* News Story ("Alex Rodriguez Confidential Drug Test Result Revealed," 2009). MLB.com, February 7, 2009.

Commissioner's Statement regarding Don Fehr (upon Fehr's retirement announcement).

Fehr, Don. MLBPA Statement on 2003 MLB Drug Test Results. February 9, 2009.

"Rodriguez Statement on Drug Use." February 17, 2009.

Court Cases and Documents

Flood v. Kuhn, 407 U.S. 258 (1972).

Silverman v. Major League Baseball Player Relations Committee, Inc., 880 F. Supp. 246 (S.D.N.Y. 1995).

New York Yankees Partnership v. Major League Baseball Enterprises, Inc., No. 97-1153-Civ-T-25B (M.D. Fla. filed May 6, 1997) (Adidas).

BMO Nesbitt Burns Inc. v. Loria, No. 1:02-cv-22061 (S.D. Fla. filed July 16, 2000) (RICO).

United States v. Comprehensive Drug Testing, Inc., 579 F.3d 989 (9th Cir. 2009).

United States v. Comprehensive Drug Testing, Inc., No. 05-10067 (9th Cir. Sept. 13, 2010) (per curiam).

United States v. Clemens, No. 1:10-cr-00223-RBW (D.D.C. 2012).

Affidavit of Jeff Novitzky in Support of Request for Search Warrants (related to Victor Conte Jr.). N.D. Cal., September 3, 2003.

Barry Bonds Grand Jury Testimony. United States v. Bonds. N.D. Cal., December 4, 2003.

Jason Giambi Grand Jury Testimony. United States v. Giambi. N.D. Cal., December 11, 2003.

Affidavit of Jeff Novitzky in Support of Request for a Search Warrant (related to Kirk Radomski). E.D.N.Y., December 2005.

Application and Affidavit of Jeff Novitzky for Search Warrant (related to Jason Grimsley). D. Ariz., May 31, 2006.

Superseding Indictment. United States v. Bonds, No. CR 07-0732-S1. N.D. Cal., May 13, 2008.

Transcript of Kirk Radomski questioning. United States v. Clemens, No. CR 09-223. May 9, 2012 (morning session).

Legislation and Government Documents

Dietary Supplement Health and Education Act of 1994, 108 Stat. 4325 (1994).

NLRB Advice Memo from Daniel Silverman to Robert E. Allen, Associate General Counsel, Division of Advice, on Major League Baseball. December 13, 1994.

McCurry, Mike. White House Press Briefing. February 6, 1995.

Baseball's Revenue Gap: Pennant for Sale? Hearing before the Subcommittee on Antitrust, Business Rights, and Competition of the U.S. Senate Committee on the Judiciary. 106th Cong., 2d Sess. November 21, 2000.

Bush, George W. Operation Enduring Freedom announcement. "Bush Announces Strikes against Taliban." Washington Post, October 7, 2001.

Fairness in Anti-Trust in National Sports (FANS) Act of 2001. Hearing before the House of Representatives Committee on the Judiciary. 107th Cong., 1st Sess. December 6, 2001.

Steroid Use in Professional Baseball and Anti-doping Issues in Amateur Sports. Hearing before the Subcommittee on Consumer Affairs, Foreign Commerce, and Tourism of the Senate Committee on Commerce, Science, and Transportation. 107th Cong., 2d Sess. June 18, 2002.

Powell, Colin. Speech to United Nations. February 5, 2003.

Bush, George W. Address before a Joint Session of the Congress on the State of the Union. January 20, 2004.

Steroid Use in Professional and Amateur Sports. Hearing before the Senate Committee on Commerce, Science, and Transportation. 108th Cong., 2d Sess. March 10, 2004.

10 Years after the Implementation of DSHEA: The Status of Dietary Supplements in the United States. Hearing before the Subcommittee on Human Rights and Wellness of the House of Representatives Committee on Government Reform. 108th Cong., 2d Sess. March 24, 2004.

Adopting a Drug-Testing Policy by Major League Baseball, 150 Cong. Rec. S3997 (statements of Sens. McCain and Dorgan). April 8, 2004.

"Milwaukee Brewers Baseball Club Finances." State of Wisconsin Legislative Audit Bureau, May 6, 2004.

Waxman, Henry. Letter to Rep. Tom Davis on Canseco book. February 24, 2005.

Brand, Stanley. Letter to Reps. Henry Waxman and Tom Davis. "Re: Major League Baseball — March 17, 2005 Letters of Invitation." March 8, 2005.

Waxman, Henry, and Tom Davis. Letter to Stanley Brand. March 10, 2005.

Waxman, Henry, and Tom Davis. Letter to Bud Selig and Don Fehr. March 16, 2005.

Restoring Faith in America's Pastime: Evaluating Major League Baseball's Efforts to Eradicate Steroid Use. Hearing before the House of Representatives Committee on Government Reform. 109th Cong., 1st Sess. March 17, 2005.

Waxman, Henry, and Tom Davis. Letter to Paul Tagliabue. March 31, 2005.

S. 1114, the Clean Sports Act of 2005, and S. 1334, the Professional Sports Integrity and Accountability Act. Hearing before the Senate Committee on Commerce, Science, and Transportation. 109th Cong., 1st Sess. September 28, 2005.

The Mitchell Report: The Illegal Use of Steroids in Major League Baseball. Hearing before the House of Representatives Committee on Oversight and Government Reform. 110 Cong., 2d Sess. January 15, 2008.

Deposition of Andy Pettitte before the House of Representatives Committee on Oversight and Government Reform. February 4, 2008.

Deposition of William "Roger" Clemens before the House of Representatives Committee on Oversight and Government Reform. February 5, 2008.

Deposition of Brian Jerome McNamee Sr. before the House of Representatives Committee on Oversight and Government Reform. February 7, 2008.

Affidavit of Andy Pettitte for the House of Representatives Committee on Oversight and Government Reform. February 8, 2008.

Drugs in Sports: Compromising the Health of Athletes and Undermining the Integrity of Competition. Hearing before the Subcommittee on Commerce, Trade, and Consumer Protection of the House of Representatives Committee on Energy and Commerce. 110th Cong., 2d Sess. (prepared statement of Donald M. Fehr, executive director, Major League Baseball Players Association). February 27, 2008.

Selig, Bud. Letter to Reps. Henry Waxman and Tom Davis (regarding Mitchell Report "tipping" allegations). June 27, 2008.

Fehr, Don. Letter to Rep. Henry Waxman and Rep. Tom Davis (regarding Mitchell Report "tipping" allegations). July 2, 2008.

Collective Bargaining

Major League Baseball team owners' drug testing proposal. June 14, 1994.

Fehr, Don. Letter to Major League Baseball team owners regarding negotiations. July 18, 1994.

MLBPA Proposals. July 18, 1994.

Ravitch, Dick. Letter to Leonard R. Gray (cc: Selig, Fehr, O'Connor, Jeffrey White) (informing players of withheld pension payment). July 29, 1994.

Fehr, Don. Letter to MLB Players (regarding owners' withholding of pension plan payment). August 3, 1994.

———. Letter to Dick Ravitch (regarding reception of letter informing MLBPA about withheld pension payment). August 3, 1994.

O'Connor, Chuck. Letter to Don Fehr (regarding exclusive representative status of PRC). February 6, 1995.

Fehr, Don. Letter to Bud Selig "Re: Joint Drug Agreement." May 1, 2005.

Other Documents

Vincent, Fay. Memorandum to All MLB Clubs "Re: Baseball's Drug Policy and Prevention Program." June 7, 1991.

Noll, Roger F. "Baseball Economics in the 1990s." A report commissioned by the Major League Baseball Players Association. 1994.

Memorandum of Understanding for the Milwaukee Stadium Project (State of Wisconsin, Milwaukee County, City of Milwaukee, and Milwaukee Brewers Baseball Club Limited Partnership). August 19, 1995.

Meet the Press. NBC, July 7, 1996. Transcript.

Selig, Bud. Memorandum to All MLB Clubs "Re: Baseball's Drug Policy and Prevention Program." May 15, 1997.

Selig, Bud, Paul Beeston, and Rich Levin. MLB Media Conference. July 23, 1997. ASAP Sports. Transcript.

Clinton, Bill. Address to the Nation. CNN.com. August 17, 1998. Transcript.

Harrington, John, Jim Healey, and Allan H. "Bud" Selig. MLB All-Star Game Media Conference. July 12, 1999. ASAP Sports. Transcript.

Steinbrenner, George. Memorandum to YankeeNets Media Committee, Harvey Schiller, and David Boies "Re: MSG Counter Proposal." March 17, 2001.

MLB. "2001 Income (Loss) by Club." Chart submitted for Hearing on the Fairness in Anti-Trust in National Sports (FANS) Act of 2001 before the House of Representatives Committee on the Judiciary. December 6, 2001.

Office of the Attorney General. "AG Reilly Announces Agreement to Bring $30 Million More to Charities from Sale of Red Sox." Press release, January 16, 2002.

Press Conference: Baseball Players, Management Reach Agreement. CNN.com. August 30, 2002. Transcript.

"Memorandum of Understanding of the New Yankee Stadium Project." City of New York, Empire State Development Corporation, New York City Economic Development Corporation, and New York Yankees Limited Partnership. June 15, 2005.

Office of the Mayor. "Mayor Bloomberg, Governor Pataki and New York Yankees Announce Plans for Area Revitalization and New Stadium in the South Bronx." Press release, June 15, 2005.

Selig, Allan H. "Bud." MLB All-Star Game Media Conference. July 12, 2005. ASAP Sports. Transcript.

Fehr, Donald, Andy MacPhail, and Allan H. "Bud" Selig. Press conference announcing new labor agreement, October 24, 2006. ASAP Sports. Transcript.

Rodriguez, Alex. Interview by Katie Couric. CBSnews.com. December 13, 2007. Transcript.

Mitchell, George. Press Conference. MLB.com. December 13, 2007. Transcript.

Rodriguez, Alex. Interview by Peter Gammons. ESPN. February 9, 2009. Transcript.

Outside the Lines. SABR Business of Baseball Committee Newsletter. Edited by Doug Pappas. Published quarterly.

Multimedia

Dykstra, Lenny. Interview. *Up Close.* ESPN. February 9, 1995.

"BB Moments: Iron Man Ripken." MLB.com. September 6, 1995.

1995 ALDS Game 5: NY Yankees vs. Seattle Mariners. Youtube.com. October 8, 1995 (posted by MLBClassics October 4, 2010).

"The Caddy." *Seinfeld.* NBC. January 25, 1996.

"BB Moments: Mac Passes Maris." MLB.com. September 8, 1998.

"Chicks Dig the Long Ball." Nike. Youtube.com. 1999 (posted by Crashdavis818 July 16, 2007).

"7-13-99: 1999 All-Star Game @ Fenway Park, Boston." Youtube.com. July 13, 1999 (posted by MLBClassics September 17, 2010).

"Baseball's Best Moments — 1999 All-Star Game." MLB.com. July 13, 1999.

"Williams' Walk-Off Homer." MLB.com. October 13, 1999.

"2000 World Series, Game 2: Mets @ Yankees." Youtube.com. October 22, 2000 (posted by MLBClassics September 21, 2010).

"Baseball Hall of Fame Members." CSPAN.org. March 30, 2001.

"Piazza's Healing Home Run." MLB.com. September 21, 2001.

"New York City Prayer Service." CSPAN.org. September 23, 2001.

"Jeter's Iconic Flip." MLB.com. October 13, 2001.

"President Bush's First Pitch." MLB.com. October 30, 2001.

"7/9/02: 2002 All-Star Game @ Miller Park, Milwaukee." Youtube.com. July 9, 2002 (posted by MLBClassics September 10, 2010).

"Benches Clear at Fenway." MLB.com. October 11, 2003.

"BB Moments: Boone Blasts BoSox." MLB.com. October 16, 2003.

"Steroid-User Canseco Names Names." *60 Minutes*. CBS. February 10, 2005.

"Steroid Use in Baseball Hearing: Players." Youtube.com. March 17, 2005 (posted by House.ResourceOrg January 7, 2011).

"Steroid Use in Baseball Hearing: Owners." Youtube.com. March 17, 2005 (posted by House.ResourceOrg January 7, 2011).

"Steroid Use in Baseball Hearing: Parents and Experts." Youtube.com. March 17, 2005 (posted by House.ResourceOrg January 16, 2011).

"Clemens Announces His Return to Yanks." MLB.com. May 6, 2007.

"Bonds' 756th Career Homer." MLB.com. August 7, 2007.

"A-Rod: I've Never Used Steroids." CBSNews.com. December 13, 2007.

"Roger Clemens on 60 Minutes." BaseballsSteroidEra.com.

"Hearing on Steroids in Baseball—Donald Fehr's Testimony." Youtube.com. January 15, 2008 (posted by Nancy Pelosi).

"Hearing on Steroids in Baseball—Bud Selig's Testimony." Youtube.com. January 15, 2008 (posted by Nancy Pelosi).

"Hearing on Steroids in Baseball—Mitchell's Testimony." Youtube.com. January 15, 2008 (posted by Nancy Pelosi).

"Hearing on Steroids in Baseball—Mitchell on Clemens." Youtube.com. January 15, 2008 (posted by Nancy Pelosi.)

"First Person: Pettitte Apologizes for HGH Use." Youtube.com. February 18, 2008 (posted by Associated Press).

"Steinbrenner Delivers the First-Pitch Baseballs." MLB.com. July 16, 2008.

Rodriguez, Alex. Interview by Peter Gammons, Parts 1-4 to 4-4. ESPN, February 7, 2009. Youtube.com (posted by xInFiNiTe7x February 9, 2009).

"A-Rod on Steroids." *60 Minutes*. CBS News, February 7, 2009.

10 Years Ago: Crane Collapses at Miller Park. Youtube.com. July 14, 2009 (posted by WISN 12 News).

"Steinbrenner's Health Worsening." CBSSports.com. October 30, 2009.

"2009 New York Yankees 27th World Series Trophy Ceremony." Youtube.com. November 4, 2009 (posted by PMS442years07).

McGwire, Mark. Interview by Bob Costas. MLB.com. January 11, 2010.

"Joe Torre Reflects on Memories of George Steinbrenner." MLB.com. February 18, 2013.

"Jeter on Steinbrenner's Passing." MLB.com. July 13, 2010.

"Jeter Honors Steinbrenner and Sheppard with a Speech." MLB.com. July 16, 2010.

"Dawson Enters the Hall of Fame." MLB.com. July 25, 2010.

"Selig on His Statue." MLB.com. August 24, 2010.

"TB@NYY: Selig Talks Steinbrenner with YES Announcers." MLB.com. September 20, 2010.

"The House of Steinbrenner." *30 for 30*. ESPN, September 21, 2010.
"9/11 Baseball Remembers: Part 3." MLB.com. January 5, 2011.
"The Case of Alex Rodriguez." *60 Minutes*. CBS, January 12, 2014.

Websites

Baseballchronology.com
Baseballprospectus.com
Baseball-Reference.com
JSonline.com (*Milwaukee Journal Sentinel*)
Mlbcontracts.blogspot.com
NYTimes.com
Opensecrets.org
Sabr.org
TheSteroidEra.blogspot.com
Thomas.gov (*Congressional Record*)

INDEX